LIVES AT THE MARGIN

LIVES AT THE MARGIN
Biography of Filipinos
Obscure, Ordinary, and Heroic

edited by
ALFRED W. MCCOY

Published in cooperation with
Ateneo de Manila University Press

University of Wisconsin-Madison
Center for Southeast Asian Studies
2000

Library of Congress Catalogue Card Number
98-061608

ISBN (cloth): 1-881261-27-1
ISBN (paperback): 1-881261-26-3

Published by the
Center for Southeast Asian Studies
University of Wisconsin-Madison
Madison, WI 53706 USA
(608) 263-1755; fax: (608) 263-3735

Edited by Janet Opdyke
Designed by Andrea L. Canfield
Cover design by J.B. de la Peña

Distributed in the Philippines exclusively by the Ateneo de Manila
University Press and nonexclusively in Asia; and in the rest of the
world, exclusively by the University of Wisconsin-Madison Center for
Southeast Asian Studies.

Contents

Introduction

BIOGRAPHY OF LIVES OBSCURE, ORDINARY, AND HEROIC

Alfred W. McCoy

B iography is a central, sharply contested form of Filipino literary and political expression. In this century's technological progress from print to film, radio, and television, biography has persisted to become a pervasive, even omnipresent, feature of Philippine life. School texts teach stories about national heroes, the Church celebrates the lives of saints, true to life stories of Filipino gunmen blaze from movie screens, and thousands of campaign biographies fill handbills and wall posters during elections.

Biography, particularly Philippine biography, is a large, diverse, hybrid field. Taking it at its simplest definition (a record of a life), it is a narrative genre encompassing confessions, diaries, letters, memoirs, family histories, genealogies, resumes, and even burial inscriptions. No one has yet surveyed the field. "From the varieties of popular tales to medieval romances, from hagiographies to the modern novel, there is," writes Resil Mojares of the Philippine narrative tradition, an "ample field for the historian and critic to move around in. The field has well-cultivated patches, early clearings, and dark districts. On dim grounds, the historian will have to mark strange growths, judge what light emanates from the native vegetation and what cast by some alien sun."[1]

Rather than trying to fill such an ambitious agenda or critique the state of Philippine biography, this volume follows what seems to be a largely unexplored path through the study of ordinary lives and obscured figures. In their canonical focus on those who built the modern nation, Philippine biographers have, with some exceptions, selected a small number of leaders and excluded many others, thereby limiting the genre's range somewhat. By stepping outside the dominant paradigm, the life histories of lesser figures can perhaps contribute to an ongoing process of innovation within the Philippine biographical canon—new subjects, multidisciplinary methods, and novel documentation. More broadly, through the close study of ordinary lives and second-tier leaders such biography can illuminate areas now obscured within the vastness of the Philippine past, allowing us a fuller view of the processes of change.

In pursuit of these aims, most of the biographies in this volume treat men and women who have emerged from the social and geographical margins of Philippine society to mobilize, through their individual talents, a mass following. Their skills have been many and varied — charisma, cunning, violence, integrity, and duplicity. Some may have been predators or opportunists, but most have acted as self-conscious agents of change, leading their constituents in a struggle for social justice. Most occupied the strategic middle strata of their society, using their skills to mediate between the state and an impoverished populace. With few exceptions, they failed in their challenges to the social order and ended their careers marginalized, impoverished, imprisoned, or dead.

History has punished them for this failure. A few were famous and some were notorious, but almost all are now largely forgotten. Their biographies do not fulfill the criteria of the heroic genre. They lack the moral example, stirring saga, or ready historical significance of textbook heroes. Nonetheless, by looking through the prism of their lives, we can view worlds now obscured at the margins of the Philippine state and its history — Iloilo's waterfront, Muslim Mindanao, Cebu City's underworld, the plantations of Negros, and the villages of central Luzon. And through these biographies of the ordinary and obscured we can begin to reexamine received wisdom about the character of the Philippine polity.

Biography and History

Biography presents historians with a problem. While it is the most popular form of history and allows the profession a mass audience, many historians have reservations about reducing the complexities of change to the actions of a few individuals, no matter how powerful or exemplary. Indeed, the modern historian might well ask: what are we to do with biography? Antonio Gramsci, in his writings about ideology and hegemony, offers some insights into the persistence and importance of biography. "Every historical act," he wrote, "presupposes the attainment of a 'socio-cultural' unity through which a multiplicity of dispersed individual wills, heterogeneous in their aims, are welded together for the same goal on the basis of a . . . common conception of the world."[2] In this vein, we might argue that biography is primarily a device that helps organize an individual's insertion into the ideological and social formations that define how, as historical subjects, men and women act or are acted upon.

If we apply this approach, then we can see, perhaps somewhat schematically, how the "life stories" of epics and ballads insert an ordinary farmer into the moral order of a community or culture group; the saint's life inserts a believer into the Judeo-Christian order; and, more recently, the heroic biography inserts a citizen into the "nation" or its subideological formations. If this schema has merit, then a colonial order based on voluntarism of the rulers and coercion of the ruled will only produce biographies of the expatriate elite, not of its colonized subjects, except as auxiliaries in the narratives of the dominant. To cite one example, the Spanish biographical register *Heroes de Filipinas,* published in 1888, included only two Filipinos among the sixty plus honored for their contributions to the colonial state. Unlike modern Philippine histories, which portray the eighteenth-century rebel Diego Silang as a national hero, this work instead celebrates "the Spanish mestizo Don Miguel Vicos," who broke this dangerous revolt by stabbing the "traitor" Silang through his "evil heart."[3] It is nationalism, then, that is most productive of biographies, as "natives" emerge as historical agents, autonomous and empowered.

Indeed, the maintenance of the nation requires a canon of model lives, while at the same time the nation creates the patterns or structures according to which actual lives are lived. But nations are also inherently unstable, ambivalent, and contested formations. These tensions are expressed in shifts in the biographical canon, debates over heroes, alternative biographies, and, of course, the persistence of hagiographical writing about national heroes. Competing ideologies, Gramsci reminds us, "come into confrontation and conflict, until only one of them tends to prevail, . . . to propagate itself throughout society — bringing about not only a unison of economic and political aims but also intellectual and moral unity."[4]

Philippine biography has a long history. One can go back to oral traditions — epics, ballads, songs, and other forms that contain, or purport to be, life stories of figures mythical or historical. Implicated in such forms are indigenous notions of self, personhood, and society, raising questions about what constitutes a life, or an exemplary life, and how this is represented.

The work of anthropologist Michelle Rosaldo has documented this relationship between social role and narrative biography. In the 1970s, she spent several years with the Ilongot of Nueva Vizcaya exploring the socialization of young males into a life cycle focused on ritual head taking as preparation for adulthood and marriage. In this exploration of self and society, she argued that in most communities "the reproduction of a given form of social life demands such continuities in discourse as would permit a shared and sensible frame for the interpretation of daily practice, so that the ways that individuals construe their actions show some relation to the orders that they recognize in the world."[5] To perpetuate the "communal joy and health" that head taking provides, elder men teach younger males "the songs and images through which . . . Ilongots celebrate the strength of violent youths."[6] As children, Rosaldo tells us, "young boys learn, and relive in their play, the headhunting encounters of their elders; they hear songs that celebrate the distances traversed by raiders; . . . and from the 'stories' told by seniors learn of slights and insults they will, if truly 'angry,' avenge when they are grown."[7] Indeed, Rosaldo transcribes several of these ballads, such at the story of the mythic Bugegiw's head taking and

marriage, which are essentially model biographies, that is, the story of a
named individual from the past who accomplished heroic deeds exemplary of Ilongot values.[8] Mojares reports that there are up to a thousand such
tales in each Filipino culture, most recounting "heroic deeds by heroes with
magical attributes."[9] As another early example of biography, one may cite
the Muslim *tarsila* or genealogy. Depending upon the particular text and its
interpretation, this form can be seen as an example of a biographical text
deployed to confirm or validate claims to status and power.

One can narrow this massive, multifaceted field by focusing on written or published lives. As the indigenous epic declined from the seventeenth century onward under the pressures of colonial rule, the Spanish
introduced metrical (verse) romances, hagiography, and the *pasyon*, the
story of Christ's crucifixion. According to critic Nicanor Tiongson, the
aim was "to mold the Filipinos into perfect colonials." Early examples of
such colonial forms are lives of saints and metrical romances *(awit* and
corrido). These are, Mojares tells us, distinct (one religious, the other secular) but not separate. Both are, in fact, called *vida (bida,* Tagalog *buhay,*
Cebuano *kinabuhi,* Ilocano *biag)*. Among the many stylistic and thematic
interactions among epics, metrical romances, and saints' lives that
Mojares has documented, the hagiography was sometimes written by
laymen as a *corrido* that "presents heroic characters with magical powers," much as the pagan myths had done. By the late nineteenth century,
the *corrido* had moved away from foreign themes "toward the treatment
of local, contemporary and common life," becoming thereby a "vehicle
for versified history."[10]

The first Filipino "biographies" were descended from the lives of
saints *(vita sancti)* as well as the metrical romance. Reynaldo Ileto has analyzed how the *pasyon* became a vehicle for the telling of Filipino lives. In
these stories, the interest is not in the person but in what the life figures.[11]
Mojares cites instances of how in the late nineteenth and early twentieth
centuries the verse romance also took on native, profane subjects such as
the lives of Father Burgos, Jose Rizal, and others.[12] All of these sources
suggest that the impulses behind Philippine biography are complex.

Secular and Religious Biography

If, as Mojares reminds us, elemental "notions of personhood . . . are not
universal," then their textual rendering through biography is indeed a
social artifact, a particular practice transmitted, and altered, through culture contact. When they arrived in the Philippines in the sixteenth century, Spanish missionaries brought an elaborate biographical form, the *vita
sancti,* or "saint's life," which was used first to inspire and then to explain
the Filipino conversion to Christianity. Indeed, the earliest known biography of a Filipino, a Jesuit account of the life of convert Miguel Ayatumo

(1593–1609), exemplifies this hagiographic genre. Following its rigid, tripartite form, the Jesuit authors narrate the life of a Filipino boy on Bohol who renounced paganism for a fervent faith, was tested when he rejected a native priestess (*bailana*) who came to cure his illness, and finally achieved his consummation at age sixteen, when, having suffered an accident, he expired peacefully reciting the names of the saints. In sum, hagiography, Mojares concludes, is a biographical genre "governed by an ideology that subordinates the historical and the particular to the ideal and the metaphysical."[13]

Through its religious and cultural ties to Spain, the Philippines was for nearly three centuries exposed to a form of European biography that by the nineteenth century articulated a conception of life, in a narrative sense, as an individual quest for fulfillment—not in the familiar world of family or locality but in a dominating institutional context, first school and church, later army and state. In nineteenth-century Europe, reflecting the doctrine of the perfectible (and thus educable) individual, both the Catholic Church and the secular state, though bitter rivals, deployed exemplary biographies to inspire emulation by students in their separate schools. In the latter decades of the century, church and state began building school systems for mass education and, as part of an explicit attempt at character formation, used biographies of those who had sacrificed for these institutions to inspire emulation.

In retrospect, the nineteenth century seems to have been the golden age of European biography. In 1854, Pope Pius IX proclaimed the dogma of the Immaculate Conception, part of a larger project of articulating and elaborating reverence for the saints and their sacrifices. Apart from pamphlets and texts, this effort led to the publication of biographical compendia of Catholic martyrs such as Father Butler's *Lives of the Saints* in 1878.[14] In England, Thomas Carlyle proclaimed history to be nothing more than "the essence of innumerable biographies" in 1830, Samuel Smiles published his didactic *Lives of the Engineers* thirty years later, and the nation's historians completed the voluminous *Dictionary of National Biography* between 1885 and 1900.[15] Despite obvious differences in the careers of, say, a medieval monk and a civil engineer, there were, in these simplified school biographies, certain structural similarities in both secular and religious narratives of heroic sacrifice.

As Spanish literacy rose in the Philippines during the late nineteenth century, the reading of European biographies became a pastime for everyone from Jose Rizal's wealthy father to the less affluent autodidact Andres Bonifacio. Sometimes Rizal's father would read aloud while showing his children pictures of Alexander the Great or Napoleon, making a deep impression upon the young Rizal. When his sisters mocked him for making a clay bust of Napoleon, Rizal is supposed to have called out: "Go on, laugh, but when I die see if they don't erect monuments in my honor!" In

Bonifacio's library of a dozen books were the *Life of the Presidents of the United States* and five novels that were essentially fictional biographies.[16]

In the nineteenth century as well, through the spread of parochial schools and printed devotional pamphlets, the lives of saints and martyrs gained a wider audience across the Philippine archipelago. In the Tagalog-speaking region around Manila, the story of Christ's life and death was popularized through reading and staging of the *pasyon*'s rich vernacular script during Holy Week.[17] There was, due to Church's requirements for canonization, an unchanging, three-part narrative structure in the lives of the great Christian martyrs. Future saints must often overcome some personal or social barrier that blocks their vocation. Then, sometimes after an epiphany, they begin their mission of good works, resisting temptations that test their faith along the way. Finally, they must meet death calmly, content to offer the ultimate sacrifice for the Church.

By 1872, when Spain executed three Filipino priests to crush the first stirrings of nationalism, the country's culture had already internalized this heroic narrative. Sentenced to die for the crime of subversion, the priests were marched to the garrote just outside the city walls before a crowd of forty thousand Filipinos. While Father Gomez, an elderly provincial priest, blessed the people and met death bravely, Jose Burgos, a popular local curate, was "weeping like a child." When it came his turn to die, Burgos called out from the scaffold, protesting, "But what crime have I committed? Is it possible that I should die like this?" Finally, when the priest calmed, the executioner knelt at his feet to ask forgiveness and the entire crowd also fell to their knees, saying prayers for the dead. Nearly twenty years later, Rizal himself, then a leader of the nationalist movement, would write: "If at his death Burgos had shown the courage of Gomez, the Filipinos of today would be other than they are."[18]

In his own life and death by firing squad in 1896, Rizal fulfilled the culture's requisites for heroism. In a prize-winning biography written for the centennial of Rizal's birth in 1961, a high tide of secular nationalism, Leon Ma. Guerrero, seemingly uncomfortable with this text of martyrdom, defied the narrative form, proclaiming that this was "not a hagiography but the story of a human being."[19] By contrast, in his 1996 biography, which was published on the centennial of Rizal's death, national artist Nick Joaquin returned to the hagiographic genre, portraying his subject as a martyr. Though past biographers had emphasized his family's wealth, Joaquin argues that Rizal succeeded after a difficult struggle "to overcome his disadvantages" of a weak body and painful shyness. The future hero's birth was marked by omens of future greatness, notably his large head, which "denotes genius." Like many saints, as a child he possessed powers of prophecy and a prescient sense of his own destiny. At the age of eighteen, he wrote a remarkable play, "uncannily envisioning the revolution, the Spanish-American War, . . . the gruesome Jap invasion, . . . the lahar plague." But, above all, Rizal died a martyr's death. After a decade of study and nationalist agitation in Europe, he returned home to detention and, following the revolution's outbreak in 1896, execution. In contrast to Father Burgos, Rizal walked calmly to the execution grounds outside the city walls and was bound, his pulse normal, facing away from the firing squad. Then, as the soldiers fired, he twisted his body, struggling to fall face upward—a "final scene so engraved in the mind that it has become a national memory," an image so powerful that it has won him "immortality."[20]

Indeed, Rizal's willing martyrdom struck a deeply responsive chord. Only two years later, the revolutionary Republic commemorated his death with speeches and parades in towns across the archipelago. After the American regime crushed the Republic, the Rizal cult continued to spread with tacit colonial support since his studious demeanor seemed to present an apt role model for Filipino students in the American public schools. In the first years of American rule, some Filipino historians suggested sharing Rizal's glory with other heroes. In his essays on the revolutionary leader Andres Bonifacio, for example, historian Epifanio de los Santos hailed the plebeian hero's "exact vision of the future," which led him to launch the Revolution. But these frail efforts failed.[21] After independence in 1946, Filipino scholars surveying the historical landscape found statues of Rizal in "almost all" of the country's twelve hundred municipalities and located more than eighteen hundred published items commemorating his life.[22]

Nationalism is thus a major force in the production of biographies. In 1920, for example, the *ilustrado* nationalist T. H. Pardo de Tavera lectured Filipino schoolteachers at Baguio on "The Heritage of Ignorance," condemning the whole Spanish colonial corpus of *corridos, pasyon,* and novenas for fostering belief that "paralyzes rather than promotes progress." He called for a "logical mentality" to replace these "frauds of a puerile nature." Heroic biography became a key element in this project of national reconstruction. Similarly, in Europe the rise of nationalism also coincided with the advent of new forms of thought, including realism in literature (notably, the nineteenth-century European novel), which influenced modern biography.[23] Modern, Western "interpretive" biography—with its bias in favor of the individual (versus the type), "warts and all," the values of texture and detail, rich circumstantiality, and psychological depth—is not of course the only possible mode of biographical writing.

Philippine nationalism was not alone in its need for a canon of heroes and exemplary lives, those of "distinguished" Filipinos. The textual production of such lives was and is part of the nationalist project elsewhere in the world. The surge of memoirs and biographies that emerged from the Philippine Revolution—those of Apolinario Mabini, Artemio Ricarte, Emilio Aguinaldo, Felipe Calderon, Teodoro Kalaw, Rafael Palma, and others—was fueled by the need of witnesses and participants to document and explain significant events as well as position themselves in relation to them.[24] These texts are shaped by—and constitute—a "national narrative." And nations require such a narrative.

Hence, the early twentieth century, as Filipino leaders laid the foundations for future independence from colonial rule, saw a surge in research and publication by such agencies as the National Library, various historical societies and commissions, and intellectuals like Manuel Artigas, Epifanio de los Santos, Rafael Palma, and Teodoro Kalaw.[25] In the preface to his memoirs of the revolution and the war against America, *ilustrado* nationalist Felipe Calderon explained his motivations in words that seem to explain this outpouring. "It is true that in the government schools they study the History of the Philippines and there exist didactic works written by Americans for these schools," he wrote, "but the understanding of the alumni of these schools on this point is from an American point of view, and there is a subjectivity in this History that is impossible to avoid."[26] Over time, all these efforts take on lives of their own within the nation-making project as knowledge is reproduced, the production of certain kinds of texts is privileged by state agencies (public schools, libraries, or government publishing), and market demand develops (through popular publishing and commercial distribution).

Paralleling the rise of a secularized hagiography, biography proliferated to become a popular form of self-expression for the Filipino elite and the middle class. Indeed, the American era saw a virtual florescence of biography. During the nineteenth century, the United States had shared the European fascination with the genre and laid the literary foundations for its own cult of heroic leaders—Washington, Jefferson, and Lincoln—later propagated through the nation's public schools. Not only did the U.S. regime in Manila lend its support to the popular reverence of Rizal during its half century of colonial rule (1898–1946), but its schools placed readers and history books on the desk of almost every Filipino child, their pages filled with stories about the exemplary lives of great Americans and Filipinos. Apart from instilling respect for particular leaders and the concept of heroic leadership, these lessons promoted mass acceptance of the biographical genre.[27] This trend also had indigenous roots, as Filipino *ilustrado* intellectuals wrote the first draft of collective memory as biography and autobiography. Most importantly, Manuel Artigas and Epifanio de los Santos produced several biographies of the revolution's fallen heroes, Antonio Luna and Andres Bonifacio.[28] In the early years of U.S. colonial rule, commercial publishers, both Filipino and American, launched the first biographical registers of distinguished Filipinos— notably, the massive *Galeria de Filipinos Ilustres,* edited by Artigas and published by the nationalist press Renacimiento.[29]

With the advent of the Commonwealth and its ten-year transition to independence, there was another outpouring of biographies and biographical registers, almost as if these Filipino writers and publishers were aspiring to agency as an integral component of the struggle for nationhood. The three major compendia of the era—by George Nellist, Zoilo Galang, and M. R. Cornejo—offer, in total, brief biographies of nearly a thousand male politicians, professionals, and businessmen. While Cornejo provides the barest of biographical detail and Galang, by contrast, paints glowing adjectival portraits, both imply that these powerful men have — by birth, education, and endeavor—laid the political and economic foundations for a modern nation. The Philippines is, they seem to say, the sum of these leading lives. In his ponderous, 2,624-page "encyclopedic directory" of the Commonwealth, Cornejo devotes nearly a third, 737 pages, to biographies of these nation builders, almost all of them wealthy or well-placed males.[30]

By the 1930s, biography had become pervasive within the Philippines. Most of the growing numbers of college graduates had short biographies beneath their photographs in their senior yearbooks. Every session of the National Assembly published a register with detailed descriptions of each legislator's education and personal life. Manila publishers launched lavish biographical registers of prominent citizens, and a number of their provincial colleagues followed suit. Trade journals like the *Sugar Central and Planters News* often featured biographies of prominent members.[31]

When independence finally came in 1946 amid the ruins of war, the initial biographical work was limited. But gradually it gained momentum to become perhaps the dominant historical enterprise of the postindependence decades. By the 1950s, the nation's historical establishment had launched itself on an ambitious project of documenting the lives of the new nation's heroes.[32] Significantly, a coincidental clustering of the birth centennials for the revolution's leaders from 1956 onward served to reinforce the biographical frame for postwar historiography. Indicative of the genre's centrality, nearly a quarter of the 279 historical markers that the National Historical Institute placed in Manila in postwar decades were for individuals.[33] "As a people desperately in search of an identity and whose unity since 1946 has been constantly beleaguered by seemingly insurmountable problems of national integration," explained historian Bonifacio Salamanca in a historiographic survey, "we Filipinos need symbols of national identification to help strengthen our sense of nationhood. Hence, our preoccupation with centennials, highlighted by the publication of biographies . . . [that] are an important integral part of Philippine historiographical literature."[34]

Written over a twenty-five-year period spanning the Commonwealth and the founding of the Republic, Gregorio Zaide's register of national heroes provides an apt index of the modern canon's standards. "The history of the Philippines reveals many names of great Filipinos, whose dalliance illumines the firmament of our storied past like the silver glow of the stars in a dark tropical night," Zaide writes in his preface. "Their achievements, which garlanded them with the mantle of greatness, are now cherished memories of the nation." Among his hundred subjects, about half, depending on how you count, are the traditional male heroes like presidents, generals, and leading professionals. Only fourteen of his subjects are women, and most are there as spouses and mothers of heroic males or nurturing figures cut from foreign molds—Marcela Mariña Agoncillo ("Maker of the Filipino Flag"), Teodora Alonso ("Mother of a National Hero"), or Mrs. Diego Silang ("Joan of Arc of Ilocandia"). Observing the demands of the heroic canon, Zaide sanitizes his subjects' lives, noting, for example, that painter Juan Luna "married the vivacious Paz Pardo de Tavera" in Paris but failing to mention that he soon murdered both his wife and his mother-in-law.[35]

While tenacious and persuasive, this postwar "national narrative"— once freed from the unifying pressure of colonial rule—proved neither stable nor homogenous. While canonical lives seem generally dominant (Rizal, presidents, great men), other trends range from the supplementary to the subversive. Above all, there have been many initiatives to enlarge and democratize the gallery of exemplary lives. An early memoir of the revolution by Santiago Alvarez incorporated messianic peasant movements in its narrative of national struggle.[36] This effort continues in the various biographical dictionaries (e.g., Zoilo Galang's *Encyclopedia*, the Cornejo *Commonwealth Directory*, the more recent *CCP Encyclopedia*, and various editions of *Who's Who*), and the National Historical Institute's multivolume *Filipinos in History*.[37]

In this regard, special mention must be made of E. Arsenio Manuel's monumental undertaking, the four-volume *Dictionary of Philippine Biography*. For more than forty years, Professor Manuel has been producing these thick tomes filled with wide-ranging biographies of politicians, revolutionaries, artists, intellectuals, and professionals who "have contributed something meaningful to the building of the Filipino nation . . . and also have distinguished themselves in the arts or creative endeavors thus enshrining the sciences and humanities." Instead of recycling the usual secondary sources, the author has shown a remarkable facility for ferreting out rare documents and unique illustrations to produce a rich source of historical information seldom available elsewhere.[38]

This national biographical effort has been replicated for various sectors and professions as well as at the regional or local levels, most notably by the *Bicol Biographical Encyclopedia*. With more than seven hundred entries for educators, professionals, and officials, this register broadens the canonical standard for significant lives by focusing on a remote region and above all by documenting the lives of middle and lower middle class people, including nearly eighty barrio officials.[39] In this vein, Luciano Santiago has run a veritable one-man crusade to publish the lives of obscured Filipino priests and *beatas* of the colonial period.[40] Beyond the immense value of these reference tools, the observation can be made that this effort does not alter the dominant national narrative; it merely incorporates more figures into an existing national hierarchy of significant lives.

Though relatively few, there are still some memorable sallies into antihagiography. Examples include Pedro Archutegui and Miguel Bernad's critical biography of Bishop Aglipay, Conchita Pedrosa's probing study of Imelda Marcos, and Pio Andrade's antiheroic account of Carlos Romulo. Each seems a response to extravagant mythmaking by or about their subjects. Through she professes to offer us a Cinderella story of Imelda Marcos's rise from a not so genteel poverty to Malacañang Palace, Pedrosa's book is in fact a searing analysis of the First Lady's profound insecurities and insatiable desire to possess.[41] After a similarly relentless pursuit of Romulo's duplicity and dishonesty, Andrade turned his fire upon the failings of a society that tolerated, even rewarded, this charlatan, damning those responsible for "the distortion of Philippine history . . . in the name of nationalism": the Manila press, the University of the Philippines, and the nation's intellectuals.[42] In this vein, Ricardo Manapat's *Some Are Smarter Than Others,* particularly its original samizdat publication, struck a major blow at the Marcos regime and its heroic propaganda—an antiheroic effort he continued with his *Smart File* once the dictatorship had fallen. Indeed, more than half of this book's densely documented 617 pages are biographies of the courtier families and individual cronies who joined the Marcoses in plundering the nation under the protection of martial rule. Beyond formal publications, if political campaign biographies are prominent then there are also counterrepresentations, scurrilous attacks against the same candidates in the form of cartoons, leaflets, and gossip.[43]

Perhaps the biographies by Nick Joaquin, Resil Mojares, and Ambeth Ocampo cannot best be styled *antihagiographic,* a term that would seem to connote, as in the Pedrosa and Andrade volumes, aggressive muckraking. They might better be styled "demystifying moves." Here one might ask whether the practice of humanizing or normalizing heroes, which Ocampo employs repeatedly, serves to reinforce or subvert the canon.[44] On a more decidedly critical note, Mojares's biography of a leading postwar politician, Serging Osmeña, uses this close study of a single career to lay "the groundwork of understanding of a political culture which is not only of the past but is still, distressingly so, as much a part of our present as well."[45] On an expressly reformist note, the Institute for Popular Democracy has used biographical research to expose the persistence of political families and bosses at both the regional and national levels.[46]

At the broadest level, Nick Joaquin's *A Question of Heroes* subverts the genre itself. Written as a mosaic of luminous fragments that form a larger picture, this extended essay arrays antihagiographic biographies chronologically to interrogate the origins of Filipino nationalism and the meaning of its revolution. The individual portraits are sharply, sometimes savagely critical, holding these national heroes to account for personal failings that blocked them from realization of their historical moment. The revolution's leader, General Emilio Aguinaldo, was "unheroic of intellect . . . anti-heroic in spirit," ultimately a "small man with little imagination" who failed to take Manila when history offered him the capital and the nation that came with it. General Gregorio del Pilar, the "hero of Tirad Pass," was simply Aguinaldo's brutal "hatchet man," whose death at revolution's end was not heroism but stupidity. In these antibiographies, Joaquin rejects a dominant historiography that thinks "heroism can cover up for our botches," arguing that "where . . . we should burn with shame for our ineptitude, there are we made to feel justified in our very stupidities—and in going on acting stupid." History's legacy, Joaquin seems to say, is too persistent, too important to be reduced to model heroes and their storybook heroism.[47]

Moreover, there are biographies that use an individual life as an axis or entry point into what is essentially a larger social, political, or intellectual history, most notably Renato Constantino on Recto, Cesar A. Majul on Mabini, and Reynaldo C. Ileto on Datu Uto.[48] In a parallel vein, biographies of opposition figures, most importantly those from the Left, are inherently subversive of the political order though they may not be anticanonical, at least as far as the genre is concerned. Examples of biographies that transform antistate revolutionaries from subversives to heroes abound: Benjamin Pimentel on Edjop, Jose Dalisay on the Lavas, Teodosio Lansang's autobiography, and Luis Taruc's two biographies. Turning back to the revolutionary era, one could include the early writings of Antonio K. Abad and Jose P. Santos on Macario Sakay and *tulisanes,* and, much more recently, Orlino Ochosa's book on Sakay, Luciano San Miguel, and Julian Montalban.[49] The interest in earlier figures can be viewed as a part of the Rizal-Bonifacio debate, the long-standing and continuing tension between official nationalism and national-popular movements. Such tension creates openings for oppositional, even marginal figures.

Recent years have seen numerous publications on women's lives, most notably the biographies of women writers by Virginia Licuanan, Edna Z. Manlapaz, Marjorie Evasco, and others.[50] The works of Manlapaz, in particular, are written from what seems to be a self-conscious feminist position that problematizes the biographical form itself. In her portraits of contemporary Filipina writers, Manlapaz probes the genre's limits, telling us in her study of poet Angela Manalang Gloria, for example, that she will use her own imagination to take us "from the orbit of fact into the orbit of fiction." She will write like a director shooting a film: "What you will see is only what the eye of the camera allows you to see. . . . This biography is not the story of the life of Angela Manalang Gloria. It is *my* story of *her* life." Indeed, going far beyond the canon's usual methods, Manlapaz juxtaposes, Rashomon-like, variant accounts of the same incident and devotes pages to examining photographs just to elicit her subject's emotions.[51]

Alongside these larger biographical forms, there are small, fledgling fields of promise. At the documentary level, several writers have published primary data, for example, the work of Doreen Fernandez and Edilberto Alegre, the Manlapaz/Evasco volume, and Ambeth Ocampo's interview with Teodoro Agoncillo.[52] Over the past half century, moreover, there have been a few efforts to collect life histories of ordinary people such as women, migrants, and workers. The tradition of "life histories" can be traced to the influence of the anthropological life history, first presented by expatriate Roy Barton in his *Autobiographies of Three Pagans*.[53] Even within the large and diverse practice of elite biography, there are sizable gaps, especially in the paucity of business biographies. Much of what is available is either commissioned (e.g., from Ed. C. de Jesus and Carlos Quirino) or thin (such as a recent La Salle University pamphlet on prominent businessmen Lucio Tan, Gokongwei, Manuel Villar, and others). Although there is a need to interrogate those with power rather than those without, unlike politicians businessmen are private and hence there is a continuing problem of transparency and access.[54]

There remain, of course, biographies that are essentially appreciative, or even laudatory, but still interesting in their defense or clarification of aspects of a controversial career (see, e.g., Jose Del Castillo's biography of Jose P. Laurel; Teodoro Agoncillo on Jorge Vargas; and even Lewis Gleeck on Harry Stonehill).[55] Among many possible contenders, Kerima Polotan's celebratory biography of Imelda Marcos stands out as a triumph of this form. Published a year after Pedrosa's critical study, this is a biography that the First Lady might well regard as a self-portrait. "For Madam wears well as a person, and endures exceedingly as a woman," writes Polotan in the book's last lines. "No one like her will come around again in a long time, and when she goes, we will all have to wait for another, but we will wait, sustained by the afterglow of everything that Madam dreamt of and reached for."[56]

Despite all this variety and creativity, the canonical form, with its heroic style and hagiographic strictures, has persisted throughout the twentieth century. Coinciding rather approximately with each of the country's major transitions during the past century, substantial, sometimes massive, biographical compilations have appeared, usually ranging from two to seven hundred entries, sharing similar standards as to what constitutes a significant life, excluding criticism, and above all expressing the didactic aim of inspiring the nation's youth with role models for service and sacrifice. Indeed, in the celebration of the revolution's centennial during the last years of the twentieth century, this classical, canonical form seemed to be ascendant again.

This centennial saw an effort to track down and honor "forgotten/lesser known" heroes, such as Muslims, women, and provincials, notably in Rafaelita Soriano's edited volume *Women in the Revolution*. Although she has broadened the biographical canon to include women, Soriano tells us that her ultimate aim is still that of her predecessors: "strengthening the moral fiber of the Filipino people."[57] Of the thirty women featured, sixteen are included simply because they were related by blood or marriage to male revolutionary leaders. For example, the national martyr Jose Rizal alone accounts for five entries—his mother, his wife, two sisters, and a niece. Only three entries are drawn from outside Luzon. Nonetheless, the balance, or nearly half the book, features women who actually fought in the revolution as agitators, couriers, spies, nurses, soldiers, and combat commanders.[58] This initiative is laudable, but one wonders to what extent and in what way this work can be viewed as an effort to incorporate the marginal into an unchanging national narrative (the large narrative in which smaller ones are embedded).

Similarly, the five-volume *Filipinos in History*, a compilation of nearly seven hundred biographies published by the National Historical Institute between 1989 and 1996, exhibits an often innovative selection within the canon's standard for significant lives, adding second-tier military officers, human rights activists, businessmen, athletes, and film directors to the past mix of revolutionary leaders, World War II heroes, and nationalist intellectuals. Even so, the volume's preface, echoing the didactic credo of past compendia, tells us that its aim is to present "biographies of noted Filipinos whose lives . . . have left lasting influences and inspiration to the present and future generations of Filipinos." Though innovative in its selections and rich in useful information, the collection still treats each subject as a hero exempt from criticism. For example, the biography of Fred Ruiz Castro, chief justice of the Supreme Court under martial law, describes his courage and fame without mentioning that he was Marcos's crony inside the court, the key figure who blocked attempts to challenge the legality of the dictatorship and its human rights abuses.[59]

There have been some parallel centennial efforts by independent writers and publishers. To inspire the nation's youth, politician Tito Guingona selected ten "brave Filipinos," six of them World War II heroes, so that readers could "hopefully draw a share of gallantry from their lifeless hands."[60] Similarly, academic Asuncion David Maramba produced two important biographical compendia that stretched and affirmed the genre's norms. Her first effort, *Six Modern Filipino Heroes*, is canonical in its heroic form (the chapter on Benigno S. Aquino Jr. is entitled "The Making of a Martyr"), its gender ratio (five men, one woman), and its aims. "Our youth need heroes," she explains, "closer to their time who will carry the torch from the heroic wave of Rizal's generation to their own era; heroes that must now figure in history." Reflecting our less reverential times, the volume does not sanitize each account, and it even details Aquino's controversial service as a CIA operative in Indonesia.[61] After publishing these biographies of the elders of the anti-Marcos movement, editor Maramba, concerned that others of "our recent heroes . . . would never be lifted from obscurity," assembled six women writers, most of them political moderates, to produce biographies of six young martyrs, five of them male and all radical leftists.[62] These latter-day heroes emerged from the student activism of pre–martial law days to struggle and die in opposition to the Marcos dictatorship. With a common plot of early brilliance, selfless sacrifice, and untimely death, the biographies, despite their unusual celebration of the revolutionary Left, follow the hagiographic form (activists come to support revolution after a personal struggle for enlightenment, like the beatified to Christ). Significantly, the authors do not question their subjects' decisions to join the Communist Party and give their lives to its strategy of armed struggle. That six skilled writers, all journalists with a proven capacity for critical analysis, would sink to such an uncritical treatment seems to indicate the persistence and significance of hagiography within the dominant canons of Philippine biography.

Heroic Biography

In 1963, at the close of a distinguished career as a legislator and history professor at the University of the Philippines, Gabriel Fabella, then president emeritus of the Philippine Historical Association, indulged in a revealing reminiscence. Looking back on his student days at Manila High School, he mused, "Until now I cannot understand why that early [1913] I was already imbued with admiration and love for our national heroes." Then, as partial explanation, he told a story. As a child, even though he had no money, he often walked to the bookstore Libreria de J. Martinez on Calle Rosario in Binondo just to look at the books. "What attracted me most in that bookstore was a picture, or rather a symbolic representation of our very illustrious great. The frame contained sketches . . . of the 'Filipino Ilustres,'" he explained. "I loved to look at the faces of the men who made our history. I judged their greatness by the position they occupied. . . . On the front row seated at center was Jose Rizal, so I thought he was the greatest of them all. On his right was Andres Bonifacio. . . . On Rizal's left was Apolinario Mabini. . . . Others on the front row were Jose Burgos, Antonio Luna, Marcelo H. del Pilar and two or three more." Despite a long career as a professional historian, Fabella admitted that he "could not improve upon that man's evaluation" although the intervening decades had produced some presidents who should be added to this framed pantheon: Manuel Quezon, Sergio Osmeña, Manuel A. Roxas, and perhaps Ramon Magsaysay.[63]

Beneath its surface charm, this anecdote is layered with insight into the influence of hagiography upon postwar historiography. As Fabella implies, in the early years of this century, not long after Rizal's martyrdom and the revolution's defeat, children seemed to imbibe an abiding respect for national heroes. Raised in such a culture of reverence, Fabella and many others in his generation of historians remained convinced that their main intellectual challenge was the ranking of heroes within that metaphorical pantheon. Probing further, we can discern an underlying religious influence that shaped the nation's agenda for historical research despite its nominally secular, even anticlerical, tenor. Just as Rizal carried a sketch of the Virgin of Antipolo on his voyage from childhood to martyrdom, so Fabella held a mental image of Rizal and his fellow heroes throughout his journey from student to professor, much like the devout within the Philippine iconic tradition who meditate not only upon a text but upon an image of a saint or martyr.

In the first decades following independence in 1946, the nation's leading historians affirmed the heroic paradigm but began to question Rizal's position at its apex. After its formation in 1956, the Philippine Historical Association devoted itself to celebrating the nation's past presidents and drafted legislation for a proposed national historical commission, which would, in the words of historian Teodoro Agoncillo, "publish the biographies and works of great Filipinos."[64] For a time, Rizal seemed tainted by the colonial embrace, and nationalist historians like Professor Fabella searched systematically for alternatives. "And who among our illustrious great," he called out, "can dislodge Rizal from his position of primacy in the national pantheon?"[65]

After a decade's research, the nation's top historians had their answer: nobody else could meet this religious standard for secular heroism. The propagandist Graciano Lopez Jaena had fled arrest and possible execution to die obscurely in Spain, thus "missing the . . . glory and immortality now enjoyed by Rizal."[66] One historian from the University of the Philippines argued in vain that the death of Marcelo H. Del Pilar from malnutrition made him the real martyr. "It is then easy enough to die by the firing squad," he wrote, "but to die of hunger is probably the hardest of all."[67] Another likely candidate, General Aguinaldo, failed on one key criterion. "His long life span," wrote Agoncillo, "robbed him of the chance to make himself the foremost Filipino hero. Had he died in battle . . . his monument today would have graced every town plaza."[68] Rizal's biographer, Leon Guerrero, seconded this view, remarking that the general's "real tragedy is that he did not die." Filipinos, he concluded, have chosen Rizal "unanimously, irrevocably" because "we reserve our highest homage and deepest love for the Christ-like victims."[69] In 1896, Rizal walked to his death calmly; in 1637, Lorenzo Ruiz, the first Filipino saint, had told his Japanese executioners, "I am now willing to give up my life for God. You can do with me whatever you please."[70]

More broadly, the postwar historians affirmed the central place of heroic biography on the nation's intellectual agenda. The two decades following independence witnessed an extraordinary outpouring of serious academic biography, book-length works and dozens of shorter biographies (in the form of single essays and special issues) that filled the pages of the *Historical Bulletin*, then the country's premier journal.[71] Although this biographical project dominated the historical agenda, in some quarters it was bitterly contested. When Agoncillo's biography won first prize in a competition commemorating the centennial of Bonifacio's birth, the Catholic Church sparked a major controversy over press freedom by successfully demanding that the government printer refuse publication of any work it deemed anticlerical. Had not the president of the University of the Philippines ordered his press to publish the book, it might have remained in manuscript.[72]

In lectures, articles, and radio addresses, this postwar generation of historians affirmed the intellectual importance of biography. At the first national conference of history teachers in 1963, Domingo Jhocson, head of National University, argued that their prime task was "the moral and spiritual uplift of the young through an analysis of personal qualities of the heroes and heroines of the past." History, he added, "should not be a mental inventory of historical facts chronologically arranged" but "an inventory of worthy impulses and lofty ideals." Since "youth is a period of hero worship," a student must identify with "commanding personalities in history" who can "greatly influence his patterns of behavior." Beyond character formation, biography, he argued, is an effective tool for teaching the past since it is "an embodiment of the customs, traditions and mores of the age" even when the subject matter is foreign, "as in world history and in the stories of the Bible."[73]

Significantly, this faith in the pedagogic power of biography found an echo in postwar Philippine religious publications. In the introduction to her oft-reprinted *Lives of Saints*, Anna Bagadiong of Manila's Pauline sisters wrote that saints are not simply those who could "predict a future event with perfect accuracy . . . or float in the air during a vision." No, she explained, saints "are very much like us," living under the same sun and through the same seasons: "When the Church canonizes a saint, She is proclaiming before the world an exemplary life which the faithful can imitate."[74]

Though professional historians have moved beyond heroic biography since the 1970s, the genre's influence has persisted in the realm of popular and public history. After the publication of the heroic biographies of the 1950s and 1960s, Philippine historians broadened the discipline's focus with explorations in social, economic, and regional history.[75]

18   Alfred W. McCoy

Simultaneously, a new generation of historians, some of them American, began to pursue a range of regionally based social and economic histories.[76] More recently, Filipino and foreign historians have produced broad national studies of crime, disease, familial politics, urbanization, and militarization.[77] Nonetheless, all of this academic research has done little to diminish the centrality of heroic biography within school curricula, popular consciousness, and public life.

Popular Biography

Under the postwar Republic, biographers worked within now well-established cultural parameters, helping to legitimate a political elite shaken by its colonial compromises and lacking a claim to aristocratic lineage. Drawing upon his comparative study of nationalism, Benedict Anderson has argued that biography is thus uniquely prevalent in the Philippines. Indeed, among the peoples of Southeast Asia, Filipinos, he argues, seem to have embraced biography and autobiography with unequaled ardor. While the causes and cultural roots of the phenomenon are complex, the source of this popular fascination may lie in the quest for legitimacy in a society in which traditional status indicators have been superseded by prolonged colonialism and an aggressive capitalism that has remade the society several times over.[78] Without the ingrained confidence that comes from traditional titles or continuity of rule, Filipino elites have compensated, using biography to attach distinction to their names.

By the 1980s, it had become possible trace the lives of prominent figures through a succession of biographies—high school and college yearbooks, professional registers, political biographies and autobiographies—and, if the individual was successful enough, a posthumous biography published by an honorary committee of family and friends. To cite a military example, we can follow the career of Commodore Ramon Alcaraz through seven biographies, short and long, published between 1940 and 1990.[79]

Just as we can track individual leaders through the arc of their lives, so we can survey whole strata of the nation's political leadership through biography. Since 1946, most presidential contenders have followed their petitions for candidacy with the well-publicized launching of a celebratory biography. And many of those in the first or second tier of the country's political life are the subjects of posthumous biographies, often written in the hagiographic tones otherwise reserved for saints and national heroes.[80] Some frame their writing in religious rhetoric, such as Olivera when he invokes a priest who calls his subject, Jose Yulo, "a saint. . . , a complete and extraordinary man."[81] In the 1980s, moreover, economically powerful families such as the Lopezes, Ayalas, and Cojuangcos began publishing genealogies and family histories clarifying their lineages, celebrating their progenitors, and seeking perhaps to legitimate their exceptional wealth at a time of political instability.[82]

Marcos and the Heroic Genre

Testifying to the genre's authority, President Ferdinand Marcos appropriated heroic biography and made it the ideological foundation for his fourteen years of authoritarian rule (1972–86). From the outset of his political career in the late 1940s, Marcos self-consciously constructed a record that would meet the canonical standard for heroic biography. While other politicians were trading in the coin of patronage and cash, Marcos took his political profits in World War II military decorations, emerging from fifteen years in the legislature with some thirty medals that supposedly made him the most decorated soldier in Philippine history.

Marcos's 1965 campaign biography, *For Every Tear a Victory,* claimed that "without Ferdinand's exploits Bataan would have fallen three months sooner. . . . In a very real sense . . . Ferdinand Marcos . . . made a contribution to the war that was of enormous consequence to the world." Protected by the "intervention of magical forces," Marcos emerged from the war's bloodiest battles unharmed, a leader destined for greatness.[83] A Filipino-language feature film based on this campaign biography, *Iginuhit ng Tadhana* (Marked for Destiny), replete with scenes depicting Marcos's wartime heroism, was released just a few months prior to the election.[84] In a deft manipulation of the heroic genre, this biography set aside the Catholic rhetoric of martyrdom and described him as divinely predestined within the martial and magical frame of the archipelago's pre-Hispanic religion.

Once elected, President Marcos summoned the country's leading artists to celebrate his wartime heroism. In 1980, for example, the last year of the formal martial law regime, first lady Imelda Marcos commissioned a four-hundred-page epic poem by E. Arsenio Manuel, a biographer and anthropologist, and Florentino Hornedo, a literary critic. By pairing the legend of "Malakas and Maganda" (Strength and Beauty) with the story of "Ferdinand and Imelda," the epic portrays the first couple as the reincarnation of ancient spirits—a sense of temporal transcendence introduced in verses celebrating Marcos's heroism in the Battle of Bataan.[85]

> He gained consciousness, his essence awakened
> In front of his confused countrymen
> At the top of Mount Samat . . .
> He sang the meaningful history
> Which was strengthened by our ancestors,
> Where each syllable is a source of strength,
> Even in a darkness with no light
> Except from the bursting of bombs
> And the bullets speeding like meteors.

Soon after taking office in 1966, Marcos promoted a soaring war memorial on Mt. Samat at the heart of the Bataan battlefield as a monument to his heroism. In 1969, after four years of construction, the president led a crowd of fifteen thousand to the summit, now crowned by a three-hundred-foot steel cross atop a lavish, marble-clad war museum.[86] Twelve years later, during his 1981 visit to Manila, Pope John Paul II boarded a helicopter and at Marcos's request flew over Mt. Samat to bless this cross. Since the Pope was in Manila to preside over the beatification of Lorenzo Ruiz, who later became the first Filipino saint, this was a small act of profound significance. With a simple blessing, the Pope made Mt. Samat a shrine, and by analogy honored Marcos as a hero, just as he would soon beatify Ruiz as a martyr.[87] At this convergence in the country's multiple heroic traditions, Marcos struggled, with momentary success, to twist the conjunction in ways that affirmed his heroism and the dictatorship that it legitimated.

Two years later, however, Benigno "Ninoy" Aquino returned home to die a martyr before military executioners, stealing the Rizal-like heroism that Marcos had so assiduously cultivated and subverting the ideological foundations of his authoritarian regime. Writing of Ninoy and Rizal, biographer Nick Joaquin has remarked that they both died "in the knowledge that their sacrifice would make the calendars of history, the altars of nationalistic devotion."[88] In one of history's ironies, the hagiographic genre ultimately defeated Marcos's heroic aura, subverting his authority and driving him into exile.

Biography from Below

Faced with the breadth and density of the genre, scholars of the Philippines are, like historians of nation-states elsewhere, confronted with a formidable task when they engage biography either critically or creatively. After decades of popularization, if not vulgarization, during the nineteenth century, historians had begun to question, and even reject, biography by the century's turn. In 1903, for example, François Simi and published an influential call for historians to abandon the "idol" of the individual in favor of a more scientific history. "The historian," G. R. Elton intoned in the mid-1960s, "should not suppose that in writing biography he is writing history."[89]

Though ambivalent about biography, other prominent historians began to problematize the genre, seeking, albeit with limited success, the intersection between Lucien Febvre's "historical individuals" and larger collective forces, the impersonal tides of economic and social change.[90] Over time, a confluence of disciplinary innovations—history's recasting of the great man, prosopography, psychohistory, and anthropology's life history—gradually revitalized academic biography. Writing in 1978 in words relevant to this volume, Robert Gittings argued that "a fruitful field lies in biography of an obscure person, who by some fortune is connected with important events or institutions, and whose history throws an unexpected, revealing light on these." By the early 1990s, biographers such as Moshe Zimmermann could proclaim with a confidence not seen for a century that "the historian should approach biography as a pivotal element of historical research." Biography, he argued, can provide broad insight into the historical process if it meets three criteria: looking not just at the person but at a larger "historical phenomenon," probing beneath the surface for a depth of motivation or complexity, and exploring not just individual idiosyncrasies but interactions with the wider society.[91] By this time, of course, the tape recorder and television camera, which made it possible to interview ordinary eyewitnesses to history, had already won biography a mass audience far beyond anything that could have been imagined in the nineteenth century.[92]

Not all of these innovations appear to be equally promising for the Philippines. Given the limited influence of psychiatry and psychology, psychohistory retains certain distinctly European resonances that may limit its acceptance. Leaving aside prosopography, which is almost antibiographical, the most fruitful approach seems to lie in exploring the lives of those whose obscurity may reveal larger historical phenomena. In their studies of otherwise ordinary individuals who have acted as agents of mass action, the essays in this volume adopt the approach that Gittings recommended more than twenty years ago.

This volume thus adopts biography to explore, above all, aspects of the country's social processes and social history. Most of the essays attempt brief biographies of figures who are ordinary or, from a national perspective, obscure, seeking through them to better understand the dynamics of Philippine society and, at the theoretical level, the interaction between the collective and the individual. More broadly, by historicizing the heroic and hagiographic forms, Resil Mojares, along with several of the other contributors, problematizes the genre's processes and politics.

In his study of the campaign for the canonization of Pedro Calungsod launched by the Cebu archdiocese in 1991, Mojares examines the meta-text of Philippine biography, arguing that hagiography is the country's "dominant structure of meaning, through which persons and lives are conferred and assured 'significance.'" While his earlier essay on the first Filipino biography, cited above, studied the narrative structure of the *vita sancti*, here Mojares examines how the Church makes a saint, that is, how it renders a human life within a particular biographical form in ways that will result in sainthood. Established in the eleventh century and systematized in the next two, the Vatican's review of candidates for canonization became the most elaborate judicial process in the world, producing only five hundred saints since 1234 and leaving a backlog of more than a thousand cases dating to the fifteenth century. In 1983, Pope John Paul II, an advocate of accelerated canonization, transferred much of the process back to the dioceses, thus making the Cebu church responsible for transforming Pedro Calungsod's little-known death on Guam in 1672 into the stuff of martyrdom. As the subsequent investigation found, his birthplace is unknown, his name is uncertain, and his life, other than his accidental death at the side of a great Jesuit martyr, is obscure. Once converts who required instruction in the lives of saints, Cebu's clergy and laity have so mastered hagiography that against great odds they can represent one of their own as fulfilling the requirements of the form. Even though Calungsod's biography is remarkable only in its "incompleteness and ordinariness," the faithful, Mojares argues, only wish to "glimpse a larger meaning" in its fragments. Thus, in the fullness of time they "will tell his story according to their desire."

Glenn May makes a similar point in his study of the hero Andres Bonifacio, which was first presented, along with these essays, at the Association for Asian Studies meetings in 1995 but was published elsewhere. Through a close examination of the documents used in biographies by historians Epifanio de los Santos and his son Jose Santos, May argues that they gave the hero Andres Bonifacio "a childhood that probably bore little resemblance to his real childhood, attributed poems and prose works to him that he likely did not write . . . and altered key events in his life beyond recognition." In trying to explain their motivation, he argues that both historians were "deeply committed to the ideal of Philippine nationhood" and thus created under the pressure of colonialism a heroic Bonifacio who could serve "as a symbol of Philippine nationalism and a model for Filipino youth." In their studies of hagiography, the process of rendering a life in a particular textual form, Mojares and May seem to argue that the two sets of Filipino biographers, the Santoses and the Cebuano clergy, though separated by many decades and very different agendas, share an underlying similarity in their pedagogical and methodological approaches to biography.[93]

While the remaining essays are for the most part narratives about the individual's interaction with the collective, some, such as Michael Cullinane's biography of Hilario Moncado, offer additional insights into the Philippine adaptation of the biographical genre. Born into a poor Cebuano family in 1895, Moncado organized a religious cult that eventually attracted thousands of Filipino followers in California, Hawaii, and the southern Philippines. As a master of spiritual syncretism, he incorporated both Catholic hagiography and Philippine heroic biography into his theology. One of his cult's "photo-graphics," which were popular with prewar members, showed Christ with his twelve disciples, Rizal with his twelve "*ilustres*," and Moncado with his twelve lodges. In another variation on the culture's exploration of the genre, the Iloilo City labor leader Jose Nava, the subject of Alfred McCoy's study, apparently internalized his childhood reading of Victor Hugo's biographical novel *Les Miserables* to plot a parallel life as a crusader against injustice, lead some of the country's largest strikes, and make a fateful decision to join the postwar communist revolt.

The core of this volume's application of biography to social analysis lies in four life histories of midstrata, working-class leaders of the middle decades of this century, the 1930s to the 1980s. In sum, these essays offer both a novel perspective on the character of the Philippine state and new insights into the mass movements that have challenged its authority. In his study of Dionisio Macapagal's half century of activism in his native central Luzon village, anthropologist Brian Fegan tries to cast light "on a submerged or subaltern politics concerned with militant nationalism and social justice," exploring linkages between diverse Philippine movements that are "dealt with in the dominant histories as if they were discrete and even distinct: millenarian movements, peasant unions, nationalist movements, and electoral parties." More broadly, Fegan found that this study "disabused me of any notion that there is a single peasant worldview or mentality or that it makes sense to talk about a dominant ideology."

Driving north on Highway 5 from Macapagal's Bulacan village for just a few hours, we would reach the town of Talavera in neighboring Nueva Ecija Province, where political scientist Benedict Kerkvliet has followed the career of Elena Santa Ana vda. de Maclang, a village-level activist some ten years younger than Mang Dionisio. Kerkvliet, like Fegan, feels that viewing peasant politics through the prism of a local leader opens him to insights obscured in broader national studies. Though Nana Elang's leadership style is "marginal to what popular media and most academics say about Philippine politics," she has nonetheless been "a central figure" in her native village for decades due to her "long involvement in land reform, economic development, and other vital social issues." Moreover, she "represents a type of political leadership that is probably more widespread in the country than mass media would suggest." At a theoretical level, Kerkvliet concludes that "patron-client and patrimonial analyses of Philippine politics are . . . limited." Relying exclusively on them obscures a whole category of community activist ignored in the Philippine studies literature.

Though sited on another island and in a later generation, anthropologist Rosanne Rutten's biography of a Negros plantation employee probes a parallel field of social interaction, reaching similar conclusions about the limitations of the current literature on Philippine politics. Through her biography of "Rafael" — a plantation clerk who became a union organizer, cadre of the communist guerrilla movement (CPP-NPA), and later an ally of the military's counterinsurgency campaign — she challenges the view of Negros as "a 'social volcano' with an amorphous mass of socially isolated and politically helpless workers suddenly exploding into violent protest." Her study

highlights the category of the enterprising poor, who have forged connections to church, state, and social movements beyond the plantation over-
lords and who, by forming an expanding stratum of community leaders,
have created a vast potential for lower-class political action in the region. At
a more theoretical level, this biography leads Rutten to view Filipino workers as part of a wider political arena in which power contenders, including
activist organizations and the state, "seek to mobilize the poor to reshape
local configurations of power." These competing mobilization campaigns —
which involve "a deliberate 'reframing' of people's perceptions about the
causes of their poverty and the solutions for which they should strive" —
have produced new opportunities for lower-class leadership and action.

Moving upward in the revolutionary hierarchy, Vina Lanzona's biography of Celia Mariano-Pomeroy, the only woman ever admitted to the
Politburo of the Philippine Communist Party, affords us an intimate view
of the Huk movement and the internal contradictions that contributed to
its collapse. Although many women fought with the guerrillas, eight of
them commanded Huk squadrons, and Mariano-Pomeroy herself reached
the hierarchy's apex, all have been obscured, and even forgotten, in subsequent histories and memoirs. Lanzona finds that biography has a
unique capacity to correct the male-centered biases of Philippine history,
rescuing these women from obscurity and thereby allowing a deeper
analysis of society and its social movements through an exploration of
gender. At the most basic level, Mariano-Pomeroy's biography makes
women visible for the first time in a general narrative history of the Huk
revolution. More broadly, her story challenges the dominant interpretations of the revolt by providing "a deeper understanding of the impact of
gender relations on the Huk movement" and exploring "how gender and
sexuality affect social . . . movements while transforming existing gender
orders . . . in society at large." Through this single life history, Lanzona
discovers the surprisingly corrosive impact of the party's contradictory
policy on gender, epitomized in its "revolutionary sex policy." In sum, the
story reveals "the contradiction between one individual's idealism and
the organization's limitations," thereby allowing a critical perspective on
the Huk movement that has sometimes eluded historians. By making the
"female experience part of the written record," biography, Lanzona concludes, forces us "to modify previously published accounts that did not
take women's experiences seriously . . . and therefore corrects the largely
male- and elite-biased Philippine historical record."

In striking contrast to Mariano-Pomeroy's idealism and Rafael's
activism, political scientist John Sidel examines two criminal careers on
the neighboring island of Cebu, an exercise that challenges a cluster of
social theories, especially Western writing on social banditry as a
precursor to rebellion and Filipino views, both academic and popular, of
crime as a form of resistance. Through his life and death history of Isabelo

"Beloy" Montemayor and Ulysses "Boboy" Alega, Sidel dismisses the heroic view of bandits as a form of academic mythology, arguing instead that these criminals were mafia, that is, "essentially predatory and conservative, their coercive resources deployed . . . in support of political domination." The state used Montemayor and Alega "as subcontracted law enforcement agents" to control the poor of a major city, "bearing witness not to the state's supposed weakness but to its strength" and thus raising for Sidel serious questions about the reigning view of the Philippine state as "chronically 'weak,' incapable of imposing 'order,' besieged by 'lawlessness' and 'unrest.'"

In their biographies of two powerful but forgotten figures from an earlier period, the essays by Patricio Abinales and Alfred McCoy lend credence to Sidel's view of the Philippine state as decentralized, even diffuse, yet resilient and paradoxically powerful. During the thirty years of direct U.S. rule, its colonial regime, a progenitor of the modern Philippine state, gradually reduced Datu Piang from a powerful local leader who controlled much of the Cotabato Valley to an instrument of the central administration. As Mindanao moved by stages "from a regional hub to an autonomous province and an integrated but peripheral fragment of the Philippines," Datu Piang, once "the most powerful Magindanao strongman of his time," slid into such obscurity that his death in 1933 passed without notice. Today his service to the colonial state has no place in a national narrative that seeks to "restore the Muslims' voice in Filipino nationalist discourse" through a myth of shared resistance to colonial rule.

This biography of Datu Piang, like each of the essays in this volume, also raises questions, both broad and narrow, that are significant within the history of its subject's time and place. Viewed from this perspective, Piang's biography shows how the Magindanaos of western Mindanao, once part of the complex, vibrant Southeast Asian trading network, were reduced to colonial "big men," living and operating in the narrow frame of the American state. Through Piang, one sees how these Magindanao *orang besar,* much like their comrades in the Malay states, sought means short of open revolt to adjust to the new colonial presence through tacit collaboration and negotiation. In the end, Datu Ali rebelled against the new American order, but Piang chose collaboration, an act that was reflective of his ability as a Malay *orang besar* to deal with more powerful forces but that also created the conditions for his transformation into a colonial big man, a servant of a rising central state that would exploit and ultimately extinguish his political autonomy. Just as Piang and his fellow *datus* were reduced, so Mindanao lost much of its autonomy and centrality in the process of state building. Viewed from a regional perspective, under the Spanish Mindanao had been a more important center than Manila because it was more fully integrated into the economic currents and political patterns of island Southeast Asia. But under the Americans the island would lose its centeredness and in the process become a mere periphery or frontier within an expanding colonial state.

Just as the Philippine state eroded the Muslim capacity for resistance at its southern periphery, so it proved equally capable of crushing militant labor and communist movements in the Western Visayas. During the depression decade of the 1930s, Jose Nava, the subject of Alfred McCoy's biography, built a mass following on the city's waterfront and used it to launch two general strikes that won workers a new social contract from the region's sugar industry. When the industry, its elite, and their gangster allies challenged his control of Iloilo's port after independence in 1946, Nava fought back with armed violence and an alliance with local communist guerrillas. Although the newly independent state was still suffering from crippling wartime damage, it nonetheless worked effectively, through its own agents and provincial adjuncts, to eliminate this threat to the reconstruction of the country's leading export industry, quickly breaking the communist revolt and banning Nava's union. In 1954, Nava, once the country's leading labor leader, died unmourned and unnoticed in a prison hospital awaiting execution.

Like most academic biography, these essays engage, at least by implication, the century-old question of agency versus structure, the individual versus the collective. Biographers of powerful leaders—whether at the head of states or revolutions—have tended to see individuals as empowered actors whose agency shapes the larger economic, social, cultural, and political processes of his or her age. With some exceptions, this biographical genre is ultimately heroic and usually celebratory of the great—saints, seers, kings, generals, and revolutionaries. Whether treating those who challenge, exemplify, or defend the social order, such biographies are similar in plot and purpose. The popular biographer within this genre often shows how the great man made his age, while the academic explores the opposite, but both share an assumption of their subject's inherent significance in the processes of change.

In contrast to this heroic view of history, there is a populist approach, not pursued in this volume, which focuses on those who remained ordinary participants in the daily life of their times. Such biography, usually oral, often avoids the activist minority and instead tries to give voice to the quiet majority by writing of ordinary lives that represent some larger cohort—soldiers, slaves, workers, women, or farmers.[94] Though this method offers much insight, it too has its limitations and should not preclude other approaches for the social historian or social scientist. To cite one obvious drawback, life history is not fully representative or egalitarian, for it cannot capture those who live truly private lives. It cannot render the resolutely inarticulate or inattentive. Historical research requires subjects industrious enough to have left some written testament or articulate enough to engage an anthropologist or oral historian. Sadly, the silent, whether rich or poor, leave no echoes for the historian and so will remain, as they have for all time, beyond biography.

Sited between these two extremes, the essays in this volume, reflecting the similarly pivotal position of their subjects, pursue a middle path between determinism and contingency by exploring the reciprocal influence of individual lives and the structures they inhabit, whether economic, ecological, cultural, or political. In the words of anthropologist Sidney Mintz, these biographies try to explain "how people are at once products and makers of social and cultural systems within which they are lodged."[95] In effect, they seem to affirm the observation of sociologist Philip Abrams that "history and society are made by constant and more or less purposeful individual action *and* that individual action, however purposeful, is made by history and society."[96]

Most of the biographers in this volume have in effect tied themselves to history's wheel, seeking to understand the process of change. As students of the Philippine past and present, they explore the dynamic of the whole, not just one part or one life. So directed, they have overlooked great men, silent spectators, and representative lives to study those whose secondary role in major events somehow lifted them out of the ordinary and then returned them to obscurity. Over the longer term, biographies of those at history's margins may encourage innovation within this genre, one day even allowing a critical reexamination of the great Filipino figures now enshrined in heroic biography.

NOTES

This essay has benefited significantly from a close reading by three anonymous readers at the Ateneo de Manila University Press and several of the volume's contributors. Most importantly, Resil Mojares drew upon his study of Philippine narrative forms to produce a critique that recast this essay and introduced a range of new sources. Similarly, Rosanne Rutten queried some of the original judgments and Patricio Abinales suggested additional points for analysis. Finally, Glenn May, who participated in the panel where the papers were first presented, offered a careful, critical reading of an earlier draft.

1. Resil Mojares, *Origins and Rise of the Filipino Novel: A Generic Study of the Novel until 1990* (Quezon City: University of the Philippines Press, 1983), 3.
2. Antonio Gramsci, *Further Selections from the Prison Notebooks* (Minneapolis: University of Minnesota Press, 1995), 156–57; Joseph V. Femia, *Gramsci's Political Thought: Hegemony, Consciousness, and the Revolutionary Process* (Oxford: Clarendon, 1981), 84–85, 162–63.
3. Pio A. de Pazos, *Heroes de Filipinas* (Santander: Imprenta Militar A. Cargo de A. de Quesada, 1888), 74–79.
4. Paul Ransome, *Antonio Gramsci: A New Introduction* (New York: Harvester/Wheatsheaf, 1992), 134.
5. Michelle Z. Rosaldo, *Knowledge and Passion: Ilongot Notions of Self and Social Life* (Cambridge: Cambridge University Press, 1980), 223.
6. Ibid., 228–31.
7. Ibid., 139.
8. Ibid., 166–68.
9. Mojares, *Origins and Rise of the Filipino Novel*, 11–15.
10. Ibid., 50–51, 52, 56–57, 60–61, 156–57.
11. Reynaldo Clemeña Ileto, *Pasyon and Revolution: Popular Movements in the Philippines, 1840–1910* (Quezon City: Ateneo de Manila University Press, 1979), 37–91.
12. Mojares, *Origins and Rise of the Filipino Novel*, 153–56.
13. Resil B. Mojares, "The Life of Miguel Ayatumo: A Sixteenth-Century Boholano," *Philippine Studies* 41 (1993): 437–55.
14. Nicholas Zafra, "Rizal and His Times," *Historical Bulletin* 1, no. 3 (March 1958): 9; Alban Butler, *Lives of the Saints for Every Day in the Year* (Rockford: Tan Books, 1995 [originally published in 1878]).
15. Barrie M. Ratcliffe, "The Decline of Biography in French Historiography: The Ambivalent Legacy of the 'Annales' Tradition," *Proceedings of the Annual Meeting of the Western Society of French History* 8 (1980): 556–57.
16. Nick Joaquin, *Rizal in Saga: A Life for Student Fans* (Manila: Philippine National Centennial Commission, 1996), 43; Epifanio de los Santos, "Andres Bonifacio," *Philippine Review*, nos. 1–2 (1918): 36.
17. Ileto, *Pasyon and Revolution*; Reynaldo C. Ileto, "The Idiom of Change in the Colonial Philippines: A 'People's Perspective,'" in *Church, State, and People – the Philippines in the 80's: Report and Papers of a National Theological Dialogue, Manila, Philippines, November 10–13, 1980,* edited by Feliciano V. Cariño, 45–59 (Manila: Commission on Theological Concerns, Christian Conference of Asia, 1981); Reynaldo C. Ileto, "Rizal and the Underside of Philippine

History," in *Moral Order and the Question of Change: Essays on Southeast Asian Thought,* edited by D. K. Wyatt and A. Woodside, 274–337 (New Haven: Program in Southeast Asian Studies, Yale University, 1982); Rene B. Javellana, S.J., "Pasyon Genealogy and Annotated Bibliography," *Philippine Studies* 31 (1983): 451–67; Rene B. Javellana, S.J., "The Sources of Gaspar Aquino de Belen's Pasyon," *Philippine Studies* 32 (1984): 305–21.
18. Leon Ma. Guerrero, *The First Filipino: A Biography of Jose Rizal* (Pasig City: Guerrero Publishing, 1998), 4–5.
19. Ibid., xiv.
20. Joaquin, *Rizal in Saga,* 2–4, 37–38, 111–14, 145, 231, 290, 299–300, 301–2.
21. Santos, "Andres Bonifacio," 34–58.
22. Eufronio M. Alip, "Jose Rizal, the Educator," *Journal of History* 5, nos. 1–2 (1957): 8; Napoleon J. Casambre, "The Forgotten Marcelo H. Del Pilar," *Historical Bulletin* 6, no. 3 (1962): 284–85.
23. Mojares, *Origins and Rise of the Filipino Novel,* 166–67.
24. Artemio Ricarte, *Memoirs of General Artemio Ricarte* (Manila: National Heroes Commission, 1963); Apolinario Mabini, *Memorias de la Revolucion Filipina* (Manila: Buro de la Imprenta Publica, 1960); Santiago Alvarez, *The Katipunan and the Revolution: The Memoirs of a General with the Original Tagalog Text* (Quezon City: Ateneo de Manila University Press, 1992); Emilio Aguinaldo, *My Memoirs: General Emilio F. Aguinaldo, President of the First Republic of the Philippines* (Manila: Crispina Aguinaldo Suntay, 1967); Teodoro M. Kalaw, *Aide-de-Camp to Freedom* (Manila: Teodoro M. Kalaw Society, 1965); Manuel Sityar, *Revolucion Filipina: Memorias Intimas* (Quezon City: Sentro ng Wika Filipino, University of the Philippines System, 1998); Rafael Palma, *My Autobiography* (Manila: Capitol Publishing House, 1953).
25. Manuel Artigas y Cuerva, *Galeria de Filipinos Ilustres,* vol. 1 (Manila: Imp. Casa Editorial "Renacimiento," 1917); Manuel Artigas, *The Events of 1872: A Historico-Bio-Bibliographical Account* (Quezon City: University of the Philippines Press, 1996); Teodoro M. Kalaw, *Gregorio H. del Pilar: El Heroe de Tirad* (Manila: Bureau of Printing, 1930); Teodoro M. Kalaw, *The Philippine Revolution* (Manila: Manila Book, 1925); Rafael Palma, *La Revolucion Filipina* (Manila: Bureau of Printing, 1931).
26. Felipe Calderon, *Mis Memorias Sobre la Revolucion Filipina: Segunda Etapa (1898 a 1901)* (Manila: Impr. de El Renacimiento, 1907), 7–8.
27. For examples of readers with biographical lessons, see Camilo Osias, *The Philippine Readers: Book Five* (Boston: Ginn, 1947); and *1940 Primer Series (Book III)* (Boston: Ginn, 1940).
28. Manual Artigas y Cuerva, *Andrés Bonifacio y el 'Katipunan': Reseña Historica Bio-Bibliográfica* (Manila: Imprenta de "La Vanguardia," 1911); *El General Antonio Luna y Novicio (Resena Bio-Bibliografica)* (Manila: Imprenta de La Vanguardia y Taliba, 1910).
29. Frank E. Jackson, ed., *The Representative Men of the Philippines* (Manila: E. C. McCullough, 1906); *Directorio Bibliográfico Filipino* (Manila: Imprenta y Litografia Germania, 1908); Artigas, *Galeria de Filipinos Ilustres,* vol. 1; Manuel Artigas y Cuerva, *Galeria de Filipinos Ilustres,* vol. 2 (Manila: Imprenta de Gabino A. Pobre, 1918); Morilla Maria Norton, *Builders of a Nation: A Series of Biographical Sketches* (Manila: E. C. McCullough, 1914).
30. George F. Nellist, *Men of the Philippines: A Biographical Record of Men of Substantial Achievement in the Philippine Islands* (Manila: Sugar News Press Co., 1931); Zoilo M. Galang, *Leaders of the Philippines: Inspiring Biographies of*

Successful Men and Women of the Philippines (Manila: National Publishing, 1932); M. R. Cornejo, ed., *Cornejo's Pre-War Encyclopedic Directory of the Philippines* (Manila: M. R. Cornejo, 1939).

31. See, for example, Narciso Pimentel, *Directorio Oficial de la Asemblea Nacional* (Manila: Bureau of Printing, 1938); Ignacio Villamor, *Industrious Men* (Manila: Oriental Commercial Co., 1930); George F. Nellist, ed., *Men of the Philippines* (Manila: Sugar News Co., 1931); Juan A. Cabildo, *Appraisals (Sketches of Outstanding Personalities)* (Manila: Philippine Herald, 1934); Nacionalista Party, *The Nacionalista Party before the Electorate* (Manila: Nacionalista Party, 1941); Andres R. Camasura, *Cebu-Visayas Directory* (Cebu City, 1932); Manuel H. David, ed., *Panay Directory and Souvenir Book* (Iloilo City: Ramon F. Campos, 1937); and *Sugar Central and Planters News* 18, no. 2 (January 1937): 40.

32. Jose de los Reyes, *Biography of Senator Isabelo de los Reyes, Father of Labor and Proclaimer of the Philippine Independent Church* (Manila: Nueva Era Press, 1947); Demerio T. Flaviano, *Business Leaders and Executives: Inspiring Biographies of Men and Women Who Became Successful* (Manila: FAL Service & Trading Co., 1950); Antonio K. Abad, *General Macario L. Sakay (The Only President of the "Tagalog Republic"): Was He a Bandit or a Patriot?* (Manila: J. B. Feliciano & Sons, 1952); Domingo Abella, *Bikol Annals: A Collection of Vignettes of Philippine History*, vol. 1 (Manila: Domingo Abella, 1954); Jose P. Laurel, *War Memoirs* (Manila: Jose P. Laurel Memorial Foundation, 1960); Elpidio Quirino, *The Memoirs of Elpidio Quirino* (Manila: National Historical Institute, 1990).

33. National Historical Institute, *Historical Markers: Metropolitan Manila* (Manila: National Historical Institute, 1993).

34. Bonifacio Salamanca, "Historiographical Literature, 1956–1993," *Philippine Encyclopedia of the Social Sciences*, vol. 1: *History* (Quezon City: Philippine Social Science Council, 1993), 87–94.

35. Gregorio Zaide, *Great Filipinos in History: An Epic of Filipino Greatness in War and Peace* (Manila: Verde Book Store, 1970), iii, 278.

36. Alvarez, *Katipunan*, 185–90.

37. Cultural Center of the Philippines, *CCP Encyclopedia of Philippine Art* (Manila: Cultural Center of the Philippines, 1994).

38. E. Arsenio Manuel, *Dictionary of Philippine Biography*, vol. 1 (Quezon City: Filipiniana Publications, 1955); E. Arsenio Manuel and Magdalena Avenir Manuel, *Dictionary of Philippine Biography*, vol. 4 (Quezon City: Filipiniana Publications, 1995), ix.

39. *Bicol Biographical Encyclopedia*, vol. 1 (Naga City: Bicol Research and Publication Center, 1968), 343.

40. Luciano P. R. Santiago, *The Hidden Light: The First Filipino Priests* (Quezon City: New Day, 1987).

41. Carmen Navarro Pedrosa, *The Untold Story of Imelda Marcos* (Rizal: Tandem, 1969), xv, 8–9. A less timely critical biography of Imelda Marcos was published by her niece, Beatriz Romualdez Francia, two years after the first family fled into exile. See *Imelda and the Clans* (Metro Manila: Solar, 1988).

42. Pio Andrade Jr., *The Fooling of America: The Untold Story of Carlos P. Romulo* (Manila: Pio Andrade Jr., 1990), 160–61.

43. Ricardo Manapat, *Some are Smarter Than Others: A History of Marcos's Crony Capitalism* (New York: Aletheia, 1991).

44. See, for example, Ambeth R. Ocampo, *Looking Back* (Pasig City: Anvil, 1990); *Rizal without the Overcoat* (Pasig City: Anvil, 1990); *Aguinaldo's Breakfast and More Looking Back Essays* (Pasig City: Anvil, 1993); *Mabini's Ghost* (Pasig City:

Anvil, 1995); *Bonifacio's Bolo* (Pasig City: Anvil, 1995); and *Luna's Moustache* (Pasig City: Anvil, 1997).
45. Resil Mojares, *The Man Who Would Be President: Serging Osmeña and Philippine Politics* (Cebu: M. Cacao, 1986), 4.
46. Jose F. Lacaba and Sheila S. Coronel, *Boss: 5 Case Studies of Local Politics in the Philippines* (Pasig, Metro Manila: Philippine Center for Investigative Journalism, Institute for Popular Democracy, 1995); Eric U. Gutierrez and Ildefonso C. Torrente, *All in the Family: A Study of Elites and Power Relations in the Philippines* (Diliman, Quezon City: Institute for Popular Democracy, 1992).
47. Nick Joaquin, *A Question of Heroes* (Manila: National Bookstore, 1981), 1-2, 21, 62-63, 69, 96-101, 123, 144-45; 160-61, 184, 202-3.
48. Renato Constantino, *The Making of a Filipino: A Story of Philippine Colonial Politics* (Quezon City: Malaya, 1969); Cesar A. Majul, *Apolinario Mabini: Revolutionary* (Manila: National Heroes Commission, 1964); Cesar Adib Majul, *Mabini and the Philippine Revolution* (Quezon City: University of the Philippines Press, 1996); Reynaldo C. Ileto, *Magindanao, 1860–1888: The Career of Datu Uto of Buayan* (Ithaca: Southeast Asia Program, Cornell University, 1971); Epifanio San Juan Jr., *Carlos Bulosan and the Imagination of the Class Struggle* (Quezon City: University of the Philippines Press, 1972).
49. Benjamin Pimentel, *Edjop: The Unusual Journey of Edgar Jopson* (Quezon City: KEN, 1989); Jose Dalisay, *The Lavas: A Filipino Family* (Quezon City: Anvil, 1999); Luis Taruc, *Born of the People* (New York: International, 1953); Luis Taruc, *He Who Rides the Tiger: The Story of an Asian Guerrilla Leader* (London: Chapman, 1967); Abad, *Gen. Macario L. Sakay*; Orlino A. Ochosa, *"Bandoleros": Outlawed Guerrillas of the Philippine-American War, 1903–1907* (Quezon City: New Day, 1995).
50. Virginia Benitez Licuanan, *Paz Marquez Benitez: One Woman's Life, Letters, and Writings* (Quezon City: Ateneo de Manila University Press, 1995); Edna Z. Manlapaz, *Our Literary Matriarchs, 1925–1953: Angela Manalang Gloria, Paz M. Latorena, Loreta Paras Sulit and Paz Marquez Benitez* (Quezon City: Ateneo de Manila University Press, 1996); Edna Z. Manlapaz, *Estrella D. Alfon: Her Life in Her Own Words/Star! A One-Woman Show* (Quezon City: University of the Philippines Press, 1997); Edna Z. Manlapaz and Marjorie Evasco, *Six Women Poets: Inter/Views with Angela Manalang-Gloria, Trinidad Tarrosa-Subido, Edith Tiempo, Virginia Moreno, Tita Lacambra-Ayala, Ophelia Dimalanta* (Manila: Aria Edition, 1996).
51. Edna Z. Manlapaz, *Angela Manalang Gloria: A Literary Biography* (Quezon City: Ateneo de Manila University Press, 1993), xi–xii, 28–32.
52. Edilberto N. Alegre and Doreen G. Fernandez, *Writers and Their Milieu: An Oral History of First Generation Writers in English* (Manila: De La Salle University Press, 1993); *Writers and Their Milieu, Part II: An Oral History of Second Generation Writers in English* (Manila: De La Salle University Press, 1993).
53. Roy Barton, *Autobiographies of Three Pagans in the Philippines* (New Hyde Park: University Books, 1963).
54. Ed. C. de Jesus and Carlos Quirino, *Earl Carroll: Colossus of Philippine Insurance* (Manila: E. Carroll, 1980); Lydia B. Echauz, Anna Isabel C. Sobrepeña, and Wilson Y. Lee Flores, *Business for All Series* (Manila: De La Salle University Press, 1997).
55. Jose Del Castillo, *The Saga of Jose P. Laurel (His Brothers' Keeper)* (Manila: Associated Authors' Company, 1949; Teodoro Agoncillo, *The Burden of Proof: The Vargas-Laurel Collaboration Case* (Manila: University of the Philippines Press for the UP-Jorge Vargas Filipiniana Center, 1984); Lewis Gleeck, *The Rise*

and Fall of Harry Stonehill in the Philippines: An American Tragedy (Manila: Lewis Gleeck, 1989).

56 Kerima Polotan, Imelda Romualdez Marcos: A Biography of the First Lady of the Philippines (Manila: Kerima Polotan, 1970), 206.

57. Rafaelita Hilario Soriano, ed., Women in the Philippine Revolution (Manila: National Centennial Commission, 1995), preface, vi.

58. Ibid., 142.

59. Filipinos in History, vol. 4 (Manila: National Historical Institute, 1994), i, 49–50.

60. Tito Guingona, The Gallant Filipino: Expanded Edition (Pasig City: Anvil, 1993), 11–12.

61. Asuncion David Maramba, Six Modern Filipino Heroes: Benigno S. Aquino, Jr., Jose W. Diokno, Estrelita G. Juco, Gaston Z. Ortigas, Joaquin P. Roces, Lorenzo M. Tañada (Pasig City: Anvil, 1993), 8, 27.

62. Asuncion David Maramba, ed., Six Young Filipino Martyrs (Pasig City: Anvil, 1997).

63. Gabriel F. Fabella, "Rizal and Bonifacio," Historical Bulletin 7, no. 3 (September 1963): 260–61.

64. Esteban A. De Ocampo, "News," Historical Bulletin 1, no. 1 (1957): 79–88.

65. Fabella, "Rizal and Bonifacio," 258.

66. Demy P. Sonza, "Graciano Lopez Jaena," Historical Bulletin 3, no. 4 (December 1959): 85.

67. Casambre, "The Forgotten Marcelo H. Del Pilar," 288.

68. Teodoro A. Agoncillo, "General Aguinaldo in History," Historical Bulletin 3, no. 1 (1959): 7.

69. Guerrero, First Filipino, 457–59.

70. Anna Bagadiong, F.S.P., Lives of Saints, rpt. (Pasay City: Paulines Publishing House, 1998), 169–72.

71. Manuel, Dictionary of Philippine Biography, vol. 1; Teodoro A. Agoncillo, The Revolt of the Masses: The Story of Bonifacio and the Katipunan (Quezon City: University of the Philippines, 1956); Majul, Apolinario Mabini.

72. Casambre, "The Forgotten Marcelo H. Del Pilar," 286.

73. Domingo L. Jhocson, "The Study of History and Moral Regeneration: Pre-Spanish and Spanish Periods," Historical Bulletin 7, no. 2 (1963): 100–102.

74. Bagadiong, Lives of Saints, 11–12.

75. See, for example, Ileto, Pasyon and Revolution; Milagros Guerrero, "The Provincial and Municipal Elites of Luzon during the Revolution, 1898–1902," in Philippine Social History: Global Trade and Local Transformations, edited by Alfred W. McCoy and Ed. C. de Jesus, 155–90 (Quezon City: Ateneo de Manila University Press, 1982); and Milagros Guerrero, "Luzon at War: Contradictions in Philippine Society, 1898–1902," Ph.D. diss., University of Michigan, 1977.

76. See, for example, John A. Larkin, The Pampangans: Colonial Society in a Philippine Province (Berkeley: University of California Press, 1972); McCoy and de Jesus, Philippine Social History; and Norman G. Owen, "The Principalia in Philippine History: Kabikolan, 1790–1898," Philippine Studies 22, nos. 3–4 (1974): 297–324.

77. See, for example, Greg Bankoff, Crime, Society, and the State in the Nineteenth Century Philippines (Quezon City: Ateneo de Manila University Press, 1997); Isagani R. Medina, Cavite before the Revolution (1571–1896) (Quezon City: College of Social Sciences and Philosophy, University of the Philippines, 1994); Ken De Bevoise, Agents of Apocalypse: Epidemic Disease in the Colonial Philippines (Princeton: Princeton University Press, 1995); Alfred W. McCoy, ed., An

Anarchy of Families: Filipino Elites and the Philippine State (Quezon City: Ateneo de Manila University Press, 1994); Daniel F. Doeppers, *Manila, 1900–1941: Social Change in a Late Colonial Metropolis* (New Haven: Program in Southeast Asian Studies, Yale University, 1984); and Ricardo Trota Jose, *The Philippine Army, 1935–1942* (Quezon City: Ateneo de Manila University Press, 1992).

78. Remarks by Benedict Anderson, discussant for the panel "Lives at the Margin: Biographies of Obscured Filipinos," Association for Asian Studies annual meetings, Washington, D.C., 7 April 1995.

79. First Class of the Philippine Military Academy, *The Sword of 1940* (Manila: The Sword, 1940); Ernesto O. Rodriguez, *Commodore Alcaraz: First Victim of President Marcos* (New York: Vantage, 1986); Ernesto O. Rodriguez, *Working with Heroes and Exiles* (New York: Vantage, 1989); Registry Committee, Association of General and Flag Officers, *General and Flag Officers of the Philippines (1896–1977)* (Manila: Association of General and Flag Officers, 1977); Jose M. Mendoza, ed., *Batch '36 Golden Book* (Manila: PMA Class '40 Association, 1986).

80. See, for example, Norberto Romualdez Centennial Committee, *Master of His Soul: The Life of Norberto Romualdez (1875–1941)* (Manila: National Historical Institute, 1975); Baldomero T. Olivera, *Jose Yulo: The Selfless Statesman* (Mandaluyong: University of the Philippines, Jorge B. Vargas Filipiniana Research Center, 1981); and Maria Kalaw Katigbak, *Few Were There (Like My Father)* (Manila: Teodoro M. Kalaw Society, 1974).

81. Olivera, *Jose Yulo*, 3.

82. Oscar M. Lopez, ed., *The Lopez Family: Its Origins and Genealogy* (Manila: Lopez Foundation, 1982).

83. Hartzell Spence, *Marcos of the Philippines: A Biography* (Cleveland: World Publishing, 1969), 7–10, 123.

84. Polotan, *Imelda Romualdez Marcos*, 123–30.

85. Remedios F. Ramos, E. Arsenio Manuel, Florentino H. Hornedo, and Norma G. Tiangco, *Si Malakas at Si Maganda* (Manila: Jorge Y. Ramos, 1980), 5–9. I am indebted to Vina Lanzona for this translation.

86. *Manila Times*, 9 April 1969, 10 April 1969; Col. Manuel A. Acosta, "Our Military Memorials," *Self-Reliance in Freedom: Speeches and Writings on Philippine Defense and National Growth* (Manila: Philippine Education Promotion, 1976), 231–36.

87. *Bulletin Today*, 22 February 1981.

88. Joaquin, *Rizal in Saga*, 273–74.

89. Quoted in Ratcliffe, "Decline of Biography," 557.

90. Ibid., 557–62.

91. Moshe Zimmermann, "Biography as a Historical Monograph," *Tel Aviver Jahrbuch fr. Deutsche Geschichte* 20 (1991): 449–57.

92. David King Dunaway, "The Oral Biography," *Biography* 14, no. 3 (1991): 256–58.

93. Glenn Anthony May, "Andres Bonifacio: Invented Hero," paper presented at the Association for Asian Studies annual meetings, Washington, D.C., 7 April 1995; *Inventing a Hero: The Posthumous Re-creation of Andres Bonifacio* (Quezon City: New Day, 1997), chap. 2.

94. Nan Hackett, "A Different Form of 'Self': Narrative Style in British Nineteenth-Century Working-Class Biography," *Biography* 12, no. 3 (1989): 208–26.

95. Quoted in Dunaway, "Oral Biography," 259.

96. Philip Abrams, *Historical Sociology* (Ithaca: Cornell University Press, 1982), xiii.

Devotional Card to support the beatification of Pedro Calungsod, ca. 1994.

THE EPIPHANY OF PEDRO CALUNGSOD, SEVENTEENTH-CENTURY VISAYAN MARTYR

Resil B. Mojares

> B ut those things which have no significance of their own are inter-
> woven for the sake of the things which are significant.
> —Saint Augustine, *The City of God*

The making of saints is a rich model for what makes for "significant" lives. It involves judgments of which lives are exemplary and which lives are not. It conjures as well the contexts in which such judgments are made and how such contexts compel belief. It is a study in the dynamics of meaning and power.

Lives assume significance through the structures of meaning through which they are lived and remembered. To expand in space, persist in time, and grow in consequence, such lives must be seen as important in constituting such structures and making them socially persuasive and dominant. The canonization of persons as "saints" in the Roman Catholic Church offers us an example of a well-articulated, institutionalized, and (in the Philippines) dominant structure of meaning through which persons and lives are conferred and assured "significance."

Hagiology, the identifying and popularizing of saints, provides us with an entry point for understanding what makes for "significant" (and, conversely, "marginal") lives. In another essay,[1] I had the occasion to dwell on hagiography, the problem of writing saints' lives (*vita sancti*), specifically in their popular form as devotional texts that aim not so much to document lives as to enhance the faith of the faithful by offering to them, in a highly conventional narrative, a model of behavior. Here I shift focus to the problem of how, in the first place, saints are determined and discovered. I shall dwell on the case of current moves in the Philippines (specifically, the Archdiocese of Cebu) for the beatification of a seventeenth-century Visayan named Pedro Calungsod.

Promoting a Cause

In 1991, the Archdiocese of Cebu initiated moves for the beatification of
Pedro Calungsod, a Visayan who was martyred in Guam on 2 April 1672
while serving as a lay catechist in the Jesuit mission in the Marianas.[2] Prior
to these moves, virtually no one in the Cebuano community knew of
Pedro Calungsod.

The beatification move was occasioned by preparations for the 1995
quadricentennial of the elevation of Manila as an archdiocese and the creation of the dioceses of Cebu, Nueva Caceres, and Nueva Segovia, and the
expected visit to the Philippines of Pope John Paul II in 1995 for both the
quadricentennial and the celebration of the Tenth World Youth Day in
Manila. The occasion was deemed propitious because Pedro Calungsod
was a youth and, so it was claimed, came from a diocese that was marking four hundred years of existence.

At another remove, there was the precedence of the beatification on
6 October 1985 of Spanish Jesuit missionary Diego Luis de Sanvitores, in
whose company Calungsod was martyred in 1672. The cause for the beatification of Sanvitores, revered as "the first apostle and founder of
Christianity in the Marianas Islands," was successfully advanced by the
Society of Jesus in 1985. Though Calungsod suffered the same death as
Sanvitores, he was not included in the 1985 petition, as "it would delay
the cause of Blessed Sanvitores" since a cause for a single person is less
complicated than a joint or group cause. Moreover, there were infirmities
in the case of Calungsod. His life is not as well documented or well
endowed with import and virtue as that of the Spaniard who headed the
mission that introduced Christianity in the Marianas.

In 1991, however, it was felt by the promoters of Calungsod's cause
that "in God's providence, his turn has come."[3] The Pope was not only
coming to the Philippines (and, it was hoped at the time, Cebu itself) for an
important and relevant commemoration, but there was the added precedent that on the Pope's first visit to the Philippines in 1981 he had presided
over beatification rites for Lorenzo Ruiz, "the first Filipino saint."

The papal visit, the precedent of the cases of Ruiz and Sanvitores, the
commemoration of the role of youth in the Church, the honors due a pioneering diocese in Asia, and not least Pope John Paul II's pronounced
interest in promoting both the role of the Church in the "Third World"
and the neglected laity — all these made a propitious context for the cause
of Calungsod, the first Visayan candidate for sainthood.

While the context was favorable, the process itself was forbidding.
Promoting the cause of an individual for beatification and canonization
in the Roman Catholic Church is an elaborate, labyrinthine process first

articulated in the eleventh century, systematized in the thirteenth, and refined and perfected thereafter.[4] Through the centuries, it has been defined and institutionalized in "judicial-administrative form," its criteria and procedures set forth in the Code of Canon Law and placed under the authority and supervision of the Pope and the Sacred Congregation of Rites in Rome (a body established in 1588 and now called the Sacred Congregation for the Causes of Saints).

Beatification, the elevation of a person to the status of a blessed, is preparatory to the process of canonization, by which the person is conferred the higher title of saint. While the basic procedures for both are the same, these are separate, sequential processes and there are important differences. Both blesseds and saints are persons who, by means of their holiness or heroic virtue, are held up for veneration by the Church as models of Christian living and divine intercessors before God. While veneration of a blessed is permitted for a determined region, nation, or religious group, the proposed veneration of a saint is universal.

Before 1983, both beatification and sainthood involved a two-stage process. The first stage, called the informative process, took place in the diocese or locality in which the cause was initiated. It aimed to gather information about the life, reputation, sanctity, virtues, miracles, and death of the candidate. It was, as it were, a preliminary investigation to determine whether it was worthwhile for the Holy See to take up the cause of the candidate. The second and more exacting stage, called the apostolic process, was conducted in Rome and began when the application for the introduction of a cause was accepted by the Pope and referred to the Sacred Congregation of Rites for examination and action. A whole body of prescribed procedures that governed both processes involved detailed prescriptions on the conduct of the investigation, the style and form of the evidence, and the qualifications of those who would participate in the process. Such entities included local tribunals, witnesses, lawyers, historical and theological consultors, Vatican commissions, and, at the center of the judicial process, a postulator (who was responsible for managing and promoting the cause) and a promoter of the faith, also known as the devil's advocate (who was responsible for finding deficiencies or infirmities in the cause).

Considered "the longest and most complicated [juridical process] in the church—and, quite possibly, in the world,"[5] the process is so elaborate that since 1234, when the right to canonize was reserved officially to the papacy alone, less than five hundred saints have been canonized. In 1988, the Congregation for the Causes of Saints had a backlog of 1,369 active causes, some of them dating to the fifteenth century.

However, as part of the Vatican Council II wave of reform the system was modified, culminating on 25 January 1983 when Pope John Paul II issued the apostolic constitution *Divinus perfectionis Magister*, mandating the most thoroughgoing reform of the saint-making process since the decrees of Urban VIII (1623–44). In effect, the process was made simpler, faster, cheaper, more collegial, and more productive.

The two processes, ordinary and apostolic, were combined and put in the hands of the local bishop. Though many of the elements of the old juridical format have been retained (e.g., witnesses giving testimony before local tribunals), much of the burden of investigation and authentication was placed at the diocesan level. The legal dialectic between defense lawyers and the promoter of the faith was abandoned. The promoter of the faith was given the new title of prelate theologian and assigned the largely administrative task of choosing the theological consultors for each cause and presiding over their meetings.

In the reformed system, the key "saint makers" are the postulators and relators (drawn mostly from the religious orders). The postulator manages, guides, monitors, and pursues the cause from inception to conclusion (down to such administrative details as meeting the considerable costs from funds raised for the purpose). The relator has the responsibility of demonstrating the truth about a candidate's life and death by producing a historical-critical account (called *positio*) of the life and qualifications of the candidate in consultation with theological and historical consultors. As in the past, the *positio* is examined by a series of commissions (historical, theological, and the congregation of cardinals) before it finally reaches the Pope.

Since 1983, the process of beatification and canonization has become more cooperative than adversarial. In essence, the scholar Kenneth Woodward says, the reforms point to a paradigm shift from the courtroom model to the academic model of critical historiography, transforming an inquisitorial process into one that aspires to be more open and inclusive.[6]

In addition to the reformed saint-making process, there is Pope John Paul II himself. Interested in broadening and strengthening the global base of the Church, the Pope has made clear his interest in bringing into the pantheon more lay saints, causes from countries that do not yet have any saints or those that have only a few, and candidates representing occupations or social groups with no saints to celebrate. In his world travels, the Pope likes to present new blesseds to the local churches, particularly in Asia and Africa. "In this way, John Paul II uses the beatification of local figures to bond these young and culturally diverse communities of Catholics to the church universal—and, of course, to the Holy Father in Rome."[7] It is thus that in his first eleven years as Pope (1978–89), John Paul

II conducted more beatifications and canonizations (268 saints and 609 blesseds) than all of his twentieth-century predecessors combined.

It was in this context that the Archdiocese of Cebu moved to have Pedro Calungsod beatified. In 1991, archdiocesan officials in Cebu sought and received permission from the Archdiocese of Guam, since it is the norm that causes of martyrdom are to be initiated by the church in the locality where the martyrdom took place. In 1992, the Catholic Bishops Conference of the Philippines (CBCP) recommended the Calungsod cause, citing its pastoral benefit and relevance in the immediate context of that year's celebration of the National Catechetical Year and its theme of "empowerment of the laity." To prepare the Calungsod *positio*, the archdiocese, under Cardinal Ricardo J. Vidal, organized an archdiocesan Committee of Experts on Historical Matters, with the Manila-based Jesuit Juan M. Ledesma (who had been involved in the preparation of the Sanvitores *positio* in 1985) as consultor-relator.

The rescue of Pedro Calungsod from obscurity was under way.

Looking for New Saints

It was in a similar context that Lorenzo Ruiz (ca. 1605–37), the first Filipino saint, was canonized in 1987.[8] A Filipino-Chinese from the Dominican-run parish of Binondo, Manila, Ruiz joined a perilous Dominican mission to Japan as a lay catechist. A pious convert and houseboy of the Binondo Dominicans, he had become embroiled in a dispute the nature of which is unclear (falsely accused, it is now assumed). Fearing arrest and reprisal, he joined the Dominican expedition not knowing that it was destined for Japan, a country then in the throes of violent anti-Christian persecution. Tortured and put to a most extreme test, Ruiz proved heroic in his devotion to the Faith. He died in the company of Dominicans in Nagasaki on 29 September 1637.

Heroic as the death of Ruiz was, he was (like Calungsod after him) just one of many Filipinos who died working with Spanish missionaries who, beginning in the sixteenth century, carried out the conversion of much of the Philippine archipelago and then used the Philippines as a staging area for the epic project of spreading the Gospel in Japan, China, Vietnam, Thailand, Cambodia, the Moluccas, and the Pacific islands. The names of many of these Filipinos came to be recorded in missionary chronicles. As auxiliaries to a "historic" European enterprise, these early converts were among the first Filipinos (or *indios*, as they were then called by the Spaniards) to enter Western historiographic records. There were, of course, many more who remained fugitive and unrecorded.

The contemporary emergence of Ruiz and Calungsod represents not only the belated recognition of virtue. It is also the product of historical contingencies. Though moves to canonize the Christian martyrs of Nagasaki (thousands of Christians died in Japan in the seventeenth century) began as early as 1637, it was not until 1867 that Pope Pius IX beatified 205 of them. Ruiz and his companions were not included. While the Dominicans continued to promote the cause of the martyred members of their order, it was not until 1977 that Lorenzo Ruiz was formally included in the cause.

In part, this was occasioned by efforts of the government of Ferdinand Marcos, desirous of healing the image of a country battered by martial law, to strengthen "understanding and cooperation" with the Holy See.[9] Enlisting the help of the Philippine church hierarchy, the Marcos government mounted a diplomatic and promotional campaign for both the beatification of Ruiz and a papal visit to the Philippines during the quadricentennial of the Diocese of Manila in 1979.

Though the cause was not completed in 1979 due to the short time frame (particularly since the cause was pursued before the reforms of 1983), it was finished in record time after it was approved by the Pope on 11 September 1980. In the company of fifteen other candidates from several countries who were martyred in Nagasaki in 1633–37, Lorenzo Ruiz was beatified in Manila by Pope John Paul II on 18 February 1981 in ceremonies attended by two million people. The rites were historic, marking not only John Paul's first visit to the Philippines but the first time rites of beatification were held outside of Rome.

It is clear that the process of beatification was aided in this case by the interest of John Paul II, who had been elevated to the papacy in 1978. Inspired by a vision of a truly global church, the Pope recognized the high symbolic value of conferring honors on "the only Christian country in Asia," a nation the Vatican has called the "Light of Christ in Asia." Even so, when the Pope visited the Philippines in 1981 he had to walk a thin line between giving legitimacy to the Marcos government (which went all out to mine the visit's public-relations potential) and performing his pastoral duty of honoring a Catholic nation and calling the attention of its leaders to the imperatives of human dignity, social justice, and freedom. It was a performance both adroit and triumphant, but the visit (including the beatification of Ruiz) was clearly an instance in which the interests of the Vatican and the Philippine government converged, if uneasily.[10]

In the wake of saint-making reforms, it was not long before Lorenzo Ruiz was elevated from blessed to saint. Rome had declared 1987 "The Year of the Laity" and a World Synod of Bishops was to be convened in Rome to discuss the role of the laity in the Church and the world. Pope

John Paul II saw a need to highlight the role of the laity by presenting at the synod blesseds and saints from the laity, a sector underrepresented in the Catholic calendar of saints. Between 993, the date of the first papal canonization, and the election of John Paul as pope in 1978, only 19 percent of canonized saints represented the laity. Of the 1,369 active causes in the files of the Congregation for the Causes of Saints as of 1988, no more than 20 percent involved lay candidates.

For three years leading up to the synod, efforts to discover and facilitate the causes of lay candidates were under way. Promoters, postulators, relators, local bishops, and papal diplomats lobbied for their favorite candidates. The result of the search was that three laypersons (a Frenchman and two young Italian women) were beatified and two causes (those of an Italian physician and the group of sixteen martyrs beatified in Manila in 1981) were presented for canonization.

Blessed Lorenzo Ruiz led the group of martyrs. In the canonization rites in Rome on 18 October 1987, Ruiz occupied a prominent place. The group cause was identified by his name, it was his portrait that dominated the group's official canonization portrait, which hung over the entrance to St. Peter's, and it was his name given special mention by the Pope to the legions of Filipinos attending the rites. Though the group included nine Dominican priests and Ruiz's death was no more heroic than those of the others, there was a special symbolism in the Filipino martyr. He was not only his country's first saint but a lay catechist. There was added significance in the fact that 18 October was Mission Sunday according to the liturgical calendar and it was the aim of the church to focus on the role of the laity in evangelization.

It was also significant that Ruiz was the only member of the group who was a married man with a family, a point highlighted by the Pope in his homily at the Manila beatification rites in 1981.[11] While Ruiz was canonized as a martyred missionary, not as a devoted husband and father, his being a *paterfamilias* was relevant to the Vatican since in the history of canonization very few married men and women have been canonized. Not one has been canonized for the virtues of married life despite the Church's teaching on the holiness of matrimony. Such is the power of reductive symbolism, however, that while the Pope's homilies and the canonization brochure pointedly referred to Ruiz as a family man they glossed over the fact that nothing is known about his virtues as *paterfamilias* and that he had abandoned his wife and three children to leave the country with the Dominicans.

Changes in the mentality of Rome had created opportunities for the promotion of "new" kinds of saints. The case of Lorenzo Ruiz, however, showed that while a new politics in the Church created fresh opportunities,

centuries-old paradigms of significance, of "holiness," remained firmly established. It is in this context that one sees the appearance, the "epiphany,"
of Pedro Calungsod.

Calungsod Appearing

The figure of Pedro Calungsod is extracted from the narrative of the
Jesuit mission to spread the Gospel in the Marianas Islands in the seventeenth century. The primary narration of events is contained in a series of
missionary reports—particurlarly the Jesuit *Anuas* or annual reports of
the missions—which recorded the activities and observations of the missionaries in the field. These reports were meant to provide a documentary record of the work of the missionaries, but woven into these
accounts were other motives, ranging from the practical (to raise logistical problems and justify support for the mission) to the theological (to
provide proof for the "presence" of God in heathen lands).

In this respect, accounts of this kind are organized around a largely
standardized plot and cast of characters. The key figure in the Mariana
story is the Spanish Jesuit Diego Luis de Sanvitores (1627-72).[12] Heir to a
noble family (his mother claimed descent from the great Cid himself) in
the city of Burgos, where he was born on 12 November 1627, Sanvitores
studied grammar at the Imperial College of Madrid and on 25 July 1640,
at the age of thirteen, joined the Society of Jesus as a novice. He professed
on 2 December 1660 and was assigned to teach philosophy in the College
of Alcala. He had his eyes set on the heroic challenge of mission work,
however, and he was assigned to the Philippines, arriving in the colony on
10 July 1662.

He quickly distinguished himself as an able and energetic missionary. In Manila, he proposed to his superiors the opening of a mission in
what the Spaniards then called the Ladrones Islands, which Sanvitores
first saw in 1662 en route to his assignment in the Philippines, the islands
being a stopover for ships traveling from Acapulco to Manila.[13] Jesuit and
civil authorities in Manila were lukewarm to the idea since a mission in
the Ladrones would be a drain on the limited manpower of the order as
well as a burden to the Manila government, which would have to maintain a garrison in the new possession.

Undeterred, Sanvitores applied to the queen regent herself, the
devout Marie Anne (Mariana) of Austria, through her Jesuit confessor,
Everard Nethard. On 4 June 1665, Marie Anne issued a royal decree
(*cedula*) approving the project, authorizing support for the new mission,
and changing the unflattering name Ferdinand Magellan had given the
tiny archipelago (*Ladrones*) to her own (*Mariana*).

On 7 August 1667, Sanvitores embarked for Acapulco to withdraw the funds and provisions authorized by the queen regent and recruit personnel for the mission. At the head of a band of five Jesuits, a group of lay helpers, and a complement of soldiers, Sanvitores left Mexico on 23 March 1668 and reached the Marianas on 15 June 1668.

The Jesuits established their main base in Agana, on the island of Guam. The most populous settlement in the Marianas, Agana had an estimated population of fifteen hundred. Under the authority of Sanvitores, a garrison of thirty-one men was set up to protect the mission. Mission work was rendered difficult not only by geography but by the active resistance of the inhabitants. A dependency of the Philippine province, the Marianas were for many years "one of the most dangerous mission fields in the annals of the Society of Jesus."[14] In the hostilities between the Spaniards and the Chamorros between 1671 and 1685, twelve Jesuit missionaries (priests and brothers) were killed, among them Sanvitores himself.

The death of Sanvitores took place against the background of what is referred to as the Great War of Guam (1671–76). Chamorro resistance to the presence of the missionaries had sparked sporadic assaults, which climaxed in a forty-day war that saw a week-long siege of the Jesuit church and residence in Agana by "some 2,000 Chamorros." While peace was eventually restored, the mission was beset by sporadic incidents of violence.

On 2 April 1672, Sanvitores was in the village of Tumon on his way to Agana, accompanied by a Visayan lay auxiliary named Pedro Calangsor. Sanvitores had stopped in Tumon to look for a mission helper, a Filipino named Esteban, who had deserted him a few days before. Learning that there was a recently born child in the village, Sanvitores asked the father, a Chamorro convert turned apostate named Matapang, to bring her out to be baptized. Matapang refused and "threatened and insulted" the priest. However, after Matapang left the scene, Sanvitores proceeded to baptize the child, since, it is told, the mother had given her consent and Sanvitores saw that the child was ill and in danger of death. This infuriated Matapang when he returned, and with the help of a native named Hirao he attacked the Spaniard's Visayan companion. The Visayan successfully evaded the first spears thrown but refused to abandon his Spanish master. Finally a spear found its mark, and with a blow of a machete to the Visayan's head Matapang and Hirao killed him. They then turned on Sanvitores, striking him with a lance and splitting his skull with a cutlass. Afterward the killers dragged the two bodies to the shore, loaded them in a boat, tied large stones to their feet, and dropped them into the sea.

Punitive action by the Spaniards after the death of Sanvitores triggered another cycle of violence. The Spanish garrison was reinforced and sterner measures adopted, especially after the first Spanish governor was installed in 1676. By 1695, the subjugation of the islands had been accomplished.

It is in this context that Pedro Calungsod appears in the historical record.[15] In the early accounts, the surname appended to his Christian name, Pedro, is variously spelled Calangsor, Calongsor, Calonsor, Casonsor, or Cassonsor. The promoters of his cause take these to be a mistranscription of Calungsod (literally, in Visayan, "fellow towns-man"), now a familiar family name in the Visayas.

The biographical particulars are extremely meager. He is referred to as *bisayo*, "a native of the Visayas," "native of the province of Visayas," and "native of these Philippine Islands, born in the Province of Visayas." He was one of the group of around twelve lay helpers who accompanied the six Jesuits and thirty-one soldiers that formed the original Jesuit mission of 1668. The lay helpers, mostly in their teens and apparently recruited in Manila and Acapulco, were mostly Filipinos. (There is a reference to one catechist from Mexico and another from India.)

It is posited that Calungsod was around eighteen when he was killed in 1672. Other inferences have been drawn to flesh out the person. He must have been recruited for the Jesuit mission in Manila (the farthest south in the Philippines that Sanvitores traveled was Mindoro, in 1665–66, an island with Tagalog and Visayan villages). He must have received literacy lessons, religious instruction, and baptism from the Spanish missionaries, as was the norm among lay auxiliaries. Nothing is known about the place and time of his birth, his parents, or the other ordinary details of his childhood and youth. No description exists of what he looked like. Even his name is not particularly helpful: a common baptismal name (Pedro) and an invented surname (surnames did not exist in indigenous Filipino society).[16]

In the violence that attended the Jesuit efforts in the Marianas, five lay catechists were killed before Calungsod himself was martyred: Lorenzo of Malabar, the Mexican Diego Bazan, and three Filipinos—the Visayan Hipolito de la Cruz, the Tagalog Damian Bernal, and the Pampango Nicolas de Figueroa. During the first seventeen years of the Jesuit mission in the Marianas, twelve priests, perhaps twenty lay helpers, and an unknown number of soldiers (probably a mix of Spaniards, Filipinos, and Mexicans) died in various assaults and skirmishes.

The death of Pedro Calungsod, therefore, was not isolated or exceptional. The importance accorded to it draws from several circumstances: he died in the company of Diego Luis de Sanvitores (the principal figure of the mission), the circumstances of his death were recorded (within a year of Sanvitores's death, a formal process was initiated in Guam—and later in Mexico and Manila—to investigate the circumstances of death as part of a move to have Sanvitores canonized), and he died in a manner that was, so it is argued, paradigmatic. Dying the death of a Christian martyr in the company of one who would be revered as blessed three centuries later, he became visible.

Imitating Christ

The key text in a cause for beatification or canonization is the *positio* (deposition). It is usually organized into three volumes, which can run to over a thousand pages: a *vita*, or documented life story, of the candidate; an *acta* (record of proceedings) containing testimonies of witnesses and supporting documents regarding the candidate's virtues, reputation, and the expected pastoral benefit from his canonization; and an *informatio*, or brief, summarizing the arguments and evidence for the existence of the requisite virtues.

In essence, the *positio* is built around a series of propositions or assertions (*articuli*) concerning the candidate's life, education, virtues, reputation, and death. The *articuli* are the very foundation on which the informative and apostolic processes of beatification or canonization are built. In the process through which a person is conferred (or denied) the title of blessed or saint, a "biography" of the person is constructed, documented, and interrogated. Together with the ordinary particulars of the person's life (birth, education, deeds), the biography must prove his or her virtues and reputation according to the standard propositions of a *positio*.

The possession of Christian virtues (such as faith, hope, prudence, justice, fortitude, temperance, poverty, chastity, and obedience) is demonstrated through an examination of the candidate's deeds and the writings and testimonies of witnesses. A reputation (*fama*) for sanctity before and after the person's death is demonstrated on the basis of certain principles: that the reputation must be spontaneous and continuous, increasing in the course of time, and still existing in the present. Miracles are documented as proof of virtues and reputation and as a "sign" of God's presence in the life of the person.

Martyrdom, however, presents a special case, one in which a certain flexibility is exercised in the application of these criteria. The requirement of miracles is dispensed with. A full investigation of the candidate's virtues is not deemed necessary, although an inquiry is considered most useful insofar as it gives a picture of the "inner disposition" of the person and thus establishes the reason that he or she willingly accepted death. In the martyr's case, *fama* refers not so much to the person's sanctity or virtue as to his or her reputation relative to the martyrdom. Less stringent requirements are applied in uncovering the full biographical particulars of the candidate. As Pope Pius XI pronounced on this point: "Sola mors est in que residet heroicitas. Ideoque vitam anteactam inquirere non expedit" (Heroism lies only in death. Hence, there is no need to inquire into his previous life).[17]

Damien Blaher cites a practical reason for treating martyrdom as a special case: "The flexibility of adaptation on the part of the Sacred Congregation in such matters seems to be prompted by the fact that martyrdom frequently takes place in missionary territories where the carrying out of the full procedural norms would often be a practical impossibility."[18] In effect, the focus of the investigation is on the act of death. It must satisfy the norm of Christian martyrdom, which is "the voluntary acceptance of death for the Christian faith." Two aspects are important; one concerns the person or persons who inflicted the death, the other the person who suffered death. The person who inflicted death must have done so out of hatred (*in odium*) for the Christian faith or some of its teachings. The martyr, on the other hand, must have suffered death willingly, "at least with habitual intent," for the Faith (*pro Fide*).

It is in this manner that the Calungsod deposition focuses on his death. The *interrogatio* conducted by the Archdiocese of Cebu asked "witnesses" and experts to answer five questions:[19]

1. Are the documents on the martyrdom authentic, reliable, and sufficient?
2. Did Pedro Calungsod die a violent death?
3. Did he die for the Faith (*pro Fide*)?
4. Did the assassin, Matapang, act in hatred (*in odium*) for the Faith?
5. Did Calungsod's fame for martyrdom subsist, at least substantially, until today?

The Calungsod deposition is based almost entirely on the primary and secondary sources amassed by the Jesuits (from archives in Rome, Spain, France, Mexico, and the Philippines) for the beatification cause of Diego Luis de Sanvitores in 1985. The promoters of the Calungsod cause argued that since Rome "accepted these documents as authentic and reliable and sufficient" for the beatification of Sanvitores, they should be so for Calungsod. The *positio* merely takes over from the Sanvitores deposition the relevant information on the history of the Mariana mission and the martyrdom of Sanvitores, extracting and highlighting the references to Calungsod. Apart from contextual data on the Archdiocese of Cebu, it does not offer new information on Calungsod except the correction of his name to Calungsod and the claim that he was Cebuano (in the sense that "his family name is used in the towns of that Island," i.e., Cebu, or "at least in the sense that he was under the jurisdiction of the Diocese of

Cebu"). The argument is specious. There is no evidence that Calungsod came from the island of Cebu (in the seventeenth century, *bisayo* had a rather loose application but mainly referred to a native of the "Visayan islands"), and the designation Cebuano (Sugbuanon in the local language) projects into the past an ethnic category that may not have been operative in the seventeenth century.[20] The local initiators of the cause, however, felt it important to claim Calungsod as their own.

On the martyrdom itself, the deposition sets out to prove the sine qua non of martyrdom: that Calungsod died a violent death, that his assassin acted out of "hatred for the Faith," and that Calungsod died "for the Faith." In fleshing out the "character and psychological state" of Matapang and the "internal disposition" of Calungsod at the time of his death, the deposition relies on the analysis of acts, gestures, and signs.[21]

In proving that Matapang was motivated by "hate for the religion" of the missionaries, the deposition situates the killings in the context of the Great War of Guam, during which priests and their companions were assaulted and killed because of the "envy, intrigue, and apostasy" of those who fomented unrest among the inhabitants. The intriguers and leaders were the native shamans (*macanas*), a renegade Chinese castaway named Choco, and local chiefs (*magas*) like Quipuha and Hurao. Though little is known of Matapang himself, except that he was a baptized convert who had apostatized, reference is made to his "violent and ungrateful" nature. Even more important are his actions: he vehemently opposed the rite of baptism, insulted and threatened Sanvitores, and stepped on the crucifix Sanvitores carried. The deposition concludes that the "true reason" for the actions of Matapang on 2 April 1672 was his "hate for the religion" of the Spanish missionaries.

Of the "internal disposition" of Calungsod, the deposition says: "We cannot see it in his own words, for he uttered none, as we gather from the documents. This disposition is manifested by his external behavior." The key act was that Calungsod did not desert Sanvitores at a time of grave danger. Evading the first spears thrown at him, *he did not run*. "As a good Catholic he preferred to die side by side with his Father and not to abandon him." He did not resist. He was unarmed, obedient to the stricture against the bearing of arms since Sanvitores's "pious heart would not allow arms on his companions." Calungsod suffered a violent death when a spear found its mark and "the barbarians" rushed toward him. With a blow of the *catana* (machete) to the head, they "finished him up." Adding a symbolic touch to the time of death, the deposition adds that by dying a few moments before Sanvitores, Calungsod was "the herald of [Sanvitores's] martyrdom in heaven." In sum, Pedro Calungsod was loyal, devoted, and obedient, "a good soldier of Christ" who willingly accepted death "for a religious cause."

In proving martyrdom, relators usually pay attention to "signs," those unusual or supernatural events that may have accompanied the martyrdom such as a brilliant light surrounding the martyr's body or a supernatural odor emanating from his wounds. With the permission of the Pope, the requirement of such signs may be waived. There is such a sign in the death of Sanvitores, as it is reported that, to Matapang's astonishment, the body of the Spaniard surfaced twice despite the heavy stones tied to its feet. When it surfaced a third time, Matapang struck the head with his paddle and speedily paddled to shore. The records are not as explicit in the case of Calungsod's body, but some accounts suggest that there was the same "sign" of the body surfacing in the case of the young Visayan as well.

Narrating a World

To narrate a life is to narrate the "world" in which the life is perceived to be embedded. In the exposition of facts (which is what *narratio* means) about a person's life, a narrator is engaged in the acts of constituting and confirming (and, in oppositional cases, interrogating and reconfiguring) that world. In this manner, the narrator offers his audience not only a life but ways of thinking about a world.

The life of Pedro Calungsod is inserted into the master text of "divine history," one that seeks to discover not so much the material causes of human events, the unique historical experience, or the idiosyncratic life as the revelation of God's presence among men and the reiteration of His enduring plan.

In retelling the life of Calungsod, his relators not only cull facts from the early missionary accounts but draw from the worldview that informed these narratives. Such narratives, as anthropologist Daniel Reff shows in his study of Spanish missionary discourse in the seventeenth century, were shaped by conventional rhetorical strategies, institutional contingencies, and, most important, a medieval epistemology that governed how their authors perceived and represented reality. In essence, Reff says, these texts were "a continual exercise in translation, of seeing beyond the immediate reality of things to their invisible, larger significance."[22]

While missionary narratives are mined today for their lode of historical and ethnographic data, they were essentially records of conversion challenges met and encounters won rather than explorations of alternative truths or histories of the precise unfolding of events. They constructed the realities of the field according to the established rhetorical and epistemological patterns of medieval Christian discourse.

In the Sanvitores-Calungsod story, this is shown in the way the history of the Mariana mission is distilled into the paradigmatic acts of a divine and timeless drama. Foregrounded are the missionaries and their labors as instruments of God. As divine instruments, their motives and aims are privileged, placed beyond the pale of critical discussion. On the other hand, the Chamorro resistance to Jesuit evangelization is depicted as the work of the devil, of Satan working through such agents as scheming heathens (the Chinese castaway named Choco), envious pagan healers (the *macanas*), and treacherous apostates (Matapang).

Such construction of villains is grounded in the belief that even the Chamorros are God's children, descendants of Adam and Eve, lost and fallen into "barbarous" customs due to centuries of isolation and ignorance of the Word of God. This theological affirmation explains the contradictory and ambivalent characterization of "natives" in missionary discourse as, on one hand, "devil-worshippers" and *barbaros* unblessed by "the light of the Holy Gospel" and, on the other, as a people "peace-loving, compassionate, and kind."[23] Villainy had to be explained as Satan's intervention through such instruments as the heathen Choco and the apostate Matapang.

Missionary discourse does not directly account for other factors behind the Chamorro resistance, that in their evangelizing zeal (it is reported there were thirteen thousand "baptisms" in the mission's first year alone) the Jesuits wittingly or unwittingly transgressed on local customs, embroiled themselves in the rivalries of chiefs and factions in the politically fragmented islands, and caused severe social dislocation. Tensions spawned acts of violence that led to the spirals of retaliation and revenge that culminated in the "Great War." Missionary reports also gloss over the fact that hard-fisted policies of suppression (particularly after a Spanish military governor was installed in the Marianas in 1676) — combined with epidemics and migration—created such a crisis that the Chamorro population was virtually wiped out. It is estimated that, between 1668 and 1710, the Marianas population dropped from around 40,000 to 3,539.[24]

Martyrdom is the core drama in the chronicles of the missionary labor to convert the "dark lands." Here the text is reduced to a simple core plot in which a believer, by the form of his death, bears "witness" (Greek *martys*) to a struggle between good and evil. In telling the story of martyrdom, the relator is not engaged in exploring "deep individuality," culturally bound notions of personhood, or contexts of social conflict, but in retracing, in the martyr's death, the passion and death of Christ, for it is only by such analogy that the martyr is recognized a saint. "To be a saint was to die not only *for* Christ but *like* him. Or, what amounted to the same thing, to be a saint was to have the story of one's death remembered and told as the story of Jesus."[25]

This is how the death of Pedro Calungsod is framed, and it is within this frame that he becomes "significant." Embracing a powerful faith, conscripted into what would be remembered as a heroic and consequence-filled enterprise, and dying "the right death," Calungsod was inscribed as part of a story that would be told again and again.

It is in sacred history, as expressed in models of sainthood, that Pedro Calungsod is located. Through the centuries, these models have included a predictable and patterned set of candidates—miracle workers, wise bishops, exemplary penitents, radical ascetics, and the martyr who dies for the faith at the hands of an enemy opposed to the Faith.

While such models have become highly institutionalized, even bureaucratized, preferences in models have not been entirely static. Through the centuries, rearticulations of doctrine as well as the changing politics of the Church have occasioned shifting priorities in "models of holiness" and classes or types of candidates. This is shown in the papacy of John Paul II, during which there has been a distinct conservatism in dealing with controversial cults surrounding miracle-working stigmatists and visionaries (like Padre Pio, the famous Italian Capuchin friar) and politically sensitive causes of "social martyrs" (like the assassinated Archbishop Oscar Romero of El Salvador). At the same time, there have been favored causes: causes involving the laity (in part because declining recruitment to the priesthood has highlighted the role of the laity in evangelization) and causes involving candidates from social groups underrepresented in the calendar of saints as well as candidates from Third World countries (not only as Rome strengthens its position as the center of a global Church but also as these countries become sending, rather than receiving, areas for missionaries).

In the saint-making reforms adopted under John Paul II, Woodward sees the beginnings of a paradigm shift from a juridical mentality imbued with an ahistorical sense of the Church as a universal institution everywhere essentially the same to a historical mentality that took saints as individuals responding by grace to the particular challenges of time and place.[26] It is clear, however, that in the practice of saint making the shift has not been evident. The models of holiness have remained firmly patterned and conventional.

This is shown in the way Pedro Calungsod has been inscribed and rescued as a text. Thomas Heffernan says: "Texts have their beginnings not in the act of composition but in a complex series of anticipations."[27] As in the case of many saints, Calungsod's "life" reveals extremely little about the person himself but much about the Church's attitudes toward sainthood and saints and the ways in which holiness is perceived, imagined, and preserved for posterity.

Constructing Fame

Significance is a function of "fame." Before it became an ecclesiastical function, saint making was a spontaneous, "democratic" act of local communities. Around exceptional persons demonstrations of public devotion developed and an oral tradition (legends, songs, and rites) grew. It was, in fact, to control the rampant proliferation of local cults, apocrypha, and devotional excess that an official saint-making system was developed and juridical procedures laid down for examining, verifying, and approving a candidate's reputation for holiness.

Yet, even as saint making was institutionalized, the cardinal rule remained — that reputation comes from the people themselves and is tested and demonstrated by how it endures through time. Hence, it is expected that a candidate's reputation for holiness must ripen for decades before a cause is initiated in his or her behalf.

In the case of Calungsod, the deposition attempts to show that his reputation as a martyr persisted through the centuries. In doing this, the deposition presents a whole set of properly annotated extracts from documents ranging from 1716 to 1994. These encompass a wide variety of primary and secondary sources (judicial transcripts, chronicles, eulogies, memorials, and articles) that were compiled for the Sanvitores cause in 1985. Only two sources (contemporary Cebu City newspaper articles that were generated by the local promotion of Calungsod's beatification) deal directly with Calungsod; the rest mention him only as an aside in the story of Sanvitores.

There is no evidence of spontaneously generated fame. In Cebu (claimed as his place of origin), Calungsod was unknown until his cause was taken up in 1991 and he was rescued from the obscurity of Spanish historical records. In Guam (the place of his martyrdom), he is virtually unknown.

In many causes, reputation is created by the promotion of the cause itself since a cause requires an organized effort (usually by a religious order or diocese) to mobilize financial and spiritual support on behalf of the candidate. A guild or promotional office is formed, money collected, reports of divine favors solicited, prayer cards printed, and articles and pious biographies published. This promotional phase is designed to encourage private and public devotion to the candidate and thus establish the candidate's reputation for holiness. Once a person is beatified and canonized, his or her reputation is further assured, as the saint's name is added to the calendar, a feast day is assigned, and devotions are encouraged.

In the case of Calungsod, the Archdiocese of Cebu set up a Pedro Calungsod Beatification Promotion Office in Cebu City, sent out appeals for letters of support, and popularized the cause by such means as newspaper articles, church sermons, and various devotional and promotional activities. A religious play on Calungsod's martyrdom was staged at the Cebu Cathedral and a local college. Prayer cards were produced, instructing the faithful to inform the Beatification Promotion Office about favors received through the intercession of "Servant of God Pedro Calungsod, Young Cebuano Catechist." In the card is the text of a prayer Catholics are asked to recite in seeking divine favor not only for Calungsod's beatification but for personal petitions:

> Lord God / through your Son / you taught us that there can be no greater love / than to lay down one's life / for one's friends. / Your servant, Pedro Calungsod / inspires us by his fidelity / in times of adversity, / by his courage in teaching the faith / in the midst of hostility, / and by his love / in shedding his blood / for the sake of the Gospel. / We humbly ask you / to raise him to the honor of the altar / so that we may count him among our intercessors / in heaven, for the glory of your name. / We ask this through Christ our Lord. Amen.[28]

On one side of the card is an artist's rendering of what the Visayan martyr must have looked like: a young man in what was imagined to be a seventeenth-century Hispanized native's garb, holding aloft a cross in his right hand and carrying the Bible in his left. In another version, there is, minimally sketched in the background, the artist's conception of two ferocious-looking "savages" about to attack the young catechist.

The lack of an authentic, spontaneous reputation is not surprising. Of largely unknown origins, Calungsod died in his teens in a distant land where he was a virtual stranger. Even if these particular circumstances were different, it is still likely that he would have remained obscure. He came out of a dominated culture without the kind of historiographic tradition toward which the Catholic saint-making process is biased.

This is shown in comparing the cases of Diego Luis de Sanvitores and Pedro Calungsod. On one hand, we have the detailed story of the Spanish evangelizer who performed deeds of high consequence (the Christianization of an archipelago). He was member of an organization, the Society of Jesus, which has effectively maintained its institutional history and presence through the centuries. We know his lineage, the particulars of his birth and early life, his character, and the details of a religious career that ended in his martyrdom. Sanvitores's prominence was such that news of his death was commemorated with masses in Manila, Mexico, and Madrid. As early as 1683, just eleven years after his death, *Vida y martyrio de el venerable Padre Diego Luis de Sanvitores*, a biography written by the Jesuit Francisco Garcia, was published in Madrid, presaging other biographies in the centuries that followed.[29] Documents written by and about Sanvitores are preserved in the Jesuit archives in Rome and in other repositories. Long before Sanvitores was beatified, he had a reputation as a heroic and holy figure. In the Cathedral of Burgos in Spain, there is an old portrait of him holding aloft a cross, his body pierced by a lance. On his head is a machete, and floating in the background is an angel poised to place a wreath on his head.[30]

He is not just an iconographic figure. There are extant descriptions of what he looked like: gaunt, ascetic, of medium height, very fair, with blue eyes and a long hooked nose on a long face.[31] We even know that he was so nearsighted he "had to be led along by a rope tied around his waist to avoid bumping into trees."[32] This detail may even suggest that on that fateful day of martyrdom our young Visayan may have been the person at the other end of that rope.

For having died at the side of the Spanish missionary as a loyal helper, Pedro Calungsod surfaced in the light of history. Yet he is present only in the elemental act of his death—he was unarmed but did not run and surrendered himself to a violent death.

Cardinal John Henry Newman laments that saints' lives offer readers "the *disjecta membra* of what ought to be a living whole. . . . [T]hey do not manifest a Saint, they mince him into spiritual lessons."[33] Calling the *positio* "a genre in search of its proper form," Kenneth Woodward envisions a form of religious biography that draws from both critical historiography and theological imagination to illuminate the hidden movement of grace in a person's life, rendering its fullness, not only its message but its unique "harmonics of holiness," its poetry.[34]

This does not account for the fact that neither the arts of memory nor the power that uses and deploys them are everywhere the same in space and time.

Retrieving Lives

Today, conscious of how colonialism has erased or obscured native lives, scholars are interested in the project of rescuing them from oblivion. It is, however, a project confounded by the politics of representation—not only the politics of what makes for "significant" lives but the historicity of modes of representation and the unequal technologies, across culture and class, for the production, preservation, and circulation of knowledge.

This is illustrated in the recently recovered story of Felipe Sonson (1611–86), who was with Sanvitores and Calungsod on the 1668 mission to the Marianas.[35] Born to a prominent landowning family in Pampanga, Sonson converted to Catholicism early. After his wife died and having provided for his son's support, he devoted himself wholly to the service of the Faith. With remarkable abasement, he offered himself as a "slave" to the Spanish missionaries, working as a carpenter, tailor, laborer, and handyman for the Augustinians in Pampanga, the Dominicans in Binondo, and finally the Jesuits in the Marianas. He identified so completely with the missionaries that he pleaded, and received permission, to wear a version of their insignias and clothing (cord, cincture, habit). (Though natives were admitted to the secular clergy beginning in the seventeenth century, it was not until the nineteenth that they were allowed to join the religious orders.) The Jesuits accorded Sonson the status of a *donado* (an auxiliary role in the community higher than that of a lay helper such as Calungsod but lower than that of a lay brother). After eighteen years of loyal and tireless labor in the Marianas, Sonson died on 11 January 1686, his death hastened by old age (he was seventy-five) and the severe physical injuries he had suffered fighting to help protect the missionaries in a Chamorro uprising in 1684. His virtues were such that he was honored with a solemn burial attended by Spanish officials and missionaries in Guam.

Shortly after his death, his story was recorded in the Jesuit *Anuas* as a testament to an "angelic" and "saintly" life. Compared to Calungsod, Sonson lived a life longer, fuller, and more richly endowed with the Christian virtues. Yet, unless the kinds of contingencies that occasion beatification causes are present, it is not likely that a cause for his beatification will be initiated. A cause for Sonson would also be more complicated. In a cause for beatification, it is easier to prove a case for martyrdom than it is for a life of holiness and virtue.

Nonetheless, the stories of Calungsod and Sonson are constructed out of the same basic assumptions about what makes a meaningful and exemplary life. In the case of Calungsod, it is a life collapsed and condensed into the simple outlines of an archetypal Christian martyrdom. In the case of Sonson, it is a life ultimately reduced and "minced" in a conventional catalogue of the scholastic virtues of humility, obedience, poverty, temperance, charity, fortitude, and chastity.

Guided by contemporary notions of personhood, today's reader is intrigued by facets of Sonson suggestive of the values of individuality, tension, and ambiguity. He was a skilled marksman who fought with the Spaniards to suppress a Chinese uprising in the Philippines (possibly the Manila uprising of 1639), a prosperous member of the gentry who turned himself into a "slave." Yet the missionary account of his life leaves these aspects undeveloped. Such disinterest is typical of the early biographies of native converts in the Philippines. Focused on tracing the workings of a universal and timeless grace in the lives of persons, these accounts slight the particularities of culture and history by producing uniform and interchangeable lives.[36]

Governed by a faith that sought to regulate human conduct in clearly prescribed ways, and narrated in the same terms, the lives of converts like Calungsod and Sonson offer us a fugitive, fitful sense of what we look for in a "life" today: psychological depth, multilayeredness, thick circumstantiality, and dramatic tension. They offer as well a veiled and heavily mediated view of "historical background," of the dialectics between an individual and the social world in which he or she is embedded.

A further example is provided by the first Filipinos (*indios*, Chinese mestizos, and Spanish mestizos) to be ordained priests in the secular clergy in the years following 1621. Historian Luciano P. R. Santiago cites these priests as "the first group of Filipinos to leave behind documentary biographies."[37] Santiago does signal work in reconstructing the lives of forty-nine pioneering Filipino priests from the period 1621–1723, yet his reconstruction also reveals the limits of the historiographic tradition out of which these early lives are rescued. In the same way that these priests were, by virtue of race, assigned a lower place in the colonial ecclesiastical order, they also occupied a marginal position in the historical record. Santiago says: "The archives were the preserve of the colonialists. The early Filipino clergymen had scarcely a voice in them save between the lines of entries of bare cold facts."[38]

Hence, Santiago's forty-nine "biographical studies" are characterized by a barren sameness and externality. It is not just that these early conscripts to the priesthood came from similar social backgrounds (sons of the "native nobility" in the most Christianized settlements of the time, particularly the Tagalog and Pampangan). The subjects surface only as they appear in lists and catalogues of education, ordination, ecclesiastical licenses, and pastoral assignments or reports of examinations, bequests, and investigations. When descriptions of character appear, they tend to be brief and formulaic ("dedicated, sincere, esteemed, exemplary, saintly").

It reflects the homogenizing Christian formation of persons at the time, as well as our modern bias for "personality," that what strikes us as the most "individual" and interesting sketch in Santiago's catalogue is that of an errant Spanish-mestizo priest, Juan Chrisostomo. Mediocre but earnest, Father Chrisostomo was assigned in 1709 to a post that no one else wanted, the hinterland parish of Lubang Island in Mindoro. Here he was suspected of keeping a woman and a child and employing too many servants. He got into serious trouble when three boys reported that the Virgin Mary had appeared to them in an abandoned chapel in the isolated barrio of Santa Rosa. Following the supposed instructions of the Virgin, Chrisostomo had the chapel rebuilt and a well dug inside it and then assigned five maidens to attend to the well. Church authorities investigated the case, decided it was a hoax, and reprimanded Chrisostomo for encouraging pagan practices and playing into the hands of "the devil." He was imprisoned in the ecclesiastical jail in Manila but was later pardoned on the grounds that his failings were less a matter of heresy than misguided zeal.[39]

The earliest Filipino "biographies" are of agents and auxiliaries in the European project of conversion and colonization. These were preserved as part of the Spanish record of missionary labor and because of their value as *exempla* of the good Christian life. They conformed to what the authors of these stories saw as the "significant" life. They have survived not only because they were incorporated into Europe's enduring archives of its presence in the world but because they are an integral part of a historical and institutional project that remains dominant to this day.

Epilogue

The process of beatification and canonization provides us with an instance by means of which a particular body of truth is preserved and renewed through time. It generates a text that reveals to us the workings of structures of authority through which significance is conferred on a person or event and through which such a person or event is "memorized" or preserved in the recollections of a community. Such a text involves the interplay of past and present since such structures of significance underlie the ways in which acts are registered as they happen and how they are remembered in the present.

In biographical sum, Pedro Calungsod may seem remarkable only in his incompleteness and ordinariness. For the Vatican, interested in retracing and renewing established paradigms of faith, the historiographic gap can be glossed over. For the Philippine Church, enamored with the symbolism of its pastoral presence in today's Catholic world, the discordant values of honoring a loyal colonial can be set aside. For the faithful, the half-formed character of Calungsod is not really what matters. What is most important is that through the traces of his life they may glimpse a larger meaning and truth. If and when he is beatified and canonized, and to the extent that popular veneration of his image grows, the faithful will tell his story according to their desires. His death will be embellished, facts will be invented, miracles told, and his "life" will grow.[40] Thus, Saint Augustine: "But those things which have no significance of their own are interwoven for the sake of the things which are significant."[41]

On 12–16 January 1995, Pope John Paul II made his triumphant second trip to the Philippines, a visit capped by the celebration of the Tenth World Youth Day, which saw at Manila's Luneta Park "the largest crowd ever gathered in a single place" in the world travels of the Pope.[42]

The visit did not witness the hoped-for beatification of Pedro Calungsod. The cause was initiated too late for the canonical process to be completed. There were delays due to infirmities of form and problems in retrieving new data about the candidate. As this was the Cebu archdiocese's first experience in promoting a beatification, archdiocesan officials had difficulty managing the cause. It was not until late in the process that a postulator (Fr. Rolando Manayon, a Cebuano priest versed in Italian and with doctorates in theology and canon law) was formally assigned to manage the cause in Rome. Perhaps more important, the historical moment did not prove too urgent: Filipinos already had a saint in Lorenzo Ruiz, and there were other candidates.[43] Moreover, the "political pressures" in both Manila and the Vatican that had hastened the beatification of Ruiz were not present in the cause of Calungsod.

The cause, however, is not dead. The *positio* was submitted to the Congregation for the Causes of Saints in Rome and received the Holy See's *nihil obstat* (decree approving the introduction of the cause). Subsequently, the diocesan examination of experts and "witnesses" was completed, and the *acta* of the Diocesan Tribunal was submitted to Rome in March 1994. The cause now awaits the judgment of the congregation and the Pope.

As it is, the cause saw researchers mobilized to recover what information still existed about the Visayan; Calungsod's name invoked in homilies and prayers; articles written about him; his "portrait" drawn; and an image of him molded in brass by the country's leading sculptor for a monumental assemblage of heroic figures of Cebuano history, which will occupy historic Parian Plaza in the heart of Cebu City.

The full epiphany of this obscure seventeenth-century Visayan may yet, "in God's providence" and in human time, come.

NOTES

I wish to thank Alfred W. McCoy and Michael Cullinane for the intellectual stimulation and support that led to the completion of this essay.

1. Resil B. Mojares, "The Life of Miguel Ayatumo: A Sixteenth-Century Boholano," *Philippine Studies* 41:4 (1993): 437–58.
2. The discussion of the archdiocesan preparations for the beatification of Calungsod is based on interviews with Monsignor Cesar J. Alcoseba, historical consultor, Archdiocese of Cebu, Cebu City, 20 February 1996; Monsignor Manuel S. Salvador, chairman, Diocesan Tribunal, Archdiocese of Cebu, Cebu City, 23 February 1996; and Monsignor Achilles Dakay, spokesman, Archdiocese of Cebu, Cebu City, 3 April 1996. Based in Cebu City, the Diocese of Cebu was established on 14 August 1595 and at one time included not only Visayas and Mindanao but the Marianas and the Palau Islands. It became an archdiocese on 28 April 1934, its territorial jurisdiction now limited to the Central Visayas.
3. *Deposition on the Martyrdom of the Servant of God, Lay Catechist in Guam, Visayan Cebuano Pedro Calungsod. +2 April 1672* (Cebu City: Archdiocese of Cebu, 1993), 4.
4. Damien Blaher, O.F.M., *The Ordinary Processes in Causes of Beatification and Canonization: A Historical Synopsis and a Commentary* (Washington, D.C.: Catholic University of America, 1949); Kenneth L. Woodward, *Making Saints: How the Catholic Church Determines Who Becomes a Saint, Who Doesn't, and Why* (New York: Simon & Schuster, 1990).
5. Woodward, *Making Saints*, 89. I am heavily indebted to this informative and well-written account.
6. Woodward, *Making Saints*, 91.
7. Woodward, *Making Saints*, 116; "John Paul Beatifies a Papuan Martyr," *New York Times*, 18 January 1995; "Brutalized in Colonial Africa, 1909; Beatified in Rome, 1994," *New York Times*, 29 January 1995.
8. Fidel Villaroel, O.P., *Lorenzo de Manila, the Protomartyr of the Philippines, and His Companions*, 3d ed. (Manila: UST Press, 1988). Father Villaroel was the historian (*relator*) in the cause of Ruiz. On Ruiz and the Dominican martyrs of Japan, see Ceferino Puebla Pedrosa, O.P., et al., *Witnesses of the Faith in the Orient: Dominican Martyrs of Japan, China, and Vietnam* (Hong Kong: Dominican Province of Our Lady of the Rosary, 1989).
9. Antonio C. Delgado, *The Making of the First Filipino Saint* (Manila: Ala-ala Foundation, 1982). As Philippine ambassador to the Holy See, Delgado was a key figure in the promotion of the Ruiz cause. Compare his account of the promotion with that in Villaroel, *Lorenzo de Manila*, 146–304.
10. On the attempts of the Marcos government (and specifically those of Imelda Romualdez Marcos) to manipulate the papal visit of 1981, see Felix B. Bautista, *Cardinal Sin and the Miracle of Asia* (Manila: Vera-Reyes, 1987), 75–92. On the visit, see *Totus Tuus: Pope John Paul II in the Philippines* (Quezon City: Vera-Reyes, 1981); and *L'Osservatore Romano* (Rome), issues of 9 February to 2 March 1981. A special edition of *L'Osservatore Romano* (16–27 February 1981) was printed in Manila to mark the visit.
11. Woodward, *Making Saints*, 342; Pedro S. de Achutegui, ed., *John Paul II in the Philippines: Addresses and Homilies* (Quezon City: Cardinal Bea Institute, 1981), 67–73. See also the homilies and articles on the 1987 canonization in *L'Osservatore Romano*, 26 October 1987, 9–10, 11.

12. See the Sanvitores deposition: *Manilen. seu Aganien. Beatificaciones seu Declarationis Martyrii servi Dei. Didaci Aloisii de San Vitores Sacerdotis Professi Societatis Jesu (+1672). Positio Super Vita et Martyrio ex Officio Concinnata* (Rome: Sacra Congregatio Pro Causis Sanctorum, Officium Historicum, 1981). See also H. de la Costa, S.J., *The Jesuits in the Philippines, 1581–1768* (Cambridge: Harvard University Press, 1961), 455–56, 469–71, 474–75, 508–11.

13. An archipelago of seventeen volcanic islands, the Mariana Islands was visited by Magellan in 1521. In 1565, Miguel Lopez de Legazpi took formal possession of the islands for Spain but took no steps to colonize them even though they were a regular provisioning stop for galleons sailing from Mexico to the Philippines. It was only with Sanvitores that the first move was made to establish a permanent Spanish presence there. See Laura Thompson, *The Native Culture of the Marianas Islands* (Honolulu: Bernice P. Bishop Museum, 1945); and *Guam and Its People* (Princeton, N.J.: Princeton University Press, 1947).

14. De la Costa, *Jesuits in the Philippines*, 457.

15. *Deposition*, 5–144. Copies of the deposition were distributed to experts and witnesses with cover letters from Ricardo Cardinal J. Vidal, archbishop of Cebu (4 February 1994), and Fr. Juan M. Ledesma, S.J., assistant chairman, Committee of Experts (4 February 1994).

16. It was not until the Claveria decree of 1849 that the use of surnames became a norm in the Philippines. The lack of written records and the problem of names make it difficult to identify persons and trace genealogies before 1800.

17. Quoted in *Deposition*, 6.

18. Blaher, *Ordinary Processes*, 236–37.

19. *Caebuana. Philippines. Acta of the Diocesan Process for the Beatification of Pedro Calungsod* (Cebu City: Archdiocese of Cebu, 1994). This is the report of the Diocesan Tribunal, containing the testimonies of fifteen experts and "witnesses," mostly Filipino scholars and priests, who received copies of the deposition and responded to the *interrogatio*.

20. *Deposition*, 5. *Bisaya* is a term of uncertain origin and etymology. It has been applied to people inhabiting parts of North Borneo (as early as the sixteenth century) and, more popularly, the inhabitants of the Visayan Islands in the Philippines. On the controversy over the word's ethnic and territorial reference, see John Carroll, "Notes on the Bisaya in the Philippines and Borneo," *Journal of East Asiatic Studies* (Manila) 8:1–2 (January-April 1959): 42–72; and Joseph Baumgartner, S.V.D., "The Bisaya of Borneo and the Philippines: A New Look at the Maragtas," *Philippine Quarterly of Culture and Society* 2:3 (September 1974): 167–70.

21. For the analysis of the act of martyrdom, see *Deposition*, 18–29.

22. Daniel T. Reff, "Contextualizing Missionary Discourse: The Benavides *Memorials* of 1630 and 1634," *Journal of Anthropological Research* 50 (1994):. 55.

23. See the descriptions of the Chamorros by an Augustinian missionary in 1586, a Franciscan lay brother in 1602, and a Jesuit missionary in 1689–90 in Emma H. Blair and James A. Robertson, eds., *The Philippine Islands, 1493–1898* (Cleveland: Arthur H. Clark, 1909), 6:138–42. See also Marjorie G. Driver, "Fray Juan Pobre de Zamora and His Account of the Mariana Islands," *Journal of Pacific History* 18:3 (July 1983): 198–216; and Domingo Abella, *Vignettes of Philippines-Marianas Colonial History* (Manila: International Association of Historians of Asia, 1962), 9–40.

24. Thompson, *Guam*, 33–34; Francis X. Hezel, "From Conversion to Conquest: The Early Spanish Mission in the Marianas," *Journal of Pacific History* 17:3

(July 1982): 115–37; Francis X. Hezel and Marjorie C. Driver, "From Conquest to Colonization: Spain in the Mariana Islands, 1690–1740," *Journal of Pacific History* 23:2 (October 1988): 137–51.

25. Woodward, *Making Saints*, 53.

26. Woodward, *Making Saints*, 95.

27. Thomas J. Heffernan, *Sacred Biography: Saints and Their Biographers in the Middle Ages* (New York: Oxford University Press, 1988), 18.

28. "Servant of God Pedro Calungsod, Young Cebuano Catechist" (prayer card, Cebu City, 1994). Two samples of letters of favors received (cure of an illness and safe release from an abduction) were printed in the newspaper of the Cebu Archdiocese (*Bag-ong Lungsoranon*, 4 June and 11 June 1995). For an example of articles generated by the Calungsod promotion, see Teodoro C. Bacani, *Preparing Our Future: The Pope and the Filipino Youth* (Manila: Gift of God Publications, 1994), 34–35.

29. *Deposition*, 93–96; Blair and Robertson, *Philippine Islands*, 37:267.

30. De la Costa, *Jesuits in the Philippines*, frontispiece.

31. De la Costa, *Jesuits in the Philippines*, 455.

32. Hezel, "Conversion to Conquest," 119. Sanvitores is shown wearing eyeglasses in an engraving by Gregorio Fosman (Madrid, 1682), published in Francisco Garcia's *Vida y martyrio de el venerable Padre Diego Luis de Sanvitores* (Madrid, 1683). See Abella, *Vignettes*, 10.

33. Quoted in Woodward, *Making Saints*, 369.

34. Woodward, *Making Saints*, 249–50.

35. The story of Felipe Sonson was recorded by the Jesuit Lorenzo Bustillo, one of Sanvitores's colleagues, in the Jesuit *Anuas* of 1686. The document was retrieved (from the Real Academia de la Historia in Madrid), translated, and published by John N. Schumacher, S.J., in "Felipe Sonson, Seventeenth-Century Filipino Jesuit: Missionary to the Marianas," *Landas* (Loyola School of Theology, Quezon City) 9:2 (July 1995): 266–85. Schumacher calls the document "perhaps the most extensive contemporary account of the life of any Filipino before the nineteenth century." See also John N. Schumacher, S.J., "Early Filipino Jesuits, 1593–1930," *Philippine Studies* 29:3/4 (1981): 281–83; and Abella, *Vignettes*, 14–15, 48.

36. Compare, for instance, the account of Sonson's life with those of the converts Miguel Ayatumo (1593–1609) of Bohol, Marcelo Banal (1632–97) of Malate, and Onofre Liban (ca. 1763–87) of Cagayan. See Mojares, "Life of Miguel Ayatumo"; Luciano P. R. Santiago, "Brother Marcelo Banal de San Augustin, O.S.A. (1632–1697): First *Indio* Augustinian Lay Brother," *Unitas* 63:1 (March 1990): 26–33; and William Henry Scott, *The Discovery of the Igorots: Spanish Contacts with the Pagans of Northern Luzon* (Quezon City: New Day Publishers, 1974), 158–60.

37. Luciano P. R. Santiago, *The Hidden Light: The First Filipino Priests* (Quezon City: New Day Publishers, 1987), 9. On the beginnings of the Filipino clergy, also see Horacio de la Costa, S.J., "The Development of the Native Clergy in the Philippines," in *Studies in Philippine Church History*, edited by Gerald H. Anderson, 65–104 (Ithaca: Cornell University Press, 1969); and John N. Schumacher, S.J., "The Eighteenth-Century Filipino Clergy: A Footnote to De la Costa," *Philippine Studies* 26 (1978): 157–73.

38. Santiago, *Hidden Light*, 10–11.

39. Santiago, *Hidden Light*, 83–87.

40. Even the written historical records, scant as they are, already show this process

of re-creation through error (Calungsod was killed by an arrow), elaboration (Calungsod was Sanvitores's "altar-boy"), or dramatization (Calungsod dodged the spears by "darting among the trees" and incensed his assassins by "preaching" the Faith to them) (*Deposition*, 103, 114, 116, 117, 119, 121). Re-creation is also illustrated in the Cebuano play about Calungsod (referred to in the main text), *Scenes from a Martyrdom* (1994), written by Monsignor Rodolfo E. Villanueva (pseud., Renato Madrid). By making Calungsod's story the centerpiece of a trilogy dealing with the travails of "overseas Filipinos," Villanueva gives the martyr's story a contemporary cast, connecting it to the phenomenon of Filipino transnational migration.

41. Saint Augustine, *The City of God*, trans. Marcus Dods (New York: Modern Library, 1950), 524.

42. On the papal visit, see *John Paul II: We Love You* (Manila: Asian Catholic Publishers, 1995), 127.

43. Another Filipino candidate for sainthood is Mother Ignacia del Espiritu Santo (1663–1748), a Filipino-Chinese from Binondo, who founded a religious congregation (now called the Religious of the Virgin Mary) in 1684, the first to be established by a Filipino woman. In 1988, the "National Movement for the Cause of the Beatification of Mother Ignacia del Espiritu Santo" was launched. The cause is pending. See Marcelino A. Foronda, Jr., *Mother Ignacia and her Beaterio* (Rizal: St. Paul Publications, 1964), 119.

In addition to Sanvitores and the Dominican companions of Ruiz, European missionary saints who worked in the Philippines include the Spanish Franciscan Pedro Bautista (1542–97), who was in the Philippines in 1584–93, martyred in Japan in 1597, and canonized in 1862; and the Spanish Recollect Ezekiel Moreno (1848–1905), who was in the Philippines in 1870–85, had a distinguished career in Colombia, and was canonized in 1992. See *San Pedro Bautista: A Saint in the Philippines* (San Francisco del Monte and Quezon City: Devotees of San Pedro Bautista, 1982); and Emmanuel Luis A. Romanillos, *Bishop Ezekiel Moreno: An Augustinian Recollect Saint among Filipinos* (Quezon City: Agustinos Recoletos, 1993).

Formal photograph of Hilario Camino Moncado distributed
in the late 1930s by the Filipino Federation of America, Inc.

THE MASTER AND JUAN DE LA CRUZ: HILARIO C. MONCADO, POLITIKO AND MAN OF MYSTERY

Michael Cullinane

Less than five months before the onslaught of the Pacific War at the end of 1941, the resident commissioner of the Commonwealth of the Philippines to the United States, Joaquin M. Elizalde, made a strong appeal to the U.S. secretary of the interior to assist his government in protecting "several thousand" Filipinos residing in California and Hawaii. The "credulity and religious fanaticism" of these Filipinos, wrote Elizalde, had led them to fall under the influence of a "faker" by the name of Hilario Camino Moncado. Elizalde sought the cooperation of the American authorities to end what he called the "exploitation of the simple" by a man practicing "fraud" under "the cloak of the Filipino Federation of America," an organization that had transformed "this impostor" into "a person of very substantial means." A short time later, Elizalde sent a personal emissary to the secretary's office to reiterate his strong desire "that some action be taken to curb Moncado's preying on ignorant Filipinos."

Possibly unknown to Elizalde, Moncado was already known to the American colonial authorities in Washington, D.C., where a rather fat file on him existed at the Bureau of Insular Affairs. Nevertheless, in the spirit of cooperation with the Commonwealth government, the Department of the Interior launched a fairly thorough investigation. In the opinion of the solicitor's office, "the nature of his operations" indicated that Moncado was "a 'front' for a scheme which has been carefully devised by someone with more intelligence than Moncado is said to have." Though seemingly convinced that Moncado and his accomplices were indeed hoodwinking large numbers of Filipino laborers, the Interior Department found no evidence of violations of the law that could be used to indict Hilario Moncado.[1]

Why were high-ranking Philippine and American government officials devoting so much attention to this man—a man who twenty-five years earlier had arrived in Honolulu as an unknown sugarcane cutter on

Michael Cullinane

contract with the Hawaiian Sugar Planters' Association (HSPA)? For some Filipinos and Americans, he was simply a clever impostor with an inexplicable influence over the lives of many Filipino laborers. Not only did he have a substantial following, but his federation extended over a wide area, being active in Hawaii, on the U.S. West Coast, and in several parts of the Philippines. For colonial officials, Moncado and his *colorum*-like followers were potential troublemakers. For the Commonwealth government, Moncado was a political nuisance, for under the banner of his Modernist Party he had the audacity to run against Manuel Quezon in the November 1941 presidential elections. More threatening, perhaps, was Moncado's advocacy of "dominion status" for the Philippines, which was popular among some Filipinos who were ambivalent about full independence, the longtime platform of Quezon's party. Above all, Moncado had succeeded in insinuating his voice and his body into a wide range of public venues that normally did not involve men of humble origins. His crime, if we must isolate one, was his pretentiousness, his quest for dignity, and his efforts to seek recognition for himself and his followers within a social and political milieu that routinely excluded them. In many of these endeavors, Moncado was highly successful.

This essay attempts to view Moncado through two angles of vision, spiritual and political—the primary elements of his charismatic authority. After a brief overview of Moncado's life and accomplishments, the essay will outline the three major arenas of his activity—California, Hawaii, and the Philippines—to present the various contexts within which the federation operated and adapted. This overview will be followed by two sections that will concentrate on more detailed discussions of the two dynamic aspects of Moncado's appeal: the man of mystery and the *politiko*. Throughout, the study will attempt to view Moncado's actions as representative of a larger movement, a movement that attracted Filipino laborers struggling to gain control over their destinies, to assert their identity within a strange and often hostile environment, and to seek a more meaningful spiritual and political explanation for their condition. For many Filipinos in America, Moncado's federation was the path they chose to achieve these ends.

Emerging from the Margin

Hilario Camino Moncado (1895–1956) was a man of remarkable achievements, all of which were made possible by his ability to establish and maintain control of an organization—the Filipino Federation of America—that attracted large numbers of loyal followers willing to acknowledge his leadership, even his divinity, and provide him with substantial resources.[2] In light of his origins, Moncado was an unlikely person to emerge as the leader of a complex organization like the federation. The son of relatively poor parents, he was raised in a remote rural barrio on the west coast of Cebu during the last years of the Spanish era and the early years of American colonial rule. The young Moncado does not appear to have stood out among his peers in anything but his height—he was unusually tall, six feet or more according to most accounts. Although he received some education in the public schools established under the Americans, he did not complete elementary school, and by the time he migrated from his village he had acquired only a rudimentary knowledge of English.[3] In 1914, at the age of eighteen, he joined a sizable number of other Cebuano youths as a labor recruit of the Hawaiian Sugar Planters' Association.[4] As a *sakada* (cane cutter) on the island of Kauai, Moncado was still rather nondistinctive, except for his athletic skills—he claims to have pitched for the Filipino baseball team that defeated the *haole* boys for the territorial championship in 1915.[5] The following year he left Hawaii, again with many of his countrymen, for San Francisco, where he hired on as a machinist with the Alaska Packers Association and spent much of 1916 processing salmon.

By the end of 1916, he was based in San Francisco, where he lived for three years. After another short employment stint in Alaska, he moved to Los Angeles in 1919. By the time Moncado arrived in Los Angeles, he had already acquired the equivalent of an American high school education. He resided in downtown Los Angeles, where he was a working student, studying law at the University of Southern California while supporting himself with two jobs, shelving books at the County Law Library and operating an elevator.[6] Like a growing number of Filipino laborers, Moncado had moved away from agricultural work, first by developing the skills of a machinist, later by parlaying his experience and seniority into more supervisory tasks (like those of a foreman), and finally by obtaining a secondary education and urban-based employment. It was in the cities that Moncado flourished and conceived of and initiated his organization. By 1925, he had lived in the two largest urban areas of California for more than eight years and was no longer the inexperienced *provinciano* who had boarded the ship to Hawaii ten years earlier.

In 1925, at the age of thirty, Moncado established the Filipino Federation of America in Los Angeles, incorporating it two years later in California as "a fraternal and semi-religious organization and non-profit corporation." In the late 1920s and early 1930s, the federation grew rapidly among Filipino laborers throughout California and Hawaii, and by the mid-1930s it was also firmly rooted in several colonies in the Philippines, especially in Mindanao. Although the number of members in the federation is at no time certain, estimates are many and varied. At its height in the early to middle 1930s, the federation's membership in California and Hawaii probably numbered between five and seven thousand, with perhaps two to three thousand living in the Philippine colonies by the end of the decade.[7]

By the early 1930s, Moncado boasted a number of academic and esoteric degrees and titles, including doctorates of Indian mystery (K.Ph.D. and N.Ph.D.) and a doctorate of law (LL.D). He was the author of several books, including his world travel memoirs, a political commentary on the United States and the Orient, a treatise on the "divinity of women," and a how-to manual on the 360-degree power golf swing.[8] Throughout the prewar years and at various intervals after the war, he published and edited a number of magazines and tabloids, including *Filipino Nation* (1924–33) — perhaps the most widely circulated Filipino magazine in the United States during its time.

Before the war, he also received considerable publicity and achieved a notable degree of success in both the American and Philippine political arenas. As the self-appointed representative of his working-class constituents in the federation, Hawaii, and the Philippines, he made frequent visits to Washington, D.C., testifying at Senate and House committee and subcommittee hearings. He appeared all over at convention and banquet tables, speaking alongside prominent Americans from chairmen of chambers of commerce to mayors and congressmen. In the Philippines, he was elected to the Commonwealth's Constitutional Convention in 1934 from his home district in Cebu, adding the title Senior Delegate to his long list of credits. As the head of his Modernist Party, he made three other bids for high political office in the prewar years: in 1934, he ran against Sergio Osmeña for Cebu's Senate seat; in 1938, he ran against the Nacionalista incumbent, Tomas Cabili, in the Senate race in Lanao; and in 1941 he ran against Manuel Quezon for the presidency of the Commonwealth. Though he was defeated in all three elections, his campaigns were covered in the press, where he was both ridiculed and depicted as a legitimate challenger to the existing political oligarchy.

Trapped in the Philippines during the Japanese occupation, he quickly negotiated a working relationship with the new rulers. At the end of the war, he was arrested as a collaborator, but he emerged in 1948, along with several others, unscathed by the postwar tribunals. Rather than suffering the censure of a suspected collaborator, Moncado surfaced after the destruction of the Philippines as Commander X, a "five-star general" in command of a 2.5 million–strong Filipino Crusaders Army, which, he claimed, had assisted in the country's liberation. When in full uniform, General Moncado was not infrequently, and not unintentionally, mistaken for General Douglas MacArthur. Although the war had separated him from his American and Hawaiian followings, he was able to reassert his leadership over the federation by the end of 1948, making it one of the few active Filipino organizations in postwar America. By the 1950s, however, Moncado was having some difficulty coming to terms with his new international status: a citizen of the new Republic of the Philippines and an alien in the United States.

Moncado died suddenly at the age of sixty in 1956 in Mexico, where he was living in exile awaiting the approval of his request for permanent residency in the United States. At the time of his death, Moncado was a wealthy man. He possessed beautiful homes in Los Angeles, Honolulu, and Manila; held property throughout California, Hawaii, Cebu, and Mindanao; was a member of a number of prestigious golf clubs; enjoyed relationships with powerful businessmen and politicians; and stocked a wardrobe that placed him among the world's best dressed. His death set off a series of feuds and eventual court actions, as some of his followers and his widow, Diana Toy Moncado, vied for control over the various branches of the federation and for ownership of the organization's assets.[9]

There can be little doubt that Hilario Moncado possessed an appealing, even magnetic, personality, one that attracted not only his followers but nearly everyone he encountered. His physical stature and attire, combined with considerable *chutzpah*, gave him a presence in almost any gathering. On a visit to Washington, D.C., in 1931, a local journalist, in an attempt to capture Moncado's persona, described his entry into a hotel lobby this way:

> Supporting his chin on a size 15 wing collar, [he] arrived here for a two-day stay at the Willard. Dr. Moncado is unusually large for a Filipino. His aspect has something of the Mongolian. When his spatted steps resounded thru the hotel lobby, guests looked up, sensing an arrival of importance. They heard a deep voice say: "Give me two rooms and a bath. I'm here to discuss the Filipino question."[10]

These personal features are not sufficient, however, to explain the hold he developed and maintained over many of his followers. Many Filipinos and Americans alike viewed Moncado as an outright charlatan, a trickster or Cebuano *tikasan* (swindler).[11] At no time is he known to have admitted to the conscious manipulation of his charismatic or divine attributes or to any grand scheme aimed at extracting money and support from federation members. Despite the lack of firsthand testimony, a close look at the evolution of his personal cult and the magnitude of his monetary acquisitions strongly suggest that he and his close associates

devoted considerable effort to the construction of a leader who was both
a spiritual and a political prophet to his followers.

With a keen sense of the spiritual and material needs and expectations of working-class Filipinos, Moncado set out to construct a fraternal
and religious organization with himself as the central figure. Between
1924 and 1930, he emerged with a set of effective attributes and accomplishments that captured the imaginations of his followers and convinced
many of them to devote their lives to the mission he defined for them.
What resulted from these efforts was a Moncado with two seemingly
contradictory personas, one as an otherworldly mystic and the other as a
modern politician. In the spiritual realm, Moncado became a man of mystery, a prophet and religious teacher with powerful supernatural attributes. He was revered as a theosophical "master" and an incarnate Christ
leading his people, in the tradition of Jose Rizal, down the path to salvation. In the material realm, Moncado became an influential *politiko*, a
highly educated lawyer and effective toastmaster with a powerful golf
swing and a low handicap. He was recognized as an effective politician
leading his people, also in the tradition of Jose Rizal, to liberation and
self-reliance. He was as adept at soiree chitchat, robust laughter, and
fashion statements as he was at proclaiming esoteric wisdom, posing in
mysterious gestures, and recounting doomsday scenarios. In one persona, he was an omniscient spirit who could simultaneously appear in
different parts of the world to observe and interact with his followers; in
the other, he boasted of his trans-Pacific voyages on luxury liners and
flights on Pan-American clipper ships. As *politiko* and man of mystery,
Moncado attracted hundreds of Filipinos who acknowledged his leadership and sustained him for more than thirty years.[12]

Arenas of Marginalization and Organization

Throughout the prewar years, thousands of mostly rural or working-
class Filipinos migrated as laborers from their villages to Hawaii and the
West Coast of the United States. Many of these sojourners eventually
returned to the Philippines after several years abroad, while others settled permanently in America. Wherever they lived and worked — in their
native villages or towns, on Hawaii plantations, on farms in California, or
in American urban areas, they found themselves on the margins, their
lives dominated by wealthier and more powerful individuals and institutions over which they had little or no influence. In the Philippines, most
were poor, uneducated, and trapped in a socioeconomic system that held
little hope for improvement. The search for a better livelihood, the promise of youthful adventure, and the dream of success led them to migrate.

As migrants to Hawaii and California, they found themselves in unfamiliar environments and circumstances where they were treated as ignorant and racially inferior. Moncado's message of ethnic and cultural dignity and the promise of liberation, not surprisingly, had considerable appeal to many of these men and women.

Among the most striking accomplishments of Moncado was his ability to recognize the varying conditions that prevailed in the three major arenas where he sought to recruit and hold members for the federation: California, Hawaii, and those areas of the Philippines where federation members returned (especially Mindanao and Cebu). Each of these operational environments presented Filipino laborers with a different set of conditions and relationships with the dominant economic and political forces, and each presented Moncado with a different challenge that led him and his close associates to devise unique arrangements.

It was not until after World War I that the number of Filipinos on the West Coast began to reach a critical mass. Most of the earliest of these migrants to the mainland came by way of the sugar and pineapple plantations of Hawaii, where Filipinos had been recruited since 1907. The general pattern of migration up to about 1920 was to hire out with the Hawaiian Sugar Planters' Association, work for at least one year in the Territory of Hawaii, and migrate as American "nationals" to the mainland to seek employment, mostly in the agricultural areas of California and Washington State or in the salmon industry of the Pacific Northwest and Alaska. With the passage of the Japanese Exclusion Act in 1924, the demand for Filipino laborers in the fields of California increased rapidly, with some 5,000 to 6,000 arriving each year at Los Angeles, San Francisco, and Seattle, and with a larger proportion of these arriving directly from the Philippines (more than 37,000 between 1920 and 1929). In 1929, there were an estimated 63,869 Filipinos residing in Hawaii, with more than 100,000 having arrived since 1907. Between 1920 and 1930, the estimated population of Filipinos in California rose from 2,674 to 30,470.[13] By 1931, there were an estimated 56,000 Filipinos residing in the mainland United States, the majority on the Pacific coast.[14]

In California, Filipinos initially worked on large farms owned and operated by individual families or corporations, which, as a rule, were linked to business interests and political power holders throughout the state. Access to work was organized through labor contractors or agents, mostly Filipinos themselves, who acted as liaisons between workers and farm owners or a variety of employers in urban areas. The agricultural work was seasonal, concentrated mostly on harvesting, and Filipino laborers migrated over considerable distances throughout the state's agricultural valleys to pick, among other things, asparagus, artichokes, cabbage, lettuce, peas, grapes, and citrus fruits. The work was exhausting and the living conditions generally substandard, with housing occasionally nonexistent. In these situations, Filipinos were often little more than beasts of burden, hired temporarily and then turned away to fend for themselves. During the off-season, many Filipino laborers migrated to towns and cities in search of employment and entertainment. The large urban areas of San Francisco and Los Angeles, as well as smaller cities like Stockton, Salinas, and Fresno, attracted large numbers of Filipino laborers. In the urban areas, Filipinos crowded into small rooms in hotels and boarding houses, found employment where they could and spent their money and time in search of more pleasurable activities, usually at dance and pool halls, gambling dens, bars, brothels, and boxing arenas.[15]

In Hawaii, Filipino labor and life were somewhat more regulated. Laborers were concentrated on plantations affiliated with the HSPA, the major recruiter of Filipinos. While in the islands, Filipinos worked on sugar and pineapple plantations under the supervision of managers in the employ of the major planters, who dominated the economic and political institutions and coercive forces of the Territory of Hawaii. In the 1920s, some efforts were made to improve living conditions for workers on the plantations and to transform them into more cohesive communities. Though there was more employment security and the potential for community formation on Hawaii plantations, wages were lower than for many jobs off the plantations, encouraging laborers to seek employment in the towns or Honolulu or, as became increasingly common, to leave Hawaii in search of better opportunities on the mainland or to return home.[16]

By far the largest number of Filipino laborers who came to Hawaii and California were young single males.[17] There were at first very few social institutions or organizations to supply the migrants with any sense of belonging or community, since most were living away from their families in unfamiliar surroundings. They led rigorous lives, full of insecurity, and suffered considerable racial discrimination, which occasionally resulted in physical attacks.

Given the migratory patterns of Filipinos in California, the larger towns and cities became the organizational centers of the federation. In Hawaii, efforts to establish the federation were concentrated on access to the plantations and their satellite camps, with branches emerging in the adjacent towns and with Honolulu emerging as the "territorial headquarters." In the Philippines, conditions were quite different. To prevent returning federation members from disappearing into rural barrios dominated by preexisting social and political conditions beyond the federation's influence, Moncado acquired land (mostly in Mindanao) and established colonies that operated as cooperative communities where followers lived and worked together and continued to devote themselves to the "Master." The "colony" was an ideal institution for the federation in the Philippines, since it functioned as a self-contained community that could operate outside the jurisdiction and scrutiny of the political-governmental system surrounding it.[18]

Moncado set out in 1925 to establish an organization of Filipinos that would permit him to transcend his marginality in American and Philippine societies and to acquire for himself a share of the relatively small surplus incomes of hundreds of Filipino laborers. To accomplish this, he and his associates invested considerable effort in the elaboration of Moncado's personal charisma and in his ultimate transformation into a grandiose figure with powerful spiritual and mystical attributes and an impressive array of political accomplishments.

The Transnational Prophet

It was Moncado's professed supernatural attributes that elicited the strongest and most frequent attacks from his critics. Moreover, over the years the belief in Moncado's divinity and the religious teachings of the federation have been the basis of a deep faith among many members of the organization. Although he at no time publicly professed his divinity, federation pamphlets and broadsides, as well as statements of devout members, clearly attributed to him a variety of spiritually potent and powerful qualities. For the faithful, Moncado was the reincarnation of Christ through Rizal. It is strongly believed by many surviving federation members (in the Philippines in general and in the federation) that "the Master" will return again (some said it would be in 1995) to redeem the world and fulfill his promise of salvation. That Moncado was actively involved in this revelation is strongly suggested by his having misrepresented the year of his birth to validate the claim of reincarnation through Rizal. Though his baptismal record states that he was born in 1895, all official biographical sources from the mid-1920s on give 1898 as the year of his birth. The change would have been necessary since Rizal was executed by the Spaniards in December 1896, nearly a year after Moncado was born, making his reincarnation chronologically improbable.[19]

It was not simply his identification with Christ and Rizal that made Moncado a person acknowledged to have supernatural powers. Moncado's charismatic appeal was rooted in a spiritual "mystery" that incorporated his personal characteristics, tales of his spiritual prowess, and a complex mix of elements incorporated into his persona from diverse religious traditions and cults operating in the Southern California of his day.[20]

Important aspects of Moncado's mystery clearly derived from his physical attributes—in particular his height, eyes, and expressions — all of which were for the faithful, as they should be, extraordinary. Throughout his career, photographs were frequently used to call attention to the supernatural elements of his body, often by adding attributes to make him seem even more unusual, such as Siva-like multiple arms and a Christ-like halo emanating from his head.[21] It was widely held that Moncado also possessed Superman-style vision and hearing and an ability to read minds and communicate with his followers when his physical body was elsewhere (a power similar to the "astral plane" of the theosophical masters). In his earliest photographs, he posed with a piercing glare—his "man of mystery" look, which was accentuated by what one biographer called "his singularly penetrating eyes."[22] "There are hidden depths in those eyes which twinkle and grow sombre by turns," observed an admirer; "Moncado the mysterious—it is that which endears him to many of his followers." This glare was reproduced on pamphlets, broadsides, and personalized pocket and wallet cards carried by followers and was integrated into a number symbolic settings that highlighted his divinity.[23]

Religious convictions undoubtedly played an important part in the decisions of many Filipinos to join and remain in the federation. It is also significant to stress that the most loyal and lasting members of the federation have been those who are deeply committed to what they perceived to be its religion. Quite a substantial number of these men and women were linked over the years with the spiritual core of the movement. During the prewar years, two spiritual centers were designated by Moncado, the first in Stockton, California (the "College of Mystery"), and later another in Honolulu. These became the headquarters of the federation's Spiritual Division and were placed under Moncado's principal spiritual adviser, Lorenzo Delos Reyes. Both centers attracted members who devoted themselves to the religious aspects of the organization. Though their numbers were relatively small (several hundred), the "spirituals" composed the esoteric core of federation religion, followed a prescribed code of conduct, and engaged in ritual acts that were not widely practiced by those members—the "materials"—outside their circle.[24] Though many spirituals remained in Hawaii, Delos Reyes transferred to the Dansalan colony in Lanao in 1932 and led the development of another center for the federation's religion until his death in 1937. With the spiritual migration back to the Philippines, the religion, after its formative years in America, returned home and began its reintegration into Filipino society, taking its place among a number of other religious movements that have been classified under the rubric of *colorum* or Rizalista cults.[25]

Though Moncado was the focal point of the federation's religion, the esoteric teachings propagated at the centers originated more from Delos Reyes, who as a youth was said to have been in close contact with "the religion of Mt. Banahaw" — the popular religion of the southern Tagalog region.[26] Moncado had not been a part of the Tagalog or the "Banahaw" tradition. He was, however, from a dynamic region of religious activity in his native province of Cebu. Although Moncado came from a Catholic family and community, there is every reason to assume that his Christianity was informed by the rich array of animistic and folk-Catholic traditions and practices of his municipality. The countryside of Moncado's youth — Cebu's *contracosta*, or west coast — was in the late nineteenth and early twentieth centuries alive with charismatic leaders and socioreligious rebels who defied Hispanized elites, resisted American rule, and established unique societies that frequently sought withdrawal from mainstream society. More than any other region of Cebu, this area was, in the view of indigenous elites and the colonial authorities, notorious for movements that were labeled *colorum*. Moncado and his family were undoubtedly familiar with several of the more prominent charismatic figures of Cebu's *contracosta*.[27] Nevertheless, when Moncado emerged as the head of the federation in Los Angeles in 1925, it was not as a traditional *colorum* or "Banahaw" religious figure but as a dynamic and complex spiritual and material personality quite different from any he would have encountered in early twentieth-century Cebu or the Tagalog area.

In the realm of interaction between the spiritual and material aspects of life, there was probably no more spectacular place on earth in the first two decades of the twentieth century than Southern California, with Los Angeles — "the city of heretics" — as its epicenter. Attempts by contemporary observers and later scholars to capture the emerging character of Los Angeles during "the dizzy decade" of the 1920s have stressed the extremes. There was an abundance of "the good life," perhaps best reflected in the tinsel world of Hollywood and the emerging automobile culture. Business and real estate speculation were booming; fortunes were being made; government offices and school buildings were rising; neighborhoods were forming; doctors, lawyers, and politicians were prospering; and people were pouring in from everywhere.[28] At the same time, religion was booming, and like business it was for some the source of considerable profit. Hundreds of religions were offering their services to the city's residents in their search for the spiritual meaning of life, making Los Angeles a city of churches, cults, and sects of all varieties: "the multiplicity and diversity of faiths that flourish," said the Works Project Administration's guide to the city, "probably cannot be duplicated in any other city on earth."[29] The majority of the successful were filling the mainstream Protestant churches, the working class was seeking salvation through a growing number of evangelical sects, and still others were involved in the hundreds of alternative religious groups scattered throughout the city.[30] Describing the city in the early 1920s, one observer wrote: "Los Angeles is the most celebrated of all incubators of new creeds, codes of ethics, philosophies — no day passes without the birth of something of this nature never heard of before."[31] Another wrote that as a "cultist paradise," Southern California was the home of "every religion, freakish or orthodox, that the world ever knew."[32]

Here, in the midst of Los Angeles in the 1920s, hundreds of Filipino laborers found employment, observed the glitter, spent their time and hard-earned money, and sought their own forms of salvation. Most resided in the downtown area in and around Main Street, which was described by one contemporary observer as a spiritual marketplace:

> Between the bookstores are little nooks where "doctors" dispensing guaranteed cures, such as tiger-fat salve, compete for customers with numerologists, astrologers, and gypsy fortune tellers. Strewn along this ungodly street one finds an occasional gospel mission.[33]

Perhaps the most striking religious change for most Filipinos in the United States was the dominant role played by Protestantism in mainstream American life. Despite their Catholic backgrounds, many Filipinos came under strong Protestant influences in Hawaii and California in the early decades of the century.[34] Three elements of Protestantism stand out in this regard: the "fellowship" or "Sunday school" model for the organization of religious services and activities; the prominence of the Bible as an authoritative text; and the overwhelming emphasis on an apocalyptic message.[35] All three were part of the federation's religion and became important components of Moncado's charismatic appeal.

Some of the earliest efforts to organize Filipinos in California were carried out by Protestant groups that sponsored religious and social welfare services in many of the larger urban areas. Perhaps the two most prominent of these in Los Angeles were the Filipino Christian Fellowship of Los Angeles and the Filipino Bible Class of Southern California. Both were organized early in the 1920s in downtown Los Angeles in close proximity to the Bunker Hill area where most Filipinos resided or boarded. The Christian Fellowship operated through the YMCA and the Bible Class was located at the Goodwill Industry Building; both provided congenial sites for social activities for Filipinos either passing through the city or residing there.[36] As a resident of Los Angeles since 1919, Moncado was active in several of the emerging Filipino organizations, in particular in the Filipino Association of Southern California.[37] Many members of the Filipino Association were also active in the Christian Fellowship and Bible Class, both of which were by late 1924 being promoted in Moncado's periodical, the *Equifrilibricum News Service*. The fellowship was one of five Filipino organizations working with Moncado in 1926 to organize the largest Rizal Day celebration held to date in the city. At that time, Moncado openly identified with the Protestants, declaring himself a Methodist in his official *Who's Who* entry in 1928.[38]

In the early 1920s, before the establishment of the federation, Moncado organized Sunday meetings where he presented sermons on a range of subjects, including Bible study, numerology, the kabala, the "moral life," the achievements of Jose Rizal, and the quest for Philippine independence. The "Sunday school" or "Bible fellowship" model for the early organization of the federation followed logically from the involvement of Moncado and his associates in these Protestant organizational activities, and the Sunday school format provided Moncado with his earliest charismatic platform. It was through these Sunday meetings that Moncado introduced his message and began to attract his following. "His religious teachings were never put in written form," wrote his biographer. Rather, "they were imparted to his followers through conversation in lecture classes, meetings, conventions, and other occasions where verbal exchanges of knowledge take place."[39]

The concept of the world coming to an end through a series of cataclysmic events (*mga gulo*) that would result in a new and better age for the chosen few was well integrated into the *pasyon*-based religious ideology of the Tagalogs as interpreted by Reynaldo Ileto.[40] This tradition, however, was based on vernacular versions of the *pasyon*, rather than on the Bible or the New Testament's Revelations.[41] The end of the world, along with the numerous signs that would portend its coming, became an even more prominent theme in Filipino Christian beliefs and practices after 1898, when a more Bible-based conception of the Apocalypse was introduced into the Philippines by American Protestant missionaries. This change was due in large part to the widespread distribution of Bibles (increasingly in the vernacular) by British and American Bible societies and Bible readings sponsored throughout the Philippines by various Protestant missionaries, as well as many of the earliest American public school teachers.[42] The greater availability of Bibles (in terms of both numbers and accessibility), especially New Testaments, and the Protestant emphasis on the Apocalypse moved the cataclysm-to-paradise theme into the forefront of popular religion in the early twentieth century.[43] It is also likely that the greater accessibility of Bibles and more popular Bible-focused interpretations of Christianity, even among

Catholics, led to the more widespread dissemination of apocalyptic themes, especially in areas like Cebu's *contracosta*, where the *pasyon*-based religion was less developed than it was within much of the Tagalog region.[44]

In the formative years of the federation, Moncado and Delos Reyes devoted considerable attention to the apocalyptic prophecy derived from their individual religious backgrounds and their exposure to fundamentalist Protestantism. For the cult of Moncado, the most pertinent aspects of the message were the impending end of the world and Christ's return to lead the chosen ones. The two obvious directions in this effort were to portend the coming end and to establish Moncado's credentials as the Messiah. In the earliest issues of *Equifrilibricum News Service,* readers were introduced to biblical passages and the language of the Apocalypse.[45] Within the emerging late-nineteenth- and early-twentieth-century popular expectation among Tagalogs, as reconstructed by Ileto, independence (*kalayaan*) from Spain (now the federation) would be as much a moment of spiritual liberation as it would be political. It would be a time (*panahon*) that would usher in a new age, an apocalyptic moment that "would bring about a condition of brotherhood, equality, contentment, and material abundance."[46] Building upon this tradition and linking it to Protestant apocalyptic precepts, Moncado and Delos Reyes identified the attainment of independence with Judgment Day and elevated Moncado to the status of the Messiah, a reincarnation of Christ through Jose Rizal, who would lead his flock to paradise. Early in the twentieth century, Jose Rizal had emerged within Filipino popular religious beliefs as the "second coming."[47]

In his early publications, Moncado prophesied the coming of independence for the Philippines, an independence that would initiate the long awaited apocalyptic moment. In less public arenas within the federation, Moncado was declared to be the Messiah. He was designated as "*omega*" in Christ's expression from Revelations: "I am the beginning and the end" (the *alpha* and the *omega*). Within this framework, federation members explain that Christ is "the beginning" (*alpha*), Rizal is the "and," and Moncado is "the end" (*omega*). Early federation symbolic representations in the form of photo-graphics (photographs displayed in a graphic format) depicted the three divine beings: Christ with his 12 disciples, Rizal with his 12 *ilustres* (prominent nationalist leaders of the late nineteenth century), and Moncado with his 144 federation members (12 lodges, each with 12 members). This photo-graphic was quite popular with federation members and showed the three messianic figures aligned in order from "*alpha*" to "and" to "*omega*."[48]

Despite his growing spiritual credentials within the realms of Protestant and Filipino popular Christianity, Moncado also drew considerably from the wide range of exotic and esoteric religious cults and organizations operating in Southern California in the first three decades of this century. Central themes of Moncado's cult were informed by a variety of mysticism associated with, among others, Vedantists, theosophists, and Rosicrucians—all of which trace their mysteries to ancient roots in India and the Middle East. Few Filipinos, including Moncado, actually joined these societies, and in fact all three were the reserve of white Americans in search of oriental wisdom, mysteries, and enlightenment. The contact point between Filipinos and these religious traditions was their literature and the various derivative interpretations of their doctrines, which sifted into the popular culture of Southern California. That Filipinos did not become Vedantists, theosophists, or Rosicrucians was significant in that the mysteries of these groups remained distant and out of context and thereby even more mysterious and more potent.

At the same time Moncado was emerging as the biblical Messiah of Revelations, Indian mystic attributes were already central to his charismatic persona. Early in the 1920s, he is said to have spent several months studying with "a Hindu holy man in Los Angeles," and one of his earliest sympathetic biographies claimed that his personal library contained a number of books on Indian religions, among them an account of Ramakrishna, the legendary founder of the Vedanta Society.[49] The Vedanta Society was established in Los Angeles in 1904, and, although it gathered a relatively small community of intellectual adherents, it served to legitimize a range of other Indian philosophical and yogic groups that had spread throughout Southern California by 1920. Among the more popular Indian yogic groups to emerge in the area was Swami Yogananda's Self-Realization Fellowship, founded in Los Angeles in the early 1920s. Los Angeles emerged as Swami Yogananda's world headquarters for the teaching of *kriya yoga*.[50] There can be little doubt that the federation's "physical culture" program, which incorporated yogic-style exercises and vegetarianism, was influenced by these readily accessible teachings.[51]

Since the century's turn, Southern California had become one of the major focal points of the Theosophical Society. Katherine Tingley, the "Purple Mother" of one of the society's popular branches, established her permanent theosophical center at Point Loma in the Imperial Valley in 1899. Soon afterward, as Carey McWilliams relates, Southern California "acquired a reputation as an occult land and theosophists began to converge upon it from the four corners of the world."[52] By the second decade of the century, all three of the main branches of the theosophical movement had headquarters in Southern California and meeting places proliferated throughout the Los Angeles area. These included the fifteen-acre Krotona ("place of promise") erected by Albert Powell Warrington, also in the Hollywood hills, and affiliated with the branch of theosophy headed by Annie Besant.[53] Theosophical reviews, tracts, and pamphlets, as well as those of various other Indian religious groups, were published and circulated widely throughout Southern California and beyond. These materials attempted to explicate a number of esoteric themes that would have been unfamiliar to most Filipinos, among them reincarnation, karma, yoga, the kabala, psychic phenomena, astral planes, and Indic forms of astrology and numerology.[54] It is not by coincidence that Moncado's earliest published biographies proclaim that he was discovered as a child and transported to India, where he acquired "degrees" in Indian mysticism and kabalistic knowledge.

Theosophy was a particularly relevant model for the federation. Though based on Indian spiritualism, the theosophical movement was promoted by non-Indian Christians, who, like Annie Besant, had little difficulty integrating her religious tradition with those of India. Within the Indian tradition, Besant also promoted vegetarianism, which, like yoga, became an important part of the food and health regime of the more spiritual members of the federation. Another prominent theosophical concept that clearly had an impact on the cult of Moncado was that of the "Masters," the great cosmic souls of "perfect beings who govern and direct the world." The most famous of the living "Masters" of the day was Krishnamurti, discovered as a child in South India and promoted by the Besant branch of the society as "the new Messiah," "coming World Teacher," or, as Besant referred to him, "our Krishna-Christ." He was the spiritual center of Besant's Order of the Star. As early as 1916, Krishnamurti made regular visits to Southern California, especially to the Krotona in Hollywood, for meetings and speaking engagements; by 1923, he had established a permanent residence north of Los Angeles at Ojai (his Arya Vihara).[55]

Significantly, in his younger days Krishnamurti was not an ascetic or even a retiring Hindu holy man; he was a man of the world, an attractive and charismatic presence. One observer described this "exotically handsome" celebrity in this way:

> Fencing with reporters in a vast suite at the Waldorf-Astoria, presiding over annual "camp" on three continents organized with military precision, speaking in French from the Eiffel Tower to a radio audience of 1.2 million—in almost all his public appearances, he was a composed and enigmatic figure, whose golf clubs and London suits, tennis rackets and aristocratic offhandedness seemed calculated to contradict every standard expectation of an Indian guru.[56]

On one of Krishnamurti's visits to Southern California, where he often arrived in his Lincoln touring car, he was reported in the *Philippine*

Republic as having "sailed from the U.S., wearing a gray lounge suit, tan shoes and spats, and reading *Elmer Gantry*, sensational new American novel."[57] This was, indeed, a man worthy of emulation, an otherworldly mystic deeply engaged in the pleasures and distractions of this world. Several of Moncado's titles (among them Master and World Teacher), his childhood discovery as a mystic sage, and his identification with the potent symbol of "the star," as well as his personal attire and flamboyant behavior, are remarkably reminiscent of Krishnamurti. In this construction, mostly by Delos Reyes, of Moncado's mysterious persona, he was the "Master of Equifrilibricum"—and in his most spiritual form was "Equifrilibricum"—combining the three qualities of equality, fraternity, and "life of liberty." Moncado was frequently, especially in textual accounts, referred to as E. F .B.—that is, Moncado as a spiritual or divine being.[58] Significantly, his first periodical, the *Equifrilibricum News Service* (1924), invoked Moncado's identification as E. F. B.

Another potent connection between the theosophy movement and the emerging federation of the late 1920s was the anticolonial struggle for independence and national identity. Annie Besant and other theosophists were outspoken proponents of the growing nationalist movement in India and strong promoters of Indian culture and religion in the West. Involved in their own movement, Filipinos were aware of the Indian struggle, and Philippine and Filipino American newspapers and magazines occasionally expressed solidarity with Indian nationalists, in particular through their representatives in the federation—the theosophists—who also expressed their sympathy for the Filipino cause. Moncado's appeal of 1926, "Wake-Up, Filipinos," clearly echoed Annie Besant's 1913 cry, "Wake Up, India," wherein she called for Indian independence and the creation of a new nation built upon strong Hindu roots.[59]

In addition, the theosophists provided the federation with a number of attractive organizational models. The various branches of the Theosophical Society were organized into lodges, each more or less self-governed, with the national and international organization being in the form of a federation of lodges. This, of course, was not unlike the Masonic organization, with which many Filipinos were already familiar and by which many Filipino organizations, including the Caballeros de Dimas Alang, were already organized. The Theosophical Society, however, also maintained an inner circle, the Esoteric Section, which consisted of the more spiritually developed members, who maintained more direct communication with the Masters, were more steadfast in their devotion and commitment to the esoteric ideas of the movement, and, as a result, wielded more influence over the movement as a whole.[60] This inner circle resembled the federation's Spiritual Division, which was, as noted earlier, initiated in Stockton and later transferred to Hawaii.[61]

The Rosicrucian Order and its mystical teachings of "ancient wisdom" appears also to have had some influence on Moncado and his associates. The two most prominent Rosicrucian groups had their headquarters in California. The Rosicrucian Fellowship was founded in 1907 by Carl L. van Graahoff (alias Max Heindel), who eventually set up a major center at Mt. Ecclesia in Oceanside, not far from Los Angeles. An even more active group, the Ancient and Mystical Order Rosae Crucis (AMORC) was established by H. Spencer Lewis in 1915 in San Jose, California. From its headquarters, the San Jose branch of the Rosicrucians grew rapidly, in part because of its organizational similarity to the Masonic movement, through systematic advertising in local newspapers and magazines, and by disseminating Rosicrucian literature by mail to anyone interested in the mystical doctrines.[62] A number of the federation's symbolic representations, as well as carefully staged mystical photographs and photo-graphics depicting both Moncado and Delos Reyes, are reminiscent of those of contemporary Rosicrucians.[63]

Moncado's earliest mystically inspired book, *The Divinity of Women* (1927), seems strongly influenced by contemporary Rosicrucian literature, which stressed the spiritual essence of women. The book's graphics, as noted, reflects a familiarity with Rosicrucian symbols, and it quotes from a number of Rosicrucian authors. One of the most intriguing connections, however, derives from the influence on the federation of the mystical and prophetic writings of the nineteenth-century Rosicrucian author Lord Bulwer-Lytton. A popular and persistent spiritual and nationalistic prophecy recounted by many federation members derives from this Rosicrucian source. Briefly summarized, the belief as reinterpreted by federation members is as follows: that a superior form of beings, the *vril-ya* (said to be of Malay, even Filipino, origin), will emerge from their subterranean domain with an extremely powerful weapon, which they will use to bring eternal peace to the world. This belief comes directly from Lord Bulwer-Lyttons's novel, *The Coming Race*, first published in 1870 and reprinted frequently during the early twentieth century.[64] The term *vril-ya*, as used by federation religious leaders, who interpreted it as "the Malay race is the light of the world," can be traced directly to this novel.[65] The concept of "the Coming Race and the Coming Christ" was also a popular theme in the addresses and writings of Annie Besant and a tradition well integrated into theosophical teachings going back to the origins of the movement under Madame Helena Petrovna Blavatsky.[66] Moncado and his associates frequently referred to Filipinos as "the coming race" and, in time, pinpointed the home of the *vril-ya* in Lanao in the federation's "promised land" in Mindanao.

Drawing from the wealth of spiritual and occult ideas prevalent in Southern California during his day, Moncado's mystery derived from diverse traditions. There was never any need for a systematic religious philosophy in the construction of Moncado's cult since his authority was rooted in mystery not doctrine. Contradictions and inconsistencies simply reinforced his mystery, enhancing his charismatic appeal. Perhaps the clearest example of this is the response of one member of the Moncado Foundation of America Church in Honolulu in 1979. In a short talk I pointed out the contradiction between Moncado's baptismal date (1895) and the date used for his birth in most official biographies (1898), the former making it impossible for him to be a reincarnation of Rizal, who was executed in 1896. What appeared to be a serious discrepancy, if not a clear example of manipulation, was of little concern to most of the members present. One man, with nearly forty years of membership in the federation, politely smiled and informed me that this so-called contradiction is simply another example of "the Master's mystery."[67] For most of his followers, Moncado possessed spiritual powers that could not be challenged by a resort to criticism based on rational argument or debate— his power was derived from spiritual forces that were beyond reason and, above all, a matter of faith.[68]

As Moncado moved from the spiritual to the earthly movement, he frequently attempted, often with much success, to make critical links between the two. One such connection appeared very early in the formation of the federation. Moncado stressed the significance of the number twelve, the unit upon which the federation was built.[69] Each lodge was to consist of 12 "matriculate" (dues-paying) members, with twelve lodges joined to form one division (144 matriculate members). When twelve divisions were established, the federation would reach its supernatural goal, or perhaps more accurately described as its apocalyptic moment: 1,728 matriculate members.[70] At the December 1927 federation convention in Los Angeles, Moncado explained to those assembled:

> The Filipino Federation hinges on these attributes, 1728. [T]he Filipino flag has three stars, which I interpret in my own knowledge—Equality, Fraternity, Liberty. The Sun is the master. He shines. I need only 1728. I have a field for you in the far corners of the world. I will not tell you where it is. [O]ur freedom depends upon these attributes, 1728 people. If you love freedom my friends, I ask you to cooperate with me. If you like to see God, I ask that you cooperate with me.[71]

82   Michael Cullinane

Pulling the convention theme together in his final speech, Moncado connected the spiritual potency of 1,728 with his prophecy concerning the Filipino political quest for independence, the central mission of his earthly activities: "We are going to tell the world that the independence of the Philippines will be granted between 1927 and 1935," and, "in that case I would like to see everyone of you a member, as that 1728 will not be far off."[72] Having established the spiritual base of the federation, Moncado turned to his political work.

The Master as Ilustrado

Although Moncado's spiritual authority contributed significantly to his hold over many federation members, he seemed much less comfortable as the "man of mystery" than as the flamboyant *politiko*. In the latter persona, Moncado was anything but the mystic or meditative sage of the Banahaw tradition. As the federation's president and political representative, he was, indeed, a highly effective politician. In the federation, he brought federation members directly into the struggle for Philippine independence and more generally into a closer relationship with the "good life" of middle-class America, a life that was denied most of them as a result of their ethnicity and low incomes.[73] In the Philippines, Moncado's political activities brought the members into electoral politics not as mere voters for distant candidates but as active campaigners and advocates of a formal political party of their own. Through Moncado's political endeavors, members of the federation were able to transcend their humble positions in both American and Philippine society and participate in activities normally reserved for the elite. In becoming a *politiko* of some renown, Moncado demonstrated remarkable skills at organization and negotiating his way through a wide range of institutions and interactions with prominent personalities.

Moncado came to Hawaii in 1914 with little or no formal education and a limited knowledge of English. Six years later he could claim to be the "poet laureate" of his class at the University of Southern California Law School. Education became an essential vehicle in his quest for recognition and leadership within the emerging Filipino community of Los Angeles. He realized the importance of education in achieving success and status in both America and the Philippines. Not surprisingly, he invested considerable effort in acquiring the necessary *títulos*, particularly the most coveted of all degrees, that of law.

While the majority of Filipinos in California were engaged in farm labor, a smaller number had come to study. The first of these were Philippine government-sponsored students, *pensionados*, sent to obtain degrees in various subjects and to return to government posts or professional careers in education or business. In time, others came on their own or were sent by their families, mainly to obtain degrees from American colleges and universities.[74] Many of the earliest Filipino social organizations in the federation were established by students and located on college campuses, often associated with the small ethnic communities that grew up around them. In the early decades of the century, as California's public and vocational school systems underwent a boom in both building and enrollments, educational opportunities expanded considerably.[75] Filipino laborers became increasingly aware of the availability of these relatively inexpensive educational opportunities, particularly in urban areas, leading a growing number to take advantage of the situation by combining work and study.[76]

By 1930, "a steady stream of young men" were described as coming directly from the Philippines to study in the federation. The number of Filipinos in colleges and universities at the time was estimated at two to three thousand, with the majority concentrated on the West Coast.[77] It is quite likely that these figures underestimate the total number of Filipinos in school, since most laborers, with little or no previous education, concentrated their schooling at the elementary and secondary levels or enrolled in vocational training programs. Moreover, these working students attended school on an irregular basis, often taking many years to obtain diplomas or degrees or, as was often the case, being forced to drop out altogether.[78] If these secondary and vocational students are added to the figures above, the number of Filipinos studying in the federation in the 1920s and early 1930s may have been as much as 10 percent of total Filipino residents (more than five thousand), with the majority of these being working students.

The "student class," as *ilustrados* in the making, assumed a degree of superiority over their working-class countrymen, some even more so as a result of their more affluent origins in the Philippines or due to their official designation as *pensionados*. Confident that their educational attainments would secure for them professional or government employment back home, most took pride in their educational achievements and saw themselves as the "true" representatives of their people in America. Although most did not stay long, they often dominated positions of leadership in the Filipino social and fraternal organizations that began to emerge during the second and third decades of the century. Significantly, they were also more assertively part of the "new Philippines," characterized by cooperation with American colonial rulers and energetic participation in the independence movement led by Filipino political elites at home. They organized events and programs that displayed Filipinos as modern, intelligent individuals worthy of self-government and freedom. When prominent Filipino politicians came on official visits or to promote the cause of independence, they often spoke on college campuses, usually at functions sponsored by the local Filipino student association. Filipino laborers found themselves paraded before such dignitaries as a voiceless mass, lending only their bodies to the cause, or they were left out of these occasions altogether. What could laborers possibly have to offer to the discussion of independence, governance, or economic development? Elite discourse on independence was the reserve of the educated; the working class was relegated to the role of spectators and followers, men too ignorant to participate in the dialogue.[79]

Although relatively little is known about Moncado's life and activities in California between 1916 and 1924, what stands out are his educational achievements, both real and fabricated. Having arrived in San Francisco with, at best, a fourth-grade education, Moncado managed to obtain enough secondary education between 1916 and 1919 to get himself admitted into the Law School of the University of Southern California in late 1919. This was no mean accomplishment. USC at the time was the premier university of Southern California, and its graduates dominated politics and the legal profession of the Los Angeles area during the prewar years.[80] Work commitments and poor grades led to Moncado's forced withdrawal from USC in 1922 but not before he had amassed about half the required credits for the degree.[81]

Sometime in 1922, after his withdrawal from law school, Moncado is reported to have disappeared for nine months. It is likely that it was at this time, as a former colleague claimed, that Moncado studied under a "Hindu holy man."[82] This experience provided Moncado with a way to short-circuit his quest for academic titles by manufacturing exotic degrees that would both contribute to his spiritual mystery and provide him with the requisite abbreviations following his name: K.Ph.D. (doctorate of kabala) and N.Ph.D. (doctorate of numerology). These titles emerged as integral parts of his early biographies and served him well for several years, but they were not sufficient to legitimize his entry into the political struggle for Philippine independence — the realm of the *ilustrados*.

By early 1927, Moncado had turned again to the educational attainments that would be necessary for him to lead a political movement. In 1927, he enrolled in the Law School of Southwestern University, a small private institution only recently established in Los Angeles but already boasting the largest enrollment of any law school on the West Coast. At the time, he was presiding over the federation, editing its newspaper, and holding down two jobs. Despite his many distractions, he was granted an LL.B. degree from Southwestern, after only a year of study, in June 1928.

In the fall, he enrolled in the same university's Graduate School of Law.[83] From this time on, published photographs of Moncado frequently show him in his cap and gown with his degree in hand.

In 1930, he transferred to another Los Angeles–based private law school, Olympic University, where in that same year he was granted LL.M. and A.M. degrees, having submitted two theses (one in law and the other in history), and an LL.D. (Honoris Causa), based on his successful lobbying efforts in the U.S. Congress in Washington, D.C.[84] In 1931, he pursued a formal doctorate of civil law at Olympic University, completing the degree (D.C.L.) that same year, as he later explained in his memoir, by taking a tour of Europe, where along the way he attended classes and conducted research at Oxford, Paris, Berlin, and the Ecclesiastical (Vatican) Universities, and by submitting a thesis entitled: "Historical Development of the Roman and Civil Laws."[85] By the start of 1932, most of his formal photographs and biographical listings identified him as: "Dr. Hilario Camino Moncado, A.M., K.Ph.D., N.Ph.D., LL.B., LL.M., LL.D., D.C.L."[86] With these academic achievements, Moncado could claim an intellectual status comparable to that of only one other Filipino, Jose Rizal, the *ilustrado's ilustrado*.

In Search of the Federation

Moncado's efforts to establish an organization in Los Angeles from the early 1920s to 1930 reveal a great deal about his motivations and the avenues available to him at the time. Although his critics would have us believe that Moncado was only after the money, it would be a mistake to assume that this was his sole motivation. Clearly, there was more at stake. As suggested earlier in this essay, among the most important contributions of Moncado and the federation to its members was to provide them with a voice and a place in the strange and often hostile worlds in which they lived. Moncado's apocalyptic and nationalistic messages held out the promise of dignity and a new relationship between Filipinos and the society that surrounded them. The federation constructed for many of them a means of improving the conditions of their existence both on earth and in the hereafter. As these messages brought in recruits for the emerging federation, they also served as the vehicle of Moncado's personal liberation.

Moncado began his efforts to seek recognition and leadership within the relatively small but growing Filipino community of Los Angeles early in the 1920s. Although the city's Filipino population fluctuated seasonally as students came and went and as agricultural laborers moved in and out in search of recreation and temporary employment, the more permanent residents at the time consisted of two to three hundred men and a very small number of women. Their livelihoods ranged from labor contractors and managers of boarding houses and restaurants to dishwashers, bellboys, and maintenance men, and their numbers included a number of individuals engaged in small-scale entrepreneurial pursuits. During the off-season of the agricultural cycle, the Filipino population of the city increased greatly, perhaps to ten times its normal size.[87]

As a working student, Moncado found himself in between, a man with working-class origins and *ilustrado* aspirations. He was neither ignorant nor interested in remaining a spectator. In addition to learning the importance of education, his long residence in California had also taught him that America was dominated by people with money and influence and that, unlike in his own society, there were more opportunities to find both. Determined to liberate himself from his lowly status, he was full of energy and ideas and was gradually becoming aware of his personal charismatic appeal. By 1921, he was firmly established in the Los Angeles area. Over the next four years, he gathered around him a small circle of other working students, most of them having come to California as laborers from the Visayan region of the Philippines.[88] In a meeting with several like-minded friends a short time before the establishment of the federation, Moncado is said to have made his quest for money quite explicit when he challenged them by saying: "What gives power to a man in America? Is it not money? Then let us get money."[89]

To his detractors, as well as to those who attempted to emulate his actions, Moncado was a charlatan who devised an efficient system to extract money and support from his docile following among uneducated Filipino laborers. He was not the only person, Filipino or non-Filipino, having this objective. Carey McWilliams put it this way: "Preyed upon by every variety of leech, kicked around by the police, the Filipinos have also been grossly imposed upon by their own countrymen." "Racketeering Filipinos," he observed,

> sell the Pinoy a bewildering variety of worthless merchandise as well as tickets for raffles, picnics, lotteries, "sweetheart contests" and cockfights; and initiate them, for fancy fees, into a bizarre assortment of lodges, social clubs, and fraternal organizations (more than 103 Filipino organizations were counted some years ago in Los Angeles)."[90]

In activities such as these, Moncado was, perhaps, one of the most successful. Like others, Moncado was aware that the large body of single Filipino males, both laborers and students, residing on the West Coast and the plantations of Hawaii had money to spend. As a part of his early feud with leaders of other Filipino fraternal and labor organizations, in particular the Caballeros de Dimas Alang, and with Chinese gambling interests, Moncado clearly revealed his awareness of the money at stake. As he wrote later in his autobiography:

> There were approximately sixty thousand Filipinos being employed by the American growers throughout California at that time [1928-29]. Each Filipino received at least a net amount of one thousand dollars in one year which would mean that gambling houses in Chinatown in California were receiving about sixty million dollars a year. The Chinese gamblers in Los Angeles were kept busy; I was responsible for the padlocking of their gambling joints in Chinatown by the city authorities.[91]

In his discussion of the exploitative institutions surrounding Filipino farm laborers in California, Carey McWilliams made a similar, though somewhat more realistic, assessment:

> It has been estimated that half of the annual earnings of Filipinos in California—and the total would run into the millions—is lost in gambling. In Stockton—"the Manila of the United States"— the "take" on Filipino gambling and prostitution has been estimated at $2,000,000 a year.[92]

Lacking capital in the early years, few Filipinos actually owned or operated such exploitative establishments. Although these operations were controlled by Chinese, Japanese, and Americans, ambitious Filipinos were quick to see the entrepreneurial opportunities and soon developed alliances with existing business interests. Advertisements for legal activities were reproduced in the emerging Filipino press of urban California (San Francisco, Los Angeles, Stockton, Salinas) and Seattle, providing publishers with modest shares of the action. To supplement their incomes, individual promoters with access to larger numbers of Filipino laborers, like labor contractors, recruited for this or that dance hall, gambling den, or brothel. Leaders of fraternal and labor organizations could establish partnerships with owners of these service industries by guaranteeing a larger clientele, allowing individuals or the organization as a whole to enjoy a share of the profits. Another common method of extracting surplus earnings from Filipino laborers was through burial and repatriation societies, often presented as a variety of insurance (or assurance) or cooperative banking schemes. Although some of these were legitimate and served valuable functions for numbers of single migrants in Hawaii and California, others were notorious for taking money and providing little or no services.[93]

It was in activities such as these that Moncado first reached out to fellow Filipinos in Southern California. His earliest known endeavor in this
direction was the promotion of Los Angeles dance halls. In the mid-
1920s, there were at least ten dance halls within a half a mile of one another in downtown Los Angeles.[94] The earliest issues of Moncado's
Equifrilibricum News Service (1924–26) regularly advertised several of
these dance halls with promotionals that catered to Filipinos. Among
them were the following.[95]

> *Claremont Dancing Academy:* Filipinos Welcome! 50 Lady
> Instructors, 50! Enjoy Good Dancing. Music furnished by
> Wilson's Jazz Orchestra. Admission 10 cents. Open from 8 p.m.
> to 12:30 a.m.

> *111 Dance Academy:* The Home Where the Filipino Boys Are
> Treated With Respect and Courtesy. 75 Girls Who Are Always
> Ready to Dance With You. Ory's Creole Jazz Orchestra. Open
> Every Night from 7:30 to 1 A.M. Except Sundays. Admission 25¢.

In 1926, even after the founding of the federation, Moncado continued to promote dance halls, but now with a greater degree of sophistica-
tion in that his newspaper was more selective. In an article entitled
"Special Attention," readers were personally encouraged to patronize the
Liberty Dance Academy, where the manager, Jack Goldberg, "is the best
friend the Filipino boys ever had in this City for many years." Elsewhere
in the same issue, Mr. Goldberg, once again labeled as "an old friend of
all the Filipino boys," was quoted, urging all eligible voters to cast their
ballots in the coming election for Charles H. Kelley for county sheriff.[96]

Ironically, as the federation grew in the late 1920s the members of its
lodges were strictly prohibited from, among other things, patronizing
dance halls.[97] Although Moncado later rationalized his opposition to
these "immoral" activities within the context of their negative effects on
the lives and images of Filipinos in America, his detractors have been
unanimous in concluding that the purpose of these prohibitions was first
and foremost to keep his followers from wasting their surplus income so
that he could collect it from them in dues, other forms of "tribute," or
simply donations to the "Master." In this way, Moncado was able to gain
direct access to the money rather than collecting only a small portion of
it through advertisements and promotional fees.[98] Given the immense
quantity of money collected by Moncado over the years, it is not difficult
to conclude that the allegations of his critics were accurate in this area.

Despite its size, the Filipino community of Los Angeles organized
at least twelve associations between 1924 and 1927, nine within the

community at large and three among Filipinos studying in the area.[99] Although his 1955 autobiography does not mention affiliations with any of these groups, other sources indicate that he was a founding member and past president of the Filipino Association of Southern California and was affiliated for a time with the Filipino Bible Class.[100] The clearest sign of Moncado's emergence as an aspiring community leader was the founding of his semimonthly newspaper, *Equifrilibricum News Service*, in November 1924. It was published predominantly in English, with occasional Filipino vernacular-language sections (mostly in Cebuano and Ilocano). The *Equifrilibricum News Service* quickly became a vehicle for promoting his personal agenda (both spiritual and material) and engaging in Filipino ethnic politics in Los Angeles. A little over a year after he established his newspaper, on December 27, 1925, Moncado announced the formation of the Filipino Federation of America.[101]

Building an Organization

Beginning as a small, intimate group of close associates, the federation remained nearly invisible for over a year. The original group, later designated the first lodge, consisted of Moncado and twelve members, most of whom were at the time working students. "The first year was a real struggle," recalled one of the early officers, with "little for the members to show for their work." The federation rented a "small office," which they "used for a club room, business office and for general gatherings."[102] Recruitment was slow, with Moncado investing his personal energy and the resources of his newspaper to solicit members. "Many a time" during the early days, as one chronicler reported, "Moncado would encounter bitter opposition even to the extent of being thrown out the door of the meeting place." The original twelve members "spent night and day campaigning for membership" and going about "by twos as the disciples of Jesus," to visit "their brother Filipinos in their own rooms and tell them of their mission." Every Sunday, Moncado lectured to the members at their office in the Stack Building, where he read from the Bible, delivered sermons, made prophetic pronouncements, and discussed recruitment strategies.[103]

While continuing to depend on key leaders within the core group, in mid-1926 Moncado was able to recruit several effective new leaders into the organization.[104] Throughout 1926, the federation's persistence began slowly paying off. "After their day's labor," dedicated members "would go to pool halls, dancing halls, gambling halls, and places of questionable character, making converts of their countrymen who frequented these places."[105] A major direction at this time was also to send Los Angeles–based recruiters out into the agricultural districts in search of members. Moreover, in an attempt to attract laborers passing through the city, the federation announced its "Free Employment Bureau," which specialized in "Hotels, Restaurants, Cafeterias, Institutions, Clubs, Domestic Homes, Apartments and Hospitals."[106] By the end of 1926, a second lodge had been established in Stockton and a third in Los Angeles, bringing into the federation "thirty-six members all told."[107] Toward the end of 1926, the *Equifrilibricum News Service* published what might be viewed as a federation apology for its "embarrassing" beginning, concluding that with more experience the organization was now on the road to success.[108]

Things began to change for the federation when Moncado succeeded in having himself chosen as the head of the organizing committee for the December 1926 Rizal Day festivities.[109] By this time, Rizal Day had become the most important event within Filipino communities and organizations everywhere within the federation, as it had in the Philippines. It was the day on which Filipinos commemorated the execution by the Spaniards of the man who was by this time their undisputed national hero. In larger communities of Filipinos, organizations and individuals joined together to honor their martyr and express their nationalist sentiments, frequently using such occasions to express their collective desire for independence.[110] Having witnessed and publicized two events of this kind in Los Angeles in 1924 and 1925 and fully aware of the growing significance they held for the Filipino community, Moncado was determined to make the 1926 festivities a moment to remember, one that would display Filipinos to the larger community and allow him, as an emerging Rizal-like figure, to appear on center stage.

The resulting Rizal Day festivities, held on December 30, were widely lauded as the best ever, the highlight being the display of Philippine flags along two downtown streets, Broadway and First, where they flew side by side with American flags.[111] The festivities included a major series of events at the Bovard Auditorium on the USC campus, complete with recitations of Rizal's writings, musical performances by a Filipino band from the *U.S.S. California*, presentations by prominent city officials, including Mayor George Cryer, and addresses by, among others, the head of Democratic Party of California, Attorney Isidro Dockweiler, scion of a prominent Los Angeles pioneer family.[112] In connection with the event, the federation sponsored an essay contest on the theme of "The 1926 Rizal Day Organization" and for months after the festivities solicited and judged the entries.[113]

The success of the festivities gave Moncado exactly what he needed, a boost to promote the federation. Early the next year, he published and distributed a sixty-four-page booklet, entitled *1926 Rizal Day Organization*

Breaks All the Records of Any Filipino Rizal Day Celebration in America,
and produced a large wall poster that included his "man of mystery"
photograph and numerous shots of the successful Rizal Day event, all
under the heading "Wake Up Filipinos, Join the Federation." The booklet featured photos of Rizal and Moncado, articles by Moncado and
William Schaefle, rapidly emerging as Moncado's most active American
promoter, and the photos and complete essays of the thirteen contest-
ants in the federation contest, all praising the work of the organizing
committee of the 1926 Rizal Day events. In the pamphlet, Moncado
appealed to Filipinos:

> I ask you not to forget the day the flag of your Mother Country
> first floated in the beautiful American City of Los Angeles,
> California. It was on the eve of December 27, 1926. I ask you also
> to remember my prophecy that between 1927 and 1935, if you do
> your part, our country will obtain her freedom.[114]

In his poster soliciting membership, where the appeal was more
direct, he proclaimed: "We, the members of the Filipino Federation of
America, believe that the Philippine Islands under the control of the
Malayan Race, will in the future rank as a 'World Power.'"[115] For many
Filipinos spending the holidays in Los Angeles, this was truly a memorable event, serving notice to the larger community that they had arrived
and that they, too, had a rich culture, an outstanding national hero, and
a desire to be free.[116]

Indicative of his success, Moncado came under serious attack from
competing organizations and individuals in the city's Filipino community. Opposition to Moncado and his style of organizing clearly made
enemies for the federation. This was evident at the end of 1926, when
another coalition of Filipino groups, led by leaders of the Filipino
Catholic Club, calling themselves the Filipino Community of Los
Angeles, convened a competing Rizal Day celebration at the city's
Knights of Columbus Hall.[117] The federation's "Free Employment
Bureau" threatened labor contractors operating in the city, apparently
leading to a lawsuit that was filed against the federation in 1926.[118] From
the federation point of view, much of this opposition came from two
main groups: "the so-called intelligent class" and the "Filipino gamblers."[119] "The student elements," noted one defender of the federation,
"called Moncado a fool, a fanatic, an idiot."[120] The "gamblers," alleged
Moncado, objected to the federation's policies against members frequenting dance and gambling halls. By 1928, much of this opposition
was concentrated in the Caballeros de Dimas Alang, a competing fraternal organization that had originated in the Philippines. The leaders of

this group challenged Moncado's claim to leadership of the community and ridiculed his apocalyptic and esoteric religious messages.

With his federation now incorporated, Moncado, in a burst of confident energy, moved in several directions at once in 1927. In July and August, he made his first cross-country tour of the federation, "personally acquainting himself with the conditions and needs of the Filipino communities" along the way. The tour included a well-publicized stay in Washington, D.C., where he was "banqueted" and visited the Philippine press offices, where, among other things, he began his critical relationship with Clyde Tavenner and familiarized himself with the operation and activities of the permanent mission working for Philippine independence.[121] The trip was in many ways an important reconnaissance operation, which convinced him that he too could engage in the independence struggle as a legitimate representative of the federation. And that is precisely what he did. Shortly after his return from this tour, he transformed his newspaper into the *Filipino Nation*, a monthly magazine in a more glossy format akin to the *Philippine Republic*. From its inaugural issue in February 1928, *Filipino Nation* was not simply a Los Angeles–based paper; it now aggresively covered Filipino community activities everywhere in the federation, in Hawaii, and back home, always placing federation events at the center of the news. As its subscriptions grew, Moncado also used the magazine for publicity, sending copies to community leaders, politicians, chambers of commerce, libraries, and schools.[122]

Encouraged by the publicity, recognition, and recruitment that resulted from his leadership activities of 1926 and 1927, Moncado, from this time forward relied on the organization of memorable events as a major technique in building and sustaining membership in the federation. Using the 1926 Rizal Day model, he and his associates organized a high-profile convention, banquet, and parade in Stockton in July 3–5, 1927, complete with Philippine and American flags decorating the streets and the use of the Civic Auditorium for speeches by Moncado and local federation officers.[123] As the reaction against Moncado and the federation grew stronger in Los Angeles, however, it was clear that he would not be selected to organize the 1927 Rizal Day festivities.[124] Determined to orchestrate another large event in Los Angeles to follow up the successful event of 1926, Moncado decided to focus directly on the federation by implementing what was rapidly emerging as his major publicity and recruitment device: conventions and banquets.

The first official convention was held in Los Angeles to commemorate the third anniversary of the federation on December 23–29, 1927, stealing the wind from Rizal Day by dominating the week leading up to the thirtieth.[125] Some seven hundred Filipinos attended a range of events held in five downtown venues with Moncado as the ever-present master of ceremonies, speaker, and facilitator. Once again, Philippine flags flew along several downtown streets and outside the Biltmore Hotel, where members and guests held their banquets. Among the prominent speakers were Rafael Palma, president of the University of the Philippines, who was visiting Los Angeles on his way to the East Coast; Charles Russell, well-known author and observer of Philippine affairs; and Clyde Tavenner, longtime promoter of Philippine independence and editor of a Washington, D.C., magazine, the *Philippine Republic*.[126]

The impact of the Los Angeles convention was immediate. By the end of 1927, the federation could claim some 550 members (by name), organized into three complete divisions, with the fourth lacking only two lodges. Drawing heavily from the Filipino laborers, the federation had by this time opened two more branches, the second in Stockton and the third in Salinas, with the membership coming from most of the major towns of California's agricultural areas.[127] In early July 1928, the Stockton branch hosted the first "state convention," advertising the event by dropping leaflets from an airplane.[128]

Conventions and banquets became institutions that regulated the life of federation members everywhere. Some were annual and others were specific to a particular anniversary or commemoration, like the Master's birthday or (after 1946) the Philippine independence day. Major conventions were convened annually in Los Angeles, Stockton, and Honolulu, and less elaborate events were held wherever a large number of members resided. Most featured formal convention proceedings, banquets, and musical performances by federation bands and string ensembles, which became integral parts of each branch headquarters.[129] Described as "gala fiestas," the national conventions in Los Angeles were said to have "a great effect on the members," who attended the event "no matter how far" they had to travel. "Sometimes," noted one promoter, "a member saves all the money he can during the year, just to be able to attend," returning "happy and revitalized, physically and spiritually."[130]

By combining conventions and high-profile events with grassroots preaching, promotional activities, and the establishment of headquarters and "homes" in the major branch areas, Moncado and his associates were able to convince increasing numbers of Filipinos that the federation was well organized and worthy of their membership and support. Clyde Tavenner attributed the remarkable growth ("in excess of 23,000") of the federation by 1930 to Moncado's "genius as an organizer of men" and "his proven ability to maintain solidarity and contentment among the members of his organization."[131]

The availability of money made it possible for the federation to over-shadow the activities of other groups and to thrust the organization into the public eye. "The large scale on which Moncado and his federation does things in the United States," explained Tavenner, "obviously costs a huge sum of money every year."[132] Moncado began to accumulate large amounts of money very early in the life of the federation. In May 1927, he acquired "a stately eleven-room house" in a well-to-do neighborhood on the city's west side, which became the residence of both Moncado and many federation officers and members. Around the same time, he also purchased a limousine, two buses, and delivery trucks, the latter used to distribute the federation's publications, as well as leasing a large house for the Stockton headquarters. By 1931, the small office in the Stack Building had expanded to ten offices.[133]

Wherever he went, Moncado had the reputation of spending lavish-ly, staying in expensive hotels, and throwing extravagant banquets.[134] During his campaigns in the Philippines in the 1930s, the belief that he had tremendous amounts of money to spread around attracted hundreds of well-wishers, among them a number of politicians and prominent members of local society. On several occasions, he publicly donated large sums to schools and charities. On his return home to Balamban in 1933, he threw handfuls of money from his open automobile as throngs of peo-ple greeted him along the streets.[135] In the late 1930s, Moncado was cited by Gregorio Zaide in his *Philippine History and Civilization* as the "richest overseas Filipino."[136]

Most observers have stressed that much of his money—"a tidy sum"—came from the initiation and monthly fees required for federation membership. In the early years, the federation recognized a hierarchy of membership, with three classifications delineated in descending order: matriculate, submatriculate, and associate. Each class of membership had a different fee structure: $30 annually for matriculate members, a $100 ini-tiation fee and $5 annually for submatriculate members, and $5 initiation fee and $5 annually for associate members.[137] Additional charges were assessed: for a federation pin, for subscriptions to its publications (espe-cially the *Filipino Nation*), and for "several fantastic pamphlets," including Moncado's own publications.[138] It is also likely that Moncado enjoyed a steady flow of income from interest and dividends on investments he made in several American businesses.[139] To get a rough idea of how much money was being passed to him through formal channels, it was reported that in 1947 his agent in Hawaii sent him a check for $162,000, representing the federation's collections there during the war years.[140]

Despite the attention given to official organizational fees and extrac-tions, it is clear that Moncado's personal income was substantially supplemented by outright gifts of money from many loyal members. Interviews with elderly members of the federation conducted in Honolulu in the late 1970s clearly indicated that many, in particular the "spirituals" residing in Honolulu, gave willingly to "the Master" during his periodic visits. These men routinely slipped money into his hand as he greeted them. Although his financial extractions were usually the focus of criticism, loyal members such as these men willingly gave him whatever money they could with no regrets. "Master did not take money from us," stressed one longtime federation member. "We gave it to him."[141]

As the federation grew, it began to take on a sprawling administrative structure, one that was on the one hand centralized under Moncado and on the other noticeably decentralized under a number of his trusted officers. A formal structure for the federation emerged at the Second National Convention in Los Angeles in December 1928, when the assembled members approved a "constitution." At the top of the federation hierarchy was a three-man board of directors elected by the matriculate members at the annual meeting. The highest administrative officer was the president, selected by the board, along with a vice president, secretary, and treasurer. Although elected, the men holding positions on the board were invariably handpicked by Moncado, who was always on the board and was repeatedly reelected as president, later assuming the title president-treasurer. In the early 1930s, the federation's central office in Los Angeles also had twelve departments, each focused on a specific task and each headed by a secretary appointed by the president.

The federation's core was composed of the matriculate members, who were organized into lodges, each consisting of twelve men or women linked to Moncado, as represented in a universally applied symbolic representation of an *equifrilibricum* (EFB) cross designed by the federation. As noted, twelve lodges composed a division, with the original idea that the federation would be complete when it had twelve divisions, or 1,728 matriculate members. Lodges and divisions were carefully designated, and all had their own elected officers. In theory, submatriculate members were to be organized by tens and associate members by sixes, with the former being limited to 144,000 members.

Although Moncado preached at the 1927 convention for the attainment of "the 1728," the federation's members exceeded this number considerably by 1930, at which time the administrative significance of the lodge-division continuum became more ambiguous. The mobility of laborers also made it difficult for lodges and divisions to remain geographically fixed, giving rise to the branch office, headed by the "branch manager." Branch managers, appointed by the president, emerged as de facto heads of their areas regardless of the numbers of lodges and divisions within their territories.[142] At the end of 1930, the federation recognized twenty-two branches in addition to the central office in Los Angeles. Twelve of these were in California (Stockton, Salinas, Santa Maria, Pasadena, Oakland, Fresno, San Fernando, Sacramento, San Diego, San Francisco, San Bernadino, and Santa Barbara), one in Seattle, five elsewhere (Chicago, New York, New Orleans, Washington, D.C., and Philadelphia), two in Hawaii (Honolulu and Hilo), and two in the Philippines (Lanao and Laoag).[143] Until after the Pacific War, all branch managers remained deeply loyal to Moncado, with revenues from their branches used for local expenses and activities and to cover all of Moncado's expenses, be they for travel, golf club fees, or entertainment. The number of branches declined in the late 1930s and early 1940s, especially in areas away from the West Coast, where few laborers resided. In the postwar period, only the major areas continued to operate as distinct administrative branches (Stockton, Salinas, Honolulu, and Hilo).

With a Little Help from His Friends

An essential component in Moncado's success as the head of the federation was the obvious role played by his loyal officers.[144] He had a distinct ability to attract and maintain the loyalty of close associates within the organization and to convince a number of Americans to lend their support by promoting him and his activities. By the 1930s, Moncado was perpetually on the road, leaving the day-to-day work to branch and office managers. There is little doubt that the success of the federation in any given area was in large part due to the labors of scores of dedicated leaders and hundreds of loyal followers who regularly attended meetings and events, which were organized on their behalf.

The central role played by Lorenzo Delos Reyes in constructing and sustaining the federation's religion has been discussed. Like many of the men who worked closely with Moncado, Delos Reyes was ubiquitous, having been involved in the early organization of the federation in Los Angeles and Stockton, as well as in Hawaii and later in the Lanao colony, where he apparently lived out his life as the spiritual head of the community. Depicted as a guru, or teacher, steeped in the traditions of Mt. Banahaw, Delos Reyes showed little interest in the political affairs of the federation, preferring to live more quietly within the brotherhood of the "spirituals."[145]

In the political and organizational arena, there were numerous luminaries among Moncado's associates. Perhaps one of the most effective was Andres Darilay, who came to America as a working student in 1919, was a member of the first lodge, and served for several years as the federation's dedicated vice president. In the 1930s, he managed the federation office in Cebu, where he served as one of Moncado's main communicators and political organizers in the Philippines and supervised the construction and management of the Lanao colony in Mindanao. Equally significant in the early days was Cornelio Clenuar, a 1921 labor migrant from Bohol, who as a member of the second lodge organized the Stockton branch, assisted Moncado with his publicity and political campaigns in Washington, D.C., and the Philippines in the 1930s, and remained throughout his life a loyal organizer and supporter of the federation, mainly in Cebu and Bohol.

From the beginning, Moncado also managed to secure strategic assistance from several Americans who for a variety of reasons were willing to assist him in promoting the expansion of the federation. Several of Moncado's critics attributed his success to the "expert American assistance" he regularly obtained.[146] The first American with whom he developed a productive interaction was Luke McNamee, an Los Angeles attorney. Moncado began his association with the firm of McNamee and McNamee in 1920, at which time he assisted the attorneys in acquiring materials from the County Law Library, where he was employed shelving books. Throughout his life Moncado maintained a close association with Luke McNamee, who served for some time as the federation's legal counsel. In 1948, McNamee even took credit for helping Moncado set up the federation and locating its office space in the Stack Building.[147]

Perhaps the most devoted American supporter was Helen Borough, who was closely associated with the federation for nearly twenty years. As a devout Protestant from Indiana, she came to Los Angeles for religious education and to pursue her calling. Before long, she was committed to missionary and social worker among Filipinos in the city. Her association with Moncado began in 1926 through the Filipino Bible Class and her work at Goodwill Industries in downtown Los Angeles.[148] In March 1927, as a student in religious studies at USC, she accepted a position as secretary of the federation's Religious and Educational Department and became "managing editor" of *Equifrilibricum News Service*, continuing to serve in the same capacity with the *Filipino Nation* for its duration. She was a strong advocate of the federation's work, defending it against attacks by its detractors and often performing on the piano at federation conventions.[149]

From 1927 into the early 1930s, Moncado's most ardent American promoters were William J. Schaefle, owner and editor of the Los Angeles–based monthly, *American Globe*, and Clyde Tavenner, a former U.S. Congressman from Illinois, who after 1923 served as the editor of the *Philippine Republic*, a Washington, D.C., monthly devoted to "Philippine affairs." Schaefle and Tavenner were instrumental in providing Moncado with the kind of positive publicity that he needed in the formative years of the federation and in legitimizing his political activities. Schaefle was the son of a Presbyterian minister from Illinois who migrated to Texas and later found employment as a journalist with several newspapers in Los Angeles. In 1903, he established the *American Globe*, a "financial and industrial monthly review" that survived for more than thirty years in its offices in the American Bank Building downtown.[150] Between 1927 and 1932, Schaefle was a staunch supporter of and publicist for Moncado and the federation, regularly using his magazine to promote Moncado's campaigns and publicize the major events of the federation. Schaefle recalled that he was introduced to Moncado in 1927 and that they hit it off from the start. At the first formal federation convention held in Los Angeles for seven days in December 1927, Schaefle was both promoter and one of the keynote speakers.[151] During that same year, Schaefle was deeply involved in the publication of Moncado's first book, *The Divinity of Women*. Schaefle wrote the introductory essay ("Biographical Sketch of the Author") and produced all the esoteric (Rosicrucian-inspired) illustrations that embellished the book.[152] In 1928, Schaefle authored a forty-seven-page booklet, *Moncado and His Mission*, published by the federation, which Schaefle included on the list of publications in his entry in the 1929 *Who's Who in California*.

Over the next several years, Schaefle wrote more than forty articles praising Moncado, many of which were reprinted in other magazines. Moncado was featured on at least eight covers of the *American Globe*, which also reproduced scores of photographs of Moncado and federation events and devoted hundreds of pages to high praise for the Master and his work, including articles written by Moncado himself.[153] In all, it can be said that the *American Globe* provided Moncado with more coverage and publicity in Los Angeles than was received by any other Filipino or Filipino organization, including the Philippine government, in the local media. In 1932, Schaefle revealed that he had contributed "many thousands of dollars worth of space" to Moncado and his causes in the *American Globe* and concluded: "We are proud to have helped smooth his rough pathway."[154]

At several junctures, Schaefle was criticized by other Filipinos, who alleged that he was only promoting Moncado for the money. Publicly Schaefle denied receiving money from Moncado, claiming that from the outset his support had been genuine, that the *American Globe* covered Moncado's exploits because they were newsworthy, and that the leader's accomplishments contributed to the cause of Philippine independence, a goal Schaefle shared. Schaefle's attraction to the federation also seems to have been based on its conservative policies, in particular Moncado's efforts to encourage federation members to avoid labor unions and lead moral and spiritual lives. During the late 1920s, when Moncado was under attack from Filipino groups in Los Angeles, Schaefle redoubled his support and accompanied him on at least one trip to Washington, D.C. Elderly federation members living in Hawaii in the 1970s occasionally brought out old copies of *American Globe* that they had preserved as examples of the Master's accomplishments and mementos of the remarkable and exciting federation conventions and banquets they had attended as young men.

An equally effective publicist for Moncado and the federation was Clyde Tavenner, editor of the *Philippine Republic*, a well-produced monthly magazine published in Washington, D.C., and circulated widely among the Filipino community, particularly among Filipinos studying in the federation. Tavenner was himself an interesting man. He began his career as a journalist in 1908 in Washington, D.C., but entered politics in 1913 and was elected to two terms in the U.S. Congress from the Fourteenth District of Illinois. In 1919, he visited the Philippines, after which time he was employed by the publicity division of the Philippine Press Bureau, established in Washington, D.C., by Manuel Quezon to promote Philippine independence. In 1923, he founded the *Philippine Republic*, which was dedicated to covering Philippine affairs and promoting the struggle for independence.[155]

Moncado first met Tavenner on his trip to Washington in August and September of 1927, by which time the *Philippine Republic* was already publishing federation advertisements in addition to reprinting William Schaefle's promotional article on Moncado, "An Answer to 'Who is Moncado?'"[156] Their relationship grew in late 1927, when Moncado invited Tavenner to be an honored guest and speaker at the federation's first seven-day convention in Los Angeles in December. In his address before the convention participants, Tavenner lavishly praised Moncado and his work with the federation. In the years to follow, his main contribution was the regular publicity he provided Moncado in the *Philippine Republic*. Tavenner depicted Moncado as one of the leading figures in the Filipino campaign for independence and by 1930 was promoting him as a skillful organizer and lobbyist and a dedicated representative of his followers — he was, as the federation leadership described him, "the man of the hour."[157] In 1931, Tavenner accompanied Moncado on his "world tour," publicizing the highlights of their trip in his magazine.

Very early in the life of the federation, Moncado realized the importance of linking his activities to chambers of commerce and their "high priests." Composed of Californians engaged in business and agribusiness,

including growers, the chambers' officials were influential, mostly conservative, white community leaders interested for the most part in maintaining the existing ethnic hierarchy and the state's supply of cheap and
docile labor. Few chamber members were associated with exploitative
enterprises (gambling, dance halls, or brothels), viewing these businesses
as potentially disruptive and a blight on their communities. Above all,
they feared organized labor. As the federation developed its ethical attack
on Filipino participation in vices and perfected its anti-union policies,
Moncado emerged as a nonthreatening Filipino leader who could do business with representatives of the chambers of commerce.[158]

Moncado's association with the Los Angeles Chamber of Commerce
began sometime in the mid-1920s and may have resulted from contacts
with his employer, attorney Luke McNamee or his publisher, J. G.
Bowman, or his developing relationship with William Schaefle. By the
time Moncado embarked on his first cross-country tour in July 1927, he
"carried flattering letters of introduction and recommendation from the
Los Angeles Chamber of Commerce."[159] By the early 1930s, Moncado
was regularly referring to himself as a "lifetime member" of this chamber. He also frequently listed himself as a member of the California
Chamber of Commerce and occasionally of that of New York.

It was as part of a Los Angeles Chamber of Commerce tour to Hawaii
in August 1928 that Moncado initiated the spread of the federation there.
As a guest at the Royal Hawaiian Hotel, representing the Los Angeles
chamber, Moncado is said to have "made quite a splurge," disseminating
his religious messages in addresses to Filipino organizations in Hilo.[160]
Although Moncado was not at first welcomed into any of the chambers of
commerce in Hawaii, by the 1950s he had developed a close working relationship with the Honolulu Chamber of Commerce. At that time, the
International Longshoremen's and Warehousemen's Union (ILWU) was
expanding its influence over Hawaii's labor force, which encouraged the
president of the Honolulu chamber to solicit the membership of Moncado,
by this time a proven anti-union figure throughout the islands.[161]

Pablo Manlapit and Other Enemies

From the outset, Moncado and the federation made enemies within the
Filipino communities in which they operated. Criticism of Moncado first
emerged among the individuals and groups that challenged Moncado for
local leadership. As such, much of the early resistance to the federation in
Los Angeles, Stockton, and elsewhere in California came from leaders of
Filipino social and fraternal organizations that competed with the federation for membership, in particular the Caballeros de Dimas Alang,

Legionarios del Trabajo, and Gran Oriente Filipino. This opposition sur-faced in Los Angeles in the late 1920s and culminated in the 1929 publi-cation by Primo Quevedo, *Read the Truth about Hilario C. Moncado*.[162] Other Filipinos who resisted Moncado and the federation were linked more closely to conventional Catholic or Protestant churches, in particu-lar Filipino ministers, lay church leaders, and members of religious organizations. The most outspoken critic of Moncado from among this group was Nicolas Dizon, who published a comprehensive attack on Moncado in Hawaii in 1931, not long after the federation began to achieve success in recruiting members there. Focused on Moncado's "peculiar teachings," Dizon's *The "Master" vs. Juan de la Cruz* was aimed at exposing his attempt to dupe Filipinos through a range of apocryphal beliefs and pronouncements that, in Dizon's eyes, both violated Christian teachings and introduced a range of esoteric and Indic elements that sub-verted the Christian message. As a Protestant minister engaged in mis-sion and church work among Filipinos in Hawaii, Dizon found it neces-sary to resist Moncado's federation in order to prevent Filipinos from veering away from the true path and to prevent "ignorant Filipinos" from being induced "to give him their hard-earned coin."[163]

In these contexts, one of Moncado's most intriguing early enemies was Pablo Manlapit, a major leader of the effective 1924–25 Filipino sugar strike in Hawaii.[164] As a result of charges related to his involve-ment in this labor struggle, Manlapit was arrested, tried, convicted, and imprisoned in Hawaii. In July 1927, he was paroled on the condition that he leave Hawaii. Released in August, he arrived in Los Angeles by early September, where he soon joined the staff of the newly established Filipino newspaper, the *Los Angeles Observer*; obtained employment with friends; and immediately became a celebrity. The *Philippine Republic* announced his arrival in Los Angeles and noted that he "promises to become a prominent figure among Filipinos here." Within two weeks, he had delivered four addresses, including a Labor Day lecture to a "crowd of 1,000 persons" at the Music Art Hall.[165] At the time of Manlapit's arrival, Moncado was emerging as an increasingly success-ful leader within Los Angeles's Filipino community. It was inevitable that they would clash.

Although details of the clash remain obscure, the story of the feud provides insight into the machinations among Filipinos aspiring to lead-ership in Los Angeles at the time. Shortly after Manlapit's arrival, it appears that there was the possibility that the two men would join forces. Moncado claims that he appointed Manlapit as head of the federation's Labor Department but soon discharged him, having discovered that he was "connected with, and was paid by, the Anti-Imperialist League of

America of New York which was a communist-infiltrated organizatioⁿ."
Moncado then claimed that Manlapit was leading a slur campaign
against him, accusing him of misusing federation funds, hiring "Filipino
intellectuals" to criticize him, and convening forums aimed against him
and the federation. "The fight was on," Moncado later declared, "and I
could not retreat."[166]

From Manlapit's side, the story takes a different twist. After the break
with Moncado in February 1928, the Los Angeles police arrested
Manlapit, searched his quarters, and "released him under surveillance."
This incident was based on an accusation that Manlapit was working
with the "Communist International" to infiltrate the U.S. Navy with
seven thousand Filipino sailors, that he was a conspirator planning a
strike of ten thousand Filipino asparagus pickers, and that he was
"attempting to undermine" the Filipino Federation of America. In addition, Manlapit was said to be receiving a stipend from the Anti-
Imperialist League as a lecturer, and it was in the context of such a lecture that he was arrested. In his defense, Manlapit stated publicly that,
although he was in sympathy with some of their objectives, "I am neither
a Communist nor a member of the Anti-Imperialist League." "As for the
Filipino Federation of America," he confessed, "it was my purpose to
undermine it, because I sincerely believe that it is a fraudulent organization—a one-man organization—and has therefore no room in a democratic country like ours." On Moncado himself, Manlapit lashed out: he
was "an utter insult to the intelligence of the Filipino people."[167]

By late 1928, as the federation was initiating its move to Hawaii, the
Hawaiian Sugar Planters' Association was particularly concerned about
Moncado's relationship with Manlapit. After some investigation into the
matter, HSPA officials were relieved to conclude that Moncado and
Manlapit had become bitter enemies. Their analysis adds another per-
spective to the story. "At one time," the HSPA secretary wrote, Moncado

> was connected up with Manlapit in Los Angeles and is appar-
> ently a much slicker bird than Manlapit is and there is some sus-
> picion, I believe, that he double-crossed Manlapit into the posi-
> tion of being a communist agitator and put the police after
> him.[168]

From yet another angle, it becomes clearer that Moncado was the
informer who turned Manlapit over to the authorities. In late 1928,
Moncado's American promoter, William Schaefle, claimed that he was
approached by a group of Filipinos who "attempted to intimidate" him
into withdrawing his support for the federation. Schaefle later wrote that
he refused, having concluded that these were "Communistic Filipinos."

He decided instead to give Moncado free publicity for the federation's Los Angeles convention to be held that December.[169]

After the 1928 encounters, reported Moncado, Manlapit joined the Caballeros de Dimas Alang and soon "headed" a group of "Filipino gamblers" connected with a weekly (the *Los Angeles Observer*, later *Ang Bantay*) that regularly attacked the federation and its president. Though Moncado claimed that the Manlapit-led group was primarily trying to steal federation members, he constructed his feud with Manlapit as a struggle against Filipino and Chinese gambling houses (and their "women of ill-repute").[170] By the end of 1929, Manlapit, now directing *Ang Bantay*, continued to attack Moncado and the federation. In December of that year, *Ang Bantay* alleged that a "gang" of angry federation members had beaten Manlapit following publication of a story criticizing Moncado.[171] This must surely have been an isolated incident and definitely out of character for Moncado, who by this time had little to fear from Manlapit, a labor agitator disliked by the local police, officials, and businessmen who attended federation banquets and sang the praises of its eloquent president.

Two things are clear from these encounters. To begin with, the efforts of Manlapit and others to destroy the federation failed. Second, their efforts succeeded in discrediting Moncado in Los Angeles, forcing the federation to base its recruitment and major operations in the urban centers of California's agricultural areas and eventually to take the federation to Hawaii. By 1928, Moncado had lost his credibility within the resident Filipino community and ceased to be a prominent figure in Los Angeles. His offices and publications remained in Los Angeles, and the federation continued to convene major conventions and banquets in the city. His influence there, however, shifted away from the Filipino community toward the American power holders.[172] As this occurred, the federation was organizing all over California, had established a strong base in Hawaii, and was beginning to set up colonies in the Philippines.

The Anti-union Friend of Hawaii's "Bigwigs"

After the organizational and membership boom of 1927 and 1928, recruitment began to fall off in California, and, although federation branches in several parts of the state remained strong and held onto loyal members indefinitely, the stronghold of the federation began to shift to Hawaii by late 1929 and early 1930.[173] In August 1928, as previously noted, Moncado visited Honolulu and Hilo as part of a Los Angeles Chamber of Commerce tour. Finding Hawaii a fertile area for expansion, he quickly moved to establish a foothold in Honolulu. Two California lodges were immediately moved there to initiate the expansion of the federation to Hawaii, where by the end of 1928 two branch offices were in full operation in Honolulu and Hilo.[174] Analyzing Hawaii's special conditions, it was clear that the federation's success there would be dependent upon its ability to convince the HSPA and individual plantation managers that they had nothing to fear from it. Still reeling from the 1924–25 strike, local business interests were at first very skeptical of the federation.

Unknown to Moncado, by late 1928 HSPA officials were already aware of the organization, having investigated its activities in California. Although John K. Butler, the HSPA secretary, stressed that the federation must be watched, primarily because of its bizarre nature, it was clear that there were also reasons to cooperate with it and refrain from becoming hostile too quickly. In a letter to each plantation owner, Butler informed them that twenty-eight "Bolshevick Filipinos" had arrived in Honolulu on board the *President McKinley* on October 18 in order to "organize the Filipinos here." These men, he noted, had come "as representatives of the so-called Filipino Federation of America, an organization in California, headed by a man named Hilario Camino Moncado who appends a large portion of the alphabet after his name and claims very mystic powers." The federation representatives informed the Philippine labor commissioner, Cayetano Ligot, that "they were willing workers at any task and that in accordance with the sacred precepts of their order, they neither smoked, nor drank, nor associated with wild women and that their principles were industry, thrift and nobility of ideals." They then met with the HSPA secretary himself and requested approval to organize on the plantations, where they would work "faithfully and well." He informed them that he could not give them this permission since this was a decision to be made by each manager. In his memorandum to the managers, Butler was careful to note that Moncado, though "a high-grade grafter, full of egotism of the most intense order," was an enemy of Pablo Manlapit, who had caused considerable labor strife in Hawaii in the 1920s. He concluded:

> It is, however, by no means certain just what form and kind of activities Moncado may develop into. In California apparently he has prospered very much by the sale of himself through his kind of bunk, but has not entered the field of labor agitation and turmoil, probably being shrewd enough to see that this would be ineffective and that his followers would be less able to pay tribute to him if disturbed by the excitement of labor strife under which he might be less able to control them.[175]

What is clear from this early encounter is that the HSPA saw some potential danger in the federation organizing in Hawaii but was aware from the outset that Moncado's objectives were not completely contrary to theirs, leaving some room for a positive interaction:

> I suspect if he does come here he would have to be watched as a supergrafter, but I am not inclined to think that he would enter the field of dangerous labor agitation because he seems to profit best by tickling the egotism of his followers who must necessarily earn money and work rather steadily to be able to pay the tributes he desires to and does get from it.[176]

Although the HSPA managers were initially wary of welcoming Moncado's agents onto their plantations, it is clear that the federation's recruiters soon gained access.[177] By 1930, as noted, the federation was growing rapidly throughout Hawaii, having opened branch offices in Honolulu and Hilo and eventually gaining access to nearly all the plantations.

During the Depression, with unemployment in Hawaii at its highest since 1891, labor militancy was on the rise. In 1932, Pablo Manlapit returned and with others began working to organize Filipinos into a more militant union. In addition, Manuel Fagel's Vibora Luviminda, a secret political-religious movement with definite tendencies toward labor unionism, had formed by 1935. The Vibora Luviminda grew into a popular Filipino ethnic movement that challenged both the planters and the federation. As "a wave of unionism" spread through Hawaii, the HSPA and the establishment press openly reached out to Moncado and the federation. It was during this period (the middle to late 1930s) that the ILWU pinpointed the federation as an anti-union organization and began systematically to collect information on the activities of Moncado.[178] After this investigation, the ILWU authorities concluded that the federation was openly anti-union and the relationship between Moncado and the leaders of Hawaii's political economy was growing closer and closer.[179] From the point of view of the labor movement in Hawaii, the federation had two negative effects: its followers were kept firmly under Moncado's control and it permitted him to promote himself among thousands of Filipinos. David Thompson alleges that the Hawaii membership of the federation peaked around 1930 (with about three thousand members at its height) and dropped in 1931 (to about fifteen hundred). By the mid-1930s, he argues, federation membership had begun to increase again, particularly due to support from the HSPA, which viewed it as a "control movement" and facilitated its growth.[180]

ILWU reports stressed that on his many visits to Honolulu in the 1930s Moncado "was royally entertained by the 'bigwigs' and greeted by prominent local business men and legislators." "He became the darling of the big employers, and the newspapers began to quote him and to acclaim him as a great leader of men," with the *Honolulu Advertiser* even labeling him the "flying laborite." His newspaper advertisements advocated proper conduct by laborers, who were instructed by their leader "to 'play ball' with the plantation managers." The ILWU claimed that Moncado "ordered his members to stay away from labor unions, ordered them not to go on strike." In October 1937, the ILWU reported that Moncado had actually sent federation agents to Molokai to assist in breaking up a strike that was taking place there.[181]

Politics of the Homeland

In the early 1930s, Moncado began to participate in the politics of his homeland. An increasingly large number of federation members were returning home at this time, in part due to the Depression's impact on California agriculture and in part due to growing hostility toward Filipino laborers and the increasingly popular movement for exclusion. In November 1929, on Moncado's orders, twenty-four federation members departed from Los Angeles to begin the development of federation colonies in the Philippines. Twelve were assigned to Laoag, Ilocos Norte, and twelve to Dansalan, Lanao, in northern Mindanao. By early 1930, new branches of the federation had been officially opened in Laoag and Dansalan.[182] Despite the return of many Filipinos to the homeland, Moncado had predicted and advocated increased Filipino migration to the United States. However, by early 1931 he was beginning to realize that most federation members would "naturally" return to the Philippines "some day."[183] From the beginning of this realization, Moncado endeavored to direct as many of them as possible to his emerging colonies in the Philippines, especially in Mindanao.

In 1932, Moncado leased a sizable tract of land near Dansalan, along Lake Lanao, and began the conversion of the area into an attractive agricultural colony, which by early 1933 had more than five hundred residents. The seriousness with which Moncado treated the move at this time is demonstrated by the fact that he sent two of his most trusted leaders to supervise the colony: Lorenzo Delos Reyes and Andres Darilay, who arrived in Dansalan in August 1932.[184] Leaving the development of the colony to Delos Reyes, the federation's central religious leader, Darilay proceeded to Cebu City at the end of the year to prepare for Moncado's political activities and to open federation subbranches around Cebu Province. By the time he returned to work in Mindanao in 1936, the Dansalan colony was prospering and federation members were beginning to establish settlements elsewhere on the island. By the late 1930s, migrants from the United States and Hawaii, as well as internal migrants from the Visayas, were adding to the growth of several other colonies in Mindanao, especially at Babak on Samal Island, near Davao City, and in Mainit, Surigao.[185]

From the outset, the Mindanao colonies emerged as spiritual centers, where the federation's religion became more institutionalized within particular locales. For the purposes of recruitment of federation members to Mindanao, spiritual justifications seem to have been particularly significant. The government's depiction of the island as the land of promise was soon converted into a spiritual revelation that had been circulating within the federation for some time: Mindanao became the place where the "coming race" of superior beings—the Malayans—would surface and lead the rest of humanity to eternal peace. As a result, the original colony in Lanao took on a powerful religious significance, which was extended to several other federation colonies established in Mindanao before and after the Pacific War.[186]

In July 1931, as part of a well-publicized world tour, Moncado returned to Cebu after an absence of more than seventeen years.[187] Having by this time familiarized himself with many of the larger issues and activities of Filipino political life, Moncado carefully prepared for his entry into Philippine politics. He began to sense the political potential of having a concentrated constituency in various parts of the Philippines, in particular in Cebu and Lanao. On this first trip, however, his political acts were limited to public donations, mainly to schools. In February 1932, he committed himself to Philippine politics by organizing a new party, the Modernist Party, dedicated to the political salvation of the Philippines through an internationalist, rather than nationalist, ideology based on independence and a continuing close relationship with the federation.[188] The Modernist Party would serve as Moncado's political organization in the Philippines. At this time, he was acknowledged in the federation as a full-fledged Filipino politician, seeking independence for his country in personal campaigns in Washington and as the head of a Philippine political party.[189]

By the end of 1932, Moncado was concentrating his political efforts on challenging Sergio Osmeña for the Tenth District Senate seat of their native province of Cebu in the election of 1934. Although there was little chance that Moncado would unseat Osmeña, he quickly familiarized himself with the growing opposition to Cebu's longtime political boss and began to work toward transforming himself into a legitimate contender. Moncado sent to Cebu two of his most trusted and competent associates, Andres Darilay and Cornelio Clenuar, and hired a full-time publicist with a Cebuano background, Diosdado Yap. The federation opened a branch in Cebu in November 1932, attempted to organize subbranches in all the

municipalities of the province, and quickly engaged in publicity campaigns in the local press. The oppositionist press of Cebu was willing to
promote Moncado's campaign to the extent that it threatened and criticized Osmeña but did not disrupt its own efforts to dislodge the senator.
The major Filipino-owned English-language newspaper of Cebu,
Progress, published the picture "Dr. Hilario C. Moncado" in October 1932
and quoted his publication, the *Modernist*, declaring that Moncado was
the "most talked about man out of public office in the Philippines."[190]

As the Moncado challenge grew throughout 1933 and into 1934, the
political turmoil at the national level between Osmeña and Manuel
Quezon over the independence bills superseded the local electoral campaign. With support from Quezon, Vicente Sotto, an old political adversary of Osmeña, entered the Senate race in Cebu, setting in motion a long-
anticipated political struggle between these two *politikos*. Nevertheless,
Moncado succeeded in capturing some attention in the Cebu press,
which moved back and forth between ridicule and guarded praise for the
Modernist candidate and occasionally provided him with coverage, even
printing his organization's promotional announcements.[191] Although
Moncado did not spend a great deal of time in Cebu during this period,
he made the most of his visits to promote his campaign, with his Cebu
agents regularly publicizing his arrivals, rallies, provincial tours, monetary donations, and grand departures.[192]

In the June 1934 election, Osmeña defeated Sotto to retain his Senate
seat, with Moncado placing third, having garnered nearly six thousand
votes throughout the province.[193] It was a credible showing that, importantly, demonstrated to Moncado that he had developed very real political support in his hometown of Balamban, where he captured more
votes than Osmeña and Sotto combined.[194] In an effort to quickly convert this local success into political office, Moncado filed his candidacy
to run for the Constitutional Convention in the July election, only a
month later. Running in Cebu's Seventh Congressional District, where
Balamban was one of the larger municipalities, he was fortunate that the
votes were dispersed among seven other candidates. In what can be
described as a remarkable political achievement, Moncado was elected
the delegate of the Seventh District by an overwhelming majority over
his next closest rival, capturing the largest number of votes in seven of
district's nine municipalities.[195]

Accounts of the deliberations of the Constitutional Convention rarely
mentioned Moncado, and when they did they generally took the form of
ridicule. When one of his biographers formally inquired from another
delegate about the role of Moncado, the response was: "I likewise regret
to state that I do not have any recollection of his having participated in

momentous debates on the floor of the convention."[196] Jose Romero, also a delegate, remembered being impressed that Moncado "had no lack of sympathizers and friends among the people whom he entertained lavishly and otherwise favored." He was, Romero recalled, the convention's "timekeeper" during debates and "always went to the session hall with a large alarm clock."[197] Historian Gregorio Zaide depicted Moncado as one of the convention's "interesting members," noting that "Dr. Moncado" had acquired much wealth in the federation and was the "best-dressed delegate."[198] In his official biography as a delegate, Moncado was reported to be serving on six committees and seeking two major reforms: the creation of a new government department of "air armada" and the changing of the name of the nation to the "United Philippines."[199] Despite his limited impact on the convention, Moncado's participation in this historic endeavor confirmed his legitimacy as a political leader for thousands of Filipinos. Throughout the remainder of the 1930s, he was introduced with the title *delegado* and, more often than not, as he described himself, "senior delegate," alleging that he had received the highest vote margin of all Cebu delegates, giving him seniority over the others. As a senior delegate, Moncado submitted a detailed (thirty-nine-page) report on "Filipino Labor Conditions in the Territory of Hawaii" directly to President Quezon in late 1936.

In November 1938, Moncado decided to run again for public office, this time for the Commonwealth's National Assembly. He must have realized that he had little chance of winning a congressional seat from Cebu, where a united Osmeña-Quezon ticket would be nearly impossible to defeat. He turned, therefore, to Lanao, where his growing colony could assist him in an electoral battle against the incumbent Tomas L. Cabili. Under the Modernist Party banner, with a revised platform calling for dominion status rather than independence from the United States, Moncado ran for delegate to the National Assembly from Lanao. Out of 45,187 votes cast, he ended up third, with 3,684 votes to Cabili's 20,003.[200]

Moncado's last prewar bid for elective office came on the eve of the Japanese invasion. In November 1941, he ran against Manuel Quezon for the Philippine presidency. As the Modernist candidate, his only real issue against Quezon and the Nacionalista Party was his advocacy of dominion status, which he vigorously publicized through print and radio, beginning at this time to adopt yet another media format for his publicity efforts. Though there was support for dominion status among some sectors of Filipino society and a few politicians, Moncado's challenge was of little significance to Quezon. Although pending warfare kept the final election results from being properly reported, Moncado later claimed that he had lost by only 10,000 votes out of 3.5 million electors.[201] Though very unlikely, it was at least clear that Quezon and his resident commissioner, Joaquin Elizalde, as was indicated in the introduction to this essay, considered Moncado enough of an annoyance to file charges against him with U.S. officials.

Moncado's abandonment of the ideal of national independence in the late 1930s in favor of dominion status represented a dramatic shift in his political message. His legitimacy had been partially based on his championship of Filipino independence. He had invested considerable energy and resources on his involvement in the independence campaign. What motivated the reversal of his policy seems to have been the realization that Philippine independence would bring an end to the U.S. "national" status enjoyed by Filipinos within the colonial relationship. Moreover, dominion status could be defended in terms of protecting the Philippines from the threat of Japan, "the Monster of the Pacific."[202] Moncado's plea for dominion status grew even louder after the war, when it became an integral part of his campaign to salvage his reputation as a Japanese collaborator and to impress American politicians who might support him in his efforts to obtain permanent residency in the United States. He declared that his support for the United States and dominion status had led to his imprisonment and torture at the hands of the Japanese military.[203] In his postwar political campaigns, Moncado not only advocated dominion status but also campaigned vigorously for parity, even after the constitutional prohibitions against it had been removed by the Philippine Congress.[204] Support for dominion status and parity permitted Moncado to posture as an ally of particular American business and economic interests, many of which he had worked with during the prewar years in Hawaii and California.

Undaunted by his string of electoral defeats and his humiliation at being charged with collaboration during the Japanese occupation, Moncado entered the political race for the presidency against Manuel Roxas in the April 1946 election. Again as the Modernist Party candidate, he was defeated, polling 8,538 votes. A little over a year later, in November 1947, he ran in the at-large election for the Senate. This time he was listed as representing the Independent Liberal Party. Though he did not win a seat in the Senate, he received an impressive 93,167 votes from around the country.[205] After this defeat, Moncado concentrated his energies on returning to the United States and rebuilding the American and Hawaiian branches of the federation, from which he had been isolated for some seven years.

Fashioning of a Self-Image

From the beginning, print and photography played a central role in the organizational structure of the federation. More so than many members of the Filipino elite, Moncado devoted a great deal of time, energy, and money to the production of printed matter and photographic renderings of federation activities and his public appearances. It is significant to recall that the federation emerged from a newspaper, *Equifrilibricum News Service*, published by Moncado in Los Angeles from November 1924 to January 1928. It was continued in 1928 by the monthly magazine, *Filipino Nation*, which was the mouthpiece of Moncado and the federation until it ceased publication in early 1933. *Filipino Nation* was one of the most informative magazines on Filipino activities in the federation, and for Moncado and his staff of writers it carefully documented the organization's contributions to a range of pertinent activities and campaigns. Subsidized by subscription payments of federation members, the magazine was widely circulated in the United States and the Philippines, with copies, as noted, systematically distributed for the purpose of publicity for the federation and its programs and activities.[206] In addition to his monthly magazine, Moncado made use of ephemeral newspapers and periodic publications throughout his career as the need arose. These publications were produced in nearly every locality in which Moncado operated and usually lasted for brief periods of time before they closed down.[207] The publication of federation newspapers or magazines was often unnecessary if other publications could be used to disseminate press releases and stories or provide regular coverage. The two most obvious magazines of this variety in the 1920s and early 1930s were *American Globe* (Los Angeles) and the *Philippine Republic* (Washington, D.C.).

In addition, both before and after the Pacific War Moncado and his local managers were able to insert federation publicity into many mainstream newspapers, in particular the *Honolulu Advertiser* and the *Honolulu Star Bulletin*; into some successful Filipino newspapers of California, among them the *Philippines Mail* of Salinas; and into Philippine newspapers, especially in Cebu City.[208] Moncado maintained a fairly articulate and assertive staff of writers who frequently submitted unsolicited stories and paid advertisements to Philippine, Hawaiian, and American newspapers. These stories and advertisements were frequently published and almost always accompanied by photographs. Moncado and his loyal writers mastered the art of the press release and had a remarkable ability to get their material into print. As one irate citizen of Hawaii complained to the governor: "Our papers are full of his ads advertising himself."[209] In this way, Moncado's stature as a leader was verified by his presence in the more mainstream press, reserving federation publications for promoting individual members and their activities.[210]

"It is a fact," wrote Clyde Tavenner in 1930, "that when Dr. Moncado testified before the Immigration Committee of Congress, he received more publicity in American newspapers than all of the other speakers, Filipino or American, combined."[211] In a positive assessment of Moncado's organizational skills, a major critic stressed that "publicity is his stock and trade."[212] By the mid-1920s, Moncado had demonstrated a sophisticated understanding and an effective application of a wide range of techniques to publicize himself and the activities of the federation. In so doing, he was also aware of constructing his publicity to suit the occasion and the audience. As another critic observed, "he makes different appeals and presents a different character to different groups, both within the Filipino community and within the larger community."[213] One of Moncado's most outspoken critics, Nicolas Dizon of Hawaii, devoted an entire chapter to the way in which he manipulated Filipinos through his use of photography. Under the title "Pictures! Pictures!! Pictures!!!" Dizon expressed dismay at how effectively Moncado and his associates utilized photos to promote "the Master" and depict him in mysterious and graphic ways that were both offensive and fraudulent.[214] From Dizon's criticism, it is clear that Moncado's publicity techniques, especially the use of "pictures," were achieving their intended goal: to convince Filipinos to join the federation. Noting "the love of Filipinos for pictures," Dizon complained:

> If one would visit any of the offices of the Federation he would see [Moncado's] photographs all about the room. Moncado's pictures appear on calendars. Pictures of Moncado, showing him in hotels, at banquets, on the train, on the globe of the world, in his office writing or phoning, in parks or hotels shaking hands with supposedly great or near great men, confront you everywhere. Pictures of conventions, banquets, parades, brass-bands, lady auxiliaries, etc., decorate the rooms of all Moncado's disciples. On their tables are to be seen copies of the Federation's magazine, "The Filipino Nation" and [William Schaefle's] "The Globe."[215]

Photographs were used in both conventional and unconventional ways. For standard publicity, Moncado was depicted at a variety of meetings and banquets, on podiums delivering speeches and expressing himself with numerous gestures, shaking hands or interacting with politicians at every level, with businessmen, and with celebrities.[216] In addition, pictures were used to reproduce and display letters of recommendation, introduction, salutation, and appreciation and clippings from newspapers and other publications. In a more unconventional way, photographs were used, even altered, to enhance Moncado's charisma and spiritual authority and to represent him as the "man of mystery" by elaborating his photographs with the addition of symbolic graphics and signs of particular significance within the federation's religious tenets.

One of the earliest, and perhaps one of the boldest, publicity stunts was carried out at the end of 1929 and early 1930, as Moncado embarked on his "independence campaign." Through a series of press releases in Hawaii and California, it was announced that Moncado had been "called by the President of the United States, Mr. [Herbert] Hoover, to discuss immediate and complete independence of the Philippine Islands" in February 1930. This was, of course, when Moncado was planning a high-publicity trip to Washington, D.C., and hoped to at least get a brief photo opportunity with Hoover. This caused quite a stir in Washington, since the president's office began to receive queries and complaints about the meeting with Moncado. Secretary of War Patrick Hurley was forced to deny the report and was asked to investigate the situation. It was at this time that the Bureau of Insular Affairs began to collect materials on Moncado.[217] Ignoring the developing controversy, Moncado proceeded to Washington to present President Hoover with a "Filipino-American Goodwill Medal" from the federation to praise the president's work toward the eventual independence of the Philippines. The trip received major coverage in the federation press and the Los Angeles–based *American Globe*, and, although the Hoover photo opportunity did not materialize, the trip resulted in substantial publicity for Moncado, including a letter of thanks from Hoover, press clippings on his activities, his photo on the steps of the Capitol consulting with Senator Hiram Bingham (Connecticut) and Congressman Joe Crail (California).[218]

Beginning in the late 1920s, Moncado was particularly successful in inserting himself into biographical directories and who's whos. His photo and biodata were included in the prestigious *Who's Who in California*, published in San Francisco in 1929. He was the only Filipino included in the volume, and the entry listed his Calcutta degrees as well as his LL.M. from Southwestern University. He was described as "one of [the] foremost moral leaders of [the] Filipino people in the U.S. and an advocate of P.I. independence."[219] Subsequently, Moncado made every effort to have himself entered into as many such directories as possible. In so doing, he was remarkably successful.[220]

It may even be argued that there was a distinct publicity angle to Moncado's marriage in his early 1940s. In 1938 or 1939 (depending on the sources), Moncado married the popular Manila-based vaudeville singer and film star, Dionisia Castro, better known to her fans as Diana Toy, occasionally as Diana Toy-Toy.[221] They had first met in California, where Diana had gone in 1937 to pursue a Hollywood movie career. Moncado, who made occasional visits to Hollywood studios in search of photo opportunities with film stars was quick to see the value of a beautiful and talented woman at his side.[222] After appearing in *The Adventures of Marco Polo* (1938), however, Diana decided to return to Manila, where she pursued her career as a popular entertainer. They met again in 1938, when Moncado hired her to join his campaign as an entertainer in Lanao, where he was running for Congress against Tomas Cabili. Moncado claims that they were married in June 1938, and it is clear that she became a more regular part of his traveling entourage after that time. The marriage was not made public, however, until more than a year later in November 1939.[223] From the beginning, their marriage appeared to be a business arrangement than a romance, with Diana's role being more the federation's muse and entertainer than Hilario's wife—the couple rarely represented themselves as engaged in anything that might be viewed as a family life.

The most remarkable publicity success of Moncado was, perhaps, the way he turned his apparent downfall as a Japanese collaborator into a great victory as a general in charge of a massive military force that aided American troops in the liberation of the Philippines. As he recounts in his autobiography, Moncado was arrested and imprisoned from April to September 1945, when he was released and then indicted by the People's Court on fifteen charges relating to his associations with the Japanese. While under indictment, Moncado filed his candidacy and ran for the office of president in 1946 and for the Senate in 1947. In late 1947 and early 1948, all charges against him were dismissed.

With his name cleared, Moncado fashioned himself as a "five-star" general. He and his associates claimed that on July 4, 1942, he had escaped from Japanese detention at Fort Santiago and was commissioned as "Commander X" of the Crusaders Army, a force of two and a half million troops. "My men," wrote Moncado, "were cooperating with the commando officers and the former officers of the United States Army Forces in the Far East (USAFFE), under the command of General Douglas MacArthur." Specializing in supplying weapons, medicine, and logistical support for MacArthur, the Crusaders Army also claimed battlefield victories.[224] Moncado explained that four of his stars had been given to him by the Crusaders and the fifth had been awarded by his wife. He flew to Hawaii as General Moncado in mid-March 1948. His success at claiming to be a hero of the anti-Japanese resistance was so complete that the Honolulu authorities that had denied the federation permission to decorate the city streets for Moncado's return from his world tour in 1931 gave his agents approval in 1948. Arriving in Honolulu in full uniform, General Moncado was even provided with a police escort as his entourage moved through the city's downtown.[225]

At the same time that Moncado was developing his image as a five-star general he was promoting himself as a golfing celebrity. In March 1948, he entered and won the Manila open golf championship. He then flew to Hawaii to enter a golf tournament there.[226] Golf had been central to Moncado's image since the late 1920s. Like Krishnamurti, he had developed a deep personal commitment to the game. In his autobiographical chronicle, *Moncado Speaks*, his annual entries from 1927 to 1954 record his increasing obsession with golf, noting that he played "whenever possible." Between 1931 and 1941, the federation sponsored an annual tournament during its national convention in Los Angeles, with Moncado emerging as the champion on every occasion. Throughout the prewar period, he was frequently photographed in golfing attire at numerous courses around the world and was a formal member of several country clubs in California and Hawaii. Upon his return to the United States after the war, golf became an even greater obsession. In the summer of 1948, the Stockton branch sponsored the General Moncado Goodwill Open—"the greatest sporting spectacle ever sponsored by the Federation." Numerous professional golfers were persuaded to participate, with Moncado's foursome finishing second. The Goodwill Open became a regular part of the federation's state conventions, held annually in Stockton up to 1955.[227] While acting as a self-professed golf promoter in Hawaii and California, Moncado published a how-to book, *360° Power Swing* (Los Angeles, 1951). On his birthday in 1954, he declared himself a professional golfer.[228]

Why golf? Moncado's interest in the game appears to have been motivated by several factors. Golf was becoming a popular sport in the 1920s, with increasing numbers of professional championships and amateur contests. Southern California was rapidly becoming one of its foremost centers, with more than twenty-six courses already constructed in Los Angeles by mid-decade.[229] The climate of Southern California made it, like Florida, an ideal locale for the new game.[230] The exclusive all-male clubs of Great Britain were giving way to the American-style country club, where husband, wife, and family could find recreation and social interaction. In addition, golf, which had been predominantly an upper-class white man's game, was emerging as an American middle-class (though still mostly white) recreational activity. As the game still excluded the working class, playing golf and being a member of a club were signs of affluence, ways to demonstrate one's place among people on the move. These were the people with whom Moncado sought identification, occasional interaction, and, if possible, a photo opportunity or outright endorsement. In the midst of his political campaign against Sergio Osmeña in 1933, Moncado's publicists managed to get a major promotional article entitled "Moncado: The Golfer and Politician" published in the leading English-language paper of Cebu City. Among the several subtitles were: "Holder of Hole-in-One Record in U.S.A." and "Member of Exclusive Clubs with Exorbitant Fees." Half the article was devoted to Moncado's achievements in golf, noting that he would represent Cebu in the upcoming Philippine national tournament.[231]

Moncado was one of a very small number of Filipinos who played golf before the war, which also seems to have been part of the game's appeal for him. His skill at golf and the prestige and publicity he gained from promoting it, donating money to clubs, and playing it with prominent Americans, including well-known professional golfers, contributed to his charisma.[232] Moncado was anything but the "man of mystery" on the greens. One of his strongest critics in Hawaii remarked: "You can be sure he doesn't toss his 'Equifrilibricum' around when playing golf or hobnobbing with the sophisticated groups in the community who tolerate him because they believe he can be of some use to them."[233]

In the postwar period, with an increasing number of public courses being opened, more and more federation members began to play golf themselves. In the late 1940s and 1950s, golf had become more than just a game for the federation; it was an ethical and sacred institution. As a clean, outdoor game, golf was free of associations with the degenerate life of gambling dens, dance and pool halls, and saloons. As a wholesome and morally uplifting form of recreation, golf was considered part of the federation's arsenal of weapons to combat evil in the world and promote social harmony—a way to follow the Master's precepts by serving humanity. As the Cold War in the United States associated communists with Satan in the mid-1950s, the federation turned to golf as a means of overcoming the diabolical message of communism. Between 1955 and 1957, the Molokai headquarters of the federation published a regular column in its monthly *Moncado and His Mission Bulletin* entitled "Fighting Communism through Golfing." By this time the Molokai branch had established the Moncado Crusaders Golf Club, whose members played golf in full military uniform around Hawaii, sponsored regular tournaments, reported their top player every month in the *Bulletin,* and eventually operated their own course.[234]

Playing golf came to be interpreted as a sacred ritual. Every aspect of the game was laden with spiritual significance. The Master's participation was compared to Christ's role as a shepherd: Jesus carried a shepherd's staff and Moncado a golf club. The second stanza of the "Crusaders Theme Song," published in the column "Fighting Communism through Golf," goes as follows:

Shepherds on the golf course
Proclaiming Christ's return
Wake up! Wake up! humanity
For here is your salvation
Be a moral being
Our motto "Watch and Pray"
Let our hearts unite together
For peace and true fraternity
Don't give up Crusaders.[235]

On April 8, 1956, on the green of the ninth hole at Agua Caliente Golf Course in Mexico, Hilario Camino Moncado collapsed and died. Noting that this "concluded his life as a man," *Moncado and His Mission Bulletin* depicted his death in a graphic showing him putting the ninth hole beside the image of Jesus crucified on Calvary during his "9th hour."[236]

Looking Back

In reviewing the life and accomplishments of Hilario Moncado, one is struck by the apparent contradictions between his two salient personas: man of mystery and *politiko*. His claim to divinity seemed to be an artificial, transparent, and fabricated spiritual addition to his natural charismatic personality. He always appeared to be most comfortable in stylish clothes at the head of banquet tables or in the latest fashionable golfing attire strolling the links. And yet the need to move in both realms was clearly perceived as necessary by Moncado and his closest officers.

Under Moncado's leadership, the Filipino Federation of America was a decisively more ambitious organization than any other to emerge among Filipinos in prewar America. Most fraternal organizations focused on a particular locale, even if they were part of a larger structure (like the Caballeros de Dimas Alang or the Legionarios del Trabajo), and, though they shared several objectives with the federation (mutual aid, promoting cultural identity and pride, and assimilation into American society), the vision and energy of their leadership paled in comparison with that of Moncado and his loyal officers. Moncado's vision for himself and the federation was grandiose. He was not satisfied with the small niche reserved for Filipinos in American society, one that was limited to such marginalized spaces of popular culture as boxing arenas, gambling dens, and taxi-dance halls.[237] Under Moncado's leadership, federation members periodically participated in large conventions and banquets held at central American buildings (first-class hotels, major urban auditoriums, and public meeting halls), in widely publicized golf tournaments at popular community courses, and in the mainstream struggle for

Philippine independence. They had their own national publications (in particular *Filipino Nation*), their own political party in the Philippines (the Modernist Party), their own uniforms for special occasions, and their own bands and orchestras. By incorporating elements of American social, religious, and political life into the federation's symbols and rituals and by combining them with more familiar elements from Filipino culture, Moncado, his leaders, and the federation's members created for themselves a more satisfying world in which to live.

In the early 1920s, Hilario Camino Moncado, in his late twenties, set out to transcend his marginality. Over the next thirty years, based on both his real and fabricated achievements, he succeeded in creating for himself and his many loyal followers a vision of a new society, one that provided him with affluence and access to status and provided his followers with dignity and the possibility of liberation from their marginal existence. Despite his manipulations and misrepresentations, Moncado succeeded in becoming the voice, indeed the embodiment, of his disenfranchised and marginalized followers in their quest for recognition and a place in American and Philippine societies.

As late as 1967, the federation was the only Filipino organization mentioned in an official publication on Asian Americans produced by the California State Department of Education. Writing specifically about the Stockton branch, the text noted that the federation was founded by General Moncado "and twelve other Filipinos" and was one of the only organizations that "recognized the many needs of the large group of young men" and "provided legal aid and fostered clean living, a sports program (notably golf), and education." "In addition," the publication continued, the federation "served as a liaison between the American public and the Filipinos."[238] Not only did the federation survive its founder, but his deeds and accomplishments, both spiritual and material, continue to be remembered in California, Hawaii, and several places in the Philippines. In his introduction to the World Leaders Past and Present series, Arthur Schlesinger wrote that "great leaders justify themselves by emancipating and empowering their followers."[239] With this as a measure for leadership, it may safely be concluded that Hilario Camino Moncado was indeed an effective leader.

NOTES

The title "The Master and Juan de la Cruz" derives from the title of a book, The "Master" vs. Juan de la Cruz, by Nicolas C. Dizon (Honolulu: Mercantile Press, 1931). The present essay is about Moncado; it is not a study of the federation or it members. The federation's story has been told by several scholars, most recently and effectively in the dissertation of Steffi San Buenaventura, "Nativism and Ethnicity in a Filipino-American Experience" (Ph.D. diss., University of Hawaii, 1990); see also her recently published essays "The Master and the Federation: a Filipino-American Social Movement in California and Hawaii," Social Process in Hawaii 33 (1991): 169–93; and "Filipino Folk Spirituality and Immigration: From Mutual Aid to Religion," Amerasia Journal 22.1 (1996): 1–30. The most comprehensive internal history of the federation is Andres A. Darilay, comp., Silver Souvenir for the Filipino Federation of America Incorporated in the Philippines (Cebu City: Barba Press, 1954); see also FFA Souvenir Book: Golden Anniversary of the Filipino Federation of America, 1925–1975 (Honolulu, 1975). My research on this project began in the mid-1970s, while doing field research for my dissertation and teaching at the University of San Carlos, Cebu City. I would like to acknowledge assistance and support from the Cebuano Studies Center, University of San Carlos, Cebu City, which during the period 1974–75 made possible several visits to the municipality of Balamban and the Moncado Colony in Sudlon, Cebu, to conduct interviews and gather data from the parish registers. Between 1976 and 1979, I worked jointly with Dr. Steffi San Buenaventura, collecting materials on the federation and conducting interviews with federation members in Oahu, Hawaii, during which time I was a research intern at the East-West Center. We were assisted in some of these interviews by Fe Susan T. Go as well as several members of the Moncado Foundation of America in Honolulu, who not only shared their stories but also made available to us valuable materials relating to federation's past and present. Support for this research was provided by Henry Luce Foundation funds awarded by the Center for South and Southeast Asian Studies, University of Michigan.

1. The letters and memoranda concerning these matters can be found in the "P" File: "Moncado, H.C.," in Record Group 350 (RG-350), Bureau of Insular Affairs (BIA), United States National Archives (USNA); see, for example, among others, Joaquin Elizalde to the Secretary of the Interior, July 14, 1941; Memorandum of Leland Graham (Assistant Solicitor) to Acting Secretary of the Interior, September 26, 1941; John J. Dempsey (Acting Secretary of the Interior) to the Attorney General, September 29, 1941; K. P. Aldrich (Chief Post Office Inspector) to Wendell Berge (Assistant Attorney General), June 6, 1942; and E. K. Burlew (Acting Secretary of the Interior) to Joaquin M. Elizalde, June 24, 1942.
2. The most exhaustive biographical studies of Moncado's early life are Larry

Arden Lawcock, "Hilario C. Moncado: Cult Leader," a chapter in his "Filipino Students in the United States and the Philippine Independence Movement, 1900–1935," Ph.D. diss., University of California, Berkeley, 1975, 356–466; Steffi San Buenaventura, "Nativism and Ethnicity in a Filipino-American Experience," Ph.D. diss., University of Hawaii, 1990; and Steffi San Buenaventura, "The Master and the Federation: A Filipino-American Social Movement in California and Hawaii," *Social Process in Hawaii* 33 (1991): 169–93. Other useful materials can be found in James Earl Wood, "Filipino Federation of America, Incorporated," typescript copy of chapter from uncompleted dissertation, n.d. [ca. 1931]) in the Bancroft Library, University of California, Berkeley; Joseph Kavanagh, "Hilario Camino Moncado," *Philippine Studies* 4.3 (September 1956): 433–40; and Francisco O. Dalumpines, "The Life of Hilario Camino Moncado and His Contribution to Education," M.A. thesis, University of the Visayas, Cebu City, 1971. Also useful are Moncado's autobiography, *Moncado Speaks* (N.p.: Hilario C. Moncado, 1955), and several biographies written by federation members and publicity agents, among them William J. Schaefle, "An Answer to 'Who is Moncado?'" *Philippine Republic* 4.6 (July 1927): 10–11; William J. Schaefle, "Biographical Sketch of the Author," in Hilario Camino Moncado, *Divinity of Women: Her Superiority over Men*, 3d rev. ed. (Los Angeles: Filipino Federation of America, 1927), 8–14; [Clyde Tavenner,] "An Attempt to Explain Hilario Moncado," *Philippine Republic*, October 1930, 4–5; Jose G. Deseo, *Moncado, the New Apostle: Filipino Federation of America*, galley proofs (Chicago: Scandia Printing Co., 1931); Cirilo T. Demetria, "The Moncado Series," *Paradise* 1.1 (December 1973) through 2.5 (May 1975); and Dominga Da. Ramos, *Moncado: The World Servant* (New York: Carlton Press, 1985).

3. According to the baptismal records of Balamban Parish, Moncado was born Hilarion Caminos Moncada on November 3, 1895 (based on his baptism at the age of one day on November 4). His family lived on the mostly rural west coast of Cebu in the barrio of Pundol just south of the *poblacion* (1903 population: 1,066, making it the fifth largest of nine barrios in the municipality of Balamban, with a 1903 population of 10,603). Balamban had always been a secular parish, with the first resident Filipino priest arriving only in the late 1870s. This part of Cebu's west coast was somewhat unsettled until the second half of the nineteenth century, when its population began to grow, mostly due to a sizable migration from Bohol. Typically, Pundol is said to have been inhabited mostly by Boholanos, who by the end of the nineteenth century grew corn for their staple crop and cultivated tobacco for sale. Moncado's parents, said to have been migrants from Bohol, were not members of the *principalía*, though there are three late nineteenth-century *cabezas de barangay* with the family names of Moncada and Caminos. In the 1950s, the teachers of Balamban recalled that it was in the old stone school building in Pundol, which dated to the Spanish times, that "Dr. Hilario Camino Moncado first learned to read and write." For this and other information, see Historical Data Papers: Cebu: Balamban: Pundol, The National Library of the Philippines; and Cornelio C. Clenuar, Looc, Panglao, Bohol, interview with Marian Diosay and Lawrence M. Liao, May 2, 1977, and June 15, 1977 (transcript available at the Cebuano Studies Center, University of San Carlos, Cebu City).

4. According to the records of the Hawaiian Sugar Planters' Association, Moncado, listed as Hilarion Moncada, signed his contract (no. 10,221) on February 1, 1914, claiming to be twenty-one years old. He arrived in Honolulu on March 5, 1914 (Hawaiian Sugar Planters' Association, Aiea, Filipino Affairs Department File, Lot no. 199). See also John K. Butler (HSPA secretary) to James Earl Wood, July 10, 1931, James Earl Wood Papers, Envelope 7, Bancroft Library, University of California, Berkeley.
5. *Moncado Speaks*, 7. On Moncado's earliest cross-cultural activity being sports, in this case baseball, see Margaret Lam, "Baseball and Racial Harmony in Hawaii," *Sociology and Social Research* 18.1 (September-October 1933): 58–66.
6. *Moncado Speaks*, 8.
7. Estimates of the federation membership vary tremendously. Using subscription data for Moncado's magazine, *Filipino Nation*, Lawcock ("Filipino Students," 373–74) estimates membership size by noting that subscriptions grew from 10,000 copies in July 1929 to 25,000 by the end of 1930; it is clear, however, that large numbers of these magazines were given away as promotions and that nonfederation members undoubtedly subscribed as well. In his testimony before the U.S. Senate in February 1930, Moncado claimed that the federation had 12,000 members on the Pacific coast and another 10,000 in Hawaii; two years later he claimed that the federation consisted of 23,000 members in the United States and Hawaii and an additional 1,000,000 in the Philippines. See U.S. Congress, Senate, *Statement of Dr. Hilario Camino Moncado, President Filipino Federation of America (Inc.), Los Angeles, Calif.*, Committee on Territories and Insular Affairs, Hearings on Independence for the Philippines, pt. 3, 71st Cong., 2d sess., February 10, 1930 (Washington, D.C.: GPO, 1930), 330; and U.S. Congress, House, *Statement of Dr. Hilario Camino Moncado, President Filipino Federation of America, California*, Committee on Insular Affairs, Hearings on Independence for the Philippines, 72d Cong., 1st sess., H.R. 7,233, January 26, 1932 (Washington, D.C.: GPO, 1932), 127.
8. Moncado's four books are *Divinity of Women: Her Superiority over Men* ([Los Angeles]: Filipino Federation of America, 1927); *World Travel Memories, Being the First Series of Illustrated Travel Stories to Be Published as Such in a Single Volume by Any Filipino* (Washington, D.C.: C. T. Clements, 1932); *America, the Philippines, and the Orient* (New York: Fleming H. Revell, 1932); and *360° Power Swing* (Los Angeles: Edendale Press for the Filipino Federation of America, 1951). In addition, Moncado claimed authorship of a number of titles, six of which were listed in his 1928 entry in *Who's Who in California: A Biographical Directory, 1928–29*, edited by Justice B. Detwiler et al. (San Francisco: Who's Who Publishing, 1929), 369, but none of them have been located in any library or in the possession of federation members. These titles are *Equifrilibricum; Sun, Moon, and Star; Matahari of India; Mikado of Japan; Re-Vizaya of the Philippines;* and *Watch, 1927–1935.*
9. This essay will not discuss the organization after the death of Moncado in 1956. Diana Toy Moncado, until her death in 1964, attempted to redirect the federation and assert herself as the central charismatic figure in the persona of Mother (Mama) Diana. For the most part, she was only successful in this effort with a number of the Honolulu-based members through the Moncado Foundation of America. On this, see San Buenaventura, "Nativism and Ethnicity," 395–407.

10. Unidentified Washington, D.C., newspaper clipping, dated December 7, 1931, in "P" File, Hilario C. Moncado, RG–350, BIA, USNA. Even one of his most virulent critics recognized Moncado's charm and "fastidious" attire, commenting on his mastery of "oratory and persuasion" and his ability to display "a manner of great sincerity in face-to-face relations." See Robert McElrath (transcript of an ILWU radio broadcast, Honolulu, February 18, 1954) in the Filipino Federation of America file, International Longshoremen's and Warehousemen's Union Archives, Honolulu (hereafter cited as McElrath-ILWU radio transcript, 1954). See also Tavenner, "An Attempt," 4–5.

11. Moncado was viewed as a charlatan by many Filipinos and Americans. See, for example, P. E. Quevedo, *Read the Truth about Hilario Camino Moncado, the Greatest Impostor the World Has Ever Known* (Los Angeles, 1930); Dizon, *"Master"*; "Rizal kun Kolorum Tikasan?" *Bag-ong Kusog*, October 3, 1930, 5; "Diwatahan ug Matuhotuhuon si Hilario Camino Moncado?" *Bag-ong Kusog*, November 14, 1930; "Kinsa ug Unsa si Hilario C. Moncado?" *Bag-ong Kusog*, April 3, 1931, 27; "May mga Kolorum sa Haway ug Amerika?" *Bag-ong Kusog*, April 24, 1931, 23; "Si Dr. Moncado Dili Kolurum ug Dili Limbungan (Tubag sa Sinulat ni J. A. Patrocinio)," *Bag-ong Kusog*, June 12, 1931, 5, 32; *Mindanao Herald*, editorial, April 2, 1932 (which describes Moncado as "that irrepressible Filipino mountebank"); "Moncado, the Hocus-Pocus Man," *Philippines Free Press*, June 4, 1932, 20; *Philippines Free Press*, June 11, 1932, 20; Edward Berman, "The Man Who Plays God," *The Voice of Labor* (Honolulu), January 20, 1938, 4; January 27, 1938, 4; February 3, 1938, 4; February 10, 1938, 4; and McElrath-ILWU radio transcript, 1954. Perhaps the most oft-repeated story about Moncado's trickery pertains to the way he claimed to read minds. Versions of the story have been passed on in various forms, but it was vividly retold by an old-timer from Hawaii who recalled the "2-story building" of the federation in Hilo, where Moncado perpetrated "his sneakiest trick [of] 'reading' peoples' thoughts. . . . He had a waiting room on the bottom floor where those who wanted to talk to him about their problems were quizzed by his assistants. And Moncado knew what was on their minds before they reached his office on the second floor because he had a hearing mike connected. Of course, the uneducated like us started believing that 'Moncado is like God!' He knows what people were going to say! And I tell you, thousands joined" ("Excerpts from Hawaii Pilipino Dream," *Hawaii Heritage News*, March 1975, 2–3).

12. The concept of "charisma" as it is applied in this essay is informed by Charles Lindholm, *Charisma* (Cambridge: Blackwell, 1993).

13. Population figures for Hawaii are from the study of Romanzo Adams reported in Bruno Lasker, *Filipino Immigration to Continental United States and to Hawaii* (Chicago: American Council, Institute of Pacific Relations, and University of Chicago Press, 1931), 30, 350–52. The Filipino population increase in California (1920–30) is reported in Eiichiro Azuma, "Interethnic Conflict under Racial Subordination: Japanese Immigrants and Their Asian Neighbors in Walnut Grove, California, 1908–1941," *Amerasia Journal* 20.2 (1994): 39, which cites 1922 and 1932 census figures. The annual migration to California after 1924 is reported in Roy Malcolm, "Immigration Problems on the Pacific Coast" (Part III), *Current History*, February 1931,

726–28, reprinted as "A Survey of Filipino Immigration," *Philippine Republic* 8.3 (April 1931): 8. In 1930, the state of California's Department of Industrial Relations published a pamphlet, *Facts about Filipino Migration into California* (Special Bulletin no. 3, San Francisco, April 1930), which estimated the number of Filipinos in the state. The report (12, 46–47) noted that according to the 1920 census there were only 5,603 Filipinos in United States and 31,092 had arrived in California between 1920 and 1929. After explaining the difficulty of determining a precise count, the report estimated that in 1930 there were between 31,000 and 34,000 Filipinos in California.

14. Lasker, *Filipino Immigration*, 21, 347–49.

15. This very brief characterization is based mostly on life histories of members of the federation, the few published personal accounts, and histories of Filipinos in the United States. The personal accounts include Manuel Buaken, *I Have Lived with the American People* (Caldwell, Idaho: Caxton Printers, 1948); Roberto V. Vallangca, *Pinoy: The First Wave (1898–1941)* (San Francisco: Strawberry Hill Press, 1977); Philip Vera Cruz, *Philip Vera Cruz: A Personal History of Filipino Immigrants and the Farmworkers Movement*, [edited by] Craig Scharlin and Lilia V. Villanueva (Los Angeles: UCLA Labor Center, Institute of Industrial Relations and UCLA Asian American Studies Center, 1992); and Benicio Catapusan, "The Filipino Labor Cycle in the United States," *Sociology and Social Research* 19.1 (September–October 1934): 61–63. Histories of Filipinos in the United States include Alfredo Munoz, *The Filipinos in America* (Los Angeles: Mountainview Publishers, 1971); Lorraine Jacobs Crouchett, *Filipinos in California* (El Cerrito: Downey Place Publishing House, 1982); Antonio J. A. Pido, *The Pilipinos in America* (New York: Center for Migration Studies, 1986); Linda Nueva España Maram, "Negotiating Identity: Youth, Gender, and Popular Culture in Los Angeles's Little Manila, 1920s–1940s," Ph.D. diss., University of California, Los Angeles, 1990, 20–65; Carey McWilliams, *Factories in the Fields: The Story of Migratory Farm Labor in California* (Boston: Little, Brown, 1939); Wallace Stegner and the editors of *Look*, "Legally-Undesirable Heroes: The Filipinos in America," in *One Nation* (Boston: Houghton Mifflin, 1945), 19–43; Carey McWilliams, *Brothers under the Skin*, rev. ed. (Boston: Little, Brown, 1964), especially 229–49; Howard A. DeWitt, *Images of Ethnic and Radical Violence in California Politics, 1917–1930: A Survey* (San Francisco: R&E Research Associates, 1975); Howard A. DeWitt, *Anti-Filipino Movements in California: A History, Bibliography, and Study Guide* (San Francisco: R&E Research Associates, 1976); Howard A. DeWitt, "The Watsonville Anti-Filipino Riot of 1930: A Case Study of the Great Depression and Ethnic Conflict in California," *Southern California Quarterly* 61.3 (Fall 1979): 291–302; Howard A. DeWitt, *Violence in the Fields: California Filipino Farm Labor Unionization during the Great Depression* (Sacramento: Century Twenty-One Publishing, 1980); and Cletus E. Daniel, *Bitter Harvest: A History of California Farmworkers, 1870–1941* (Ithaca: Cornell University Press, 1981).

16. Ruben Alcantara, *Sakada: Filipino Adaptation in Hawaii* (Washington, D.C.: University Press of America, 1981); Roman B. Cariaga, "The Filipinos in Hawaii: A Survey of Their Economic and Social Conditions, 1906–1936," M.A. thesis, University of Hawaii, 1936; Ronald Takaki, *Pau Hana: Plantation*

Life and Labor in Hawaii, 1835–1920 (Honolulu: University of Hawaii Press, 1983); Edward Norbeck, *Pineapple Town Hawaii* (Berkeley: University of California Press, 1959); Edward D. Beechert, *Working in Hawaii: A Labor History* (Honolulu: University of Hawaii Press, 1985); John E. Reinecke, *The Filipino Piecemeal Sugar Strike of 1924–1925* (Honolulu: University of Hawai'i, Social Science Research Institute, 1996).

17. Based on his data, Lasker (*Filipino Immigration*, 23–24) estimated that 90 percent of the migrants were males, 80 percent of the men were single, and slightly more than 10 percent of the women were married.

18. There are several studies of the federation's Philippine colonies, among them: Victoria V. Flores-Tolentino, "The Moncado Believers: A Case Study in Religious Typology," M.A. thesis, Xavier University, 1979; Victoria F. Tolentino, "The Moncadistas of Mindanao," *Kinaadman* 4 (1982): 1–36; Leonor Miranda, "A Study of the Educational Training of the Moncadistas of Samal Island, Davao del Norte," M.A. thesis, University of Santo Tomas, 1969; Julita M. Chio, "A Historical Study of the Filipino Crusaders World Army, Inc., in Sudlon, Cebu," M.A thesis, De la Salle University, 1973; and San Buenaventura, "Nativism and Ethnicity," 274–80. The most comprehensive account by a federation member is Andres Darilay, *Silver Souvenir*, a 266-page compendium continuing numerous short biographies of returning migrants in the various Philippine colonies, especially in Mindanao. See also Andres Darilay, "Developing the Wilds of Lanao," *Progress*, May 28, 1933, 6. The colony in Surigao in the 1940s and 1950s is described in Emilio Alcutse Aninao, "Mga Pilipinhon Pagmata na Kamo," *Bag-ong Kusog*, November 22, 1940, 10; Emilio Alcutse Aninao, "Bakwi," *Bag-ong Kusog*, November 29, 1940, 31; Emilio Alcutse Aninao, *Our Master* (Mainit, Surigao: Surigao Branch, No. 9, Filipino Federation of America, [1954]); and Emilio Alcutse Aninao, "The Voice of Moncado," *Philippines Free Press*, July 3, 1954, 22. The growth and development of the federation colonies was covered in the Philippine press; see, for example, Federico D. Alferez, "Moncado Colony in Lanao," *Philippines Free Press*, February 11, 1933 (reprinted in *Progress*, February 12, 1933); F. Sionil Jose, "A Moncado Colony," *Sunday Times Magazine*, April 10, 1955; F. Sionil Jose, "1,000 Moncado Followers Lead a Frugal Life in Cebu Colony," *Manila Times*, February 13, 1957; Restituto del Rosario, "Moncado's Colony Keeps Up Expansion Work," *Progress*, February 26, 1933; Amador P. Moriles, "A Visit to the Moncado Colony [Cebu]," *Philippines Free Press*, May 19, 1956, 28; and "Moncado Federation Turns 60 Dec. 17," *Freeman*, December 22, 1985, 3.

19. The entry for Moncado in the baptismal registers of the parish of Balamban is fully integrated with the other entries for that year, making it quite certain that his baptism took place in 1895. This date is also verified in Dalumpines, "Life," 14, 166. Moreover, when Moncado signed his labor contract on February 1, 1914, the agent recorded that he was twenty-one years old, indicating that he was born sometime in 1893 or 1894—at least a year before his actual birth. See Filipino Affairs Department File, Lot No. 199, HSPA, Honolulu. Finally, the registrar of Sacred Heart High School, where Moncado was enrolled between 1916 and 1919, has his correct date of birth (November 4, 1895) recorded; see Vera Phillips to Francisco O. Dalumpines, November 17, 1970, as cited in Dalumpines, "Life," 150. By

1922, when Moncado withdrew from the University of Southern California (USC), his birth date was recorded as November 4, 1898. See Registrar (USC) to James Earl Wood, July 14, 1931, in James Earl Wood Papers, Envelope 7, Bancroft Library, University of California, Berkeley. In his autobiography (*Moncado Speaks*, 7), Moncado gives 1898 as his year of birth, a date that by the middle to late 1920s was used in all Moncado-sanctioned accounts of his life.

20. See Schaefle, "Answer," 10–11.

21. These physical attributes were frequently depicted through photographs of Moncado. One shows him entering a luxury liner amid a crowd of people, making it seem as if he had four or more arms. This photograph clearly was touched up to erase the other people, leaving Moncado alone and multi-armed. Another common photograph of Moncado in the early years depicted him with a halolike glow radiating from his head.

22. Lawcock ("Filipino Students," 357–58) describes Moncado in this way: "He impressed people with his abundant nervous energy, his singularly pene-trating eyes, his charming manners and, particularly, by his lavish use of money."

23. Deseo, *Moncado*, 30–31. "Moncado was a mystic of the first order," wrote Deseo, and "this statement needs no verification—one has only to look into the depth of his eyes and find there the soul of a mystic philosopher" (22).

24. See San Buenaventura, "Nativism and Ethnicity," 262–72.

25. San Buenaventura ("Nativism and Ethnicity," 36–37, 253) interprets the fed-eration's religion within the framework of "Filipino nativism," that is, as being "clearly an extension of the *colorum* tradition." For brief references to the federation within this religious continuum, see Leonardo N. Mercado, *Christ in the Philippines* (Tacloban: Divine Word University Publications, 1982), 31, 40–43, 76; Douglas J. Ellwood, *Churches and Sects in the Philippines* (Dumaguete City: Silliman University, 1968), 91; Amador P. Moriles, "A Visit to the Moncado Colony," 28; and Filemon V. Tutay, "The Colorum Today," *Philippines Free Press*, December 8, 1956.

26. Andres A. Darilay, "Biographical Sketch of Lorenzo Delos Reyes," in *Every Day New and Wonder* (N.p.: 1931 [blue copy]), 9–11. An updated biogra-phy under the same title was published in Darilay, *Silver Souvenir*, 27–30. See also San Buenaventura, "Nativism and Ethnicity," 254–59. The indigenous religion that developed in the Tagalog region of the Philippines during the Spanish era has been associated with Mt. Banahaw, the slopes of which reach down into two provinces—Quezon (Tayabas) and Laguna—and are home to a number of contemporary reli-gious groups. For discussions of the complex of religious beliefs that have existed and continue to exist in this region, see Reynaldo C. Ileto, *Pasyon and Revolution: Popular Movements in the Philippines, 1840–1910* (Quezon City: Ateneo de Manila University Press, 1979); Prospero R. Covar, "The Iglesia Watawat ng Lahi: An Anthropological Study of a Social Movement in the Philippines," Ph.D. diss., University of Arizona, 1975; Prospero R. Covar, "General Characterization of Contemporary Religious Movements in the Philippines," *Asian Studies* 13.2 (August 1975): 79–92; Vicente Marasigan, *A Banahaw Guru: Symbolic Deeds of Agapito Illustrisimo* (Quezon City: Ateneo de Manila University Press, 1985); and Vitaliano R. Gorospe, *Banahaw: Conversations with a Pilgrim to the Power Mountain*

(Makati: Bookmark, 1992).

27. Among the most prominent leaders of *colorum* groups on the *contracosta* of Cebu were the Tabal brothers, who led the Pulahanes from the 1890s to 1906 (they were considered heroes in Balamban, as reported in the Historical Data Papers at the National Library of the Philippines); Claudio Bakus, a popular rebel in the Toledo area in 1898–99; Capitan Eloy, who fought "Spaniards" in Pondol (Moncado's barrio) in the late 1890s; Emilio Verdeflor, a popular revolutionary hero who resisted the American occupation at the beginning of the twentieth century; Roberto "Mintong" Caballero, leader of a *colorum* society pursued by the Constabulary in 1902; Justo Templador, a popular healer and cult leader driven out of Cebu City around 1910, who established a spiritual colony in the mountain barrio of Lamak, Aloguinsan, about 1917; and Dikoy Saludar, founder of a popular spiritual society that flourished in the 1920s in Colonia, Tuburan. See Resil B. Mojares, "The *Pulahanes* of Cebu: Case Study in Human Geography," *Philippine Quarterly of Culture and Society* 4.4 (December 1976): 233–42; Michael Cullinane, "Rebellions in Cebu, 1898–1906: A Preliminary Analysis," paper presented at the conference Philippine Local History, University of the Philippines, Quezon City, July 1975; and Michael Cullinane, "Social Movements in the Central Visayas, 1800–1940," paper presented at the conference The Role of Social Movements in Philippine History, University of the Philippines, Quezon City, November 1975.

28. See Carey McWilliams, *Southern California Country: An Island on the Land* (New York: Duell, Sloan & Pearce, 1946), which uses Frank Fenton's phrase (269) "city of heretics." See also Kevin Starr, *Inventing the Dream: California through the Progressive Era* (New York: Oxford University Press, 1985); Kevin Starr, *Material Dreams: Southern California through the 1920s* (New York: Oxford University Press, 1990); Gregory H. Singleton, *Religion in the City of Angels: American Protestant Culture and Urbanization, Los Angeles, 1850–1930* (N.p.: UMI Research Press, 1979); and John D. Weaver, *Los Angeles: The Enormous Village, 1781–1981* (Santa Barbara: Capra Press, 1980), who notes that Los Angeles since 1915 has had more automobiles per capita than anywhere else in the world (201).

29. Quoted in David Reid, "The Possessed," in *Sex, Death, and God in L.A.*, edited by David Reid (Berkeley: University of California Press, 1992), 175.

30. See Richard Mathison, "California, Mecca for Cultists," in *Faiths, Cults, and Sects of America: From Atheism to Zen* (Indianapolis: Bobbs-Merrill, 1960), 125–219, where he notes (125) that "civic boosters have been trying to forget one of the area's questionable superlatives: that 'crackpot religion' rivals agriculture, movies, and aircraft manufacture as a major industry."

31. J. S. McGroarty, quoted in McWilliams, *Southern California Country*, 249. See also Singleton, *Religion in the City of Angels*, especially chapter 6; and Reid, "The Possessed."

32. H. Birney, quoted in McWilliams, *Southern California Country*, 250; see also Reid, "The Possessed"; and Elmer T. Clark, *The Small Sects in America* (Nashville: Cokesbury Press, 1937), 140. Clark has also noted (286–88) that not only was mainstream religion on the rise in America during the late teens and 1920s but cults of all varieties were among the most rapidly growing religious movements in the country.

33. Quoted in Severino F. Corpus, "An Analysis of the Racial Adjustment Activities and Problems of the Filipino-American Christian Fellowship of Los Angeles," M.A. thesis, University of Southern California, 1938, 20.
34. Jose Deseo, "The Filipinos in America," *Missionary Review of the World* 57.6 (June 1934): 288–89. The three most influential evangelical, or fundamentalist, sects in Southern California that confronted resident Filipinos were Aimee Semple McPherson's Four Square Gospel Church, Rev. Bob Shuler's Trinity Methodist Church, and the Seventh Day Adventists, each with large followings of mostly white working-class migrants. Though Filipinos heard and read their readily accessible messages, they rarely became members of their congregations. See Daniel Mark Epstein, *Sister Aimee: The Life of Aimee Semple McPherson* (New York: Harcourt Brace Jovanovich, 1993); Robert Barr, *Least of All Saints: The Story of Aimee Semple McPherson* (Englewood Cliffs, N.J.: Prentice-Hall, 1979); Williams, *Southern California,* 259–62, 343; Starr, *Material Dreams,* 136–39; Weaver, *Los Angeles,* 100–103, 117; Reid, "The Possessed," 193–95; Singleton, *Religion in the City of Angels,* 168–69; and Clark, *The Small Sects,* 26–27, 30–68, which reported that in the early 1930s the Seventh Day Adventists published "215 different periodicals," had an extremely active foreign missionary program, and were spending more than 11 million dollars annually on "evangelistic work" (55–56). Dizon (*"Master,"* 100) argued that the federation's "belief in an impending world cataclysm" was borrowed from the Adventists. Surviving members of the federation in Honolulu in the late 1970s still possessed copies of old religious tracts from these and other sects, some with vivid depictions of the horrors of Judgment Day and the alternative paths, one leading to salvation and the other to hell.
35. San Buenaventura ("Nativism and Ethnicity," 231–35, 328–34) has outlined the influence of American Protestantism on the federation's religion, particularly with regard to Bible reading and citation and the adoption of the Sunday school model.
36. For examples of activities and members of the Los Angeles branch of the Filipino Christian Fellowship, see the occasional reports filed in the *Philippine Republic,* February, September, November, and December 1926; and *Equifrilibricum News Service,* November 1, 1926, 7. The fellowship's activities included regular Sunday Bible studies, with singing and testimonies and social events, including Rizal Day programs, oratorical and declamation contests, lectures, and debates.
37. See the biography of Moncado included in the long caption under his large photo in *Equifrilibricum News Service,* March 1, 1925, 1.
38. *Who's Who in California* (1928–29), 369. Moncado's direct association with the Christian Fellowship and the Bible Class was also confirmed when in 1926 one of the active American volunteers of both organizations, Helen Borough, was employed by the federation. See *Equifrilibricum News Service,* October 1, 1926, 7; *Equifrilibricum News Service,* November 1, 1926, 1, 3; *Philippine Republic,* April 1931, cover, 6.
39. Deseo, *Moncado,* 22. In a rare account of federation religious services, a reporter who visited the Moncado Colony in Lanao in 1933, noting that the congregation gathered informally in a small chapel and began their service with readings of messages sent to them by Moncado, commented: "They use the *Holy Bible* and sing hymns similar to those of the Protestants" (*Philippines*

Free Press, February 11, 1933, 40).

40. Ileto, *Pasyon and Revolution*, 77, 94, 168–69, 261. It is perhaps important to point out that the religious ideology discussed by Ileto operated within the Tagalog region and that a similar *pasyon*-based ideology may not have been as old or as deeply rooted in other regions of the Philippines. See, for example, Alfred W. McCoy, "*Baylan*: Animist Religion and Philippine Peasant Ideology," in *Moral Order and the Question of Change*, edited by David K. Wyatt and Alexander Woodside, Southeast Asia Monographs, no. 24 (New Haven: Yale University, 1982), 338–423.

41. Although New Testament Bibles existed within the Philippines during the Spanish period, Spanish Catholicism did not have a tradition of using the Bible. See Stanley G. Payne, *Spanish Catholicism: An Historical Overview* (Madison: University of Wisconsin Press, 1984), 105, 193. See also San Buenaventura, "Nativism and Ethnicity," 329–31. The apocalyptic concepts embedded in the religious ideology of the Tagalogs, as analyzed by Ileto in his *Pasyon and Revolution*, derived from the *pasyon* text rather than from the Scriptures, or Bible, per se.

42. Arthur J. Brown, *The New Era in the Philippines* (New York: Fleming H. Revell, 1903), 183–84, 186, 216–18, 279–80; Charles W. Briggs, *The Progressing Philippines* (Philadelphia: Griffith & Rowland, 1913), 125–28. Briggs notes that by 1912 the two Bible societies (British and American) operating in the Philippines had distributed 1,439,938 Bibles and that these were particularly popular with members of the Philippine Independent Church. See also Kenton J. Clymer, *Protestant Missionaries in the Philippines, 1898–1916* (Urbana: University of Illinois Press, 1986), 4–5.

43. It is significant that one of the earliest Filipino Protestant faiths, the Iglesia ni Cristo (founded in 1914), emerged from its founder's (Felix Manalo's) readings of the Bible and that the initial revelation at its creation was that Manalo was the angel (messenger) coming to fulfill the apocalyptic prophecy (see Mercado, *Christ*, 39). Manalo, who was profoundly influenced by Protestant missionaries in the early years of the twentieth century and at the time he founded his new church was a Seventh Day Adventist, was thoroughly familiar with the New Testament and its Book of Revelations, which became integral parts of his religious discourse. See Fernando G. Elesterio, *The Iglesia ni Kristo: Its Christology and Ecclesiology* (Quezon City: Ateneo de Manila University, 1977), 6–12, 89–108.

44. In this context, it is interesting to note that the father of Manuel Buaken, Nicolas Buaken, became a Methodist minister in Manila after "he felt the call to propagate the new American doctrine of the Open Bible" (Buaken, *I Have Lived*, 17–18). In general, very little has been done by social or religious historians to study the early impact of Protestantism in the Philippines, an influence that may have been far more widespread than suspected.

45. An example of this is a regular editorial section authored by Moncado himself, wherein he quoted from the Bible and frequently gave commentaries. See, for example, his editorial "Glorious Coming of Christ," *Equifrilibricum News Service*, July 1, 1926, 8.

46. Ileto, *Pasyon and Revolution*, 144 and passim.

47. See for example, Mercado, *Christ*; and Marcelino A. Foronda, Jr., *Cults Honoring Rizal* (Manila: De La Salle College and R. P. Garcia, 1961).

48. This photo-graphic was widely reproduced in federation literature by 1925

and was reduced to small wallet-sized cards that were (and are) carried by members. The concept of the twelve *"ilustres"* was well developed by the early part of the twentieth century and the photograph widely known and circulated; a copy of it is reproduced, for example, in Evaristo C. Pecson, *Bitter Tears of Mother Philippines,* 2d ed. (Stockton: Muldowny Publishing, 1945), 61 (Pecson was an early leader of the federation in Los Angeles, Stockton, and elsewhere). In addition to these, a number of other apocalyptic images and symbols were propagated to promote Moncado's Christ-like credentials: the "Brown Christ"; the 1910 "sign" of Halley's comet (Delos Reyes and the graphic of the falling star with Moncado, the messenger, returning with the star); proclamations regarding the coming end (representing *panahon* or "independence/liberation") — "Watch for 1927-1935"; and a variety of photo-graphics depicting Moncado as *equifrilibricum* leading his flock to paradise. For a more systematic account of this and the religion of the federation, see San Buenaventura, "Filipino Folk Spirituality."

49. See Lawcock, "Filipino Students," 365, 402; and Deseo, *Moncado,* 19, 22.

50. Singleton, *Religion in the City of Angels,* 168-69; Peter Washington, *Madame Blavatsky's Baboon: A History of the Mystics, Mediums, and Misfits Who Brought Spiritualism to America* (New York: Schocken Books, 1995), 320-21; Robert S. Ellwood, Jr., *Religious and Spiritual Groups in Modern America* (Englewood Cliffs, N.J.: Prentice-Hall, 1973), 81-83, 219-31; Mathison, *Faiths, Cults, and Sects,* 184-95. Mathison noted (190) that "Indian mystics in flowing robes and with wondrous tales were no oddities in Los Angeles in 1925. The theosophy stir had brought scores of them, ranging from crude opportunists to famed holy men."

51. Indian and theosophical beliefs and practices were not the only influences on the federation's eating habits (vegetarianism, raw food, fasting, and other dietary/nutritional practices) or physical culture (yoga and other yogic forms of exercise). Numerous Western-based health, food, and nutritional innovations, including those of the Seventh Day Adventists, were circulating at the time, especially in Southern California, and clearly had an impact on Moncado and his associates. For a discussion of some of these, in particular the influence of Arnold Ehret's *Mucusless Diet System,* see San Buenaventura, "Nativism and Ethnicity," 340-45.

52. McWilliams, *Southern California,* 254. For an account of Katherine Tingley's role in the theosophy movement, see Washington, *Madame Blavatsky's Baboon,* 108-14. Moncado and his associates were not the only sojourners in Southern California to find inspiration and to borrow from the theosophy movement. The Los Angeles-based cult Mighty I Am (with more than 350,000 members in the 1930s) drew heavily from the occult doctrines of theosophy as well as from the Rosicrucians; see Reid, "The Possessed," 196-97.

53. McWilliams, *Southern California,* 254-55; Washington, *Madame Blavatsky's Baboon,* 216; Bruce F. Campbell, *Ancient Wisdom Revived: A History of the Theosophical Movement* (Berkeley: University of California Press, 1980), 113-46; Mathison, *Faiths, Cults, and Sects,* 142-59; Jan Karel Van Baalan, *The Chaos of Cults: The Study of Present Day Isms,* 7th ed., rev. (Grand Rapids: Wm. B. Eerdmans, 1948), 48-65; R. Ellwood, *Religious and Spiritual Groups,* 88-103.

54. All branches of the theosophical movement published regular reviews (usually monthly): *The Path* (the original organ of the society), *The Theosophist* (of Besant), *Theosophy* (of Tingley), and *Theosophy* (of the United Lodge of Theosophists).

55. Mary Luytens, *Krishnamurti: The Years of Awakening* (New York: Avon, 1976), 10 (including quote on "perfect beings"). His first public address in the United States was delivered at the Hollywood Bowl on May 15, 1928, when more than sixteen thousand people came to hear the "new Messiah" (276). Among the many tracts circulating at the time was Annie Besant, *The Masters* (Krotona, Hollywood, and Los Angeles: Theosophical Publishing House, 1918). See also Reid, "The Possessed," 187–92.

56. Reid, "The Possessed," 189.

57. Quoted in Luytens, *Krishnamurti*, 41, 60, 182–83. On his Lincoln, see 201–2. The movements and activities of Krishnamurti were periodically reported in the Filipino press in the United States. The account mentioned here derives from the *Philippine Republic*, June 1927, 19. Other selected accounts in this magazine may be found in the issues of October 1926, 11; January-February 1927, 13; March 1927, 4; and May 15, 1928, 9. In the Philippines, see, for example, "'I Come to Those Who Want Happiness,'" *Philippines Free Press*, April 24, 1926, 36 (on Krishnamurti, Besant, and theosophy); and Mima de Manziarly Porter, "Man Krishnaji," *Philippines Free Press*, May 29, 1926, 17, 49–50, both of which reproduced photos of the "new Christ, from India." See also Reid, "The Possessed," 187–92.

58. See San Buenaventura, "Nativism and Ethnicity, 284–85. She draws her material in this case from Lorenzo Delos Reyes's *Every Day New and Wonder*, and from interviews with spiritual members of the federation.

59. Campbell, *Ancient Wisdom Revived*, 122; see the federation broadside "Wake-Up Filipinos, Join the Federation, '1926 Rizal Day Organization,' Lodge #1, housed at the Pioneer Museum and Higgins Galleries, Stockton, California.

60. Ellwood, *Religious and Spiritual Groups*, 98–99.

61. San Buenaventura, "Nativism and Ethnicity," 262–72.

62. Mervyn Jones, "The Rosicrucians," in *Secret Societies*, edited by Norman MacKenzie (London: Aldus Books, 1967), 130–51. See also Ellwood, *Religious and Spiritual Groups*, 110–13; and Van Baalan, *Chaos of Cults*, 66–89, 318. The latter describes the literature produced by the San Jose headquarters of AMORC.

63. See, for example, the illustrations in Moncado's *Divinity of Women* (1927), which are attributed to one Duke Schaefle (quite likely the son of one of Moncado's publicity agents at the time, William Schaefle), and the graphics and photos in Delos Reyes's *Every Day New and Wonder* and Leon G. Vaguios's *Ang Agi-anan Ngadto: "Ang Basahon nga Naga Sulti Alang sa Caayohan sa Mga Taw"* ([Honolulu: Filipino Federation of America, 1930]).

64. Edward George Earle Lytton Bulwer-Lytton (Lord), *The Coming Race*, rpt. (Santa Barbara: Woodbridge Press, 1979); originally published 1870–71.

65. See Vaguios, *Ang Agi-anan Ngadto*. In several interviews with federation members, the phrase "the coming race" was used. See also Deseo, *Moncado*, 96, where the explicit connection is made as follows: "We the members of the Filipino Federation of America, Inc., friends of humanity, believe that the Malay race is the light of the world, as pointed out in Bulwer Lytton's work, 'The Coming Race.'" For a more detailed summary

of the origins and depth of this belief among federation members, see San Buenaventura, "Nativism and Ethnicity," 346–51. See also pages 300–302, where her interviews reveal that the concept of the *vril-ya* was for some members merged with the Cebuano belief in *ingkantu*, a form of supernatural being or spirit.

66. Reid, "The Possessed," 190. The co-optation of the belief in a powerful subterranean "race" was not unique to Moncado and his followers, as witnessed (197) by the popular Southern California cult, Mankind United, of the 1940s, which designated its spiritual guides to be "a superhuman race of little men with metallic heads who dwell in the center of the earth."

67. Arcadio Amper, interview with the author, Honolulu, September 9, 1979.

68. See, for example, Ramos, *Moncado: The World Servant.*

69. On the symbolic use of "*doce-doce*" (12-12), a significant mystical concept promoted by Moncado and Lorenzo Delos Reyes, see San Buenaventura, "The Master and the Federation," 172-73; and San Buenaventura, "Filipino Folk Spirituality," 7–11.

70. *American Globe*, January 1928, 25.

71. *American Globe*, January 1928, 12.

72. *American Globe*, January 1928, 28.

73. Reference is made here to Philip Vera Cruz's phrase — "so close to the good life" — characterizing the place of Filipino laborers in the United States, constantly within view of a "good life" that remained out of reach. See Vera Cruz, *Philip Vera Cruz.*

74. Aquilino B. Obando, "A Study of the Problems of Filipino Students in the United States," M.A. thesis, University of Southern California, 1936, 4–10. The thesis was published by R&E Research Associates, San Francisco, in 1974. See also Lawcock, "Filipino Students," 86–97, 123-28. Although the term *pensionado* technically refers to the earliest government-sponsored students (through 1905), the term was applied to all sponsored students during the prewar years. On the *pensionados*, including short biographies of each, see William A. Sutherland, *Not by Might: The Epic of the Philippines* (Las Cruces, N.M.: Southwest Publishing, 1953). The most comprehensive study of Filipino "students" in the prewar United States is Lawcock, "Filipino Students."

75. Between 1900 and 1940, elementary and secondary school enrollments increased from 272,000 to about 7 million, with public school expenditures jumping from $7.2 million to near $200 million. See Robert Glass Cleland, *California in Our Time (1900-1940)* (New York: Knopf, 1947), 142–43.

76. Obando, " Study," 11-17.

77. Malcolm, "Immigration Problems," 726-28; Obando, "Study," 21-25; Lawcock, "Filipino Students," 241-355.

78. Malcolm ("Immigration Problems," 728) noted that "quite a number [of Filipinos] registered in American high schools." Though they were in the minority, some Filipino laborers had already obtained full or partial secondary educations in the Philippines before coming and were as a result able to attend college. For personal accounts of problems faced by Filipinos pursuing educational objectives, see Vallangca, *Pinoy*, 14–15; and Obando, "Study," 9, 12-16.

79. In this context, it is significant to mention an entry in Moncado's 1955 autobiography (*Moncado Speaks*, 9), where he briefly describes an early conflict

with Carlos P. Romulo, at the time a *pensionado* at Columbia University in New York City. Although he does not detail the causes of their feud, Moncado attributes the conflict to Romulo's referring to "self-supporting students" as "riffraff" not worthy of being legitimate representatives of the Philippines in America. Moncado alleges that he defended the working students to *pensionados* such as Romulo. For a stimulating essay on the political interaction between the elites and masses at about the same time in the Philippines, see Reynaldo C. Ileto, "Orators and the Crowd: Philippine Independence Politics, 1910–1914," in *Reappraising an Empire*, edited by Peter W. Stanley (Cambridge: Harvard University Press, 1984), 85–113, 326–33.

80. On Moncado, see *Moncado Speaks*, 7–9. On lawyers and politicians from USC, see Starr, *Material Dreams*, 151–56; and Bruce Henstell, *Sunshine and Wealth: Los Angeles in the Twenties and Thirties* (San Francisco: Chronicle Books, [1993]), 46.

81. On Moncado's failing grades at and withdrawal from USC, see James Earl Wood, "Filipino Federation of America, Incorporated" (manuscript), 3; and Arnett F. Hanley (Registrar, University of Southern California, School of Law) to James Earl Wood, July 14, 1931. Both documents are included in the James Earl Wood Collection, Bancroft Library, University of California, Berkeley.

82. Lawcock, "Filipino Students," 365, citing an article in the Filipino newspaper *Three Stars* (Stockton), September 15, 1928.

83. *Moncado Speaks*, 13. This degree was confirmed by the Registrar of Southwestern University in a letter to Francisco Dalumpines on November 19, 1970. See Dalumpines, "Life of Moncado," 148. On the size of Southwestern University's College of Law, see Lawcock, "Filipino Students," 362. In an article written by a Filipino law student who was at Southwestern with Moncado published in *Three Stars* (October 1, 1928) and cited by Lawcock (362), Moncado was said to have been a poor student. By fostering "friendships" and paying out "great sums of money," he was able to obtain his degree.

84. Moncado stated that his LL.M. was granted for a thesis on "History and Development of the Corporation Law in the United States" and his A.M. degree for a thesis on "The Immigration of Filipinos into the United States." See *Moncado Speaks*, 14–15. Olympic University was in 1930 the new name for the Pacific Institute, which drew most its law students from the Polytechnic Evening Law School, described as "one of the largest in the nation," with twenty-seven instructors on its faculty. See *American Globe*, November 1930, 20. In his effort to locate information about the school, Francisco Dalumpines was informed by the State of California Committee of Bar Examiners on May 7, 1971, that Olympic University apparently ceased to exist after 1933 and they have "no information about the structure or the faculty of the school" (Dalumpines, "Life of Moncado," 154).

85. *Moncado Speaks*, 15.

86. It is significant to note that his two Indian degrees in kabala and numerology (K.Ph.D. and N.Ph.D), allegedly obtained as a youth in Calcutta, were normally integrated with those he obtained in the United States. Moncado's law degrees were always the most important within the Philippine context, and photographs of the his diplomas were frequently displayed and distributed

by sympathetic biographers and federation members. See, for example, Dalumpines, "Life of Moncado," appendixes.

87. In 1927, George E. Cryer, mayor of Los Angeles, estimated that "among our citizens" there were "several hundred Filipino" residing in the city. See Cryer to Moncado, December 7, 1927, reproduced in the *American Globe*, January 1928, 6. In its May 1929 issue, the *Philippine Republic* reproduced an article by Evaristo C. Pecson (reprinted from the *Filipino Nation*) in which he described the growing Filipino "colony" in Los Angeles: "Today there are at least seven Filipino barber shops, six restaurants, three pool room parlors and shoe stands, four employment agencies, three corporations, a tailor shop and several other partnerships" (6).

88. Wood, "Filipino Federation of America, Incorporated," 4.

89. Quoted in Dizon, "*Master*," 50–51. The quote is from a former associate of Moncado before the establishment of the federation.

90. McWilliams, *Brothers under the Skin*, 236–41 (quote from 238–39). Filipino labor contractors were often blamed for cheating laborers. A particularly virulent attack against "unscrupulous Filipino 'capitalists' who make a practice of acting as middlemen" can be found in Eliot G. Mears, *Resident Orientals on the American Pacific Coast* (Chicago: University of Chicago Press, 1928), 272–73.

91. *Moncado Speaks*, 13. A brief description of the gambling and prostitution operations in the Los Angeles Chinatown is given in Starr, *Material Dreams*, 145–46; and Henstell, *Sunshine and Wealth*, 88–93. Contrary to Moncado's boast about closing down Chinese gamblers, they continued to flourish for many years after this time.

92. See McWilliams, *Brothers under the Skin*, 238, which cites the *Proceedings of the First Official Filipino National Convention in America* (1938, 82). McWilliams made a similar estimate in his introduction to Carlos Bulosan's *America Is in the Heart* (Seattle: University of Washington Press, 1975), xi.

93. For an example of such a society, see Oriental Benevolent Association, *Constitution and By-Laws, December 10, 1937, Territory of Hawaii* (Wailuku, Maui: n.p., 1937).

94. The names and locations of these dance halls appeared regularly in advertisements in the *Philippine Republic* (1924–26) and Moncado's *Equifrilibricum News Service* (November 1, 1924, through December 15, 1926).

95. *Equifrilibricum News Service*, December 1, 1924, 4. Along with those for dance halls, there were ads for insurance companies and Japanese and American businesses (photography studios, tailor's shops, medical services, restaurants, and the like).

96. *Equifrilibricum News Service*, July 1, 1926, 1, 12.

97. As one leader of the federation in Mindanao put it: "The members are not allowed to dance, smoke, drink alcoholic beverages, use drugs, to gossip, or indulge in vices" (Aninao, *Our Master*, 20).

98. Dizon ("*Master*," 56–57) alleged that Moncado targeted the laborers rather than the students since they were both more ignorant and better able to pay the fees and make contributions to the federation as a result of their more regular employment. In this context, Moncado received much criticism for his efforts (in 1924) to organize the Filipino National Bank of America, a cooperative banking scheme promising investors large returns on their money. This bank scheme was abandoned on the eve of the establishment

of the federation with no apparent accounting or refunding of deposits to investors. See *Equifrilibricum News Service,* November 1, 1924, 4 (most of the back page). In an article in *Ang Bantay* (Los Angeles), January 24, 1930, G. F. Aceveda attacked Moncado in a letter that stated: "And you would not deny the fact that before the inception of your Federation, you organized the so-called Filipino-American Bank, that was not incorporated with any laws of the United States, yet you had accepted several hundred if not thousand dollars from different depositors and then dissolved the Bank. As to what happened with the money, nobody knows." This article is quoted in its entirety in Dizon, *"Master,"* 98–99. In other accounts, published in *The Three Stars* (Stockton), September 15 and November 1, 1928, Moncado was accused of deceiving subscribers to his bank, which was said to have been a scheme devised in collaboration with an American partner. See also Lawcock, "Filipino Students," 365.

99. These organizations were regularly publicized and promoted during this period in Moncado's Los Angeles–based *Equifrilibricum News Service* and the Washington, D.C.–based *Philippine Republic.* Among the groups discussed in these publications are the Boholano Brotherhood Association, Caballeros de Dimas Alang, Filipino Association of Southern California, Filipino Bible Class, Filipino Brotherhood, Filipino Catholic Club, Filipino Christian Fellowship, Filipino Club of California, Gran Oriente Filipino, "The Ten Club," and the three student groups: the Filipino Club of Polytechnic High School, Filipino Club of UCLA, and Filipino Students at Automotive and Electrical School.

100. *Equifrilibricum News Service,* March 1, 1925, 1; Wood, "Filipino Federation of America, Incorporated," 4; Lawcock, "Filipino Students," 364–65, 375.

101. Although the federation was not officially launched until December 1925, advertisements soliciting members were published as early as March (*Equifrilibricum News Service,* March 1, 1925, 3).

102. Evaristo Casiano Pecson, "The Federation and Its Objects," in *Those Who Serve* ([Stockton: Muldowney Publishing, 1945]), 23.

103. See Deseo, *Moncado,* 37–39 (quotes from 34, 38). The titles of several of his lectures have been recorded: "The Coming Race," "Watch 1927 to 1935," "The World Coming Teacher," "Filipino as a Power," and "Morality."

104. Two among the original group of twelve who stand out as central figures in the federation's management are Lorenzo Delos Reyes and Andres Darilay. Among the most effective new recruits in 1926 were Evaristo C. Pecson and Cornelio Clenuar.

105. Deseo, *Moncado,* 39, which also reports that federation recruiters were often refused entry into several of these establishments when their "mission" became known.

106. See the federation's ad in *Equifrilibricum News Service,* June 1, 1926, 11.

107. *Equifrilibricum News Service,* November 15, 1926, 1. Lists of the members of the first three lodges can be found in the November 1, 1926, and December 1, 1926, issues. The quote is from Deseo, *Moncado,* 40. *Equifrilibricum News Service,* November 1, 1926, 2, lists fifty-four "members who regularly attend all the meetings."

108. *Equifrilibricum News Service,* December 15, 1926. 2. For a somewhat more detailed account of the federation's first year, see Deseo, *Moncado,* 34–40.

109. *Equifrilibricum News Service,* November 15, 1926, 1, 7.

110. See, for example, Howard A. DeWitt, "Philippine Independence: Dr. Jose Rizal and the View from California," paper presented at the International Conference on the Centennial of the 1896 Philippine Revolution, Manila, August 12–23, 1996.

111. For praise of the event, see *Philippine Republic*, January-February 1927, 16; Deseo, *Moncado*, 40–42; and San Buenaventura, "Nativism and Ethnicity," 173–78.

112. *Moncado Speaks*, 11; see also *Philippine Republic*, January-February 1927, 16; and Deseo, *Moncado*, 41–42.

113. See *Philippine Republic*, September 15, 1927, 14, in which there is a letter written by the judge of the contest, USC professor Claude Douglas, in praise of Moncado. The letter was also printed in the *Equifrilibricum News Service*.

114. *1926 Rizal Day Organization Breaks All the Records of Any Filipino Rizal Day Celebration in America* (Los Angeles: West Coast Publishing, [1927]), 20.

115. "Wake Up Filipinos, Join the Federation" (poster, [1926]), located in the Pioneer Museum and Higgins Galleries, Stockton, California.

116. This sentiment is clearly expressed in the context of the 1926 Rizal Day event in Deseo, *Moncado*, 41–42.

117. *Philippine Republic*, March 1927, 10.

118. Deseo (*Moncado*, 38) claims that two federation members, Andres Darilay and Victor Aranjuez, had to appear in court, where the charges were dismissed.

119. Deseo, *Moncado*, 35; *Moncado Speaks*, 12–13.

120. Deseo, *Moncado*, 39.

121. *Philippine Republic*, August 15, 1927, 5; September 15, 1927, 13.

122. One of the most complete sets of the magazine can be found in the collection of the Library of Congress, where it was regularly deposited by the publishers.

123. *Philippine Republic*, September 15, 1927, 20.

124. *Philippine Republic*, December 15, 1927, 11.

125. Before long, the Los Angeles and other conventions ran for the whole last week of December, overlapping with Rizal Day and often incorporating it within the federation's schedule of activities during the convention period.

126. The event was well publicized in the *Philippine Republic*, December 15, 1927, the front cover of which displays a photo of Moncado shaking hands with Los Angeles mayor George Cryer, who is said to be "congratulating" Moncado; both the front and back covers of the issue advertise the federation's Los Angeles convention and highlight the speakers.

127. Deseo, *Moncado*, 40. *Philippine Republic*, October 15, 1927, 16–17, published the names of all the officers of the first thirty-one lodges, indicating that two other branches were already open by this time: Stockton and Salinas.

128. The Stockton convention featured all the requisite activities: an elaborate parade, musical entertainment, a major address by Moncado, and a banquet. See *Philippine Republic*, May 15, 1928, 20 (back cover), which includes a photo of the federation's orchestra, at the time under the direction of the renowned conductor Emilio A. Aninao, a veteran musician who was earlier a member of the Philippine Constabulary Band. In the early days, he had helped Moncado organize the federation's musical groups in Los Angeles. His son, Quintin Aninao, joined his father after studying music in Hong Kong and Illinois. When Emilio returned to the Philippines in the 1930s, he helped

establish the colonies in Mindanao, while Quintin eventually headed the federation's President Moncado Band, which—among other things—played at
the Golden Gate Exposition. See also Lawcock, "Filipino Students," 378,
quoting the story in *Filipino Nation*, March 1928, 3.

129. In Los Angeles in the early 1930s, the federation maintained three bands, two
orchestras, and a number of vocal soloists who were used for federation
events and hired out to entertain around the city. See Lawcock, "Filipino
Students," 389–90.

130. Deseo, *Moncado*, 96–97.

131. Tavenner, "An Attempt to Explain Hilario Moncado," 4.

132. Tavenner, "An Attempt to Explain Hilario Moncado," 4.

133. Lawcock, "Filipino Students," 373, 385. Lawcock also notes that by 1930 the
federation owned and operated a grocery store in Stockton, having already
leased a "21-room, three-story home" for members there (377). A third
large house had been obtained in Fresno by 1930. See *Filipino Nation*,
January 1930, 23, where all three "Federation Homes in Sunny California"
are pictured.

134. An editorial in the *Mindanao Herald* (April 2, 1932) charged Moncado with
collecting large sums of money from his followers, money that "makes it
possible for him to travel *de luxe* and put up at the bridal suites of the best
hotels." For Moncado, the editor argued, the federation was "better than a
beer racket." In the 1950s, Moncado was attacked for his opulence by labor
leaders: "He throws money around as though his funds are unlimited"
(McElrath-ILWU radio transcript, 1954). In a report on Moncado written
more than a decade after his death ("Moncado's Dream Is Still Alive,"
Honolulu Star-Bulletin, December 25, 1967, A4), Hawaii journalist Ligaya
Fruto wrote: "No one knows how much money was poured into his private
coffers by his adoring subjects, but it enabled him to live in a manner befit-
ting a potentate. It was reported that for two visits in 1955 within a 3-month
period, he spent $70,000." Eventually, of course, Moncado acquired a beau-
tiful house in Honolulu and no longer needed to stay at the Royal
Hawaiian Hotel.

135. An eyewitness to Moncado's triumphant return to Balamban recalled that
he threw a large amount of money from his car, causing considerable
chaos (Nicolasa M. Nacar, interview with the author, San Francisco,
California, September 13, 1980). In his memoirs, Jose Romero recalled
many of his fellow delegates to the Constitutional Convention of 1934.
What stood out in his recollections of Moncado was the large fortune he
seemed to have collected "from fees paid by the laborers affiliated with
the labor organization he had formed" (*Not So Long Ago* [Manila: Alemar,
1979], 59). For examples of local perceptions in Cebu regarding
Moncado's wealth and his charitable gifts to institutions in the province,
see "Si Moncado Mihatag Usa ka Libo ka Pisos," *Bag-ong Kusog*, April 17,
1931, 13; "Kalandrakas," *Bag-ong Kusog*, July 17, 1931, 15; "Dr. Moncado
Gipasidunggan," *Bag-ong Kusog*, December 18, 1931, 16; "Moncado Dili
Mobubug Sapi," *Bag-ong Kusog*, August 12, 1932, 21; "Si Moncado sa
Balamban," *Bag-ong Kusog*, August 11, 1933, 26; and "Kalandrakas," *Bag-
ong Kusog*, December 15, 1933, 31. For the national perception of Moncado
as a wealthy Filipino from the United States coming home to buy a political office, see "Moncado's Candidacy a Big Joke," *Philippines Free Press*, July

23, 1932, 46; and "A 'Mammoth Political Carnival,'" *Philippines Free Press,* August 13, 1932, 48–49.

136. Gregorio F. Zaide, *Philippine History and Civilization* (Manila: Philippine Associated Publishers, 1939), 695.

137. "Constitution of the Filipino Federation of America" (December 27, 1928), reproduced in Deseo, *Moncado,* 121, 123.

138. See also San Buenaventura, "Nativism and Ethnicity," 443–45.

139. See the statement of Horace C. Curry (said to have been an old friend of Moncado), published in *Philippine NEWSPIC* and quoted in Alconi, "His True Mission in Life," *Moncado and His Mission Bulletin* 2.10 (October 1956): 3–4, where the author claims that, other than his "vast properties scattered all over [the Philippines]," Moncado "has investments in many of the multi-million dollar corporations in the United States. He is a stockholder to reckon with in airline companies, railroads, banking institutions, oil wells, and real estate. Dividend checks arrive regularly, giving him an income worth a king's ransom, allowing him a prince's existence, if not actually surpassing the luxuries enjoyed by royalty." Curry alleged that Moncado spent "half a million pesos" on his campaign in favor of parity in 1946.

140. "Moncado Received $162,000 from Followers in '47," *Honolulu Star-Bulletin* September 12, 1958, 4. Collection receipts and copies of cablegrams transferring these and other funds to Moncado in the Philippines have been preserved in the Benigno "Benny" Escobido collection, currently in the possession of the author. Dizon ("*Master,*" 71) claims that earlier, in 1931, in one Honolulu bank alone "the amount of $50,000 is deposited in Moncado's name."

141. Statement of Alfonzo Nagal, quoted in San Buenaventura, "Nativism and Ethnicity," 445. A rare glimpse of federation collection and distribution procedures can be reconstructed from records in the Escobido collection cited in the previous note. These records, mostly from the Honolulu, Kauai, and Maui branches in Hawaii in 1938 and 1939, provide detailed accounts of the collection of fees for the various levels of membership existing at the time, of costs for pins sold by the federation, of money for "voluntary support of Master" for his political campaign in the Philippines, and of "donations for Master giving a lecture" to the members of the Maui branch. After deducting small amounts for branch expenses, the bulk of the money collected was wired directly to Moncado in Manila.

142. All the formal administrative structures described here and above come from the "Constitution of the Filipino Federation of America" (December 27, 1928), which is reproduced in Deseo, *Moncado,* 119–128. Though the geography of the federation did not correspond to lodges and divisions, an individual matriculate member's lodge and division number remained an important designation (e.g., EFB Division 1, Lodge 9) and was the means of identifying each link in "the 1728."

143. *Filipino Nation,* December 1930, 49.

144. For a discussion of the role of some of Moncado's "lieutenants," see Lawcock, "Filipino Students," 369–80.

145. Andres A. Darilay, "Biographical Sketch of Lorenzo Delos Reyes," in Lorenzo Delos Reyes, *Every Day New and Wonder* (blue copy) (N.p.: 1931), 9–11.

146. Editorial, *Mindanao Herald,* April 2, 1932.

147. *Moncado Speaks*, 9, 19; San Buenaventura, "Nativism and Ethnicity," 227–28; Lawcock, "Filipino Students," 461–62. For a photo of Luke McNamee in Manila in 1948, together with Filipino Crusaders Army officers (in uniform), see Darilay, *Silver Souvenir*, 35, 126–27.

148. *Equifrilibricum News Service*, October 1, 1926, 7.

149. *Philippine Republic*, March 1931, 16; April 1931, cover, 6; *Equifrilibricum News Service*, January 1, 1927, 1; San Buenaventura, "Nativism and Ethnicity," 174–76. San Buenaventura used valuable information from a 1984 interview with Helen Borough. See also Lawcock, "Filipino Students," 379–80.

150. *Who's Who in California* (1928–29), 571–72.

151. *American Globe*, January 1928 (twenty-seven-page coverage).

152. Moncado, *Divinity of Women*, 8–14. The illustrator was identified as "Duke Schaefle."

153. Among the most influential of Schaefle's articles on Moncado was his earliest, reprinted in the *Philippine Republic*, the glossy Washington, D.C.–based Filipino public relations magazine backed by the Philippine Legislature to lobby for independence. The article, "An Answer To: 'Who is Moncado?'" (*Philippine Republic*, July 1927, 10–11), lavishly praises Moncado at a time when the federation was beginning to gather momentum in recruiting members. The number of pages devoted to the federation in selected issues of the *American Globe* was as follows: January 1928, 27 pages; March 1930, 29; June 1930, 31; November 1930, 22; January 1931, 32; April 1931, 7; October 1931, 5; February 1932, 15. See also William J. Schaefle, *Moncado and His Mission* (Los Angeles: Filipino Federation of America, 1928); and *Who's Who in California* (1928–29), 571–72.

154. William J. Schaefle, "Why the American Globe Publisher Has Backed Dr. Hilario Camino Moncado and Filipino Federation of America, Inc.," *American Globe*, February 1932, 5.

155. *Philippine Republic*, December 1926, 20.

156. The earliest federation advertisement appeared in the May 1927 issue of the *Philippine Republic*, with Schaefle's article appearing in the July 1927 issue. The first notice of Moncado in the magazine seems to have been in the January–March 1927 issue, when he was praised as the organizer of the successful Rizal Day festivities held in Los Angeles in December 1926.

157. See the various reports on Moncado in Tavenner's *Philippine Republic* throughout 1930, in particular Tavenner's "An Attempt to Explain Hilario Moncado," October 1930, 4–5. See also Harry H. Beall, "President Moncado: The Man of the Hour," *American Globe*, June 1930, 5–9.

158. An example of the array of Americans who participated in federation events can be seen in those attending the Fourth National Convention, held in Los Angeles in December 1930. Some twenty Americans took part, including Edgar Parson, president of the San Fernando Chamber of Commerce (and manager of a Veteran's Administration Hospital that employed many Filipinos); Helen Holt, "an active member of the California Chamber of Commerce" (of the state of California's Safety, Street, and Highway Department); Dr. Harold E. Peterson, president of the San Fernando Rotary Club; Judge Charles Haas of the Los Angeles Municipal Court; Col. Le Roy F. Smith, director of the Speakers' Bureau of the Better America Foundation; Samuel Rosenkrantz, director of the Los Angeles National Automobile School; Dr. Frederick P. Woellner, UCLA professor of

education; Marceline Day, "movie star" of "the Fox Motion Picture Industry"; and one Sergeant Johnson "of the Los Angeles Police Department." See *Filipino Nation*, February 1931, 21–36; *American Globe*, January 1931, 1–33, and *Philippine Republic*, January-February 1931, 12.

159. *Philippine Republic*, August 15, 1927; September 1927, 13.
160. John K. Butler to Wallace R. Farrington, September 18, 1928, Wallace H. Farrington Papers, Hawaii Archives.
161. Richard H. Wheeler to General Hilario Moncado, FFA ("Dear General Moncado"), October 11, 1954, ILWU Library, Honolulu. Wheeler enclosed his business card in the letter.
162. Quevedo, a law student residing in Los Angeles at the time, was associated with organizations competing with Moncado for leadership of the Filipino community. Quevedo's pamphlet, along with a letter attacking Moncado, a Los Angeles community resolution (dated December 22, 1928) condemning Moncado for defacing the Philippine flag in his symbolic representations, and a 1929 poster advertising Quevedo's pamphlet are part of the James E. Wood Papers, Bancroft Library, University of California, Berkeley. Quevedo continued his efforts to discredit Moncado and the Federation for several years, and in late 1929 he was contemplating a formal legal suit against Moncado. See *Ang Bantay* (Los Angeles), December 7, 1939, and articles by Quevedo in *The Three Stars*, December 1931, January 1932, and April-May 1932. As the Federation moved into the Central Valley of California, especially Stockton, Moncado's organizing efforts were opposed by a group calling itself the Anti-Kolorum League, which, among other things, criticized his "Filipino Hindu" teachings. Resistance to the Federation was led by members of fraternal organizations already operating in the area: the Caballeros de Dimas Alang, Mga Anak ng Bukid, Gran Oriente Filipino, and Legionarios del Trabajo. See *The Three Stars*, September 1, October 5, October 15, November 1, and December 1, 1928. One attack on Moncado referred to him as *talagang sira ang ulo* (a true cracked head); elsewhere, in an effort to belittle his title of "Master," he was referred to as Maskaluko Moncado (Impostor Moncado); see *The Three Stars*, September 15, 1928, December 1, 1928, January 1, 1928, and February 1929. See also Deseo, *Moncado*, 39, for an account of these attacks by a Moncado promoter.
163. Dizon, *"Master,"* 7, 11. At the time he wrote this book, Dizon was the pastor of the Filipino Community Church in Honolulu. For a brief account of Moncado's critics in Stockton, especially Damiano Marcuelo, the longtime editor of the Filipino newspaper *Three Stars*, see Lawcock, "Filipino Students," 417–18. See also San Buenaventura, "Nativism and Ethnicity," 432–45, for a discussion of a range of Moncado and federation critics; and Dizon, *"Master,"* 7, 11. At the time he wrote this book, Dizon was the pastor of the Filipino Community Church in Honolulu. For a brief account of Moncado's critics in Stockton, especially Damiano Marcuelo, the editor of *The Three Stars*, see Lawcock, "Filipino Students," 417–18. Issues of *The Three Stars* from mid-1928 through 1932 frequently published attacks on Moncado. See also San Buenaventura, "Nativism and Ethnicity," 432–45, for a discussion of a range of critics of the Federation and its leader.
164. The most comprehensive account of this strike and Manlapit's role in it can be found in John E. Reinecke, *The Filipino Piecemeal Sugar Strike of 1924–1925*

140 Michael Cullinane

(Honolulu: University of Hawai'i, Social Science Research Institute, 1996); and Melinda Tria Kerkvliet, "Pablo Manlapit's Fight for Justice," *Social Process in Hawaii* 33 (1991): 153–68.

165. *Philippine Republic*, August 15, 1927, 15; October 15, 1927, 19. See also Reinecke, *Filipino Piecemeal Sugar Strike*, 110.

166. *Moncado Speaks*, 12–13. On the feud between Manlapit and Moncado in Los Angeles, citing the Filipino press of San Francisco and of the Philippines, see Lawcock, "Filipino Students," 419–21.

167. This paragraph is extracted from Reinecke, *Filipino Piecemeal Sugar Strike*, 110–11, 174–75, where the author cites information and quotes from the Honolulu newspaper *Hawaii Hochi*.

168. John K. Butler to Wallace R. Farrington, September 18, 1928, Wallace H. Farrington Papers, Hawaii Archives.

169. Schaefle, "Why the American Globe," 5.

170. *Moncado Speaks*, 13.

171. *Ang Bantay*, December 29, 1929, and January 24, 1930, attacking Moncado, as cited in Dizon, *"Master,"* 93–94.

172. On the changing Filipino community of Los Angeles in the mid-1930s, see Valentin R. Aquino, *The Filipino Community of Los Angeles* (San Francisco: R&E Research Associates, 1974); and Benicio T. Catapusan, "The Filipino Occupational and Recreational Activities in Los Angeles," M.A. thesis, University of Southern California, 1934. In the context of the discrediting of Moncado in the Filipino community of Los Angeles, and in the educated Filipino community in general, see Lawcock, "Filipino Students," 425–26, which briefly describes the defection of three early federation leaders, M. P. Orlanes, Jose Deseo, and Primitivo Alonzo.

173. Deseo, *Moncado*, 40.

174. *Filipino Nation*, December 1928, 19; January 1929, 20; February 1929, 14–15.

175. John K. Butler to Each Plantation Manager, October 20, 1928, Wallace H. Farrington Papers, Hawaii Archives, Honolulu.

176. John K. Butler to W. R. Farrington, September 18, 1928, Wallace H. Farrington Papers, Hawaii Archives.

177. See *Filipino Nation*, March 1929, 17, which reproduces a formal letter, dated January 24, 1929, from the manager of the Maui Agricultural Company granting the federation representative unrestricted access to the laborers on the plantations under his jurisdiction.

178. See Beechert, *Working in Hawaii*, 226–32.

179. Edward Berman, "The Man Who Plays God," *The Voice of Labor* (Honolulu) 3.11 (January 20, 1938): 4; 3.12 (January 27, 1938): 4; 3.13 (February 3, 1938): 4; 3.14 (February 10, 1938): 4.

180. Thompson, "Filipino Federation of America," 32–35.

181. Similarly, Moncado openly condemned labor unions and strikes in California. See, for example, his criticism of a strike staged by Filipino workers in the Central Valley in 1939 published in the *Philippines Mail*, August 30, 1939.

182. See Darilay, *Silver Souvenir*, 9–10, where photos of the twenty-four pioneers are reproduced; and *Filipino Nation*, January 1930, 11. The best overall description of the federation's move to various locations in the Philippines, especially in Mindanao, is Darilay, *Silver Souvenir* (see especially 9–27).

183. See Moncado's statements in *American Globe*, April 1931, 7.

184. Darilay, *Silver Souvenir*, 12–14; Federico D. Alferez, "Moncado Colony in

Lanao," *Progress*, February 12, 1933, 5. The *Progress* article also appeared in *Philippines Free Press*, February 11, 1933, 7, 40. Other reports on the growth of the Lanao colony can be found in Restituto del Rosario, "Moncado's Colony Keeps Up Expansion Work," *Progress*, February 22, 1933; and Andres Darilay, "Developing the Wilds of Lanao," *Progress*, May 28, 1933, 6. Delos Reyes would remain as the director of the Moncado colony at Dansalan until his death in 1937.

185. See Darilay, *Silver Souvenir*, 19–27. Although federation groups also formed in Cebu and the Ilokos area, the Mindanao colonies were clearly more substantial during the prewar years. After the war, the Cebu colony at Sudlon, along the central ridge of Cebu's interior, grew in size around an active leadership that maintained close contacts with Cebu's west coast towns, in particular Moncado's birthplace, Balamban, and nearby Asturias.

186. Mindanao became the home of the *vril-ya* of "the coming race," now associated with Malayans (Filipinos) and directly linked to Mindanao, especially Dansalan. See, for example, Vaguios, *Ang Agi-anan Ngadto*; Aninao, *Advent of the Master*, 2–6, 24–32, 35–38; and Aninao, *Our Master*, 17, 46. It should be noted that the concept of Mindanao as a "promised land" or "new Jerusalem" was not unique to the federation. From the 1920s, and perhaps earlier, northern Mindanao had been the site of a number of so-called *colorum* movements, which called upon pilgrims from all over the Visayas to come to the island to prepare for the Judgment Day.

187. See *Bag-ong Kusog*, July 10, 1931, 23; *Ang Freeman*, July 15, 1931, 4; and, in particular, "Si Moncado Miabut, Misulti ug . . . Mibomba," *Bag-ong Kusog*, July 17, 1931, 11.

188. On the establishment of the Modernist Party and its relationship with the federation, see Hilario C. Moncado, *America, the Philippines, and the Orient*, 197–205; and Darilay, *Silver Souvenir*, 39–40. See also Lawcock, "Filipino Students," 453–54.

189. See, for example, how his statements criticizing U.S. congressional delays of the date of Philippine independence are treated in "Moncado Assails Philippine Bill," *New York Times*, February 28, 1932; and "Filipino Leader Assails Senate Self-Rule Plan," *Herald Tribune*, February 29, 1932.

190. *Progress*, October 23, 1932, 6. For an even more favorable article, see Andres R. Camasura, "Osmeña and Moncado: A Political Forecast," *Progress*, November 27, 1932, 9, 21. Moncado is reported to have been the first to file his candidacy for the Senate race. See *Philippine Herald*, November 21, 1933 (clipping), deposited in "P" File: Hilario C. Moncado, RG–350, BIA, USNA. For a firsthand account of the activities of the federation's Cebu office, see Darilay, *Silver Souvenir*, 15–19.

191. See, in particular, the regular column "Siling Kulikut" on political developments in the weekly newspaper *Bag-ong Kusog* throughout 1933. See also, as examples of the variety of coverage, "Moncado's Technical Adviser Praised by United Press," *Progress*, March 12, 1933, 7; Andres Darilay, "Developing the Wilds of Mindanao," *Progress*, May 28, 1933, 6; "The Moncado Campaigning Method," *Progress*, August 13, 1933, 7; "Ikaduhang Pahayag ni Dr. Hilario C. Moncado," *Bag-ong Kusog*, September 1, 1933, 28; Andres Darilay, "Moncado Feted on Birthday Anniversary," *Progress*, November 12, 1933, 12; and Andres Darilay, "Moncado, the Golfer and Politician," *Progress*, November 26, 1933, 6.

192. One account pictured Moncado arriving at the Cebu wharf by boat from Manila being met by more than ten thousand people (*Bag-ong Kusog*, September 1, 1933, 29). See also, for example, *Progress*, April 29, 1934, 14.

193. Osmeña received 42,389 votes to Sotto's 31,976 and Moncado's 5,814. See *Bag-ong Kusog*, June 22, 1934, 13, 17, 21, 24–25.

194. Moncado received 948 votes in Balamban, while Osmeña garnered 525 and Sotto only 76. See *Bag-ong Kusog*, June 22, 1934, 13, 17, 21, 24–25.

195. With more than 15,149 voters in the district, Moncado received 6,095 votes. His closest rival, Juanito Maramara, received only 1,919. See Francis Sayre to Chief, BIA, Radiogram, Manila, August 14, 1941, in "P" File: Hilario C. Moncado, RG–350, BIA, USNA. For the details of the municipal vote breakdown, see *Bag-ong Kusog*, July 13, 1934, 3, 6, 30.

196. Jesus Y. Perez to Francisco O. Dalumpines, September 15, 1970, in Dalumpines, "Life of Moncado," appendixes, 167.

197. Romero, *Not So Long Ago*, 59.

198. Zaide, *Philippine History*, 690. See also *Philippine Commonwealth Chronicle* (Honolulu), January 15, 1938, 3, especially the article "Noted Historian Confirms Dr. Moncado's Contribution to Constitutional Convention," which makes it clear that Zaide's familiarity with Moncado was established through contacts with the federation in Hawaii at this time.

199. Bustos and Fajardo, *New Philippines*, 216.

200. See Francis Sayre to Chief, BIA, Radiogram, Manila, August 14, 1941, in "P" File: Hilario C. Moncado, RG–350, BIA, USNA.

201. *Moncado Speaks*, 20. The *Philippines Mail*, November 17, 1941, reported that Moncado "was third" behind the overwhelming winner, Manuel Quezon, and "his nearest opponent," Juan Sumulong. The article, however, presents Moncado's challenge as part of a legitimate opposition to Quezon.

202. Hilario C. Moncado, "Dominion Status" (a 1941 radio talk), reproduced in Darilay, *Silver Souvenir*, 41–42.

203. *Moncado Speaks*, 20.

204. Hilario C. Moncado, "Dominion Status Plan" (pamphlet, 1946: address at the Modernist Party headquarters, Manila, April 5, 1946); "The Dominion Status Favored in America" (pamphlet, 1946: address at Modernist Party headquarters, Manila, April 19, 1946); "The Last Call" (pamphlet, 1946: address at the Modernist Party headquarters, Manila, April 22, 1946); "Parity and Charity" (pamphlet, 1946: address at convocation at University of Santo Tomas, Manila, October 16, 1946); "Cebu-Manila Students Association Inaugural Address of General Hilario Camino Moncado" (pamphlet, 1946, Manila, n.p.); "For Parity: Quezon and Parity Rights," *People's Review* 1.43 (1946): 7–8, 21–22; "21st Anniversary of the Founding of the Filipino Federation of America, Inc. Subject: F.F. of A. Anniversary Address" (pamphlet, 1947[?]: Honolulu); "The Republican Victory and Parity Rights" (pamphlet, 1947: address on radio station KZRH, Manila, January 5, 1947); "Billions of Pesos and Parity Rights" (pamphlet, 1947: address on radio station KZRH, Manila, January 12, 1947); "Report to President Roxas on My Campaign for Parity Rights over Visayas, Mindanao and Sulu, February 6, 1947" (pamphlet, 1947). For reproductions of Moncado's speeches and transcripts of his radio broadcasts between 1946 and 1948 in favor of dominion and parity, see Darilay, *Silver Souvenir*, 46–64, 75–104.

205. The election results for both postwar elections are from Rufino Tusit (Commission on Elections statistician) to Francisco O. Dalumpines, September 18, 1970, cited in Dalumpines, "Life of Moncado," appendixes, 157.

206. Lawcock ("Filipino Students," 373) attempts to estimate the size of *Filipino Nation*'s distribution using the monthly subscription numbers published in each issue: July 1929, 10,000; August 1930, 15,000; December 1930, 25,000; and December 1931, 25,000.

207. Examples of publications of this kind that have been located and used in this essay are *FFA Convention News* (Los Angeles, 1949); *FFA News* (Los Angeles [?], 1938, 1950); *Federation Bulletin* (Los Angeles, 1954); *Filipino Eagle* (Los Angeles, 1940); *Filipino Eagle Sentinel* (Honolulu, 1936–38); *Filipino Federation Frontier* (Honolulu, 1954); *General Moncado News Express* (Manila, 1948); *The Moncadian* (Los Angeles, 1949); and *Moncado and His Mission Bulletin* (Honolulu, 1955).

208. Clippings praising Moncado and featuring photos of him meeting with various dignitaries were frequently reproduced in *Filipino Nation* as well as in all the publications promoting Moncado and the federation. See how pages of clippings were displayed in *American Globe*, March 1930, 4, 6, 8 ,10, 12, 14, 16, to publicize "Moncado in Washington."

209. Mrs. R. H. Sweet to Governor-General Farrington, July 26, 1928, Wallace H. Farrington Papers, Hawaii Archives.

210. *Filipino Nation* and other federation publications are rich sources of information and depictions of Filipinos in the United States during the prewar period. *Filipino Nation*, in particular, published a great many photographs of the members themselves, often showing large gatherings, selected groups of leaders (all carefully referenced in the captions), and a wide range of events. In addition, federation publications provide useful biographical information on large numbers of Filipinos who migrated to the United States as laborers during this period.

211. Tavenner, "An Attempt to Explain Hilario Moncado," 4.

212. Editorial, *Mindanao Herald*, April 2, 1932. The piece continued in a less flattering vein: "He will say or do anything that will attract the spotlight, whereby he lives and enjoys the fleshpots."

213. McElrath-ILWU radio transcript, 1954

214. See Dizon, "Master," 42–48.

215. Dizon, "Master," 42–43.

216. One of the most effective photographs depicting Moncado as a political emissary for Philippine independence shows him standing before a large globe in the Washington, D.C., office of Sen. William H. King. Reproduced on the cover of *American Globe* (April 1931), the caption describes Moncado as "impressively explaining" to the senator "the vital necessity" for "immediate, absolute and complete independence of the Philippine Islands and urging the co-operaton of Senator King" to assist in "laying the foundation of the only Christian nation in the Orient—a new republic." A month earlier, a similarly effective shot appeared on the cover of the *Philippine Republic* (March 1931), showing King and Moncado sitting in the senator's office behind a large pile of documents and papers discussing "plans for the coming big independence drive." For two other examples from the Filipino press, see the *Philippines Mail*, November 13, 1933, and February 22, 1937, the former depicting the former general superintendent of the

Salinas-based Spreckels Sugar Company giving the keynote address at the
Federation's birthday celebration for Moncado and the latter featuring a
front-page photo of Moncado standing beside Manuel Quezon, who had
just arrived in Los Angeles, with an accompanying article praising the campaigns for independence of Quezon and Moncado. On the latter meeting,
see the striking photo spread published in the *Filipino Eagle Sentinel*
(Honolulu), February 27, 1937.

217. See letters and clippings from February and March 1930 in "P" File: Hilario
C. Moncado, RG–350, BIA, USNA, especially H. C. Moncado to P. Hurley,
Telegram: Hollywood, California, March 14, 1930; and P. Hurley to H. C.
Moncado, Letter: Washington, D.C., March 18, 1930.

218. For a full account with many photos, including reproductions of clippings
and Hoover's letter, see *American Globe*, March 1930, cover, 3–27. During this
well-publicized visit to Washington, Moncado used a Hollywood publicity
agent, Harry H. Beall, to supervise press releases and the distribution of photographs and to assist him in making appointments with congressmen and
other Washington notables. See also the cover story in the *Philippine Republic*,
June 1930, cover, 3, which displays the medal itself and a copy of President
Hoover's note acknowledging receipt of the letter. The gold medal reproduced the federation's "1728" symbol at its center.

219. *Who's Who in California* (1928–29), 369. Before this, Moncado had already had
his biography published in "'Who's Who' among Filipino Clubs in U.S.,"
Philippine Republic, October 15, 1927, 16–17. Realizing that a great deal of status went along with even a formal telephone listing, Moncado was among
the first Filipinos (if not *the* first) in Los Angeles to have himself and his
offices entered into the official directory. See *1927 Los Angeles Telephone
Directory: Extended Area* (Los Angeles, 1927). It was under his personal entry
that the Filipino Federation of America was listed.

220. Among the many biographical directories that included entries for
Moncado were the following: the *Cebu-Visayas Directory*, 147–48; *New
Philippines: A Book on the Building Up of a New Nation*, compiled and edited
by Felixberto G. Bustos and Abelardo J. Fajardo (Manila: Carmelo &
Bauermann, 1934), 216; *Handumanan: Mga Punoang Lungsodnon* (1935), 70;
Who's Who of the Island of Hawaii (1939), 126–27; *Cornejo's Commonwealth
Directory of the Philippines* (Manila: Miguel R. Cornejo, 1939), 1952; *The
Philper, or Philippine Personalities and Other Features*, compiled and edited
by Pedro C. Melicor (Manila: Melicor Enterprises, 1947), 1:15–16; and
Encyclopedia of the Philippines: Builders, edited by Zoilo M. Galang, 3d ed.,
vol. 18 (Manila: Exequiel Floro, 1958), 302. The importance of these entries
to Moncado was emphasized in a 1933 controversy, when Andres
Camasura, the compiler of the *Cebu-Visayas Directory* (1931), filed charges
against Moncado for nonpayment of fees. As the case unfolded, it was
revealed that Camasura had agreed to dedicate the directory jointly to
Moncado and Sergio Osmeña by placing their full-page photos and biographies at the front of the volume side by side and by supplying Moncado
with a large number of copies for publicity purposes. At the time,
Moncado was planning to run against Senator Osmeña, and the suit
exposed the entire operation as an elaborate publicity stunt. See
"Moncado Files Counter-Charge," *Progress*, October 15, 1933, 7; "Demanda
Contra el Dr. Hilario Moncado," *La Opinion*, October 17, 1933 (clipping);

"Osmeña's Son-in-Law in Moncado Camp," *Progress*, October 22, 1933, 11; and "Moncado Sued in Cebu," *Philippines Free Press*, November 11, 1933, 22–23.

221. In *Moncado Speaks* (18), he claims to have married Diana Toy on June 9, 1938, in Reno, Nevada. Other accounts claim that the couple was married in November 1939 in Manila. See *Philippines Free Press*, November 25, 1939, 29; *Honolulu Advertiser*, November 15, 1939; and *Honolulu Advertiser*, December 15, 1939.

222. During the early 1930s, Moncado's visits to Hollywood were recorded in both his magazines and those of others. For one of his most successful forays into the nearby celluloid world, see "Real People," *Screen Mirror: The Magazine from Hollywood*, January 1931, 18. A regular column in this issue profiled Moncado and published an ad for the federation (27). Moncado's 1937 meeting with Diana in the company of Hollywood celebrities is reproduced in a photograph published in *Filipino Eagle Sentinel* (Honolulu), November 1937, 13. Diana was not, it seems, the first attractive partner pursued by Moncado. One of his earliest involvements with a beautiful woman ended in his hospitalization as the result of an "uncharacteristic fisticuff" with Marion G. Antenocruz, the president of the Catholic Filipino Club of Los Angeles in 1929. The fight, as reported, was over Carmen de la Peña, the "Doughnut Queen," daughter of the owner of the popular Manila Bakery. See Lawcock, "Filipino Students," 395–96. For another rare account of Moncado's romantic adventures, see *Philippines Free Press*, November 25, 1939, 29.

223. Diana Toy was identified as Moncado's "campaign manager" in 1938 (see *Bag-ong Kusog*, September 30, 1938, 31; October 7, 1938, 31). In a photo caption of late 1938, Diana Toy is clearly on tour with Moncado but not identified as his wife (*FFA News*, August 1938, 3).

224. *Moncado Speaks*, 20–25.

225. For accounts of Moncado's return to Hawaii, see "Moncado Planning United States Visit," *Honolulu Advertiser*, February 16, 1948, 3; "Moncado Free of All Charges," *Honolulu Advertiser*, February 20, 1948; "Followers in Noisy Greeting to Moncado," *Honolulu Advertiser*, March 16, 1948, 2; "Moncado Will Arrive Tonight, Welcome Planned," *Honolulu Star-Bulletin*, March 15, 1948, 16; "Crowd Greets Hilario Moncado at the Airport," *Honolulu Star-Bulletin*, March 16, 1948, 12; "Moncado Tells How His Guerrillas Stole Medical Supplies from Enemy," *Honolulu Star-Bulletin*, March 19, 1948; and "Moncado is Guest at FFA Banquet," *Honolulu Star-Bulletin*, March 22, 1948. Before leaving the Philippines to come to Hawaii, Moncado formally incorporated the Filipino Crusaders World Army in the Philippines (July 1947), assigning members a range of military ranks and titles. By the time of Moncado's death, for all intents and purposes, the crusaders had merged with the federation in most of the places where it maintained branches. See Filipino Federation of America, *FFA Souvenir Book: Golden Anniversary of the Filipino Federation of America, 1925–1975* (Honolulu: Filipino Federation of America, 1975), 77–93.

226. *Moncado Speaks*, 26–31.

227. *Moncado and His Mission Bulletin* 1.4 (April 1955): 4; 1.8 (August 1955): 4; 2.11 (November 1956): 4; 3.1 (January 1957): 4. In his autobiography, Moncado states: "In 1927, I learned to play the game of golf under golf

professional Marvin Clawson who was manager of the Sunset Fields Golf
and Country Club in Los Angeles," adding that Clawson later became "my
playing partner" (*Moncado Speaks*, 12–19). A particularly attractive photograph of Moncado in his golfing garb, published in the *FFA News* (August
1938), carried the caption: "FFA National golf champion Dr. H. C.
Moncado receiving the handsome trophy from lovely Diana Toy of Radio
Fame while pro. Marvin Clawson . . . looks on." Lawcock ("Filipino
Students," 397) stresses that golf "became an increasingly passionate
obsession" for Moncado and that "he belonged to several California country clubs and spent his vacations at Catalina Island country clubs playing
golf." His golfing exploits were well covered in the Filipino press in
Hawaii and California as well as in the Philippines; see, for example,
reports on his Manila victories in the Salinas newspaper *Philippines Mail*,
April 22, 1930, and April 7, 1939.

228. *Moncado Speaks*, 30–33.
229. See, for example, Henstell, *Sunshine and Wealth*, 117. Krishnamurti was also
an accomplished golfer who took pride in his "plus two" handicap. See Reid,
"The Possessed," 191; and Luytens, *Krishnamurti*, 112.
230. In an attempt to describe "Mr. and Mrs. Los Angeles" of this era, Harry Carr
writes: "All members of the Angeles family play golf—sometimes at the
beautiful Municipal golf-links on the old Los Feliz rancho and sometimes at
private country clubs, of which there are many" (*Los Angeles: City of Dreams*
[New York: Grosset & Dunlap, 1935], 386). See also Ross Goodner, "America
Gets the Bug," in *The World of Golf*, edited by Gordon Menzies (London:
British Broadcasting Corporation, 1982), 65–94.
231. *Progress*, November 26, 1933, 6.
232. In 1935, on one of his political visits to Cebu, Moncado made a large ($5,000)
donation to the only golf club in the city at the time, the Club Filipino, in
order to sponsor the construction of a tee house near the sixth hole. The Club
Filipino was at the time frequented mainly by American and other foreign-
ers residing in the area. The tee house was constructed (displaying the name
of its donor), but it "was destroyed during the last war" (N. P. Crowe to
Francisco O. Dalumpines, May 15, 1971, quoted in Dalumpines, "Life of
Moncado," appendixes, 155).
233. McElrath-ILWU radio transcript, 1954.
234. See, for example, Andres A. Darilay, "Moncado, the Golfer and Politician,"
Progress, November 26, 1933, 6 (with a large photo of Moncado in modern
golfing garb swinging through a drive shot); "FFA National Golf Champion
Dr. H.C. Moncado Receiving the Handsome Trophy from Lovely Diana Toy
of Radio Fame While Pro. Marvin Clawson of Sunset Fields Golf Course, Los
Angeles, Cal., Looks On," *FFA News*, August 1938, 3; "Moncado Will Send
$500 Check for Golf Clubhouse Furniture," *Hilo Tribune Herald*, April 6, 1954;
"Golf Activities of General Hilario Camino Moncado," in his *360° Power
Swing*, 69–76. On golf and communism, see *Moncado and His Mission Bulletin*
1.1 (January 1955): 4, as well as nearly every issue published between this
date and April 1957.
235. *Moncado and His Mission Bulletin* 1.12 (December 1955): 4.
236. See *Moncado and His Mission Bulletin* 2.5 (May 1956): 1.
237. For an innovative thesis that argues that prewar Filipinos in California created a vibrant popular culture for themselves on the margins of American

society, see Maram, "Negotiating Identity."

238. Ed Ritter, Helen Ritter, and Stanley Spector, *Our Oriental Americans* (Sacramento: California State Department of Education, 1967), 95–96.

239. Quoted in the introduction to John Beilenson, *Sukarno* (New York: Chelsea House Publishers, 1990), 11.

**Ulysses "Boboy" Alega shortly after he was killed
in a shoot-out with police at Cebu in June 1987.**

FILIPINO GANGSTERS IN FILM, LEGEND, AND HISTORY:
TWO BIOGRAPHICAL CASE STUDIES FROM CEBU

John T. Sidel

Over the years, a set of consistent images regarding crime and its role in society has endured in popular discourse in the Philippines: the Philippine state as besieged by rebels and outlaws, struggling to overcome endemic rebellion and lawlessness; crime as a form of social protest or "primitive rebellion" against the capitalist transformation of a predominantly agrarian society; and the outlaw as a "primitive rebel," peasant hero, and "social bandit." Time and again, these images have cropped up, in newspaper and tabloid stories, comic books, novels, and especially in movies, where film biographies of gangsters have commanded considerable profitability and popularity. Even the limited scholarly literature on crime has tended to replicate and reaffirm popular discourse in this regard.

Against the backdrop of these images, this essay offers a set of preliminary revisions and explorations with regard to crime in the Philippines. First, the essay outlines the structure of the conventional representation of crime in Philippine society. Second, it provides an alternative, revisionist conceptualization of criminality in the archipelago, drawing on the extensive literature on mafia and organized crime elsewhere in the world. Third, and finally, it reexamines the conventional representation of crime in the Philippines against the backdrop of this revisionist account, linking the structure of representation to that of the distinctive political economy of criminality in the archipelago. The essay illustrates these points through case studies of the two most successful outlaws in the postwar history of Cebu Province, Isabelo "Beloy" Montemayor and Ulysses "Boboy" Alega, drawing on film biographies and popular legends as well as documentary and press sources and interviews conducted in the course of the author's fieldwork in the province in 1991–92.

Viewed historically and compared to its counterparts elsewhere in Southeast Asia, the Philippine state has appeared chronically "weak," incapable of imposing "order," and besieged by "lawlessness" and "unrest." Indeed, frequent disturbances variously described as uprisings, revolts, millenarian rebellions, and banditry plagued both the Spanish and the American colonial regimes.[1] The Sakdalista uprising swept the environs of Manila in 1935, and peasant "unrest" in central Luzon beginning in the late 1930s crystallized after independence in 1946 in the Huk rebellion of the late 1940s and early 1950s, subsequently echoed in the communist and Muslim insurgencies of the 1970s and 1980s.[2] Even in the intervening years, highway robbery, cattle rustling, piracy, car theft, kidnapping, and smuggling have, according to official and newspaper accounts, almost always been "rampant." Philippine society, it appears, is in a perpetual state of "lawlessness."

In this context, historians and other chroniclers of the Philippines have tended to align "crime" with "resistance" against the encroachments of a predatory colonial or post/neocolonial state and the intrusions of capitalist production relations upon the countryside. Inspired in large part by the British historian Eric Hobsbawm,[3] the American scholar David Sturtevant, for example, recast criminality in the Spanish Philippines as an "archaic form" of class struggle, a peasant-based "social movement," a kind of "primitive rebellion":

> Known as *tulisanes* or *ladrones*, outlaws disrupted the countryside throughout the Spanish era. The problem, however, became acute during the developmental sequence of the late nineteenth century. After 1850, lawlessness of a new type started to disturb provincial officials. Depredations could no longer be attributed to ancient blood feuds. Solitary murders and assaults, moreover, could not be dismissed as tragic results of frustrated passions. Rural crime began to take on class connotations. Rustlers, highwaymen, extortionists, and cutthroats preyed increasingly upon estate owners, lawyers, usurers, friars, and itinerant Chinese merchants — all the emerging enemies, in short, of the troubled peasantry.[4]

Disputing official U.S. government accounts of so-called *bandolerismo* in the first decade after the Philippine-American War, nationalist Filipino scholars have likewise championed famous early twentieth-century *tulisanes* like Macario Sakay and Julian Montalan as popular figures, peasant heroes and participants in a long and laudable tradition of resistance to colonial domination over the archipelago.[5] Throughout the twentieth century, in fact, popular legends, comic books, novels, radio dramas, and movies have frequently portrayed bandits and gangsters as rebels and folk heroes.[6]

From this perspective, Filipino outlaws appear as classic examples of what Hobsbawm has described as "social bandits," peasant outlaws whom the lord and state regard as criminals, but who remain within peasant society, and are considered by their people as heroes, as champions, avengers, fighters for justice, perhaps even leaders of liberation, and in any case as men to be admired, helped and supported.[7]

In the late Spanish colonial era, for example, Sturtevant claims:

> Villagers came to look upon the largess-dispensing outlaws as defenders and frequently elevated them to the status of folk heroes. Their exploits, embellished and romanticized to swash-buckling heights by admirers, created persistent Robin Hood myths in the barrios. Spain, accordingly, found it impossible to eradicate banditry.[8]

Even in the postwar era, commentators have often described Filipino gangsters as latter-day "Robin Hoods" whose success in evading the law depends on the support they enjoy among the poor and downtrodden.[9] The exploits of a long list of slain "outlaws" have been celebrated in tabloid headlines, comic books, and action movies and etched in the popular imagination: Nicasio "Asiong" Salonga of the 1940s and 1950s;[10] Arturo Porcuna, alias "Boy Golden," of the 1960s;[11] Benjamin Garcia, alias "Ben Tumbling," of the 1970s;[12] and numerous others.[13]

In the Philippines, moreover, the legitimacy of these outlaws has allegedly rested to a considerable extent on popular beliefs in their intrinsic personal power and charisma, most commonly expressed through reference to their martial prowess and possession of amulets or magical powers known as *anting-anting*. In the Spanish period, for example, according to Sturtevant:

> Almost without exception, brigands claimed miraculous attributes. Outstanding chieftains were widely reputed to be protected by potent *anting-anting*. The wonder-working talismans — ranging from simple amulets and charms to elaborate uniforms bearing mystical designs or quasi-Latin formulas — allegedly shielded their owners from malign sorcery and physical misfortunes. Famous ladrones often maintained they were immune to death. Some even averred they possessed the capacity to extend invulnerability to followers. Less pretentious tulisanes asserted they could resurrect dead comrades. The most influential outlaws, however, posed as reincarnations of divine beings or deceased popular champions. On a limited scale, their appeal was comparable to that exercised by prophets of old and new religions. Bandit leaders, in brief, gained prestige among their supporters, and notoriety among their adversaries, by surrounding themselves with supernatural auras.[14]

References to *anting-anting* similarly crop up in accounts of charismatic guerrilla leaders in the revolution,[15] World War II,[16] and various postwar insurgencies.[17] Likewise, postwar bandits and gangsters have also allegedly drawn strength from magically endowed amulets in their possession.[18]

According to popular beliefs in the Philippines, these *anting-anting* evidently absorb, tap into, or afford privileged access to external sources of power but ultimately depend upon the inner qualities—*loób* in Tagalog—of the bearer. In the Catholicized lowlands, various items associated with Holy Week rituals—icons, scapulars, rosaries, crosses, holy water—are frequently used as *anting-anting*, while Latin verses or *orasyon* are said to empower the amulets.[19] In Muslim areas, verses from the Koran likewise serve as empowering *ajimat*.[20] Though often derived from the paraphernalia of organized religion,[21] *anting-anting* serve merely as a mode of access to intrinsic power (Tagalog: *kapangyarihan*), and their efficacy depends on the state of the bearer's inner self or *loób*.[22] According to one scholar:

> For the power that is concentrated in an amulet to be absorbed by its wearer, the latter's loób must be properly cultivated through ascetic prayer, controlled by bodily movements and other forms of self-discipline. For an amulet to take effect, the loób of its possessors must have undergone a renewal and purification.[23]

As the most thorough study of *anting-anting* in the Philippines concludes:

> [A]ccording to ordinary folk, someone who has an *anting-anting* is helpful, devout, humble, and quiet, but brave if put to the test. . . . There is a close connection between an anting-anting and the "loób" of a person, the sturdiness and beauty of her/his character.[24]

In short, both scholarship and the culture industry in the Philippines concur on a view of "crime" as reflecting certain features of Philippine society. In particular, scholars and screenplay writers alike portray criminality in the archipelago as a form of societal "resistance" to injustices unpunished—or perpetrated—by predatory agents of capital and the state. Bandits and gangsters thus appear as authentic local heroes of the poor and downtrodden, "social bandits" whose success in evading "the law" is attributed to their Robin Hood–like popularity; to their intrinsic powers, *anting-anting*, and charisma; and to the "weakness" of the state.

While numerous scholars, comic book writers, and movie producers have concurred in these depictions of "primitive rebellion" and "social banditry" in the Philippines, their accounts raise questions about the relationship between "crime" and its social representation in the archipelago.

Indeed, revisionist scholars have already cast considerable doubt upon conventional wisdom about the origins, dissemination, and social signifi-cance of the English ballads that first brought Robin Hood to popular cul-ture.[25] Similarly, Hobsbawm's "social bandit" has come under attack from critics who see crime less as a form of popular protest and class conflict than as a mode of economic accumulation and political domination.[26] In this vein, recent scholarly accounts have portrayed bandits in such settings as China,[27] the Mediterranean,[28] and Latin America[29] as playing complex and multifaceted roles in state formation, class conflict, and popular cul-ture. Elsewhere in Southeast Asia, a reconsideration of Burmese dacoits,[30] Javanese *jago*,[31] Malay *penyamun*,[32] and Thai *nakleng*[33] is already well under way. In light of this rich and nuanced literature, a reexamination of "crime" and its social representation in the Philippines is clearly in order. What fol-lows below constitutes a preliminary step in that direction.[34]

Compared to its counterparts elsewhere in Southeast Asia, the Philippine state is virtually unique in its highly decentralized, politicized, and priva-tized administration of law enforcement, a legacy of the American colonial period.[35] Since the first years of this century, elected municipal mayors in the Philippines have by law enjoyed considerable discretion over the appointment, transfer, payment, and removal of municipal policemen,[36] who thus, in the words of the director of the Philippine Constabulary (PC) in 1908, have typically functioned as the "messengers, muchachos, and ser-vants" of the towns' chief executives.[37] Provincial governors, moreover, have long held the authority to appoint "special agents," security officers, and jail wardens and have consistently intervened over the years in the appointment, promotion, transfer, and removal of provincial commanders of the Philippine Constabulary.[38] In addition, members of both houses of Congress have, through the powerful Commission on Appointments, retained a measure of influence over the promotion and transfer of high-ranking Constabulary/police officers, thus diluting the otherwise unim-peded discretion of the president in his control over the nation's primary law enforcement agency. Attempts to centralize and bureaucratize law enforcement under a national police agency included a short-lived experi-ment with a State Police in the 1930s, the establishment of a National Police Commission (Napolcom) in 1966, and the creation of an Integrated National Police subordinated to the Philippine Constabulary (PC-INP) and the Armed Forces of the Philippines (AFP) in 1975. From 1975 through 1990, policemen throughout the archipelago served as members of the PC-INP/AFP, their assignments, promotions, and transfers determined by ranking PC/AFP officers instead of elected officials.[39] Today, however, due to key provisions of legislation enacted in 1990, elected officials at the municipal, city, provincial, and national levels have regained significant discretionary powers over the supervision and appointment of Philippine National Police (PNP) personnel.[40]

Viewed as a set of apparatuses geared for the maintenance of "order" and the administration of "justice," the decentralized, politicized, and personalized law enforcement agencies of the Philippine state constitute a structural "weakness" highly favorable to criminal activity. The limited capacities of national police agencies and the subordination of police forces to municipal and provincial elected officials allow criminals to exploit the parcelized jurisdictions of local law enforcement authorities in the archipelago. As Eric Hobsbawm has noted:

> The ideal situation for robbery is one in which the local authorities are local men, operating in complex local situations, and where a few miles may put the robber beyond the reach or even the knowledge of one set of authorities and into the territory of another, which does not worry about what happens "abroad."[41]

Viewed alternatively, however, as predatory apparatuses geared not for the suppression of crime and the administration of justice but for the regulation and exploitation of illegal economies, these police forces appear less unsuccessful in stemming lawlessness and more successful in imposing their own self-serving version of the law upon Philippine society. After all, Philippine policemen have figured most prominently over the years not as the defenders of justice but as the protectors of bandits, car thieves, cattle rustlers, illegal loggers, *jueteng* (illegal lottery) operators, smugglers, the organizers of bank robberies and kidnappings, and the distributors of illegal firearms and narcotics. Through their selective and discretionary enforcement of the law, the police have perhaps not so much failed to eradicate crime as they have managed to exact monopoly rents from the proceeds of illegal commerce. Through their command of coercive resources, moreover, the police have retained the powers necessary to wield "the law" as an instrument of their predations: the National Police Commission itself has recently admitted that "more than half of the murder cases in the Philippines involve policemen, either as protectors or perpetrators."[42] By contrast, killings of policemen by criminal elements (rather than by other policemen) have proven much less common in the Philippines. In their enforcement of the law, the police — and the elected officials to whom they are responsible — are thus quite successful *as racketeers*.

Reexamined against this backdrop, much of what has passed for "resistance," "primitive rebellion," or "social banditry" in the Philippines no longer appears so decisively in opposition to the state. Outlaws, ironically perhaps, have often relied heavily upon the law and its selective enforcement. Bandits and gangsters have often depended for their survival not upon the popularity they enjoy among subaltern communities of peasants and the urban poor but upon the informal franchise and protection they receive from the police and the elected officials to whom the police are responsible. In general, as Anton Blok, a leading critic of Eric Hobsbawm's "social bandit" formulation, notes: "This yields the following hypothesis, which may be tested against data bearing on all kinds of robbery: *The more successful a man is as a bandit, the more extensive the protection granted him.*"[43]

Insofar as Filipino gangsters have served as the subcontracted agents of an essentially predatory state, they resemble not so much Hobsbawm's social bandits as what Blok and other scholars define as mafia: entrepreneurs who use private, formally unlicensed violence as a means of social control and economic accumulation.[44] Engaged in what some authors see as the production, promotion, and sale of "private protection"[45] and others view as organized extortion,[46] these mafia work to achieve and maintain a monopoly of violence within a given territory[47] from which they extract "predatory incomes"[48] through appropriation by force and collection of "protection rents."[49] In their monopoly of violence and provision of so-called protection, mafia thus assume the position of police, even as police take on many features of mafia.

Overall, this symbiotic relationship between mafia and police sustains various forms of criminal monopoly. In smuggling and other so-called black market activities, for example,

> [t]here must be an "optimum degree of enforcement" from the point of view of the criminal monopoly. With no enforcement—either because enforcement is not attempted or because enforcement is not feasible—the black market could not be profitable enough to invite criminal monopoly (at least not any more than any other market, legitimate or criminal). With wholly effective enforcement, and no collusion with the police, the business would be destroyed. Between these extremes, there may be an attractive black market profitable enough to invite monopoly.[50]

Within these parameters, however, the maintenance of criminal monopoly is always contingent upon the interplay of institutional structures and illegal economies of scale and mediated by the use and threat of violence. Within a given police jurisdiction, for example, law enforcement authorities may in fact extend sponsorship and protection to several mafia who compete for market share on the basis of their respective economic and coercive resources. Competition between rival law enforcement agents or, more importantly, turnover in the elected officials to whom law enforcement agents are responsible, may also disrupt criminal monopoly. Alternatively, where criminal economies span multiple or overlapping police jurisdictions, mafia may achieve monopoly and a measure of autonomy irreducible to the protection of a single law enforcement body. In the final analysis, however, the law enforcement agents of the state ultimately retain the upper hand, as the bloodied corpses of numerous famed gangsters amply attest.

In this context, the mythology surrounding many prominent Philippine outlaws works not only to legitimate the power of these mafia bosses but also to obscure the essential origins of their power. Depictions of bandits and gangsters as providers of protection and material rewards to grateful peasants and urban poor folk mask these predators' roles as extortionists who impose their will by means of violence. Cast as subaltern champions of primitive rebellion and everyday forms of resistance, mafia play down their role in "primitive" capitalist accumulation and everyday forms of oppression and domination.[51] Likewise, accounts that emphasize the martial prowess, charisma, and *anting-anting* of Philippine outlaws help to explain away putatively "unsuccessful" law enforcement efforts and permit the outlaw to claim authority on the basis of popularly acclaimed and intrinsic — rather than externally imposed and derivative — power. However reminiscent of precolonial charismatic authority, Filipino mafia bosses' claims to legitimacy thus work to obscure their close links to the very state against which they purport to counterpose themselves.

The Mafia Bosses of Cebu

To illustrate the arguments sketched out above, the remainder of this essay examines the changing patterns of criminality in postwar Cebu, a province where the author undertook extensive fieldwork in 1990-92. Case studies focus on the two most famous and successful outlaw figures in postwar Cebu history, Isabelo "Beloy" Montemayor and Ulysses "Boboy" Alega. Drawn from two successive periods in the history of Philippine law enforcement — the heyday of localized, civilian control over policing (1946-72) and the era of centralization and military integration (1972-90) — these case studies suggest clear patterns of change and variation in the geography, organization, and social representation of crime in the province. Together these studies underscore the interplay between coercion, crime, the state, and an evolving capitalist economy in Cebu and throughout the Philippines.

The distinctive pattern of criminality observed in postwar Cebu has reflected the peculiar geography of the Central Visayan island province. Of all the provinces in the Philippines, Cebu is unique in that corn rather than rice has long constituted the primary subsistence crop and staple food of the population due to unusually low rainfall levels, minimal forest cover, and the prevalence of limestone in the soil.[52] Moreover, mountainous and hilly terrain comprising more than three-quarters of Cebu's total land area bisects the province, limiting the possibilities for agriculture and rendering communication and transportation within the island difficult. As one historian of the province has noted:

> In many respects Cebu presents an unlikely environment for extensive human settlement. The long narrow island possesses a rugged interior with very few lowland plains, even along its coast. A porous limestone base and a limited rainfall have made Cebu unusually dry for a tropical setting. On only a few coastal lowland areas have Cebuanos been able to produce wet rice; their staple food has always been a dry crop (mainly millet and corn). Deforestation and subsequent erosion over the centuries have left much of the island unsuitable for agriculture.[53]

Indeed, with the exception of fertile tracts in a few eastern coastal towns and a small sugar plantation belt near the northern tip of the island, Cebuano farmers have cultivated only corn and coconuts in significant quantities. Fishing and, to a lesser extent, mining have supplemented agriculture as means of livelihood for the rural Cebuano population.

Unsurprisingly, Cebu's distinctive geography has failed to generate patterns of rural criminal activity comparable to those observed in more bandit-rich Philippine provinces.[54] Cattle rustling, for example, has never promised significant rewards in a province lacking a concentrated zone of wet-rice cultivation where carabaos would be found in abundance. For most of the postwar period, highway robbery has proven similarly unattractive, given the meager traffic, poor provincial roads, and virtual absence of "unprotected" passenger buses or cargo trucks from neighboring Visayan islands traversing Cebu Province. Only during periods of intense social ferment and state breakdown has Cebu witnessed significant upsurges of rural outlaw activity, and even these remained largely confined to the province's rugged and mountainous interior: *pulahanes* during the Revolution and early American occupation,[55] guerrilla bands in World War II,[56] and the New People's Army in the 1980s.[57]

Cebu Province, however, does feature a major urban center, which in the course of the twentieth century has provided the site for an increasing concentration of capital, labor, and crime. A major entrepôt since the late Spanish period, Cebu City evolved in the twentieth century into the Visayas' premier center for the processing and export of coconut and corn products, for educational institutions and government agencies, and in recent years for tourism and manufacturing.[58] In the postwar era, as population growth, rising landlessness, and the steady depletion of marine and mineral resources in Cebu Province and on neighboring islands have swelled the ranks of the rural poor, migrants have flocked to Cebu City in increasing numbers. Since 1945, the population of Metro Cebu—encompassing Cebu City, Lapu-Lapu City, Mandaue City, and Talisay—has more than quintupled and today stands at more than one million residents.[59]

As a major hub for interisland commerce and transport, a privileged zone of intensive production and circulation of commodities, and a growing market for the consumption of various legal and illegal goods, Cebu City has also evolved into the center of predatory and criminal activities in the province. With law enforcement agencies' manpower and resources likewise concentrated in the metropolis, the authorities in Cebu have enjoyed the spoils of predation through subcontracting, selective regulation, and the exaction of "monopoly rents" on illicit economic transactions.[60] Where criminal economies spanned multiple and overlapping police jurisdictions, moreover, Cebuano outlaws have achieved monopoly, autonomy, and occasionally fame.

Piracy on the High Seas: Isabelo "Beloy" Montemayor

Of all the outlaws in the history of Cebu Province, none is more famous than Isabelo "Beloy" Montemayor, the notorious "pirate" whose exploits in the 1950s, 1960s, and early 1970s—chronicled over the years in newspaper accounts, radio commentaries, and movies—remain to this day etched in the popular memory. Several years after Montemayor's death in 1975, a Manila-based film studio released *Montemayor: Tulisang Dagat*, with action star Rudy Fernandez playing the slain Cebuano outlaw.[61] In the film's opening scene, a Tagalog folk song introduces Montemayor and the legend surrounding his life and exploits:

> Dito sa dalampasigan ng alaala
> Buhawi ng buhanginan ng gunita
> May ibubulong sa inyo—ang hanging habagat
> Ang kasaysayan ng tulisang dagat
>
> Kapalarang kinagisnan ang pagkatulisan
> Nangahas mangarap maging pangkaraniwan
> Isang araw ang dagat niya'y nilisan
> Sinikap baguhin ang kapalaran
> Ito ang kasaysayan ng tulisang kaibigan
> Sa buhay at pag-ibig niya sa dalampasigan
> Alaalang ibinaon sa buhanginan ng panahon
> Gunitang nasa bawat lampas ng alon

Habang patuloy ang habagat
Habang ang alon ay bumabalik sa dagat
Habang ang tubig niya'y maalat
Patuloy ang alaala ng tulisang dagat. . .

[Here on the seashore of reminiscences
A whirlwind on the sandbanks of memories
The southwest monsoon breeze whispers to you
The tale of the bandit of the seas

Piracy was his fate since birth
He dared to dream of an ordinary life
One day he abandoned the seas
He worked hard to change his fate
This is the story of the bandit friend
Of his life and love on the seashore
Reminiscences buried in the sandbanks of time
Memories in every breaking of the waves

As long as the southwest monsoon breeze blows
As long as the waves roll back to the sea
As long as the sea's waters are briny
Memories of the bandit of the sea will live on . . .]

As these verses suggest, the legend of Montemayor involves a particular *geography*, a picturesque and rustic setting in which the rhythms
of man and nature remain harmonious and free from the pressures and
intrusions of the urban-centered cash economy. The gently blowing breeze
and the lapping of the waves on the seashore form a backdrop dominated
by the natural elements. Indeed, the film follows Montemayor's exploits on
the proverbial "high seas," in dark island caves, and on shores dotted with
small nipa huts and coconut trees, without a single scene of urban life. The
common folk are fishermen and subsistence farmers whose wealth is measured in pigs and sacks of rice. The only hints in the film of a larger market
economy emphasize predation and ruthlessness: local toughs at a beer
house in a coastal town, garishly dressed flunkies of a big-time "smuggling
lord," and bandits who abduct fishermen's daughters and sell them to
prostitution houses in the city.

As the song asserts, Montemayor also appears in the film as a folk
hero of sorts, a *social bandit* forced to take "the law" into his hands to seek
justice and protect poor fishermen and coastal townsfolk from outside
predators. The only "piracy" he seems to engage in is the hijacking of
contraband foreign cigarettes from smugglers' passing sea traffic. When
Montemayor's men discover illegal narcotics aboard a hijacked smugglers' vessel, he orders them to unload the drugs into the sea. When a
rival pirate gang starts to divest coastal villagers of pigs, sacks of rice, and

local women, the townsfolk implore Montemayor to protect them. In the end, he dies avenging his wife, who has been held hostage, maltreated, and almost raped by the smugglers.

A final feature of the Montemayor legend elaborated in the film is the virtual absence of the law enforcement agents of the state. Neither Montemayor's group nor the rival pirate gang nor the smuggling syndicate confront any policemen or Coast Guard officers in the course of the film. Smuggling operations briefly cease, not in response to a government crackdown but because the smuggling lord's unsuspecting daughter is home on holiday from college in the United States. Only in the final scene do police officers make an appearance, but by that time Montemayor, the leader of the rival pirate gang, and the smuggling lord are dead.

This portrait of Beloy Montemayor as a heroic social bandit protecting poor fisherfolk from various predators on distant and lawless shores, while hardly based on fact, sheds considerable light on the Cebuano pirate's life and times. The central elements of this legitimating myth — a pristine rural setting, a popular folk hero, and an ineffective and largely absent state — in fact systematically obscure the contours of the Montemayor phenomenon. A reexamination of the historical record reveals both the distinct geography, economics, and political connections of Montemayor's outlaw activities *and* the specific logic of the Cebuano pirate's social representation.

In terms of *geography*, Montemayor's origins were less rural and remote than suggested by the mythologized version of his life. Born in 1930 in a small island off the coast of the neighboring island province of Bohol, Isabelo "Beloy" Montemayor grew up helping his parents gather shells and sell them in nearby Cebu City. As a teenager, he found himself working in the Carbon market — the main retail street market in Cebu City — selling fish and shells from nearby islands. By the early 1950s, he was already married and residing in Barrio Ermita, Cebu City, where the Carbon market is located, and where he owned a small tailor shop.[62]

Ermita and the neighboring barrio of Pasil formed a natural base for certain forms of predatory and criminal activity. These two adjacent barrios were (as they remain today) central to Cebu City's economy, Pasil serving as host to the wholesale fish market for the entire metropolitan area and the Carbon market in Ermita functioning as the city's premier retail center for everything from vegetables and poultry to pots and pans.[63] Increasingly densely packed with "squatters," the Ermita-Pasil area in the postwar era grew dirty and overcrowded and became identified as a haven for "smugglers, gambling syndicates, organized crimes, gangsters and convicts."[64] The transit of goods in massive quantities through a small and crowded area not only attracted pickpockets and petty thieves but encouraged organized rackets in "protection" and smuggling as well.

Montemayor's central base of operations was thus the very heart of Cebu's market economy rather than some remote Visayan islet. According to former police and military officials, as well as longtime residents of the Ermita-Pasil area, Beloy evolved into the "protector" of those trafficking in smuggled foreign cigarettes and other contraband in the two barrios in the 1950s and 1960s.[65] Fishing boats and other cargo-laden vessels landed regularly on the beaches of Ermita and Pasil, bringing a variety of goods—legal and illegal—for distribution in the nearby main markets and consumption in the rapidly growing metropolis. Montemayor, as the leader of a motley gang of local toughs, "taxed" (and often escorted) the incoming contraband and, according to several sources, came to enforce a monopoly on smuggling in Ermita by a well-heeled close relative of his wife. Moreover, he appears to have "protected" the two major markets (Carbon and Pasil) from rival predators, in one celebrated case killing two thugs who were harassing Carbon market vendors.[66] Finally, Montemayor used the Ermita-Pasil area as a safe haven from which to prey upon nearby sources of cash through occasional robberies of banks, other businesses, and the homes of wealthy residents of Cebu City and nearby towns.[67]

While Montemayor's base in Ermita-Pasil placed him at the center of traffic in fish, contraband, and human cargo in the Visayas, Cebu-centered transportation routes for interisland commerce provided a variety of pathways for highly mobile forms of crime. The widespread availability of inexpensive U.S. Army surplus engines (two to five horsepower) in the early postwar years had motorized sea travel, dramatically facilitating journeys between various points in the Visayas and drawing coastal villages closer to hitherto distant fishing grounds and urban markets for their produce.[68] Thus, fishermen from numerous coastal towns in Cebu, the Camotes islands, and the neighboring island province of Bohol; commercial operators based in Iloilo City, Bacolod City, and Cadiz City on the islands of Panay and Negros; and fish carrier boats from as far afield as Masbate, Leyte, Samar, and northern Mindanao came to bring their catches to Pasil for sale in Cebu City's wholesale fish market.[69] The dramatic expansion of metropolitan Cebu in the postwar period spurred the growth of numerous Visayan coastal towns supplying fish to the swelling urban market. By the early 1970s, the annual volume of fish passing through Pasil exceeded ten million kilograms.[70] Yet the resultant prosperity spread unevenly across Visayan coastlines, as large-scale purse seine and trawler operators, together with a few selected Pasil-based brokers, came to dominate Cebu's fish trade by the early 1970s, marginalizing small-scale operators.[71] Those employed by the big-time commercial fishing outfits increasingly supplemented the meager shares of the catch (in cash and kind) allotted them by the owners through clandestine midsea sales of freshly netted fish to itinerant dealers operating in motorized "pumpboats" — double outrigger canoes with inboard engines — under the cover of darkness.[72]

The constant flow of sea traffic between Pasil and the various towns in this market network facilitated smuggling and piracy from Montemayor's base in Pasil. A number of coastal towns provided markets for smuggled "blue-seal" cigarettes from distributors under Montemayor's protection or as targets for "strikes" from Ermita-Pasil beaches or the small islands off Bantayan Island northwest of mainland Cebu, where relatives on his mother's side resided.[73] Some merchants in coastal towns in Negros, Masbate, Leyte, Samar, Camiguin, and northern Mindanao established links to Montemayor and the smugglers he "protected"; others suffered raids on their homes and stores by heavily armed men arriving and departing in high-speed motorized pumpboats.[74] Fish carrier boats and other interisland vessels were also vulnerable to "pirate" attacks, hijackings, and extortionist demands by Montemayor's well-equipped and expertly manned small fleet.[75] In a particularly memorable incident in the early 1960s, Montemayor and several close associates held up an interisland passenger vessel off the coast of Cebu, speeding away with more than a hundred thousand pesos.[76] Moving — often by night — between various coastal towns and among numerous fishermen, "Beloy" Montemayor established a reputation for such daring exploits throughout the Visayas.

Thus, shades of the folk hero portrayed in *Montemayor: Tulisang Dagat* are also prominent in the memories of those who shared the same seas and shorelines as the famed Cebuano outlaw. Longtime residents of Barrio Ermita, Cebu City, recall an incident that took place in the 1950s and catapulted Montemayor to local fame. During a major fiesta at the Carbon market, a dried-fish dealer of Waray extraction well known for his tendency to engage in brawls when inebriated attacked the unsuspecting tailor (*mananahi*) Montemayor with a bolo (*pinuti*). A sizable crowd formed and watched the ensuing fight with an enthusiasm usually reserved for cockfights. Armed only with a hunting knife, Montemayor received numerous wounds but finally succeeded in killing his drunken assailant.

This incident appears to have established Montemayor's reputation in crucial respects. First of all, the mild-mannered tailor had defended himself against an unreasonably aggressive outsider — a Waray speaker from Samar or possibly Leyte[77]—who was arrogantly throwing his weight around and exploiting the overwhelming martial advantage afforded by his bolo. Second, Montemayor successfully defended himself and, despite the disparity in weapons, slew his opponent, thus establishing before the attentive crowd his evident martial prowess. Finally, among the wounds the tailor/pirate suffered from this encounter, one in particular marked him for life—the slicing off of a sizable portion of his earlobe, earning him the nickname *palong* in Cebuano. This distinctive marking, along with a permanent limp,[78] led Montemayor over the years to assume a variety of disguises, most notably a wig and a pair of platform shoes that masked his slashed earlobe and obscured his lameness. Legend has it that Montemayor often dressed up as a woman or an old man in order to evade "the law" and that he was in fact "in drag" when shot to death by Constabulary troops in Ermita in 1975.[79] This skill in self-disguise appears as the most prominent personal trait in the Montemayor myth, far more important than his supposed martial prowess. In fact, longtime acquaintances of Montemayor recall that he was not particularly fond of violence and relied heavily on close associates such as Patricio Baltazar—alias Tarzan—and Patricio Barrera—alias Tambok (Fatso)—for physical intimidation and "muscle."[80]

As for the social banditry aspect of the Montemayor myth, the popular memory appears more ambiguous. Residents of Ermita do not recall the pirate enjoying a particularly widespread reputation for Robin Hood–like exploits, though he certainly rewarded those who joined him in his criminal activities and was generous to his relatives. Nonetheless, Montemayor is remembered as having observed a certain moral code. For example, he turned against a nephew who had raped his sister, and he killed two ex-convicts who were harassing vendors in the Carbon market. Overall, Ermita residents recall that Montemayor "did not make enemies or steal here among us [the residents of Ermita]."[81] Some element of mystery about the pirate seems to have remained throughout his outlaw career. Fishermen's wives on a tiny island off the coast of northern Negros told the author in late 1992 that when Montemayor was killed a crowd of onlookers sliced open his torso in order to see what kind of heart the pirate had. Though dismissed as hearsay by those present at Montemayor's death, this story highlights the degree of uncertainty surrounding the Cebuano outlaw in the popular imagination.

Despite such ambiguities, it is clear that Montemayor's rise, long survival, and eventual fall depended far less on his reputation among the fisherfolk of the Visayas than on the protection he enjoyed from law enforcement officials and local politicians in Cebu City and elsewhere in the province. Most importantly, Montemayor had close and long-standing

links with the political machine of Sergio "Serging" Osmeña, Jr., who
served at various times as Cebu provincial governor (1952–55), Cebu City
mayor (1956–57, 1963–65, 1972), congressman (1958–60), and senator
(1965–71) and who dominated Cebu politics in the pre–martial law period.[82] The pirate's relations with the Cebu City Police Department (CCPD)
were so cordial that he often ate breakfast with the commander of the
detachment assigned to the Carbon market. The police force turned a
blind eye to Montemayor's activities and through selective enforcement
allowed him a monopoly on the "protection" of cigarette smugglers in
Ermita. This arrangement with the police came as part of a larger "pack-
age" with Osmeña and his minions, who controlled the CCPD through the
Office of the City Mayor. According to various sources, Montemayor
enjoyed close personal relations with the barrio captain of Ermita; knew
José Briones, the Osmeñista Cebu provincial governor (1955–61) and
Second District congressman (1961–69); and met with Osmeña himself on
several occasions.[83]

In exchange for such protection, Montemayor provided two crucial
services to Osmeña's political machine. First of all, the proceeds from his
smuggling, piracy, and various other illegal activities — doled out
through partnerships, percentage payments, and election contributions —
helped to oil the machine with a constant flow of cash. Second,
Montemayor played an important role during elections by engaging in
what has euphemistically been described as "campaigning" for the
Osmeña ticket. Such electoral support involved much more than just rallying his own personal following to vote for Serging or sharing some of
his popularity with Cebu's premier politician. Rather, it entailed the
mobilization of tough-guy characters from Ermita and Pasil for election
day activities such as ballot box stuffing, precinct watching, and intimidation to back up various forms of electoral fraud. Barrios Ermita and
Pasil were themselves rich sources of votes,[84] but Montemayor's
seaborne mobility allowed him and his hired goons to "influence" the
electorate in remote areas on the outskirts of Cebu City (e.g., on Olango
Island off Mactan) and elsewhere in the province.

Meanwhile, Montemayor also enjoyed a similar relationship with
local police and politicians in the town of Bantayan on the island of the
same name off the northwest coast of Cebu. Blessed with proximity to
rich fishing grounds, Bantayan was a major supplier of fish to the Pasil
market and one of the most prosperous towns in Cebu Province.[85]
Relatives on Montemayor's mother's side lived on the small islet of
Botiguis, which lay within Bantayan's municipal boundaries, and the
pirate was a frequent visitor to the place. Much of the land on Botiguis
was owned by a certain Rafael Escario, whose brother Isidro dominated

town politics for the duration of the pre–martial law period. Isidro
Escario served as town mayor from 1938 through 1959, followed by his
wife Remedios (1960–67) and his eldest son Jesus (1968–80).

Over the years, Montemayor developed close ties with the Escario
family. Whenever the pressures of life in Cebu City exceeded
Montemayor's liking, he could hide out in Bantayan, where he enjoyed
the goodwill of the town police force under Chief Salvador Abello, the
brother of Remedios Escario.[86] Montemayor also engaged in smuggling
and gunrunning in partnership with the Escarios and offered his "campaigning" services to the family during elections. Moreover, the Escarios
and their minions clearly played a role in Montemayor's acts of "piracy."
For example, Rafael Escario, one of Bantayan's municipal councilors, and
the barrio captain of Botiguis were all implicated in Montemayor's New
Year's Eve 1967 raids on the stores of wealthy merchants in the towns of
Toboso and Cadiz in Negros Occidental.[87]

Political connections and police protection not only sustained
Montemayor's criminal career, but they determined his rise and fall as
well. In fact, Montemayor's emergence in the 1950s as Ermita's most
notorious criminal owed as much to his links to Cebu City politicos as to
his early exploits. After the celebrated knife fight in Carbon market in
the 1950s, Montemayor surrendered to the police, but once released he
skipped bail and went into hiding. At this point, he offered his services
as bodyguard and flunky (*bata-bata*) to an aspiring politician, the scion of
a family with extensive real estate holdings in Cebu City, who shielded
him from legal troubles. It was this series of events that established both
his privileged political connections and his involvement in the criminal
underworld.

In the 1960s, the ebbs and flows of Cebu politics determined
Montemayor's ability to evade the agencies of the law. For, while he
enjoyed consistent police protection in Cebu City, Philippine
Constabulary cooperation was less reliable, especially in the mid-1960s
when a politician unaffiliated with Osmeña assumed the provincial governorship.[88] Thus, Montemayor fell to PC troops and landed in prison
soon after the M/V *Doña Pacita* hijacking in 1963, but he escaped with
Osmeñista assistance in 1965 and again in 1967 in time to provide assistance during crucial election campaigns.[89] In 1969, Serging Osmeña's
decision to run for the presidency against incumbent reelectionist
Ferdinand Marcos led to an extensive PC-led manhunt for Montemayor
under the rubric of "Task Force Kingfisher." Through a trusted aide, III
PC Zone Commander Brigadier General Vicente Raval,[90] Marcos secretly
offered Montemayor amnesty in exchange for surrender, but the Osmeña
loyalist refused,[91] leading Marcos to raise the reward for Montemayor's

capture.[92] On October 21, 1969, a contingent of 250 PC troops descended upon Pasil and after a long fight captured Montemayor.[93]

Ultimately, local political circumstances in Cebu proved decisive in the final episode of Montemayor's life. Sentenced to life imprisonment following his arrest and conviction in 1969, he languished for several years in New Bilibid Prison, Muntinlupa. In August 1975, however, he managed to "escape," using money supplied by Isidro Escario to secure the cooperation of prison officials.[94] Yet upon his arrival in Cebu City Montemayor found his political connections considerably weakened, with Serging Osmeña in exile in the United States and civilian and military officials loyal to President Marcos overseeing the pirate's former turf under a martial law regime. Moreover, the trusted associate in Cebu City who met him at the pier and offered him lodging in Pasil—a certain Joe Ledesma—soon proved unreliable. Ledesma, a major Pasil fish dealer (and smuggler) whose brother served as a *barangay* official in Ermita, had been holding more than two hundred thousand pesos in cash for Montemayor since his arrest in 1969. Unenthusiastic about parting with the money and supposedly concerned about recent investigations into his illegal activities, Ledesma alerted the local authorities to Montemayor's presence in Cebu City.[95]

Thus, on the evening of November 2, 1975, Montemayor finally met his demise. Characteristically disguised in a wig, sunglasses, and an elevator shoe, he was passing by the Pasil *barangay* hall and basketball court on the way back to his temporary place of lodging. According to newspaper and eyewitness accounts, the court was filled with undercover PC intelligence operatives, one of whom tossed a basketball in Montemayor's direction. Catching and returning the ball with ease, the Cebuano outlaw inadvertently revealed his identity to the onlooking crowd of Constabulary agents, who immediately opened fire, killing him on the spot.[96]

Thus, the famed Cebuano outlaw's career came to a close as colorfully—and as violently—as it had begun. Tellingly, Montemayor's demise came not as the result of declining popular support but through his fatally weakened connections to local agents of the state. Revealingly also, his outlaw career concluded—as it had commenced—not in some remote Visayan islet but in the very heart of the region's cash economy in Cebu City. Moreover, in terms of criminality in Cebu, Montemayor's death marked the end of an era. Since 1975, smuggling has continued in Ermita and Pasil, but improved road connections between Cebu City and other towns in the province have diversified the pathways of this illicit commerce. Meanwhile, increasing economies of scale and technological innovations (e.g., rural banks and two-way radios) in interisland trade and travel have reduced the rewards—and increased the risks—of seaborne piracy. On land, by contrast, the continuing growth of metropolitan Cebu has multiplied the opportunities—and expanded the markets—for certain criminal activities. Thus, in the 1980s the most notorious and successful outlaw in all of Cebu was not a pirate but the leader of an urban slum gang.

The Alega Gang and the Urban Slums of Cebu City

In contrast to the romanticization of rural outlawry in the film version of Montemayor's life, the 1988 action movie *Alega Gang: Public Enemy No. 1 of Cebu* vividly depicted urban poverty and state oppression in its dramatization of the life and times of Ulysses "Boboy" Alega, the most notorious criminal in Cebu since the time of the celebrated pirate. The film, which played to packed movie theaters in Cebu City and elsewhere in the country,[97] stars Ramon "Bong" Revilla, Jr., the son of the action star who portrayed Beloy Montemayor in an earlier film of the same genre.[98]

The film begins with a depiction of Boboy Alega's life in Cebu City as a young man trying to get by under difficult circumstances. He drives a passenger jeepney[99] but has only a temporary license, which in the film's first scene is ripped up by an officious and offensive traffic policeman. Like his fellow jeepney drivers, Alega must pay a regular *tong* (protection money) to the policemen who monitor his route and to a gang of toughs who control (with police collusion) the flow of traffic through a jeepney terminal, exactions which eat away at the drivers' meager earnings. To add to these occupational hazards, Alega has to watch over his father, a drunkard and gambler who is discrediting the family and wasting money that could be spent on the education of Boboy's kid sister.

It is against these forms of everyday oppression that the young Alega eventually rebels. First, he takes on a local gang leader, the burly "Logan," who is throwing his considerable weight around the neighborhood beer house, his *territorio*. Defending a fellow driver who has failed to pay "parking fees," Alega ends up mauling Logan until the fat gang leader's protectors, local policemen, arrive on the scene. Soon thereafter he tries to kill Logan in a downtown Cebu movie theater with a gun obtained from a drug dealer he has met. Arrested by the cops, Alega is beaten and urinated upon. But he persists, gathering a group in the slum area and riding in on motorcycles to a pool hall where Logan and his buddies are holding court. Single-handedly, Alega reduces Logan to a whimpering heap of blubber, crying for mercy and clearly unable to retain his grip over the neighborhood.

Similar acts of social bandit–style heroism soon follow. After Boboy's sister complains of obscene comments being made at her expense (*binabastos ako*) at the beer house where she works as a waitress, the Alega Gang motorcycles in to dispense with the offending thugs. More importantly, one of Boboy's pals beats up a *tong* collector at the jeepney terminal, who goes to the *barangay* captain, a certain Abling Cabrera, who runs this racket, to complain. Cabrera rallies his goons, who pick up the uncooperative driver and take him off in a jeep for "salvaging" (summary execution) in the dead of night, a plan foiled only by the fortuitous arrival of a police patrol. Alega responds by driving his motorcycle up to the *barangay* hall and spraying it with machine-gun fire. Soon thereafter he breaks up a "Cabrera for reelection" rally by killing the *barangay* captain before a crowd of his supporters. Finally, Alega seeks his revenge on the traffic policeman who had ripped up his temporary license, shooting him to death before a frightened but no doubt grateful motorist.

Predictably, the forces of the law rally the troops to capture the offending outlaw. Without much fuss, they kill or capture most of the members of the Alega Gang, including Boboy's younger brother Eddy, who is packed off to jail. Boboy is forced to flee to Davao, where he stays for a year, returning in late 1986 to Cebu City, where he is soon captured by the police. Tortured, his head stuffed down a vomit-filled toilet bowl, he is imprisoned in the Cebu provincial jail, where he finds himself among his old gang. Restless, Alega successfully engineers a jailbreak, killing in the process the policeman who had tortured him after his arrest. On the run, Alega spares a brief moment to visit his family and soon finds himself hunted by Constabulary troops. After a prolonged gunfight, the outlaw falls dead, the film ending with Boboy's younger sister sobbing and wailing as she holds his blood-spattered body in her arms.

Though less romanticized than the film version of Montemayor's life, *Alega Gang: Public Enemy No. 1 of Cebu* portrays the gang leader as the defender of his family's honor, courageous underdog, and avenger of injustice. Throughout the film, Boboy is concerned about his family — his father's drinking and gambling, his younger sister's safety, chastity, and education, and his younger brother's well-being. Confronted with a world of powerful predators, he must defend himself — and those dear to him — in order to survive with his — and their — honor intact. His misdeeds consist largely of efforts to avenge the injustices that he and his loved ones have suffered.

Unlike *Montemayor: Tulisang Dagat*, the film dramatization of Alega's life and times demonstrates the inability of the outlaw to rise above the moral squalor against which his rebellion initially rages. Alega fails to keep his younger brother out of the gang and neglects his own wife and son, "Junior," who after a particularly poignant scene leave Cebu for rural Leyte to escape the trouble that Boboy's outlaw escapades have brought them. Moreover, Alega's underdog status comes into question when he loses a *manu-mano* (hand-to-hand) barroom brawl and then shoots to death his victorious opponent in a fit of cowardly rage. Finally, after Alega eliminates parasitic local toughs, corrupt *barangay* officials, and brutal police officers, his original quest for justice dissipates into a rampage of random robberies and desperate efforts to survive. By the end of the film, the audience sees not only the triumph of the predatory state but the destructiveness of the outlaw rebel.

Unlike the film version of Montemayor's life, *Alega Gang: Public Enemy No. 1 of Cebu* maintains a closer relationship to the real circumstances surrounding Ulysses "Boboy" Alega and the gang he led to great notoriety in Cebu City in the mid-1980s. The film accurately depicts the social setting in which Alega emerged as well as the nature of the local agencies of the state. What the film obscures, however, is the evolving relationship between Alega and the forces of "the law" and his role as a subcontracted agent of the state.

As in the film, the real-life Ulysses "Boboy" Alega was a product of the emergence of an urban poor population in Cebu City. As early as the 1960s, local officials had begun to note the growing presence of "squatters" and "slum dwellers" in Cebu City,[100] their numbers approaching 70,000 by the end of the decade.[101] Continuing migration to the metropolis from the increasingly impoverished countryside only enhanced this problem, as the city's population swelled from nearly 350,000 in 1970 to more than 600,000 by 1990.[102] By the late 1980s, the number of Cebu City's urban poor ranked second only to Metro Manila's indigent population.[103] Over the years, squatters' colonies of densely packed shanties (*barong-barong*) expanded inland and south from the waterfront district and the Ermita-Pasil zone, edging along the coast and interior corridor of the metropolis several kilometers south into the neighboring municipality of Talisay. Residents of these areas, many of whom were recent migrants to Cebu City, filled the ranks of the burgeoning lumpen proletariat, from relatively well paid jeepney drivers to construction laborers and desperately poor cigarette and newspaper vendors, beggars, and garbage scavengers.[104] As elsewhere in urban slum areas in the Philippines,[105] neighborhood street gangs emerged in Cebu City,[106] engaging in distribution of drugs, protection rackets of various sorts, and syndicated control over land rights.[107] These gangs typically operated in collusion with law enforcement officials, who provided protection in exchange for regular payments of shares in their "take."[108]

Born (ca. 1962) and raised in Labangon, an increasingly crowded and predominantly poor *barangay* in the southern section of Cebu City, Alega faced many of the harsh realities of urban poverty depicted in the film version of his life. As in the film, his father, a custodial employee in the

Office of the City Engineer, is in real life something of a drunkard, who today can still be found a bit groggy and grumpy lazing around Cebu City Hall. Heavyset and strong, Boboy worked while still a teenager in Cebu City's main abattoir (slaughterhouse) on Lorega Street[109] but later became a jeepney driver. In the early 1980s, he lived together with his common-law wife, the daughter of a retired police sergeant, and their infant son in Labangon.

As a jeepney driver, Alega inevitably found himself subject to the predations of policemen empowered with the regulation of traffic and public transportation.[110] Passenger jeepney drivers in Cebu City had long been easy targets for police extortion.[111] As early as the 1950s, rival armed gangs had fought for control over various jeepney terminals in the city, using "service" as "dispatchers" as cover for exactions from the hapless drivers.[112] These gangs enjoyed close links to the Cebu City Police Department, collecting *tong* as protected and subcontracted agents of the city police.[113] Despite periodic complaints, this arrangement has remained in force to the present day.[114]

Driving a jeepney regularly between *barangay* Tabunok, Talisay, and Labangon, Cebu City, Alega had to pay his "dues" in two separate police jurisdictions. In the early 1980s, urban expansion southward toward Talisay and the construction of the Cebu South Expressway — an ill-named two-lane road linking the metropolis to southern towns in the province — made Alega's jeepney route one of the most frequently traveled in Metro Cebu. The increasingly heavy flow of traffic reduced the number of round trips each jeepney driver could make, while guaranteeing the local authorities a steady income through the extortion of *tong*. According to complaints of jeepney drivers voiced in a media exposé in 1983, regular *tong* collection by patrolmen attached to the Talisay Police Station reached hundreds of pesos a day, a practice sanctioned by a higher ranking police official who shared in the proceeds.[115] In the context of rising inflation, these exactions cut sharply into the jeepney drivers' paltry income, which consisted only of the passenger fares collected over and above the "boundary" (daily rental fee) paid out to the vehicles' owners.[116]

It was against this backdrop of economic hardship and police oppression that Alega emerged as a local outlaw in the slum areas of southern Metro Cebu. In 1983, he engaged in a face-to-face shoot-out with members of the Talisay Police Station in Tabunok, killing one patrolman and wounding several others in what is remembered today by some local residents as retribution for police abuses against jeepney drivers. Police records, however, mention in passing that Alega was a primary suspect in the November 1982 hacking to death of a person on Katipunan Street (a main thoroughfare in Labangon), suggesting that the former abattoir employee already had a criminal record and dealings with the authorities before the incident in question. In any event, Alega subsequently established a reputation for daring and violent crimes, most of which he committed in Talisay in 1984–86. Police records and newspaper accounts detail numerous motorcycle thefts, which provided Alega and his gang a high degree of mobility as well as a source of cash through resale via local "fences." Alega also "held up" local businessmen, in more than one instance killing his victim during the robbery. Moreover, he robbed the major gasoline stations in the Talisay-Labangon area, milking these vulnerable urban cash cows in rapid raids on his motorcycle.[117] These criminal activities pitted Alega against the Talisay police force, whose members he on several occasions encountered—and in more than one instance gunned down—in armed confrontations.[118]

Aside from these newsworthy exploits, Alega formed a regular gang of sorts and established his domain in the slum areas of Cebu City. Drawing on relatives and childhood friends, Alega surrounded himself with streetwise tough youths, most notoriously Nestor "Kingkong" Gomez, whose capacity for violence was said to outstrip even that of Alega. This gang imposed its "protection" over Labangon and the neighboring *barangay* of Punta Princesa, shaking down local businessmen and forcing neighborhood *sari-sari* stores to extend gang members lenient credit lines and provide them a constant flow of beer and refreshments. Uncooperative store owners and other offending residents met untimely ends at the hands of the gang on several occasions. Meanwhile, the gang secured a monopoly on the distribution of illegal drugs such as marijuana in these slum neighborhoods, a trade that guaranteed a steady flow of income.[119]

In fact, this involvement in the illegal trade in marijuana suggests that the gang enjoyed links with law enforcement officials. Beginning in the late 1970s, marijuana plantations had emerged in the mountainous area stretching from Guadalupe, Cebu City, to the town of Balamban on the island's western coast, a remote and largely uninhabited zone that soon earned a reputation as Cebu's "Golden Triangle." A variety of armed groups—ranging from government paramilitary units to New People's Army (NPA) platoons—held sway over these hinterlands, imposing production quotas on those who planted the crop within their spheres of control.[120] Yet ultimate control over the transport and distribution of the marijuana rested in the hands of military officials based in Cebu City.[121] Similarly, the authorities controlled the dissemination of the imported illegal narcotic methamphetamine ("*shabu*"), widely used in the slum areas of the metropolis.[122]

Significantly, the birth of the Alega Gang also coincided with the emergence of leftist revolutionary forces in the Metro Cebu area. By the mid-1980s, the NPA had established a presence in several *barangays* of Talisay. NPA "sparrow units" (urban assassination squads) liquidated so many policemen and other "enemies of the revolution" that residents began to describe the town as "The Killing Fields" after the widely shown film of that name.[123] In Cebu City, Communist Party of the Philippines (CPP) cadres organized students, farmers, and urban poor for "mass actions," while the radical labor confederation Kilusang Mayo Uno (KMU), or May First Movement, undertook a rapid unionization drive and led numerous strikes.[124] These efforts accompanied the CPP's acceleration of the revolutionary struggle in urban areas throughout the Philippines, as reflected in its activation of urban NPA units and promotion of labor militancy, squatters' movements, and "people's strikes" (*welgang bayan*).[125] In Talisay and Cebu City, the party was no doubt hoping to replicate its recent successes in southern Mindanao's metropolis of Davao City, where

> Communist organizing teams conducted nightly political teach-ins in lower-class neighborhoods. Communist tax collectors filled Party coffers with "donations" solicited from businesspeople, some of whom were sympathetic, others simply fearful of reprisals. Communist-influenced trade unions paralyzed business operations, while armed sparrow units answered labor repression or abusive police and military actions with bloody retribution. Government propaganda in the local press and on radio was matched word for word by communist propagandists positioned in legal fronts and by sympathizers in the media. During the November *welgang bayan* [people's strike], communist partisans in the sprawling Agdao slum district jubilantly hoisted the CPP's flag—a white hammer and sickle emblazoned on a field of red.[126]

To stem the rising tide of Communist activity in Metro Cebu, the government launched a counterinsurgency campaign noteworthy for its brutality and extralegal methods. Suspected leftists in Cebu City found themselves the targets of harassment, detention, and summary execution—known as "salvaging"—at the hands of military intelligence agents and their accomplices.[127] Overseeing counterinsurgency and law enforcement efforts throughout Cebu City and the neighboring towns, the Metropolitan District Command (Metrodiscom)—in coordination with the Region 7 Command also based in Cebu City—organized and armed paramilitary units and anticommunist vigilante groups, forces that became associated with well-documented instances of human rights abuses and illegal activities.[128]

Scattered evidence links the Alega Gang to Cebu Metrodiscom's counterinsurgency operations. For example, eyewitnesses noted Alega's presence during the abduction by military intelligence agents of a leading student activist in Cebu City according to human rights lawyer Alfonso Surigao, Jr.[129] An investigation into the student's "disappearance" faltered, however, and Surigao himself fell victim to an assassination evidently ordered by the commanding officer of the Regional Security Unit (RSU-7), an entity attached to the Cebu Metrodiscom and heavily involved in counterinsurgency operations.[130] The Cebu Provincial Command of the New People's Army asserted publicly in 1986 that Alega served as a military intelligence "asset,"[131] while the Cebu Metrodiscom chief made statements before the press in June 1987 denying widespread rumors that Alega had been killed because he had "outlived his usefulness" to the authorities.[132]

In fact, Alega's criminal career was closely linked to that of a key law enforcement official in Cebu City, PC-INP Major Eduardo Ricardo, who headed the General Investigation Service and the Special Operations Division (SOD) of Cebu Metrodiscom in 1984–87. According to ranking police officers familiar with the period, Alega enjoyed a special relationship with Ricardo wherein he received "protection" from Metrodiscom in exchange for regular shares of his "earnings" in crime.[133] Hints of this relationship periodically surfaced in the press, as when SOD operatives released members of the Alega Gang from custody under suspicious circumstances in January 1985[134] and when weapons found on Alega's body at the time of his death in June 1987 were traced to a patrolman detailed to the SOD.[135]

Alega's criminal career in fact closely paralleled that of Major Ricardo. According to police officers familiar with the period, Ricardo was in fact tolerating a wide variety of illegal activities in Cebu City in exchange for regular payments of "protection money." Yet the widely publicized upsurge in criminality in 1984 eventually forced him to take measures against the city's most notorious criminal gang. In early 1985, Ricardo led SOD operatives in the arrests of several peripheral members of the Alega Gang, who were conveniently charged with the gang's murder of a Talisay policeman in December 1984.[136] While Boboy fled to Davao, core members of his gang—Nestor "Kingkong" Gomez and Gerry Alega (Boboy's brother)—remained active, as a series of unpublicized motorcycle thefts and killings attested.[137] Thus, Boboy returned to Cebu in 1986, no doubt eager to reassert his position in Labangon and Punta Princesa.

Local political circumstances, however, dictated against Alega's survival. The civilian authorities installed in Cebu City by the newly inaugurated Aquino administration worked for Ricardo's removal, and by the fall of 1986 he was "kicked upstairs" to a largely ceremonial post. In his stead, a young police officer who had been named "Most Outstanding Policeman" of 1986—INP Lieutenant Rogelio P. Yap—took over as chief of SOD. Just two weeks after he assumed command, Yap made headlines by capturing Alega and the remaining members of his gang in a police operation in Labangon.[138] Imprisoned in the Cebu Provincial Detention and Rehabilitation Center (CPDRC) for several months, Alega and his fellow gang members seized a number of high-powered firearms in the CPDRC armory and escaped in June 1987,[139] evidently with the collusion of prison officials.[140] Yet Alega's freedom was short-lived, as the Cebu Metrodiscom mounted a massive operation to hunt him down. Just three days after the escape, a helicopter gunship, two truckloads of Constabulary troops, and scores of Cebu City policemen surrounded Alega's hideout in Labangon and after a two-hour firefight decimated the ranks of his gang.[141] As a newspaper commentary accompanying published photographs of armed Metrodiscom operatives in Labangon concluded:

> Boboy Alega, leader of the most dreaded gang here, and two other members were slain while a fourth member was critically wounded in the firefight. Later in the evening, two more members of the gang were nabbed, virtually ending the gang's reign of terror in the city.[142]

Conclusion

In a recently published essay, anthropologist Brian Fegan recalled the setting in which he conducted fieldwork in Central Luzon in the 1970s and early 1980s.

> [T]he literature on relations between landowner and tenant, or politician and electorate, had omitted the bailiffs and strong-arm men who manage relations between them. In a system of absentee landowners, one characterized by resistance and at times rebellion, it struck me forcefully in 1980 that these crucial men in the middle had been overlooked. The literature on rural violence instead had focused, romantically, on the deeds of millenarian rebels, social bandits, unionists, and for the brief periods when they were active, peasant rebels. Yet the overseers and armed guards of the landowners and local politicians had always been present and their use of force was usually more effective, though less newsworthy, less inspiring to radicals, or less disturbing to conservatives.[143]

Against the backdrop of such ubiquitous, everyday coercion in Philippine social relations, Fegan resituates the much romanticized Filipino outlaw

among the "bailiffs and strong-arm men," the "overseers and armed
guards of the landowners and local politicians," whom he, following
Anton Blok, calls "entrepreneurs in violence," aligning criminality not
with the resistance and rebellion of subalterns but with the oppression
and predation of dominant classes and agents of the state. In the
Philippines, Fegan notes:

> We often find social bandits and former rebels, along with dis-
> charged guerrillas and former soldiers, among landlords' rent
> and debt collectors, or working as guards of their crops, cattle,
> houses, businesses, and bodies; employed as strikebreakers and
> goons carrying out evictions of tenants and squatters; among the
> armed followings of members of the elite in their political con-
> tests; working as ward heelers and poll watchers, intimidating
> voters and guarding, seizing, or stuffing the ballot boxes; serving
> as agents charged with persuading, intimidating, eliminating, or
> spying on potential peasant leaders; or otherwise serving one or
> more members of the dominant classes as guardians of their per-
> sons, property, or incomes, controllers of the poor, or supporters
> in intra-elite contests.[144]

Crime thus constitutes not a form of primitive rebellion but a particular
mode of political domination and economic accumulation. Criminals
resemble Hobsbawm's "social bandits" less than they do Blok's "entrepreneurs in violence" and aspiring mafia bosses.[145]

Following Fegan, this essay has examined various forms of mafia in
Cebu, paying particularly close attention to the most successful and
enduring mafia bosses in the province during two consecutive historical
periods, 1946–72 and 1972–92. As the case studies of Isabelo "Beloy"
Montemayor and Ulysses "Boboy" Alega have made clear, these mafia
bosses have been essentially predatory and conservative, their coercive
resources deployed in pursuit of economic accumulation and in support
of political domination. Whether in the service of gangster politicians or
in league with kleptocratic Constabulary officers, these mafia bosses have
exacted "monopoly rents" and "predatory incomes," first by reproducing
and imposing conditions of economic insecurity and limited access to
scarce resources upon—and then by selling "protection" and illegal
goods and services to—a captive population of rural and urban poor.

Moreover, as the two case studies have suggested, the rise and fall of
Cebu's most successful mafia bosses, and the longevity and scale of their
criminal empires, have depended heavily upon privileged access to politicians and agents of the state's law enforcement apparatuses. Emerging
where illegal economies of scale spanned multiple and/or overlapping

police jurisdictions, these mafia bosses' petty empires and monopolies on violence achieved a measure of autonomy irreducible to the protection of a single politician or law enforcement agency. Ultimately, however, Cebu's criminals rose and fell, flourished and faded, lived and died, at the sufferance of those controlling the coercive levers of the Philippine state, its courtrooms and prisons, enforcers and executioners. Imposing not *lawlessness* but *the law* upon society, criminals in this province have served essentially as subcontracted law enforcement agents, their successes in some ways bearing witness not to the state's supposed weakness but to its strength.

As the case studies have illustrated, crime and predation in Cebu have intersected with the workings of an evolving capitalist economy in a systematic pattern. In the early postwar period, pirates "taxed" commerce on the sea lanes linking various coastal towns to Cebu City and smugglers coveted access to the Ermita-Pasil area, a major point of entry into Cebu City and the site of its major markets. By the 1980s, Cebu City had evolved into a major market for illegal drugs and had become a center for distinctly urban mafia in the form of slum syndicates. In sum, the geography of crime has paralleled local demographic patterns and market flows in Cebu, with concentrations of criminality found at nodal transportation choke points and in privileged zones for the consumption or production of illegal commodities.

Moreover, the rise and fall of Cebu Province's most successful mafia bosses and the longevity and scale of their criminal empires have depended heavily upon privileged access to politicians and agents of the law enforcement apparatuses of the state. Montemayor, for example, emerged and endured as Cebu's most notorious pirate and smuggler in the 1950s and 1960s thanks to his close ties to the political machine of Serging Osmeña, and he disappeared in the course of Osmeña's political demise. Alega, by contrast, owed his more ephemeral success in the mid-1980s to the protection he enjoyed from high-ranking officials in the local police and military commands based in Cebu City, who enjoyed considerable autonomy from local elected officials in the Marcos and early post-Marcos era.

Finally, the case studies of Beloy Montemayor and Boboy Alega have highlighted changes in the geography, organization, and social representation of crime in Cebu. Over the course of the postwar period, the tremendous growth of Metro Cebu has shifted the locus of violent criminal activity and monopoly from the center of Visayan maritime commerce in Ermita-Pasil to the densely packed urban poor communities on the southern fringes of Cebu City, from piracy and cigarette smuggling to motorcycle theft, drug dealing, and violent forms of social control. Meanwhile, however subtly, the organization of criminal activity also changed, from Montemayor's loosely knit pirate band and political/police protection in the pre-martial law era to Alega's well-defined "gang" and Marcos-era links to various elements of the regional military command based in Cebu City.

As the geography and organization of crime in the province evolved over the years, so too did the social representation of crime, as the contrasting movie "careers" and popular myths of Montemayor and Alega amply illustrate. In emphasizing the colorful personalities of Cavite's most successful mafia bosses, the film biographies of both Montemayor and Alega have obscured the economic and political bases of their success, their roles in capitalist exploitation, and their links to—and dependence upon—the law enforcement apparatuses of the state. Viewed sequentially, moreover, the two films represent a shift from the romanticization of the *picaro* waging a rearguard battle against the onslaught of capitalist transformation of rural society to the melodrama of the mafioso escaping urban poverty through entrepreneurship in violence and crime. In the earlier film, *Beloy Montemayor: Tulisang Dagat*, the famed Cebuano pirate appears as a quintessential "noble robber," whose picaresque exploits, charismatic features, and Robin Hood–like services in a bucolic setting counterpose themselves against the capitalist transformation of rural society and the predatory apparatuses of the state, thus providing some hope for resistance against social injustice and political oppression. The more recent *Alega Gang: Public Enemy No. 1 of Cebu*, by contrast, portrays the slum gang leader as a tragic figure, whose response to the hardships and humiliations of urban poverty lies in criminal and violent entrepreneurship and fails to offer any promise of redemption or liberation.

In short, the construction of such picaresque and popular outlaw heroes has moved onto shakier ethical grounds. With memories of Montemayor fading fast by the 1980s, Cebu has witnessed the disappearance of the "noble robber," the victim of injustice, who, like Robin Hood, rights social wrongs, enjoys the admiration and support of the poor, and, "invisible and invulnerable," kills only in self-defense or for just revenge. He "dies invariably and only through treason, since no decent member of the community would help the authorities against him."[146]

In his stead, less honorable "avengers" the likes of Alega have taken center stage:

> They are heroes not in spite of the fear and horror their actions inspire, but in some ways because of them. They are not so much men who right wrongs, but avengers, and exerters of power; their appeal is not that of the agents of justice, but of men who prove that even the poor and weak can be terrible.[147]

Thus, the shift from Montemayor to Alega has entailed the eclipse of the classic local "hardman," the bare-fisted street fighter, who in bygone days defended a close-knit neighborhood but enjoyed a wide and long-lasting reputation, who "fought to attain a personal visibility" and whose personal singularity and prowess, as in Montemayor's well-remembered and mythologized knife fight at the Carbon market in Ermita (and his much celebrated skill as a master of disguises), received affirmation in the performative acts of violence.[148] This reputation, after all, buttressed the coercive power that underlay his monopoly on "protection" in the Ermita-Pasil area.[149] As one scholar of mafia has noted: "[A] reputation for credible protection and protection itself tend to be one and the same thing. The more robust the reputation . . . the less the need to have recourse to the resources which support that reputation."[150]

In the hardman's stead, Alega appears as a "gunman," who, clad in dark sunglasses and a black leather jacket, heavily armed and seated on a motorcycle, becomes an increasingly impersonal figure, more attached to his gun than to the family and friends he once vowed to defend. This change in the moral economy of violence in Cebu is perhaps most dramatically apparent in the scene in *Alega Gang: Public Enemy No. 1 of Cebu* in which the famed gang leader, losing in the barroom fistfight, grabs his gun and shoots his opponent to death. Mechanized and depersonalized, violence appears not as an affirmation of the outlaw's individual prowess but as an instrument of his power over and oppression of the community.

The changing social representation of Cebu's most notorious outlaws reflects not only the evolving geography and organization of crime but shifts in the demography of the province. The image of the carefree, popular pirate holed up on some remote tropical isle has become less and less plausible over the last twenty years in the face of population growth, economic integration, and expansion of the repressive agencies of the state. Moreover, the romanticization of rural social banditry, of "piracy on the high seas," which conjured up a certain popular nostalgia in the 1970s, has lost its evocative power in the face of the increasing rural poverty, depletion of natural resources, and impoverishment of common fishermen now found in Cebu and throughout the Visayas. Hardened by the realities of urban poverty, police oppression, and criminal predation, Cebuanos in the 1990s appear to have largely forsaken the myths of the "noble robber" and the street-fighting man previously affirmed in popular recollections of Beloy Montemayor. Disenchanted and disillusioned, Cebuanos today seem unwilling or unable to recast Boboy Alega as a freedom-fighting hero worthy of emulation. Instead, they recall his widely publicized outlaw escapades and his largely imagined acts of vengeance and rebellion against the authorities as fleeting moments of violent self-empowerment for the common Cebuano. In Cebu Province, so the old joke goes, nostalgia is not what it used to be.

Nevertheless, the continuing popularity and profitability of Filipino gangster films — unsurpassed in Southeast Asia — remain to be explained. As suggested above and elsewhere,[151] the social representation of criminality in the Philippines is in fact closely linked to the objective circumstances under which illegalities are exploited in the archipelago. Millions of ordinary Filipinos, as the preceding pages have illustrated, live in the context of everyday violence and predation personified by gangster-politicians, mafiosi policemen, and their subcontracted "outlaw" agents. Against this backdrop, the specificity of the Filipino experience is worthy of note. As Piven and Cloward have argued with regard to the American working class,

> people experience deprivation and oppression within a concrete setting, not as the end product of large and abstract processes, and it is the concrete experience that molds their discontent into specific grievances against specific targets. Workers experience the factory, the speeding rhythm of the assembly line, the foremen, the spies, the guards, the owner, and the pay check. *They do not experience monopoly capitalism.*[152]

In this regard, the peculiarly decentralized, politicized, and privatized administration of law enforcement in the Philippines, a legacy of the American colonial era, has spawned a plethora of local predatory mafia rather than a single monolithic predatory state. Thus, if, as Hobsbawm claims, all agrarian societies make the distinction between the "good" robber and the "bad,"[153] Philippine society has a great abundance of the *former* and, unsurprisingly, a rich history of yearning for the *latter*.

As for the apparent disappearance of the "noble robber" and *picaro* from Filipino films, *komiks*, and popular legends in recent years, this development may well be viewed as portending more politically threatening yearnings among ordinary Filipinos. Length notwithstanding, this suggestive passage from Peter Linebaugh's seminal study of crime in eighteenth-century England seems particularly worthy of citation:

> To sum up, we may compare the picaro and the proletarian. Like the picaro, the proletarian has nothing: neither a mess of pottage today nor the land and tools to work with that he or she may fill his or her bowl tomorrow. Unlike the picaro, who is defined by shunning work, the proletarian is defined as being a worker. The scene of action of the picaro is the road, the market, the inn or the tea-garden — places of public exchange. The proletarian in contrast operates in places of private production: beneath decks or in

a garret. Like the proletarian, the picaro is held in contempt by those who lord over him or her. While the picaro's stance towards the world is active and resourceful — qualities promoted by the literary forms that arose from the individuality of the protagonist — the proletarian as an individual is often left passive and dumb by the historical records, more like a drone or a brute. However, since the proletarian's experience in life is dominated by cooperative action in the production and reproduction of the world, it is within collective experience that his or her individuality is realized. That the world can be hostile and capricious the proletarian knows, but he or she also knows that this need not always be so, because it is the work of his hands and the labour of her body that have created it in the first place. Therefore, destiny does not arrive as the necessary corollary of axiomatic forces. On the contrary, history is made by a series of collective battles, now defeats, now victories . . .[154]

In short, the popular image of the "noble robber" in the Philippine imagination is, as illustrated in the case of Ulysses "Boboy" Alega, clearly on the wane for the reasons outlined above. Yet whether this trend portends, as Linebaugh's premature and romanticized triumphalism suggests, the emergence of more broadly based and politically potent forms of subaltern consciousness — or simply a continuing pattern of brutal and depressing Filipino gangster movies — remains, of course, to be seen.

NOTES

1. David R. Sturtevant, *Popular Uprisings in the Philippines, 1840–1940* (Ithaca: Cornell University Press, 1976).

2. Benedict J. Kerkvliet, *The Huk Rebellion: A Study of Peasant Revolt in the Philippines* (Berkeley: University of California Press, 1977); Gregg R. Jones, *Red Revolution: Inside the Philippine Guerrilla Movement* (Boulder: Westview Press, 1989).

3. E. J. Hobsbawm, *Primitive Rebels: Studies in Archaic Forms of Social Movement in the 19th and 20th Centuries* (New York: W. W. Norton, 1959).

4. Sturtevant, *Popular Uprisings in the Philippines*, 115–16.

5. See the thoughtful and provocative discussion of Sakay in Reynaldo Ileto, *Pasyon and Revolution: Popular Movements in the Philippines, 1840–1910* (Quezon City: Ateneo de Manila University Press, 1979), 173–86. See also Orlino A. Ochosa, "Cavite's Peasant Hero: Shattering the Myth of Julian Montalan as Bandit and Scamp," *Diliman Review* 37, no. 2 (1989): 45–53.

6. "The Outlaw and His Manifestations in Popular Culture," in *The Romance Mode in Philippine Popular Literature and Other Essays*, edited by Soledad S. Reyes (Manila: De La Salle University Press, 1991), 290–94.

7. Eric Hobsbawm, *Bandits* (New York: Pantheon, 1981), 18.

8. Sturtevant, *Popular Uprisings in the Philippines*, 116.

9. See, for example, "Tondo 'Robin Hood' Gunned Down in Daylight," *Malaya*, October 1, 1985, 1, 3.

10. Macario Vicencio, "Nicasio Salonga Slain!" *Manila Times*, October 8, 1951, 1, 14; Santiago S. Pangan, "Salonga, Tondo Gunman, Killed," *Manila Chronicle*, October 8, 1951, 1, 10; "Manila Crime Chieftain Killed," *Philippines Free Press*, October 13, 1951, 10.

11. Rufino Rogel, Jr., "Porcuna, 2 Aides Shot Dead by Foes," *Manila Chronicle*, December 24, 1963, 1, 8; Edward R. Kiunsala, "The End of Boy Golden," *Philippines Free Press*, January 4, 1964, 6, 63.

12. P. N. Abinales, "Where, Oh Where Is Ben Tumbling?" *Who*, March 28, 1981, 16; J. Ma. Bartolome, "Ben Tumbling: Hero or Anti-Hero, He Thrilled the Masses, Was Feared, Applauded, Hated, and Loved. . . ," *Who*, March 28, 1981, 14–16, 38.

13. In general, see Carolyn I. Sobritchea, "Banditry in Cavite during the Post World War II Period," *Asian Studies* s 22–24 (1984–86): 10–27.

14. Ibid., 118.

15. See, for example, Santiago V. Alvarez, *The Katipunan and the Revolution: Memoirs of a General with the Original Tagalog Text* (Quezon City: Ateneo de Manila University Press, 1992): 211, 447; and Similor, "Amuletos Guerreros De La Pasada Revolucion," *Renacimiento Filipino*, October 7, 1910, 17–18.

16. See, for example, the discussion of two World War II guerrilla leaders in Brian Fegan, "Folk-Capitalism: Economic Strategies of Peasants in a Philippine Wet-Rice Village," Ph.D. diss., Yale University, 1979, 62–73.

17. See, for example, Lorenzo-Abrera, *Ang Numismatika*, 39.

18. Reyes, "The Outlaw," 293.

19. See, for example, Ma. Bernadette G. Lorenzo-Abrera, *Ang Numismatika ng Anting-Anting: Panimulang Paghawan ng Isang Landas Tungo sa Pag-unawa ng Kasaysayan at Kalinangan Pilipino* (Quezon City: Unibersidad ng Pilipinas, Programang Kaalamang Bayan, Tanggapan ng Dekano, Dalubhasaan ng Agham Panlipunan at Pilosopiya, 1992); Prospero R. Covar, "Potensiya, Bisa,

at Anting-Anting [Decoding System Encoded in Folklore]," *Asian Studies* 18 (April, August, December 1980): 71–78; and Ileto, *Pasyon*, 23.

20. Lorenzo-Abrera, *Ang Numismatika*, 38.

21. Recent scholarship has traced this linkage back to the Spanish colonization of the Philippines in the sixteenth century: "Faced by a superior physical/spiritual power, the islanders understandably comprehended colonial conquest in terms of the Spaniards' rapport, alliance and support derived from *their* spirit world. . . . The paraphernalia used by the friars in their shamanic ensemble were thereby seen as potent objects . . . [which] became novel media for the transference of power from the spiritual to the human domain" (Filomeno V. Aguilar, Jr., "Phantoms of Capitalism and Sugar Production Relations in a Colonial Philippine Island," Ph.D. diss., Cornell University, 1992, 39–43).

22. See Reynaldo C. Ileto, "Rizal and the Underside of Philippine History," in *Himalay: Kalipunan ng mga Pag-aaral kay José Rizal,* edited by Patricia Melendez-Cruz and Apolonio Bayani Chua (Manila: Sentrong Pangkultura Ng Pilipinas, 1991), 285.

23. Ileto, *Pasyon*, 25. Ileto notes the similarity to the Javanese notions of power cited by Benedict Anderson: "the direct relationship between the state of a person's inner being and his capacity to control the environment" ("The Idea of Power in Javanese Culture," in *Culture and Politics in Indonesia,* edited by Claire Holt [Ithaca: Cornell University Press, 1972], 16–17).

24. The original text reads "ang taong may anting-anting, ayon sa mga karaniwang tao, ay matulungin, madasalin, mapagpakumbaba, at tahimik, subalit matapang kung magkasubukan. . . . [M]ahigpit ang pagkakaugnay ng anting-anting sa 'loób' ng tao, sa katatagan at kagandahan ng kanyang pagkatao" (Abrera, *Ang Numismatika*, 63–66; translation by the author).

25. See R. H. Hilton, "The Origins of Robin Hood," *Past & Present* 14 (November 1958): 30–43; J. C. Holt, "The Origins and Audience of the Ballads of Robin Hood," *Past & Present* 18 (November 1960): 89–110; Maurice Keen, "Robin Hood—Peasant or Gentleman?" *Past & Present* 19 (April 1961): 7–15; J. C. Holt, "Robin Hood: Some Comments," *Past & Present* 19 (April 1961): 16–19; T. H. Aston, "Robin Hood," *Past & Present* 20 (November 1961): 7–9; and J. R. Maddicott, "The Birth and Setting of the Ballads of Robin Hood," *English Historical Review* 93, no. 367 (April 1978): 276–99.

26. Anton Blok, "The Peasant and the Brigand: Social Banditry Reconsidered," *Comparative Studies in Society and History* 14, no. 4 (September 1972): 494–503.

27. Phil Billingsley, *Bandits in Republican China* (Stanford: Stanford University Press, 1988); Jonathan Marshall, "Opium and the Politics of Gangsterism in Nationalist China, 1927–1945," *Bulletin of Concerned Asian Scholars* 8, no. 3 (July–September 1976): 19–48.

28. Stephen Wilson, *Feuding, Conflict, and Banditry in Nineteenth-Century Corsica* (Cambridge: Cambridge University Press, 1988).

29. See, for example, Gilbert M. Joseph, "On the Trail of Latin American Bandits: A Reexamination of Peasant Resistance," *Latin American Research Review* 25, no. 3 (1990): 7–53; Richard W. Slatta, ed., *Bandidos: The Varieties of Latin American Banditry* (New York: Greenwood, 1987); and Paul J. Vanderwood, *Disorder and Progress: Bandits, Police, and Mexican Development* (Lincoln: University of Nebraska Press, 1981). See also the various articles published in *Latin American Research Review* 26, no. 1 (1991): 145–74.

30. Michael Adas, "Bandits, Monks, and Pretender Kings: Patterns of Peasant Resistance and Protest in Colonial Burma, 1826–1941," in *Power and Protest in*

the Countryside: Rural Unrest in Asia, Europe, and Latin America, edited by Robert P. Weller and Scott E. Guggenheim, 75–105 (Durham: Duke University Press, 1982).

31. See, for example, Benedict R. O'G. Anderson, *Java in a Time of Revolution: Occupation and Resistance, 1944–1946* (Ithaca: Cornell University Press, 1972), 5–9, 156; Robert Cribb, *Gangsters and Revolutionaries: The Jakarta People's Militia and the Indonesian Revolution, 1945–1949* (Sydney: Allen & Unwin, 1991), 18–20, 26–30, 52; Henk Schulte Nordholt, "The Jago in the Shadow: Crime and 'Order' in the Colonial State in Java," *Review of Indonesian and Malaysian Affairs* 25, no. 1 (Winter 1991): 74–91; Onghokham, "The *Jago* in Colonial Java, Ambivalent Champion of the People," in *History and Peasant Consciousness in South East Asia,* edited by Andrew Turton and Shigeharu Tanabe, 327–43 (Osaka: National Museum of Ethnology, 1984); and James R. Rush, *Opium to Java: Revenue Farming and Chinese Enterprise in Colonial Indonesia, 1860–1910* (Ithaca: Cornell University Press, 1990), 115–18.

32. Cheah Boon Kheng, "Hobsbawm's Social Banditry, Myth, and Historical Reality: A Case in the Malaysian State of Kedah, 1915–1920," *Bulletin of Concerned Asian Scholars* 17, no. 4 (October-December 1985): 34–51; *The Peasant Robbers of Kedah, 1900–1929: Historical and Folk Perceptions* (Singapore: Oxford University Press, 1988).

33. David B. Johnston, "Bandit, *Nakleng,* and Peasant in Rural Thai Society," *Contributions to Asian Studies* 15 (1980): 90–101.

34. For a recent reevaluation of criminality in the Spanish colonial Philippines, see Greg Bankoff, "Crime, Society, and the State in the Nineteenth Century Philippines," Ph.D. diss., Murdoch University, 1990; and "Redefining Criminality: Gambling and Financial Expediency in the Colonial Philippines, 1764–1898," *Journal of Southeast Asian Studies* 22, no. 2 (September 1991): 267–81.

35. For a comparison with the British legacy in Malaysia, for example, see Zakaria Hin Haji Ahmad, "The Police and Political Development in Malaysia: Change, Continuity, and Institution-Building of a 'Coercive' Apparatus in a Developing, Ethnically Divided Society," Ph.D. diss., Massachusetts Institute of Technology, 1977.

36. See "Brief History of the Municipal Police," in Emmanuel A. Baja, *Philippine Police System and Its Problems* (Manila: Pobre's Press, 1933), 202–21.

37. "Report of Acting Director of Constabulary, Department of Commerce and Police, Bureau of Constabulary, Manila, P.I., August 8, 1908," in Bureau of Insular Affairs, War Department, *Report of the Philippine Commission to the Secretary of War, 1908,* pt. 2 (Washington, D.C.: Government Printing Office, 1909), 372.

38. On this point, see Cicero C. Campos, "The Role of the Police in the Philippines: A Case Study from the Third World," Ph.D. diss., Michigan State University, 1983, 205–6.

39. Ibid., 166–69, 211–30.

40. See, in particular, section 51 of Republic Act No. 6975, in Rod B. Gutang, *Pulisya: The Inside Story of the Demilitarization of the Law Enforcement System in the Philippines* (Quezon City: Daraga Press, 1991), 164–65.

41. Hobsbawm, *Bandits,* 21.

42. Stella Gonzales and Jerry Esplanada, "Napolcom Report: Cops behind Half of Murders in RP," *Philippine Daily Inquirer,* March 11, 1994, 1.

43. Blok, "The Peasant and the Brigand," 498 (italics in the original).

44. Anton Blok, *The Mafia of a Sicilian Village, 1860–1960: A Study of Violent Peasant Entrepreneurs* (New York: Harper & Row, 1974), 6.

45. See, for example, Diego Gambetta, "Fragments of an Economic Theory of the Mafia," *Archives Européennes de Sociologie* 29 (1988): 127–45; and *The Sicilian Mafia: The Business of Private Protection* (Cambridge: Harvard University Press, 1993).
46. See, for example, Thomas C. Schelling, "What Is the Business of Organized Crime?" in *Choice and Consequence*, 179–94 (Cambridge: Harvard University Press, 1984).
47. Pino Arlacchi, *Mafia Business: The Mafia Ethic and the Spirit of Capitalism* (London: Verso, 1987), 14, 21; Hobsbawm, "Mafia," in *Primitive Rebels*, 30–56, esp. 33, 51; Mary McIntosh, *The Organisation of Crime* (London: Macmillan, 1975), 50–58.
48. Max Weber, *Economy and Society: An Outline of Interpretive Sociology*, vol. 1 (Berkeley: University of California Press, 1978), 204–6.
49. On "protection rents," see Frederic C. Lane, "Economic Consequences of Organized Violence," *Journal of Economic History* 18, no. 4 (December 1958): 401–17.
50. Thomas C. Schelling, "Economics and Criminal Enterprise," in Schelling, *Choice and Consequence*, 174.
51. On "routine repression," see James C. Scott, *Weapons of the Weak: Everyday Forms of Peasant Resistance* (New Haven: Yale University Press, 1985), 274–78. On the related notion of "everyday forms of oppression and domination," see Andrew Turton, "Patrolling the Middle-Ground: Methodological Perspectives on 'Everyday Peasant Resistance,'" *Journal of Peasant Studies* 13, no. 2 (January 1986): 36–48.
52. Canute Vandermeer, "Corn on the Island of Cebu, the Philippines," Ph.D. diss., University of Michigan, 1972, 13, 15–17, 51, 71.
53. Michael Cullinane, "The Changing Nature of the Cebu Urban Elite in the 19th Century," in *Philippine Social History: Global Trade and Local Transformations*, edited by Alfred W. McCoy and Ed. C. de Jesus (Quezon City: Ateneo de Manila University Press, 1982), 251–52.
54. The most comprehensive study of Cebu under Spanish colonial rule, for example, does not include a single mention of crime in the province. See Bruce Leonard Fenner, "Colonial Cebu: An Economic-Social History, 1521–1896," Ph.D. diss., Cornell University, 1976.
55. Resil B. Mojares, "The *Pulahanes* of Cebu: Case Study in Human Geography," *Philippine Quarterly of Culture and Society* 4, no. 4 (December 1976): 233–42. See also Hagahaw, "Kinsa ba si Luis Flores sa Kagubut sa Sugbu?" *Bag-ong Kusog*, December 23, 1938, 27, 51, 64–65; and Fer, "Ang mga Pulahan Lain sa mga Rebolusyonaryo," *Bag-ong Kusog*, October 14, 1932, 1, 24–26.
56. See, for example, Silvano Jakosalem, "Mahal Pa ang Kinabuhi sa Manok kay sa Tawo," *Bisaya*, April 9, 1947, 9, 23; Celestino Rodriguez, *Episodios Nacionales: Horas Tragicas De Mi Patria*; Manuel F. Segura, *Tabunan: The Untold Exploits of the Famed Cebu Guerrillas in World War II* (Cebu City: M. F. Segura Publications, 1975); Celerino V. Uy, *Karon Mosulti Na Ako: Basahon sa Gubat* (Cebu: Mercer Book Company, 1947); and Jesus Villamor, "Capt. James Cushing and the Cebu Guerrillas," serialized in *Variety*, March 15–April 26, 1964.
57. Godofredo M. Roperos, "The Armed Groups That Roam Our Mountains," *Sun-Star Daily*, July 9, 1985, 7, 14; "The Cowed Mountains," *Sun-Star Daily*, November 7, 1985, 7–8, 14.
58. As the provincial governor noted in 1990: "Cebu is the only major island in the Republic where the majority of its population is engaged in manufacturing and services rather than agriculture" (*Republic of the Philippines, Province*

of Cebu: Socio-Economic Profile CY 1990 [Cebu City: Provincial Planning and Development Office, 1991], 3).

59. *1990 Census of Population and Housing: Cebu: Report No. 2-28G: Population by City, Municipality, and Barangay* (Cebu City: Provincial Planning and Development Office, 1991).

60. Over the years, Cebu daily newspapers have chronicled, however selectively, the involvement of the police in the "exploitation of illegalities." For representative examples of such reportage, see "Mga Polis Gisumbong sa Pagkakawatan ug Pagkabugaw," *Bag-ong Kusog,* February 8, 1929, 13; "Agents Frequenting Gambling Dens," *Republic News,* June 6, 1962, 1, 8; and "17 Cops Involved in Drugs—Ayap," *Sun-Star Daily,* July 24, 1991, 1, 19.

61. An earlier (1976) film, *Beloy Montemayor,* featured Ramon Revilla, the famous action film star who depicted "Nardong Putik," the famed Cavite gangster, as the Cebuano pirate.

62. Vicente R. "Longlong" Kyamko, retired detective sergeant, Cebu City Police Department, interview with the author, Office of the Vice Mayor of Cebu City, Cebu City Hall, September 7, 1992.

63. Numeriano A. Cuyos and Alexander Spoehr, "The Fish Supply of Cebu City: A Study of Two Wholesale Markets," *Philippine Quarterly of Culture and Society* 4 (1976): 160-98.

64. Visayas Human Development Agency, *A Study of Urban Poor Dwellers, Their Attitudes and Responses to Government Initiated Development Programs: The Case of Four Selected Communities in Cebu City* (Cebu City: Visayas Human Development Agency, 1987), 6.

65. On cigarette smuggling in Cebu City in the 1960s, see, for example, Ramon D. Abellanosa, "Widespread Smuggling: Bigtime Vices in Cebu," *New Day,* December 20, 1961, 1, 5; "'Blue seals' worth P10,000 Seized," *Cebu Afternoon Tribune,* December 16, 1966, 1; and "Experts Tag Cebu Cities, Province as Citadel for Smugglers!" *Cebu Afternoon Tribune,* June 21, 1967, 1, 6.

66. Kyamko interview; Felixberto Rosito, *barangay* captain, interview with the author, Ermita, Cebu City, February 8, 1992; Rudy Ticle, interview with the author, Ermita Beach, Cebu City, February 18, 1992.

67. See, for example, "Argao Resident Held Up, Robbed," *New Day,* November 21, 1961, 1, 5; "Argao Hold-Up, Robbery Solved, 4 Men Arrested," *New Day,* January 5, 1962, 1, 5; "Suspects Reenact Escaño Lines Robbery," *New Day,* January 6, 1962, 1, 5; "250-Man PC Bags Montemayor after Gun Battle," *Morning Times,* October 21, 1969, 1, 12; and Balt V. Quinain and Orlando C. Sanchez, "Beloy Montemayor Shot Dead by PC," *The Freeman,* November 3, 1975, 1, 2.

68. On this development, see, for example, Alexander Spoehr, *Protein from the Sea: Technological Change in Philippine Capture Fisheries* (Pittsburgh: University of Pittsburgh, Department of Anthropology, 1980), 43-44; and David L. Szanton, *Estancia in Transition: Economic Growth in a Rural Philippine Community,* Institute of Philippine Culture Papers, no. 9 (Quezon City: Ateneo de Manila University Press, 1972), 30-31, 39.

69. Cuyos and Spoehr, "The Fish Supply of Cebu City," 164-66.

70. Ibid., 161.

71. Ibid., 171, 175-76; Szanton, *Estancia,* 30-34, 105.

72. Szanton, *Estancia,* 39-40.

73. Judge Alfonso B. Baguio, "Decision," promulgated March 21, 1970, in *Criminal Case No. CCC-XII-27 Negros Occidental, for: Robbery in Band with Multiple and Less Serious Physical Injuries, People of the Philippines, Complainant, versus*

Carlos Caramonte, Accused (Bacolod City: Republic of the Philippines, Circuit Criminal Court, Twelfth Judicial District, 1970).

74. See, for example, "Banditry Drive in Visayas Losing Steam," *Morning Times,* May 23, 1968, 1, 8; "Pirates in Misamis Raid Flee to Cebu," *Republic News,* May 31, 1968, 1; "Cebuano Bandit Wanted since 1963 Arrested in Zamboanga," *Morning Times,* June 7, 1968, 1, 9; "4 Pirate Suspects Arrested," *Republic News,* June 7, 1968, 1, 6; "Camiguin Sacked by Cebu-Based Pirates," *Republic News,* June 19, 1968, 1, 8; and "Montemayor Foils Arrest at the Back of Carbon Market," *Morning Times,* March 19, 1969, 1, 9.

75. See, for example, "Pirates Hijacked, Stripped Motorboat," *Morning Times,* May 11, 1968, 1, 2.

76. See "Montemayor Escapes Anew!" *Republic News,* May 27, 1967, 1, 5.

77. A study of slum dwellers in Cebu City in the mid-1960s noted the reputation of Waray speakers for being "rather temperamental in character" (Fermin A. Dichoso, "A Study of the Life in the Slum Areas in Cebu City," M.A. thesis, University of San Carlos, 1965, 36).

78. While commonly assumed to be the result of some combat wound, Montemayor's limp was more likely the product of his years of work as a tailor. As Bernardino Ramazzini, the great early eighteenth-century scholar of industrial pathology, noted in his 1713 classic, *De Morbis Artificum*: "Tailors are often subject to numbness of the legs, lameness, and sciatica, because while they are sewing garments they are almost of necessity obliged to keep one of the legs back against the thigh." Thus, Ramazzini concluded, tailors are generally "stooping, round-shouldered, limping men" (*Diseases of Workers* [New York: Hafner Publishing, 1964], 283).

79. However, the Constabulary officer who headed the operation leading to Montemayor's death recalls that the outlaw was not dressed as a woman but was clad in eyeglasses, a wig, and a special shoe to correct his limp (*kimpang*) (Retired Brigadier General Cesar G. Villarin, interview with the author, Economic Intelligence and Investigation Bureau [EIIB], Region 7 Office, Cebu City, October 7, 1991).

80. For accounts of other close Montemayor associates, see Balt V. Quinain, "Death of a Gunman," *The Freeman,* February 15, 1968, 6, 12, 18–18A; and "Posse Kills Montemayor Gang Member," *The Freeman,* June 18, 1974, 1, 9.

81. "Wa siya mangitag kaaway, wala siya manulis diri sa amu" (Interview with Felixberto Rosito, *barangay* captain, Ermita, Cebu City, February 8, 1992).

82. On Osmeña, see Resil B. Mojares, *The Man Who Would Be President: Serging Osmeña and Philippine Politics* (Cebu City: Maria Cacao, 1986).

83. Sources on Montemayor's relationship with Cebu City politicians and police officials include Dioscoro P. Alesna, retired PC colonel, interview with the author, Cebu Provincial Detention and Rehabilitation Center, Cebu City, September 24, 1991; Florencio Villarin, National Bureau of Investigation regional director, Region 7, interview with the author, Cebu City, October 1, 1991; Felixberto Rosito, *barangay* captain, Ermita, Cebu City, interview with the author, Cebu City, February 8, 1992; Rodolfo Ticle, longtime Ermita resident, Cebu City, February 8, 1992; and Vicente R. Kyamko, Jr., retired Cebu City police detective sergeant, interview with the author, Cebu City, September 7, 1992.

84. Mario Ortiz, "Serging's Mightiest Weapon: City Votes," *Daily News,* December 6, 1959, 1, 10.

85. Cuyos and Spoehr, "The Fish Supply of Cebu City," 164.

86. See "Bantayan: Terror Grips Bantayan Islet," *The Freeman*, February 1, 1968, 5, 9, 20–21.

87. See Judge Alfonso B. Baguio, "Decision," promulgated March 21, 1970, in *Criminal Case No. CCC–XII–27 Neg. OCC, People of the Philippines, Complainant, versus Carlos Caramonte, Accused* (Bacolod City: Circuit Criminal Court, Twelfth Judicial District).

88. See "The Feud between the City Police and the Cebu PC Provincial Command," *The Freeman*, February 8, 1968, 9–10, 23.

89. See "Montemayor Escapes Anew!" *Republic News*, May 22, 1967, 1, 5.

90. On Raval, see "Col. Raval Is New III PC Zone Boss," *Star Monthly*, January 1966, M; and Tereso Cañares, "The Integrity of Raval," *Star Monthly*, August 1966, 6, 36.

91. Kyamko interview, September 9, 1992.

92. "P20,000 Prize Is Tagged by PC on I. Montemayor," *Morning Times*, October 4, 1969, 1, 10.

93. "250-Man PC Team Bags Montemayor after Gun Battle," *Morning Times*, October 21, 1969, 1, 12.

94. Letter of August 31, 1975, from Nicanor D. Marquez, Plant Industry Secretary, to Superintendent, New Bilibid Prison, Muntinlupa, Rizal. Further details of Montemayor's "escape" from New Bilibid were supplied by prison guards Dante Cruz and Diomedes Dador in interviews conducted by the author in November 1992.

95. Police Captain Rogelio P. Yap, Philippine National Police inspector general, RECOM 7, interview with the author, October 9, 1991, Cebu City.

96. Balt V. Quinain and Orlando C. Sanchez, "Beloy Montemayor Shot Dead by PC," *The Freeman*, November 3, 1975, 1, 2.

97. According to one report, *Alega Gang* was such a hit in Cebu City that "the crowd broke the glass wall of the box office during a scramble for tickets." See "Bong Stars in 'Manong Gang,'" *Philippine Daily Inquirer*, September 24, 1991, 27.

98. See note 61.

99. The jeepney is a distinctively Filipino passenger vehicle that emerged in the early postwar years as a convenient remodeled version of the widely available surplus U.S. Army Jeep. With seating for more than a dozen passengers, jeepneys dominated urban passenger transportation in the Philippines throughout the postwar period.

100. See, for example, "Squatter Houses Demolition Pressed," *Republic News*, February 2, 1961, 1, 6; and "Ortiz Acts on Railway Squatters, Assures Road Project Start," *Republic News*, December 5, 1963, 1, 5.

101. John H. Osmeña, *The Squatter Problem* (Cebu City: Department of Housing and Development, 1968), 2.

102. *1970 Census of Population and Housing: Cebu* (Manila: Bureau of the Census and Statistics, 1972), 2; *1990 Census of Population and Housing Report No. 2–29G: Population by Barangay: Cebu City* (Manila: National Statistics Office, 1990), 1.

103. Pilar Ramos-Jimenez, Ma. Elena Chiong Javier, and Judy Carol C. Sevilla, "The Poor in Philippine Cities: A Situation Analysis," *Sojourn* 3, no. 1 (February 1988): 81.

104. Joseph Fernandez and Amalia de la Torre, "Scavengers of Cebu City: A Case Study of Urban Poverty," in *Faces of Philippine Poverty: Four Cases from the Visayas*, edited by Ricardo G. Abad, Rowe Cadeliña, and Violeta Lopez-Gonzaga, 139–62 (Quezon City: Philippine Social Science Council Visayas Research Consortium, 1986).

188   John T. Sidel

105. Officials of the Presidential Commission for the Urban Poor estimated in 1987 that syndicates victimize 75 percent of the three million squatters in the Philippines, earning a total of P25 million a month, or P2.7 billion a year, through extortion and land fraud. See Ernesto Lim, Jr., "Syndicates Making P2.7b Annually by Fleecing Squatters," *Manila Chronicle*, September 28, 1987, 1, 6.

106. See, for example, Felix W. Lamarte, "Child, 3 Others, Hurt in Rival Gang Shootout," *The Freeman*, September 22, 1971, 1, 2; and "Gangs Surrender Various Weapons," *Sun-Star Daily*, March 15, 1983, 1, 2.

107. For scholarly descriptions of neighborhood gangs and criminal syndicates in the Philippines, see, for example, Ricardo G. Abad, "Squatting and Scavenging in Smokey Mountain," *Philippine Studies* 39 (1991): 263–86; F. Landa Jocano, *Slum as a Way of Life: A Study of Coping Behavior in an Urban Environment* (Quezon City: New Day Publishers, 1975), 100–22; Philip C. Parnell, "Time and Irony in Manila Squatter Movements," in *The Paths to Domination, Resistance, and Terror,* edited by Carolyn Nordstrom and JoAnn Martin, 154–76 (Berkeley: University of California Press, 1992); Richard L. Stone, "The Squatter and the Law," in *The Politics of Public and Private Property in Greater Manila,* Special Reports, no. 6 (De Kalb: Northern Illinois University, Center for Southeast Asia Studies, 1973), 69–80; and Richard L. Stone and Joy Marsella, "Mahirap: A Squatter Community in a Manila Suburb," in *Modernization: Its Impact in the Philippines III,* edited by Walden F. Bello and Alfonso de Guzman II, 64–91, IPC Papers, no. 6 (Quezon City: Ateneo de Manila University Press, 1968).

108. See, for example, "Law Agents Involved in Labangon Gang War," *The Freeman,* March 26, 1970, 1, 6; Wilfredo A. Veloso, "Campaign against Swindlers Should Include Police Cohorts," *Sun-Star Daily,* September 20, 1991, 8, 13; and Irene R. Sino Cruz, "Cebu Cops Face Shabu Raps," *Philippine Daily Inquirer,* August 5, 1992, 21.

109. Questionable health conditions have at various times made the city's slaughterhouse the focus of considerable controversy. See, for example, Balt V. Quinain, "'Hot Meat': Authorities Face Serious Problem of Uninspected Meat Being Smuggled into the City's Markets," *The Freeman,* February 15, 1968, 5, 20, 22; and "Only 40% of Meat Sold in Cebu Untainted," *Philippine Daily Inquirer,* August 18, 1991, 20.

110. On the prevalence of police extortion of jeepney drivers throughout the Philippines, see Richard L. Stone, "'Lagay' and the Policeman: A Study of Private, Transitory Ownership of Public Property," in *Modernization: Its Impact in the Philippines V,* edited by Frank Lynch and Alfonso de Guzman II, 142–66, IPC Papers, no. 10 (Quezon City: Ateneo de Manila University Press, 1971); and Medardo Roda, "Ang mga Manggagawa sa Industriya ng Dyipni [The Workers in the Jeepney Industry]," in *Labor and the Transport Industry in the Philippines,* edited by V .A. Teodosio, P. B. Bandayrel, Jr., and G. L. Labastilla, 125–30 (Quezon City: University of the Philippines, School of Labor and Industrial Relations, 1989).

111. According to a 1983 study, jeepneys carry nearly 86 percent of all public commuters in Metro Cebu (Visayas Human Development Agency, *The Cebu Labor Situationer: Base to Societal Change* [Cebu City: VIHDA, 1983], 39).

112. See "5 Wounded as Rival Gangs Shoot It Out," *Daily News,* March 11, 1959, 1, 6; and "Gang Rivalry Ends, Leaders Sign 'Treaty,'" *Daily News,* March 20, 1959, 1, 2.

113. "Link 2 EMs in Gang War," *Daily News,* March 12, 1959, 1, 2; "Lozada Wants Gang Rivalries, Rackets Stopped," *Daily News,* April 5, 1959, 1, 2; "Ordinance

on Dispatches OK'd," *Daily News*, April 7, 1959, 1, 2; "Dispatchers Measure Inked," *Daily News*, April 15, 1959, 1, 4.

114. See "Cop Denies Ties with Terminal Extortionists," *Sun-Star Daily*, September 17, 1991, 8, 14; and "Cebu Central Police to Revive Campaign v. Tong Collection," *Sun-Star Daily*, November 24, 1991, 4.

115. Cris Diaz, "2 Cops 'Defy' Court Order, Face Arrest," *Sun-Star Daily*, May 28, 1983, 1, 2; "Olano Orders 'Tong' Probe," *Sun-Star Daily*, June 1, 1983, 1, 2; "Manila Probers Due," *Sun-Star Daily*, June 3, 1983, 1, 2.

116. On the boundary system, see Ruperto P. Alonzo, "The Informal Sector in the Philippines," in *The Silent Revolution: The Informal Sector in Five Asian and Near Eastern Countries*, edited by A. Lawrence Chickering and Mohamed Salahdine (San Francisco: International Center for Economic Growth, 1991), 57; Brian Fegan, *Rent-Capitalism in the Philippines*, The Philippines in the Third World Papers, no. 25 (Quezon City: Third World Studies Center, University of the Philippines, February 1981), 25–26; Quintin C. Mendoza, "Should We Abolish the 'Boundary' System?" *Philippine Labor* 1, no. 4 (August 1962): 14–15; and Michael Pinches, "'All That We Have Is Our Muscle and Sweat': The Rise of Wage Labor in a Manila Squatter Community," in *Wage Labor and Social Change: The Proletariat in Asia and the Pacific*, edited by Michael Pinches and Salim Lakha (Quezon City: New Day Publishers, 1992), 121.

117. See P/Lt. (INP) Rogelio P. Yap, Chief, Special Operations Division, "After Operations Report re Arrest of Ulysses 'Boboy' Alega and Nestor Gomez, alias Kingkong," November 7, 1986, Cebu Metropolitan District Command Headquarters, Cebu City Police Station, 2–4.

118. See, for example, Edward M. Gutang, "Cop Blasted Dead in Hunt for Rob Gang," *Sun-Star Daily*, December 23, 1984, 1, 2; and "Cop, Girl Injured in Gunbattle," *Sun-Star Daily*, January 6, 1985, 1, 2.

119. "Sworn Statement of Eleazar Tabar y Carmilotes, Taken at the Office of the Investigation Section, Cebu City Police Station, Camp Sotero Cabahug, Gorordo Avenue, Cebu City, by PFC Desiderio B. Operario in the Presence of P/Sgt Francisco Magalzo This 10th Day of January 1985," in *Criminal Case No. CB-4460, People of the Philippines, Plaintiff, versus Eleazar Tabar et al., Accused* (Cebu City: Regional Trial Court of Cebu, 7th Judicial Region, Branch 21).

120. Godofredo M. Roperos, "Special Report: The Cebuano under Siege," *Sun-Star Daily*, July 8, 1985, 5, 12; Godofredo M. Roperos, "Special Report: The Armed Groups That Roam Our Mountains," *Sun-Star Daily*, July 9, 1985, 7, 14; Godofredo M. Roperos, "Special Report: The Military Response," *Sun-Star Daily*, July 10, 1985, 4, 11; Godofredo M. Roperos, "Special Report: The Cebuano under Siege," *Sun-Star Daily*, July 11, 1985, 5, 12; Godofredo M. Roperos, "Special Report: The Cowed Mountains," *Sun-Star Daily*, November 7, 1985, 7, 8, 14; Xenia P. Tupas, "Cebu's Golden Triangle," *Veritas*, August 14–20, 1986, 14.

121. See, for example, Cris Diaz, "Marijuana 'King' Dies in Gangland Style Liquidation," *Sun-Star Daily*, July 5, 1983, 1, 2; "PC Men Did Gangland Style Killing?" *Sun-Star Daily*, July 7, 1983, 1, 2; and "3 in Shootout Confirmed RSU Agents," *Sun-Star Daily*, July 8, 1983, 1, 2.

122. Jim Falar, "Sitio Bato, Barangay Ermita," *Sun-Star Daily*, December 20, 1991, 9, 12; Thea C. Riñen, "Sitio Bato, Shabu Retail Center, Uses Children as Drug Runners," *Sun-Star Daily*, December 21, 1991, 1, 2; Irene R. Sino Cruz, "Cebu Cops Face Shabu Raps," *Philippine Daily Inquirer*, August 5, 1992, 21.

123. See "NPA Now Active in Laguna, Ilocos Norte, and Cebu City," *Ang Bayan*

(published by the Central Committee of the Communist Party of the Philippines) 17, no. 7 (September 1985): 12–13.

124. The New People's Army also established a presence in Guadalupe and Sapangdaku, two mountainous *barangays* on the remote westernmost fringes of the city's administrative boundaries.

125. See, for example, "People's Strikes: A High Tide in Popular Urban Struggles," and "People's Strikes in Mindanao, Bataan Draw Widespread Support," *Ang Bayan* 16, no. 10 (December 1984): 2–4, 15–16; "Militant Workers' Movement Chalks Up Unprecedented Gains," and "Squatters Are Major Potential Force in Advancing Revolution," *Ang Bayan* 17, no. 3 (May 1985): 1–4, 11–15.

126. Gregg Jones, *Red Revolution: Inside the Philippine Guerrilla Movement* (Boulder: Westview Press, 1989), 138.

127. Lawyers Committee for Human Rights, *"Salvaging" Democracy: Human Rights in the Philippines* (New York: Lawyers Committee for Human Rights, December 1985), 74.

128. See Lawyers Committee for Human Rights, *Vigilantes in the Philippines: A Threat to Democratic Rule* (New York: Lawyers Committee for Human Rights, 1988), 69–89; and *Out of Control: Militia Abuses in the Philippines* (New York: Lawyers Committee for Human Rights, 1990), 80–81, 136–39. See also Solitaire T. Suico, "Sergeant, Cafgus Jailed for 'Raid' on Police Station," *Sun-Star Daily*, April 4, 1991, 1, 2; Fred C. Espinosa, "'Tigbakay—Crazy' Cops Running Wild in the City?" *Sun-Star Daily*, February 17, 1991, 7, 8; "Mountain Folks Flee Homes Scared of Mad Killer Band," *Sun-Star Daily*, October 7, 1992, 5; and "Campos Confirms Harassment but Denies Mass Evacuation," *Sun-Star Daily*, October 9, 1992, 4, 14.

129. "Lawmen Asked to Pursue Alega 'Link' to Kidnap," *Sun-Star Daily*, November 15, 1986, 1, 2; "Status Report on Romano Case Asked by Capitol," *Sun-Star Daily*, June 30, 1987, 4, 19.

130. "Pa Says His Son Killed Surigao," *Sun-Star Daily*, July 10, 1988, 1, 2; Elias L. Espinoza, "Palcuto Keeps His Silence on Charges," *Sun-Star Daily*, July 12, 1988, 1, 2; Thea C. Riñen, "'Dead' Gunman Surfaces, Owns Surigao Slay," *Sun-Star Daily*, July 12, 1988, 1, 2; Allan D. Soroño, "NBI Sets Raps v. Palcuto, 3 Others," *Sun-Star Daily*, July 12, 1988, 1, 2; Thea C. Riñen, "Palcuto Assails Alan Confession, Denies He Ordered Surigao Killing," *Sun-Star Daily*, July 28, 1988, 1, 2.

131. "Local NPA Disowns Boy Alega Gang," *Sun-Star Daily*, November 7, 1986, 1, 2.

132. "Avenido Denies Talks on Alega," *Sun-Star Daily*, June 26, 1987, 3, 20.

133. Former chief of Special Operations Division, Cebu Metrodiscom, interview with the author, RECOM 7 Headquarters, Camp Sergio Osmeña, Jones Avenue, Cebu City, October 9, 1991.

134. "Where Are Raiders' 3 Arrested Suspects?" *Sun-Star Daily*, January 7, 1985, 1, 2.

135. "Alega Encounter: Guns Traced to SOD Cop," *Sun-Star Daily*, June 21, 1987, 4, 25.

136. Edward M. Gutang, "8 More Fall in Anti-crime Operations," *Sun-Star Daily*, January 8, 1985, 1, 2; "Alega Gang Member Falls," *Sun-Star Daily*, March 7, 1985, 1, 2; "Alega's Gang: 4 More Members Arrested," *Sun-Star Daily*, March 29, 1985, 1, 2.

137. Yap, "After Operation Report," 2.

138. Leo S. Enriquez, "Gang Leader in Metro Rob, Killings Falls," *Sun-Star Daily*, November 3, 1986, 1, 2. Yap's "After Operation Report" describes in painstaking detail the events leading up to Alega's arrest.

139. The circumstances of the escape are described in PC Major Prudencio G. Erfe, "After Operation Report," June 26, 1987, Cebu City, Camp Sotero Cabahug, Headquarters, 341st Constabulary Company, Metropolitan District Command. See also Allan D. Soroño, "Inmates Bolt Jail, Loot Armory of Firearms," *Sun-Star Daily*, June 15, 1987, 1, 2.
140. See "Probe Warden, Guards on Escape," *Sun-Star Daily*, June 16, 1987, 1, 2; and "Alega Took Phone Call before Escape," *Sun-Star Daily*, June 18, 1987, 1, 2. Retired PC Colonel Dioscoro P. Alesna, CPDRC provincial warden, confirmed in a September 24, 1991, interview with the author that prison officials had colluded in the escape.
141. Erfe, "After Operation Report"; Edward M. Gutang, "Alega Gang Falls," *Sun-Star Daily*, June 19, 1987, 1, 2.
142. "Longest Firefight," *Sun-Star Daily*, June 19, 1987, 4.
143. Brian Fegan, "Entrepreneurs in Votes and Violence: Three Generations of a Peasant Political Family," in *An Anarchy of Families: State and Family in the Philippines*, edited by Alfred W. McCoy (Madison: University of Wisconsin, Center for Southeast Asian Studies, 1993), 36.
144. Ibid., 44.
145. Blok, *The Mafia of a Sicilian Village*, 6.
146. Hobsbawm, *Bandits*, 42–43.
147. Ibid., 58.
148. In the usage and definition of the term *hardmen*, this passage borrows heavily from Allen Feldman, *Formations of Violence: The Narrative of the Body and Political Terror in Northern Ireland* (Chicago: University of Chicago Press, 1991), 46, 52–56.
149. For an influential discussion of "men of prowess" in precolonial Southeast Asia, see O. W. Wolters, *History, Culture, and Region in Southeast Asian Perspectives* (Singapore: Institute of Southeast Asian Studies, 1982).
150. Gambetta, *The Sicilian Mafia*, 44.
151. See John Sidel, "The Philippines: Languages of Legitimation," in *Political Legitimacy in Southeast Asia: The Quest for Moral Authority*, edited by Muthiah Alagappa (Stanford: Stanford University Press, 1995).
152. Frances Fox Piven and Richard A. Cloward, *Poor People's Movements: Why They Succeed, How They Fail* (New York: Vintage, 1977), 20; also cited in Scott, *Weapons of the Weak*, 43 (emphasis added).
153. Hobsbawm, *Bandits*, 140.
154. Peter Linebaugh, *The London Hanged: Crime and Civil Society in the Eighteenth Century* (Cambridge: Cambridge University Press, 1992), 151–52.

**Dato Piang and his children with some of his people,
Cotabato.**

FROM ORANG BESAR TO COLONIAL BIG MAN: DATU PIANG OF COTABATO AND THE AMERICAN COLONIAL STATE

Patricio N. Abinales

A ny study . . . can not but bring forth convincing arguments that it is to the material and greatest interest of the Philippines that Luzon and the Visayas make whatever present sacrifices may be necessary in order to extend such financial aid to the public services in Mindanao-Sulu that the latter may quickly be made in fact a part of the Philippines. At present, commercially and socially, southern and central Mindanao and the Sulu group pertain rather to Singapore than to Manila, and must be acknowledged as little more than politically Philippine territory.
—John Pershing

In his memoirs as an observer in the Moro Province, the political tourist Vic Hurley noted an incident in which, during the intense negotiation between the Americans and the sultan of Sulu over the contents of what was later to become the Bates Treaty, the latter insisted that the new colonizers allow him "to hoist the American flag together with his own" when he traveled around and beyond his domain with his entourage. The Americans, as expected, denied the request, and the sultan's decline as an important personage in "Moroland" proceeded in earnest.[1] While this royal persistence merited only a casual reference by Hurley, a closer examination of this request symbolizes something more significant than a mere supplication, for at the core of this plea lies the nature of the Muslim response to American colonialism's intrusion into their lives.

This essay looks at the life of Cotabato's Datu Piang, believed to have been the most powerful Magindanao strongman of his time. In the national narrative Piang is hardly mentioned, while in the smaller domain of "Muslim-Filipino" studies he has often been identified with Muslim collaboration with American colonialism. This relative obscurity and captious description of Piang conceal one of the most important processes that came about in southern Philippine political development. I refer here to the changes that Muslim *datus* experienced as their Southeast Asian world began to be replaced with two narrower domains: first, the Moro Province, an administrative unit administered by the U.S. Army that sought to maintain an existence autonomous from Manila; and later the formal integration of southern Mindanao into the larger colonial and Filipinized state.

Muslim reaction to American rule was founded on the experiences and historical memories Muslims had as participants in the Southeast Asian trade network and not as inhabitants of a Philippine territory let alone members of an incipient nation. Upon the consolidation of American rule, this Southeast Asian context was displaced by a new framework — the Moro Province. It is in the narrowing of their horizons that one can better understand Muslim resistance and collaboration. With access to the Southeast Asian world effectively shut off by the colonial reconfiguration of southern Mindanao's borders, *datus* were left with very little choice but to accept a narrower, district-bound standing as "big men." While it did impose constraints, this transmutation of *datu* collaborators nevertheless solidified Muslim support for the Moro Province.

The mutation, however, did not stop with the Moro Province. When the U.S. Army's term ended, so did the existence and autonomy of the Moro Province. A colonial state, now dominated by Filipinos who had been demanding the integration of the "Moros," began to extend its administrative and political reach into southern Mindanao. Muslim *datus* whose powers had been weakened under army rule were once again forced to adapt to a new order. This time, however, many of them — Datu Piang included — had become too enfeebled and old to once more alter their politics. They would "retire" from politics and be succeeded by a younger generation of Muslim leaders whose fidelity, aspirations, and political educations would be tied closely to the Filipinized colonial state. With their passing, a period in which southern Mindanao's Muslim communities had their own history — separate from that of Manila — had ended.

The Muslim Response to American Colonialism: A Reconsideration

Studies on Muslim responses to American colonialism base themselves on one unquestioned premise, that is, that Muslims, like other groups confronted with a superior power, either revolted against or collaborated with it. This premise is hardly debatable given its logic and its seeming self-evidence. When applied to Muslim societies, however, the premise becomes problematic. For one thing, there is the motivation underlying the premise. This notion of a dichotomy between Muslim resistance and

Muslim collaboration derives from a postwar intellectual effort to restore the Muslims' voice in a Filipino nationalist discourse that addresses the country's relationship (conflictual or not) with its two colonial powers, Spain and the United States.[2] In this national(ist) version, the "Moro masses" led by anticolonial leaders fought the Spanish and later the Americans just like the rest of the Filipinos.[3] Some of the Muslim elites likewise collaborated, very much like the *caciques* of the northern provinces did when the nationalist revolution of 1896 began to unravel. While Islam and Catholicism may have kept Muslim-Christian relations in constant tension, this separation hardly nullified the fact that the obvious parallelism of their responses to colonialism had secured the foundations of their emergence as one people.[4]

Two peculiar issues are evident when we examine this premise more closely. First is the rigidity of the dichotomy. Historical evidence shows that the divide between collaboration and resistance tended to be less distinct than what these scholars try to suggest. Indeed, these two responses overlapped as Muslims tried to cope with a U.S. Army intent on subduing them. The case of a Datu Tahil of Sulu is illustrative. He was a leader at the "Battle [and massacre] at Bud Bagsak," where his wife and child were killed. Later he was appointed third member of the Provincial Board after his pardon in 1915, and he was one of those groomed for the governorship of Sulu. A parallel case was that of Datu Santiago of Parang, Cotabato, who was an avid supporter of Governor Leonard Wood until 1923 when he led a revolt against the imposition of the head tax (interestingly, a late response, as the head tax had been imposed more than two decades earlier). Santiago later surrendered and was reappointed by Wood as district *lider* (leader) of the area.[5]

The second issue is the framing of the premise itself. Driven by the desire to integrate Muslims into the national narrative, many scholars assume that Muslim responses were no different from the Filipino elite's reaction to colonialism. Again, the empirical evidence shows the contrary. The Muslims, who never really imagined themselves as part of the Philippines, were kept administratively separate by the Americans. And the distinct nature of the Moro Province as colonial authority nurtured rather than dissolved this sense of separateness.[6] One cannot simply adduce that the revolts were Muslim versions of the great anticolonial resistance. The causes behind most of them point to narrow, rearguard, and unsuccessful attempts to stave off colonialism. None indicated any forward-looking, anticolonial, or nationalist perspective, and the ease with which these "rebels" were subdued showed not only American military superiority but the lack of unity that unsurprisingly characterized these localized acts of defiance.[7]

It might be less contentious to associate *datus'* cooperation with the "general" collaboration of Filipino "elites" by pointing out the opportunist habit that both groups appear to share.[8] The difference, however, lies in the setting in which this collaboration took place. A long history of conflict with the Spanish proves that these *datus* historically opposed a colonial presence when it became an obstacle to their trade. But intrinsic to that conflict was also a supercilious attitude toward Spain's Filipino allies. The Muslim *datus* never regarded them as equals, referring to them as inferiors worthy only of being slaves. It would therefore be presumptuous to assume that these Muslim "elites" transformed themselves overnight from putative slave masters into nationalist soul mates of Filipino *caciques*.[9] This disdain carried over into the American period, and mutual hostility was kept at bay only through the buffer zone that was the Moro Province. The Americans themselves maintained the segregation with their policy of a lengthy civilizing process prior to Muslim integration into the rest of the Philippines.[10] This "gap" between the Muslims' anti-Filipino sentiments and their 180-degree acceptance of their northern neighbors as allies and brothers sharing the same experiences as part of a colonial-national community remains unexplained by nationalist scholars.

The essential error here is in accepting the Philippine frame as a "given" at the onset of American colonial rule in Mindanao. The nationalist imagination that underpins most of the scholarship is based on this orientation. Yet, if one stands on a hill in Cotabato and turns one's back on Manila, one is drawn into an expanse in which the colonial Philippines was but a minor cog—the Southeast Asian trading zone Anthony Reid calls "The Lands below the Winds."[11] It is this constantly changing zone that initially framed the way Muslims related to the American colonial process. Muslims viewed their responses to the Americans in terms of their experiences in Southeast Asia, not just in the Philippines.[12] The issues of resistance and collaboration would be better understood using this zone, rather than the twentieth-century Philippines, as the original frame. And it is in the transformation of this frame, not toward a Muslim-Filipino identity but toward a more colonial but provincial "Moro" identity, that one can further understand the nature and evolution of Muslim collaboration with American colonialism.[13]

Magindanao as a Southeast Asian Society

Scholars of Southeast Asia generally agree that a regional trading network existed in precolonial times, extending from China to Africa, of which various Southeast Asian "ports and polities" were a part. The center of this network often changed based on the ability of the trading states to maintain military superiority as well as in the accessibility and control of the commodities being exchanged.[14] The Magindanao Sultanate figured prominently in this trade in the seventeenth century when it emerged as part of a "new generation of port-states [whose role] was to keep the indigenous network of trade alive in the face of European challenges."[15] It supplied the trading centers with a variety of forest and sea products, and, most important of all, it supplied slaves for the various pepper plantations set up all over Southeast Asia.[16] This involvement was propitious for Magindanao, as it facilitated unification under one sultanate. Once the Europeans became dominant players in the network, the Magindanaos merely adjusted to the new period. The sultanate even managed to expand commercial ties to include the more hostile Spanish, exporting cinnamon to Manila for inclusion in the Manila-Acapulco galleon trade. This contribution continued despite the efforts of the Spanish to suppress it and the shift of the network's center toward the increasing domination of British-controlled Singapore at the turn of the century. The English even planned a settlement in Magindanao territory to compete with the Dutch. European rivalry proved handy to a sultanate that had declared itself neutral, and Magindanao benefited from the presence of these three competing colonial powers.[17]

This brief description of the Magindanao Sultanate's part in the trading network brings to the fore two factors previously underemphasized in the historiography. First, the link involved Magindanaos not only in trade but in the ethos of the network itself. Through their participation, Magindanao *datus* developed an "internationalist" outlook. As O. W. Wolters reminds us:

> [O]ne still knows very little of the early history of the Philippines but one should not conclude that these islands remained on the fringe of early Southeast Asia. Their inhabitants did not perceive their map in such a way. They are more likely to have looked outward to what is the Vietnamese coast today or to southern China for the more distant worlds that mattered to them. Every centre was a centre in its own right as far as its inhabitants were concerned, and it was surrounded by its own group of neighbors.[18]

Ruurdje Laarhoven likewise suggests that Magindanao *datus'* intellectual curiosity transcended even their "own group of neighbors." Kudrat enjoyed discussing "religious matters" with a "Jesuit slave" and engaged "foreign visitors" in conversations about "European life and governance" as well as "the habits and customs of other nations." Kudrat was said to be fluent in Spanish and could converse in "Chinese, English and Dutch."[19] Spaniards and Americans, therefore, "confronted" neither an isolated society nor a parochial set of leaders. On the contrary, what they saw was a "port-state" with a sophisticated organization led by people who were quite aware of their place in a regional trading network and the world beyond it.[20]

Second, as members of this network the Magindanaos invariably displayed a habit that suggested less the uniqueness of their society than its affinity with the archetypal Southeast Asian community. Let me cite two significant comparisons here. The basic division among Magindanaos described by scholars — a conflict between "upstream" and "downstream" communities over control of forest products and slave power — was typical of polities all over Southeast Asia. Barbara Watson-Andaya's classification of *hulu* (upstream) and *hilir* (downstream) communities in Jambi echoes the Magindanao's *sa-ilud* and *sa-raya*. Both Jambi and Magindanao were typical models of riverine commercial posts all over the region in which "forest products" were important trading commodities.[21] Under Sultan Kudrat, the divided Magindanao communities — those belonging to *sa-ilud* (the lower valley and coastal area), of which Cotabato town was the known capital, and those in *sa-raya* (the upper valley), of which Dulawan was the capital — were unified under Kudrat's sultanate.[22]

The shape and character of Magindanao authority also corresponded to the coastal Malay *orang besar*. Magindanao *datus* conformed closely to "men of prowess," whose powers lay not in the span of territory under their domination but in their ability to project armed power to gain control of slave labor and a monopoly over tradable products. Like most *orang besar*, Magindanao *datus* engaged in constant interaction with their communities, their fellow *datus*, and outside forces to maintain precarious positions that were always subject to challenge.[23] They founded their power on cognatic kinship bonds strengthened by alliances formed through intergroup marriages, very much like other *orang besar*. They continually accumulated what Wolters calls "political intelligence" about their rivals, valued the importance of having an entourage, and were involved in "diplomatic" negotiations, particularly with forces stronger than they.[24] When their power base was stable enough, they engaged in war with each other or against other powers in pursuit of slaves and products.

Especially significant in this regard were the "treaty systems," which obliged mutual armed assistance when either of the signatories needed help. Magindanao *datus* concluded such an agreement with Spain (while maintaining informal trade ties with the Dutch) to enhance their power and attempt to destroy their Sulu rivals. The insistence of the sultan of Sulu that he must fly the American flag, keep his entourage, and be able to secure American protection if he encountered "trouble with European nations" was obviously intended to project a sense of power and importance not only within his realm but throughout Southeast Asia. All this should not be read as grasping by a petty ruler operating within a confined environment but as an almost always successful behavior that was routinely employed by rulers in the region.[25] Thus, when they encountered the Americans the Magindanaos were not as inexperienced a group as scholars suggest.[26] There already existed a tradition of dealing with the Dutch, the Spanish, and the English. When they either cooperated with or opposed American rule, their actions were informed more by the historical memory of their Southeast Asian experiences than by some affinity with Filipino nationalism or a nebulous notion of "Muslim ethnic pride." The Magindanao *datus'* attitude toward the Americans was just like the one any other *orang besar* would adopt toward powerful outsiders. The Americans were allies and business partners, to be relied upon in their trading in Southeast Asia. For a time, it was this *mentalité* that was the guidepost by which they would assess their relationship with the new colonizer.[27]

Yet there was something also specifically Magindanao in these turn of the century encounters with the Americans. This had to do with the steadily diminishing fortunes of the sultanate, a decline that began soon after Kudrat's death. The rise of Sulu as the new entrepôt and the defeat of the Magindanaos by this new rival combined with increasing Spanish manipulation of their treaty system to signal the general decline of the Magindanaos.[28] The rise to power of Datu Uto was an attempt to resurrect the glories of old, but by the 1880s, with the Spanish successfully fueling division among the Magindanaos, the Uto years merely witnessed the last attempts to reverse the process.[29] The Americans thus confronted a Southeast Asian society considerably weakened by local and colonial rivalries and constant internal divisions. The Magindanao *datus* reacted much like the *orang besar* of the Malay coasts, but their weakened condition gave them very few options in dealing with the Americans. The extent to which the once powerful Magindanao sultanate had declined was vividly described in a 1905 newspaper account. The sultan of Magindanao,

> whose ancestors were once the most powerful chieftains of the Island of Mindanao, is utterly without means of support. Though having no following, he is respected by the Moros [only] on account of his "royal" birth, and is virtually living the life of a tramp. Having no home of his own he spends his time visiting the various chieftains, stopping at each place until his presence ceases to be a novelty, [then] he moves in on some neighboring chieftain.[30]

It is with this in mind that we can better understand Datu Piang's encounter with the Americans.

From Parvenu to Magindanao Orang Besar

Datu Piang was a mestizo — the youngest of six children born to Tan Toy, a trader from Amoy, southern China, and "Mora" Tico from Sillik village. His father died when Piang was only eleven, but he left the family well established in Magindanao society. Tan converted to Islam and became "minister of lands" and an economic adviser to the most powerful Magindanao *orang besar* of that time, Datu Uto.[31] He further reinforced his ties with Magindanao *datus* by marrying Tico, the daughter of Uto's ally Datu Ayunan.[32] Tan's actions were hardly unique; they were in fact part of the "normal practice" of the Chinese in Southeast Asia. As one author put it: "The Chinese become converts, not that their . . . souls are in any degree susceptible to the influence of the Christian religion, but in order to obtain material advantage."[33] Tan clearly saw his links with the Magindanaos as providing both a business opportunity and a place to raise his family.

Piang, who inherited his father's business and political acumen, took over where Tan had left off. He established an alliance with Datu Ali of Kudarangan, a village located at the fork where the Bacat River diverges from the Pulangi and flows into Liguasan Lake.[34] This was north of Piang's village, which was located where the Cotabato River flows into Illana Bay. Together these two towns controlled the traffic in commodities and slaves between the hinterland and the coast, placing Piang and Ali in an enviable position to profit from the trade. They cemented their relationship further through marriage when Piang gave his favorite daughter, Minka, as wife to Ali. Both *datus* then sought to protect their fortunes by joining the entourage of Datu Uto. Piang married the daughter of Uto's top adviser, Datu Ayunan. An aging Uto also gave Piang and Ali extensive control over the trade in commodities and slaves and allowed them to strengthen their armed followings.

Uto later suffered for his actions when his two subordinates, aided by Ayunan, switched their support to the Spanish in the late 1800s.[35] Piang and Ali capitalized on their relationship with the Spanish to take over Uto's lands "by shrewd tactics" and further weaken their old patron.[36] He also entered into a business arrangement with the Spanish, supplying them with "men and materials [for the construction of Spanish forts in the Magindanao area] and offered other services [armed support?] for which he was recompensed."[37] When the Spanish withdrew from Cotabato after their defeat in Manila at the hands of the Americans, they left Piang and

Ali with sufficient weapons to ensure that there would be a peaceful transition to American rule. Both used this expanded firepower to crush
Filipino settlers who were planning to establish a Cotabato local government under the Malolos Republic.[38] By the time the Americans arrived,
Piang and Ali had become the new strongmen of Magindanao, reuniting
the *sa-ilud* and *sa-raya* communities last unified under Kudrat.

Before continuing with the story, it is worthwhile to step back and
consider what Piang did. The manner in which he rose to power has been
noted by observers of Magindanao society. The missing element in these
accounts, however, was the appropriate context in which to understand
Piang. What is notable about his actions is that they were hardly unique.
They were in fact common practice among Southeast Asian strongmen.[39]
Marriage alliances were frequently concluded by Maluku sultans for
political purposes as well as to establish stability through consensus.[40]
The conspiracy that Piang concocted with Ali to undermine Uto was also
vintage *orang besar*. One historian notes that in Southeast Asia "in the
absence of firm rules for royal succession, access of the elite to social
advancement through acquisition of wealth and manpower could jeop-
ardize the ruler's position. Men of wealth and commanding influence
were often the initiators of court intrigues."[41] Finally, by supporting the
Spanish against Uto, Piang and Ali appeared to be doing what any Malay
strongman would do when faced with someone more powerful. Instead
of fighting, they cooperated but in such a way that their power and
resources within Magindanao society were enhanced.[42]

The same basic principle was carried over to the early American
period, when once again Piang and Ali, despite their stature, acknowledged the superior firepower of the new arrivals. They welcomed the
Americans and, like the sultan of Sulu, were hoping to cash in on the new
order.[43] The only problem was that the Americans had a different notion
of who was in charge. Once they began to exercise their colonial prerog-
atives, the Piang-Ali alliance broke down.

Parting of Ways, Changing of Perspectives

One of the first acts of the army was to declare the formal abolition of the
practice of "slavery" throughout southern Mindanao. The decree instant-
ly drew opposition from Muslim *datus*; some protesting to their overseers, but others seeking to cut off ties with the Americans through
armed revolt. Datu Ali was one of those who revolted, assembling his
men in early 1903 at his *cotta* (fort) and daring the Americans to attack.[44]
The *cotta* fell under relentless American attack, and Ali withdrew to the
jungle where he engaged the army hit-and-run battles. He eventually

died at the hands of a special unit of Philippine Scouts sent to his Davao hideout to surprise him on October 22, 1905.[45]

A biography of Ali contends that his revolt resembled similar acts of defiance by both Muslims and Filipinos. It argues that Ali's audacity was prompted by the Magindanaos' determination "to free themselves from western colonizers' control." Thus, his "ascendancy may have been accidental but he dared to unify the divided sultanates to fight against a common aggressor [prompted by] his astuteness and love for his native land."[46] This explanation, however, flies in the face of the evidence. In reality, Ali acted more like an *orang besar* seeking freedom from American colonialism because he was losing the foundation of his power: the right to acquire and trade slaves. Ali erroneously thought that the Americans would allow him to continue his trade. When they refused, his options became limited, for to concede meant an end to his status as a man of prowess in his territory.

With the establishment of new borders by the Americans, the world of the *orang besar* became increasingly marginalized. The regional trading network once dominated by the different port-states gave way to a commercial system dominated by the various colonial powers and linked to the economies of Europe and the United States. The entrenchment of various colonial boundaries and the growth of the customs and immigration agencies of the colonial states likewise reinforced this displacement of the Southeast Asian network by world capitalism. Moreover, the new colonial map meant a different notion of boundaries as well as rules of access and passage. In the specific case of the Magindanaos, this new border was fixed by the establishment of the Moro Province.[47] Ali's resistance was a futile attempt to prevent the irreversible process of disengaging Magindanao society from its Southeast Asian base and relocating it within Philippine "boundaries."[48] In doing so, it shared the fate of an earlier revolt by Perak Malay chiefs, who rebelled after being informed that a "British protectorate" would deprive them of their power and their slaves. Their defiance and the ensuing arming of the *cotta* were repeated many years later, this time by a Magindanao man of prowess. Like the Perak chiefs, Ali's act of defiance would also fail.[49]

Yet American tenacity in pursuing Ali was not the main reason for his death. Rather, it was the betrayal of his own father-in-law, Datu Piang, that brought about his end. Piang had earlier masterminded the divorce of his daughter from Ali on the grounds of spousal abuse.[50] With his daughter back in his home, Piang had no qualms about giving Ali to the Americans.[51] Piang's betrayal not only marked the end of an alliance that had effectively ruled Cotabato in the last years of Spanish rule, but it marked the beginning of a collaborative relationship between the more astute Piang and the new power in Cotabato.

The Collaborator

Unlike Datu Ali, the Americans were more congenial to Piang not only because of his instant support but because many were sympathetic to his "humble" nonroyal origins and rags to riches life story.[52] The American perception of Piang was typified by this official account:

> He is very shrewd, has brains and is self-made, being now quite wealthy and a power in the valley, as he controls all of Dato Ali's influence over the tribes and adds to this his own brain. He is the only prominent Moro who seems to appreciate what the American invasion means and the business opportunities it brings with it. The Chinese blood in him makes him a shrewd businessman, and he has accumulated quite a fortune and is daily adding to it. He practically controls all the business of Cotabato, especially exports, through his Chinese agents in that place; has complete control of the Moro productions, and working with the Chinese merchants makes it practically impossible for a white firm to enter into business in the Rio Grande, even with much capital behind them.[53]

Piang quickly exploited this positive perception to firm up his hold over the Magindanaos. He saw to it that he would become richer. By the late Spanish period, Piang had already amassed a fortune through control of the trade between communities in the interior and the coastal areas. This wealth was aided by ties with the local Chinese, who traded in wax, coffee, rubber, and gutta percha.[54] Under the Americans, this partnership blossomed further when Piang and his associates gained full control of the trade in gutta percha, an insulating material for the trans-Pacific cable that was then being laid.[55] They also took over the "Moro Exchanges," an internal marketing system set up by the army to facilitate trade between communities without Chinese middlemen.[56] Piang convinced the Americans that instead of excluding the Chinese it would be more productive to include them in the exchanges, especially since they would be paying a big portion of the sales tax. The exchanges thus fell under the control of and was eventually subordinated to the interests of the Cotabato Merchants' Association, the organization joined by the Chinese, aspiring American entrepreneurs, and Datu Piang.[57] Army officials acquiesced to all this since Piang kept Cotabato peaceful.[58] Piang branched out into other ventures, notably the budding timber and rubber industries and rice milling.[59] When the army mandated the need to have land titled, Piang was one of the first to take advantage of the policy and amassed much land.[60] He also became a moneylender, netting four to five thousand pesos a month.[61] By the decade's end, Piang was the wealthiest *datu* of Cotabato. He had very few rivals; Ali was dead, and Datu Uto had retired, "sulking in the back country, refusing to have anything to do with the Americans though not averse to borrowing from Piang the money that the crafty Oriental won at trade from the invader."[62]

Access to colonial state followed economic bounty. As one of the many rewards for his cooperation, Piang was appointed tribal ward leader of Dulawan. The position was created to help in the collection of the head tax and so that its appointee could convey and interpret colonial laws and policies to his constituents. Piang dutifully fulfilled his responsibilities but also took advantage of the opportunity to pursue his own interests. For example, he convinced the Americans to give him a say on tribal ward selections. This enabled him to get members of his entourage appointed, among them his old allies Datus Balabadan and Kali of Pandapatan and even the half-brother of Datu Ali, who had helped Piang betray his former brother-in-law. He also convinced the Americans to appoint as ward leader the weak Datto Mastula, heir to the Magindanao Sultanate.[63] This appointment not only enhanced Piang's standing among the Magindanaos, for it restored some credibility to the old sultan, but it also fit in well with American intentions to use Magindanao royal families for pacification purposes.[64]

Piang did not hesitate to abuse his power, knowing fully well that his indiscretions would be ignored by the Americans. The latter looked the other way when Piang used force against those who opposed him and to collect taxes for the state and tribute for himself.[65] With American consent, he also

> designated himself "Chief of the Central District of Cotabato." . . .
> [He] moved towards Dulawan and attacked Pikit, Reina Regente
> and Tumbao, thereby adding these places to his sphere of influ-
> ence and making the heads of these areas pay tribute to him.
> Having increased his power over the two mouths of the Pulangi
> River, he gained stature among the datus of the valley.[66]

He did not hesitate to expropriate assets, even those of other pro-American *datus*, knowing that in the final analysis the Americans would continue to support him. Thus, when a certain Datu Bakki protested to the Philippine Commission that Piang had "stolen 73 of his carabaos," destroyed his fields, stole his rice harvest, killed his nephew and cousin, and carried off "one hundred and eighty three of his people," the commission promised to investigate. Nothing came of it since army officers refused to testify against Piang.[67] Piang was also exempted from antislavery laws. He was allowed to keep his old slaves, although he was prohibited from acquiring more.

The Americans were not entirely comfortable with Piang's actions. Sometimes they had to step in and disapprove some of his antics, such as when he "repeatedly requested to be placed in charge of [collecting the taxes of] all the dattos in the valley, saying that he alone could preserve order and collect taxes without difficulty."[68] In general, however, Piang was allowed to exercise his political power among the Magindanaos provided that it did not disturb the peace.

In power, he carried himself with bravado, not missing an opportunity to display the marks of his dominance. Thus, for the marriage of his daughter Narig to the son of his ally Datu Balabada (Balabaran?) of Taviran, Piang ordered the construction of a royal barge complete with "Moro paraphernalia," including twenty to thirty *agongs* (brass drums) and *lantakas* (small cannons). He announced that he would give his son-in-law P800 in coins and "goods," and at the ceremony he was "dressed in an undershirt with buttons made of Spanish gold pieces and a white sarong."[69] With wealth and political influence, came the opportunity to reinvent and be reinvented. Piang had himself declared the sultan of Mindanao despite his nonroyal status.[70] He had his *tarsila* (genealogy) rewritten to indicate royal blood, justifying his claim to the leadership of Cotabato.[71] This *tarsila* was rumored to resemble closely the bloodline of an admired idol, the seventeenth-century Kudrat.[72] The Americans contributed to Piang's reinvention through constant references to his role in keeping Cotabato peaceful. Annual official reports, as well as the accounts of those who met him, were littered with guarded praise.[73] The American fixation on Piang's "prowess" even extended to the mythical: one admirer wrote a novel about his youth, complete with episodes recounting battles with the supernatural.[74]

What became increasingly important for Piang, however, was that in the recasting of his persona he needed to be linked not only with the past but with the present. It was not enough to declare himself Kudrat's heir or even to claim as a relative one of the Prophet's disciples. He also needed to show that his prestige was broader because of what he had assimilated from the Americans. Thus, though accepting the tribal ward leadership was a demotion, he turned it to his advantage by weaving tales to the Magindanaos about how he was using the Americans to administer Cotabato "at his request."[75]

Transition to Colonial Big Man

As mentioned, Piang's story has often been associated with Filipino politicos who collaborated with the Americans instead of continuing the nationalist revolution. I also argued that Piang's actions were informed by a different political frame. Likening Piang to his Filipino counterparts puts the cart before the horse. Indeed, he did become known as a local strongman in what would eventually become a special province of Philippines. But in the encounter with the Americans, it was his Southeast Asian context that underpinned his actions as *datu*. To what extent was Piang's power indicative of this context? Malay modalities of "men of prowess" were clearly operating when Piang first sought to break Datu Uto's power by creating his own faction, when he entered into marriage alliances with Ali, and when he relied on a loyal entourage for support against Uto.[76] Even stories of his sexual prowess, a quality associated with power in Southeast Asia, were deliberately spread to magnify the extent of his power.[77] Piang's agreement with the Spanish and cooperation with the Americans can likewise be understood through a Southeast Asian prism. Wolters notes how Muslim polities joined forces with certain European "country traders" to "thwart the monopolistic plans of other Europeans."[78] It was also within the norm for *orang besar* to seek the assistance of more powerful foreign forces to alter the internal balance of power in their favor. Perak's Datu Abdullah, for example, accepted British protection because the British "would make him Sultan" and force the other *datus* to recognize him as such.[79] Abdullah's actions occurred at almost the same time that Piang and Ali were seeking Spanish aid in their struggle against Datu Uto.[80]

Piang's relationship with the Spanish and later the Americans helped him keep his power and prestige stable at home. Like other Southeast Asian strongmen, he used colonial firepower "to exert influence in the peripheries" and avoid stories of "instability at the centre [which] traveled quickly and reduced his outreach."[81] With the Americans also came the opportunity to further enrich himself by playing the ingenious role of the broker who kept the balance between community and authority and among the different groups inside the community itself.[82] To the Magindanaos, he projected himself as their link to the colonizers, a representative who could keep the Americans responsive to their needs. To the Americans, he promoted himself as the only person who could preserve Magindanao loyalty to the Moro Province. The result of acting like a *penghulu* (sole leader) was the reinforcement of his own power. There was therefore no doubt that Piang's decision to collaborate was very much influenced by his being a man of prowess. It would be erroneous to ignore this context—the experiential foundation of his actions—in order to dramatize the similarity of his actions to those of Filipino *caciques*. The similarities cannot be denied, but neither should one reify Piang's actions out of a world that had—until the Americans arrived— very little in common with the rest of the colony.

The next question to ask, then, is at what point Piang ceased to think like an *orang besar* and opted to become part of the colonial state. I would suggest that this occurred when Piang, even as he tried his *orang besar's* best to cope with the Americans, realized that the new order represented a major change in the lives of the Magindanaos. Piang may have attained unprecedented control over Cotabato, but he also knew that his power remained precarious. With prodding from his Chinese allies, who wanted a return to stability, he requested American troops to ensure the maintenance of peace and order in Cotabato.[83] Although Piang and Ali's Christian rivals had been crushed, other Muslim men of prowess had not. On the northern periphery of Magindanao society, Lanao *datus* were threatening to defy and do battle with the Piang-Ali alliance.[84] American firepower provided the opportunity for Piang and Ali to unify Magindanao society once again.

Yet this request for aid from an outside power was different from earlier appeals to the Spanish. For one thing, it came at a time when Magindanao was past its prime as a trading center, its once dominant position in southern Mindanao already upstaged by Sulu.[85] Piang may have become "the most powerful man in Cotabato," but he was also aware that his power rested on very weak foundations and his choices were limited. Trade in gutta percha had declined as the supply dwindled due to excessive harvesting.[86] The slave system, the most important base of any *orang besar's* power, was gone, and those, like Ali, who defied the new regulations were systematically destroyed by the Americans.[87] Colonial taxation likewise signified not only loss of income but submission to a higher authority, which was a demotion in stature for a man of prowess. Piang not only had to pay the Americans for allowing him to engage in trade—a hitherto unheard of practice—but his payment signified recognition of their preeminence.

Finally, with the creation of districts with explicit boundaries, there was a redefinition of what the Magindanao understood as their territory. They became attached to and bounded by a well-defined area called Cotabato District. With this reclassification, the earlier Southeast Asian notions of domain had changed; the *sa-ilud* and *sa-raya* (or *hulu* and *hilir*) were giving way to district, municipal, and village councils. Even the "tribal wards"—thought by the Americans to be the best way to reorganize non-Christian groups—were administrative mechanisms alien to Magindanao society.[88] American colonialism also created a barrier that cut Magindanao off from the rest of the Southeast Asian trading network. It did so by setting up barriers to regulate and control a trade that was once "free" and administered by the *orang besar*. American colonialism thus sealed off Magindanao society, albeit not thoroughly, from the trading system on which much of its earlier history was based.[89] Those who continued to operate under the old system were declared illegal traders and were liable to be prosecuted. Magindanao traders either had to operate under the new perimeter rules (and likewise submit to the extractions attendant to it, i.e., customs and revenue taxes) or be declared "smugglers" and be subjected to relentless pursuit by the Americans.[90]

Piang was not blind to these changes. With the slave trade over, he knew that trade in goods had become the crucial basis of his wealth.[91] Land was also a new source of wealth, especially once the Americans declared their intentions to "open up" and exploit the resources of Mindanao. Piang adjusted accordingly and with considerable success. By 1926, he had diversified,

> accumulat[ing] so much wealth during the three or four decades of his power: 42,000 coconut trees (they are good for $1 per tree each year), thousands of carabao, thousands of hectares of rice, land, horses, cattle, buildings, boats and what not—to say nothing of the tithe paid him by his loyal subjects. He is also reputed to have a huge hoard of gold coins.[92]

The setting up of administrative borders within and around southern Mindanao also meant a redirection of trade inward, that is, toward the Americans and Manila. Most important of all, Piang became aware that to keep his power and influence he had to accept the conditions imposed by the new colonial reality. He could not rely any longer on Southeast Asian–style alliances with fellow *datus*; the downfall of his predecessor had taught him that no one could be "lord" of the Magindanao as Kudrat had been.[93] In order to survive, he had to depend on the Americans. Members of his entourage were likewise drawn to American power. They were more and more likely to seek out his opponents and together try to draw the Americans away from him for their own purposes.

There was little choice but to alter the old notion of prowess and suit it to the terms preferred by the Americans. This meant acquiring the necessary "official" pedigree associating him with the colonial state. The pedigree in turn brought new opportunities to enhance his influence through the use of the powers associated with his office. It was in this context that one can understand why this purportedly most powerful Magindanao *datu* welcomed the American presence. Piang may have inherited firepower from the Spanish, but he also acknowledged American military superiority; he needed the Americans to remain in power, especially after betraying his own son-in-law.[94] This act ironically became another reminder of the fragility of the sultanate, which had led to the downfall of Datu Uto. Unlike Uto, however, Piang saw a way out of the dilemma by placing all his bets with the new power. It meant, in turn, accepting that the Magindanaos had become a part of the colonial territory. Piang henceforth had to play a different role, one that combined aspects of the old with features of the new. He was still a man of prowess among the Magindanao, but it was a title set upon entirely different foundations. With Piang, the era of the *orang besar* in southern Mindanao came to a close; he remained a big man, but this time he was operating in a more constricted world.

Filipinization and the Constriction of the Colonial Big Man's World

No sooner had Piang accustomed himself to his new world than it underwent yet another modification. This time the source of change came from an authority beyond Piang's reach—in Manila and Washington. By the second decade of American rule, the ambiguity of U.S. imperial policy had given way to a consensus with Filipino leaders that the business of colonial administration should increasingly be taken over by Filipinos.[95] The Filipinization of the colonial state also called for the hastening of the integration of the "special provinces," including the Moro Province of southern Mindanao. Army leaders who still believed that President McKinley's doctrine of "Benevolent Assimilation" meant two generations of close supervision of their "Moro wards" resisted Filipinization and integration as best as they could.[96] Mindanao Americans likewise agitated for a separation of Mindanao on the grounds that no bond existed between its inhabitants and the rest of the Philippines except perhaps warfare.[97] However, they failed in the face of their own inadequacies, the failure to muster enough "popular" support among Mindanao communities, and the dogged insistence of Filipinos that Mindanao was an intrinsic part of the Philippines.[98]

Muslim leaders responded differently to Filipinization. Many sided with the Americans and even mobilized their followers for separation—and when this appeared not to be feasible for the autonomy of Mindanao from the state.[99] On the eve of the formal transfer of power, however, it was clear that the Muslims themselves were unable to unite behind their military mentors. Pro-Filipinization forces managed to gain the support of most of the *datus* of Lanao, and even the sultan of Sulu was eventually swayed in their favor.[100] By 1913, the Moro Province was formally abolished and Cotabato, together with Davao, Lanao, Sulu, and Zamboanga, were reclassified as new "special provinces" under the Manila-directed Department of Mindanao and Sulu.[101] Manuel Quezon, leader of the Filipino politicos, declared that the Muslims had the same "racial identity" as Filipinos and, although they lived in "primitive conditions," they were ready for Filipinization.[102]

Datu Piang's first response to Filipinization was to support the Americans.[103] But once it became clear that Filipinization was inevitable he hedged his bets. He declared his allegiance to Manila after the establishment of the Department of Mindanao and Sulu. And to prove his loyalty to a skeptical Filipino leadership he gave his blessing to the expansion of public education in the Muslim areas, a controversial subject, as the majority of Muslims regarded the program as part of a Filipino conspiracy to eradicate Islam in Mindanao.[104] Piang also encouraged his children's involvement in the integration process, ordering them among other things to represent him in delegations to Manila organized by the department. He likewise agreed to send his two sons to the colonial center for higher education.[105] In 1915, Piang was rewarded for his cooperation with an appointment to the lower house of the Philippine Assembly.[106]

Piang, however, remained sensitive to who wielded the ultimate power and made sure that he had a foot on the other side. After the Department of Mindanao and Sulu was established, he continued to secretly support the separatist plans of other *datus,* including his sons. He promised to help fund a Muslim delegation to Washington, which would lobby for the separation of Mindanao and compete with Quezon for the attention of Congress.[107] His actions were replicated by other *datus,* who were aware of the increasing likelihood of Filipinization but remained hopeful that anti-Filipino Americans would stage a comeback and reassert control over Mindanao. But, since the U.S. Army had rendered them powerless, they had few resources with which to fight Manila. Once the army left, their options narrowed further; the only way that the status quo ante could return was for the *datus* to convince the Americans in Washington to set the clock back.[108] This is the reason Piang supported the idea of a Muslim delegation.[109] Yet Piang had enough experience to recognize that the likelihood of Filipinization succeeding was also strong. Thus, even as he tried to play off one side against the other, it was making his life difficult. He described this dilemma to his American friends, complaining that Filipinization had placed him in the "difficult position" of maintaining dual loyalties.[110]

The chances that the Americans would reverse Filipinization improved in 1921 when a presidential victory by the Republican Party brought about a change of regime in the Philippines and the appointment of "Datu" Leonard Wood as governor-general. Wood's appointment caused reverberations in southern Mindanao, especially after he expressed his opposition to the forced Filipinization and integration of Mindanao.[111] Wood proceeded to undo the structures and policies of Filipinization, including reorganizing the administration of southern Mindanao to strengthen his influence in it.

Wood pushed for changes in the jurisdiction of the Bureau of Non-Christian Tribes and intervened in provincial affairs to challenge Filipino control over the Muslims. He proposed that the bureau be transferred to the American-controlled Department of Public Instruction. He also summarily replaced Filipino officials with Americans under the pretext that *datus* were more at ease working with "los Americanos" than the detested Filipinos. Wood kept himself closely informed about Muslim affairs. He took two trips a year to Mindanao and received Muslim leaders who visited Manila. All the while, he assured the Muslims that Philippine independence was not in the offing and the United States was not contemplating withdrawal from the colony.[112] His claims were later backed up by the recommendations of a special investigator sent by Washington to restore some autonomy in Mindanao.[113]

Wood's actions were resented by the Filipinos but raised hopes among the Muslims.[114] The latter's optimism was further invigorated by the introduction of a bill in the U.S. Congress to separate Mindanao from the Philippines and restore the "Moro Province," which would be governed by officials directly appointed by the American president with Senate concurrence.[115] The ensuing battle between Wood and his sympathizers, on the one hand, and the Filipinos on the other were interpreted by many *datus* as signs of a weakening center. This, in turn, precipitated acts of disloyalty from below.[116] The excitement of a possible return to American direct rule was reflected in a meeting between Wood and the *datus*:

> When General Wood asked all of those present desirous of continued American rule to raise their hands, every Moro in the room threw up first one hand and then the other until pandemonium broke loose, the only unenthusiastic observers being a few representative Filipinos who stood looking on grimly with folded arms. The foremost datus began to execute a dance, and the cheering and stamping rose in volume until two sultans danced forward and each of them embraced one of the two members of the mission.[117]

Datus also began to be more open about their true intentions. Those in favor of integration were the first to support Wood and criticize what they called the excesses of Filipinization.[118] Hadji Butu, who voted for Philippine independence in the Senate, switched sides to advocate the retention of American rule in Mindanao even if the Philippines became independent.[119] Others followed suit; the rivals Datu Mandi and Hadji Abdulla Nuno set aside their differences and declared themselves firmly in support of American rule.[120] The separatist spirit was eventually embodied in a "Declaration of Rights and Purpose" manifesto addressed

to President Coolidge demanding the creation of an "independent constitutional sultanate" for "the Moro nation."[121]

Datu Piang himself was enthusiastic about the changes. Although he
did not express this in public, in a rare interview with Vice Governor
Joseph R. Hayden, Piang, who had aged considerably, expressed his real
views. He was particularly optimistic that the Bacon Bill would be able to
correct the betrayal of a promise made by the U.S. Army.

> The American Army officers who governed us then were good
> men and just. They gave us assurance that they would protect us
> and not turn us over to those whom we do not trust. Whether
> those officers had the power to make those promises we do not
> know. But we trusted them. But year after year, slowly, they have
> given the Christian Filipinos more power over us. Their laws are
> too complicated for us; the Moros need a simple government.
> Our own is more simple, ours are laws that have been handed
> down from father to son for many centuries. My sons have told
> [me of] one of the bills presented to Congress by Mr. Bacon of
> New York. They tell me that this is to separate Mindanao, Sulu
> and Palawan from the rest of the Philippines. That would be bet-
> ter. Perhaps not the best solution but better than present condi-
> tions. . . . My sons tell me that if this bill of Mr. Bacon becomes a
> law then more capital would come to Mindanao. That would be
> good. Then we would have those roads and telegraphs. My old-
> est son has been in the United States. He tells me that the farm-
> ers there have those things and are happy and prosperous.[122]

With advancing age, Piang had to pass the responsibility for conducting
his family's politics to his children, Abdullah, Gumbay, and Ugalingan,
although he remained the final arbiter in any major decision.[123] With
Piang's blessing, they joined the chorus, championing the Bacon bill and
signing the manifesto.[124] They likewise sought to bring the different
Muslim *datus* and the sultan of Sulu to a "conference" that would "present a solid front against the Christians."[125] With the assistance of a former American soldier, Piang's sons had also created a "Moro
Commission on Separate Government," with headquarters in Cotabato,
which committed itself to establishing a newspaper to promote sepa-
ratism and spearheading the organization of the planned delegation to
Washington.[126]

This animated resurgence of anti-Manila sentiments among the very
datus who earlier had claimed allegiance to Filipinization ended abruptly when Wood died. Suddenly the *datus* were without their purported
guardian, and when Wood's successor, Henry Stimson, declared himself
in favor of a return to "Filipino-American cooperation" their minirevolt

was doomed.[127] A despondent and now ailing Datu Piang wrote a letter to President Coolidge, mourning the death of Wood. The letter also expressed what may have been the general sentiment of the Muslim *datus* with regard to Wood's passing. He wrote:

> After our mastery by the Americans, we expected to be ruled by them. This was vouchsafed and promised us. To that end, there was set up by your able military commanders a government simple, clear of understanding, and suited to our position and condition. The Moros were a large part of the government. Enforcement of its edicts was by Americans assisted by Moros. All was moving well when suddenly it was decreed from Washington and Manila that "the government was to be changed for one complex in organization, 'soothing' in its operation, effective in its results" (the intent in Washington was apparently not to the detriment of the Moros). And, from Manila, it has been carried out in a manner the most humiliating to the Moros . . . ever imposed by a great power upon a loyal and helpless people. Early there swarmed over our country, under the aegis of the American flag, buttressed by bayonets (who never dared come otherwise) an array of Filipino office holders . . . and pressing closely in their wake [were] civilians, all equally indifferent of our welfare and equally greedy of spoils. Remote was the dream of the Moros from degradation, to extortion, he was soon to become the victim.[128]

Datu Piang lived for another six years with his wives and forty-one of his children.[129] He witnessed his sons' reintegration into a Filipino-dominated colonial politics. His eldest son Abdullah was appointed to the Philippine Assembly, while Ugalingan became a member of the Dulawan Municipal Council and a strong advocate of public education.[130] At midnight on August 23, 1933, Datu Piang died at the age of eighty-seven, leaving a legacy that reflected the extent to which Magindanao society had blended with the new colonial order.

What informed Piang's responses to Filipinization? Were they reflective of a growing knack for opportunism that had become the norm in Philippine colonial politics? If such was the case, did this mean that integration had begun to work? Or were these rearguard actions of an indigenous leadership further weakened by Manila's reach? If one goes by motive alone, these questions have their respective answers. Yet, if we add the context, the image becomes a bit more variegated. Rather than merely attributing these *datus'* actions to opportunism or desperation, we can see in their overlapping and contradictory responses an effort by Muslim elites to negotiate their way through political change.

The switching of sides, the discrepancy between public declarations and private assurances, and the attempt to play Americans against Filipinos were less the actions of astute operators or small-time conspirators than of a "local elite" unsure of its fate. In the *datus'* eyes, the Americans appeared to give way to the Filipinos, but even this was not definite, as the return of Leonard Wood seemed to portend.

It was only when Filipinization was restored in the post-Wood period and was sure of becoming permanently established in Mindanao that these political ambiguities were clarified. Anti-Filipino and separatist sentiments steadily diminished in rhetoric and influence as more *datus* accepted Filipino rule.[131] These *datus* grudgingly recognized a change in their fortunes and had to—if only to survive—accommodate themselves to it. While many quickly learned the art of working with the Filipinos, others perceived that the new system might be beyond their capabilities. They had neither the wherewithal, the knowledge, or the experience to deal with Filipinization. A new generation of leaders, more familiar with the new order, had to emerge, and the more forward-looking of the old *datus* were perceptive enough to recognize this.

Piang was one of them. He was clearly unhappy with Filipinization. He despised the Filipinos and was aware that Filipinization would eventually have a regressive impact on Magindanaos. He complained that with Manila's blessing lands in Cotabato would eventually be taken over by Christian settlers and the "shrines [where] once his ancestors gathered in solemn worship [would be] converted into pig-wallows or drinking shops."[132] His estrangement was not only based on his fears of what would happen to his community. He was also clearly unable to deal with his new role as "representative of the Moro people" in the colonial state. Elliot smugly wrote that when he was appointed to the Philippine Assembly Piang appeared more concerned with "soliciting government aid to retrieve one of his wives who had run away from the over-populated home" than thinking about how best to represent the Muslims.[133] He was unfamiliar with the assembly's procedures, and life in Manila during the regular sessions was alienating. Harrison had this description of how Piang and other Muslim leaders fared in the legislature.

> Senator Hadji Butu and Representatives Dato Benito, Dato Tampugaw and Dato Piang regard their residence in Manila during the sessions as a sort of exile. I remember seeing Dato Piang, the powerful "boss" of Cotabato Valley, sitting one afternoon at the window of his residence in Manila. His old face was expressive of unhappy longing for his wide rice-fields and herds of carabao [water buffalo] in the Cotabato Valley. To these older

men, the "Manila Government" is something far away from the needs and realities of Moro life.[134]

Yet Piang was cognizant that Filipinization might have its political benefits, though this time to a new generation of Muslim leaders. This explains why he opted to send his sons to school and worked to get them involved in the Philippine Assembly. Piang understood that the world of the *orang besar* had ended with the demise of American rule, and he came to accept the narrowing of his boundaries to those of the Moro Province. He resisted Filipinization because it threatened this constricted world protected by the Americans, but he also began to see the possibility of working his way out of this predicament by linking up with Manila, albeit this time through the activities of his sons. Again, Harrison notes:

> [These datus] have, however, a wholesome respect and admiration for their young men who are educated in the American school system. Behind all their self-assertion there is a safe and sane understanding that their followers must perforce forever abandon the old life of incessant warfare, and that now the only way for them to protect their rights is to square themselves with modern conditions and a modern system of government.[135]

Piang did not live to see this change in attitude. His children, however, picked up where he left off. One month after his death, his eldest son Abdullah, once a leading coconspirator in the plan to convince Washington to grant autonomy to Mindanao, declared in his first legislative speech that if the Bacon bill was passed "I will reside during the rest of my life in Manila because I do not want to separate from you." He added: "Look at my skin. The blood that runs in my veins is not different from that of you Christian Filipinos."[136]

Conclusion

Datu Piang's death on August 23, 1933, went largely unnoticed. There were no announcements of his passing, no half-mast flags even in Cotabato, and no statements of condolence by politicians—American, Filipino, or Muslim—Manila's newspapers, or the public. This slide to obscurity in a way mirrored the diminution of Mindanao from a regional hub to an autonomous province to an integrated but peripheral fragment of the Philippines. The story of Piang is the story of Mindanao as it became bound to the colonial body politic and transformed into a local unit whose history is subordinated to the larger Philippine narrative.

Scholars of the Philippines accept without question the peripheral character of Mindanao. As I have tried to show in this essay, this condition was not intrinsic to the island but the product of politico-historical changes under American colonial rule. Mindanao and Muslim leaders like Piang could have easily moved in other directions. Had the Magindanaos succeeded in keeping the Spanish and Americans out of southern Mindanao, their relations with the Southeast Asian regional trading network would have continued. Later, had the U.S. Army succeeded in keeping the Moro Province autonomous from Manila (or, perhaps better, separated), Magindanaos and others might today live like the residents of Hawaii, Guam, and the other American Pacific territories. That these events never took place is a truism, but their possibility showed that there was nothing immutable about Mindanao as the Philippine periphery.

Muslim political involvement did not end with Piang's death. A new generation, which Harrison predicted would "square themselves with modern conditions and a modern system of government," began to make its presence felt in colonial politics, albeit in a limited role. Age and education were the most obvious differences between these new leaders and their antecedents. But there was more. In his first speech before the convention created to draft the constitution of the Philippine Commonwealth, Aluya Alonto, representative from Lanao, implored his fellow delegates to stop referring to all Muslims as "Moros."

> We do not like to be called "Moros" because when we are called "Moros" we feel that we are not considered as part of the Filipino people. You also know that the name "Moro" was given to us by the Spaniards because the Morocco had been under the rule of Spain like Mindanao and Sulu. *So that I would like to request the members of this Convention that we prefer to be called "Mohammedan Filipinos"* and not "Moros," because if we are called Moros we will be considered as enemies, for the name "Moro" was given to us by the Spaniards because they failed to penetrate into the Island of Mindanao.[137]

NOTES

Research for this essay was supported by funds from the Social Science Research Council Dissertation Fellowship and the Mellon Foundation–Cornell University Department of Government Dissertation Write-up Fellowship. I am grateful to Donna Amoroso, Benedict Anderson, Alfred McCoy, Vivienne Shue, Takashi Shiraishi, and O. W. Wolters for their comments and criticism of this work in its present and previous forms. All shortcomings of this essay are solely mine.

1. Vic Hurley, *Swish of the Kris: The Story of the Moros* (New York: E. P. Dutton, 1936), 154–56.
2. See Reynaldo C. Ileto, "The 'Unfinished Revolution' in Philippine Political Discourse," *Southeast Asian Studies* 312, no. 1 (June 1993): 62–82. Teodoro Agoncillo and Renato Constantino, regarded as the two foremost advocates of Philippine nationalism, have in their respective works given only cursory attention to the Muslims: Agoncillo a mere four pages and Constantino only five. See Teodoro Agoncillo and Milagros Guerrero, *History of the Filipino People* (Quezon City: R. P. Garcia, 1973); and Renato Constantino, *The Philippines: A Past Revisited* (Quezon City: Tala Publishing, 1975). The nationalist "right" shares the same proclivity. See O. D. Corpuz, *The Roots of the Filipino Nation,* vol. 2 (Quezon City: AKLAHI Foundation, 1989), 329–30.
3. Samuel K. Tan, "Unity and Disunity in the Muslim Struggle," in *Selected Essays on the Filipino Muslim* (Marawi City: Mindanao State University Research Center, 1982), 62–69; Alunan Glang, *Muslim Secession or Integration?* (Quezon City: R. P. Garcia, 1969), 47; Cesar Adib Majul, "The Role of Islam in the History of the Filipino People," *Asian Studies* (August 1966): 304.
4. Melvin Mednick refers to American colonialism as having brought together two parallel sociocultural streams in Philippine society — the "Islamized Malays" of southern Mindanao and the "Hispanized Christian Malays" of the central and northern Philippines (except the northern regions of the Cordilleras). He adds: "It was not until the assumption of colonial jurisdiction of the Philippines in 1898 and the resulting pacification of the Moros that the separate streams of development came together" (*Encampment of the Lake: The Social Organization of a Moslem-Philippine [Moro] People* [Chicago: Department of Anthropology, University of Chicago, 1965], 4).
5. Samuel K. Tan, *The Filipino Muslim Armed Struggle, 1900–1972* (Manila: Filipinas Foundation, 1977), 39 (on Tahil), 41 (on Santiago). The Americans were well aware of the ambiguity of Muslim responses, noting that even those who professed to be their "allies" and "friends" could be the first to break into revolt, especially in the volatile district of Lanao. See Edward Bowditch, "Military Taming of the Moro," n.d., Capt. Edward Bowditch Papers, Rare Manuscript Collection, Carl A. Kroch Library, Cornell University, 31, 35–36.
6. On the "wars" between the Muslims and the north, see James Frances Warren, *The Sulu Zone, 1768–1898: The Dynamics of External Trade, Slavery, and Ethnicity in the Transformation of a Southeast Asian Maritime State* (Quezon City: New Day Publishers, 1985). American colonial perceptions of Muslim

"distinctiveness" were aided by such studies as Najeeb Saleeby, *Studies in Moro History, Law, and Religion,* Department of the Interior Ethnological Survey Papers, no. 4 (Manila: Bureau of Public Printing, 1905); and *The History of Sulu* (Manila: Filipiniana Book Guild, 1963).

7. Some scholars argue that Muslim "ethnic pride, a keen sense of freedom and consciousness of individualism" prompted the revolts. Again the historical evidence shows the unreliability of these factors as rallying symbols for a united Muslim opposition. Muslim alliances broke down as fast as they were created because of both the effective "divide-and-rule" policy of the Americans and the disunity among the *datus* themselves. The American "hands-off" policy toward Islam also hindered any effort to use religion as a unifying theme (see Tan, "Unity and Disunity," 25).

8. Majul echoes the "nationalist" Constantino in this, partly attributing the failure of a unified Muslim anticolonialism to the fact that "certain influential sultans and *datus* were given gifts, salaries and flatteries" (Cesar Adib Majul, *The Contemporary Muslim Movement in the Philippines* [Berkeley: Mizan Press, 1985], 20). Tan regards this collaboration as historical and aimed at preserving "feudal" authority, in a sense very much like the Filipino *caciques'* use of American rule to preserve and expand their land-based wealth and power (*Filipino Muslim Armed Struggle,* 95, 105).

9. It is often said among Muslims that the word for slave is *bisaya,* attesting to the regard the former had for the Visayan communities in the Central Philippines.

10. Tasker Bliss, "The Government of the Moro Province and Its Problems," *Mindanao Herald,* February 3, 1909, 4.

11. Anthony Reid, *The Lands below the Winds,* vol. 2 of *Southeast Asia in the Age of Commerce, 1450–1680* (New Haven and London: Yale University Press, 1988).

12. Majul actually made this observation when he argued: "At bottom, the Muslim resistance against Spain in the Philippines was not an isolated or insignificant phenomenon *but an essential part of the general resistance of all Muslim peoples in Malaysia against Western Imperialism, colonialism and Christianity. In an important sense, the sultanates were articulations of a wider social entity, the Islamic society in the Malaysian world. It is within this context that the history of the Moro Wars should be seen to be better understood and appreciated."* Unfortunately, he failed to extend this argument into the American period, preferring to look at the Muslim reaction to the Americans as now a "part of the heritage of the entire Filipino people in the history of their struggle for freedom" (*Muslims in the Philippines* [Quezon City: University of the Philippines, 1973], 346).

13. It is especially interesting to note that nationalist scholars appear to ignore even the most obvious observations made by Americans. For example, consider this description of the Muslims: "They use titles similar to those of the Malays of Borneo and Johore. Tuang, the headman of the village; Cuano, a Justice of the Peace; Lamudia, Nacuda and Timuay, 1st, 2nd, and 3rd class judges; Gangalia, a constable; Baguadato, a principal, or Cabeza; Maradiadina, eldest son of a principal. . . . Like the Malays, they call the heir of a rajah the Rajah-muda; the nephew of a sultan uses the epithet Paduca; the son of the sultan calls himself Majarasi, the pure or mighty . . . Orang-Kaya corresponds to a magnate; Cachil, to a prince of the blood" (Frederick H. Sawyer, *The Inhabitants of the Philippines* [New York: Charles Scribner's Sons, 1900], 368).

14. Reid, *Lands below the Winds*. See also the following literature, invariably an incomplete listing: Anthony Reid, ed., *Southeast Asia in the Early Modern Era: Trade, Power, and Belief* (Ithaca and London: Cornell University Press, 1993); Jennifer Wayne Cushman, *Fields from the Sea: Chinese Junk Trade with Siam during the Late Eighteenth and Early Nineteenth Centuries* (Ithaca: Cornell University, Southeast Asia Program, 1993); Kenneth R. Hall, *Maritime Trade and State Development in Early Southeast Asia* (Honolulu: University of Hawaii Press, 1985); and J. Kathirithamby-Wells and John Villiers, eds., *The Southeast Asian Port and Polity: Rise and Demise* (Singapore: Singapore University Press, 1990).

15. J. Kathirithamby-Wells, "Banten: A West Indonesian Port and Polity during the Sixteenth and Seventeenth Centuries," in Kathirithamby-Wells and Villiers, *The Southeast Asian Port and Polity*, 120.

16. Magindanao sent wax, slaves, gold, tobacco, and rice to a variety of other port-states, most notably Ternate and Melaka. It came as a surprise to the Americans, then, that the sultan of Sulu's "strongly built [Singapore] house in Balester road" was a far cry from "his decrepit home at Maymbun [*sic*], the capital of Sulu" (*Mindanao Herald*, June 15, 1907). See also John Villiers, "Makassar: The Rise and Fall of an East Indonesian Maritime Trading State, 1512–1669," in Kathirithamby-Wells and Villiers, *Southeast Asian Port and Polity*, 151.

17. Ruurdje Laarhoven, "Lords of the Great River: The Magindanao Port and Polity during the Seventeenth Century," in Reid, *Southeast Asia in the Early Modern Era*, 175–79.

18. O. W. Wolters, *History, Culture, and Region in Southeast Asian Perspectives* (Singapore: Institute of Southeast Asian Studies, 1982), 3.

19. Laarhoven, "Lords of the Great River," 163.

20. Datu Sirongan's awareness of "regional colonial politics" led him to try to placate the Spaniards by "writing a conciliatory letter to [the Spanish governor-general] begging him for pardon [for allowing the Dutch to trade in his area] and hoping thereby to avoid a fate similar to Ternate [which the Spaniards attacked in 1663]" (Laarhoven, "Lords of the Great River," 165). The case of Datto Ayunan of Cotabato was also illustrative. As one American put it: "The Datto Ayunan, who resides in the same neighborhood, also came over to the Spaniards, and learned to understand and speak Spanish very fairly. He had at least three thousand followers, and in the fighting on the Rio Grande in 1886–87 he took the field, supported the Spanish forces against the other dattos, and rendered important services" (Sawyer, *Inhabitants*, 370).

21. Barbara Watson Andaya, "Cash Cropping and Upstream-Downstream Tensions: The Case of Jambi in the Seventeenth and Eighteenth Centuries," in Reid, *Southeast Asia in the Early Modern Era*, 91–95.

22. Both areas were connected by the Pulangi River, and their conflicts structured control over the flow of goods up and down the river (Laarhoven, "Lords of the Great River," 164–68). See also Laarhoven's larger work, "From Ship to Shore: Magindanao in the 17th Century from Dutch Sources," M.A. thesis, Ateneo de Manila University, 1985.

23. Wolters, *History*, 6, 8–9, 17. Wolters's observation was "confirmed" by Philippine scholars like Mednick, who noted that among the Maranaos, a Muslim group close to the Magindanaos, "neither leader nor led were automatically fixed in their relationship to the political system by birth. An

individual could change the political group and a group could change its relationship to the hierarchy either in the physical or social sense" ("Encampment," 7).

24. Wolters, *History*, 18–19. Treaties and diplomacy were also observed among the Rotinese of eastern Indonesia and the western Malay states. On the Rotinese, see James J. Fox, "'Standing' in Time and Place: The Structure of Rotinese Historical Narratives," in *Perceptions of the Past in Southeast Asia*, edited by Anthony Reid and David Marr (Singapore: Asian Studies Association of Australia, 1982), 11. On the Malay states, see J. M. Gullick, *Indigenous Political Systems of Western Malaya* (New York: Humanities Press, 1958), 15, 106, 113, 125.

25. Hurley, *Swish of the Kris*, 154–56. The Magindanao and Joloano treaties recalls the attempt of the Malay Temenggongs to play the Dutch and British against each other while retaining control over the port of Singapore. See Carl A. Trocki, *Prince of Pirates: The Temenggongs and the Development of Johor and Singapore* (Singapore: Institute of Southeast Asian Studies, 1979), 40–60.

26. Constantino — in a typical Manila-centric fashion — thus errs when he suggests that the "Muslim south became a beleaguered fortress, a sizable segment of indigenous society that tenaciously resisted Hispanization and colonization. Because of its consequent isolation [*sic!*], it was able to preserve indigenous customs and cultures as well as to continue to receive Muslim influences" (*The Philippines: A Past Revisited*, 26).

27. Sultan of Sulu to Col. Sweet, Governor of Jolo, July 7, 1901, asking to borrow a gunboat and/or arms to "fight those who are opposed to the welfare of my country and my people," reprinted in *Affairs in the Philippine Islands*, in *Annual Report of War Department* (hereafter ARWD), 1902, 2147–48.

28. Sulu's rivalry proved especially costly, as it drew the Chinese and other traders away from Magindanao (Laarhoven, "Lords of the Great River," 179). See also James F. Warren, "Sino-Sulu Trade in the Late Eighteenth and Nineteenth Centuries," *Philippine Studies* 25 (1977): 67–78.

29. Reynaldo Ileto, *Magindanao, 1860–1888: The Career of Datu Uto of Buayan* (Ithaca: Cornell University, Southeast Asia Program, 1971).

30. *Mindanao Herald*, June 17, 1905.

31. Ileto, *Magindanao*, 8.

32. Datu Piang Biography, Joseph Ralston Hayden Papers, Bentley Historical Library, University of Michigan, Box 28–24 (hereafter JRH).

33. Frederic H. Sawyer, *The Inhabitants of the Philippines* (New York: Charles Scribner's Sons, 1900), 375.

34. The Pulangi River is one of the largest of the Philippines, and its importance as a trade and military route cannot be understated. See Miguel A. Bernad, "Five Letters Describing the Exploration of the Pulangi or Rio Grande de Mindanao, 1890," *Philippine Historical Review* 1, no. 2 (1966): 17–62.

35. On the concept of "entourage," see O. W. Wolters, "Southeast Asia as a Southeast Asian Field of Study," *Indonesia* 58 (1994), 7.

36. Ileto, *Magindanao*, 63. Ileto cites Saleeby as stating that Piang "learned his method" from his father-in-law. Ayunan was the first to "betray" Uto by transferring his support to the Spanish. The son-in-law followed suit.

37. Ruth Cabanero-Mapanao, "Maguindanao, 1890–1913: The Life and Times of Datu Ali of Kudarangan," M.A. thesis, University of the Philippines, 1985, 21.

38. Peter Gowing, *Mandate in Moroland: The American Government of Muslim Filipinos, 1899–1920* (Quezon City: New Day Publishers, 1983), 23.

39. Even Piang's father was not an exception. The ties he established with Uto and other Magindanao leaders resonated in Indonesia as well. See Denys Lombard and Claudine Salmon, "Islam and Chineseness," *Indonesia* 57 (1993): 117–20.

40. Leonard Andaya, "Cultural State Formation in Eastern Indonesia," in Reid, *Southeast Asia in the Early Modern Era,* 37. See also Gullick, *Indigenous Political Systems,* 15; and Trocki, *Prince of Pirates,* 36.

41. Jeyamalar Kathirithamby-Wells, "Restraints on the Development of Merchant Capitalism in Southeast Asia before c. 1800," in Reid, *Southeast Asia in the Early Modern Era,* 132. Kathirithamby-Wells adds: "Titles and positions were, strictly speaking, not hereditary, so that winning the personal favour of the ruler was the only guarantee of security of status and office."

42. Wolters, *History,* 18–19. This practice found resonance all over maritime Southeast Asia. See Fox, "Standing in Time and Place," 11; and Gullick, *Indigenous Political Systems,* 15, 106, 113, 125.

43. Gowing, *Mandate in Moroland,* 55.

44. Leonard Wood, "Report of the Governor-General of the Moro Province [hereafter RGMP]," *Report of the Philippine Commission,* in ARWD, September 1, 1904, 9–10.

45. In May 1904, Ali successfully ambushed pursuing American troops, killing seventeen men and two officers of the Seventeenth Infantry (*Mindanao Herald,* May 28, June 25, October 22, 1904).

46. Mapanao, "Magindanao," ix, 2.

47. The same conflict of "perceptions" may have underpinned the bargaining between the sultan of Sulu and the Americans over the right of the former to fly the American flag when he visited Singapore. The notion of border, sovereignty, and boundaries was, I believe, an issue over which the Muslims and the new colonizers were at odds. On probable Magindanao notions of "boundaries," see Wolters, *History, Culture, and Region,* 16–17.

48. These sentiments were shared by Sulu Muslims, who initially saw the formation of the Moro Exchanges as a means by which trading access to Borneo would be denied them. See Douglas Hartley, "American Participation in the Economic Development of Mindanao and Sulu, 1899–1930," Ph.D. diss., James Cook University, 1983, 27.

49. Gullick, *Indigenous Political Systems,* 106–8. But this was true not only of Perak. Trocki cites late-eighteenth-century Malay resistance to the British presence in Riau as having been aggravated by the slide to destitution of this once prosperous port (*Prince of Pirates,* 34–35).

50. The divorce—not surprisingly—coincided with Ali's revolt. See Glang, *Muslim Secession,* 47.

51. As reported one soldier, Piang's "assistant talked lucidly about the precise location and armaments of Ali's *kota.*" His own ambitious brother, Tambiluan, would also abandon him (Mapanao, "Maguindanao," 113–14).

52. He was, after all, a commoner, who rose through the ranks through the adept use of this talent.

53. ARWD, 1902, 528, as quoted in Beckett, "The Defiant," 401.

54. ARWD, 1902, 111. Piang, who maintained close relations with local Chinese entrepreneurs by virtue of his "Chinese blood," also contrived to restore some form of economic normalcy to Cotabato, which the Americans appreciated (Gowing, *Mandate,* 55).

55. RGMP, 1904, 573; Helen Taft, *Recollection of Full Years* (New York: Dodd,

Mead, 1914), 174–75. On the use of gutta percha as insulation for underwater cables, as well as the competition among Malay chiefs to monopolize its harvest and trade, see Trocki, *Prince of Pirates*, 76–77, 82, 88.

56. Gowing, *Mandate*, 127–29.
57. *Mindanao Herald*, November 16, 1907. The February 3, 1909, issue of the *Herald* listed the following leading merchants of Cotabato: Sui Funero, reputedly the wealthiest of all the Chinese, having been in Cotabato for forty years; Ya Deco, who had controlled the gutta percha trade with Datu Piang since the Spanish period; and Chin Kai, owner of the largest lumber store and agent of the shipping line Compania Maritima. Others mentioned were Messrs. Chao Sua, Celestino Alonzo (Christianized), Ty Kongco, Cua Consuy, Quipo, Ong Lee, Tan Cacao, Tan Opon, Te Liongco, Lim Peu, Ong Baco, Chu Yuqui, Dy Toco, and Tan Se Tun, all described by the *Herald* as "businessmen."
58. ARWD, 1902, 111.
59. Herman Hagedorn, *Leonard Wood: A Biography*, vol. 2 (New York: Harper and Brothers, 1931), 19. See also Jeremy Beckett, "The Defiant and the Compliant: The Datus of Magindanao under Colonial Rule," in *Philippine Social History: Global Trade and Local Transformations*, edited by Alfred W. McCoy and Ed. C. de Jesus (Quezon City: Ateneo de Manila University Press, 1982), 402.
60. Ileto, *Magindanao*, 63–64.
61. *Mindanao Herald*, November 6, 1907.
62. Hagedorn, *Wood*, 2:19. See also Mapanao, "Maguindanao," 39.
63. See *Mindanao Herald*, August 4, 1906, and August 25, 1906, on Pandapatan and Mastula, respectively. Before his appointment, the latter had been "reduced to tending store for a livelihood" (Gowing, *Mandate*, 183).
64. The *Mindanao Herald* observed that the sultan of Magindanao "is held in deep respect by the lesser Moros, and could, had he the inclination, be of great assistance to the government in keeping peace among the tribes in that section." The article continued: "It is now proposed to build him a residence at Margosa Tubig, and endeavor to make that place his headquarters, where trivial questions among his people will be settled by him. This, it is expected, will do much to inspire the Moros with confidence in the Government, as much as they prefer to remain under the Sultan's rule" (June 17, 1905).
65. *The American*, July 13, 1900.
66. Mapanao, "Maguindanao," 38–39. By extending his influence, Piang also helped facilitate American pacification efforts in Cotabato. He even volunteered his own men to help American troops conduct slave raids and mediate with other *datus* on their behalf. See Gowing, *Mandate*, 83–84; and Harold Hanne Elarth, *The Story of the Philippine Constabulary* (Los Angeles: Globe Printing, 1949), 110–11.
67. Daniel R. Williams, *The Odyssey of the Philippine Commission* (Chicago: A. C. McClurg, 1913), 199–200.
68. The reporter added, mistakenly, that Piang's "real object is presumed to be to secure an open field for 'graft'" (*Mindanao Herald*, May 19, 1906).
69. *Mindanao Herald*, March 31, 1907.
70. Ileto, *Magindanao*, 63.
71. *Tarsilas* are genealogical accounts that show the links of *datus* and sultans with past personalities whose bloodlines suggested ties to the Prophet Muhammad

or any of his relatives. These are secret, "kept securely by trusted members of a Muslim clan" lest they turn out to be invented, thus rendering the clan's claims to royal descent illegitimate. See Mohammad Fatthy Mahmoud, "The Muslims in the Philippines: A Bibliographic Essay," *Asian Studies* 12, nos. 2–3 (1974): 173.

72. Judge Japal Guiani, interview with the author, Cotabato, April 1991.

73. J. R. Hayden, "Biodata of Datu Piang," JRH, Box 28–24.

74. F. P. Stuart, *Piang: The Moro Chieftain* (New York: Julian Messner, 1941).

75. Hagedorn, *Wood*, 19.

76. Andaya, "Cultural State Formation," 37.

77. In 1907, Piang was reported to have had six wives and twenty children (*Mindanao Herald*, March 31, 1907).

78. Wolters, *History*, 25. See also Laarhoven, "Lords of the Great River," 165.

79. Gullick, *Indigenous Political Systems*, 13. On the transformation of the Perak strongmen brought about by their alliance with the British, see R. J. Wilkinson, *A History of the Peninsular Malays, with Chapters on Perak and Selangor* (Singapore: Kelly and Walsh, 1923), 124–40.

80. Ileto, *Magindanao*, 62–63. See also a discussion of the alliance that Abu Bakar, successor of the Temenggong, sought with British Governor Cavenagh as a means of "establishing himself as the major force in neighbouring Pahang and Negri Sembilan" in Carl A. Trocki, *Opium and Empire: Chinese Society in Colonial Singapore, 1800–1910* (Ithaca and London: Cornell University Press, 1990), 131–32.

81. Wolters, *History*, 20.

82. Kathirithamby-Wells, "Restraints," 137.

83. Michael Mastura, "American Presence in Mindanao: The Eventful Years in Cotabato," *Mindanao Journal* 8, no. 104 (1983), reprinted in *The Muslim-Filipino Experience: A Collection of Essays* (Manila: OCIA Publications, 1984), 78–79.

84. Mapanao, "Maguindanao," 43.

85. James Warren, "Slavery and the Impact of External Trade: The Sulu Sultanate in the 19th Century," in McCoy and De Jesus, *Philippine Social History*, 415–44.

86. "The native gutta percha supply, it is believed, is fast disappearing before the destructive methods employed by the natives and avaricious datus in gathering it" (*Mindanao Herald*, August 10, 1907).

87. Mastura, "American Presence in Mindanao," 83. In Zamboanga, provincial officials cheerfully reported that Tribal Ward 3 was "practically weapon-less" and that the "Moros [there] are in pretty bad shape" after having been banned from raiding neighboring Subano communities for slaves (*Mindanao Herald*, June 17, 1905).

88. RGMP, 1904, 6–7.

89. This sealing off was never totally successful. As the following description of a Magindanao market shows, the network still continued to reach into Cotabato Valley: "One of the largest markets in the Rio Grande Valley is held at Duluan on Tuesdays and Thursdays of each week. Almost every article of value to a Moro, from *buyo nut* to Singapore cloth of many colors, may be purchased on these days. Several Chino merchants do a thriving trade in cheap prints, silk thread, knives, buttons, etc. All kinds of money is accepted in the market; a Straits Settlements cent or a Spanish silver piece being equal in value to a centavo or peseta. An examination of 10 copper cents taken from the hand of a passing Moro showed coins from the following countries:

British North Borneo, Sarawak, Hongkong, India, Straits Settlement and the
Philippines" (*Mindanao Herald,* April 13, 1907).

90. By this time, Zamboanga-based ships owned by Americans, Filipinos,
Chinese, and even Japanese had taken over from the *praos* of the Sulu and
Magindanao sultanates as the main vehicles of trade throughout the ports
around Asia, from Singapore to Shanghai (Hartley, "American
Participation," 28). Manila, however, imposed a ban on allowing passengers
from these ports to enter the Philippines through Zamboanga or Jolo, a reg-
ulation that Mindanao governors tried to have rescinded due to the potential
loss of revenue. See Frank W. Carpenter, Department of Mindanao and Sulu,
"Report to the Governor-General, Philippine Islands, January 10, 1917, in
Report of the Governor-General of the Philippine Islands, 1917, 90.

91. Mastura, "American Presence," 84.

92. J. R. Hayden to Dr. Barr, September 21, 1926, cited in Beckett, "The Defiant
and the Compliant," 401–2.

93. Ileto, *Magindanao,* 58–63.

94. The report of the murder of one Hadji Tahib, the minister of war of the sultan
of Sulu, for being too close to the Americans may also have pushed Piang
toward this colonial option (*Mindanao Herald,* September 17, 1904).

95. On the politics of Filipinization, see Peter W. Stanley, *A Nation in the Making:
The Philippines and the United States, 1899–1921* (Cambridge: Harvard
University Press, 1984); and Michael Cullinane, "'Ilustrado' Politics: The
Response of the Filipino Educated Elite to American Colonial Rule,
1898–1907," Ph.D. diss., University of Michigan, 1989.

96. Zamboanga Americans engaged their Filipino rivals in a propaganda war, the
most vicious attack being an article in the *Mindanao Herald* with the title "A
Los Filipinos." See the reprint in *Philippines Free Press,* June 8, 1912.

97. One American columnist even recommended that all Muslim groups be transferred to Sulu so as to leave Mindanao to those Filipinos and Americans
"who cared to settle." In Sulu, a "quasi-independent sultanate could be
organize [sic] with an American Resident after the manner of the Malay
states." This, accordingly, would solve the problems of continuing anti-
Christian sentiments among the Muslims, of settling Mindanao, and, most of
all, of keeping the Muslims out of Filipino *cacique* control (*Philippines Free
Press,* August 17, 1907).

98. Nationalist agitation had reached Mindanao as early as 1906. It increased as
Filipino leaders in Manila began to broaden their power. See *Mindanao
Herald,* August 18, September 15, and September 22, 1906; and *Philippines Free
Press,* August 31, 1907.

99. Gowing, *Mandate,* 250–51; Howard T. Fry, "The Bacon Bill of 1926: New Light
on an Exercise in Divide-and-Rule," *Philippine Studies,* 3d quarter (1978):
257–73.

100. Gowing, *Mandate,* 254. In 1910, the sultan of Sulu, Jamalul Kiram, drew con-
siderable attention when, after his return from the United States, he declared
his support for integration, contending that this would strengthen his hand
against his Tausug rivals. See Wayne Wray Thompson, "Governors of the
Moro Province: Wood, Bliss, and Pershing in the Southern Philippines,"
Ph.D. diss., University of California, San Diego, 1975, 5, 198–99, 206–7; and
"Por la Isla de Mindanao, Un Gran Convencion," *Philippines Free Press,*
November 12, 1910.

101. *Philippines Free Press,* July 25, 1914.

102. Manuel L. Quezon, "The Right of the Philippines to Independence," *The Filipino People* 1, no. 2 (October 1912): 4–5.
103. Beckett, "The Defiant and the Compliant," 402.
104. Muslim *datus* who ingratiated themselves with Quezon cited Piang's construction of two public schools and his support for the primary education of Magindanao children at his own expense as proof that "the Moros [have] realized the value of public schools" (*Philippines Free Press*, May 11, 1915). See also *Philippines Free Press*, January 19, 1918.
105. On Piang's children being part of the Mindanao delegations to Manila, see *Philippines Free Press*, May 6 and October 15, 1915. Piang's second son, Ugalingan, was sent to the Central Luzon Agricultural School to study "trade and exchange" and English. According to one account, Piang became "the most advanced" among the Cotabato students (*Philippines Free Press*, January 6, 1917).
106. Charles Burke Elliot, *The Philippines to the End of the Commission Period: A Study in Tropical Democracy* (Indianapolis: Bobbs-Merrill, 1917), 443.
107. Interview with Datu Piang," in JRH, Box 28–33.
108. Florence Horn, *Orphans of the Pacific: The Philippines* (New York: Reynal and Hitchcock, 1941), 155. Many Muslims regarded their relationship with the Americans as intimate and personal, and their loyalties rarely went beyond their immediate superiors. The only exception may be the Muslim deference to Leonard Wood, which resulted from his frequent visits to the districts. See H. H. Elarth, "With Moro Soldiers," *Bulletin of the American Historical Collection* 14, no. 2 (1991): 4–6. Muslims were said to be ecstatic about the return of Wood because he renewed his close ties with them (Thomas, "Muslims but Filipinos," 100).
109. See the petition prepared by a Committee of Petitions and Communications that was part of a "Declaration of Rights and Purposes" allegedly signed by various Muslim leaders warning of "bloodshed and disorder" if Mindanao was not kept separate from the Philippines (Tan, *Critical Decade*, 47–48).
110. Hagedorn, *Wood*, 392.
111. Wood asserted that the Moros "are a unit against independence and are united for continuance of American control and, in case of separation of the Philippines from the United States, desire their portion of the islands to be retained as American territory under American control" ("Conditions in the Philippine Islands: Report of the Special Mission to the Philippine Islands to the Secretary of War," 67th Cong., 2d sess., 1922, H. Doc. 325, 21). See also Tan, *Critical Decade*, 74.
112. In a cable, Wood expressed his hope that such messages would "rectify" and "neutralize" Quezon's speeches to Muslim leaders regarding independence (November 14, 1923, Bureau of Insular Affairs, file no. 4865–150).
113. Carmi A. Thompson, "Conditions in the Philippine Islands Together with Suggestions with Reference to the Administration and Economic Development of the Islands, December 22, 1926," 69th Cong., 2d sess., 1926, S. Doc. 180, 7. The report also criticized Wood's "authoritarian" style of leadership and warned of irreparable damage to Filipino-American cooperation. Journalists sided with Wood in the effort to "expose" Filipino chicanery. See Katherine Mayo, *The Isles of Fear: The Truth about the Philippines* (New York: Harcourt, Brace, 1925), 298–99.
114. *Philippine Herald*, August 1 and 18, 1925.
115. Fry, "Bacon Bill," 267. See also "Remarks of Hon. Robert L. Bacon of New

York in the House of Representatives, February 9, 1926," in JRH, Box 28–24. Bacon, a childhood friend of Wood, led a "fact-finding" mission to the Philippines on behalf of American business. The mission was guided through Mindanao by Wood. Back in Washington, Bacon was aided in the preparation of his bill by David Barrows, former education director of the Philippines and a Wood ally.

116. Thomas, "Muslims but Filipinos," 85.
117. Forbes, *The Philippine Islands*, 47.
118. R. Joel de los Santos, "Reflections on the Moro Wars and the New Filipino," in *Understanding Islam and the Muslims in the Philippines*, edited by Peter Gowing (Quezon City: New Day Publishers, 1988), 102.
119. Hadji Butu also demanded that the Americans accord him power and prestige similar to that given the sultans of Johore and Perak by Britain (Fry, "Bacon Bill," 260, 267).
120. Forbes, *The Philippine Islands*, 2:44–45.
121. Tan, *Critical Decade*, 47–48. This movement was by no means unanimous. In Lanao, *datus* were split between the "pro-independence" and "pro-American" factions, raising fears of renewed violence in what had always been regarded as the most volatile of the Muslim provinces. See *Manila Daily Bulletin*, August 22, 1926.
122. "Interview with Datu Piang of Dulawan, 1926," in JRH, Box 28–24.
123. Joe (Hayden) to (wife) Betty (Hayden), September 12, 1926, Cotabato Province, in JRH, Box 28–24. Piang was believed to be "past seventy."
124. Thomas, "Muslims but Filipinos," 132; Fry, "Bacon Bill," 267.
125. J. R. Hayden to Betty Hayden, September 17, 1926, in JRH, Box 28–24.
126. J. R. Hayden to Dr. Bauer, September 21, 1926; Ugalingan Piang, Chairman of the Moro Commission on Separate Government, Dulawan, Cotabato, to the Governor-General, November 26, 1926; and Charles S. Cox, Publicity Manager, Moro Commission on Separate Government, to J. R. Hayden, November 18, 1926. All three letters are in JRH, Box 28–24.
127. Without Wood, the U.S. Senate also lost interest in the Bacon bill and the question of retaining the Philippines as a colony. Quezon and Osmeña reasserted their control over the colonial state and worked for the creation of the Philippine Commonwealth as a transition to full independence.
128. Datu Piang to President Coolidge, on the Occurrence of the death of Leonard Wood, August 26, 1927 [a translation], in JRH, Box 28–33.
129. Wood cynically noted that "Piang has apparently progressed in the matter of children. He has some forty-one (or forty-four; he can't remember) and about sixty dead" (quoted in Hagedorn, *Wood*, 392). The same reaction came from his successor, Tasker Bliss. See Frederick Palmer, *Bliss, Peacemaker: The Life and Letters of Tasker H. Bliss* (New York: Dodd, Mead, 1934), 91. Hayden had the number of Piang's children pegged at thirty-three with twenty dead. He also had "a number of wives" ("Biodata of Datu Piang," 2).
130. Open Letter of Gumbay Piang to his Parents and Relatives, November 20, 1934, attached to G. Piang to J. R. Hayden, December 6, 1934, in JRH, Box 27–30.
131. Kalaw, "The Moro Bugaboo," 74.
132. Mastura, "American Presence," 84.
133. Elliot, *The Philippines to the End of the Commission Period*, 443.
134. Harrison, *Cornerstone of Independence*, 118.

135. Harrison, *Cornerstone of Independence*, 118.

136. *Philippines Free Press*, October 21, 1933.

137. "Speech of Aluya Alonto on the Problem of Mindanao (Interpreted from Moro to English by Datu Marigan Saramain Alonto), August 21, 1934," in *Proceedings of the Philippine Constitutional Convention, 1934–1935* (Manila: Bureau of Printing, 1935), 420 [italics mine].

Celia Mariano-Pomeroy the day after her capture by the
Armed Forces of the Philippines, April 1952.

ROMANCING A REVOLUTIONARY: THE LIFE OF CELIA MARIANO-POMEROY

Vina A. Lanzona

I watch Celia, sitting on the floor of the hut, preparing her lesson plan. . . . There is so much of love in this wife of mine, and so much of loyalty to all that she holds dear. She is so soft and feminine that one would not think on first meeting that so much strength and determination is in her. Before I met her I had been told about "Lydia," and her four years with the Huk guerrillas . . . and I had expected a toughened woman. Then this gentle creature entered the room and put her tiny hand in mine in greeting.
— William Pomeroy, *The Forest*

William Pomeroy, an American who fought with communist guerrillas in the postwar Philippines, wrote *The Forest* (1963) not only as a memoir of his extraordinary experiences but also as a declaration of love for his wife Celia.[1] In this tale of his adventures and political convictions, Pomeroy talks at length about Celia Mariano, first and foremost as a partner and second as a revolutionary. By the end of the book, we feel that we know Celia, perhaps as well as we know Pomeroy himself. Still, what we know about her is not enough. There is much more to discover about Celia Mariano-Pomeroy, a leading revolutionary and pioneering *feminista*. Celia was the only woman ever elected to the Politburo (Political Bureau), the policy-making organ of the then Communist Party of the Philippines, the Partido Komunista ng Pilipinas, or PKP. She was involved in two revolutionary battles in her life: first, in a struggle against the Japanese during World War II and, second, in a communist-led, peasant revolution during the postwar decade. These two periods in Philippine history are also termed the Hukbalahap, or Huk, revolt after the peasant armies that fought the Japanese and then the Philippine Republic—the Hukbo ng Bayan Laban sa Hapon (or People's Anti-Japanese Army) and the Hukbong Mapagpalaya ng Bayan (the HMB or National Liberation Army). No other woman achieved a comparable position in the history of the movement and, arguably, in Philippine revolutionary history.

William Pomeroy was and still is a romantic revolutionary. His wife Celia similarly was and is a revolutionary and a romantic. But Celia admits that she was not born a revolutionary, nor does she believe that she was destined to become one. Unlike many prominent political men and women in the Philippines, Celia was not a daughter of a politician, and she had no relatives or close friends who were involved in politics. Yet she became intimately involved in the political and social changes of her time. The events and people around her inspired and shaped Celia—to become an idealist, a guerrilla, a communist, and a revolutionary. She was court-ed by the Communist Party and trained as a rebel. From the time she dis-covered her own lack of understanding of her country's situation, she was enticed to become more involved, ever so patiently, by people, mostly men, eager to make her a comrade. The changing political situation also seemed to compound Celia's politicization, although her transformation did not occur overnight. It took her three years to embrace communism, another two to become a member of the Central Committee of the PKP, and another six to rise to the Politburo. Beginning as an involved student in her college years, she worked as a courier, secretary, editor, writer, edu-cator, feminist, and intellectual in the movement. How did this "soft and feminine" woman, as Pomeroy described her, become the consummate revolutionary? This essay traces Celia's development from an "innocent girl" (as she would describe herself) to a determined woman who gave herself entirely to a revolutionary cause.

Unfortunately, Celia Mariano remains at the margins of the Philippine historical record. Although she was the highest-ranking woman in the Huks, she is barely mentioned in the major works on the Huk rebellion.[2] In presenting the life history of Celia, I also present a social history of a popular movement in the Philippines whose history may be well known but remains incomplete. Women such as Celia Mariano do not figure prominently in the literature on the Huk rebellion, despite the general perception that women were vital to the struggle. Their participa-tion—from subsidiary "helping" roles as educators, organizers, and party members to combatants and commanders—has scarcely been noted let alone perceived as something that needs to be explained. Although we have no records of the precise number of Huk women, there is no doubt that their participation was considerable in both the Hukbalahap and HMB movements. The number of Huk women commanders was also extraordinary and significant. At least six women became commanders in the seventy-six squadrons that existed as of 1944.[3] The emergence of women leaders and commanders among the Huks was unprecedented in Philippine revolutionary history. These women were comparable to and perhaps as exceptional as women in other revolutionary movements and modern armies, such as those in China and Vietnam.[4] It was indeed significant that the army of the Huks incorporated women at a time when they were not prominent actors in the Philippine political arena and were excluded from official military activities. This unique feature of the Huk movement alone calls out for alternative explorations of the rebellion.

Sketching the life of Celia Mariano-Pomeroy and narrating her story is therefore a crucial step toward enhancing our understanding of the Huk rebellion. Her biography, which is obscured within the various histories of the Huks, can likewise address more general issues about women's mobilization and contribute to the understanding of how gender shapes collective action in Philippine society.

The Huk Biography

The Huk rebellion can be seen as the culmination of years of unrest and scattered incidents of peasant uprisings that can be traced back to the late Spanish colonial period in the Philippines. The heart of the rebellion, central Luzon and some parts of southern Luzon, particularly Quezon Province, underwent dramatic transformations in response to the economic pressures of modernization that characterized the country's late-nineteenth-century colonial economy.[5] Subsistence agriculture was transformed into an export-oriented economy, making rice a cash crop. The process of utilizing land, labor, and capital to its maximum in order to satisfy the domestic and international markets similarly led to a deterioration of the once mutually beneficial, paternalistic relationship between landlords and tenants.[6] Under American rule, the state became more centralized and responsive to the interests of landlords and political elites. Indeed, the gap between landlords and their tenants intensified. While the landlords enjoyed the rewards of their economic and political power, the peasants barely met their subsistence needs and incurred heavy debts. During the 1930s, significant numbers formed peasant organizations and staged mobilizations to ensure that these grievances would be addressed by the authorities.

The Huk rebellion emerged through two separate, peasant-based struggles in the Philippines. The first, which led to the formation of the Hukbalahap in March 1942, was initiated by the Communist Party of the Philippines to resist the Japanese Army during World War II. Peasants, particularly from central Luzon, joined the guerrilla bands in great numbers, attacking and organizing raids against the Japanese. Adopting a policy of not conducting peasant-landlord confrontations to develop a broad anti-Japanese united front, the Huks nevertheless liberated the peasantry, some of whom obtained land and did not pay rent to landlords and collaborators. By the end of the Japanese occupation, the Huks came very close to establishing a civilian government in central Luzon, with the support of a large peasant base.[7]

The second stage of struggle, from 1946 to 1954, involved a revolution, a serious attempt to seize state power. Under the new Philippine Republic, then under the tutelage of the United States, the Huks were initially encouraged to operate within the framework of the constitution. Fighting did cease for a while, limited agreements were concluded, and efforts were made to secure the surrender of Huk arms. But the Philippine government made no serious effort to solve peasant problems or implement a real land reform program through either legislation or the initiation of improvements in the working conditions of the peasantry. Instead, it launched a series of actions aimed at disempowering the Huks, delegitimizing their leadership, and harassing their supporters.[8] By the end of August 1946, the PKP leadership was convinced that no truce or political reform could be achieved. Soon afterward, the movement went underground and peasants reorganized in the forests of Luzon to launch a massive resistance movement against government troops and landlords. This mobilization revitalized the Huk organization, which now became known as the Hukbong Mapagpalaya ng Bayan (HMB) or People's Liberation Army.

The peasant rebellion grew in size and organizational strength between 1946 and late 1948, with armed Huks numbering eleven to fifteen thousand, including large numbers of peasant supporters. They were able to capture more villages, driving out landlords and redistributing land among the tenants, while at the same time launching successful surprise attacks against the Philippine Constabulary.[9]

Despite its historical importance, the secondary literature on the Huk rebellion remains meager. Individual biographies of the Huks themselves therefore provide rich sources of historical material. There are currently three published memoirs written by two members of the Politburo:[10] William Pomeroy's *The Forest: A Personal Record of the Huk Guerrilla Struggle in the Philippines* (1963) and Luis Taruc's *Born of the People* (1953) and *He Who Rides the Tiger* (1967).[11] Alfredo Saulo, another prominent leader, offered his personal narrative of life as a "wanted man" in articles and a book on communism.[12] Personal histories of other Politburo leaders, particularly Jesus and Jose Lava and Casto Alejandrino, are currently being written.[13]

William Pomeroy, an American historian who joined the Huk movement in 1950 along with his wife Celia, testifies that he was attracted to the cause of national liberation and social justice. His account is moving and emotional, full of idealism and vivid experiences. He incorporates the peasants' views and perceptions of their roles in the movement in his personal notes and recollections. Luis Taruc, in contrast, claims to articulate the peasantry's views in his memoir. As the leader of the rebellion, and with a peasant background himself, Taruc considers his articulation of Huk origins and the peasant struggle as representing the views of the rebels, particularly the peasants. In language with religious overtones, he describes how the disgruntled Huks and peasants went to the hills to fight for justice for the poor, a democratic government, and greater freedom for the Philippines.

While these memoirs provide a more intimate and deeper look at the rebellion than do the strict military and political treatments, they are incomplete. Undoubtedly, the perspective of the leaders, not ordinary peasant members, is recorded in these accounts. But it can be argued that ordinary peasants and members of movements do not necessarily share the views of their leaders. As other histories of the rebellion suggest, a schism of perception developed between the party leadership and the membership of the communist movement at various times during the rebellion.[14] Not only is the peasantry's viewpoint inadequately presented in these accounts; what is even more invisible is the presence of women in the Huk movement. While Pomeroy writes extensively about Celia, her struggles and thoughts are interpreted through his own. She remains silent in his story.

It is easy to see why biographies of women such as Celia Mariano remain unwritten. Philippine history has always been rich in biographies of heroes and great leaders, but it remains almost exclusively male-centered. The few women who are immortalized in history books, such as Tandang Sora and Gabriela Silang, both heroes of Philippine revolts against Spain, have incomplete biographies and are treated as secondary figures alongside the great male leaders. Huk women such as Celia are not given their proper recognition and eminence in Philippine history. Certainly, their absence marginalizes Huk women not only within the history of the movement itself but even within historical memory. Only through the writing of life histories can these remarkable women be rescued from obscurity and a deeper understanding of the rebellion be gained.

Combining Social History and Life History

In recent decades, feminist scholars have pointed out the general neglect of women actors in history, and this has led to a reexamination of the social scientific and historical disciplines and the writing of women's histories.[15] Since most history is written by men, and features men, women's history has lacked the theoretical and methodological development of the predominant historical studies. Even social history, which attempts to give a voice to the marginalized in society, has failed until recently to seriously consider the question of women and their agency.

Perhaps the most valuable methodology that feminist scholars have utilized to tell "women's stories" is the biography, or life history. Generally undertaken through in-depth oral history interviews, these biographies provide an intimate look at participants in the making of history. The stories of these actors not only provide insight and inspiration, but they enhance our understanding of major historical events. Through biographies and oral histories, history becomes not only a presentation of events in society but a series of narratives of people and their interactions with society. Women's stories, because of their intimacy, detail, and unique perspective, provide a fuller and more accurate picture of the past, especially when combined with other historical narratives.[16]

The development of women's history also has served to empower women since it provides a voice for those whose stories would otherwise go unrecorded.[17] Sociologist Sherna Gluck explains that "women's oral history is a feminist encounter because it creates new material about women, validates women's experience, enhances communication among women, discovers women's roots, and develops a previously denied sense of continuity."[18] However, feminist historians' attempts to develop women's history as a separate entity perhaps has contributed to another type of marginalization within the discipline. As feminists, these researchers value biographical work because it not only develops feminist theories and explores the meaning of historical events in the eyes of women but serves the political purpose of expressing affinity and admiration for other women while simultaneously promoting social justice.[19] But treating women's biographies solely as a feminist, political endeavor disconnects them from other types of histories and fails to broaden the discipline of historical writing.

Focusing on the story of Celia as a revolutionary leader should be seen not only as a means of advocating women's issues but as an attempt to arrive at a deeper understanding of the processes of political and social change. Narrating the story of Celia is therefore an attempt to combine one woman's biography with the social history of her time. Her life story, which unfolded during the turbulent years of the Japanese occupation and the Huk rebellion, provides a unique perspective on these.

The presentation of Celia's life, and the Huk woman's experience in general, goes beyond what most feminist studies explain: that women are not invisible in history even though they are not the main protagonists in many historical works. While introducing Huk women into the written record is an important step toward correcting the gender-blind practice of Philippine historical writing, this study goes beyond that aim. I do not attempt to separate men and women in the Huk movement by writing a version that deals only with women. Instead, I am attempting to bring Huk men and women together.[20]

The presence and participation of women among the Huks over-turned many of the usual conventions of running a revolutionary organization. The Huks knew that having women in their movement reinforced their strength and at the same time challenged both their preconceived notions about gender roles and the cohesion among their members. While advocating an egalitarian ideology, the Huk movement was undercut by the participants' own patriarchal assumptions about appropriate gender roles and sexuality. In the end, the rebellion may have failed in part because the Huk organization was unsuccessful in addressing both the immediate needs and the deep-seated aspirations of their participants, especially women. Through Celia's life story, I probe this relationship between gender and collective action by looking at how the roles of Huk members, female and male, affected the organization's dynamics.

More broadly, Celia's story can also enhance our understanding of the processes of social change in the Philippines. At a time of great trans-formations in Philippine society, the presence of a significant number of women fighting in the hills against the state threatened the established social and gendered order within the larger society. From the outside, these women seemed both admirable and confusing. Women's involve-ment in the Huk rebellion thus marks an important transition, seldom noted, of the status and role of women in Philippine society. As is evident from Celia's life, Filipina women were capable of leaving the comfort of their homes to embrace a revolutionary cause. Despite the limitations and strict roles society imposed upon her, a woman in the Philippines could still contribute to the development of her society.

The Story of Celia: Beginnings

Celia Mariano was born a middle child of six children on 18 June 1915 in Tondo, the historical home of Manila's working class.[21] Unlike many of her Huk women comrades, she did not grow up poor or a peasant but as a member of a middle-class family in Manila. Her father was the treasurer-registrar of the University of the Philippines, while her mother worked as a dressmaker and later gave up her job to devote herself to her home and her children. Calling herself a "city girl," Celia understood early what it meant to belong to a social class. Living among proletariat families in Tondo, she understood that her family was not poor but was not considered rich. Like many middle-class families, hers subsisted on her father's salary but man-aged to invest in two small homesteads in the town of Tanay, Rizal, then a hilly farming community about two hours from Manila by bus.

Celia did not trace her political beginnings to her nonpolitical family, close relatives, or friends — a common reason why men and women joined political organizations and revolutionary movements. In hindsight, she had reason to believe that her father was a nationalist since he baptized all his children in the Aglipayan, or Filipino Independent, Church and became a member of the Nacionalista Party. But he did not mention or explain these actions to her. When Celia recalls her childhood, she maintains that her political convictions stemmed from her own observations:

> When I was ten years old, I used to come with [my mother around Tondo] and at that stage already I began to be appalled by the poverty of the people [there], and I always wondered, "Why are there so many poor people here while we live in better circumstances?" I began to wonder why there are poor people, why there are middle-class people, and why there are so very few rich people. That was a question in my mind that tugged on my conscience for a long, long time.
>
> As early as age ten, I began [to be] conscious of this disparity in the lives of people in the Philippines. I was conscious of the fact that these people live in such outrageous conditions. But how could they tolerate it? They had no running water, no electricity, no toilets. How could they live that way? For me, these basic needs are so important that life will just be miserable without them. I began to wonder, but I did not know how to answer my own questions.

Her own comfortable situation, however, did not initially lead her to actively seek answers to these questions. For much of her development, Celia benefited from an excellent education obtained at the Philippines' premier university, the University of the Philippines (UP), then located on Padre Faura Street in Manila's Ermita district, where she studied from 1931 to 1935 and obtained a bachelor of science in education. As a college student in the early 1930s, she regarded her education as both a means of achieving social mobility and an opportunity for intellectual advancement. At the same time, it provided a political awakening, as her university life was marked by intense political discussions on the vital issues affecting the country at that time, in particular, the growing fascism in Asia, with Japan's imperialist designs and alliance with Germany clearly posing a threat in the region. At the UP, Celia began to think about political problems but realized that their solution was far more complex than she had at first thought. Moreover, she came to realize that she must understand not only domestic issues but international events. She fondly remembers her study of sociology and history, subjects taught by progressive professors who stimulated her interest in learning about the world around her. She recalls that two professors, Professor Macaraig in sociology and Professor

Padilla in psychology, "opened my mind. They made me think, they stimulated my thinking, they made me get out of myself, not to think only of
myself, but to think of other people." [22] It was at the UP that Celia became
both an activist and a nationalist. Despite her expanded academic knowledge, she felt as if she was still the same ten-year-old Celia who did not know
how to respond to her growing number of questions about her country.

After graduating in 1935, Celia became a high school teacher and
took the civil service examinations a year later. Civil service posts were
much sought after, especially among women; thus, the examinations
were difficult. Despite the intense competition, Celia acquired a superior
grade, which led to a post as an examiner in the Bureau of Civil Service.
After a few months, she was promoted to senior examiner, correcting the
examination papers of applicants who wanted employment in government posts. Although she was devoted to her career as a government
bureaucrat, Celia continued to seek answers to the questions that had
haunted her since childhood. In 1936, after she attended a lecture on the
situation in the countryside delivered by Pedro Abad Santos, a peasant
leader who founded the Socialist Party of the Philippines, members of the
Philippine Youth Congress (PYC) urged her to join their organization.
The invitation was prompted by Celia's apparent enthusiasm and curiosity about social and political issues, asking most of the questions following the lecture. Though she knew little about the PYC, she agreed to
attend the meetings.

Thus began the political courtship of Celia. After several meetings,
she joined the PYC formally in 1937, where she became concerned with
issues relating to the country's youth. She was appointed treasurer of the
PYC and met with senators and congressmen to solicit donations to the
organization. At the same time, her friends at PYC immersed her in lectures and readings on political issues. In this period, she attended a lecture by a Japanese-American visiting professor at the UP, Kenneth
Kurihara, on imperialism, socialism, and communism—her first exposure to these concepts. Her friends also lent her readings on fascism and
the Philippine Communist Party. Celia remembers that her earliest education about fascism and communism was derived from reading two
books given to her by fellow PYC members: Amleto Vespa's *Secret Agent
of Japan* (1938) and Edgar Snow's *Red Star over China* (1939). As she
immersed herself in these subjects, she never imagined that understanding such concepts would also mean a unique path of action and lifestyle.

In a way, Celia did not have to exercise her own imagination. Her colleagues at the Philippine Youth Congress made sure she understood that
fulfilling her assignments was just the beginning. Soon, five of her PYC
colleagues, all men—including Jesus Lava, Jorge Frianeza, Bayani Alcala,

and Pacifico Puti—began to visit regularly at her home to discuss political issues, particularly the impending threat of fascism in Asia. At that time, Celia was in awe of these young people who seemed to know a great deal about politics and international issues. She welcomed them in her home and fraternized with them, not realizing that their visits were part of a plan to recruit her to the Communist Party.

According to Celia, she was at the PYC for four or five years in the late 1930s before her colleagues told her about the PKP. Before this revelation, she admitted that she was anticommunist, believing most of the government's propaganda. But if communism was evil, she thought, then how could these decent people, who enlightened her on important questions, embrace such an ideology? When her friends told her that they were communists, she began to change her mind:

> They counteracted all my beliefs about anticommunism. They told me what communism really is and why Catholics and the press are always hammering communism. I can understand why— because the press . . . even our president of the Philippines . . . and the Church were controlled by imperialists. And they explained to me so many things about the blind, mistaken thoughts I have . . . and I can believe them because I can see they are true, in real life they are true, so this feeling of anticommunism vanished away, and in fact I felt sympathy for the Communist Party.

Sympathy, yes. But still not commitment. True to herself, Celia needed to learn more about the party before joining. Again, her friends worked tirelessly to win her to their cause, encouraging her to attend their meetings as an observer. This phase of the courtship did not take long. The coming of the war hastened and deepened Celia's involvement. Two months before war broke out in 1941, after one year of studying the Communist Party, Celia decided to join. In hindsight, however, she admits that joining the party then did not make her a full-fledged communist. As in the past, Celia's commitment to the party and its cause had to grow, while the people around her nurtured her development.

On 8 December 1941, the Japanese attacked the Philippines. As a member of the Philippine Youth Congress, Celia had already discussed the rise of fascism in Asia and the world with her fellow congress members. She relates that "we were convinced that the rise of militarism in Japan would lead to a Japanese invasion of the Philippines."[23] In the party's meetings, her understanding of fascism became more sophisticated. On 18 December, in the midst of the chaotic conditions in Manila, Celia's supervisor at the Bureau of Civil Service announced that government offices would close indefinitely. All employees, including Celia, were given three months' advance pay. Along with her mother, father, and a brother and sister, she hastily evacuated Manila for the family farm in Tanay, Rizal.

The war did not disrupt Celia's political activities. Very soon after settling in Tanay, Manila comrades such as Geruncio Lacuesta and Isabelo Caballero began to visit her. During one of their visits, they began to devise a plan of action as a response to the war. Celia narrates: "My colleagues and I decided, with the cooperation of my parents, to organize the farm as a base from which we would establish a guerrilla unit against the Japanese." She immediately contacted her comrades at the PKP, who had already begun the most visible and organized revolutionary movement in the country. The party then sent leaders such as Pedro Penino, a veteran of the International Brigade that had fought in Spain against Franco, and Mariano Balgos, a well-known trade union leader, to assist the nascent revolutionary organization in Rizal. Subsequently, a meeting of the "United Front" (UF) was held at Tanay, with middle-class people like Celia and parish leaders in attendance. Celia recalls:

> We asked the people of Tanay for assistance, stating that a guerrilla movement would require money, food, medicine, clothing, and arms. The guerrilla unit would be kept secret, and therefore needed to be self-sufficient. The people of Tanay were very positive.

In the following weeks, Tanay would become a strong United Front base, harboring guerrillas and acting as a center from which the party could direct anti-Japanese offensive actions.

In the ensuing months, Celia's leadership and dedication to the movement did not go unnoticed. Dr. Vicente Lava, then the secretary general of the PKP,[24] invited her to move to central Luzon to formally join the guerrilla movement there, the Hukbo ng Bayan Laban sa Hapon, or Hukbalahap, the anti-Japanese army formally established on 29 March 1942. Lava believed in Celia's ability to communicate and assigned her the role of an educator of the movement. He explained that education was critical in a resistance movement, not only for the guerrillas but for the masses. According to him, hundreds of people had already joined the Huks, but very few members had the ability to organize and educate them. Celia was indeed the ideal choice. Lava also informed her that he would recommend to the Military Committee the recognition of the guerrilla unit in Tanay as part of the Hukbalahap. Celia, who considered herself a young and inexperienced political worker, was pleased with this achievement.

Under the alias "Loleng," Celia proceeded to go to Bulacan in central Luzon. She took up residence with the Lavas and later was introduced to Ida Santos, a good friend of the family who served as chief campaign officer of Jesus Lava when he ran for councilor of Bulacan. Along with other

PKP colleagues, Celia recruited members and supporters of the resistance movement and organized meetings composed of eight to ten people. In these meetings, she lectured on the nature of Japanese fascism, the need for the United Front, the tasks to be performed by the resistance movement, and tactics the UF members should employ to prevent capture. Together with Ida Santos, Celia traveled, usually on foot, to the villages of Meycauayan, Plaridel, Taal, Guiginto, Paombong, and Hagonoy to fulfill her duties to the movement.

Not long after this first assignment, Celia was ordered to educate members of the resistance movement in Nueva Ecija. This time, alias "Lydia," she visited towns in central Luzon, including Cabiao, Cabanatuan, and San Carlos. She recalls that these areas were highly organized in a Barrio Unit Defense Corps (BUDC), which protected each village. In borrowed peasant clothing and with uncut hair, she resembled a barrio lass—concealing her Manila origins and avoiding the suspicion of Japanese soldiers and their Filipino collaborators.

In a major promotion, Celia became editor of the revolutionary newspaper *Katubusan ng Bayan* (Redemption of the Nation). During a meeting with "Dading," the son of Mateo del Castillo, whom she succeeded as editor, the Japanese Army entered the barrio where they were staying. Celia recalls: "I had to hide in a bamboo grove in order to escape capture. Dading was also warned of the approaching Japanese by the BUDCs but was caught on his way to Manila and was later tortured to death." During her life as Hukbalahap guerrilla, Celia would come face to face with the Japanese on many occasions, often narrowly escaping arrest and torture. She encountered the Japanese on the streets of Manila and in the villages of central Luzon, but she always managed to elude them. At different times, Japanese soldiers came looking for her at home or in the village, but she was always one step ahead of them. Her family was even forced to move back to Manila around 1943 because of increasing surveillance and harassment by the Japanese. But Celia trusted the people around her, and, indeed, they were the ones who distracted the Japanese in order to protect her, often at great risk for their lives.

One of the highlights of her involvement with the peasants of central Luzon was what Celia calls the "Harvest Struggle." During each harvest, the Huks promulgated slogans such as "No rice for the enemy!" and "Keep the food of the people." Under the protection of the guerrillas, the peasants would harvest and hide the rice in the hollow bamboo poles of their houses, in concealed warehouses, or buried underground to keep the supply away from the Japanese collection agency. Celia still remembers how such acts increased her nationalist fervor and gave her tremendous faith in the Huks and their peasant followers.[25]

With a new role as editor of *Katubusan* and a new alias, "Alicia Garces," Celia became more deeply involved in the movement. At one point, she walked all the way to Pampanga to instruct peasants on how to fight the Japanese. As she says, "I stopped at houses along the way for food and rest. All the villages were organized. At one point, I hid out in the Candaba swamps — that area had creeks in a mazelike formation — and the BUDC built for me a small hut that could not be detected in the swamps." By 1943, Celia's daily routine consisted of talking with and instructing people, writing *Katubusan*, and translating documents given to her by the Huk leaders from English to Tagalog for use by the regional committees.[26] In 1944, she was reassigned, this time, as educational secretary of the Central Luzon Bureau, a body that supervised five Huk provincial committees in Bulacan, Nueva Ecija, Pampanga, Tarlac, and Pangasinan. She was responsible for directing schools in the region and spent time in San Juan, Pampanga, and Paombong. In the latter town, she operated a school for thirty students — fifteen women and fifteen men — between the ages of sixteen and thirty-five. As part of her task, she summoned different comrades to deliver lectures on such topics as Japanese fascism, the United Front, and the Communist Party. Even now, Celia counts her early experiences as an educator as her most memorable. She prides herself on having taught Huk men and women who later achieved prominence in the movement, including Remedios Gomez, who became "Kumander Liwayway," and other heroic fighters.

By early 1944, the party knew that the Americans, under the command of Gen. Douglas MacArthur, were advancing toward the Philippines. Celia, however, insists that it was the Huks — then the strongest, most militant guerrilla organization in the country — who paved the way for liberation. According to her, they

> sustained, augmented and increased their resistance campaign against the Japanese from the fall of Manila, unlike other movements who were attached to MacArthur's forces. . . . The Huks had engaged in ambushes, sabotage, and attacks on Japanese property with the support of the Philippine peasantry and had earned a fearsome reputation among the Japanese. The Huks had such control over the population that, for example, they would supervise rice harvests, distributing the rice among the people before the Japanese would have the opportunity to appropriate it.

On 22 September 1944, the Americans bombed Manila. Lava, the party's general secretary, decided that Celia should inform the leaders of the Southern Luzon Bureau of the outcome of an earlier conference that had clarified the position the Huks should take upon the arrival of the Americans. She was to relay the message that Huk squadrons would be joined by the Chinese squadron, who were then Huk allies, to fight against the Japanese and therefore facilitate the entry of the Americans in the country. As she later explained:

> Conveying this message was a most important assignment. I had to relay that there was a certain date, time, and place for certain guerrilla squadrons to meet the Chinese squadron—Squadron 48 or Wa Chi—in the southern Luzon forest in order to establish a route between central and southern Luzon. Above all, Lava told me, "you must not allow yourself to be caught."

With her reliable courier, Ely, Celia was able to deliver the message. On the way to her destination, she stopped in Manila to warn her family that the city would soon become a battleground between the United States and Japan and urge them to leave. The Marianos were brought to San Juan, Pampanga, where Celia's comrades took care of them. Months later, she recalled how surprised and touched she was when "the peasants said that, as 'Lydia' educated them, they should look after the Marianos." In part through Celia's success in delivering her message, the Huks were strengthened in the coordination of their northern and southern forces. In the end, "the Huks fought the Japanese to clear the way for the U.S. forces throughout central Luzon until the Americans reached Manila," she recalls with intensity.[27]

The end of the war was a cause for great celebration throughout the Philippines, as the Huks claimed victory in their war against the Japanese. The country believed that its united efforts against imperialism had contributed to the ending of the war. For the Huks, peacetime also meant an end to chaotic lives; they welcomed the new government that would lead the country to prosperity. Celia dreamed of going home to her family and starting a new life in Manila. The celebration, however, did not last long. What was in store for Celia after the war was far from the blissful life she had envisioned.

Romance and Revolution

By the time the war ended, Celia could no longer be considered a political novice. Through firsthand experience, she understood the concepts that she had studied—fascism, imperialism, and communism. In the party schools she had attended and directed, she had acquired intimate knowledge of such topics as dialectical materialism, political economy, the state, revolution, Marxism, Leninism, and the Communist Party.

Even today, she can still recite and discuss the tenets of the communist ideology. Yet, when asked to explain, she talks about her political convictions in simple, unadorned language:

> What influenced me to join the Communist Party is its emphasis on ridding the country of poverty—which was what really had disturbed me since the age of ten—the poverty in the Philippines. And it is the CP, the only party where I heard that they want to get rid of poverty. And they explained how to do it. You have to fight imperialism. You cannot fight imperialism frontally; you have to do a lot of organizational work, political work, propaganda work, writing, talking, delivering speeches, to make people understand.
>
> We are poor, and our people did not know that they are poor because they are being exploited by these imperialist forces— what we know today as multinational corporations. You do not see, it's invisible, but the manipulations, and how they control— they can control people, even the most important people in the Philippines. They deprive people. They are so rich, so influential, so powerful—the average person does not see it. I did not see it at first. It is only when I began reading, when these Communists began explaining to me and when I began to think about it myself. All these influences made me think that I must work with the Communists. These are the people who will really help me conquer poverty. To me, poverty is the greatest scourge in our country and all countries in the world.

Even at that time, Celia could not believe that these words could be uttered and clearly understood by someone like her, who was once an innocent and naive person with the needs and desires of an ordinary woman. But Celia was forever changed—by a horrible war and the people and comrades who were with her in central Luzon, who had taught her and fought with her to defend the causes of freedom and equality. She yearned to go back to a normal life, but she still wanted to fight the battle against poverty. Although she rejoined her family after the war, she knew that her commitment to the Communist Party was not ending but in fact intensifying.

Soon after the Philippines won its independence in 1946, Celia, along with her comrades, had to leave Manila for the mountains and the life of a revolutionary. They had come to realize that the United States would never support the Huks, a nationalist and anti-imperialist force led by communists. Celia's comprehension of the movement's decision to launch a revolution is compatible with the party's own version. According to her, as the campaign of suppression against the masses in central Luzon ensued, with harassment, intimidation, and arrests of members, the Huks had no choice but to take up arms again in self-defense.[28] At this point,

Celia did not need to be educated; she had become an ideologue and intellectual, and she no longer had to look for answers to her questions. She explicitly understood the situation of the country and the institutions and political systems that had led to the Huks' repression. She never questioned the party's decision to launch another rebellion. Although she realized that a difficult path lay ahead, she stood by her party.

Yet the romantic in Celia had not died. Although she knew the hard concepts of imperialism and communism, her personal reasons for continuing the struggle were articulated in a much more idealized way. In a lecture delivered many years after the Huk rebellion, she recalled:

> The war and my experiences in central Luzon had changed my whole outlook. Gone were my dreams of building for myself someday a big beautiful house and travel abroad to see lovely places. What was disturbing me then was the plight of those kind, hospitable peasants, who even in their poverty shared with me the last bit of rice they had in their pantry. At the back of my mind I felt the drabness and emptiness of their lives, the hopelessness of their futures. Working with the cadres of the Hukbalahap, I sensed that their thrust was to alleviate and eventually eliminate the deprivation and wretched misery of workers and peasants who are the underdogs of society. I felt a strong identification with them and thereby I decided I would stick it out with the Hukbalahap.[29]

Although this was a most difficult decision for Celia, she was prepared for what lay ahead. As a Hukbalahap, she had experienced peasant life, a life considerably different from her middle-class origins, yet she was humbled by the unity and kindness of the peasantry. While political maturity led Celia to devote herself to the ideals of communism, it was always her relationship with the peasants who took care of her in central Luzon that anchored her commitment. She saw how barren their lives were; yet they shared what little they had with her and her family. The peasant leaders also impressed her — they were not educated formally, yet they had an intimate and broad knowledge of how to improve life in their communities. In the end, she says, "I developed a new purpose in life: you must serve society. Working with people with the same objectives, one can get somewhere. I decided to become a full-time revolutionary and to dedicate my life to working to improve the life of the peasants."[30]

Such noble sentiments came at a high emotional cost. Celia always cried herself to sleep, as she missed her parents; it was clear that life would never be the same again.[31] But she had been transformed. Communism did not frighten or confuse her anymore, and even today she believes that it was her embrace of this ideology that allowed her to understand politics and how society works. She described herself as a quiet, reticent, "sort of lethargic" person who did not know how to talk with people. When she became a communist, she says, "I felt very alive; there was a lot of vigor in myself, as though the learning of these things was stimulating me as a person." Celia wanted to learn much more. She read a lot, engaged in discussions, and became sociable. Finally, in a unique way, she felt connected to the people and events around her.

Indeed, Celia did not return to her "normal" life after the war. She remained a communist and worked full time for the party. Her family also experienced a tragedy — they lost their home and possessions in Tanay; their land was burned by the Japanese, who suspected that it was a guerrilla base. They eventually settled in Manila, but they lived in its poorest neighborhood. Celia stayed with her family in a one-room house with no toilet, electricity, or running water. She did not need to adjust to this life; she had already lived it among the peasants of central Luzon. Her resolve to help improve the lives of the poor was strengthened even more.

The Communist Party knew that a dedicated revolutionary such as Celia was a valuable asset to the movement. Although Celia was encouraged to assume a normal life in Manila while working for the party, its members always looked after her and asked her to perform important tasks. And yet it was clear that the party did not know how to deal with someone like Celia, a woman of unquestionable commitment and intelligence. A man with an equal or even lesser grasp of the concepts that guided the Communist Party would surely have assumed a leadership position. Celia recalls her discomfort and awkwardness in being the only woman at the many party meetings she attended. Even after many years of being a party member, Celia was unable to decide what to do. Nor could she advance her own ideas of what the party's agenda should be. Although such treatment began to frustrate her, she accepted her place in the party and patiently waited for an opportunity to be of greater influence. The party, for its part, continued to nurture her, educating her and giving her important responsibilities.

At the end of World War II, it was another party task that brought Celia and her future husband Bill Pomeroy together. Bill came to the Philippines in October 1944 with MacArthur's forces in the Leyte invasion, moving in the course of the campaign from Leyte to Mindoro and then to Fort Stotsenberg, Clark Field, in Pampanga.[32] Before reaching Pampanga, he had become aware of the Hukbalahap. By then, he was a member of an army historical team working on the war's history, and therefore he had access to military intelligence reports mentioning the Hukbalahap.[33] Being a member of the Communist Party of the United

States, he closely identified with Hukbalahap soldiers he met in the town of Arayat that led him to germinate the idea of writing a book about the conditions in central Luzon. Pomeroy fell in love with the country and returned to the Philippines in 1947 to work as a freelance journalist, writing for American magazines and the *Philippines Free Press*.[34] As he writes in *The Forest*:

> In 1944 I came to the Philippines as a soldier myself. It was in the midst of a war against fascism, a war in which I believed deeply. We had come, I thought, as liberators, to oust an invader that was ravaging the country. I was not prepared for what I found.[35]

What Bill found was the "finest of all Filipino guerrilla movements, the Hukbalahap," whose leaders had been arrested by the U.S.-supported Philippine government and whose squadron members were regularly shot to death. He also saw American military forces acting in the interests of big landlords to suppress the peasant movement. And Bill found an additional reason to stay:

> To my intense shame, I was not a member of an army bringing freedom; I was a member of an army reestablishing an imperialist rule. I swore to myself then that I would not rest until I had done all that I could to correct that wrong, until I had wiped from my own hands the moral stain that had been placed there, until I had put my American strength on the side of those who had suffered from American imperialism.[36]

Bill wanted to write about the history of the Hukbalahap movement, and Celia was assigned by the Communist Party to accompany him as his interpreter around central and southern Luzon to interview the Huks. During that trip, Bill fell in love with Celia. Before long, he had embraced the cause of the Huks and joined its underground struggle. And he also proposed marriage to Celia. Although reluctant to marry someone before she had a chance to get to know him better, Celia trusted Bill. She was moved by someone who promised to be her partner in everything—in the home, in their chores, in their work, and, most importantly, in the struggle. After many years of interaction with men in the movement and a number of marriage proposals, Celia was afraid that marriage would mean compromising her duties to the party. With Bill, she found a comrade and a partner. After working together in the party for more than a year, Bill and Celia married in 1948. Celia would later state: "In those days of tremendous unrest, upheavals, tension, and turbulence in my country, my marriage to William Pomeroy was to become the most stabilizing and vivifying factor in my life."[37]

From the beginning, the two believed that part of their commitment to each other was their commitment to the country, the party, and its cause. Bill Pomeroy's book *The Forest* relates one of the most intimate moments of their lives:

> I think of the day when I proposed. We sat on a patch of grass, in front of a house destroyed in the war, on Dewey Boulevard, looking out over a Manila Bay that was crimson at sundown.
>
> Do you know what it would mean to marry me? she said. These are not normal times, or, rather, in my country people like us cannot live normal lives. Already I am wanted. You know that. We may have a short time together, of real peace and of the happiness known by others. But sooner or later, there will be decisions to make: I cannot go to your country for I am known as Huk; you could not stay in mine if your sympathies for us are discovered. If we would want to stay together, there would only be the mountains for us. Do you know that? Are you ready for that?[38]

Finding an answer to this question was not hard for Pomeroy. He said "I know. I love you. I am ready for it." Pomeroy continues his elegy of love:

> I think of how we were twice-wedded, once by a justice of the peace, and once by the movement to which we belong, in a little ceremony in a small house in Manila, to which the leaders of the movement came and where the principal leader spoke the words that bound us closer than any document of the state, and how we swore in the name of the Philippine national liberation movement to be loyal to each other but never to let our own relationship stand in the way of our loyalty to the cause of the people.[39]

For Celia, too, the question of marriage to a person and a cause was not complicated. She had always wanted a balance between her commitment to the struggle and her personal happiness, and with Bill she did not feel she had to prioritize one over the other. Regarding family and children, however, Celia was more torn. Bill writes of

> how we decided, advisedly, to postpone the having of children until the struggle is won. So many women in this country, we were told, were drawn to the movement and have had their contribution ended by marriage and by the having of children too soon. There must be examples.
>
> I lean forward and touch Celia's hand. She looks up and smiles. She understands.

The struggle proved to be a long one for Celia and Bill. Not until many years later did they assume a normal life as husband and wife. They had to endure years of separation and lost moments of intimacy. They wanted to have children but decided that life in the forest was neither the place nor the time to raise them. They decided that until the situation became normal, until they could live a normal life, they would not have children. Nor did Celia consider the option of having her siblings assume the responsibility of taking care of her child. This was a common practice among Huk women, who left their children with relatives while they continued to fight the war in the forest. By the time their situation normalized, however, it was too late for Celia to have a child. Sometimes, forty years after these decisions were made, Celia still pines for the child she and Bill never had.

And yet Celia rationalizes her choice since this meant dedicating herself fully to the struggle. During the first years of her activism, Celia was uncertain about her commitment to the Hukbalahap, but by the HMB period she knew she would give everything for the struggle. She never believed in giving only a part of herself to the party and its ideology. Having a child would mean that she had to be ready to compromise. This situation would only create conflict for Celia and Bill. Explaining this choice, Celia says:

> We are totally dedicated to the movement. And we use all our spare hours for the movement. If you have children, you will give a lot of time for the children and I am very particular how my child will be brought up. I will probably use a lot more time for my child than for the movement. So it is better that we did not have any children.

During their first years of marriage, Celia and Bill lived in Manila, she working full time for the party and he studying at the University of the Philippines. By the end of the 1940s, the armed struggle of the Huks had shifted from a defensive to an offensive strategy and the guerrilla army had assumed a new name, the Hukbong Mapagpalaya ng Bayan (HMB). Although they lived a relatively normal life in Manila, they both understood that working underground for a cause outlawed by the government left them with little freedom and a dangerous existence. With the situation in Manila becoming more volatile for the PKP's top intellectuals, Bill and Celia were assigned to work in the Education Department, which had its headquarters in the guerrilla camps in the mountains of Laguna Province. Soon after, they abandoned their home in Manila to live in the forest.

Pomeroy's book, *The Forest*, begins with the couple packing their belongings in Manila en route to the mountains of southern Luzon. In

April 1950, Celia and Bill went from the "open world" into the dense
forest of Laguna and took up residence in a small hut made of forest material where they, along with other comrades, mapped out a long-term plan.
Bill, alias "Ka Bob," was placed in charge of the Propaganda Division, and
Celia, who became known as "Ka Rene," was made the head of the
National School Division. In the two years that Celia and Bill were in the
forest, their commitment to the struggle and to each other deepened as
they faced numerous challenges—malaria, hunger, cold, wet weather,
leeches in the forest, and, of course, the enemy. Yet, those years were also
the most productive for Celia:

> For a period of two years, 1950 to 1952, working under very
> rough conditions in small makeshift huts and living on very
> scanty rations of rice and dried fish or rice and mung beans,
> which our HMB comrades transported on their backs over long
> distances from towns below, we turned out leaflets and pam-
> phlets and a newspaper called *Titis* (Spark). We conducted
> month-long schools that frequently had to move from place to
> place to avoid enemy raids. We wrote our own textbooks. Our
> educational materials were distributed to the far-flung various
> regional organizations of our movement.[40]

Celia as a revolutionary and a woman was torn between her commitment to the movement and her personal desires. The cause, the movement, her marriage and family, all these desires led to internal conflict.
Because of her unique position as a woman leader, Celia had to act in the
same way as most Huk men. Whatever she wanted in her personal life
had to be abandoned for the demands of the revolution.

Celia always had to exhibit strength, no matter how much physical
or emotional pain she endured. She had to be decisive, even in moments
of utter confusion. Not only were her mind and emotions conflicted, but
her body, "soft and feminine," as Pomeroy described, also endured suffering. At a time when intimacy was important, when expressions of
love were as important as expressions of principle, Bill and Celia had to
suppress their emotions. While they lived in the forest, they were careful not to show affection in front of their comrades. They slept apart so
that they would not arouse their jealousy. In one story from *The Forest*,
Bill relates:

> A day of rest. . . . This is the first time that we have been alone
> in all these months. There is no privacy in the camp, where we
> sleep with others like one giant body upon the floor, and where
> we move always in the vision of others. Now we have found a

room of our own in the forest, a green wall of trees on either
side, a blue ceiling, a white floor with a strip of blue carpet running upon it.

   We take off our clothes and are strangely pale, like the
growth under leaf mold on the forest floor. . . . We splash in the
water and our laughter echoes along the forest wall. . . . We sit
closely, talking quietly of our lives together. . . . It is not long. . . .
The shadows of the trees creep over the beach toward us,
reclaiming us. Our afternoon is over. We rise and go, back into
the forest and affairs and all.[41]

This is the only entry evoking intimate moments between Celia and Bill.
Most of Pomeroy's account focuses on the larger purpose that defined
their existence in the forest. At times, Celia had her doubts. Does intimacy also count as a higher purpose? During the revolution, however, such
thoughts were better put aside.

   Just like her marriage and her relationship, Celia did not own her
body. Whatever her body needed had to be evaluated, as her commitment was always measured by her ability to go on with the struggle.
While moving more deeply into the forest, escaping the enemy, Bill and
Celia, along with other Huks, endured days without food and sleep, having no strength. The miracle in the forest was not that they were able to
evade the enemy but that they remained alive. As Bill narrates one of
their encounters:

   It is two weeks now since we have eaten anything of substance.
   Prior to that there were months of semi-starvation. . . . Celia is a
   wasted figure, dark loops beneath the eyes, the full breasts
   almost disappeared; for two months, in the cold rivers, her men-
   struation has not occurred. For weeks neither of us has had a
   bowel movement. I did not know that the human body could
   take such a punishment.[42]

   But, like her other needs and desires, Celia had to suppress her most
basic needs and sometimes exert herself beyond what her body could
bear. In living up to what she believed to be the standards of a true revolutionary, Celia was not allowed to show her vulnerability. She whole-
heartedly, and perhaps credulously, believed what her top comrades
preached—that the cause the Huks were fighting for was far greater than
her individual desires. The Huks' defeat would mean the loss of freedom
and equality in the country. Life in the forest for Celia was therefore an
unending test of her strength and commitment. While there were many
things she valued in her life—Bill, her family, her future—she was also
ready to give it all up for a revolutionary cause.

A Leader and Feminist

As Celia became more involved in the movement, exceptionally performing her tasks, her leadership qualities were honed and became apparent to everyone. The party wanted her to be more active and gave her increasingly challenging tasks. And yet, with relatively little experience in dealing with women, the party gave her few leadership responsibilities for many years. After some time, she had to assert herself, and the party finally had to take notice of a woman who was good enough to be a leader. It was an uphill battle.

Celia first became a member of the Bulacan Provincial Committee of the Hukbalahap during wartime. For the first time, she met with other leaders of the party, including Pedro Castro and Jose Lava, who later became general secretaries of the Communist Party. Although no major responsibilities were given to her at this time, she attended meetings where the group strategized against the Japanese. It was also at this time that she was sent to the National Party School, where she was trained according to the principles of communism. Toward the end of the war she finally was admitted to the core of the party, the Central Committee.

In 1944, a general meeting of the Communist Party was called to plan how the movement would act at the end of the war and conduct itself in front of the Americans and the soon-to-be Philippine Republic. Twenty-five important leaders and cadres came, and Celia was one of three women in attendance. An election was held after the meeting. When asked who among the cadres would be willing to be sent anywhere to perform any task, Celia did not hesitate to raise her hand. She was then elected to the Central Committee on the basis of her commitment to the party. Her first major task was to unite the Hukbalahap's southern Luzon squadrons with the Chinese squadron, which together defeated the Japanese Army in Laguna. As described earlier in the essay, this move facilitated the entrance of the Americans into Luzon.

After the war, Celia continued to be the only female member on the Central Committee. She became more deeply involved in the Huk organization and headed various committees, including the Women's Division. As a Central Committee member, she was able to promote different issues and make suggestions concerning the implementation of the party's policies. When Celia was in the forest in 1950, she continued to play a leadership role in the party. In a Central Committee meeting in 1951, she was elected to the Political Bureau (Politburo) of the PKP, the policy-making organ of the party. This move was unprecedented, for never in the history of the Communist Party in the Philippines had a woman been elected to the Politburo. For Celia, the fact that a woman had assumed a position of power in the movement was a liberating act for herself and for the party as well.[43]

It was clear from the beginning that Celia was an extraordinary woman. She was different. To this day, none of her Huk comrades has ever questioned why she became a Politburo member.

How could Celia have become a member of the Politburo? Christina Kelley Gilmartin's study on women and the Chinese Revolution reveals that many top female communists in China did not achieve their status in the party on their own. Rather, their roles were legitimated through their husbands, all of whom were prominent party leaders.[44] According to Gilmartin, the unwritten requirement for the advancement of Chinese women was marriage or consensual unions with important communist leaders. Thus, most of the key women figures in the Chinese Communist Party were partners of male communist leaders. As such, women were never able to command the status and legitimacy of male leaders in the informal structure, in part because their access to the reins of high authority were dependent on their sexual partnerships. The most important criterion for a woman's high political status in communist institutions was rarely her political accomplishments but the political rank of her partner.[45] Can Celia be compared to these Chinese communist women? In the first place, her partner, Bill Pomeroy, was a top intellectual in the party. Since he was a member of the Communist Party of the United States, which had enduring ties with the Philippine communists, Pomeroy was respected by his Huk comrades. Bill was someone whose convictions were never doubted. The trust and position accorded to him were even strengthened when Pomeroy officially became a member of the PKP. The same kind of status may have been extended to Celia, who after her marriage was given a more prominent role in the party.

But Celia's ascension to the party leadership was more complicated than having an important partner. Before Bill Pomeroy joined the Huks, she already had achieved prominence and was considered a wartime hero by her comrades. Bill only became a formal member of the PKP late in the Huk rebellion, in 1951. Some might even argue that it was because of Celia that Bill was accepted as a leader and intellectual in the movement.

Celia therefore cannot be seen simply as an appendage to a powerful and influential man. She believes that she earned the role of a Politburo member by means of her dedication to the movement. When asked why she thought she was elected, she replied:

> It depends on your achievements and on what you have done for the movement—that is always the criteria. If you have done enough to get the attention of the Politburo and the higher organs, they will notice you. They will promote you, as they have

promoted me. You are chosen because of what you have done, whether you are a man or a woman. If a woman has not risen to the rank that I have, it is because she did not do as much work as I or she did not show enough talent to help the movement as I did.

Certainly, another important factor in Celia's promotion was her education. She had graduated from the University of the Philippines, the country's most prestigious school; she wrote and spoke in English; she could comprehend the sophisticated dogma of communism; she spoke eloquently; and she was smart, thorough, and articulate. In a movement in which the average level of education reached by its members, both male and female, was the fourth grade, Celia stood out. While peasant men with no education still had the access to power due to their organizational skills, women in the movement, who were mostly from peasant backgrounds, stood at the margins. Celia explained:

When I became a Central Committee member, there were two other women who were present in the CC meetings—Remedios [Liwayway] Gomez and Teofista Valerio. But when we sat in the meetings, they didn't say anything, while I gave contributions. I questioned what they said, I disputed with the other members, I gave suggestions. And these two women, they just sat there and said nothing. So, who will be noticed? I was also the one who took minutes of meetings. They could not do that. They did not have education. Even Liwayway—maybe only seventh grade, and Teofista only fourth grade. The women were also deterred by the attitudes of society, of men, towards them. I was not deterred by that, because I had already emancipated myself.

Celia understood that it was not the fault of Huk women that they were undervalued in a movement that obviously needed them. Many women never questioned the fact that they were mostly followers, rather than leaders. Some even remained passive despite opportunities for deeper involvement. For Celia, these women were brought up to believe that they were to be subservient to men. Celia was also fighting a bigger battle within the Huk organization. She believed that her dedication and life could stand as an example for Filipina women who decided to break free from their traditional roles to commit themselves to a higher cause. But like her development as a cadre and communist, Celia's growth as a feminist also took years. Although her comrades were successful in politicizing her and introducing her to the concepts of dialectical materialism, political economy, and the state and revolution, no one ever discussed with her the "woman question." Celia learned, initially through experience, how different women's issues and concerns were from those accepted by men.

When she attended her first party school, Celia had an experience that she would never forget:

> In the party school, we were about twelve who were studying there, only two women, the others men. One thing that happened was that the men built a toilet outside the house. But when you squat in the toilet, your body could be seen down to the chest. I thought, My God, how can we women go in there?
>
> So, what we did was to go a little way out to a stream. You had to cross a log so that you could hide among the bushes. One day, when we were having classes, I felt that I had to respond to the call of nature, so I left the room and went there. And when I crossed the log, I fell into the water. Of course, I shouted. So all the comrades came out and fished me out of the water.
>
> After I changed my clothes, I began to criticize these comrades. I said, "You people, you only think of yourselves as men, you do not think of our situation as women. You expect us to use that toilet. You did not even think of building a toilet for us. You just think of yourselves as men. You don't think of the women. You don't bother with the needs of women."

After Celia complained, her male comrades became reticent and admitted that it was their fault that they were not sensitive to the needs of women. After the school session had finished that day, all of her male comrades built a toilet for the women. Celia believed that the incident served as a lesson to the men. She continues:

> Another lesson they learned from me was in the evening; when we are already sleeping, lying down, we could hear them telling sex jokes. It was lurid, they made me sick. The next day, we had our lessons first, but always at the end there was a part called "Criticism–Self-Criticism" or "Comments." I told the comrades, "I don't want to be rude or abominable to you, but your conduct last night was to me outrageous. You were talking and telling sex jokes. I don't understand how you communists can behave in that manner. You should know by this time what is wrong, what is good, and what is bad. For you to talk in that way in the presence of your comrades who are women shows no sensitivity at all as to how we feel about these jokes. Do you want your wives to listen to these jokes? You would not even tell your wives these jokes; would you like your sisters to hear these jokes? Do you want your mothers to hear these jokes? And if you behave this way in the future, we will not think of you as comrades. You are not worthy to be communists."

Once again, Celia's male comrades bowed their heads in embarrassment. They accepted the criticism, which for Celia was a small but significant step toward emancipating both the men and the women in the movement. While Celia was already sensitive to the issues that separated her from her male comrades, she did not pursue the question of women's rights any further until the HMB period.

As she became more central to the Huk organization, Celia became increasingly frustrated with her role and those of other women in the movement. During meetings, for instance, she noticed how the men waited for the women to do the cooking and washing up. Although she managed to avoid them, other women were obliged to do such tasks. In her mind, she had many questions: why is this work always delegated to the women and why can't the men cook?

Celia's search for answers did not stop. Early in her involvement in the Huk rebellion, she read two works that would drastically influence her views. The first, by Clara Zetkin, a leading figure in German socialism, was a pamphlet called "The Woman Question," which discusses the problems of women in general and shows how they are considered inferior and are oppressed and exploited in many societies. Celia also read Lenin's "The Emancipation of the Working Woman":

> And these stirred my imagination. It brought me a new outlook—I began to see how we women in general have been exploited and oppressed. And I also saw how the Communist Party and all the parties allowed this to happen and even went along with this custom. Women must fight for equal rights with men because you cannot generally say that men are more intelligent than women. That's why from the time I read these two books I became a feminist. I was always trying to see how women were treated in the party and elsewhere. I became very sensitive to the question of the treatment of women.

These works helped Celia formulate her own feminist ideology. From the beginning, she understood that there was a disparity between men's and women's roles in the movement. Although she did not pay particular attention to recruiting and educating women, she noticed how women could be as dedicated as the men but were relegated to roles such as cooks, laundresses, nurses, first-aid workers, and couriers. She fraternized with many women in the camps during the Japanese occupation and the HMB period, but she never discussed political issues with them. Most of her time at leadership meetings was spent with men.

During 1946–47, Celia began to raise the question of women in Central Committee meetings. Without criticizing her male comrades, she proposed forming a Women's Division in the party, which would be responsible for recruiting and educating women. At that time, she recalls, the party was not responsive and even the women were indifferent to her proposal, but she nevertheless volunteered to lead this effort. In the next few years, she supervised and was solely responsible for this division. She continues:

> The first thing I did was to look around for the women I knew in the party who would be willing to form with me a Women's Committee—Ka Sophia, Rosenda Torres, Nene Mallari, and Isabel. We met once a week in my house, and I discussed all these questions with them to politicize them, to open their minds to the oppression of women. It did not take just a week or a month; it had taken a long time for me, too. They understood it, but it did not excite them. They did not become dynamic about it.

But Celia did not give up. She continued to politicize these women, displaying the same dedication as the male comrades who tirelessly educated her. At Celia's urging and under her leadership, this core of women decided to form a women's organization in Manila and central Luzon. While four female colleagues went to the provinces to organize the rural women, who were mostly the wives and daughters of peasant organizers, Celia's group in Manila set up the Women's Forum, a venue where women could come together and discuss the issues that affected them, including issues of international political significance. Eventually, the Women's Forum became a women's organization with professionals and intellectuals as members. Under Celia's supervision, these women lobbied Congress for price controls in the late 1940s, a time when inflation was a major problem. They also campaigned for more job opportunities for women and the provision of child care facilities. Celia remained in the Women's Division for three years, from 1947 to 1950. For her, the most important result of the formation of the Women's Division was the increasing involvement of women in party work and their rise to responsible posts.

By this time, Celia had become an advocate for women's issues, but she still had not managed to articulate a feminist ideology that the party could embrace. For a long time, she was unable to criticize the party leadership for their stance on the treatment of women.

Celia's frustration with relations between men and women in the movement intensified as the "sex problem" among the Huks became more pronounced.[46] Much later in life, she spoke of this problem with passion:

> The particular problem of men-women relationships arose very often. We were leading abnormal lives under abnormal circumstances, and there were times when relationships between men and women contradicted the traditional conservative norms of

Filipino customs. Many of our guerrillas were far away from their wives for long periods of time, and loneliness sometimes drove them into amorous relations with some women in the camps.

It became a social problem, which we had to solve, because wives whose husbands developed mistresses complained to us from the villages of their mates' unfaithfulness.[47]

These came to be called "*kwalingking* cases," occasions when Huk and communist cadres engaged in extramarital relations with young women in the camps while their wives were left behind in cities and barrios.[48] The affairs were carried out through deception — the men hiding the relations from their wives and deceiving their mistresses and even their comrades. Although the problem arose during the Japanese occupation, it became more pronounced during the postwar revolt. During the war, male Huk fighters could live in the barrios with their wives and children. After the war, their participation in the HMB forced them to live in the forest and prevented them from visiting their homes. The need for intimacy was therefore satisfied with women in the forest.

These extramarital relations posed a moral and political dilemma for the Huk organization. The men, particularly those Politburo members who engaged in sexual relations, became targets of criticism, especially since they were supposed to set a moral example for others. The "mistresses" were also seen as inferior, even in the eyes of the womanizers themselves. The situation created tensions within the movement, threatening its popularity with the local population and weakening the solidarity and discipline among its ranks.[49] The Huks' reputation was jeopardized, as the local people, often villagers of a very conservative morality, were beginning to resent the seemingly immoral behavior of its members.[50] Moreover, most of the *kwalingking* offenses were committed by high Huk commanders and leaders, whose prominence in the movement made them more desirable to the women there. Ordinary soldiers and the rank-and-file did not have easy access to women and were severely punished when caught in an extramarital affair. This discrepancy weakened guerrilla solidarity, as the fact that leaders had more access to women replicated the norm in the Philippines, where higher status ensured preferential access. This weakened the movement's claim that it was promoting social reform and equality of the sexes among both the soldiers and peasant supporters. Taruc later wrote in his memoir that the "sex problem" reflected the immorality and "transient sex relationships common among the Communist leadership":

Thus, despite our favorite claim that, to use Stalin's words, "Communists are people of a different mold," we were no different from our "class enemy." Indeed, in a sense, we were worse; we exploited our own class sisters and comrades, taking

advantage of their hero-worshipping loyalty, their trusting sim-
plicity and credulity.[51]

For Celia, embracing a feminist viewpoint and belonging to a movement that clearly did not understand women created an inner conflict
that had no easy resolution. Finally, she saw an opportunity to make herself heard—and that event became a turning point in her life. She recalls:

> In February 1950 the HMB held a big two-week conference in
> the Laguna forest of leaders and the most dedicated cadres of
> our movement, forty men with me as the only woman. We dis-
> cussed the problems of the movement and decided on our tasks
> for the immediate future. On the last day of our meeting, com-
> rades who wanted to raise any question not covered were given
> ten minutes each to talk. I requested to be given half an hour to
> speak on the woman question. Somebody in the crowd asked,
> "What is the woman question?" I turned to the questioner and
> said, "I am asking the chair to give me half an hour to speak so
> that I can explain to all of you the importance of understanding
> the woman question." But the chairman conceded only fifteen
> minutes to me.
> I spoke about the woman question—the problem of women's
> inequality with men, about women being considered inferior to
> men in all aspects of living. I pointed to examples of capable
> women, active in our movement, who after being married to our
> men comrades became mere housekeepers. I cited cases of many
> women in our camps that were looked upon as just sex objects,
> not treated with [the] respect and dignity that they deserved. I
> said I was not proud of the fact that I was the only woman in that
> conference. It was no indication that women couldn't play an
> important role in the movement. It showed the failure of the
> movement's leaders to recognize that women deserved the same
> rights and opportunities as men.[52]

Although Celia was vociferous and made her points clearly, she did not
expect the party to change overnight. But she made her mark that day, the
first time in the history of the Huk movement that the woman question was
presented and discussed. She followed up by writing articles on women's
issues in the movement's journals and newsletters, most notably several
pieces in *Titis*, the party's official paper. Her articles were devoted to the
problems of women, to explaining why women were treated as inferiors in
the movement, and to suggesting what could be done. She tried to educate
not only party members but the rank-and-file as well. Indeed, by 1950 Celia
was not only a committed communist but a full-fledged feminist.

For the first time, the party began to confront gender and sex issues in the movement, in particular, the *kwalingking* cases. The sex question was becoming increasingly problematic, threatening the movement's solidarity and reputation in the villages. Its resolution became urgent. Even today, it continues to puzzle and chagrin Celia. On her own, she has tried to understand how this problem posed such a serious threat to the Huk movement's strength. She still asks why Huk men engaged in these affairs and offers an explanation:

> Men have to fulfill their sexual instincts. They need sex. How could they have sex unless they got it from a woman? And of course they got the consent of the woman first. They seduced the women first. There were a few women in the camps and in the party, and because these men were charming and attractive, so the women fell for them.
>
> There was a need for them—that is what they told me. They could not get along for a month without sexual intercourse. When the urge came, they had to fulfill it. It was not because they wanted to oppress a woman; it was because they wanted to answer the urges in their body.

Although Celia has tried to understand these men, she refuses to accept such excuses. She insists that one can control his or her sexual instincts, as she did.

The party decided to appoint a committee composed of five people, including Celia and Bill Pomeroy, to study and solve this problem. After long, acrimonious debates, the committee agreed upon a document entitled "The Revolutionary Solution to the Sex Problem."[53] Since this was considered a moral problem, the committee offered a solution that tried to guide the comrades. Briefly, the document states that men and women are born with sexual and emotional needs that cannot be eliminated "short of actual removal of the organs from which the desire is generated."[54] It is acknowledged that the removal of such organs or celibacy produces "abnormal results not conducive to the full development of one's faculties." Moreover, the work of a man or a woman for the movement could suffer as a result of prolonged sexual frustration.[55] Since "biological necessity" compels such behavior in men, extramarital relationships were deemed permissible by the party. Thus, the party would allow a man to take a "forest wife"—but only if he observed strict regulations. The solution allowed a married man to take a forest wife as long as his legal wife was informed about it and he agreed to settle down with one woman at the end of the struggle.[56] In addition, before entering into an extramarital relationship, the "frustrated cadre" must present his problem to his Regional

Committee (Reco) and convince its members that either his health or his work was being adversely affected by the absence of his wife.[57] Celia elaborated the final requirements:

> (1) a married man entering a relationship with a woman comrade in a camp must inform her of his married state and let her know whether their relationship would be temporary or permanent; and (2) the man must inform his wife of his relationship with another woman, explaining the circumstances, and let her know whether his relationship with the other woman would be temporary or permanent.[58]

Celia recalls how this solution created quite a stir in the movement. The document was circulated among party members, with some agreeing and most disagreeing with the solution. Celia is quick to defend this document as "very fair," especially for the women—both the wife and the mistress. She believes that

> the man who is the *kwalingking* originator will not be satisfied with this. He will think it is unfair to him because it is difficult to tell your wife about your affair and it is difficult to tell your mistress that she is only temporary, that they will only live together while he cannot live with his wife.

Ultimately, in Celia's opinion, the solution must come from the man himself through honesty and a change in his outlook on women. According to her, "He must look at women as human beings, and not as sex objects, because women have feelings . . . they have sentiments, they can be hurt and can feel oppressed." Agreeing with her male comrades, Celia knew that the requirements laid out by the party were rigid but fair.

According to Bill Pomeroy, the regulations were strictly followed.[59] However, in reality the party had no way of measuring their success, nor is there any certainty that they were ever implemented.[60] What the document did accomplish in Celia's mind is that it made the party more conscious of gender and sex. It demonstrated the rift between men and women in the movement. The party's inability to address crucial problems and its failure to understand women's issues further alienated its male and female members, intensified existing divisions in the movement, and may have contributed to the failure of the revolt.[61]

Even today, Celia can understand and justify why, even though the Communist Party espoused an egalitarian ideology, it was patriarchal. While the party advocated equality in society, it failed to recognize the equality between men and women. But for Celia these attitudes cannot be attributed solely to the party or her male and female comrades. Rather, they were products of the society in which they lived. The men and women in the movement, although they were communists, could not break away from the traditions and lifestyles that had guided them throughout their lives. In Philippine society at that time, women were supposed to work and remain at home. Men were supposed to make all the decisions, especially in public and political life. As Celia explains:

> Women in the Philippines are brought up to believe that they are inferior to men, that their chief work is to become a housewife, and to take care of children. Women are not trained or made conscious of the fact that they can be useful as citizens who can work outside the home. So there are very few women who are interested in working outside the home; instead most think that their work is inside the home — that they must be good housewives, train their children, and always follow the wishes of their husbands.

Almost regretfully, Celia admits that this mentality was reproduced in the party and the Huk movement. Similar to ordinary Filipino men, most Huks did not concern themselves with treating women as their equals. Even when living in the camps, Huk men expected the women in their families to stay at home, cook and wash, and take care of their homes and children. Although the party did not discourage women's involvement, it did not encourage it, either. Also, women did not assert themselves or question their treatment. Like that of the men, women's mentality was a reflection of the attitudes that pervaded society. As Celia states:

> I don't think the men would stop any woman from using her abilities; it is just that the women are backward. They are brought up that way. From the time you are a child, you are given dolls; you are not even taught how to ride a bicycle. . . . [Y]ou are brought up to be a woman — to learn only embroidery and prayers. And you are taught how to cook, how to keep your house clean, all the housework. That's all what women are taught.

Although the Huks came to recognize how vital women were to the struggle, the movement did not alter women's status. As in the larger Philippine society, where there was no woman who held a prominent position in business or in government at that time, most Huk women did not occupy leadership positions or have opportunities for advancement. Coming from a feudal society, it was expected that party members would espouse the belief that men should work outside the home and women should take care of it.

Bill Pomeroy writes that both he and Celia insisted "that many men would have no problem if they had overcome their feudal outlooks and had involved their wives in the struggle beside them."[62] In addition to the sex problem, another source of conflict was the so-called family and baby problem, the reluctance of cadres, both women and men, to become more active in the rebellion—and, more particularly, to join "expansion teams" that attempted to spread the insurgency beyond its traditional stronghold in central Luzon—because this would force them to neglect their spouses and children.[63] The party's proposed solution to this problem was to call for integration of spouses (especially wives) and older children into the movement and for the distribution of younger children to friends and relatives who were not involved in the rebellion. According to Celia, those wives who also washed clothes and cooked for the members were allowed to stay in the camps. However, eventually most of them had to go home, as the party would not tolerate women who were merely "decorations," who stayed just to be near their husbands. Women who bore children were also sent home, as children in the camps threatened the security of everyone. In fact, in many Huk areas the solution of integration was not all that successful.

Throughout most of the Huk rebellion, therefore, women's issues were consistently treated as "problems" that required political and strategic solutions. Celia informally became an advocate for women's rights, but she would not see significant changes as a result of her efforts. No systematic reeducation or changes in policy that would promote women's participation were ever undertaken by the party. Women's issues remained secondary to the bigger issue of national liberation. Party leaders who engaged in illicit relationships were not punished. Women consistently left the movement after marrying or becoming pregnant. And yet, however late or imperfect, Celia believes that the party attempted to recognize the disparities that disadvantaged women within the movement. She strongly believes that, once informed, it wanted women to play a more active role.

The path to complete transformation, however, was not easy. And certainly this goal could not have been achieved in a short period of time. As an educator within the HMB movement, Bill Pomeroy describes this specific battle for Celia:

> After a long discussion that gets heated it is decided that the older men, who are peasants, suffer from a feudal outlook that makes them less ready to accept youth and women as equals. Celia has to point out the role of women in the struggle, and that a woman who can stand on her own and argue should be encouraged rather than repressed. One old peasant is stubborn about accepting his weakness; he wants to study the matter.[64]

Celia at one point believed that the promotion of women's rights in the movement meant acting like a man. Being a woman in a predominantly male movement, she was always careful that her actions should not set her apart from her male comrades. Pomeroy recalls another incident, when Celia, even in an extremely difficult situation, did not display vulnerability in front of her comrades:

> There is a morning when the comrades in a security unit say they cannot stand, cannot go any further. Celia, my wife, her face like a frail flower on a thin stalk, hardly able to walk herself, goes into their shelter. What are you? she says. Do you call yourselves men? Must I, a woman, carry you? They look at her with weak pained expressions, holding to the rifles with the butts upon the ground. Ka Rene, they say. Please don't say those things. They pull themselves up, stagger into line, and we go on.[65]

Numerous times during her involvement Celia occupied herself with the question of "how to change this situation—the inequality between men and women." Herself harboring conflicted views, she could not blame the Huks for this condition. It is clear, listening to Celia, that despite her feminist viewpoints she remained deferential and at times submissive to the movement and its leaders. She recalls moments when she harshly criticized the party as times when she acted impulsively and therefore became ineffective. Even at present, she is reluctant to express derogatory opinions about her comrades and even justifies their mentalities and the decisions they made. Discussing why the party treated women the way it did, she could only blame society. While she tried to influence the party, she always followed its directives, somehow accepting the supposition that its male leaders knew more than she did. When she married Bill, she found someone she could look up to, someone she believed to possess a more sophisticated understanding of world affairs. Celia went forward, but she also accepted her place in the movement, partly due to the indifferent treatment she had received from her male comrades. Even though the party nurtured Celia's political development, its members did not fully recognize her talents and achievements or encourage her further. Undercut by their own patriarchal assumptions, many did not respond to the aspirations and capabilities of women comrades such as Celia. As a result, Celia is hesitant to claim her political achievements as her own. Thus, while acting as a leader she remained first and foremost an ardent follower and supporter. Although the treatment of women did not significantly improve in the movement, she continued to believe in the Huks and the party that claimed her allegiance. Unfortunately, her further efforts to advance women's rights were interrupted.

Years later, Celia exclaimed: "For me, those years with the peasants of central Luzon and in the forest enriched my outlook, educated me as no other experiences had done for me, and gave my life meaningful memories that I shall always treasure."[66]

There was never a time when the romance died for Celia.

Always the Romantic

In the early 1950s, the Huks believed that the possibility of victory was real. However, with the U.S. government's military aid the Philippine Army was built into a counterinsurgency force that launched systematic attacks against the guerrillas. The government's expanded military operations led to wholesale arrests of Politburo leaders in October 1950. Intelligence units simultaneously raided twenty-two Manila homes and apartments and captured six officers in the HMB-PKP's national leadership, including PKP general secretary Jose Lava. Hundreds of other Huks and Huk sympathizers, as well as hundreds of Politburo documents, were also captured by government soldiers.[67] After its first great success, the anti-Huk campaign intensified. Other Huk leaders at the forest headquarters immediately felt the loss and perhaps the revolution's imminent defeat. The Huk movement was eventually thrown on the defensive. It was becoming impossible for Celia, Bill, and their comrades to stay for more than a week in one place. The armed forces of the Philippines formed Battalion Combat Teams (BCTs) specifically to confront the Huks, and they scoured the forests on a daily basis, their airplanes continually overhead. In one surprise attack on their camp, Celia and Bill were nearly killed, and they were temporarily separated while fleeing into the forest. Within a few months, in April 1952, they would sustain another attack, and this time they would not escape. Celia narrates:

> Subsequently, in a second surprise attack that we experienced many months later, we suffered disaster. Around noontime a volley of gunfire descended on our huts and sent us dashing down a hillside. Some of our comrades, including women, were killed. William was captured; he lost his glasses and could not manage without them. I was able to dart into the thickness of the dense forest. However, five days later I was also captured— exhausted, starving, feeble, and frightened.[68]

Celia and Bill were reunited at the headquarters of the Philippine Army. The challenge to the Huks' strength, however, was not just external; internally the movement was breaking apart. From 1950 on, the party leadership remained divided over policy issues, while the government performed the double tasks of launching mock agricultural reform programs and intensifying repression. The support of the peasantry in the towns and barrios wavered, which led to the Huks' surrender in late 1954. With the surrender of the last Huk leaders and followers, this phase of peasant revolution ended in the Philippines.

On Celia's thirty-seventh birthday, on 18 June 1952, she and Bill faced a judge in a Manila courtroom who declared them guilty of "rebellion complexed with murder, robbery, arson, and kidnapping" and sentenced them both to life imprisonment. Five years later, due to pressure from many lawyers, the Philippine Supreme Court ruled the charge illegal and declared that it be reduced to one of "simple rebellion," which carried a maximum penalty of twelve years.

Even so, the Pomeroys spent the next ten years of their lives in prison. Celia was initially incarcerated, along with seven other Huk women, in the men's prison where Bill and other Huk men were being held. Influenced by the anticommunist propaganda that branded them as bandits and terrorists, the authorities feared that the Huk women were too dangerous to be quartered in a women's prison. After three years, on 19 July 1955, the eight Huk women were moved to the Correctional Institution for Women, where they were separated from the other two hundred inmates because they were political prisoners. Although still without freedom and separated from Bill, Celia found this prison "less austere" and "more cheerful looking."[69]

Celia continued to be a romantic and idealist in prison. She speaks of some positive outcomes of that experience—she was able to read a lot, she wrote poems for Bill, and she discovered a talent for painting. But perhaps her most important experience was teaching many of her Huk companions, almost all of whom had only elementary schooling, the basics of English grammar, arithmetic, civics, geography, health, and sanitation. Celia writes: "By the time we parted from one another, my companions could read newspapers in English and could carry on easy conversation in English."[70]

In January 1962, Bill and Celia were released from prison. They were granted a presidential pardon by President Carlos P. Garcia, who responded to the pressures of an international campaign on their behalf. Upon their release, Bill was immediately deported to the United States and to this day cannot return to the Philippines. Celia, on the other hand, was not allowed to enter the United States. Thus, the two have made their home in England, though Celia continues to campaign for Bill to be allowed back into his beloved Philippines.[71]

In Britain, where they moved in 1963, Bill worked as a correspondent for a leftist newspaper, the *Guardian*, and later for the *People's Daily World*.[72] Celia earned a living as a teacher, first at the Harry Gosling Primary School, located in the East End, and later at the Joseph Tritton

Primary School in the southwestern part of London. She undertook this task with the same perseverance that marked her as a political leader. Whenever she had the chance, Celia would talk to her children about the Philippines and "People of other Lands."[73] She took evening classes to improve her skills and joined the National Union of Teachers. Later she became the representative of her union at the school, directing its attempts to improve the pay and conditions of teachers. In 1977, she retired after twelve years as a teacher. She was later informed that she had been the first Filipino teacher in the British schools.[74]

Throughout her years in Britain, Celia has never abandoned her revolutionary ideals. In 1975–76, she went to several British libraries to give a series of one-hour lectures and conduct discussion sessions on the Philippines. She also became a devoted member of the National Assembly of Women (NAW), a British women's organization, founded in 1952 to work toward full equality for women in all areas. For eleven years, between 1978 and 1989, she served as a member of NAW's Executive Committee and represented the organization at international women's conferences held in Berlin, Prague, Budapest, and Moscow.[75]

Echoing her days with the Huk movement, Celia also worked for six years as an editor for NAW's journal, called *SISTERS* (Sisters in Solidarity to End Racism and Sexism), where she wrote about women's issues and struggles around the world. In 1984, she organized a branch of NAW in West London and has served as its secretary to the present day. As a member of NAW, she is often invited to give lectures about the Philippines in different parts of Britain.

Celia has stated that "the turbulence of the armed struggle, our capture by the Philippine Army, our imprisonment, and our efforts to be reunited in another country blurred for me for a long period the pursuit of improving the lot of our women in the home country."[76] Still she did not waver in her nationalist commitment and in Britain resumed her connections with the nascent and dynamic women's movement in the Philippines. Although she was far away, she renewed her ties with the PKP and has relentlessly encouraged its leaders to promote women within its ranks.[77]

In early 1974, Celia learned that the Women's International Democratic Federation (WIDF), an organization closely aligned with the United Nations, was to hold an international conference in conjunction with the U.N. Decade for Women in Sofia, Bulgaria, in March 1975. She wrote to the PKP's secretary general, Felicisimo Macapagal, and several comrades, emphasizing the need to send delegates from the party to this historic and important event. She also sent a document explaining the need for an organization that would mobilize women to take up the revolutionary cause. Her efforts were not in vain. In the latter part of 1975, she was informed by the party that a women's organization had been founded that year called the KaBaPa, or *Katipunan ng mga Bagong Pilipina* (Federation of the New Filipino Women). Two delegates, one of whom was Aida Lava, were sent to Bulgaria to attend the conference, and their organization eventually became affiliated with the WIDF. KaBaPa also became the peasant women's organization of Central Luzon that included many Huk women veterans, and in 1976 Celia was invited to join. She prides herself on being part of this women's movement, which now claims about twenty thousand members and is, according to Celia, the "strongest, biggest and the most progressive" women's organization in the Philippines.[78]

During trips to the Philippines in 1982 and 1985, Celia saw the KaBaPa in action. The party had placed its most capable women cadres in the KaBaPa, whose emphasis was the mobilization of women in the provinces. She saw primers published to educate ordinary women in the barrios and towns of central Luzon and masses of literature distributed on women's issues. The KaBaPa also discoursed on political issues such as removal of U.S. military bases and agrarian reform. Regular meetings and discussion sessions were held, and KaBaPa was always successful in organizing two to five thousand women to join in antigovernment demonstrations in the 1980s. Celia could only have dreamed of such things when she was still a Huk. Most importantly, she was pleased to see "how the recruitment of many women into the party and into mass organizations had strengthened their struggle for national liberation" — a reversal of the party's earlier policy.[79] She knows that the groundwork for all these accomplishments was laid during the Huk struggles.

Today Celia and Bill enjoy a peaceful existence in Britain, a world away from their turbulent lives during the Huk rebellion. Although they are no longer leading a revolution, they still spend time reading and writing about matters of political and personal significance. After fifty years of marriage, they savor every moment together. Celia finds pleasure in narrating stories from her Huk days, even though these were also the times when she experienced much hardship. She does not call herself a hero. She considers herself fortunate to have known dedicated comrades who nurtured her political maturity. She never questions the fact that while her male Huk comrades are already in the history books she remains obscure.

Lessons from the Huk Rebellion

The biography of Celia is more than a presentation of a remarkable and extraordinary life; it also offers a different perspective on the Huk movement and the state of gender and social relations in Philippine society. Celia was a product of her society, and yet her struggles challenged the values of both the Huk movement and Philippine society. She was surrounded by people who persuaded her to become a revolutionary. But, more significantly, her life was shaped by momentous events, especially the war. Thus, Celia's political development grew out of her relationships with people, especially her comrades, and her response to the political and social forces around her. By looking closely at Celia's life, we can gain insights not only into the society she lived in but more directly into the Huk rebellion, arguably one of the most significant events in modern Philippine history.

Philippine society during the period of the Huk rebellion segregated men's and women's labor. Women dominated the domestic economy and were responsible for housekeeping, child care, and income generation.[80] Though many women were agricultural workers, Filipino men controlled the national and political economies. Women felt most comfortable with decision making in the household, while men usually managed public decision making.[81] Although public educational opportunities were readily available to women from the early 1900s on, only women from specific classes were able to study.[82] Women were not allowed to vote until 1938, and until more recent decades they rarely entered formal politics. Until 1963, the armed forces banned women from its ranks.[83] The structure of the Philippine Army in the 1930s reflected an engendered division in society that defined "men as the protectors and women as the protected."[84] Military men, from their initiation rites throughout their training, promoted a strict ideal of masculinity. In this definition, women stayed in the background, primarily acting as "muses" to these valiant men. The military was but a reflection of the kind of engendered divisions occurring in Philippine society at the time.[85]

Indeed, for a politically motivated woman of the 1930s and 1940s such as Celia, radical movements provided the most readily available venue for political involvement. In many ways, the Huk movement subverted the existing social and gender inequities in Philippine society. The Huks promoted a social revolution, bringing together peasants, workers, members of the middle class, professionals, and intellectuals in support of causes such as land reform, equal rights, and social justice. The Huk organization created a classless structure in which everyone, in principle, had an opportunity to influence the movement's decisions and actions. Male peasants, even those without formal education, were able to assume leadership positions. The movement similarly attempted not to discriminate according to class or religion. Cadres democratically selected members of the party who protected and advanced the movement's ideals. Finally, by recruiting women as soldiers and combat commanders, the movement subverted the larger societal roles of men as protectors and women as protected. However limited its efforts may have been, the party was determined to address the gender issue—perhaps for the first time in Philippine history—by recruiting women cadres and developing their abilities. The Huks attempted to create an alternative society, promoting the ideals of brotherhood, equality, compassion, and justice within their organization. These are the same principles that the Huks believed to be missing in the unjust, divided, and repressive Philippine society. Although the Huks advocated such radical policies, this presentation of the life history of Celia shows how ingrained the inequities (and especially sexual divisions) were in Philippine society and how they shaped the Huk revolutionary movement.

As demonstrated by Celia's experiences, women's role in the Huk movement reflected and even reproduced the larger sexual division of labor that pervaded Philippine society. Their relegation to the domestic sphere and their role in reproductive activities indicate that women were, even within a radical movement, likely to perform tasks consistent with their gender. Indeed, in the Huk rebellion women generally assumed supportive rather than leadership or combatant roles. Ranging in age from sixteen to twenty-eight years, most women found themselves on support and service committees—propaganda, medical, communications (courier), intelligence, secretarial, education, and youth and women's organizing. Sofia Logarta explained that women in the Huk movement did the "cooking, washing and sewing," but she qualified this complaint with the observation that men sometimes helped out when they had the time.[86] Since women in Philippine society then were largely relegated to the domestic sphere, such work was readily accepted, tolerated, and willingly performed by the Huk women.[87] Logarta concludes that "women performed traditional tasks of females," although sometimes they also "did things not tied to their sex role."[88]

Women not only joined the movement to increase the numbers of the Huk rebels. They joined to protect themselves, to fight, to care for their comrades, to follow, and to lead—to make their presence felt both within the movement and outside of it. Celia's biography shows that the Huk women joined the movement with roles and cultures ascribed to them by their families, communities, and society, yet some of them tried to venture beyond those roles. In a highly segregated society and a nonfeminist movement such as the Huk, the fact that a woman became a leader, a commander, and a member of the Politburo challenges the dominant paradigms that dictate what women should do. These women were both the protected and protectors, cooks and fighters, comrades and lovers. Like the men, women received ideological and practical training. Many risked their lives for the movement. Perhaps most unexpected was that this very participation altered the movement and changed the dynamics of the rebellion.

Most women, and even Celia at one point, seldom understood their significance. They were not supposed to assume positions that were reserved for men, particularly combat and leadership positions. In general, Huk women, although seen as vital to the struggle, remained subordinate and dominated by men, and their roles were considered "subsidiary" and not crucial to the movement's success. The party, at different periods during the rebellion and even after, has been unwilling to analyze the discrepancies within the movement, as is amply demonstrated by its treatment of the sex problem. Perhaps echoing what the male comrades believed, Logarta states that women, "aside from facilitating life within the movement and making it more joyful," also "formed part of the strong link between the guerrillas and their mass support."[89] Celia herself, despite having leadership responsibilities, remained mostly deferential to the male leaders of the Huk movement. Even today, she believes that the revolutionary solution to the sex problem was the best the party could produce, even though it clearly did not empower women. The solution in the end gave men control, allowing them to have two women during the struggle and then choose one after the revolution. The solution also explicitly guided men but ignored the possibility that women might enter into similar relations. Although Celia admits that there were times when the party's decisions conflicted with her own, she consistently stood by it. For her, the bigger battle was for social justice and national liberation — everything else, including women's equality, came second.

For Celia, the gender divisions in the movement cannot be attributed solely to the attitudes of the party and the Huks themselves. Speaking with her idealism and dedication intact, she believes that the party and the members were products of their societies, bringing with them some of its prejudices. In many ways, Celia's romanticism and devotion to the movement blinded her and her comrades to the hard reality of the party's myopic analysis of Philippine society, including gender relations, which led them to blind persistence in a doomed strategy. The Politburo launched an armed revolution that had, in retrospect, limited chances of success, wasting many lives and exhausting the resources of the movement in an ill-advised armed struggle. The party similarly was unsuccessful in addressing the needs and aspirations of its followers, especially women. The Huk movement was undercut by its own patriarchal assumptions about appropriate gender roles and sexuality, despite its egalitarian ideology. Thus, the Huks not only diminished the potential contribution of women, but they failed to take into consideration the extent to which the process of women's participation was transforming the gendered norms, practices, and aspirations of all their participants, female and male.

These internal social dynamics — the relationships between women and men, leaders and members — profoundly affected the outcome of this revolutionary struggle. In lieu of an explicitly political agenda, sexual and moral norms were tacitly imposed that turned out to be inimical to the members' immediate needs and deep-seated aspirations. By recruiting many women yet relegating most to support roles and by advancing a few to command yet allowing others to serve the sexual needs of powerful male leaders, the party fostered serious contradictions within its ranks. The presence of women confronted the Huk organization with new challenges to incorporate women's desires and interests into the movement's goals and necessitated a strict code of discipline and morality among both its female and male members. But the leadership's ineptitude in both understanding and addressing these issues led to restrictions on women's roles and serious problems of solidarity among the movement's members. In a certain sense, the Huk movement suffered from its own hesitant steps toward a more progressive policy on gender.

Ultimately, the Huks failed from their limited analysis of objective social conditions, aggressive yet unrealistic military and political tactics, divisions between peasant members and the intellectually distant leadership, and a contradictory policy toward women cadres. All these weakened the movement from within and destined it to fail with or without the effects of the government's counterinsurgency measures. Celia knew that the party and the movement were not without their flaws, and yet she gave herself to the Huks, never wavering in her commitment. Her involvement was marked by inner conflicts between the cause she was fighting for and the movement to which she gave such devotion — although perhaps it did not truly deserve her. Her romanticism resolved these tensions for Celia, as she looked beyond the Huk movement's failures and limitations to give her whole life to its cause.

Conclusion

The life of Celia Mariano-Pomeroy, almost invisible in the current historical works on the Huk rebellion, offers a serious challenge to the prevalent paradigms regarding gender and collective action in Philippine society. Not only did she leave her comfortable life at home, but she joined a military and revolutionary organization that not only was outlawed but historically excluded women. She responded to the events and people around her by working for national liberation during the war and for social justice and equality at times of ostensible peace. The daily realities

of her life and the challenges she faced at the time of her involvement
were unique and certainly extraordinary. By joining the Huks, she freed
herself from the limitations imposed by her culture to become an active,
political member of society. In a significant, though limited, way, her
efforts to make the Huk movement itself a site for revolutionary change
constitute an important contribution to the structural transformation of
Philippine society.

Unfortunately, even forty years after the revolt we still have only a
conventional account of this important period in Philippine history. The
dominant narrative of the Huk rebellion is still that of a movement that
began during the Japanese occupation, won the support of central Luzon
peasants, and was led by the Communist Party. Much of the recorded
history of the Huk rebellion thus remains essentially a sociopolitical
account of a peasant revolution. By witnessing Celia's life, we can begin
to see that there are dynamics within the rebellion that cannot be
explained by politics, just as there are many aspects of the movement
that have not yet been explored. Celia's biography provides an intimate
look at a movement that was not only threatened by external factors but
challenged from within. The issue of gender imbalance and sexual
exploitation, hereby opened through Celia's biography, allows us to
understand how these contradictions, although not the main cause for
the movement's defeat, nonetheless weakened the guerrillas' solidarity
and military capacity and played a significant, though unquantifiable,
role in the Huks' ultimate downfall. Moreover, Celia's life demonstrates
the conflicts between one individual's idealism and the organization's
limitations, leading us to a more critical analysis of the party and a deeper understanding of the Huk movement. Unless biographies of individuals, such as that of Celia, are incorporated in the rebellion's history, the
Huk story will never be complete.

Individual biographies of Huk women can remedy the largely gender-
and sex-blind literature on the Huk rebellion and other histories of movements in the Philippines. Biographies have the unique potential to bring
women into history and make the female experience part of the written
record. This form of research thereby revises history by forcing us to modify previously published accounts that did not take women's experiences
seriously.[90] Indeed, biographical work such as that presented here
becomes all the more significant, and necessary, because it draws actors
and actresses out of obscurity and corrects the largely male- and elite-
biased Philippine historical record.

NOTES

This essay has undergone numerous changes, including a complete revision of the original presentation made at the Association for Asian Studies annual meetings in 1995 in Washington, D.C. I would like to thank, first of all, Al McCoy, who stood by this project in many ways. He meticulously edited my draft (in all its versions) and made substantive comments that challenged me to deepen my analysis. Many people have also helped me since my presentation at the AAS conference. I would like to thank especially Mike Cullinane, Amy Golden, Jeff Goodwin, Joyce Hermoso, Friedrich Huebler, and Rosanne Rutten, who assisted me as friends and colleagues. Thanks also go to Jan Opdyke for editing my overly long manuscript. Many people in the Philippines also helped in invaluable ways. Since there are too many of them to mention here, I limit myself to thanking the remarkable Huk men and women in Manila and central Luzon who treated me very warmly, accommodated me, and patiently answered all my questions. Finally, I would like to thank Celia and Bill Pomeroy, who welcomed me in their home, gave me their undivided attention, fed me, and reminisced with me about their years as revolutionary fighters and leaders. Ka Celia offered her life story in remarkable detail, and it is because of her that I wrote this essay.

1. William Pomeroy, *The Forest: A Personal Record of the Huk Guerrilla Struggle in the Philippines* (New York: International, 1963), 30.
2. See especially Benedict Kerkvliet, *The Huk Rebellion: A Study of Peasant Revolt in the Philippines* (Manila: New Day, 1979); Eduardo Lachica, *Huk: Philippine Agrarian Society in Revolt* (Manila: Solidaridad, 1971); Alfred Saulo, *Communism in the Philippines: An Introduction* (Quezon City: Ateneo de Manila University Press, 1990); and Alvin Scaff, *The Philippine Answer to Communism* (Stanford: Stanford University Press, 1955).
3. The number of commanders was elicited in the course of my interviews. On the total number of squadrons, see Kerkvliet, *Huk Rebellion*, 87.
4. At the time of the Huk rebellion, women had begun to assume major roles in other revolutionary movements such as those in China and Vietnam, although their inclusion in their countries' histories has only been advanced by feminist historians since the late 1970s and early 1980s. For China, see Judith Stacey, *Patriarchy and Socialist Revolution in China* (Berkeley: University of California Press, 1983); Elisabeth Croll, *Feminism and Socialism in China* (New York: Schocken Books, 1978); Kay Ann Johnson, *Women, the Family, and Peasant Revolution in China* (Chicago: University of Chicago Press, 1983); and Christina Kelley Gilmartin, *Engendering the Chinese Revolution: Radical Women, Communist Politics, and Mass Movements in the 1920s* (Berkeley: University of California Press, 1995). For Vietnam, see Arlene Eisen, *Women and Revolution in Vietnam* (London: Zed Books, 1984); and Tran Tu Binh's memoir *The Red Earth: A Vietnamese Memoir of a Life on a Colonial Rubber Plantation* (Athens: Ohio University, Center for International Studies, Center for Southeast Asian Studies, 1985).
5. The most comprehensive accounts of the social and economic transformation of the Philippine economy since the late nineteenth century are found in Alfred W. McCoy and Ed. C. de Jesus, eds., *Philippine Social History: Global Trade and*

   Local Transformations (Manila: Ateneo de Manila University Press, 1976).
6. This statement is one of the main themes of Kerkvliet's authoritative *The Huk Rebellion* (see especially 250–52, 254–55, 266).
7. Ibid; Bill Pomeroy, letter to the author, 15 March 1999.
8. The repression of the Huks took many forms. Harassment by landlord guards and government authorities of Hukbalahap veterans and peasant union participants intensified. The headquarters of the Pambansang Kaisahan ng mga Magbubukid, or National Peasants' Union (PKM), the largest peasant organization in the country's history, was frequently ransacked and meetings of its chapters curtailed. On the national level, upon the commencement of Roxas's presidency and the Philippine Congress in 1946, the six central Luzon congressmen-elect on the Democratic Alliance (DA) ticket, as well as another sympathetic congressman from Bulacan, were prohibited from taking their seats following false allegations that they had used terror and other illegal means to win. The refusal to seat these representatives, coupled with the Roxas administration's zeal for military force, resulted in increased violence and more peasants going underground. But perhaps the most immediate cause of the Huk rebellion was the disappearance and killing of Juan Feleo, a popular and highly effective peasant leader (Kerkvliet, *Huk Rebellion*, 92ff.).
9. Ibid.; Secretariat, Communist Party of the Philippines (CPP), "Milestones in the History of the CCP," Politburo Exhibit no. O-180F, n.d., Court Exhibits, University of the Philippines Archives. See also Kerkvliet, *Huk Rebellion*.
10. The Politburo, or Political Bureau, was the policy-making organ and think tank of the Communist Party of the Philippines, which comprised the leadership of the Huk movement.
11. Taruc in his second book disowns the authorship of the first, claiming that it was edited by another Politburo member before it was sent to the United States for publication and that many important sections were added without his knowledge. It is now an established fact that William Pomeroy wrote the book but placed Taruc's name on the cover for various complex reasons.
12. Saulo wrote *Communism in the Philippines* as well as numerous articles narrating his personal experiences as a Huk guerrilla.
13. This information is based on numerous conversations with Alejandrino and Lava. For a treatment of the Lava Brothers, see Jose Dalisay, Jr., "The Lava Brothers: Blood and Politics," *Public Policy* (University of the Philippines), July-September 1998, Vol. II. No. 3, and his new book, *The Lavas, A Filipino Family* (Pasig City: Anvil, 1999).
14. This statement is one of Kerkvliet's conclusions in *Huk Rebellion* (262).
15. For feminist historical works, see, for example, Joan Scott, *Gender and the Politics of History* (New York: Columbia University Press, 1988); Jane Atkinson and Shelly Errington, eds., *Power and Difference: Gender in Island Southeast Asia* (Stanford: Stanford University Press, 1990); Louise Tilly and Joan Scott, *Women, Work, and Family* (New York: Routledge, 1989); Micaela di Leonardo, ed., *Gender at the Crossroads of Knowledge: Feminist Anthropology in the Postmodern Era* (Berkeley: University of California Press, 1991); Guida West and Rhoda Lois Blumberg, eds., *Women and Social Protest* (New York: Oxford University Press, 1990); and Cynthia Enloe, *Does Khaki Become You? The Militarization of Women's Lives* (London: South End, 1983).
16. Shulamit Reinharz, with assistance from Lynn Davidman, *Feminist Methods in Social Research* (New York: Oxford University Press, 1992).
17. Jennifer Scanlon, "Challenging the Imbalances of Power in Feminist Oral

History," *Women's Studies International Forum* 16, no. 6 (1993): 639–45.

18. Quoted from Reinharz, *Feminist Methods*, 132.

19. Ibid., 134.

20. This essay on Celia Pomeroy is part of a larger dissertation project on the role of women in the Huk rebellion in the Philippines. My main aim in this essay, as well as in the dissertation, is to bring men and women together in history, but the space constraints of a biographical essay limit the number of characters, male and female, of this essay beyond the subject herself.

21. Most of the material for Celia's biography was obtained through a series of interviews (conducted in English) with her in Twickenham, England, in October and November 1998. Her words, unless otherwise stated, are extracted directly from the transcripts of the interviews.

22. Celia Mariano-Pomeroy, interview with the author, Twickenham, England, October 1998.

23. Celia Pomeroy, "WWII Forgotten Heroine," *Kamusta*, no. 2 (1995): 11 (interview with Diana Reed).

24. The PKP, led by Crisanto Evangelista, merged with the SPP—the Socialist Party of the Philippines—which had been founded by Pedro Abad Santos in 1938. At the beginning of the war, these two leaders were caught and tortured by the Japanese. Thus, Vicente Lava became the secretary general of the PKP.

25. Speech by Celia Mariano-Pomeroy delivered at the Malibongwe Conference for South African Women, Amsterdam, 11 January 1990.

26. Pomeroy, "WWII," 2.

27. Ibid., 3.

28. Celia Mariano-Pomeroy, "Experiences as a Guerrilla in the Philippines," lecture delivered at the Centre of Southeast Asian Studies, University of Kent, 17 May 1991.

29. Ibid.

30. Celia Mariano-Pomeroy, interview with the author, October 1998.

31. Pomeroy, "WWII," 2.

32. Bill Pomeroy letter to the author, 15 March 1999.

33. Ibid.

34. William Pomeroy, interview with the author, October 1998; Candy Gourlay, "Happy Birthday Celia and Thanks," *Filipinos in Europe*, summer 1995.

35. Pomeroy, *The Forest*, 21.

36. Ibid.

37. Mariano-Pomeroy, "Experiences as a Guerrilla."

38. Pomeroy, *The Forest*, 31.

39. This quote and the next one are from ibid., 31.

40. Mariano-Pomeroy, "Experiences as a Guerrilla."

41. Pomeroy, *The Forest*, 82–83.

42. Ibid., 204.

43. The other woman who reached a position of leadership in the party as a member of the Hukbalahap Military Committee, though she was never a member of the Politburo, was Felipa Culala. Popularly known as "Dayang-Dayang," Culala was the first known female to command guerrilla detachments against the Japanese. She became well known for her victories over the Japanese military, including the capture of the municipal building in Candaba, Pampanga, on 8 March 1942, during which prisoners were freed and the Japanese and their allied Filipino soldiers were killed. Her victories, however, were known to have driven her to abuses such as stealing food, carabaos, money, and other valuables

from villagers. She was summoned by the Politburo, court-martialed, and executed by a firing squad. The story of Dayang-Dayang still captivates the people of central Luzon and comprises many of the myths regarding Huk women commanders, although there is little written or known about her. See Luis Taruc, *Born of the People* (Westport, Conn.: Greenwood, 1953), 128–30; and Celia Mariano-Pomeroy to Jeff Goodwin, 26 February 1993 (cited by permission). Other female military commanders were Remedios Gomez, Simeona Tapang, and Gloria Sagum. Some women held positions as leaders in the Education/Organization Department, including Rosenda Torres and Manuela Maclang.

44. Christina Kelley Gilmartin, *Engendering the Chinese Revolution*, 101.

45. Ibid., 108–9.

46. Undoubtedly, the most explosive internal problem in the movement was that of sex opportunism, also known as the "sex problem," terms that referred to the affectual dynamics of men-women relationships within the movement (Secretariat, "Milestones").

47. Mariano-Pomeroy, "Experiences as a Guerrilla."

48. Although most of the Huk men and women knew about the "*kwalingking* cases," no one seems to know the origin of the term. It is not a Tagalog or Kapampangan word. Nonetheless, almost everyone in the movement understood what *kwalingking* meant.

49. For an in-depth discussion of the sex problem and its effects on the Huk movement, see Jeff Goodwin, "The Libidinal Constitution of a High-Risk Social Movement: Affectual Ties and Solidarity in the Huk Rebellion, 1946–1954," *American Sociological Review* 62 (February 1997): 53–69.

50. This information is derived from interviews with several Huk women, including Celia, Rosenda Torres, and Lily del Castillo.

51. Luis Taruc, *He Who Rides the Tiger: The Story of an Asian Guerrilla Leader* (London: Geoffrey Chapman, 1967), 64; Goodwin, "Libidinal Constitution," 62.

52. Mariano-Pomeroy, "Experiences as a Guerrilla."

53. Secretariat, CCP, "Revolutionary Solution of the Sex Problem," Politburo Exhibit no. I-15, 12 September 1950, Court Exhibits, University of the Philippines Archives.

54. Ibid.

55. Pomeroy, *The Forest*, 143.

56. The so-called sex problem was not a unique Philippine revolutionary experience. In the Nicaraguan revolutionary movement, Dora Maria Tellez, a military commander, recalls that "the problem of male chauvinism was evident among the comrades. . . . Some men harboured distinctly sexist attitudes toward women. They believed that women were for domestic tasks alone, and that they shouldn't go beyond being messengers. Some even said women were no good in the mountains, but they were only good 'for screwing,' that they created conflict — sexual conflict (Enloe, *Does Khaki Become You?* 171).

57. Secretariat, "Revolutionary Solution"; Pomeroy, *The Forest*, 144.

58. Celia Mariano-Pomeroy, interview with the author, October 1998.

59. Pomeroy, *The Forest*, 144.

60. Many of my Huk interviewees, including Celia, did not know whether the solution was implemented or how successful it was.

61. Using sociological and psychological explanations, Jeff Goodwin argues that such affectual relationships eroded the solidarity of the Huk movement and undermined the collective identity and discipline of communist cadres ("Libidinal Constitution," 53–69).

62. Pomeroy, *The Forest*, 144.
63. Goodwin, "Libidinal Constitution," 63–64; Secretariat, CPP, "Letter to PB (Out) from SEC," Politburo Exhibit no. O–321, 27 May 1950, Court Exhibits, University of the Philippines Archives.
64. Pomeroy, *The Forest*, 34.
65. Ibid., 204.
66. Mariano-Pomeroy, "Experiences as a Guerrilla."
67. Kerkvliet, *The Huk Rebellion*, p. 218.
68. Mariano-Pomeroy, "Experiences as a Guerrilla."
69. Ibid.
70. Ibid.
71. Gourlay, "Filipinos in Europe."
72. Bill still writes for this newspaper, now called *The People's Weekly World*.
73. Celia Mariano-Pomeroy, "Personal Experiences of Integration in Britain" (transcript of a speech delivered in 1993).
74. Ibid.
75. Celia Mariano-Pomeroy, letter to author, 3 April 1999.
76. Celia Mariano-Pomeroy to Jeff Goodwin, 26 January 1993.
77. This Communist Party (the PKP) should be distinguished from the other "new" Communist Party of the Philippines (the CPP-MTT), which was founded by Jose Maria Sison in 1968. Celia's affiliation continues to be with the "old" PKP of the Huks.
78. Pomeroy, "Personal Experiences." Celia's assessment is somewhat overstated, ignoring other prominent women's organizations such as Gabriela, which is connected with the rival CPP-MTT. Although KaBaPa did have a considerable following, Gabriela has more members and has been much more influential in the advance of the women's movement in the Philippines.
79. Celia Mariano-Pomeroy to Jeff Goodwin, 26 June 1993.
80. Cristina Montiel and Mary Racelis Hollnsteiner, *The Filipino Woman: Her Role and Status in Philippine Society* (Manila: Ateneo de Manila University Press, 1976).
81. Ibid., 16.
82. Encarnacion Alzona, *Social and Economic Status of Filipino Women, 1565–1932* (Manila: University of the Philippines Press, 1933).
83. See Alfred McCoy's analysis of the construction of the male identity in the Philippine military in *Closer Than Brothers: Manhood at the Philippine Military Academy* (New Haven: Yale University Press, 1999); and "'Same Banana': Hazing and Honor at the Philippine Military Academy," *Journal of Asian Studies* 54, no. 3 (August 1995): 689–726.
84. McCoy, *Closer Than Brothers*.
85. Ibid.
86. Sofia Logarta, "The Participation of Women in the Huk Movement," in *Women's Role in Philippine Society: Selected Essays* (Diliman: University Center for Women's Studies, 1996), 138.
87. Jesus Lava, former secretary general of the PKP, explained that such appropriation was not the fault of the women. He attributed it to the "feudal relations" that prevailed in the countryside and to the nature of society in general. Women were simply not considered equal to men, and such prejudice existed among the cadres themselves (Jesus Lava, interview with the author, Manila, November 1993).
88. Logarta, *Women's Role*, 138.
89. Ibid., 139.
90. Reinharz, *Feminist Methods*, 134.

Jose Ma. Nava presenting a portrait that he had painted of
President Elipidio Quirino at a mass rally,
Iloilo City, ca. 1949.

A DYING DREAMER:
JOSE NAVA AND THE DRAMA OF CLASS STRUGGLE

Alfred W. McCoy

Y ou are now in Iloilo," union *supremo* Jose Nava told a Philippine labor convention on May Day 1951. Speaking in the thundering baritone that had won him fame on the local stage, he celebrated his union's historic role in the country's class struggle. "You are the guests of this great city," he continued, "a queen by its own right, the bulwark of freedom and democracy, the bastion of freemen, the Bethlehem of workers and peasants who 22 years ago proclaimed the emancipation of the workingman with the advent of the Federacion Obrera de Filipinas."[1]

With language and gesture, Nava presented himself as the powerful leader of a miliitant union that controlled an entire city. Through his loaded words — *advent, Bethlehem,* and *emancipation* — he seemed to portray himself as a latter-day Moses, leading his people out of a socioeconomic wilderness. Moreover, his image of a militant, unified Ilongo working class was matched by his union's organizational chart showing 100,000 members in 114 branches spread across the southern Philippines — 46 in Iloilo, 4 in Capiz, 14 in Negros Occidental, 27 in the Eastern Visayas, and 23 in Mindanao.

Yet these were false images. The Federacion Obrera de Filipinas (FOF) had launched several impressive general strikes under Nava's leadership in the early 1930s. But, riven by ideological, factional, and family fissures, the union was now crumbling from within.[2] Few of the chapters outside of Iloilo forwarded their monthly dues to the union's headquarters. In 1948, for example, the total remitted was only P8,362 — barely enough to cover the costs of electricity and rent and leaving little for staff salaries.[3] At the end of World War II, Nava's sons had rebuilt the union's influence on the Iloilo waterfront, but they did so with a violence that alienated loyal crew bosses and angered the city's elite. Moreover, Nava himself failed to grasp the primacy of electoral politics after independence in 1946 and mismanaged his factional alliances, alienating both regional and national patrons.

Only two days after Nava delivered this defiant address, Constabulary troopers arrested him on charges of subversion—beginning a prosecution that would bring the dissolution of the union, the imprisonment of his sons, and his own death in prison. During the three years that elapsed between his arrest and his death, once loyal union leaders turned away, the rank and file remained silent, and elite allies abandoned him.

Although the FOF was the largest and most militant labor union in the prewar Philippines, its history remains obscure. Jose Nava led the largest strikes in the history of the country's labor movement, but he is little known beyond his native Iloilo. Even there he is remembered as a demon who destroyed the city's prosperity with his unbending demands and extreme violence. If the world knows anything of Jose Nava today, it is only through a harsh portrayal as Tio Sergio, the ruthless waterfront boss in Stevan Javellana's novel *Without Seeing the Dawn*.[4] Beyond recovering a lost chapter in the country's labor history, Nava's biography opens us to the world of prewar Filipino intellectuals who combined literary careers with working-class mobilization to launch the modern Philippine labor movement.

Looking at the past through the prism of Nava's eyes, we can glimpse, albeit faintly, Philippine provincial life in an era before Manila's relentless rise stripped the outlying islands of their vernacular culture, political autonomy, and intellectual vitality. Most importantly, Nava's life is exemplary of a generation of Filipino literati who used reputations from journalism and drama to inspire the country's first trade unions. As a self-taught artist and writer, Nava, like other union leaders of the colonial era, was an active participant in the prewar florescence of vernacular literature as poet, playwright, and journalist. Moving beyond the narrow nationalism of the colony's political elite, these vernacular literati identified with working-class aspirations for social justice and used their credibility to organize both laboring brotherhoods and trade unions. Their fusion of literary eloquence and political radicalism played a catalytic role in an early, critical phase of lower-class mobilization.

Among this generation of activist literati, Jose Nava was the most successful and controversial, for he not only built a union but he destroyed a city. From his base on the Iloilo waterfront, Nava built the FOF into the colony's largest trade union. He led the country's only general strikes. He rewrote the social contract between the city's sugar brokers and stevedores. He became the most powerful labor leader of his generation. But his hold over the Iloilo waterfront was so tenacious and his union's labor charges were so high that exporters were forced to move their cargoes elsewhere, hastening, after 1930, the city's relentless economic decline. If history is indeed written by the victors, then it is not surprising that Nava is remembered today not for building a militant labor movement but for destroying a city.

Elusive Subject

This attempt at biography has both problems and promise. Over the past fifteen years, I have written separate articles about the region's theater, politics, and unions, using Nava as an exemplar or actor in these histories. By subordinating his life to larger analytical tasks, I could only present a single fragment of his complex, multifaceted career. By contrast, in preparing this biography I have tried to see Nava's life from his own perspective. Not only have I come to understand his personality, and its contradictions, more fully, but I have been able to see his role in these larger events more clearly than before. This narrowly focused biography offers new insights about the larger issues that first attracted me to him, and he emerges from it as a more significant historical figure than I had imagined.

In writing his story, I will use Nava's words whenever possible and try to make him, in one sense, the narrator of his own life. Instead of simply recounting his biography as a seamless narrative with all the contradictions and confusion sorted out, I will pause to reproduce verbatim extracts from documents that he somehow created — his birth certificate, diaries, autobiographies, union history, letters, and speeches. Inserting these passages into the text slows the narrative pace, but it also forces us to engage his life and its meaning on his terms.

Yet this subjective method is not without its problems. By focusing on Nava as an individual, I found that his role in shaping the events that revolved about him was sometimes less than what he would have had us believe. As an accomplished playwright, he fictionalized his own life, investing it with a sense of historical drama that often sacrificed detail for effect. In short autobiographies and union histories, Nava wrote himself into the narrative as the central figure, the moving force in great events — in a word, the hero. Yet when looking beyond his words to other sources, oral and documentary, we find that his account suffers from an obvious bias. Not only did he embellish events, sacrificing fact for effect, but he often twisted facts in his favor — forgetting dates and details or leaving out embarrassing incidents. To cite but one example, Nava's arrest and death makes him seem, in his own public statements, the victim of repression by reactionaries trying to crush his militant union. Examining his words critically through an objective biography allows us to see these same events with all the blunders that made him, in one sense, the author of his own demise.

Even though we might wish to let Nava tell his own story, we cannot trust him fully on either the facts or their interpretation if we wish to understand the significance of his life. To resolve this apparent conflict between the objective and subjective, we can combine both approaches, letting Nava's words narrate his life, whenever possible, but intruding, whenever necessary, to comment or even correct.

The dramatic flair that makes Nava an unreliable narrator of his own life was both an asset and a liability in the living of that same life. All his thespian graces—the strong voice, romantic imagination, gift for words, and the following that these won him—gave him the means and motivation for mobilizing the city's poor against powerful social pressures. Indeed, without his romantic vision of class struggle, Nava might never have dared to venture beyond the narrow middle-class confines of his conservative city. Instead, driven by his heroic self-image as a leader of the oppressed, he sacrificed a conventional career and chances for self-advancement to pursue his ideals beyond the tolerances of society's limits. Nava always chose principle and confrontation over convention and compromise. Indeed, his heroic self-image drove him to acts of moral courage and historical import. Yet the same romantic vision that inspired his work as a labor leader ultimately ensured its failure. Indeed, it is this tension, even contradiction, between Nava's idealism and pragmatism that lends a tragic air to an extraordinary career.

Colonial City

Nava's life as a union leader followed the economic rhythms of his native city, rising with Iloilo's brief florescence as a major sugar port and declining with the contraction of its cargo volume after World War II. Indeed, to understand Nava's multifaceted career as a dramatist, newspaper editor, and radical activist we have to understand something of the city that was his stage.

By century's turn, Iloilo City was already well established as the regional entrepôt for the islands of Panay and Negros, known as the Western Visayas region. While Iloilo Province was one of the archipelago's richest rice granaries, Negros Occidental, facing Iloilo City across the Guimaras Strait, supplied some 60 percent of Philippine sugar production in the 1930s.[5] Negros held the region's largest sugar plantations, but Iloilo City provided all the industry's support services—warehouses, banks, retail shops, theaters, bakeries, and social clubs.

At the apex of Iloilo's urban society were the *casas*, or foreign commercial firms. Usually numbering about a dozen, these Spanish, British, American, and Swiss firms were involved in every aspect of the city's break and bulk trade. Lining the city's Calle Progreso (now De la Rama Street) a block from the waterfront, the *casas* controlled the sugar exports, and ultimately the destiny, of Iloilo City. It was the *casas*, not the colonial state, that were the region's most powerful institution.

As Jose Nava was finishing high school, the sugar industry was passing through a major industrial transformation. From 1912 to 1922, investors capitalized the construction of sixteen modern centrifugal mills, called *centrals*, capable of grinding up to 5,000 tons of cane per day into raw brown sugar. By upgrading the quality of sugar exports, the *centrals* saved the region's industry from extinction. In so doing, however, they initiated major changes with far-reaching ramifications for the industry, its workers, and their port city.

Most importantly, the modern factories built ten docks along the Negros Occidental coast, allowing direct offshore loading and eventually rendering Iloilo City's warehouses redundant. The process of change was slow, complex, and even contradictory. At first, the mills greatly expanded the amount of sugar passing through Iloilo, producing a corresponding increase in the size of the city's waterfront work force. Between 1903 and 1939, the city's population more than doubled from 52,000 to 116,000. As cargo volume grew, local brokers abandoned their fleets of small sail craft and shipped sugar to Iloilo via a single tug and lighter corporation, the Visayan Stevedore Transportation Company (Vistranco). On the Iloilo waterfront, this concentration meant lower wages and harsher working conditions, which eventually encouraged unions and strikes. In Negros, the new mills employed up to a thousand factory workers and created an opening for organized labor. In the midst of this change, it was Jose Nava who fused these elements into social ferment.

Beneath these broad structural influences of class and city, microsocial relations among Iloilo's narrow elites played an critical role in shaping Nava's career and life choices. From his adolescence in the early years of American colonial rule, Nava belonged to a group of intimate, middle-class friends who shared a concern for the city's working class, a passion for local politics, and a commitment to national independence.

Prisoner Parents

With his birth and background, Jose Nava seems at first glance an unlikely agent of social change. Born into a prosperous merchant family at the end of the Spanish era, he enjoyed a childhood free of menial labor and full of enrichment. Beneath this surface of gentility and success, however, Nava's family had a history of social conflict that hinted at a strain of volatility, if not instability, impelling them over the span of three generations into conflict with the social order.

At the time of his birth in 1891, Jose Nava's family had been established as urban merchants for at least three generations and traced its origins to the Chinese mestizo community of Manila's Binondo District. His grandfather, Simplicio, was a Tagalog merchant who had migrated to Iloilo in the 1860s and established himself in the booming sugar port as a successful small-scale broker. He prospered and eventually built the family home on Aldeguer Street in the heart of Iloilo's business district.[6]

In 1883, however, Simplicio died suddenly, leaving his widow Timotea with heavy debts, six young children, and no liquid assets to support them. This adversity has left some revealing documents for the historian. According to notarized documents in the Philippine National Archives, the family was forced to cover Simplicio's debts with the sale of a prime lot in Iloilo for P2,700 and the home of his mother, Regina Que-Jongco, in Manila's Binondo District.[7]

In February 1884, Timotea Legaspi viuda de Nava signed a deed of sale for her husband's lot at the corner of Calles Iznart and Tres Reyes at the heart of Iloilo's busy commercial district. Since she was a woman and was disposing of her children's property, Spanish law required a formal justification. At the top of the deed, Timotea identified herself as being thirty-eight years old, an "*india*," or pure Malay-Filipino, born in Manila, and a resident of Iloilo. She swore that the capital of her deceased husband was tied up in commercial debts difficult to collect and products difficult to sell. Simplicio had left P1,503 in debts—including one for P977 to Jose Figueras, a leading Spanish sugar broker. Hence, she sold the lot for P2,700 to Don Vicente Gay, aged forty-two, a peninsular Spaniard who was becoming one of Iloilo's major landholders.[8]

Beneath the legal formalities, the document tells us a good deal about the family. Although he was a Chinese mestizo, Simplicio had married out of that closed community to a woman of purely "Filipino" background. After only a decade or so in Iloilo, Simplicio had managed to purchase valuable real estate worth P2,700—substantial assets that placed him just below the city's major sugar brokers.[9] Born a Chinese mestizo, married to a Malay-Filipino, and an associate of Spanish merchants, Simplicio Nava seemed well integrated into the multiethnic, merchant society of his adopted city.

Despite the debts, the family preserved enough capital for its eldest son Mariano to inherit the business, marry the daughter of a local merchant, and build his own home only a few blocks away on Iznart Street. There he and his sons would live for the next twenty-six years until the house was destroyed by fire in 1917.[10]

Our next document indicates that the circumstances of Jose Nava's birth were unexceptional. On 15 August 1891, Fr. Jesus Fernandez, a Spanish priest at Iloilo's San Jose Church, baptized Jose Maria Nava, a legitimate child of Mariano and Estefa Nuñal born two weeks before on 31 July. The entry in the parish registry shows that all four grandparents, unlike the child's maternal great-grandmother, had "*indio*" or "Filipino" surnames—indicating that the families had moved beyond the confines of the Chinese mestizo ghetto into the wider Malay-Filipino community.[11]

When Nava was only two, his parents were arrested on charges of murdering a Spaniard and were imprisoned in the local garrison, Fort San Pedro. The incident had a gothic colonial quality, and our information about it, all gleaned from the city's Spanish newspaper *El Porvenir de Bisayas,* is biased and incomplete. The facts are few. On the night of 15 November 1893, a nineteen-year-old Spaniard named Miguel Ortigas y Barcinas, "well known in this city where he had many friends and relatives," stumbled into the Dulceria Bocaccio on Calle Sto. Niño. Though he remained conscious for about ten minutes, he did not name his attackers before he passed out and died, apparently of poison. Three days later, despite the apparent lack of evidence, Spanish authorities arrested Mariano and Estefa Nava at their home on Iznart Street and imprisoned them incommunicado at Fort San Pedro. Although the couple denied any involvement, their arrest and the publication of their names as suspects stigmatized the family as felons.[12]

Several days later, a reporter from *El Porvenir* visited the accused's mother, Timotea Legaspi, in her home at 37 Iznart Street. In this house, which was "not of great value," the reporter found Timotea suffering from "prolonged nervous stress" caused by her son's imprisonment and surrounded by his children, her grandchildren, one of whom may have been the two-year-old toddler Jose Nava. She recalled that on the night of the murder "she heard Mariano's servant shouting at him into his house repeatedly, in a sudden and bewildering manner, for a lamp." But she had no explanation for this need "at such an extraordinary hour."[13]

Gaps in the extant copies of Iloilo's local press conceal the outcome of this case. A year later, the mystery still had not been solved. On the first anniversary of the death, the victim's relatives published an accusatory notice in the local Spanish press:[14]

R.I.P.
FIRST ANNIVERSARY OF THE DEATH OF
D. MIGUEL ORTIGAS Y BARCINAS
Who was treacherously murdered in this locality on
15 November 1893 at the age of 19 years.
His siblings and other relatives, absent and present, mourn you
and remember you
to God in their prayers.

When the Philippine Revolution swept Iloilo in 1898, Mariano Nava fought with the local insurgents as a senior officer and was later a member of the Veteranos de la Revolucion. When U.S. troops occupied the city and defeated the Filipino forces, Mariano, though captured and confined, refused for months to take an oath of loyalty to America, becoming one of the last among the local elite to accept the new colonial order. Nonetheless, Mariano, stigmatized as a suspected murderer under Spain, now prospered under the new regime and became a respected community leader—treasurer of Iloilo's annual Rizal Day festival, municipal councilor, and accountant for the city's Chinese merchants.[15]

Mariano, unlike the wealthy planters and merchants who clung to Spanish, enrolled his four sons in the American public schools and encouraged their use of English. His eldest son, Leon, an outstanding student, was among the first awarded a government scholarship for study in the United States. In June 1907, Leon graduated in law from the National University in Washington, D.C., a distinction that marked him for a rapid rise in the U.S. colonial government.[16]

Leon returned to Manila marked as a young man of promise and immediately won an influential post in the office of the U.S. executive secretary at Manila. Three years later, however, the family's aspirations were blighted when he died of tuberculosis in the government hospital at Baguio. In reporting the death, Iloilo's newspaper *El Nuevo Heraldo* described him as an official "who was much appreciated by his superiors for his good qualities both intellectual and moral."[17] Had Leon survived, his American patrons might have provided scholarships and positions for his three younger brothers, Jose, Jesus, and Mariano, Jr., thereby setting them on a path to power in the emerging Philippine state.

Thundering Baritone

Even as a child, Jose Nava revealed an artistic and combative temperament. Like his older brother Leon, he studied the American curriculum in the public schools and became fluent in English. But he also showed an extraordinary assertiveness by leading a student strike in elementary school to protest the beating of a classmate by an American teacher. In a talk before the FOF Workers' Institute many years later, Nava described this incident, in his dramatic manner, as a turning point that "started me on the way to organizing a laborer's union":[18]

> One of my classmates, Rafael Consing (Paeng), was the poorest student in our class. He was the smallest boy. One day our American teacher, without any plausible reason manhandled Paeng, raining blows on him and kicking him while he was down. This enraged me: I drew my knife and threatened to use it on the teacher if he continued maltreating the poor boy. The whole class stood behind him.

After classes I gathered my classmates below and harassed them: "these Americans are treating us like beasts, because they think they are racially superior." The whole student body joined me in filing protest that the teacher be transferred resulting in bringing the case before Judge Bates.

Nava got his real education outside the classroom through private lessons in art and music and, above all, as a voracious reader of Spanish and American novels. "I tell you," recalled his younger brother, Mariano, Jr., in a 1974 interview, "he knew all the authors, Spanish and English. From the time he was young, his head was like a dictionary. When we were playing, he was always reading." Not only did Nava's indulgent father buy him the latest Spanish novels from the local bookstores, La Editorial and La Aurora, but his elder brother sent back a stream of English-language fiction from America, including translations of Hugo, Dumas, and Tolstoy. "Victor Hugo became Jose's favorite author, especially *Les Miserables*," said Mariano. "He read it many times and so when he wrote plays and *zarzuelas* his inclination was always to *Les Miserables*. I tell you, Mr. McCoy, you should read that book to help you understand my brother and to inspire your sympathy with the poor."[19]

As a student at Iloilo High School, then an elite institution, Jose Nava first showed his talent for acting. In December 1907, Nava, now sixteen, played the leading role of "Mr. Longhead, President of the Company" in C. T. Denison's play *The Great Doughnut Corporation*.[20] Bored with his studies, he quit high school and left for Manila to pursue a career in the arts. In 1917, three years after his return to Iloilo, he gave an interview to Ms. Encarnacion Gonzaga, a student from the University of the Philippines who was writing her master's thesis on Visayan literature. Her brief biography sums up Nava's years on the road in phrases that seem to echo his own expansive manner of self-description:[21]

From childhood Nava had already shown himself unusually fond of theatrical life. At the age of thirteen he organized a Spanish Vaudeville known as the "Progreso Infantil." This company had for its members boys and girls from six to fourteen years of age. Three years later he became a member of "Lirico Dramatica," then one of the most famous societies in the Bisayan Islands. His membership to this society had done him a great deal of good. It taught him Spanish and it developed his literary taste more and more.

In 1902 Nava began his study of English. He attended successively the Iloilo Central School, the Iloilo Normal School, and the Iloilo High School. In all these schools he showed himself to be a Bisayan Macaulay. With what a heavy heart did he use to enter his classes in mathematics! He detested the subject more than anything else. Tired with his studies in Iloilo High School, Nava sailed for Manila to study painting, first in the school of Fine Arts, then at "Raspall's Studio," and still later in "Antonio Torres' Studio."

In the year 1914 Nava returned to Iloilo to devote his life once more to theater. He was made the principal actor of "Cristobal's Theatrical Company" which made a several months tour to the different Bisayan Islands, and later principal actor again of the "Betia Theatrical Company." In Iloilo too Nava organized the "Nava Liliputian Company," and it is this very company which acted his plays, "Si Luding" and "Carnaval." Still one year later he with Antonio Salcedo (a dramatist) and Narciso Bantegui (an actor) formed another company popularly called the "Nasalbanti Company."

In 1914 our young author married in Pulupandan, Negros Occidental. His wife was the principal soprano of the "Nasalbanti Company."

As an actor, Nava distinguished himself with his thundering baritone, his bearing, and "his ability to interpret roles intelligently."[22] After writing ten known *zarzuela*, or musical dramas, and appearing in countless more, Nava's theatrical career on the stage peaked and ended in 1917 with two disturbing events. On 13 April, during the middle of the local *carnival* celebrations, a fire swept down Ledesma Street, destroying three shops and seven substantial homes. Not only did Mariano Nava, Sr., lose his house and furnishings worth P7,000, a substantial sum, but all of Jose's scripts—six *zarzuela* and two dramas—were destroyed.[23] Only a week later, one Julio Peña of Hinigaran, Negros Occidental, sparked controversy in the local press when he wrote the editor of *Makinaugalingon*, which was then serializing Nava's play *Si Datu Palaw*, asking why its story seemed so close to Jose Ma. Ingalla's *Dumut kag Huya*.[24] Nava, as he often did, reacted emotionally to the implied plagiarism:[25]

Mr. Julio Peña:

Why? That's a long story. One thing, if I am to recall, it makes my heart bitter. . . . Why [are the two plays so similar]? I don't know. But if you have doubts about why I cannot explain it, and if you think I "plagiarized" it, then I can tell you I would rather throw my pen away than do something like that.

Mr. Peña, if you could read one of my *zarzuela* you could study the movement of its style. Each writer, like a painter or composer, has a style that distinguishes him from his fellows.

Since you were concerned to ask, buy one of the *zarzuela* of Mr. Ingalla if you can and see for yourself his style, his preferences, his aesthetic, and his staging.

Since the script of "Si Datu Palaw" was burned, I am writing the concluding part three. At the end there is a wedding. I understand Muslim weddings, and if you wish to as well then see the play when it appears as announced at the Opera House. I can tell you it will suffice because I actually witnessed a Muslim wedding in Zamboanga, not to mention what I have read in the Koran.

No matter what questions you have, I will answer.

[signed] Jose M. Nava

When the musical was staged at Iloilo's Opera House in August, it attracted large, unruly crowds. One reporter for *Makinaugalingon* noted that "not even a single seat was without someone seated in it." The music was sensational and the painted scenery spectacular. "That night they were selling librettos of *Datu Palaw* to the audience for 20 cents each and, we heard they sold 50 copies that night," wrote a local reporter. "Jose M. Nava has shown that not only is he a writer but he also has a head for business."[26]

Whether it was the fire, the controversy, or married life, Nava abandoned the theater after this success and devoted himself during the next decade to local politics and journalism, supporting his growing family as a multilingual editor in the city's booming newspaper industry.

Fighting Editor

When Nava gave up the life of a traveling thespian and settled in Iloilo, he was able to rebuild ties to boyhood companions. Throughout 1917, as he was staging *Datu Palaw*, his close friends Dr. Fermin Caram, attorney Felipe Ysmael, and attorney Vicente Ybiernas finished their schooling in Manila and returned to launch their careers.[27] Two years later, the circle was closed when the poet Flavio Zaragoza Cano came home after years in Luzon. Educated, talented, and dynamic, this small group of middle-class professionals in their mid-twenties rapidly came to dominate the city's political and cultural life. Not until the Lopez brothers came back a decade later to form a political faction with their wealthy relatives was there a group that could equal their energy, intellect, and vision.

Within this circle, Nava's closest friend was Dr. Fermin Caram (b. 1888), a second-generation Lebanese. Educated in Spanish at the Colegio

de San Agustin, Caram earned a medical degree from the University of
Santo Tomas and came home in 1917 to set up his practice. He served rich
and poor regardless of their ability to pay, winning a mass following that
facilitated his rapid political rise—to municipal councilor (1925), provincial board member (1931), Constitutional Convention delegate (1934),
and National Assembly legislator (1940).[28] On the thirteenth anniversary
of the founding of the FOF in 1941, Caram turned his pro forma "message" into a celebration of their intimate friendship:[29]

> [T]here exists between us, the labor leader Pepe Nava . . . , and
> me, a great length of deep friendship for many years, so it is nat-
> ural that I should interest myself sincerely in the good fortune of
> the workers' organization that he founded, finding myself happy
> and satisfied with his successes and saddened, depressed by his
> defeats. This is the reason that I celebrate this anniversary . . . :
> because I identify spiritually with Pepe Nava, his Federation,
> and all the workers of my country.

Attorney Felipe Ysmael, a wealthy second-generation Lebanese (b.
1895), was one of the most erudite lawyers in the region. After graduating
as valedictorian in the University of the Philippines law class of 1917, he
placed first in the national bar examinations—distinctions that should
have assured his success. Instead of joining one of Manila's major firms
and aspiring to the Supreme Court, Ysmael came back to Iloilo and
opened a small law office.[30] Though he once considered a campaign for
the Senate, Ysmael, alone among the group, lived a largely private life and
was drawn into politics only through his close friendship with Dr. Caram.

In contrast to Ysmael's faint public presence, Flavio Zaragoza Cano
won fame with his rich corpus of Visayan and Spanish poetry. Born in
Barrio Jinipa-an, Cabatuan, in 1892, Cano was educated at the Spanish-
language Institute de Molo. In 1909, he migrated to Luzon, where he spent
a decade writing poetry and organizing labor unions in Bicol and
Manila.[31] After his return to Iloilo in 1919, he dedicated himself to Spanish
poetry while working as secretary to local politicians, notably Dr.
Caram.[32] Cano, writing in regional and colonial languages that were being
superseded, slipped into an unwilling obscurity that was only momentar-
ily relieved by his notoriety at the Commonwealth literary awards in 1936.
Outraged that he had not won first prize for his nationalist epic *De Mactan
a Tirad*, he tore up his third-prize check in front of President Manuel
Quezon and stormed out—a bold, even spectacular, act, but also one that
spoke eloquently of his growing cultural and political marginalization.[33]

For this intimate circle, poetry was a vehicle for friendship. In 1923,
Nava published a love poem in the vernacular newspaper *Makinaugalingon*,

which he dedicated to "My brother writer, Mr. Flavio Zaragoza Cano, the Shakespeare and the Hiligaynon poet without equal in entire Visayan region."[34]

> Your eyes are as dark as the night,
> your hair is pure loveliness,
> your brow is the most dazzling white,
> If you were mine, I would be most selfish.
>
> Your eyebrows are like rainbows, your movements so graceful,
> teeth the most beautiful,
> your figure precious perfection of perfections,
> All made to make one enslaved to you.
>
> Of all the flowers, you are the chosen,
> Of all the beauties, you are the precious,
> you are the only one on my altar,
> You are the owner of this fate.

Within this tight circle, a break had lasting repercussions. At the start of his career as a union activist, Nava's closest ally was Vicente R. Ybiernas (b. 1890), a classmate at Iloilo High School, who shared his background in the city's merchant community. After graduating from the University of the Philippines and passing the bar in 1917, Ybiernas opened law offices in Iloilo and launched his political career by organizing a militant waterfront union with his friends, Nava among them. But the two, according to Nava's account, soon broke over union matters, and Ybiernas pursued a conventional career, winning election as mayor of Iloilo in 1919 and later marrying a wealthy planter's daughter. With the support of both his powerful in-laws and working-class clients, Ybiernas won three terms in the National Assembly, making him a prominent figure in local politics.[35] Significantly, in his last race, in 1934, Ybiernas defeated Dr. Caram after a bitter campaign that marked a complete break with his former friends.[36]

Nava, like others in his circle, had political ambitions, but he never advanced beyond a marginal role in local government. Between 1919 and 1931, he ran for Iloilo's Municipal Council five times, scoring three losses and two victories. In 1919, the year his *compadre* Ybiernas was elected city mayor, Nava won a council seat for the first time, placing fifteenth among the eighteen elected with only 331 votes, far below the top candidate's 1,219. After two successive defeats, Nava returned to the council in 1928, again placing low, at twelfth, with 454 votes opposed to 1,219 garnered by the number one councilor, his rival and fellow playwright Serapion Torre. In 1931, when Ybiernas was reelected to the Assembly,

Nava lost his seat for the last time. While Ybiernas's younger brother
Fortunato won 1,005 votes to capture the second seat, Nava slipped to a
lowly twenty-fifth place, with only 273 votes—a humiliation that forced
his retirement from local politics.[37]

While his political career was, on balance, a failure, Nava enjoyed
considerable success as a crusading newspaper editor, creating a form of
advocacy journalism that broke the mold of genteel discourse that had
characterized the city's Spanish press for nearly half a century. Toward
the end of his journalistic career in 1932, he described this phase of his life
for a local biographical dictionary:[38]

> NAVA, JOSE: *Newspaperman; Founder, Federacion Obrera de
> Filipinas, Iloilo.*
>
> Educated at the public schools of his native city and thru home
> self-study, Mr. Nava has risen to the first file of the intellectual
> class in this place. His unique and colorful career in the public
> service as newspaperman and political and social leader is a glo-
> rious triumph of the laboring class of the Philip. community to
> which cause he had recently devoted the best years of his life. A
> writer of note, well-known as the fighting editor for his fearless
> campaigns against vice and corruption in the government which
> cost him libel suits . . . , no wonder that Mr. Nava thruout his
> public career has always wielded tremendous influence in the
> realm of public opinion and civic leadership.

Nava's prominence in the local press began when he assumed the edi-
torship of *El Tiempo,* a daily founded in 1901 by the sugar planter and politician Benito Lopez. After Lopez was assassinated in 1908 while serving as
provincial governor, his business partners managed the paper for a number
of years.[39] In March 1921, Nava and his younger brother, Mariano, Jr.,
signed a five-year lease with the governor's widow, giving them the right
to publish the paper and use its presses.[40] Nava ran the paper with flair,
courting controversy and hosting lavish dinners for the city's journalists.[41]
This brief success ended when the founder's wealthy widow, Presentacion
Hofileña Lopez, was deeply offended by an article about an "altercation"
involving her second husband and filed suit to rescind the lease. Acting on
behalf of her children, Eugenio and Fernando Lopez, she won a court order
in March 1922 directing the Nava brothers to turn the paper over to a receiv-
er. When she quickly sold the paper's assets for P500, the Navas counter-
sued, unsuccessfully, for P29,000 in damages.[42] As the litigation dragged on
to the Philippine Supreme Court, *El Tiempo,* then the city's oldest paper,
closed in July 1922 after more than two decades of continuous publication.[43]

A few days after the *El Tiempo* folded, Nava announced the opening of his own newspaper, *La Prensa*. With capital from their father, Jose's brother and partner Mariano, Jr., set off for Manila to purchase a press.[44] Although *La Prensa* closed in 1925, its successor *Prensa Libre* achieved daily sales of 3,027 six years later—the city's second highest after a revived *El Tiempo*, now owned by the city's rising young entrepreneurs, Eugenio and Fernando Lopez.[45]

As editor of *Prensa Libre*, Nava had the freedom to practice an aggressive advocacy journalism, attacking local officials and fighting for the city's poor. From the time that Iloilo's first Spanish newspapers had opened in the 1880s, editors had favored long, literary essays written in an elegant, ambling style. Coverage was erratic, writing flowery, factual references oblique, and controversies few. In contrast, Nava's staff wrote in a direct, factual style; his pages offered comprehensive local coverage; and, above all, his reporters conducted independent investigations. In reporting the controversies that sprang from articles in *Prensa Libre*, the Hiligaynon press often described Nava's reporters as *tiktik*, that is, "detectives" or "investigators"—indicating that he had created something akin to investigative journalism.

In October 1922, for example, *La Prensa* exposed illegal *jueteng* gambling and police corruption, a major embarrassment to city mayor Vicente Ybiernas, Nava's former friend.[46] Some months later, the paper continued its attacks on the local police, charging that officers were beating prisoners "cruelly" at the station to extract confessions.[47] Since most of Iloilo's workers depended upon the public markets, Nava paid particular attention to their prices and sanitation. In 1926, *Prensa Libre* exposed a syndicate of "*comisionistas*" who were collecting an illegal fee from all fishermen, thereby raising the price of basic protein for the city's laborers.[48] When inspectors failed to enforce health standards, *Prensa Libre's* headlines blasted: "Putrefied Meat Sold in the Public Market."[49] Moving into the slums, the paper's reporters exposed loan sharks who were charging workers in the Lapus District a usurious interest of 10 percent a week.[50]

Reflecting his father's involvement with Iloilo's Chinese, Nava was aggressive in his defense of this minority community. Throughout his long career as a merchant, Mariano Nava, Sr., had worked as a bookkeeper and political broker for the city's Chinese, a relationship he passed on to his son Jose. During Chinese New Year, their dining table was covered with imported hams and Chinese delicacies from grateful clients.[51] When two police officers beat the Chinese proprietor of the El Naval general store in July 1926, the front page of *Prensa Libre* erupted in banner headlines: "Decolongon and His Buddy Suspended. Dismissal of Those Who Attacked Mr. San in the Recent Fire. Mayor Torre Issued the Executive Order Yesterday."[52]

At the height of these civic crusades, Nava's parents died only months apart, leaving him to raise his growing family without their support. After a long operation for cancer in March 1926, Estefa Nava died in Mission Hospital at the age of fifty-six. A year later, Mariano, Sr., died at age sixty-five. As a member of the Municipal Council, he was honored with a wake at City Hall, and as a veteran his coffin was escorted to the cemetery by the local chapter of Veteranos de la Revolucion.[53]

With Mariano's death, Nava and his brothers divided their parents' modest estate—a farm in Lambunao, a large house and lot between Valeria and Iznart Streets, a few urban properties, and a small amount of capital. No longer the traveling thespian, Nava, now thirty-six, was head of a family and burdened with responsibilities—two brothers without professions, ten young children, and aging in-laws. Without his father's earnings as a bookkeeper for the Chinese merchants, expenditures would soon exceed income. But, just as his father had made his career as agent for the city's Chinese, so the son would prosper as a patron of its workers.

The Supremo

In the story that he told and retold, Jose Nava was an accidental labor leader. As his political fortunes declined, his reputation as an editorial advocate for the workers had grown. Although few laborers could read about Nava's crusades in his Spanish-language newspaper, the vernacular *Makinaugalingon* followed his exposés with short Hiligaynon summaries, providing him a following among the poor. In July 1928, a group of waterfront workers crossed the river from the slum district of Lapus and petitioned Nava to organize a union. Thirteen years later, after the Federacion Obrera de Filipinas had become a power in Philippine labor, Nava wrote a short, celebratory history of its founding for a commemorative volume:[54]

THE FEDERACION OBRERA DE FILIPINAS—
A POTENT FACTOR IN PHILIPPINE LABOR

Redemption of the Workingman Was the Battle Cry of the Federation's Supreme Head, and Won against Great Odds

In January 1928, Jose M. Nava, then editor of the *Prensa Libre*, a daily paper in Iloilo, was busy in his office when an unknown visitor arrived, with a bandage over one eye. The newcomer was Gerardo Chaves who lost the sight of one eye as a result of an accident while working in the dry-dock of the Visayan Stevedoring Company. Although he has sought the services of a number of lawyers, Chaves saw no hope in his claim for compensation for the permanent physical injury he sustained. . . .

Nava immediately sent a wire to the Bureau of Labor in Manila, and following an exchange of communications, Chaves was awarded a compensation of P1,700 from the Visayan Stevedoring Company.

When Chaves was finally paid by the respondent company . . . the first thing he did was to go to Nava and offer him P400 for his services. This Nava turned down. Instead he asked Chaves about the status of his family. The latter disclosed that he had 8 children to support aside from his wife, mother and two sisters for whom he spent P1.00 a day.

"In that case," Nava told him, "you better keep the P400 and give your family the satisfaction of knowing that they are assured of support for at least another 400 days."

Nava's good deed was amply rewarded when Chaves arriving in his home town in Lapus recounted to the laborers there how Nava succeeded in fighting for his rights. A few weeks later, Chaves, together with 50 other dry-dock laborers, arrived in Iloilo and immediately called on Nava.

That was on July 31, 1928, during which Nava was celebrating his birthday in his house. The Lapus delegation brought along with it a list containing the signatures of 470 laborers advocating the organization of a legitimate labor union. The signers were mostly dry-dock workers and employees in industrial firms in Iloilo.

Right on that day, with the late Mrs. Adela Caranieta Nava, Alfonso Palmejar, Eugenio de la Cruz, Mariano Mijares, Demetrio Preja and eight others, the FEDERACION OBRERA DE FILIPINAS bloomed into life. The constitution was drafted and publicly announced in Iloilo.

Aside from the useful narrative detail, this story is revealing for its plot and above all its omissions. The story has the structure of an Old Testament parable: a virtuous man does a good deed for a stranger, refuses to accept a reward, and then is given the gift of trust by countless poor who are persuaded of his virtue. Then, shifting to the New Testament, Nava and his fourteen friends, like Christ and his twelve apostles, strike out on a pilgrimage seeking salvation for the masses. There is no mention of any personal motives on Nava's part—neither his frustrated political ambitions nor the financial pressures of his growing family. As the account moves on to detail the union's later strikes, Nava portrays himself as a crusader against oppression, omitting his compromises with the companies and their oppressive waterfront foremen, the *cabecillas*.

It is significant that the impetus for the union's formation came from Lapus, an isolated working-class slum separated from the city by the

Iloilo River. Built on swampy land, Iloilo's downtown was a city of hollow squares. Substantial shops and homes were built on high ground fronting the elevated roadbeds, while most workers lived in clusters of bamboo shacks on rented plots inside each block. This peculiar urban morphology placed most of the city's workers in close proximity to their more educated, affluent neighbors. Those among the elite with political ambitions often acted as advocates for the poor with the local bureaucracy and then courted their votes during elections.

By contrast, Lapus was a homogeneous sprawl of workers' huts without a local street-front elite. Squeezed between Vistranco dry dock and the Philippine Railway yards, Lapus's only links to the city and its political leaders were the small ferries that crossed the Iloilo River. Instead of a society of poor masses and an educated elite, Lapus was a slum of laborers and their waterfront foremen. In effect, its masses were unattached to local patrons and thus free to support a purely class-based union. Like other local politicians in Iloilo, Nava had played the patron to the interior cluster of lumber and copra workers across the street from his Valeria Street home. But he had no contact with Lapus residents before they arrived with their petition. In this union of patron and clientele, mass and leader, the FOF was born.

Judging from the few articles about the union's early progress in the pages of *Prensa Libre,* the FOF concentrated its initial organizing in Lapus.[55] Most of the organizers who Nava cited in his union history were, like himself, merchants distant from the rough milieu of waterfront toil.[56] Significantly, in this chronicle Nava did not mention his alliance with the *cabecillas.* Indeed, in its first two years the FOF was able to take control of the waterfront only with the support of these powerful labor bosses. Through their influence, the six thousand stevedores on the Iloilo waterfront began paying the FOF a fixed percentage of their daily earnings through union branches called *gremio*—thereby sustaining the national office and financing its later expansion across the southern Philippines. In effect, the FOF's power was based on an oppressive social institution: the so-called *cabo* system or its Iloilo variant, the *cabecilla* system.

Nava may have been reluctant to celebrate his alliance with the *cabecillas* since they were hard, even unsavory, characters who often maintained control over their crews through violence and intimidation. Playing a Janus-faced role on the waterfront, the Ilongo *cabecilla* was in essence a labor contractor—responsible for handling all the cargo in the company's warehouse and acting simultaneously as spokesman for his workers. Before the formation of the FOF in 1928, most *cabecillas* retained 25 to 50 percent of the crew's income and distributed the balance to their men, Despite their status as employers and the exploitative relationship with their crews, the *cabecillas* did have a personal interest in raising cargo rates. When the merchant *casas* cut stevedoring rates in 1929, the *cabecillas* supported the union as mediators in the negotiations. After the FOF's general strikes of 1930–31, the *cabecillas* also agreed to pay 3 percent of their income to support the union inspectors who would enforce the contract with the companies.[57]

While Nava was dependent on the *cabecillas* at the outset, he was aware of their excesses and tried to reduce their percentage of the workers' income. Retiring *cabecillas* were replaced by younger men who agreed to a reduced percentage. Incumbents who refused a lesser share were eased out, and the central office gradually assumed control of their contracts. By the late 1930s, a typical division at one of the city's warehouses provided for a more modest *cabecilla* share—3 percent for the FOF *centro*, 20 percent for the *cabecilla* and his subordinate *cabo*, and the balance divided among the workers.[58]

In his successive accounts of the union and his role in it, Nava came to see himself as a world-historical leader. Over time, he wrote and rewrote his life story to portray himself as a man of destiny, ordained almost from childhood to lead the city's workers. The first instance of such invention came in 1932 when he described his career for a local biographical register:[59]

> Born a leader of men and affairs, he founded the first labor union in Iloilo and the Visayas with now Rep. Ybiernas in 1910 with a total membership of more than 6,000 . . . ; and founder in 1929 and General President until now of the powerful labor federation, "Federacion Obrera de Filipinas," having an actual membership of about 70,000 with branches scattered thruout the Visayas, Mindanao and Luzon.

In his later accounts, Nava depicted Ybiernas as an opportunist who used the union for his rise to wealth and power—in effect, making his friend's vice a foil for his own virtue. During a street rally in downtown Iloilo in 1937, Nava made his first use of this story in a bitter attack on his former friend:[60]

> This is the Ybiernas who is presented as your defender and leader. This same Ybiernas who is defending you abandoned your brothers, the poor workers who joined the Union Obrera, to rise to the heights of glory ignoring them once he was at the peak. This Ybiernas, once a leader of the workers, is now a *hacendero* [sugar planter], a capitalist. And what has he done for you? Nothing. A Comedy, a *"moro-moro,"* is being acted out in front of you.

After World War II, Nava drew these two tales into a single parable of idealism and opportunism. In a volume commemorating the twentieth

anniversary of the FOF's founding, Nava made an oblique reference to
this incident to portray himself, not Ybiernas, as the real founder of the
region's labor movement:[61]

> In 1909 he [Nava] organized the first labor organization "Union
> Obrera de Iloilo in Iloilo. In 1910 Vicente Ibiernas (the present
> mayor of Iloilo) and others joined him after paralyzation of all
> newspapers in Iloilo and stoppage of the Iloilo port. Nava was
> the pioneer organizer of labor unions on the island of Panay and
> the Visayas and Mindanao.

A week later, Nava gave a speech to the rank and file attending the Iloilo
Workers' Institute, again portraying himself as the true leader and
Ybiernas as an opportunist.[62]

> Later thru entreaties of friends the Union de Tipografos was
> founded with me as president. There were about seven newspa-
> pers then; Iloilo was then governed by a municipal president and
> 18 councilors. The union grew but it broke up when Vicente
> Ybiernas, a classmate, used the union for his political ambitions.

What can we make of these stories, with their changing details and constant structural tension between opportunism and idealism? First, let us
turn to the facts as they were recorded in Iloilo's prewar press to see if
there is any basis for Nava's version of events.

After a prolonged hiatus in union activity, the city's leading journalists formed the Union Obrera de Iloilo in 1914 at a "monstrous meeting"
of workers at the Teatro Malhabour. Nava, still dedicated to his stage
career, was not among them.[63] After these first meetings, the union quickly faded. Three years later, in November 1917, workers gathered in a city
cockpit and formed a new Union Obrera, electing Vicente Ybiernas as
president. The articles in *Makinaugalingon* describing the event do not
name the organizers, so we cannot judge Nava's role. Unlike earlier
unions, which had failed for want of mass support, the new Union Obrera
created a network of workplace branches for seamen and stevedores.[64]

In August 1918, a press report about the current campaign for the
municipal mayoralty listed Vicente Ybiernas as "the candidate of the
Union Obrera" — thus confirming a key element of Nava's story.[65] When
the union held new elections for officers in September 1918, Ybiernas won
the post of "general president," but Nava's name does not appear among
the union's ten leading officials.[66] Was he still an informal adviser or had
he broken with Ybiernas? Or had he never been one of the union's leaders?

In the 1919 mayoral elections, Ybiernas won the mayoral race by a
wide margin and Nava himself captured a seat on the Municipal Council.

The campaigning proceeded in the midst of a rice shortage that had brought hunger to the city's working class, and Ybiernas's prominent role in relief efforts had strengthened his candidacy.[67] Significantly, he scored his winning margins in downtown districts with large concentrations of workers (1,147 votes to 410) but lost badly in less impoverished districts such as Molo (34 votes to 674).[68]

Two years later, the Union Obrera launched the city's first dock strike. Reacting to a drop in the world sugar price, Iloilo's brokers had cut wages and dismissed their weighing crews—one of three teams at each water-front warehouse.[69] In years past, it had been necessary to weigh each hand-woven palm sack, but now the mills filled standardized Calcutta jute bags uniformly, making the task and its workers redundant. After a two-week strike, the union was forced to settle with few concessions.[70] In the wake of this defeat, the Union Obrera collapsed under the pressure of infighting.

As the campaign for the 1922 local elections began, Nava's *El Tiempo* published a report that Mayor Ybiernas, the union's official candidate three years before, was now claiming that he had won the earlier election on his own. The mayor's claim outraged many voters and prompted angry letters to the vernacular newspaper *Makinaugalingon*. One voter wrote accusing the mayor of exploiting the poor to advance his political career:[71]

> Do you recall how many of you poor have been used as ladders and how many of you have been used with a foot planted on you so that somebody can climb to the top. Now, Mayor Ybiernas has clarified the truth by telling *El Tiempo* he planted his own foot on the ladder to reach the top and saying that he ran as an individual for mayor.

In the June balloting, Mayor Ybiernas lost his bid for reelection and retired, albeit temporarily, from politics. Although we can only speculate, the collapse of the union and his refusal to identify with it may have played a role in his repudiation by the voters.[72]

Several months after his defeat, Ybiernas married Estrella Mapa, daughter of a wealthy planter, in a lavish church ceremony. The local press reported that the new couple had received P20,000 in wedding gifts—a vast sum in an era when a working-class family needed only a peso a day to survive.[73] In the 1925 elections for the National Assembly, Ybiernas had the means to run a conventional, cash-driven campaign and won a seat, joining the nation's political elite. On balance, Nava's allegation that Ybiernas had used the union as a stepping stone to wealth and power seems borne out by the facts.

There is a final, sad note to Nava's history of his union. In the long extract quoted above, he listed his wife as one of the founders of the FOF.

Above that page her photograph appears with the caption: "Mrs. Adela Carineta de Nava (Deceased), Co-Founder, Federacion Obrera de Filipinas."[74] In December 1929, only a year after the union's founding, Mrs. Nava suffered heart failure while delivering her eleventh child in fifteen years. Despite his tireless efforts, Nava's close friend Dr. Caram could not "snatch her back from death." The child survived and Nava became a widower responsible for the rearing of eleven children.[75] Her funeral was celebrated with "very long processions" from the family home to the burial at the Catholic cemetery.[76] After a period of deep mourning, Nava married Adelina Aldeguer of Iloilo, who bore him, in quick succession, nine more children.[77]

Strike Leader

It was the Iloilo general strikes of 1930 and 1931 that catapulted Nava to fame and made him a powerful labor leader. The FOF's first strike began in April 1930 as a localized response to retrenchments by the *casas* in their waterfront warehouses. Although the city's elite saw Nava as something of a labor dictator, he remained, as this strike indicates, merely a broker for his union's *gremios*. The strike, involving some three thousand stevedores, was one of the longest in the colony's history and froze all sugar loading in the port for twenty-eight days. Aside from some short-term concessions, the strike forced the *casas* to accept the union as a legitimate representative of the dockworkers, a fundamental change in the city's social contract. But this concession proved to be little more than a tactical retreat. In the months following the strike, the *casas* cultivated political alliances and developed logistical alternatives that would allow them to either recapture the waterfront or abandon the city as a sugar entrepôt. The union's victory thus carried within it the germ of later defeat.

The strike began as a localized dispute in the warehouse of the Compañia General de Tabacos, or Tabacalera. Unlike the other Iloilo warehouses, Tabacalera had not reduced its piece rates nor eliminated the weighing crew, or *banda pesada,* following the Union Obrera's 1921 strike. As the world sugar price fell in 1930, all *casas* slashed wages, but Tabacalera compounded the crisis for its workers by adding the wage cuts the others had made years earlier. In April, the company's Spanish warehouse manager dismissed the weighing crew and reduced piece rates in line with the other warehouses. Significantly, Tabacalera's crews were organized in ways that made them capable of translating workers' discontent into resistance. While most *cabecillas* supervised their crews in a symbolic jacket and tie, the foreman of Tabacalera's stacking crew (*banda pasaka*), Teofilo Castillo, carried a sack in the line and took only a single share of his crew's income. When Tabacalera announced its cuts, *cabecilla* Castillo and his workmates met with Nava and urged him to call a strike.

Following consultations with the *cabecillas* and *gremio* officers, Nava ordered a work stoppage at all sugar warehouses and demanded a substantial increase in stevedoring rates. On 19 April, some three thousand stevedores struck against the city's nine *casas*. All loading on the two foreign freighters in port stopped. Initially, the *casas* did not treat the strike with any seriousness. Writing to the head office in Manila, Ynchausti's local manager dismissed Nava as a petty politician: "The director of this newspaper [Nava] is nothing more than an instrument in the senatorial candidacy of Felipe Ysmael and the gubernatorial candidacy of Dr. Caram, both forming a Syrian-Ilongo ticket for future elections."[78] By 10 May, the strike's twenty-first day, the situation was at a turning point of confrontation or resolution. Instead of settling, Nava met with the *cabecillas* in control of interisland shipping and declared a general strike on the waterfront. Reacting to his escalation, the *casas* urged the provincial governor to seek Constabulary protection for their scabs working at the North Negros Company's warehouse.[79]

Despite repeated attempts by Nava to mediate a settlement between the *casas* and his membership, he could not bring the rank and file to accept their offer. To break the deadlock, Nava suggested that the *casas* meet directly with the strikers. On 20 May, the *casas* convened a mass meeting of several thousand stevedores at the La Carlota warehouse. In a show of hands among the workers, the "very great majority" agreed to accept a new payment system that represented a compromise. The next morning, thirty-one days after the start of the strike, work resumed on the waterfront. On the next Sunday, the FOF staged a massive victory parade with floats, banners, and thousands of workers marching through city streets shouting union slogans.[80]

The next conflict on the waterfront erupted three months later after the midyear lull in sugar exports. Pleading losses from the general economic crisis, the Visayan Stevedore Transportation Company (Vistranco) announced a 20 percent wage cut at its Lapus dry dock, the Iloilo Dock & Engineering Company (Ideco). With Nava's support, the workers countered with a demand for a 10 to 20 percent increase in all wages.[81] The strike spread quickly to Vistranco's stevedores and from there to the entire waterfront. Within a week, three thousand sugar stevedores had imposed bans on all Vistranco cargoes.[82]

Determined to break the union, the Vistranco management worked through the company's *cabecillas* to recruit 150 scabs. Unlike the waterfront *cabecillas*, who shared their crew's piece-rate payments, Vistranco's foremen worked for wages and made extra money by exploiting their men.

During the week of 18 August, there was protracted fighting between mobs of strikers and the scab crews led by the company's *cabecillas*. After two weeks of fighting, Vistranco was finally forced to capitulate.[83] Instead of a 20 percent wage cut, the company conceded a 5 percent increase and agreed to an impartial rotation of workers under union supervision.[84] The settlement was a major union victory, consolidating FOF control over the workplace and banning the most inhumane conditions in the port.

In these weeks of high drama, the FOF's reputation spread beyond the city to Negros, Cebu, and Mindanao. After the union's victories of May and August, Negros workers crossed the Guimaras Strait to Iloilo seeking approval for branches in their home districts. By late 1930, the FOF had an extensive network in Negros Occidental. Apparently emboldened by his expanding membership on both islands, Nava attempted a general strike against the sugar industry in the whole of the Western Visayas region. In the end, his bold attempt failed and the FOF retreated into a defensive position on the Iloilo waterfront.

While the political balance in a port city like Iloilo had allowed a union victory, conditions in Negros were less favorable. Through sheer numbers and uniformity of interests, Iloilo's stevedores had the strength to prevail in a strike. In Negros, by contrast, laborers were divided into mill workers and field hands scattered across the length of a large province. Hoping to split the Negros elite by playing planters against millers, Nava launched a limited strike on 20 January 1931 along the Negros docks but soon found himself facing a phalanx of Constabulary troops. A week later, he suddenly changed tactics, declaring a general strike on the Iloilo waterfront and a walkout at a single Negros mill, Central La Carlota. A mass meeting of union members at Iloilo's Teatro Lyric approved a strike motion, and three thousand stevedores stopped work that same day.[85] In Negros, the strike spread beyond Central La Carlota to other mills along the coast. But the Constabulary intervened at each *central*, breaking the FOF's picket lines.[86]

With strike action contained by the Constabulary in Negros, the focal point of conflict shifted back to Iloilo City. As in 1930, the FOF stopped all shipping on the Iloilo waterfront with the support of Nava's political allies—the Lopez newspaper *El Tiempo*, the Chinese community, and the city's working class. Instead of making local demands that the *casas* could concede, Nava was striking on the Iloilo waterfront for union recognition in Negros. In effect, Nava had conceded tactical initiative to the *casas*. Determined to break the union's power in Iloilo, the *casas* employed three tactics: recruitment of strike breakers, support for company unions, and an accelerated shift to offshore sugar loading, beyond the reach of Nava's union. Within a week, over a thousand strikebreakers had arrived in Iloilo and were working under Constabulary protection. As the general strike entered its second week, the *casas* tried to put their strikebreakers on a permanent footing by sponsoring sympathetic unions. With the *casas'* support, Vistranco's manager, Mr. A. H. Taylor, organized a company union, the Katilingban Sang Inanak Sang Pangabudlay (Children of Toil.)

But the strike was still disruptive, and on 7 February the management at Central La Carlota advised its regional headquarters in Iloilo that its staff was "at the breaking point." Several days later, the *casas* began talks with Nava and soon reached a tentative agreement.[87] Supported by a monthly payment of P1,000 from the nine *casas*, the FOF would retain eight inspectors to supply labor and resolve disputes. In the end, however, the hard-line *casas* refused to deal with Nava and the deal dissolved. Finally, on 25 February, his strike collapsing, Nava was forced to settle on the *casas'* terms. Wages would remain unchanged, and the union waived its demand for inspectors to supervise work in the warehouses.[88] Though they refused to recognize the FOF, the *casas* agreed to make voluntary payments of P1,000 per month for the union's inspectors. In exchange, Nava promised a ban on further strikes. As Ynchausti Iloilo explained to its head office in Manila: "[Nava] understands that at the slightest move against these *casas*, that will be the end of it forever."[89]

Although the strike was a defeat, Nava emerged with his hold on the waterfront strengthened and a de facto division of labor in the port of Iloilo. FOF controlled the waterfront and all its warehouses, while the rival company union, Katilingban Sang Inanak, handled all cargo on freighters at anchor in the harbor.

The FOF continued to organize almost every laborer in Iloilo City who moved goods on the waterfront. Beyond that bastion, however, the union had only a limited success. After an eight-day strike against Panay Autobus in 1933, the FOF won concessions but then lost control of the shop to the rival Inanak after months of violence.[90] Realizing his limitations, Nava began a skillful game of patronage politics to protect and advance his union's influence. After more failed attempts at strikes against plantations and mills in Negros, Nava finally won a collective bargaining agreement from Central La Carlota in 1938—significantly, by playing upon his close friendship with the firm's regional manager in Iloilo City.[91] Through his courtship of powerful local allies like the Lopez brothers, publishers of the influential *Tiempo/Times* newspapers, Nava kept local antagonists at bay, reducing the threat of political pressure on his union. Indeed, when bitter competition over bus routes erupted into a political battle for control of Panay Autobus, Nava maneuvered deftly within the complexities of local politics.

The competition over Panay Autobus began in 1937 when Eugenio and Fernando Lopez, the city's leading entrepreneurs, decided to extend their urban bus franchise into the countryside by buying out the island's largest firm, Panay Autobus. To force its owner, Miguel Borja, to sell out on their terms, the Lopez brothers manipulated a coalition that ranged from the Iloilo docks to Malacañang Palace. The conflict soon dominated provincial politics, and Iloilo's labor unions backed the Lopezes against a populist coalition of five City Council candidates called the "Banwa Boys" (town boys), who were campaigning on a platform opposed to the Lopez interests.

The December 1937 local elections intervened at midpoint in this struggle, making Panay Autobus the dominant campaign issue. In the course of 62 mass rallies on city street corners in the two weeks before the voting, the pro- and anti-Lopez rhetoric grew intense.[92] Nava was bitter over the failure of his union's strikes against Panay Autobus and joined the Lopezes in attacking the Banwa Boys, his longtime enemies in local politics. According to a partisan account in the Lopez newspaper *El Tiempo*, Nava's speeches drew an enthusiastic response. At one street-corner meeting in downtown Iloilo, his aides held up a placard reading "Banwa Boys" and then, with a dramatic flourish, changed one word to make it read "Borja Boys":[93]

> "This," shouted Nava in the midst of frenetic applause and numerous shouts, "is the real meaning of Banwa Boys. . . . They are candidates of Mr. Miguel Borja of Panay Autobus. This is the other side of the story that [the candidate Eulogio] Garganera and his comrades do not want to reveal. Those so-called 'Banwa Boys' are candidates financed by Panay Autobus as a tool for vengeance against the Lopez family since they have competed with his transport business."

Drawing on popular support built up during the past decade, the Banwa Boys captured five of the seven City Council seats in the December elections.[94] Nonetheless, the Lopezes could still count on the support of the mayor and governor in their campaign against Panay Autobus. As the violence against the company's buses escalated over the next two months, Borja's group finally capitulated and accepted an offer for their shares from investors led by Eugenio Lopez.[95] Most importantly for the FOF, Nava had guided the union skillfully through a complex, multilayered, political battle in ways that preserved his relations with Commonwealth president Manuel Quezon and affirmed his alliance with the city's new powers, the Lopez brothers.

On the eve of war in August 1941, Jose Nava celebrated his fiftieth birthday with lavish party. Coverage in Nava's own *Prensa Libre*, a copy of which is preserved in Dr. Caram's private papers, allows us to assay the *supremo*'s social standing after a decade as Iloilo's top labor leader:[96]

BRILLIANT SOCIAL FIESTA IN THE HOUSE OF J. M. NAVA FOR HIS 50TH BIRTHDAY

Gathered that night were the distinguished representatives of commerce, industry, and finance, as well as the labor element from different parts of the archipelago who were meeting in the city for the joint convention of the Federacion Obrera de Filipinas and the Collective Labor Movement. From 7:00 pm onward, the many friends of the host arrived to wish him much happiness and many years of life and happiness. There was as well in the lovely mansion of Don Jose another display of the splendid hospitality in the abundant buffet which was served to the innumerable guests. During the gathering as an entertainment for the guests, Miss Adela Nava and Benjamin Nava, sons [*sic*] of Don Jose, sang modern songs accompanied by an orchestra.

The guest list is a tribute to the social dexterity that allowed the FOF to survive for over a decade as a radical union in a conservative colonial city. Nava had gathered wealthy planters, including Fernando Lopez and his ally Mayor Oscar Ledesma, in the same room with the militants of the Collective Labor Movement, notably the communist Guillermo Capadocia. Looking at this guest list from the vantage point of historical hindsight, it hints at a delicate, even volatile, political balance. To draw these contradictions even more starkly, after the war Ledesma would become president of the Asian People's Anti-Communist League and Capadocia would lead a communist revolution on Panay Island.

Guerrilla Captain

World War II, with its ideological passions and ethos of violence, split Nava's close circle and pushed him toward confrontation with the social order in ways that led ultimately to the destruction of his union. Reflecting the position of Quezon's Commonwealth government and his own ideology, Nava took a staunch pro-American position at the outset of the war.

On the Fourth of July 1941, Nava's FOF staged a large loyalty parade, which featured speeches by Dr. Caram, Governor Tomas Confesor, and Mayor Oscar Ledesma. The rally ended with Nava's reading of an emotional pledge: [97]

>We declare our faith in Democracy which is a way of life that insures freedom in all it forms and upholds human dignity and personality.
>
>We declare our attachment to civilization, which is the full flowering of the human spirit in the atmosphere of liberty.
>
>We declare our grateful loyalty to the great American nation, under whose generous policies we Filipinos are preparing ourselves for complete independence in 1946.

Despite his apparent loyalty to America, Nava was not abandoning his anticolonial ideology. Instead, he saw the United States as an ally in an antifascist struggle to which he was deeply committed. In the late 1930s, Nava had played a leading role in Iloilo's antifascist campaigns. During the Spanish Civil War, Iloilo's local Falange movement, supported by Mayor Ramon Campos and Bishop James P. McCloskey, staged fascist demonstrations at the Casino Español and sent P100,000 and three hundred local Spaniards to aid Franco's armies.[98] In the pages of *Prensa Libre*, Nava supported the region's Republicans, mostly Basques employed as managers on the sugar haciendas.[99] Similarly, Nava sided with the Chinese community during the Japanese invasion of China, and his subordinate in the FOF, Severino Ronquillo, was a leader of the local boycott of Japanese retail bazaars.[100] This overarching antifascism is evident in Nava's introduction to the Fourth of July program: "Show your loyalty to the United States of America, the bulwark of Democracy, by joining the parade especially nowadays that the Totalitarian Powers — Nazism and Fascism — are intending to destroy Democracy."

In the first months of war, the political circle around Dr. Caram managed to preserve its unity. On 1 December 1941, Caram, the appointive governor of Iloilo Province, designated Nava as his deputy governor. With all the passion he could command, Nava became a leading advocate of guerrilla resistance to the impending Japanese invasion.[101] During the Japanese bombing of Iloilo City on 18 December, the Navas and their Valeria Street neighbors sniped at the enemy aircraft with rifles and later organized the Parashooters' Brigade "to meet the Japanese who according to reports will invade Iloilo thru their airborne troops."[102] The unit included Nava's brother Mariano, the president of the Iloilo Rifle Association, and Mariano's sons, who were skilled marksmen.[103]

In the following weeks, Nava's family joined the general elite exodus from the city. After the bombing, his circle established evacuation sites near the association's rifle range in the mountains of Alimodian, evidently planning to resist the invaders. On 22 February, Nava wrote in his diary: "Everything moved from Iloilo to the [rifle] range."[104] By "everything," he meant his presses, which continued to print *Prensa Libre*; his wife and children, eight of whom were now men of military age; and some thirty-six armed men who were either Valeria Street clients or union members. This evacuation into the Alimodian foothills kept him close to Caram and Ysmael, who later followed him to the town's nearby center, or *poblacion*.[105] Reflecting his adamant opposition to collaboration, Nava's diary entry for 5 February reads: "Published names of 34 TRAI-TORS in Manila"—a reference to the Executive Commission of Filipino leaders appointed by the Japanese.[106]

In late February 1942, while continuing to take medications for heart and prostate conditions, Nava wrote to General Bradford Chynoweth, local commander of the U.S. Armed Forces in the Far East (USAFFE), in a prose reflective of his heroic, and even messianic, self-image:[107]

> *My Object:* To volunteer the services of the FOF and the whole Nava clan as soldiers in the USAFFE with no ranks and compensation. The FOF thru my initiative has already approved this move when the war broke out on December 8, 1941. Immediately we the Nava Clan and the FOF rallied behind America, indignant over the cowardly attack on Pearl Harbor by a blood thirsty aggressor. Democracy is threatened, our hard-won freedoms are at stake in this war . . .
>
> In the island of Panay alone, I am putting under your command fifty thousand followers of the FOF and the Nava Clan. The FOF in other provinces had already been notified by me to fight for Democracy which they have complied with immediately.

As the Battle of Bataan raged and Panay awaited invasion, the local USAFFE command tried to mobilize the entire island for resistance. General Chynoweth replied on 6 March, ignoring the overblown rhetoric but assigning Nava a series of military missions. Five days later, Lieutenant-Colonel Macario Peralta inducted Captain Jose Nava and twenty-seven of his men into USAFFE at the Alimodian rifle range. After arming Nava's group with choice automatic weapons, General Christie, Chynoweth's successor, dispatched the unit on missions into Japanese-occupied Masbate, Romblon, and Mindoro Islands. Nava's eldest son, Lieutenant Leon Nava, led a two-week expedition to southern Mindoro and returned to Panay with fifty-five American aviators who had been stranded behind the Japanese lines.[108]

During this period of waiting, Nava met frequently with Caram and Ysmael in Alimodian. While Caram lived in a private home with his family, Ysmael moved himself and his law library, reputedly the city's best, into the priest's residence, or *convento,* near the town's Catholic church. Two days after the Japanese landed in April, Captain Nava reported to USAFFE that the Alimodian *convento* had hoisted the "Fascist Spanish

Flag" and that the local parish priest, Father Mariano, was a "rabid Nazi propagandist and fifth columnist."[109] On 22 April, when some nineteen truckloads of Japanese troops drove into Alimodian, their officers were received at the *convento* by Ysmael and Father Mariano. In a gesture of cooperation, the group turned over some firearms.[110] In a later report, Nava recorded his retribution: "April 23, '42 — Capt. Jose M. Nava raided the Alimodian Catholic Convent where Japs stayed for the night." In the attack, two Japanese soldiers died and two more were wounded.[111] After the Japanese evacuated these civilian refugees to the city, Ysmael included, Nava attacked Alimodian again on 27 April and burned the *convento*, destroying Ysmael's law books and all of Caram's possessions.[112]

The following day, Ysmael accompanied a Japanese motorcade to Alimodian, inspected the ruins of the *convento*, and guided the Japanese troops to look for his friend at the rifle range.[113] The next day, Nava wrote in his diary: "Wednesday — Distributed bulletin that will pay 5,000 [pesos] to whomever can capture Ysmael dead or alive for his treason and espionage."[114]

Ysmael returned to the city, and Nava continued his raids, which were some of the first experiments with guerrilla warfare on Panay. Significantly, these combat operations gave Lieutenant-Colonel Peralta, the island's future guerrilla commander, his first experience in nonconventional warfare. After conferring with Nava in Alimodian on 6 May, Peralta led Nava's men and thirty-six of his own troops in a series of successful guerrilla raids and ambushes against the Japanese along the Panay Range from Maasin to Passi. In what would become a pattern for the duration of the war, the Japanese retaliated by burning 150 houses and killing forty-six civilians in the Alimodian area.[115]

While Nava was fighting these battles in the hills, his friend Dr. Caram, always a reluctant evacuee, decided he could not survive outside the city. The Japanese invasion of late April had caught him in Iloilo City, but he had escaped to his family's evacuation site at Alimodian after refusing Japanese requests to address their rallies. Then Corregidor fell and Panay's local USAFFE forces surrendered, allowing bandit groups to proliferate and making the mountains dangerous for those members of the city elite who had taken to the hills. Threatened by marauding gunmen and seeing no point in resistance, most decided to return to the city's safety and collaborate with the Japanese.[116] One of the few who remained in the mountains was ex-governor Tomas Confesor, Dr. Caram's political ally, who began organizing civil resistance and invited him to join. Caram refused and instead descended to the city, where, on 14 July, he assumed the chairmanship of the Japanese-sponsored Executive Commission of Iloilo.

When the Japanese decided to form a provincial government, Dr. Caram became governor, making the local administration a wartime haven for his political allies. For much of the war, Caram's close friend Flavio Zaragoza Cano served as his executive secretary and took up the Japanese cause with an exceptional enthusiasm. Seeking to balance local factions, the Japanese made Iloilo City's government a refuge for the opposing Lopez-Ledesma faction. Oscar Ledesma served as city mayor, and his close ally Fernando Lopez opened a pro-Japanese newspaper, the *Panay Shu-ho.* [117]

While his friends enjoyed the city's comforts, Nava, despite his age and illness, remained in the mountains with the anti-Japanese resistance until liberation in early 1945. Although he had played a major role in the formation of Panay's guerrillas, by late 1942 his influence had begun to wane and his unit was integrated into the Sixty-Third Infantry Regiment. Now part of the regular army, or its guerrilla variant, his family-based unit was broken up. Several of his sons found themselves facing disciplinary charges, and Nava himself was given a minor staff post as chief of propaganda.[118]

Nava tried periodically to recapture his influence by proposing a mass uprising of FOF dockworkers inside the Japanese-occupied city. In September 1942, Colonel Peralta wrote his executive officer, Leopoldo Relunia, instructing him to "back up Nava's project for sabotaging Iloilo City as much as possible." But Japanese attacks on guerrilla bases in the mountains soon made the project impracticable.[119] In February 1944, Nava, angered by Japanese atrocities, revived the plan in a letter to Peralta, "asking for his approval for the movement which was already prepared to start with the wholesale assassination of the Japs and sabotage in Iloilo City, but the DC [District Commander Peralta] keep [sic] quiet on this matter." As U.S. forces approached Panay in late 1944, Nava again suggested sabotage, using "as the nucleus of this underground movement 1,000 of his members in the Philippine Labor Federation who were then holding key positions in . . . [the] storing of Jap ammunitions." Again, the colonel did not reply.[120]

While Nava had once plotted strategy with Peralta, by September 1943 his letters to the guerrilla commander were dwelling on complaints about lack of supplies for his unit and promotions for himself and his family members.[121] Gradually, Nava's poor health worsened from lack of food and harsh living conditions. By the end of the war, he was relegated to a remote rear area, publishing a propaganda paper. Ever the social activist, he used his time to train the non-Christian hill peoples, the Bukidnon, in guerrilla tactics.[122]

Despite his reverses, Nava maintained an unswerving commitment to the resistance through three years of guerrilla warfare. In March 1943, he refused Governor Caram's offer of P50,000 to establish a printing press under Japanese control, arguing that the war presented clear moral choices. In his reply to Caram, he characterized Iloilo's collaborators as "the scourge of humanity, moral lepers," and a collection of "petty politicos, traitors, opportunists, spies, fifth columnists, cowards, hypocrites, flatterers, bandits, and defeatists."[123] These were harsh words directed at a close friend who was, of course, chief among these scoundrels.

After the U.S. Army landed on Panay in March 1945, Nava put aside the passions of global war and returned to the realities of local politics. As soon as American troops secured the city, Nava and his sons came down from the hills and stood guard outside Dr. Caram's house to protect him from vengeful guerrillas. Some months later, Captain Jose Nava was mustered out of the U.S. Army, without promotion or recognition, at his original rank. In the coming months, twenty-five of his close kin were recognized as U.S. Army veterans with accompanying educational and medical benefits. In 1947, the FOF's national convention voted the Navas the "labor union family that served most during the resistance movement." This self-commendation was the only recognition Nava ever received for his wartime services, something that would embitter him in later years.

Waterfront Warrior

After the war, Nava adopted a more militant, ideological position in city politics, allying himself with the Communist Party and later backing its armed revolution. Instead of courting local elites to preserve a social space for his union, Nava attacked them and used violence to defend the FOF's position on the waterfront. While the *supremo* turned his attention to national politics, his sons assumed control of the FOF's central office and engaged in bitter infighting to supplant prewar officials. Embattled from within and without, the Navas and their union descended into conflicts that consumed them all.

These problems were compounded by postwar dislocations in the city's entrepôt economy and delays in postwar reconstruction. Although Iloilo City did not suffer from systematic Allied bombing like Manila and Cebu, some key aspects of its port and transport facilities were badly damaged. Almost all of its gasoline storage tanks were bombed by the Japanese in the early months of war, some sugar warehouses were destroyed, and wartime neglect left the Iloilo River blocked with silt and wreckage. While the oil tanks and warehouses were repaired by late 1946, the river was not dredged for another two years, forcing shippers to load at the mouth of the river and pay extra handling charges.

Adding to these short-term problems, the economic ties between the Negros sugar industry and Iloilo's port, attenuated during the 1930s, were severed after the war. During months following liberation, the city's working class suffered from the collapse of public services and escalating inflation. Relief goods were insufficient, and most items were sold on the black market at prices ranging up to 1,000 percent above prewar prices.[124] Prices declined gradually, but rice was still selling for P1.50 per *ganta* in July 1946—more than seven times the prewar rate of P0.20.[125] Pressed by inflation, the city's stevedores demanded wage increases through their union. The FOF responded by imposing the highest cargo-handling charges in the Philippines. Calculating his charges on the basis of a "living wage," which combined inflation and the city's decreased cargo volume, Supremo Nava increased most labor rates 1,000 percent in late 1945. He reduced the charges as living costs declined in 1946–47, but the cost of hauling one sack of sugar from *bodega* to truck was still P0.50—far above the prewar rate of P0.02 and five times the rate in the rival port of Cebu.[126] These costs made lightering between harbor and waterfront prohibitive, and by late 1947 none of Negros's bulk cargo was transiting through Iloilo City.

Vistranco's management tried to cope with this crisis by denying FOF any work on the waterfront and transferring all its labor to a new company union, the Consolidated Labor Union of the Philippines (CLUP). Vistranco recruited attorney Pascual Espinosa, a prewar vice president of the FOF, who now broke with Nava to join the Lopez faction and lead the new union.[127] The scarcity of cargo forced the city's stevedores to intensify their competition for the little work that remained. By 1947, the two unions were engaged in a war for the city's waterfront punctuated with spectacular incidents of arson, gunplay, and murder. This violent, six-year battle along Muelle Loney was a central factor in the city's postwar politics: union leaders sought the support of politicians and candidates allied with rival unions to win votes. The postwar decade thus witnessed a spectacle of armed violence that aging stevedores would later recall as Iloilo's "mga Dodge City days."

For most of the postwar decade, Fernando Lopez and his rival Jose Zulueta, a perennial congressman, defined the poles of allegiance at the highest levels of Iloilo politics. Next came the urban factions and their allied unions, the FOF and CLUP. Operating within both organizations were small, intimate groups of young guerrilla veterans who mixed gunplay with union work. Supremo Nava's son Flavio, an FOF general inspector and leader of its Cadets, was then in his early twenties. He passed his leisure hours in the city's nightclubs with a tight group of friends, a *barkada*, composed of skilled gunmen ready for a fight with their rivals, the Espinosa and Victoriano brothers. The CLUP's president, attorney Pascual Espinosa, was the eldest of six brothers, all of fighting age, and his ally Angel Victoriano was the one of the city's few prewar gladiators who remained an active force on the waterfront.[128]

Both unions had their spiritual and ideological patrons. Following his mentors in the Lopez faction, Espinosa's CLUP paid symbolic homage to the Catholic Church. The archbishop of Jaro, Jose Ma. Cuenco, was militantly anticommunist and praised the CLUP publicly while his newspaper, *Veritas*, sniped constantly at Nava's union and its ideology of class conflict.[129] During the 1949 elections, Espinosa denounced presidential candidate Jose P. Laurel as a communist. By contrast, Supremo Nava retained Guillermo Capadocia, a former Communist Party leader, as his union's chief spokesman.

Embittered by the war and the postwar exoneration of collaborators, Nava became more militant and less sensitive to the protocol of local politics. As he moved leftward through his alliance with the Communist Party and its local organizer, Capadocia, he alienated his upper-class allies and exposed himself to political reprisals. During the early 1930s, Capadocia, the only Ilongo in the Politburo, had made frequent visits to Iloilo, trying to organize a communist presence amid the region's labor ferment. His success had been limited, and on the eve of war the Communist Party's local affiliate, Katipunan nga Mga Anak Pawis, had only a hundred members.[130] But in mid-1945 Supremo Nava went to Manila for six months to negotiate war damage payments for his properties, freeing himself for a protracted interaction with the country's leading radicals. He renewed his friendship with Capadocia, a former secretary general of the Communist Party now prominent in Manila's labor movement, and invited him to Iloilo as the FOF's general inspector.[131] Arriving in Iloilo in early 1946, Capadocia soon became the FOF's chief field representative, a friend and de facto spokesman for the ailing Nava, and a prime mover in the radicalization of the local labor movement. While Nava's opposition to Capadocia during the 1930s had won him a reputation as an independent radical, their open alliance now branded him a communist. In August 1946, a "Class A source" reported to Philippine Army intelligence at Camp Murphy in Manila that the "FOF with other allied organs as Tigbatas, Chinese Democratic Alliance, and Second World War veterans headed by Maj. Francisco Offemaria are having communistic leanings. Jose Nava as per intelligence report is having honorary rank of Colonel of the Huks [communist guerrillas]."[132]

While the details were inaccurate, this report still captured the essence of these relationships. Through Capadocia, Nava had become involved with the Communist Party and its Huk guerrilla army. Though secretary general of the party before the war, Capadocia had been expelled for his wartime cooperation with the Japanese and now was working tirelessly to win reinstatement by extending the party's reach into the Western Visayas. Nava was Capadocia's fulcrum for this regional expansion, and in long conversations he tried to persuade Nava that communism could help him realize his historic destiny as a leader of the Filipino working class. Listening to Capadocia, a brilliant and persuasive speaker, Nava may have come to feel that he could at last transcend the growing frustrations of his life and achieve greatness. Without any extant documents or letters, we can only imagine the subtlety of this political seduction. Our only evidence for the tenor of these conversations, aside from Flavio's recollections, is Nava's subsequent march to self-destruction.[133]

Nava's alliance with this leading communist ruptured relations with the groups that had been central to his success before the war. In the late 1930s, Elizalde & Co. had allowed the FOF to organize in its La Carlota mill district. But once the company learned that Capadocia was organizing for the FOF in Negros, the management decided to battle the union at all costs.[134] Similarly, Capadocia's reputation as a ranking communist aroused considerable opposition from the FOF's conservative provincial leaders, most notably Florentino Tecson of Cebu and Manuel Palacios of Negros Occidental. In the debates over Capadocia's draft of a new constitution at the FOF's 1947 national convention, both Tecson and Palacios fought its approval, in vain, with sharply divisive rhetoric.[135] Moreover, most provincial chapters refused to forward their monthly dues to the national office, leaving Nava's staff short of funds and dependent upon the Iloilo waterfront for their salaries.[136]

As Nava moved leftward, he expended his political capital on national issues remote from the union's base on the Iloilo waterfront. In late 1946, President Manuel Roxas announced a plebiscite on a Constitutional amendment granting Americans parity with Filipinos in exploitation of the nation's resources. Though the issue admittedly struck at the core of Filipino national identity, Nava's principled antiparity position pitted him, in the context of local politics, against his one-time patrons in a Quixotic crusade. Roxas's local supporters—Fernando Lopez and Oscar Ledesma—led the bandwagon for approval with the enthusiastic support of rich and poor alike. Their opponents were political marginals: notably, Tomas Confesor, the local communists, and the FOF.[137] The leader of the union's Cebu branch, Florentino Tecson, joined his local allies in supporting parity, in effect dividing the FOF.[138] Despite a tireless effort by Supremo Nava and his local leaders, Iloilo City's voters approved the parity amendment by a wide margin—12,212 votes to 979. Even in the city center, where many of the FOF's six thousand members resided, parity won by 4,855 votes to 290.[139] Clearly, Nava's influence over his members was declining. Indeed, in October 1947, when Nava called a union

rally to protest Philippine diplomatic recognition of the Franco regime in
Spain, the FOF's branch at the Philippine Railway Company boycotted.
In the words of the company manager's letter to President Roxas: "They
did not even allow their Railway Union flag to be displayed during the
celebration. Some of the officers are frank to tell the FOF Supremo that
they are 100% behind Your Excellency's administration."[140]

After the war, Nava also attacked his former allies, the Lopez brothers, a tactic that proved unwise in light of their rapid political rise. In the
heady months following liberation, Nava excoriated the Lopez brothers
for their wartime collaboration in the pages of his newspaper, the
Liberator. During the 1946 elections, Nava gave speeches at FOF rallies,
attacking the Lopezes and accusing Fernando's eldest daughter of a
wartime liaison with a Japanese officer.[141] As Lopez power grew apace,
Nava realized his blunder and scrambled, without success, to repair the
breach. Although he supported Fernando Lopez for vice president in the
1949 elections, the restoration of harmony was superficial. After his arrest
in 1951, Nava blamed the Lopezes, albeit obliquely, for the "political persecution" that sent him to prison:[142]

> Shortly after the liberation [of March 1945] I put up the *Liberator*
> out of what remained of my newspaper, the *Prensa Libre*, that was
> destroyed by the war. The paper was bitter against traitors, col-
> laborators, and buy-and-sell tycoons who raked in huge profits
> over the blood and sacrifices of their fellowmen in the resistance
> movement. It hurt those people and I knew it because I received
> many anonymous letters threatening my life and those of my
> family. Many of those collaborators and tycoons are now high in
> the public life.

As Nava involved himself in national issues, his sons assumed
responsibility for daily management of the FOF's central office. Before
the war, only Nava's eldest son, Leon, had held a union office, and even
that was a minor position as head of a waterfront local. After the war,
however, another six sons by his first wife came of age and, lacking any
professional skills, joined the FOF to provide for their families. By 1947,
six of Nava's sons and two sons-in-law held six out of the twenty posts
in the central office and led six of the waterfront *gremios*. Their growing
influence aroused hostility among veteran *cabecillas*, who were justifiably
concerned about losing their contracts. Adding to the sense of threat,
Nava's sons organized the union's paramilitary units and caroused with
the city's toughest waterfront gangsters.

After liberation, Flavio Nava and his *barkada*, or male alliance group,
soon emerged as the city's most feared gunmen. All were guerrilla veterans

skilled in the use of infantry weapons. The war had effectively terminated prewar labor contracts, and the situation was chaotic as *cabecillas* secured work at random. Backed by a group of six guerrilla veterans, including the notorious gunmen Hugo Peregil and Pablito Gepana, Flavio quickly reestablished almost all of the FOF's stevedore *gremios*. However, Vistranco's award of an exclusive contract to the CLUP blocked him from organizing the city's largest bloc of stevedores.[143]

Several months later, Vistranco challenged FOF's control of the waterfront by transferring gasoline handling to the rival union. On the morning of 13 March 1946, the *S.S. Tucson Victory* dropped anchor in the Guimaras Strait and a Vistranco lighter began shuttling the cargo of 5,332 gasoline drums down the Iloilo River to the Caltex oil depot at Lapus Sur. The FOF *cabecilla* Elias "Insik" Torres was standing by with his crew, but city police, without any notice, escorted forty CLUP men to the lighter and stood guard while they began unloading the drums.[144] One of the FOF *cabos*, Restituto "Moros" Sumili, reported the events to the FOF's Valeria Street offices. From Nava's perspective, Vistranco had unilaterally breached a long-standing, hard-won division of the city's waterfront between the FOF and the company's union. Shortly before noon, Supremo Nava and his son Flavio drove over to Lapus to discuss the matter with the Caltex manager, David H. Scott, a twenty-one-year-old Canadian new to Iloilo. As Flavio recalled the meeting, Scott was arrogant:[145]

> I went into the office and had a talk with Mr. Scott, the Caltex manager.
> He said: "I have no contract with your union. I can give the work to anyone whom I want to. And if you make any trouble, I will have you arrested."
> And I answered him: "You cannot just deprive those men of their work. They have been holding it for 15 years and without it they will starve."
> But Mr. Scott refused to listen to me. Since it was close, I went to meet my father at the home of his mother-in-law in Lapus. He asked me the result of my conference, and I said Mr. Scott refused to listen to me.
> Father looked at me and said: "Can you not do anything?"
> And I answered: "I will try something."

Flavio gave his trusted man "Moros" Sumili a U.S. Army fragmentation grenade and detailed instructions. Unseen by police or the CLUP stevedores eating lunch on the dock, Sumili slipped into the water some distance from the depot, swam under the lighter's hull, and tossed the grenade into its hold with an arching throw.[146] As he dove underwater, the 816 drums of gasoline in the lighter exploded, sending up a high column of flames and smoke that drew thousands of spectators from downtown offices across the river. The damage was estimated at P120,000 to P145,000 for the gasoline and P75,000 for the lighter.[147] The next morning, the corpse of Ariston Balad-on, a CLUP stevedore who dove from the lighter and fractured his skill on a submerged piling, was found floating in the Iloilo River.[148]

The spectacular explosion had the desired effect. Less than twenty-four hours after the incident, the Department of Labor convened a meeting of the rival unions and the CLUP agreed to back down. As *El Tiempo* reported: "Atty. Espinosa . . . agreed to give the work of loading and unloading on the waterfront to the Federacion Obrera in conformity with the earlier [1931] agreement between the Federacion and the Union Inanak."[149] When the regular Caltex manager, Genaro Barberan, returned to Iloilo, he gave Nava, an old friend, a permanent contract with the company.[150] Moros Sumili was arrested and tried for arson, but Caltex did not press the suit and the court later found him innocent.[151]

Although CLUP had lost the waterfront, Vistranco rewarded its leader with a lucrative contract to supply laborers for construction of the new U.S. Navy base in Guam. Between 1947 and 1955, Espinosa maintained some four thousand Iloilo workers on Guam, making him one of the city's wealthiest politicians. According to a later investigation of union corruption, between 1946 and 1953 the CLUP collected P1.4 million in dues from the laborers, although it could account for only P453,000.[152] By contrast, Nava's central office collected only P8,362 in dues for the whole of 1948 and an additional P2,552 as its monthly share of the *cabecillas'* percentage liquidation in the peak months of 1949.[153] In sum, Nava's disposable income, whether for politics or warfare, was but a fraction of that of his rivals.

The outcome of a dispute over Bureau of Customs cargo handling, or *arrastre*, was another setback for Supremo Nava and his union. After negotiations with the bureau in August 1948, Nava was forced to divide the work with an Espinosa ally named Ben Villanueva. In 1948–49, Villanueva's *arrastre* service earned a gross of P215,306, while the FOF central office had a maximum income of P30,665.[154] The CLUP's Guam contract and Villanueva's *arrastre* gave Nava's enemies a formidable financial base.

In the first two years of competition between the unions, there was not a single incident of direct, armed confrontation. From 1947 to 1950, however, the city's downtown was divided into armed camps and union warfare dominated Iloilo's politics. The confluence of election campaigns with labor competition raised tensions that erupted in eight major incidents of armed violence.

The violence began in November 1947 when CLUP's President Espinosa was elected to the Iloilo City Council as number one councilor. Running as a Liberal Party candidate with the Lopez-Ledesma faction, Espinosa scored a major upset against Nava's allies, beating the strongest FOF candidate, Cirilo Mapa, Jr., by a count 10,637 votes to only 6,018.[155]

The election results increased tensions between the city's rival unions and led to the most famous incident of the period—the 18 November 1947 shoot-out at the Bachelor's Bar & Grill on J. M. Basa Street. At 10:00 P.M., FOF Inspector Ricardo Nava walked into the bar where three of the Espinosa brothers were drinking and the notorious gunman Pablito Gepana, one of Flavio Nava's friends, was seated by himself. Sitting down at a table near the Espinosas, Ricardo poured his beer and banged the bottle on the table, saying: "Na-anad lang kamo diri!" (You are used to lording it over here). After an exchange of insults, Jerson Espinosa stood up and Ricardo Nava spat in his hand. Drawing a .45 pistol from his belt, Jerson shot Nava in the chest and kept firing as he fell. Seeing that Jerson would not stop until Nava was dead, Pablito Gepana fired lethally with his .45—hitting Benny Espinosa in the left leg, Jerson in the back, Amalik in both legs, one CLUP bodyguard in the hip, and another in the neck. The latter died in the hospital a short time later.[156]

Warned of Ricardo Nava's arrival a few minutes before, a CLUP security squad had set out from the Espinosa compound on Blumentritt Street only nine hundred yards away. Arriving after the shooting, they raked the bar with Thompsons and a .50 caliber machine gun for thirty minutes before police arrived. For the next few hours, trucks loaded with armed FOF and CLUP members patrolled the city streets until Constabulary troopers began confiscating firearms—three Thompson submachine guns from the CLUP men on Blumentritt Street and an M–2 carbine and a grenade from an FOF sentry on Valeria Street.[157] There were rumors that the CLUP's men had used, among other infantry weapons, a U.S. Army flame thrower smuggled in from Guam. Supremo Nava had not only been outvoted; he had been outgunned.[158]

An angry and grieving Jose Nava wrote Interior Secretary Jose Zulueta four days later, charging that the shooting was part of a systematic campaign by the CLUP and local Constabulary to "liquidate" members of his family.[159] Nava concluded by demanding an investigation of the Constabulary's Captain Santiago and the disarming of the Espinosas before they "stage an orgy of ruthless and bloody killings." Since Nava published his letter on the front page of the Liberator, attorney Pascual Espinosa complained. The city fiscal then charged Nava with criminal libel, further inflaming tensions.[160]

Reluctant Revolutionary

Two years later, the violence of the 1949 elections pushed Nava and his allies toward revolution. Threatened by CLUP goons and his union crumbling, Nava decided to support the communist revolution. Determined to win the balloting at any price, the incumbent president, Elpidio Quirino, sanctioned coercion by Constabulary troopers and private goons, producing an election notorious for fraud and intimidation. With Iloilo's own Fernando Lopez running for vice president on Quirino's ticket, the province became a cockpit of violence. In the vice presidential race, Nava was an active Lopez supporter. But in the local campaign for Congress, the Lopez-Ledesma faction backed the CLUP's Espinosa, Nava's worst enemy, against Dr. Caram, his best friend. As Nava was well aware, Lopez influence allowed Espinosa the full use of Constabulary troops and the governor's Special Police (SP). Since city mayor Vicente Ybiernas, Nava's former friend turned enemy, was closely allied with Lopez, Espinosa could also count on the support of Iloilo's police.

Preoccupied with the national race, the Lopez faction left control of the Iloilo campaign to Espinosa, who combined anticommunism with gunplay. In early September, he denounced Dr. Jose Laurel's presidential candidacy, saying: "A vote for Laurel is a vote for the communists. It is also a vote against the CLUP!"[161] Several days before the election, Dr. Caram's rally in Pavia was broken up when Espinosa gunmen fired at the speaker's platform, dispersing the crowd in panic.[162] Although the Lopez-owned *Times* called the balloting "peaceful," Nava and Caram denounced their opponent's use of force.[163] Despite his prestige as a veteran political leader, Dr. Caram lost to Espinosa, a neophyte, by a humiliating margin of 10,574 votes to 16,829.

After protecting his friend with his union's bodyguards during the elections, Nava now ran a series of articles in the *Liberator* attacking Espinosa's campaign. On 12 November, for example, his headline charged "Force, Fraud Defeat Dr. Caram," claiming that at least a thousand Caram supporters had been driven away from the polls at gunpoint.[164] Refusing to concede, Dr. Caram claimed that "blanket terrorism, wholesale frauds, brute force" had cheated him of victory.[165] Several days later, Nava's *Liberator* carried an inflammatory headline denouncing the government goons deputized as Special Police: "SPs Poised to Bathe City in Blood, Espinosa Cohorts Provoke FOF Men to Battle in Guise of SPs."[166]

This postelection tension erupted in a shoot-out between Sixto Acap, a Nava loyalist, and several Constabulary soldiers—an incident that would force Flavio Nava and his *barkada* to seek refuge with the Huk guerrillas in the mountains. At 11:00 P.M. on 7 December 1949, just a month after the elections, Constabulary troops under Sergeant Manuel Patriarca exchanged fire with a dozen of Acap's gunmen at a dance enclosure on Oton's town plaza, leaving both the sergeant and Acap fatally wounded. After the firing subsided, Acap was taken to Dr. Caram's Polyclinic, where he expired the following day. A *Liberator* editorial described the shooting as "reaping the whirlwind" of official terror, and Supremo Nava, along with Dr. Caram and poet Flavio Zaragoza Cano, led the mourners at Acap's funeral.[167] While Acap's friends were still grieving, the Constabulary mounted a series of "punitive drives" in his home area. Labeling the operations as "undeclared martial law," the *Liberator* denounced the manhunt for Acap's men and claimed it was forcing them into hiding.[168]

This repression was also the catalyst for an alliance between the FOF's central office and the Communist Party's guerrilla army, known popularly as the Huks. During the 1949 elections, the Communist Politburo had decided to expand its combat operations beyond Luzon and ordered Capadocia into the mountains of Panay to open a new guerrilla front. Convinced by Acap's death that they were marked men, Flavio Nava and his allies fled to the mountains for refuge and revenge.

At this moment of confrontation between state and revolution, Jose Nava cast his lot with the fledgling guerrilla forces, risking all to serve as a secret agent for a revolt that was already on its way to defeat. In the weeks before his departure for the hills, Capadocia met with Nava, now a good friend, arguing with great conviction that they should ride the historic tide that was carrying communists to victory in Korea and the Philippines. Capadocia continued this dialogue from the hills, playing upon Nava's heroic self-image and writing: "You could have been a much better and greater man if you had been a communist. And I know too all your frustrations under the present system of government."[169] This appeal to greatness came at a desperate time in Nava's life—health failing, household mired in strife, union collapsing, and repression rising. More immediately, his beloved son Flavio was caught between death in the city or disaster in the hills, a choice that intensified these long-term pressures.

Even as the drama of this moment pushed him toward danger, Nava still sided with the revolution reluctantly, aware of the enormous risk of discovery. In a later interview, Flavio recalled the agonized precautions his father attempted even as he sent him into the hills to join the Huk guerrillas:[170]

> Before we left for Tigbauan the next morning, Capadocia met with my father and they agreed that Capadocia would write the FOF a declaration that he was joining the Huks postdated November 30, 1949, instead of November 29, the day we actually

went into the mountains. My father had the minutes of the FOF Executive Meeting, which expelled Capadocia several days later, typed up before I went to the mountains so I could sign the minutes even though I would not be in attendance. So you can see that everything was well planned to protect my father.

With his cache of automatic weapons, Flavio was a prime recruit, taking command of one of the Huk's four squadrons and using his union followers to form an urban underground. Once he joined the guerrillas, his father put aside any reservations and supported the revolt as fully as his difficult circumstances would allow.

The Huk underground in Iloilo City was a vital source of arms, supplies, intelligence, and funds for the guerrillas in the hills. With the exception of food, which could be procured in the barrios, the Huks' entire logistics was based in the city. At first, the communist element within Iloilo's Chinese community provided cash and supplies, but it quickly backed away.[171] With Chinese support reduced to a mimeograph machine and a few T-shirts, the Huk relied on the FOF to manage its logistics and serve, in effect, as its entire urban underground.

Not only did this alliance provide critical support for the Huks, but it was responsible for Nava's arrest and the union's dissolution. Flavio feels his father's commitment was qualified and limited. But he admits that his father maintained regular contact with Capadocia through a special courier, a series of prearranged codes, and a hidden typewriter used only for his communications with the Huks.[172] As it turned out, Jose Nava was an amateurish secret agent and made mistakes that led to his arrest and trial.

Indeed, Nava's role in the execution of an alleged spy, Captain Guillermo Parreño, provided the crucial evidence for his eventual prosecution on capital charges. In July 1950, a Huk patrol captured Parreño wandering in the mountains of Maasin not far from the guerrilla headquarters where Flavio Nava was in command. Claiming that he wanted to join the Huks, Parreño was brought to Flavio's camp, where he was placed under arrest and interrogated on 28 July.[173] Since he had known Parreño since their childhood on Valeria Street and had served with him in the wartime resistance, Flavio accepted his story. But other communist cadres were suspicious. Only a year before, Parreño's brother Roberto and his patron, Colonel Francisco Offermaria, had arranged the assassination of the island's Huk commander, Juanito Sandoy. As the interrogation continued, Capadocia wrote Jose Nava asking for information. On 12 August, the *supremo* replied: "I have received damaging reports against Guimo Parreño who is now under your custody. I suggest that before he can do any harm to the movement and incriminate everyone connected with it, he must be liquidated immediately upon receipt of this note."[174]

In the midst of these investigations, Capadocia wrote to the Huk's new commander on Panay, Felicisimo Macapagal, recommending execution on the basis of Nava's report: "As to Parreño, the letter of Kabesang Tales [Jose Nava] to me is clear. He is a 'stooge' to join and make harm to our organization. In my opinion, he should be given a 'pass' to Korea soon."[175] After weeks of deliberation, the Huk regional command voted in mid-August to execute Parreño. Several days later, a Huk "trigger man," one Conrado Canto, alias "Sweetheart," shot Captain Parreño.[176]

Aside from this injudicious involvement in Huk operations, Nava risked exposure in countless other ways. Constant indiscretions, combined with his reputation as a radical, produced a steady stream of intelligence reports about communist infiltration of the FOF. In September 1951, just as Nava's trial was opening, the National Intelligence Coordinating Agency (NICA) reported to the President Quirino that "the FOF . . . is the reserve force of the HMB [Huks]." The report warned that "FOF members will be armed in due time when arms could be made available for a general HMB operation."[177]

Apparently aware of his vulnerability once his son joined the Huks, Nava tried to repair relations with powerful patrons and moderate his radical image. Only two months after Flavio left for the hills, a notice appeared in the 8 February 1950 edition of the *Liberator*: "Jose M. Nava, after a long absence, has resumed full responsibilities as Editor." That same day, in a marked change of tone, international coverage condemned "Russian obstinacy and duplicity" and local news praised Vice President Lopez's work in the anti-Huk campaign.[178]

In August 1950, Nava staged a mass baptism of seven children by his second wife in what seems in retrospect a desperate caricature of the ordinary *compadre* ritual. Born during the period of their father's radicalism, several Nava children bore names with clear ideological overtones—Sumakwel, Lenin, and Josef Stalin. Seeking to rebuild his alliance with the Lopezes, Nava invited several of them to stand as sponsors and thus become his *compadres*, or ritual siblings—Mrs. Mariquit Lopez, wife of Vice President Fernando Lopez; Ramon Lopez, the vice president's nephew; and Vicente Arenas, local manager of the Lopez enterprises. Other powerful figures who stood as sponsors included Secretary of Labor Jose Figueras and Iloilo's mayor, the retired general Rafael Jalandoni.[179]

After Flavio's arrest in October 1950, Jose Nava could see that his own was imminent and began to flail desperately for a survival strategy. On the occasion of President Quirino's sixtieth birthday, the Nava family hired Radio DYRI in Iloilo to broadcast a special tribute: a march "dedicated to President Quirino by the Nava Kids Cumbacheritos," a poem by

Flavio Zaragoza Cano entitled "Long Live Quirino," another poem by
Nava himself in Visayan, and "Happy Birthday" sung in English by the
FOF chorus.[180]

These gestures had no effect. On 1 November 1950, some three hundred Constabulary troops in full battle gear cordoned off Nava's
Valeria Street neighborhood for eight hours and conducted a rigorous
search, without success, for the union's weapons cache. Nava ridiculed
the raid in the columns of the *Liberator*, describing himself as happily
leading the troops from room to room and opening each cupboard or
carton for their inspection.[181]

Despite his bravado, Nava knew that he was in serious trouble. Six
weeks later, he telegraphed President Quirino, offering his entire family
as frontline troops in the fight against communism:[182]

> Due to uncertainty of world situation in announcement today by
> President Truman state of emergency and considering danger fac-
> ing the Philippines I and all my sons, brother, cousins, nephews,
> grandsons numbering one hundred . . . and all leaders Federacion
> Obrera de Filipinas offer all resources and manpower of this
> organization.

In April 1951, Nava sent a similar telegram to U.S. Ambassador Myron
Cowen, supporting his call for a "constructive resolution to fight communism" and again offering the services of the entire Nava clan.[183] Then,
on May Day, Nava again lurched to the left, lashing out at his enemies in
a messianic voice that echoed the country's rhetoric of heroism:[184]

> Because of the proven militancy of the FOF, the reactionaries, the
> gods of imperialism, are now smearing the FOF as a
> "Subversive" and "Communistic" movement. The leaders of the
> FOF are included in the blacklist of the local brand of Gestapo.
> All are being shadowed. I myself am closely watched and fol-
> lowed. They tell people not to go to my house. Shall we step
> backward and let our enemies weaken our movement? Our
> answer is NO, NO, and NO. If I die as a martyr for the Cause of
> the Masses, I am ready for the sacrifice.

Two days later, Constabulary troops arrested Jose Nava, his son
Ricardo, and a son-in-law, Alfredo Palmejar, at the FOF offices on Valeria
Street and imprisoned them in the provincial jail, a dank remnant of
Spanish rule. Nava sent a telegram to his new *compadre*, Labor Secretary
Jose Figueras. The secretary wrote a restrained note to President Quirino
stating that he did "not have the slightest intention to question or criticize
the action taken by the military authorities in the case of Mr. Nava." In

future, he suggested, such arrests might be reviewed by a committee of some sort.[185]

After two weeks in prison, Nava issued a public statement denouncing the Lopez faction by transparent innuendo. This text reveals a self-image bordering on fantasy. Locked in a prison cell and facing a possible death sentence, he still played the popular hero, the chained labor titan in possession of powerful information:[186]

> From very good sources I know that all this persecution is backed by POLITICS. Three political figures are the masterminds whose names I'll later reveal. Because of my popularity among the people in Iloilo and outside of Iloilo plus the FOF they want to eliminate me so that they can have all the political power they want. But in 1949 I helped one of them [Vice President Fernando Lopez], in 1947 the other [Governor Mariano Peñaflorida] and the other was able to be "elected" by means of guns [Congressman Pascual Espinosa]. You add to this certain PC officers who are tools of the trio.

But there was no protest from the waterfront. The only FOF local leaders who rallied to Nava were the presidents of the large industrial concerns, the Philippine Railway and Panay Electric, that were exempt from paying a percentage of their income to the central office and thus free from conflict with Nava's children. These branches offered to launch protest strikes, but Nava ordered them to avoid any confrontation with the authorities.[187] In September, Secretary of Labor Jose Figueras, Nava's supposed *compadre*, canceled the FOF's permit, effectively suppressing the union. In a letter to the union's central office, he explained: "Jose Nava of the Federacion Obrera de Filipinas had been in constant communication with Guillermo Capadocia of Reco 6 of the Communist Party."[188] With its leaders in prison and its members alienated, the FOF collapsed quietly. Nava's prosecution would proceed without protest.

The Accused

Questions of guilt or innocence were only secondary matters in the trial of Jose Nava. While Huk guerrillas guilty of murder and rape were given amnesty or nominal sentences, Nava, who never fired a shot, was the only one of the 178 Huk suspects in Iloilo sentenced to death. Though we know now from Flavio's admissions that his father was active in the Huks, the evidence presented at Nava's trial was rather weak. Indeed, all Nava family members who appealed their convictions eventually won reversal in the higher courts.

The suspension of habeas corpus during the Huk revolt had removed legal safeguards and opened the Nava cases to political influence. Writing in his prison diary in 1952, Nava would note with bitterness that he, the innocent, remained behind bars while Muslim rebels and murderous Ilocano politicians had been freed after serving only a fraction of their sentences.[189] The question at the root of Nava's reflections is an important one: why was he, a major labor leader once courted by the powerful, given such a harsh sentence? And why, once convicted, was he not paroled for reasons of failing health or pardoned through the influence of his patrons?

Simply put, Nava was without friend or patron by the time of his trial. During the war, he had offered a reward for Ysmael's death, and later he had denounced Fernando Lopez for wartime collaboration. Indeed, two weeks after his arrest Nava issued a public letter, implying, without mentioning names, that Lopez was the "mastermind" of his downfall.[190] His sons had split the union and alienated its veteran organizers. The violence of his war with the CLUP had outraged Iloilo's civic leaders. And his alliance with Capadocia and the communists had marked him as a threat to a fragile, newly independent Philippine state.

Nava and his sons spent more than a year before the courts on charges of subversion. Flavio was sentenced to life in prison in April 1951, and Nava himself was subjected to a lengthy trial. In both cases, the prosecution's star witness was Rodrigo de Jesus, the prewar leader of the Communist Party in Iloilo and the political supervisor of Flavio's Huk unit. The defense tried to challenge his credibility by arguing that de Jesus had once been expelled from the FOF for supporting a rival union and thus harbored a grudge against Nava.[191] Though the court found him credible, de Jesus had in fact shown extraordinary determination in collecting evidence against Nava. He had participated in the Huk investigation of Parreño in August 1950, buried Nava's incriminating report in the mountains, and later led Constabulary troopers to this cache. Since Nava had broken his own security procedures by adding a postscript to the typed note in his distinctive hand, prosecution handwriting experts were able to implicate him in the murder.[192]

After months of hearings, Judge Magno S. Gatmaitan convened the court in April 1952 and read his decision. Calling Nava "a man of culture, . . . one in whom the Executive had placed his trust and given the responsible position," the judge declared him a traitor to his class and sentenced him to death.[193] In a diary entry later that day, Nava described his sentencing like a playwright sketching a dramatic courtroom climax. Even at the moment when he received his death sentence, Nava could not confront his errors and retreated into language that Victor Hugo might have used for Jean Valjean in *Les Miserables*, playing the fictional hero whose virtue will, in the end, overcome all:[194]

> About 8 a.m. unexpectedly a guard tells me to go to the court at 9 a.m. because we were wanted there for something he didn't know. . . . [Judge] Gatmaitan was pale, livid, the mask of death & fear in his countenance. I was steadily looking at him, straight in the eye to seek the mystery he was so crudely & clumsily trying to cover. He was avoiding my eyes. He dared not look at me . . .
>   He pronounced my death sentence with a yellow face, trembling voice & the words cut as if he could not swallow the crime he was committing with immunity & impunity under the sacred mantle of justice. Inday [Nava's daughter], shocked at the impact of such savagery, cruelty & vindictiveness which contradictions of justice, held me as if to find support, looked at the judge in disbelief & sobbed. I smiled with disdain & felt pity for this little man so-called judge who in complete disregard of truth had connived w/ PC [Constabulary] to kill me in cold blood . . .

Dying Dreamer

After his conviction, Nava was transferred to the Muntinglupa Prison near Manila. There, under a sentence of death, he began to confront the reality of his failings. Abandoned by his closest friends, he was forced to spend his last years alone, writing and reflecting.

In his dreams and his diary, Nava searched for answers. He focused on his relations with friends and patrons, trying to understand why they had abandoned him. Slowly, the sense of anger and betrayal gave way to a tentative realization that he may have somehow betrayed himself. In his diary, he still denied responsibility, but in his dreams he seemed to engage his failings.

In retrospect, one of Nava's critical failings was his ambiguous position in the 1949 elections, particularly his failure to forge a close alliance with President Quirino. Even though Nava had fought the colonial state before the war, it had been insulated from the interests of the Filipino economic elite and thus provided union leaders with a narrow social space for radical maneuver.

After independence, however, a Filipino executive would be much more responsive to elite interests and would act forcefully to crush any industrial disruption that threatened the nation's economic recovery. Political miscalculation would now court disaster. Nava had begun cultivating President Quirino after he assumed office in 1948, but he transferred his support to Laurel's hopeless candidacy when the campaign began. In his prison diary entry of 1 May 1952, Nava reviewed his relations with Quirino:

> In 1948 thru Jesus [Nava] gave Pres. Quirino at Rizal Memorial
> Sta.[dium] a historical 300-yr. Moro Battle Kris in formal cere-
> mony w/ Sultan & Datus. I w/ Inday in Cebu arrived 6 p.m.
> from PT boat w/ debaters. I broadcast Labor Day speech. In 1949
> gave Pres. Quirino his oil portrait painted by me, in platform in
> front Legis. Bldg. after parade w/ Mary where he, Lovina, & I
> spoke. . . . In 1950 I offered him Main Dance in Manila Hotel
> Nactu Convention. In 1951 I gave him Samurai Sword & Jap Flag,
> C.C.C. Nactu Convention.

Despite this elaborate courtship, Nava had failed the critical test of loyalty in the 1949 elections. At the start of the campaign in March, President Quirino's confidential agent, Colonel Agustin Marking, observed a rally in Iloilo and, in a report to the president, quoted Nava's attack: "What kind of administration is this now when the Veterans are not well taken care of?" Nava was later seen demonstrating for a rival presidential candidate, Senator Jose Avelino.[195] By associating with all three candidates during their visits to Iloilo, Nava had failed to identify fully with Quirino and could not be considered a follower after his reelection.

Under a death sentence from state and body, Nava gradually dropped his dramatic artifice in a search for answers. His health, declining for several years, suffered further in prison. He began experiencing breathing problems and violent coughing spasms. His finances were exhausted by the trial and the dissolution of the union, and he began selling off his house and other properties. In the midst of this personal crisis, Nava reconsidered his deepest beliefs. On 24 May, his diary noted, apparently with approval, that: "Radio Peiping Broadcast vs. Quirino govt. for having condemned me to death for being a Communist 'SUSPECT.'"[196] But on 18 June Nava, long a staunch opponent of the Church, made his confession for the first time in years. The following day, he took communion: "When I received the wafer I was so moved that spontaneously tears poured from my eyes. I felt I was not ready for the great event."[197] A month later, Nava had a dream, the first recorded in his prison diary:[198]

JUL 18—QUEZON DREAM

> Cloudy whole day and very warm in later afternoon.
> —Nobody came [to visit me] this afternoon. This was Flavio's turn.
> —With the intention of resting and sleeping more, I laid down in bed 7:30 p.m. was not even able to join the evening

prayer as usual. I must have slept at 8. At about 11 woke up and resumed sleeping. From this time I had a dream. I was with Pare Cente Ybiernas went up a nipa house where I found two old people (man and woman) lying down asleep. Then Pres. Quezon came out from a room and chatted with us merrily. I ordered a man to take some old fotos on the wall. In these pictures were I and Ybiernas during our youth way back in 1910. Quezon laughed heartily at our figures. Then Ybiernas left and Quezon and I remained talking and laughing.

What do we make of this remarkable dream? In this reverie's cast of political characters, Nava seemed to admit that he was the victim of his own postwar blunders. First, the mention of Vicente Ybiernas and the date 1910 seem significant. One of Nava's oft-told stories about the local labor movement involved their formation of the Union Obrera in 1917 and Ybiernas's later opportunism. As political pressures mounted in 1949, Nava had recounted the incident twice, once without specifying a date and another time with this version: "In 1910 Vicente Ybiernas . . . and others joined him [Nava] after paralyzation of all newspapers in Iloilo and the stoppage of the Iloilo port." In both the dream and this earlier recounting, Nava gave an incorrect date, 1910 instead of 1917. Similarly, Nava's earlier speech used the full, formal name "Vicente Ybiernas," while the dream text revives the warm, familiar term of address that he had once used for his ritual sibling, his *compadre* "Pare Cente," before their bitter break in the 1920s.

President Quezon's appearance in the dream indicates that Nava may have been reflecting on his more recent relations with President Quirino. The intimacy of Nava's dream-state feelings for Quezon stood in stark contrast to his diary's cool, even hostile feelings for Quirino. During the 1930s, Nava had supported Quezon faithfully and launched massive strikes without state harassment. After the war, however, Nava had failed in his most important role as a union leader—the cultivation of influential protectors, local and national, beyond the social resources of its rank and file. By spurning the chief executive, Quezon-cum-Quirino, and breaking with local elites, Ybiernas-cum-Ysmael, Nava had denied his union the political patronage it needed to survive in the postwar years.

Despite his dreamtime intimations, the waking Jose Nava still felt unjustly persecuted. In the months following this dream, his sense of social ostracism deepened and he lashed out. After two rank and file organizers from Mindanao visited him in November, Nava compared them to his fickle elite friends: "These people altho uneducated are very loyal, true and honest better than my rich and influential friends."[199] In the next few months, the contrast between their visit and Dr. Caram's distance was striking. The refusal of his closest friend to visit forced Nava to confront the loss of this intimate, lifelong relationship. In his diary entry of April 1953, one of his last, Nava still denied his own responsibility for the loss:[200]

> *Dr. Caram with FEAR.*
>
> Jesus [Jose's brother] was able to get a pass for Mrs. and Dr. Caram but the DR. had to leave for Baguio for FEAR of being involved in a rebellion case. Poor Doc, until now he is in the grip of the nightmare of fear which dominated Iloilo since 1941.

If Nava had been more honest with himself, he might have seen that Dr. Caram's distance was understandable. After all, Nava, as he knew all too well, had tried to draw his friend into an armed revolution, a crime punishable by death. He could hardly blame Caram for refusing to join him as he plunged onward on the path to self-destruction.

The conscious diarist still blamed his fate on plots and persecutors, but the dying dreamer seemed to admit that his predicament was, at least in part, of his own making. Inspired by the drama of class struggle, whether general strike or armed revolt, and a heroic self-image as leader of the oppressed, Nava had put aside political pragmatism and pushed himself beyond the tolerances of his society. In spurning the country's chief executive, Quirino, and breaking with local elites, Ybiernas and Lopez, Nava had denied himself the political allies he needed to survive within the rising violence and repression that marked the postwar Philippines.

On 14 January 1954, while on hospital leave from Muntinglupa Prison, Jose Nava died in the Manila Sanitarium.[201]

NOTES

I am indebted to many in Iloilo City who assisted me during the research for this essay, most notably the family of Rosario and Caridad Formoso and their daughter Glenita, who hosted me during my three-year stay, and the hundreds of workers who consented to my long interviews. During the writing phase of this work, Dr. Doreen Fernandez of Ateneo de Manila University was a constant source of encouragement and insight about the Iloilo stage. At the University of Wisconsin-Madison, where I teach, Dr. Michael Cullinane, Dr. John Roosa, and Professor Dan Doeppers provided detailed and useful comments on earlier versions of this essay.

1. Jose Nava, "Workers and Peasants Clamor for Justice," 1 May 1951, Nava Papers.
2. Flavio Nava, interview with the author, 19 August 1974; Manuel Palacios, interview with the author, Ilog, Negros Occidental, 27 August 1975; minutes of the eighteenth anniversary and general convention of the Federacion Obrera de Filipinas, 6 April 1947, Flavio Nava Papers.
3. Alfredo Palmejar, Statement of Income and Expenses, 1 January 1948 to 31 December 1948, Federacion Obrera de Filipinas, Flavio Nava Papers; Alfredo Palmejar, FOF Treasurer, 1945–51, interview with the author, 21 August 1974.
4. See Stevan Javellana, *Without Seeing the Dawn* (Quezon City: Alemar-Phoenix, 1976), 100–10, 129–31, 134–36. Originally published in 1947 when Nava was at the peak of his power, the novel is set in Iloilo during the years 1930 to 1944. Reflecting the bias of Iloilo's established families, Javellana portrays the union as a mafia-like organization. Ruling the waterfront by force, Tio Sergio (a thinly disguised Jose Nava) and his organizers force unwilling workers to join with threats and beatings. Through a network of spies, Tio Sergio stifles anti-union dissent among his members and forces them into an arbitrary general strike that they neither understand nor support.
   Within this fable of good and evil, Javallana, a member of a local elite family, crafts several chapters that seem, in the context of Iloilo politics of the 1940s, a political polemic. In Javellana's view, there were no social grievances dire enough to justify the FOF or its 1930–31 general strikes. While there are poor in his novel, there is no poverty. There is then no social justification for any sort of collective action in the form of unions, strikes, or working-class solidarity.
5. Commonwealth of the Philippines, Commission of the Census, *Census of the Philippines, 1939: Summary for the Philippines and General Censuses of Population and Agriculture* (Manila: Bureau of Printing, 1941), 2:42–46, 1184.
6. Interviews with the author: Mariano Nava, Jr., brother of Jose, Iloilo City, 20 April 1974; Alfredo Palmejar, son-in-law of Jose Nava, Iloilo City, 9 December 1973; Flavio Nava, son of Jose, Iloilo City, 19 August 1974.
7. Dn Mariano Nava poder a Dn Severino Nava, 17 October 1885, Protocolos-Yloilo 1593, and Doña Timotea Legaspi, Venta Real a Don Vicente Gay, 20 February 1884, Protocolo 1,589, Philippine National Archives.
8. Doña Timotea Legaspi, Venta Real a Don Vicente Gay, 20 February 1884, Protocolo 1,589, Philippine National Archives.
9. For information on Jose Figueras, see *Witton's Manila and Philippine Directory,*

1904 (Manila, 1905), 518, 654.

10. *Makinaugalingon* (Iloilo), 18 April 1917.
11. Jose Maria Nava, 15 August 1891, Bautismos, vol. 11, San Jose Church, Iloilo City.
12. *El Porvenir de Bisayas* (Iloilo), 21 November 1893, 15 November 1894.
13. *El Porvenir de Bisayas*, 21 November 1893, 15 November 1894.
14. *El Porvenir de Bisayas*, 15 November 1894.
15. *Makinaugalingon*, 10 May 1927, 13 May 1927; *El Adalid* (Iloilo), 19 June 1911; Mariano Nava, Jr., interview with the author, Iloilo City, 20 April 1974.
16. *El Tiempo* (Iloilo), 8 July 1907.
17. *El Nuevo Heraldo* (Iloilo), 29 April 1910.
18. *Liberator* (Iloilo), 28 May 1949. Henry C. Bates served as a judge in the Iloilo Court of First Instance from June 1901 until December 1905. See *Witton's Manila and Philippine Directory, 1904*, 406.
19. Mariano Nava, Jr., interview with the author, Iloilo City, 20 April 1974.
20. *El Tiempo*, 17 December 1907.
21. Encarnacion Gonzaga, "Bisayan Literature (from Pre-Spanish Times to 1917)," M.A. thesis, University of the Philippines, 1917, 162–65.
22. The definitive study of the Iloilo theater contains a richly detailed section on Nava's career as a dramatist. See Doreen G. Fernandez, *The Iloilo Zarzuela, 1903–1930* (Quezon City: Ateneo de Manila University Press, 1978), 74–78.
23. *Makinaugalingon*, 14 April 1917, 18 April 1917, 21 April 1917.
24. *Makinaugalingon*, 21 April 1917.
25. *Makinaugalingon*, 25 April 1917.
26. *Makinaugalingon*, 11 August 1917.
27. *Prensa Libre* (Iloilo), 5 April 1929.
28. Abe S. Gonzales, *Dr. F. G. Caram, Jr.: Grand Old Man of Iloilo* (Iloilo City: Yuhum Press, 1969), 1–51.
29. Federacion Obrera de Filipinas, *Ivory Book: 13th Anniversary Souvenir Federacion Obrera de Filipinas, July 31, 1928–July 31, 1941* (Iloilo City: FOF, 1941), 7.
30. Filemon Poblador, ed., *The Panay Yearbook of 1951* (Iloilo City: E. C. Villanueva Associates, 1951), 198.
31. Ramon Lagos, "History of Duenas," manuscript, 1 February 1960, 275–77; Gonzaga, "Bisayan Literature," 167–70.
32. Flavio Zargoza Cano, *Cantos A Espana* (Estanzuela, Iloilo: Lix Publishing, 1936), vii, xvi.
33. In a recent interview, historian Carlos Quirino, who was present at the ceremony in 1936, recalled: "Flaviano Zaragoza, with whom I used to work before the war in the Department of Interior which was founded by my uncle, former President Elpidio Quirino, . . . had written a masterpiece of a poem in Spanish entitled *De Mactan a Tirad* [From Mactan to Tirad Pass, 1940]. It was an epic story in verse of the Filipino nation. Zaragoza was given only third prize which I disagreed [with] because I think it was good. It was praising the Filipino courage and yet he was given only the third prize. In the awarding of the prize, Zaragoza angrily tore up his prize check in front of the surprised Quezon. Afterward, he left the room" (*Sunday Chronicle* [Manila], 28 May 1995, 5).
34. *Makinaugalingon* (Iloilo City), 13 March 1923.
35. Manuel H. David, *Panay Directory and Souvenir Book* (Iloilo City: Manuel H. David and Dr. R. F. Campos, 1937), 117–18; *El Tiempo*, 11 December 1937; Ricardo Gonzalez Lloret, *Directorio Oficial de la Camara de Representantes* (Manila:

Bureau of Printing, 1926), 88; Andres R. Camasura, *Cebu-Visayas Directory* (Cebu City, 1932), 160–61; *Makinaugalingon* (Iloilo City), 9 January 1923.

36. Eulogio Benitez, *Directorio Oficial de la Camara de Representantes* (Manila: Bureau of Printing, 1938), 94–95.

37. *Makinaugalingon,* 11 June 1919, 2 June 1922, 13 June 1922, 19 May 1925, 12 June 1925, 12 June 1928, 6 May 1931, 15 June 1931.

38. Camasura, *Cebu-Visayas Directory*, 399.

39. *Makinaugalingon*, 5 June 1920.

40. *Jose M. Nava and Mariano N. Nava, Jr., plaintiffs, v. Presentacion Hofileña et al., defendants,* no. 27,764, 31 December 1927, *Philippine Reports*, vol. 53 (Manila, 1928), 739–40.

41. *Makinaugalingon*, 18 May 1921.

42. *Makinaugalingon*, 17 September 1921; *Nava v. Hofileña*, 739–45.

43. *Makinaugalingon*, 17 September 1921, 5 January 1922, 11 July 1922.

44. *Makinaugalingon*, 23 July 1922.

45. Camasura, *Cebu-Visayas Directory*, 51, 399.

46. *Makinaugalingon*, 17 October 1922.

47. *Makinaugalingon*, 23 February 1923.

48. *Makinaugalingon*, 23 April 1926.

49. *Makinaugalingon*, 25 November 1927.

50. *Makinaugalingon*, 19 March 1929.

51. Mariano Nava, Jr., interview with the author, Iloilo City, 20 April 1974.

52. *Prensa Libre*, 20 July 1926.

53. *Makinaugalingon*, 10 May 1927, 13 May 1927.

54. Federacion Obrera de Filipinas, *Ivory Book*, 17.

55. *Prensa Libre*, 5 April 1929.

56. For details on one such leader, Manuel Mijares, see *Makinaugalingon*, 22 November 1919, 4 May 1918.

57. Alfredo Palmejar, son of prewar inspector Alfonso Palmejar and postwar treasurer, interview with the author, Iloilo City, 17 and 19 April 1974.

58. Alfredo Palmejar, interview with the author, Iloilo City, 17 April and 19 April 1974.

59. Camasura, *Cebu-Visayas Directory*, 160–61, 399.

60. *El Tiempo*, 11 December 1937.

61. Federacion Obrera de Filipinas, *Twenty Years Struggle for Democracy* (Iloilo City: FOF, 1949), 23–24.

62. *Liberator*, 28 May 1949.

63. *El Tiempo*, 7 March 1903; *Makinaugalingon*, 25 April 1914; *Nuevo Heraldo*, 2 May 1914.

64. *Makinaugalingon*, 17 November 1917.

65. *Makinaugalingon*, 14 August 1918.

66. *Makinaugalingon*, 24 September 1919.

67. *Makinaugalingon*, 11 January 1919.

68. *Makinaugalingon*, 4 June 1919.

69. *Makinaugalingon*, 28 November 1921.

70. *Makinaugalingon*, 8 December 1921.

71. *Makinaugalingon*, 26 May 1922.

72. *Makinaugalingon*, 9 June 1922.

73. *Makinaugalingon*, 9 January 1923, 12 January 1923.

74. Federacion Obrera de Filipinas, *Ivory Book*, 18.

75. *Makinaugalingon*, 17 December 1929.

76. *Makinaugalingon*, 24 December 1929.
77. Fernandez, *Iloilo Zarzuela*, 76.
78. Kauffmann to Miguel M. Yrissary, 30 April 1930, Ynchausti y Cia., Iloilo City (hereafter, YCO).
79. Ynchausti Iloilo to Kauffmann, 13 May 1930; Yncahusti Iloilo to Kauffmann, 6 May 1930; Kauffmann to Yrissary, 7 May 1930, YCO.
80. Ynchausti Iloilo to Kauffmann, 23 May 1930, YCO.
81. Ynchausti Iloilo to Kauffmann, 16 August 1930, YCO; *Makinaugalingon*, 13 August 1930; *Tribune*, 17 August 1930; *Progress* (Cebu), 19 August 1930.
82. *Makinaugalingon*, 20 August 1930.
83. *Makinaugalingon*, 20 August 1930, 22 August 1930; Kauffmann to Ynchausti, 3 September 1930, YCO.
84. *Progress*, 24 August 1930; *Makinaugalingon*, 8 September 1930; "Twenty Second Annual Report of the Bureau of Labor," Quezon Papers, Philippine National Library.
85. *El Tiempo*, 27 January 1931.
86. *Tribune*, 6 February 1931; *Progress*, 6 February 1931, 27 February 1931; *Makinaugalingon*, 13 February 1931.
87. Ynchausti Manila to Gifford Stower, 28 January 1931, YCO.
88. Lopez to Miguel Yrissary, 20 February 1931, YCO; Miguel Yrissary to Ynchausti Iloilo, 21 February 1931; Ynchausti Iloilo to Joaquin Elizalde, 11 February 1932, YCO.
89. Ynchausti Iloilo to Kauffmann, 9 June 1931, YCO.
90. *Makinaugalingon*, 29 December 1933, 5 January 1934, 30 January 1934, 10 April 1934.
91. Manuel Palacios, President, FOF Negros Occidental Chapter, interview with the author, Barrio Dancalan, Ilog, 27 August 1975; Bernardo Gareza, Vice President, FOF Negros Occidental Chapter, interview with the author, Barrio Bacuyungan, Hinoba-an, 28 August 1975.
92. *El Tiempo*, 2 December 1937.
93. *El Tiempo*, 11 December 1937.
94. *El Tiempo*, 22 December 1937, 24 December 1937.
95. *Makinaugalingon*, 2 March 1938.
96. *Prensa Libre*, 2 August 1941, Caram Papers.
97. Federacion Obrera de Filipinas, "July 4th, 1941 (1776–1941), 165th Anniversary of the Independence of the United States of America," Caram Papers.
98. "La Falange en Visayas y en el Bicol," *Arriba España* (Manila, n.d.).
99. *Prensa Libre*, 30 December 1936.
100. Severino Pineda Ronquillo, "Affidavit," 24 September 1942, vol. 76, World War II Collection, Central Philippine University (hereafter CPU-WWII).
101. Fermin G. Caram, Sr., to Jose Nava, 21 October 1941, Nava Papers.
102. Jose Ma. Nava to Commanding General, 61st Division, USAFFE, 24 February 1942, Nava Papers.
103. David, *Panay Directory*, 100–101, 325.
104. Jose Ma. Nava, "Diary," Sunday, 22 February 1942, Nava Papers (hereafter Nava Diary).
105. Sigfredo Nava, son of Jose Ma. Nava, interview with the author, 2 December 1973.
106. Nava Diary, Thursday, 5 February 1942.
107. Jose Nava to Commanding General.
108. Officer's Record, Jose Maria Nava, 28 February 1945, Nava Papers; Leon

Nava, interview with the author, Iloilo City, 2 December 1974.
109. J. M. Nava, Intelligence Report, n.d., Nava Papers.
110. Nava Diary, Wednesday, 22 April 1942.
111. Officer's Records, Nava; Nava Diary, Thursday, 23 April 1942.
112. Officer's Records, Nava.
113. Nava Diary, 28 April 1942.
114. Nava Diary, Wednesday, 29 April 1942.
115. Officer's Record, Nava; Nava Diary, Saturday, 9 May 1942.
116. Confidential Memorandum from Fermin G. Caram, Sr., to Col. Frank X. Cronan, C.I.C. U.S. Army, 20 April 1945, Caram Papers.
117. Confidential Memorandum from Fermin G. Caram, Sr.; Memorandum: Background of the Men Who Occupied Ranking Positions with "Puppet" Government, n.d., File: Collaboration, Manuel Roxas Papers, Philippine National Library.
118. Recommendation for Promotion, HQ 1st Bn., 63rd Inf., Maj. Francisco Offemaria, 1 November 1942, Nava Papers; Mac to Poldo, 8 November 1942, vol. 3, CPU-WWII.
119. Letter from Mac to Poldo, 3 September 1942, vol. 9, CPU-WWII.
120. Nava, Officer's Record.
121. Joe [Jose Nava] to Capt. Santos, 12 September 1943 and 20 August 1943, Nava Papers.
122. Andres L. Loot, Governor of Non-Christian Tribes to District Executive Officer, 14 June 1944, Vol. 18, CPU-WWII; Nava, Officer's Record.
123. F. Caram to J. Nava, 2 March 1943; Jose Nava to Dr. Fermin G. Caram, 2 May 1943, Nava Papers.
124. *Tigbatas* (Iloilo), 22 May 1945.
125. *The Times* (Iloilo), 23 July 1946.
126. Labor Rate Statistics — Iloilo City, n.d., International Chamber of Commerce, Iloilo.
127. Pascual Espinosa, interview with the author, Iloilo, 29 November 1974.
128. Angel Victoriano, interview with the author, Iloilo, 4 December 1974; Flavio Nava, interview with the author, Iloilo, 19 August 1974.
129. *The Times*, 12 March 1948, 7 December 1948; *Veritas* (Jaro), 27 January 1946, 29 September 1946, 6 October 1946, 17 November 1946, 10 December 1946, 9 February 1947, 8 October 1950, 7 January 1951, 1 April 1951, 13 May 1951, 16 September 1951.
130. Salvador Bas and Felicia Palmejar de Bas, prewar members of Anak Pawis, interview with the author, Iloilo City, 2 December 1974.
131. Evidences of the Case, 10 May 1942, Personal File: Guillermo Capadocia, Intelligence Service Armed Forces of the Philippines (hereafter ISAFP).
132. Subject: NAVA, Jose Ma., CAPADOCIA, Guillermo, DIONES, Jose Fuentes, Labor Leaders, 31 August 1946, Office of the AC of S, G–2, Army Headquarters, Personal File: Guillermo Capadocia, ISAFP.
133. Flavio Nava, interview with the author, Iloilo, 19 August 1974.
134. Francisco Ordoñez, prewar employee of Elizalde & Co. and postwar manager of Central La Carlota, interview with the author, Bacolod City, 9 September 1975; Emilio Severino, assistant to Jose Yulo, interview with the author, Makati, Manila, 11 December 1974.
135. Manuel Palacios, interview with the author, Ilog, Negros Occidental, 27 August 1975; minutes of the eighteenth anniversary and general convention of the Federacion Obrera de Filipinas, 6 April 1947, Flavio Nava Papers.

136. Alfredo Palmejar, Statement of Income and Expenses, Jan. 1, 1948 to Dec. 31, 1948, Federacion Obrera de Filipinas, Flavio Nava Papers.

137. *The Times*, 14 March 1946, 21 November 1946.

138. *Pioneer Press* (Cebu), 22 December 1946, 7 March 1947.

139. *The Times*, 12 March 1947.

140. Magin Bautista to President Manuel Roxas, 2 October 1947, File: Iloilo 1947–48, Roxas Papers.

141. Flavio Nava, interview with the author, Iloilo, 7 September 1974.

142. Jose Ma. Nava to Capt. Blumentritt Jumuad, Interrogation Team, Military Intelligence Service, 16 May 1951, Nava Papers.

143. Flavio Nava, interview with the author, 19 August 1974.

144. *People v. Sumili*, CFI Iloilo, Criminal Case 463 (1946), transcript, 162–66.

145. Flavio Nava, interview with the author, 19 August 1974.

146. Flavio Nava, interview with the author, 19 August 1974.

147. *The Times*, 14 March 1946, 16 March 1946.

148. *People v. Sumili*, CFI Iloilo, Criminal Case 463 (1946), Nicomedes Laborte, Autopsy Protocol, 15 March 1946.

149. *El Tiempo*, 18 March 1946.

150. *Kirab* (Iloilo City), 19 August 1947.

151. *People v. Sumili*, CFI Iloilo, Criminal Case 463 (1946), Sentencia, 15 April 1948.

152. *Philippines Free Press*, 10 July 1954.

153. Alfredo Palmejar, Statement of Income and Expenses, Jan. 1, 1948 to Dec. 31, 1948, Federacion Obrera de Filipinas, Flavio Nava Papers; Percentage Liquidation, Mar. 1–15, April 15–30, May 1–15, 1949, Federacion Obrera de Filipinas, Nava Papers.

154. F. M. Espino, Iloilo Collector of Customs, to Ben Villanueva, 28 April 1955, Iloilo City, Bureau of Customs.

155. *The Times*, 15 July 1947, 7 August 1947.

156. *People v. Jerson Espinosa*, CFI Iloilo Criminal Case 1,426 (1948), Decision; Pablito Gepana, Arevalo, interview with the author, Iloilo City, 26 November 1973; *The Times*, 19 November, 20 November, 21 November 1947.

157. *The Times*, 21 November, 22 November, 27 November 1947; Leon Nava, interview with the author, 2 December 1974.

158. Confidential source, interview with the author, 4 September 1974.

159. *People v. Jose M. Nava*, CFI Iloilo Criminal Case 1,336 (1947), Pascual Espinosa, 1 December 1947, Complaint.

160. *People v. Jose M. Nava*, CFI Iloilo Criminal Case 1,336 (1947), Pascual Espinosa, 1 December 1947, Complaint, 10 December 1947, Information.

161. *The Times*, 12 September 1949.

162. Dr. Caram to President Quirino, telegram, 5 November 1949, President Elpidio Quirino Papers.

163. *The Times*, 9 November 1949.

164. *Liberator*, 12 November 1949.

165. *The Times*, 19 November 1949.

166. *Liberator*, 19 November 1949.

167. *Liberator*, 10 December 1949, 14 December 1949.

168. *Liberator*, 10 December 1949.

169. Flavio Nava, interview with the author, 19 August 1974, 12 May 1975.

170. Flavio Nava, interview with the author, 19 August 1974, 12 May 1975.

171. Chinese Bureau to Capadocia, 20 November 1949, Personal File: Capadocia, ISAFP.

172. Flavio Nava, interview with the author, 19–20 August 1974.
173. *People v. Amado Hernandez et al.*, CFI Manila, Criminal Case 15,841, Panaysayon ni Gg. Guillermo Parreño Gin Kuha ni Louise Kroll [Rodrigo de Jesus] Sa Atubang Nanday S. Golez, Santiago Apostol, kag Goyo Karon Hulio 28, 1950 Halin Sa Alas 5:50 pm.
174. *People v. Jose Nava et al.*, CFI Iloilo Criminal Case 2,878 (1951), Decision; Flavio Nava, interview with the author, 19–20 August 1974.
175. HB to Abra, 11 August 1949; HB to Abra and K. Alunan, 14 August 1940, both in Personal File: Capadocia, ISAFP.
176. *People v. Jose Nava et al.*, Decision; Flavio Nava, interview with the author, 19–20 August 1974.
177. NICA, Subject: HMB Reco "6" (Visayas), 27 December 1951, Personal File: Capadocia, ISAFP.
178. *Liberator*, 8 February 1950.
179. *The Times*, 21 April 1950, 2 August 1950.
180. Special Radio Program Dedicated . . . to President Elpidio Quirino, 16 November 1950, Nava Papers.
181. *Liberator*, 4 November 1950.
182. Jose Nava to President Quirino (telegram), 16 December 1950, Flavio Nava Papers.
183. Jose Nava to Myron Cowen (telegram), 5 April 1951, Flavio Nava Papers.
184. Nava, "Workers and Peasants."
185. Secretary Jose Figueras to President Elpidio Quirino, 4 May 1951, Department of Labor, Records Section, Manila.
186. Jose Nava to Capt. Blumentritt Jumuad, 16 May 1951, Nava Papers.
187. Sigfredo Nava, FOF Secretary, interview with the author, Iloilo City, 7 May 1974.
188. *The Times*, 1 September, 20 September 1951.
189. Nava Diary, 20 November, 25 November 1952.
190. Jose Nava to Capt. Blumentritt Jumuad, 16 May 1951, Nava Papers.
191. *People v. Flavio Nava et al.*, Transcript, 1054–98.
192. *People v. Jose Nava et al.*, CFI Iloilo Criminal Case 2,878, Decision, Defense Memorandum, 193–217; Flavio Nava, interviews with the author, 19–20 August 1974, 22 August 1975.
193. *People v. Jose Nava et al.*, Decision.
194. Nava Diary, 5 April 1952.
195. Col. Agustin Marking, Subject: Digest and Observations Made on the Different Speeches Delivered by Sen. Avelino & Party in Iloilo, To: His Excellency President of the Philippines, 21 March 1949, Quirino Papers.
196. Nava Diary, 24 May 1952.
197. Nava Diary, 11, 19, 20, 29 June 1952; Jose M. Nava to Jose Ponce de Leon, 24 March 1952, Nava Papers.
198. Nava Diary, 18 July 1952.
199. Nava Diary, 11 November 1952.
200. Nava Diary, 16 April 1953.
201. *The Times*, 15 January 1954.

Mang Dionisio Macapagal shaking hands with President
Diosdado Macapagal, who had just signed titles to
homesteads in Barrio Manaul, Candaba, Pampanga Province
for *Mang* Dionisio and ten of his kin and neighbors,
Malacañang Palace, Manila, early 1960s.

Dionisio Macapagal: A Rebel Matures

Brian Fegan

A life has some coherence: the person who lived it was designing it as he or she went along. A biography has even more coherence if the subject tells it, shaping it with his or her own imagination. This essay is less tidy. Some parts were virtually dictated to me by its subject. Other elements came from his kinsmen, allies, and enemies. Some events I observed directly, from the first time I met Mang Dionisio Macapagal during two years spent in his village from July 1971 to May 1973 and in five later visits between 1979 and 1995. One reason this story is messy is that I did not collect material consistently with an eye to writing a biography. Instead, I began by looking at the social and political history of a locality that is a part of wider systems, trying to understand where its present was located on the trajectory of change. For me, that present began in 1971. Over the span of what has now become a full human generation, the "present" itself has become elastic and historic. Through the course of my visits to this village, Mang Dionisio Macapagal gradually emerged as one of the most interesting people in both its past and its multiple presents.[1]

When I first met him in the 1970s, Mang Dionisio was a prominent village elder and faction leader in his mid-sixties. I lived in his village for two years, trying to make sense of its changing social and economic life. At this time, he presented himself as a lifelong *oposisyonista*, always siding with those out of power. He was oppositionist in three senses: as a patriot against the *compromisario* elite who worked with the U.S. colonial government, as a peasant against the proprietors, and as a voter against the dominant factions of landed families that were contending for municipal and national offices. This stance led him to support everything from millenarian nationalist conspiracies to peasant unions and radical minority parties.

Mang Dionisio's account of his political alignments casts light on a submerged or subaltern politics concerned with militant nationalism and social justice. It shows how he and many other Central Luzon peasants

tried to reconcile these often contradictory ideals. His account makes linkages between a number of organizations that have been dealt with in the
dominant histories as if they were discrete and even distinct: millenarian
movements, peasant unions, nationalist movements, and electoral parties.
Philippine electoral politics is usually analyzed as if Carl Lande's atom-
istic model of shifting alliances between elite families and patron-client
relations was all-explanatory.[2] "Nationalist" histories tend to be unilineal
and teleological, dismissing the millenarian and radical conspiracies as
superstitious or "rightist" deviations from the main line toward a Marxist-
Leninist revolution. Taking the viewpoint of one member of these marginal groups reveals continuities that have been neglected, in part because
the teleology of hindsight relegates history's losers to oblivion.

   This biography is based on interviews with Mang Dionisio and his
neighbors, family, faction allies, and enemies. Some details I have witnessed, and others have been corroborated by family, letters, public documents, newspapers, court reports, and published sources. I enjoyed
spending time in his house as guest and observer. It was at times a
munisipyong munti, or mini–city hall, where kin, faction mates, neighbors,
and allies called for advice and support on matters that ranged from family and neighborly disputes to planning for weddings and funerals.
Villagers often sought his intervention in securing favors from outsiders
or avoiding penalties imposed by them. These efforts included manipulating village and municipal governments, land reform policies and programs, landlords, the National Irrigation Authority, the government-sub-
sidized crop loan system, police, politicians, courts, and employers. Some
came, of course, out of curiosity or boredom. Until the electrical grid was
extended to the village around 1979, bringing television into villagers'
homes, people knew more about local affairs than the lives of film stars
in Manila. In sum, Mang Dionisio's home was a center for the creation
and dissemination of local knowledge.

   Oral history, however, has well-known limits. Memory is slippery, apt
to be encoded in set-piece narratives, revised by hindsight, and often self-
serving. As a courteous and intelligent colleague, Mang Dionisio undoubtedly directed and edited his memories in the directions he perceived to be
of interest to me—such as social history. In our conversations, Mang
Dionisio showed a scholarly bent for accuracy. His oral accounts made
scrupulous use of the Tagalog enclitic *daw* (it is/was said) to distinguish
rumor or report from facts, to signal that he did not vouch for its accuracy,
or, sometimes ironically, to indicate the foolishness or dishonesty of another's version of a story. Several times he referred me to an "original source,"
a document, or more often a person who had directly participated in or
observed an event that he had not. When he could not supply a name or

some significant detail, he would say so, distinguishing *ewan ko* (I do not/did not know) from *di ko natatandaan* (I cannot remember).[3] Even so, I do not pretend that this biography is the truth or that it is only Mang Dionisio speaking. Looking over this text, I realize now that this is an accidental biography, pieced together from fragments of interviews that were focused on my earlier interest in economic and political matters. Where the voice is mine or that of someone else, I have usually said so. After finishing this account, I was not able to check with Mang Dionisio to confirm that what I have made of his life corresponds to what he makes of it.

Mang Dionisio is at times didactic and, as his enemies used to say, *makahari*, or "imperious." His personality is far from Frank Lynch's stereotype of the Filipino as a smooth chameleon guided by *pakikisama*, a social norm for "fitting in with others" or a concern with maintaining "smooth interpersonal relations."[4] Mang Dionisio wears that mask when it suits him, but beneath it is a strong-willed and at times abrasive man. Some say he is *matigas ang ulo*, or stubborn: he sticks to his position at the risk of giving offense, even when relating to a class superior or a majority in a meeting.

In this account, our central character seems to move through three conventional life stages: the youthful rebel, who joined movements to fight injustice; the mature farmer, with sideline businesses that put his youngest daughter and granddaughters through college, the political elder of his numerous kindred, and a village influential; and the retired elder, who has distributed his land but is faced with succession disputes among sons who compete with each other in politics. This three-stage simplification reflects only part of the reality. I am most aware of the period since 1971 when I first came to know the landscape, some of the people, and had the chance to observe some of these events.

Although he was a youthful revolutionary, Mang Dionisio, by the time I knew him in his later years, supported the incremental and often frustrating process of reform. I don't know how to judge in what proportion his impatience for justice had been tamed by the usual mellowing that comes with age and experience or by being compromised by relative success in the everyday system, within which he used his contacts, talents, and energy to secure available resources for his kin and allies.

Mang Dionisio's weapons in pragmatic politics have always been his keen intelligence, his knowledge of how organizations work, his ability to approach the right people, his ready comprehension of legal procedures, his persuasiveness, and his energy. As an individual, he has never used violence as a means in competition for position or resources within the system. In pragmatic politics, however, he was allied for fifty years with a related family, the de Guzmans, who for three generations did maintain a reputation for the effective use of violence.[5] Moreover, from the 1920s through the 1940s Mang Dionisio was also a member of organizations that advocated violence to achieve collective nationalist and class ends. In nearby municipalities, branches of those organizations actually joined abortive risings. His local branch organized for insurrection but balked at suicidal gestures when promised arms failed to arrive.

While this account focuses on Mang Dionisio's political and economic life, it is not possible to really know the man through these important but narrow domains alone. He was also a good husband, father, grandfather and great-grandfather, neighbor, friend, and *kumpadre*. I have ignored those private relations except where they shed light on the public man. Though I refer to him here as Mang Dionisio, in his village I address him as Tata Dionisio or Tata Desing. At some point, our relationship became such that I began to call him Tatang, or "Father." He and his wife, Nana Pitang, are kind enough to refer to me as their *anak kwenta*; their children address me as *kuya* or, when their real eldest brother is present, *Kuya* Brian. Mang Dionisio has my respect and affection as both a mentor and colleague. I deliberately use the term *colleague* since he is intelligent, reflective, and articulate. In retrospect, I have come to see that we are each trying to understand what it means to be a Filipino and a small farmer in Central Luzon. He has tried all his life to learn how his society works and why it is unjust.

We are now both a generation older. Each of us has changed, as have the times and our relationship. When last I spoke to Mang Dionisio, in January 1995, he was almost eighty-nine but still clear minded. He was no longer strong enough to walk beyond the pool of shade linking his *bakuran* houseyard to those of his sons and close neighbors. Death, senility, and retirement had removed all of his own generation and most of the next from active participation in village affairs. That had opened succession struggles within the *angkan* (led kindreds), and precipitated realignments of *angkan* as village factions. When he was younger, he had wanted to change the system radically. Even in the twilight of his life, he retained a lively interest in village, town, and provincial political figures and factions as they maneuvered for position in the upcoming May 1995 elections.

Early Life

Dionisio Macapagal was born in 1906 in Buga, then a *pook*, or hamlet, of Barrio Pinambaran, municipality of San Miguel, the northernmost town in the Tagalog-speaking province of Bulacan, Central Luzon, Philippines.[6] Dionisio was the fourth and youngest surviving son of Fulgencio Macapagal and Maria Baltasar. His parents told him that his father's father, a Kapampangan speaker, had come upstream to Buga from Candaba Swamp sometime in the nineteenth century.

Mang Dionisio's first memories of his father are as a share tenant of a rain-fed, but bunded and leveled, wet-rice farm. This farm ran in a narrow strip from the bank of the Ilog Bulo River to Ilog Bakod Creek, just downstream of the *ferrocarril*, the Manila-Cabanatuan railway. The railway bridge over the Bulo River was built the same year Mang Dionisio was born. The Macapagal house stood on stilts on the natural levee of the river. Its walls were of *sawali* (split bamboo), and it was thatched with *kogun* (*Imperata cylindrica*) grass. His family carried household water from the river in bamboo.

Under the Spanish, San Miguel's only school was in the township, seven kilometers away. After about 1904, the U.S. regime established a public school system, which conducted its classes in English. By 1920, there were schools in the township and at barrios Sibul Springs and Salacot. As a boy, Dionisio Macapagal went to school a couple of kilometers downstream from Buga on the Daang Real, now Highway 5, at Barrio Salacot, where he finished the fourth grade. He recalls that the teachers whipped children who spoke Tagalog at school. Somehow he managed to learn usable English.

The landlord Don Felix de Leon lived in a big house at Barrio San Vicente in the town center. Sometimes, around harvest in dry season, Don Felix rode around his estate on a big "Australian" horse. Mang Dionisio's older brothers said that tenancy conditions on Don Felix's land were then 50/50 crop sharing—after deduction from the still undivided harvest of the standard allowances for seed, reaping, and threshing. Don Felix charged *takipan*, or 100 percent interest, on rice loans for subsistence, payable at the next harvest. Effectively, the interest rate was about 120 percent because the estate equated one sack of rice with two sacks of paddy, or unhusked rice, though the milling recovery rate was actually about 60 rather than 50 percent. For money loans, Don Felix charged no visible interest, but at harvest he valued paddy well below the market rate. The tenant was expected to provide the work animals and tools; to plow, harrow, and make seedbeds; to supervise, pay, and feed the transplanters; to retransplant flooded areas, regulate the water, and try to control pests for the growing crop; to manage reaping and gathering the sheaves; to supervise threshing by cattle and horses treading the sheaves on a prepared clay floor; and to winnow and bag.

Tenants were required to cart the owner's share to his *bodega*, or warehouse, in town, about seven kilometers away. They were also required to provide extra services unconnected with the farm, which they often resented. For instance, the men could be required to cut and deliver one buffalo cartload of firewood. The landowner could require his tenants' womenfolk to work as maids and cooks in the big house at fiesta or when he was entertaining. Old people in 1971 complained that in the 1920s some landowners had misused such household service and employed the threat of eviction to seduce or rape tenants' daughters with impunity.

The wars of 1896–1902 against the Spanish, then the Americans, and the recurrent rinderpest epidemics from 1898 to 1916 made buffaloes scarce. In those disturbed years, many peasants had lost their buffaloes, a basic qualification for tenancy, and hence the capacity to farm their own land. Don Felix, like several other rich townsmen, had a ranch in the *parang* grasslands at the receding forest fringe, where his men raised cattle and buffaloes. He rented buffaloes to his tenants at the rate of ten *cavans* (five hundred kilos) of paddy per beast per year, or about 60 percent of the tenant's share of the normal net harvest from one hectare of a two- or three-hectare farm.

The Landscape of 1906–19

In 1906, when Dionisio Macapagal was born, the forest was close and people were "scarce," as the local agricultural frontier had not yet closed. During his lifetime, Dionisio saw the forest recede to the highest ridges of the Sierra Madre. He played a role in its destruction and suffered the floods and dry streams that were its effects. On the flat, fertile, clay loam on the north bank of the Bulo River, there was a labor and buffalo shortage, with much *tiwangwang* (waste or idle land) under *parang*, a tangled mix of coarse grasses and scrub. On the river's southern bank, toward the Sierra Madre, there are low rolling hills of poor, stony, clay soil. There the forest fringe receded gradually as the big trees were logged, followed by firewood cutting and pioneer swidden farming. In their wake, these processes left stretches of *parang* grasslands where dense forests had once stood. These coarse grasses, when mature and long, are low in nutrition and unpalatable to livestock. Stockraisers maintained grazing by means of fires set in the dry season to encourage edible new shoots. The rolling *parang* slopes were gradually terraced into rain-fed paddies, a transformation of the landscape that was complete for the area nearest Buga by the 1960s. In the early years of the century, rich landowners like Kapitan Pepe de Leon, Don Felix de Leon, Kabesang Vicente Morales, Pioquinto Tecson, Kapitan Gorio Marquez, and Don Catalino Sevilla had cattle ranches in the *parang* zone.

When Mang Dionisio was a boy, there were still *buri* (sugar palms) in low areas, tapped for palm wine and sugar. Men cut the fronds, and women softened, sized, and bleached them to weave *banig* (sleeping mats) for sale. As late as 1927, when Dionisio married, it was only an hour by buffalo cart (three kilometers) from Buga to the fringe of the forest to get lumber, firewood, wild bamboo, and rattan or to make charcoal or hunt wild pig and deer. When Mang Dionisio was in his teens, there were still big trees close to the river. Some were barged down the San Miguel River for lumber. The *bahay propiyetaryo*, or large houses, of the landlords, with an upper story made of Philippine hardwoods, were built or rebuilt in township barrios like San Vicente between 1900 and 1920 after the Americans burned parts of the township in 1899.[7] Some have floor planks of polished *narra*, or Philippine mahogany, a meter wide, twelve meters long, and five centimeters thick.

Tales of Land-Grabbing

Don Felix de Leon's son, attorney Don Cecilio de Leon, told me that around the turn of the century his father acquired two extensive lots for the Hacienda de Leon by foreclosure on a mortgage from a Macapagal. One lot included the land on which Dionisio Macapagal was born, some fifty hectares upstream of the railway. The deed showed that it included a private earth-walled dam.[8]

Mang Dionisio's mother told him that his grandfather's first cousin, "Paka" Macapagal, had owned three large lots that became part of the Hacienda de Leon and Hacienda Sevilla de Leon. Though illiterate, Paka Macapagal could count and calculate in his head and was successful in business. He was an aficionado of cockfights. Don Pelagio de Leon took Paka to Manila, entertained him in cabarets, introduced him to *bailarina* (taxi dancers), encouraged him to gamble, and lent him money. Paka made his "X" on a duly witnessed document of *sanglang bili* (mortgage with the option to repurchase) for a sum less than the market value of the land.

During the three-year term of the loan, Don Pelagio had usufruct of the land as mortgagee, in this case the right to collect the rents from its tenants and run his cattle on the *parang*. On the *taning* (due date), Paka Macapagal went to Don Felix's house with the money. Don Pelagio had gone to Manila. The contract specified that to redeem the land Paka Macapagal must pay in full, on the due date, to Don Pelagio in person. Don Pelagio had instructed his relations and lawyer to not disclose his Manila address, to insist on the "in person" clause, and to refuse to accept payment on his behalf. Protesting that he had been cheated, Paka Macapagal tried to recover the land in a legal suit in which he was represented by attorney Simeon Payawal. Don Pelagio's son, Don Felix, won the case. Paka Macapagal was ruined by the costs.

The oral accounts of the two sides roughly tally, but the details cannot be documented; Bulacan's Registry of Deeds had burned down in the 1970s, as had several other provincial registries during the controversy over Marcos's 1972 land reform decree. Two matters are important: first, there is ample evidence that since the Spanish period legally skilled members of the educated landlord-moneylender-lawyer class have used the law to take out legal title over the heads of less legally skilled landowners and peasants with customary or homestead title. Widespread peasant memory confirms colonial officials' complaints that then, as now, particularly after the United States introduced the Torrens title system, the rich used lawyers' dodges to acquire lands.

Second, and more importantly, the smallholder, tenant, and landless families cherish such narratives of expropriation. They recount them to account for their own poverty, to justify claims for a greater share of farm production or even for ownership, and to dismiss the legal title of the landowners as unjust, having its roots in land-grabbing by force and fraud.

Troubles with the Landowner

When Mang Dionisio was still small, his father fell sick. As none of the four boys was yet big enough to plow and harrow, their family lost the tenancy. The family called upon their kin and neighbors to carry their house upstream of the railway to a site also on de Leon land. There they lived as farmless laborers for two years. Then Don Catalino Sevilla took on the eldest son, Emiliano, as tenant, to clear and bund for paddy some wasteland across the river, just upstream of the railway. The place was called Makabaklay, after a story that in the Spanish times a man was found *nakabaklay* (hanged) from one of the *balete* (fig trees) by the swamp.

That land belonged to Capitana Dariang (Eladia de Leon). The law and custom required equal division of property among all legitimate children. The wealthy de Leons pursued an aristocratic strategy of discouraging their daughters from marriage in order to restrict the number of heirs among whom the estate would be divided in the next generation.

De Leon men married late, by arrangement, often to cousins — to reunite lands divided by inheritance. Members of elite families say the strategy was *para huwag kumalat ang kayamanan*, intended to prevent wealth from being scattered. The men had few children by their legal wives, but some sired several noninheriting children with the daughters of their tenants or other nonelite mistresses.[9] Don Felix was unusual in that, having no legitimate children, he legally recognized several of his village children as heirs.

Catalino Sevilla and his brother Regino were tough smallholder peasants from Pinambaran (of which Buga was part until 1964). Employed as overseers on the de Leon estate, they perceived the opportunity presented by the spinster heiresses. The Sevilla brothers covertly courted a sister of Kapitan Pepe (Don Jose) de Leon and of his wife, Doña Sisang (Narcisa Buencamino). That success converted management of their wives' shares of de Leon lands into conjugal property. Most of Buga's land north of the Bulo River thus became part of the Hacienda Sevilla de Leon.[10] The brothers went on to open cockpits, where they encouraged the heirs of wealthy families to gamble. About 1918 or 1919, Regino Sevilla introduced steam threshing machines, which collected an extra 10 percent of the crop, a share that formerly went to the peasants. Ruthless in business but with the common touch, the Sevilla brothers became the flag-bearer candidates for the de Leon faction in municipal politics against the rival Tecson faction. The de Leons themselves campaigned for nothing lower than provincial and national offices.

The older Macapagal brothers, Emiliano and Guillermo, worked the tenancy on Don Catalino's estate. The third, Miguel, while still a lad, took buffaloes to pasture and cared for them on *iwihan* terms — receiving every second calf as payment. Most of the land within the farm boundaries was at first *tiwangwang*, or wasteland. The brothers cleared as much as they could each year, cutting down trees and grass in the dry season, burning off the debris before the first rains in June or July, and then farming each section first as swidden for maize. In the wet season, when the clay-loam soil was soft, they would excavate to expose the roots of stumps and then in dry season pile wood around them and burn them out. In the following wet season, they would wait until the soil was soaked in July, then plow, bund, and level it to add a new section to existing paddy fields. In 1912, their father died there. When that farm was broken in, Don Catalino shifted Guillermo to break in another further upstream. There they built a house and remained tenants of Don Catalino Sevilla for about ten years.

The Macapagal brothers broke with Don Catalino in 1918 or 1919 when he changed the conditions of tenure from what they had come to think of as just. The brothers had broken in the farms on the usual condition of no share to the land for the first two years during conversion to paddy field and thereafter a low fixed rent. They had their own buffaloes by then and got neither work nor calf from the estate buffaloes.

Tenants resented the difference between the "just" peasant system of *iwihan*, in which the herder received payment in calves, and the compulsory *pakalabaw* system, in which the herder had no claim on the buffaloes but had to care for them 365 days a year, even though they only used them for 30 or 40 days to prepare the fields. The annual rent was enough to buy a *kalabaw* in three years.

Resentment came to a head when, in 1918 or 1919, Don Catalino demanded a change from the low fixed rent to 50/50 crop share, 100 percent interest on rice or paddy loans for subsistence, and repayment of money loans (*kakabiguin*) to be valued in paddy at one peso per *cavan*, well below the market price.[11]

Emiliano Macapagal did not respond within the dyadic norms of the tenancy relation. He took the unusual step of leading a delegation to negotiate a better contract. He and his brother Guillermo led a delegation of about ten Sevilla tenants to Don Catalino's house in the township, asking him to reconsider. Don Catalino refused the proposals, saying: "Well if you do not like the new conditions, vacate the farms!" He then repeated his own new conditions. The Macapagals said that if he would not agree to their counterproposals they would leave him.

The Early Unions

Dionisio Macapagal, who was not present, would have been about twelve years old at that time. His account gives a version of the events that must have been a set piece in Emiliano Macapagal's later reputation as a local peasant union leader. The narrative can be read to indicate spontaneous reaction to a rationalizing landlord who withdrew previous favorable conditions and failed to fulfill the just or traditional expectations of peasant clients. This resembles the moral economy interpretation, applied to accounts of peasant responses in Talavera in the adjacent province of Nueva Ecija in the 1930s, suggested by Ben Kerkvliet.[12] But Mang Dionisio says that before that incident, around 1918, two men came to the Macapagal *bakuran* and spoke at length with his eldest brother, Emiliano. I neglected to ask why they chose the Hacienda Sevilla de Leon and Emiliano Macapagal. But other sources confirm the role of these two in spreading the new idea of a peasant union.

These two visitors were Lope de la Rosa from Barrio Mandile/Batasan, and Jacinto Manahan, an official of the radical Union de Impresores de Filipinas (Printers Union [UIP]) from the town of Bulacan. In the Historical Data Papers, several barrios credit Manahan and either Lope de la Rosa or Benigno Cristobal with founding a branch of the Union ng Magsasaka (Farmers' Union) for "farmers and field workers" in 1918 or 1919.[13] The HDP town history also reports that Manahan set up the Confederacion del Trabajo, (Confederation of Labor) "for tenants" there in 1920. The Philippines' first director of the Bureau of Labor wrote:[14]

> In 1917, a union of tenants called "*Pagkakaisa ng Magsasaka*" was organized in Matungaw, Bulacan. A few months had hardly elapsed when the name was changed to "*Union ng Magsasaka sa Filipinas*." Notwithstanding this alteration, the name did not appeal to the tenants of Pampanga, Ilocos, and Pangasinan who considered it regional.... [T]he name was again changed to *Union de Aparceros de Filipinas*.

It is significant here that the union as an organizational form was new to peasants and only a decade old in Manila. Manahan, who introduced it, was a member of the radical UIP. In a document from about 1950, tracing the early labor movement, Communist Party (PKP) secretary Capadocia says that Manahan was sent by Crisanto Evangelista, president of the UIP, "to help the peasants."[15] The place where the first peasant union began was a barrio of Manahan's hometown. The next year, peasant unions were seeking collective bargaining contracts, a procedure again introduced by the UIP printers. Manahan organized branches in other Bulacan towns and Nueva Ecija and in 1922 formed the first confederation of peasant unions. In this account, radical Manila unionists, who would in 1930 become foundation members of the Communist Party, introduced in 1917–18 new ideas, forms of organization, and leadership styles that spread peasant unionism out from Manila, first to Bulacan then into the interior. This differs from Kerkvliet's account of Nueva Ecija in the 1930s, which holds that individual peasants spontaneously joined with their fellows as terms of trade with landowners worsened during the Depression.

Electoral Politics in the Early Twentieth Century

When the Jones Law of 1916 dropped the property qualification and extended the franchise to vernacular-literate males over twenty-one years of age, it threatened to breach the monopoly over electoral politics held by town-dwelling property owners. Elite politics in San Miguel municipality had been dominated since at least 1896 by two rival family-based factions—the de Leons and the Tecsons. Holding different political assets, each faction devised appropriate tactics to organize votes. These strategies worked down to the 1950s. By then, the Tecsons had exhausted their wealth, the de Leons had shifted to Manila, and changing times had made openings for new powerful men.

Several of the Tecsons had been officers with revolutionary forces in the wars against Spain and the United States. They retained the respect of, and contacts with, peasant veterans, nationalists, and *barako* or *magaling na lalaki* (tough-guy local leaders). In prewar elections, the Tecsons were able to control the village vote through alliances with these toughs. The de Leons had very large amounts of land and many tenants. No known member of the family had distinguished himself in the revolution, and they were allied by marriage to the family of Felipe Buencamino, excoriated by patriots as a *compromisario* and founder of the Federalista Party of collaboration with the U.S. colonial state. The de Leons' manners were resented by peasants as *ugaling Kastila*, "Spanish ways." They were aristocratic, married to cousins or members of similarly wealthy families, and moved in exclusive social circles with families of their own wealth and standing in Manila and at San Miguel's Sibul Springs, the summer resort of the Manila elite. They had overseers to deal with tenants or they dealt with them in the yard.

Dionisio Macapagal says that Don Felix de Leon did not evict tenants for voting against his candidates but did seek out compliant ones who would pay a premium for the tenancy by shouldering the debts of the outgoing tenants. But the Sevilla brothers used their estates as political assets: they often would give, withhold, or withdraw tenancies and credit to control the vote and punish tenants for joining militant unions. Among the tougher estates were the Candelaria holdings downstream and the Sevilla de Leon estates controlled by Don Catalino, Don Regino Sevilla, and Doña Sisang's brother, Don Gomercindo Buencamino. Peasants refer to the period from about 1925 to the Japanese invasion as *panahon ng buhat-bahay*, "the era of carrying houses," as kin, neighbors, and union brothers helped move the houses of tenants evicted for voting against their landlord's wishes or for joining a union.

After the Eviction

Surrendering their tenancies to Don Catalino Sevilla, the Macapagal brothers quickly found two nearby farms owned by medium-sized landowners with scattered holdings: Veronica Morales and Pioquinto Tecson, who was married to Petra Morales. The farms had a total area of about six hectares. The brothers avoided accepting an advance of *palag-utan* (cutoff pay), which must be repaid before leaving. The term seems alternative to the more common *pasunod*, which tenants resented, as it bound them to a compulsory annual loan at 50 percent interest. The Morales's conditions were more favorable: 60 percent of the crop to the farmer, with the bonus that a 20 percent allowance for reaping and threshing would be deducted from the harvest and the net divided, so that those costs were in effect equally shared. They were not forced to rent buffaloes.

By then, Miguel Macapagal was old enough to farm. The brothers called together kin, neighbors, and friends and carried their house to the new site, where they later built a large lumber house. While the brothers remained single, they shared the farm work and pooled the income from the two farms.

The household composition constantly changed. Dionisio's mother had died when he was ten years old and his father two years later. In 1923, his newly married second brother, Guillermo, took on a tenant farm across the river on the Hacienda de Leon. Their late mother's sister and her invalid husband came to join the brothers in 1917 from San Leonardo, Nueva Ecija. Her four children grew up in the Macapagal house. In 1925, the third brother, Miguel, married and acquired sole tenancy of the farm owned by Veronica Morales. When the cousins had grown, they built and moved into their own house. Dionisio stayed with the eldest brother, Emiliano, who was by then sick with tuberculosis, and took over tenancy of the farm owned by Pioquinto Tecson. In June 1927, Emiliano died.

Mang Dionisio stresses that until he married he had no other *hanapbuhay*, or means of living, but farming and that this left him very poor. In the 1920s, as now, it was normal and necessary for a rice farmer to have a number of skills, to try to expand them, and to seek nonfarm income. As there was no irrigation until 1935, there was no farm work once the harvest was threshed. After threshing, it would be June before the next significant farm work, and rice and cash had to be budgeted for the twelve months until next harvest. Virtually all men of his generation and the next learned carpentry and worked in logging, sawmills, or construction during the dry season. Many kept buffaloes and worked as carters or used horses to operate taxis.

Men of Mang Dionisio's age went as far afield as Taguig Rizal and various towns in Nueva Ecija with threshing machines owned by Don Catalino Sevilla or Don Mariano Tecson. Young members of many families went away as hired laborers in season following the transplanting, reaping, and threshing. A number of marriages record the places where they worked.

Mang Dionisio Elopes

In March 1927, Dionisio Macapagal eloped with his sweetheart, Felisa "Pitang" Morales, against the wishes of her parents, who thought him a poor match. That branch of the Morales then owned its own farm, but Dionisio's father-in-law later gave his Torrens title to his first cousin, Vicente Morales, as security for a debt and was unable to redeem it. At that time, Dionisio was farming the land of Veronica Morales. The nominal tenant was his brother, Emiliano, who was already ill.

Nana Pitang told me that when she was a *dalaga* (maiden) her mother feared she might attract the attention of landlords Don Catalino Sevilla or Don Felix de Leon, notorious for sexually abusing the village girls. If word came that one of the landowners was around, her mother would rub dry buffalo dung on the girl's face to roughen and dirty it. On one occasion, she made the girl hide in a *matong* (granary basket).

In March, already the middle of the dry season, Dionisio had only P2.20 (U.S.$1.10) left, since medicine for Emiliano had used up their cash. The couple sneaked out about 2:00 A.M., with Felisa's cousin as chaperon, and began to walk toward Gapan, Nueva Ecija, about sixteen kilometers away. About 5:00 A.M., they reached Malimba, a barrio of Gapan, and woke a *kalesa* (driver), a stranger until then. For twenty centimos he took them to the house of an American Protestant pastor. The driver served as their witness, becoming the *ninong,* or godfather, of their wedding.

Dionisio paid the pastor one peso for the wedding. Then they invited the driver to breakfast, which for the four cost ninety centimos. He had ten centimos left. Dionisio decided that on their wedding day, rather than walking the dusty sixteen kilometers back and passing the house of Felisa's parents, who would be angry, they should hire a *kalesa.* The driver wanted a peso, but Dionisio had only his ten centimos. His new bride, Felisa, paid the driver from two pesos that she had concealed. Dionisio tells the story as if this set the auspices for their married life: Felisa would handle financial emergencies from hidden reserves. In my experience, thrift and prudence are the stereotypical virtues of Tagalog women, as generosity and fiscal nonchalance are those of men.

When Dionisio's brother Emiliano died, the couple had the house to themselves. Felisa's parents did not reconcile with them until their first child was born. By then, the in-laws had forfeited their land and Dionisio's father-in-law had taken a job as *kapatas* (foreman) of a gang maintaining the railroad tracks. Later, when the old couple became ill, Dionisio and his wife *nagsakripisyo,* or underwent severe hardship, to have them treated.

Political Life, 1925–45

In an interview conducted a week before President Marcos's declaration of martial law in 1972, Mang Dionisio said:

> What I sought was that we, the poor, should progress by means of our joining together. We farmers live by tilling the soil. For example, people like us by means of farmers' associations can change the [tenancy] conditions of the proprietors, to give advances to the farmers. That was my starting point.

In 1926, at the age of twenty-one, he was already running the farm for Emiliano, who, though sick, still headed the village chapter of the Kapatiran Magsasaka, or Peasant Brotherhood. Dionisio had been initiated at a secret gathering at night. The initiates were blindfolded and instructed in Kapatiran rules. They swore to uphold unity, never take up the tenancy of a farmer evicted for asking for better conditions or for voting against his proprietor's instructions, and never reveal the names of the Kapatiran members. The blindfold was removed to reveal the assembled brothers around a fire in which was heated the *panaklayan*, a triangular iron eye projecting from the high center of a yoke-shaped wooden cross-bar to which the traces from the yoke join a meter or so behind a buffalo. A hook on the plow fits into the eye. The assemblage resembles alpha and omega, the first and last letters of the Greek alphabet, which appear in the Catholic liturgy. Those symbols are prominent on the Paschal Candle, lit outside the dark and mourning church at the Easter Vigil ceremony, where the new fire kindled with flint and new light is brought in to symbolize Christ's resurrection. The candle is then used in the annual making of holy water and in the baptism of catechumens. They likewise die to their old life, are questioned on their new faith, have a sign made on them, and are reborn as children of God, hence brothers.

The Kapatiran Magsasaka initiation owes details to the Masonic and Catholic traditions but also to rural symbols. When a boy is superincised at about age twelve, he becomes a *binata* and is expected to begin to behave responsibly and learn how to farm. When a buffalo bull calf is castrated and branded at about four years of age, it becomes *bagun-tao*, a "new person," and thereafter is trained to accept the yoke, to plow, and to haul, that is, to forsake the freedom of youth and shoulder the responsibilities of an adult. The Kapatirang Magsasaka initiates were symbolically branded on the shoulder with the heated iron triangle (or "alpha") of the buffalo harness. They symbolically saw the light of brotherhood, becoming moral new persons. The new ritual brothers were supposed to act for the common good with *kaisahan*, or unity/union, as should siblings.

The Kapatirang Magsasaka, or Union Magsasaka, was founded by General Teodoro Sandiko and attorney Vicente Almazar. From nearby Baliwag, Almazar was heavily involved in legal cases, representing tenants in their complex struggles with the *inquilinos* of the Hacienda Buenavista church estate in San Ildefonso. The Kapatiran's *patron*, or president, was revolutionary general Teodoro Sandiko, an early governor of Bulacan, who was allied with Judge Sumulong and Angelo Suntay, a leader of the nationalist-populist wing of the opposition Democrata Party.[16] The Kapatiran's agrarian demands were that landlords abolish *takipan*, or 100 percent interest, on subsistence loans, the maximum interest to be *talindua*, or 50 percent; to repay money loans, they should value the *palay* at only 20 percent below the market price; and they should share the crop 60/40 in favor of the farmer and share costs equally.

Mang Dionisio insists that Kapatiran's field organizers in the villages were Jacinto Manahan, Lope de la Rosa, and Mateo del Castillo, who would later be important in the Kalipunan Pambansa ng Magbubukid sa Pilipinas (KPMP) peasant union confederation, founded by Manahan in 1922 and known under a series of names in Tagalog, Spanish, and

English. He also says that the Kapatiran of Almazar became a member of the Kalipunan of Manahan and de la Rosa, as they had the same agrarian goals, although the Kapatiran was earlier and more radical in its nationalist objectives. About 1929, as a member of Kapatiran, Dionisio went on to join Tanggulan.

In 1972, almost all the Buga men who had been adults in the late 1920s proudly rolled up their sleeves to show the Kapatiran brand. Some of their accounts make little distinction between the Kapatiran and the KPMP, whose agrarian goals and provincial leaders often overlapped. But the Kapatiran, or some elements in it, focused on another issue: radical nationalism.

Since Dionisio was a boy, there had been stories about the diehard revolutionary general Artemio Ricarte, who was put in solitary confinement for several years rather than kiss the American flag on his return from exile in Guam. Repeating the same intransigence on release, he was sent into exile in Japan. To peasant patriots, Japan was the only imaginable source of guns for insurrection. The patriot imagination had been disposed since the 1890s to embroider the theme of guns from Japan with the mythic return of a liberator coming from the sun rising in the east. Moreover, Ricarte himself kept contact with a stream of visitors and encouraged patriots to form and drill a secret army to await his return from the rising sun with guns.

Dionisio Macapagal says there was no Ricartista organization locally until "1929," and that lasted only one year. This local unit included himself as second lieutenant as well as others from neighboring barrios. Among his family, Emiliano Macapagal was dead and Guillermo refused to join. Emiliano's successor as Kapatiran leader, Kardeng de Guzman, also did not join.

Nevertheless, there were many Ricartista units in San Miguel and Nueva Ecija in the late 1920s. Members practiced *escrima* (fencing), *arnis* (bolo fighting), and marching in formation. They collected whatever firearms they could, mostly homemade shotguns. In 1972, Mang Dionisio showed me among his treasures a pair of *pang-arnis*, hardwood staves for fencing practice. Members drilled with wooden rifles.

The Ricartista organization was promised that Japanese ships would land a cargo of guns at Baler on the east coast of Luzon. The movement planned a transport route from Baler through the pass near Bongabon, organizing safe houses and relays of buffalo carts by night. The guns were to be distributed before the rising. But the seditious organizing and drilling did not last long, as the Constabulary and the police chased and arrested high-level leaders. The members and village-level leaders soon went over to the Tanggulan.

Dionisio Macapagal's account of the Tanggulan of Patricio Dionisio was that in San Miguel it was an inner nationalist conspiracy whose outer movement was the Kapatiran Magsasaka peasant union led by Vicente Almazar and General Sandiko. Entry into the secret organization was by the familiar rite: blindfolding, questioning, taking an oath of unity and secrecy, then initiation. Dionisio signed with blood from his left hand in 1929 or 1930. San Miguel peasants regarded the organization as a version or continuation of the Ricartistas. Some bought its expensive uniform, modeled on that of the Kataas-taasang Kagalang-galang Katipunan ng mga Anak Bayan (KKK) of Bonifacio. The shirt and breeches with leggings were of *rayadilyo*, a coarse, shiny, ridged silk with fine stripes. They wore a sombrero turned up at the front with a triangle insignia. In 1972, Dionisio Macapagal showed me, carefully unwrapping them from oil-cloth, his uniform shirt and breeches. He said wryly that after the Tanggulan national leaders were rounded up in December 1931 it was not the sort of clothing that was likely to deteriorate from frequent wear.

Both national leaders and ordinary followers of radical societies were disposed to be members of diverse movements, some with apparently contradictory ideas. Thus, some members of the leftist Kapatiran Magsasaka/Union ng Magsasaka and/or the KPMP unions were also members of the ultranationalist Ricartista-Tanggulan-Sakdal series. Capadocia reports that in the early 1930s Crisanto Evangelista, head of the PKP communist party; Patricio Dionisio, head of Tanggulan; Eusebio Godoy of Palihan ng Bayan; and Benigno Ramos of Sakdal met and debated weekly at the printing shop that produced their diverse papers.[17] Several members of the PKP's Politburo were arrested in the December 1931 roundup of Tanggulan, in which they were active members.

Although the Kapatiran/Union ng Magsasaka was decapitated nationally by 1932, Buga members continued to follow Kardeng de Guzman, who had been its local leader since the death of his cousin, Emiliano Macapagal, in 1927. Jose Hernandez and Ben Zafra, both Kapatiran members, saw the transition more starkly: first there was the Kapatiran, which was pursued by the police "because of Tanggulan," then they joined the Kalipunan. Andron de Guzman, brother of Kardeng, was not a member of the Kapatiran, as he "objected to people being branded." But he was a member of the Kalipunan. He says Kapatiran members, including his brother Kardeng, joined the Kalipunan when the Kapatiran dissolved at higher levels.[18]

Dionisio Macapagal was initiated into the KPMP by Jose Manuzon of the adjacent barrio of Cambio. He signed with blood from the left elbow. Members of the KPMP wore the symbol of the yoke (or omega) on their sleeves. In Macapagal's view, the KPMP/Kalipunan and the Kapatiran differed only in the degree of priority they gave to agrarian versus nationalist issues. But to join the landowner-organized Katipunan Mipanampun was to betray the brotherhood and one's oath. Indeed, only one member of Buga's Kapatiran is known to have done so; the orator Yalong, who began as a strong member.

By the early 1930s, paddy had fallen to P1.50 per *cavan* and there was little off-farm work as the Great Depression hit. Peasants were buried in debt. As a result, peasant organizations that had begun a decade before the Depression grew in size and militancy.

Demonstrations and strikes became frequent and large in San Miguel and throughout Central Luzon. In 1932, the Kalipunan campaigned for written tenancy contracts, abolition of the compulsory annual *pasunod* loans at high interest and of buffalo rent, reduction of interest to the legal rate of 12 percent, and paddy delivery against debt to be valued at not less than 80 percent of the current market value.

Another cause of peasant grievances was the big steam threshers, which were by then almost universal. They had changed the nature of farm work and took the 10 percent of the crop that formerly remained in the villages. After reaping, the tenant had to bundle the stems, tie them into sheaves, dry them on the stubble, then haul them in a buffalo cart to the roadside.

There, he had to make a *mandala*, or great conical stack of all the sheaves of one variety, sited at the road end of his farm, to await the landowner's thresher. This might take three months to reach his farm, as the landowner scheduled it to thresh first on other estates, where his machine faced competition. In the meantime, overseers prevented the tenant from threshing to get grain to eat, pay creditors, or sell.

To Dionisio Macapagal, the agrarian and national problems in the 1930s were two faces of the same coin. If peasants protested, demonstrated, and organized against oppressive and unjust agrarian conditions, they faced repression from the municipal police controlled by Nacionalista Party (NP) landlord-mayors and backed by the American-controlled Philippine Constabulary. If they organized as patriots against the colonial power, then they ran up against the police of the landlord-mayor, the collaborator Nacionalista government of Quezon, and the Constabulary. Macapagal was a member of Almazar and Sandiko's Kapatiran, which had its greatest strength in San Ildefonso—the next town south, and center of the Catholic Church's Hacienda Buenavista.

When Dionisio Macapagal was in the Tanggulan in early 1931, he read guest editorials of the Tanggulan leaders Vicente Almazar and the journalist Patricio Dionisio in *Sakdal*, the newspaper of Benigno Ramos's party of the same name.[19] When the Tanggulan was suppressed in December

1931, Mang Dionisio shifted to Sakdal, which was then strong in
Pinambaran and its *sitios* of Buga and Cambio. In interviews, he listed
Leonardo Victorio as San Miguel municipal president. Victorio became a
pro-Axis Ganap during World War II, and he accompanied the Japanese to
Quiangan, where he was killed. In 1934, Mang Dionisio himself went on
Sakdal business to Penaranda to arrange transport for the Japanese guns
that were supposed to be landed at Baler and then carted through
Bongabon to the Central Plain.

Dionisio Macapagal says that the program of Sakdal was to seize all
the *municipios* in Bulacan, Tarlac, and Nueva Ecija. As with the Ricartistas
and Tanggulan, the Sakdals prepared for an armed insurrection. They
collected a few shotguns, drilled with wooden rifles, and practiced fencing, but they looked forward to the modern rifles and machine guns that
were to arrive on the east coast from Japan. The recurring narrative, that
kalayaan freedom would be achieved by a brotherhood of marked initiates who had seen the light, bearing guns landed on the east coast and led
by a pure hero returning from the land of the rising sun, and the visual
connection between the sun rays from the heads of images of the risen
Christ, the sun on Bonifacio's KKK flag, and the sun of the Philippines
flag is made powerful by the assembly of symbols of millennial renewal.

In 1935, as the referendum on the Commonwealth approached,
Benigno Ramos remonstrated that it would "delay" independence for
another ten years. Rural patriots prepared again for insurrection. Word
came that Ramos had flown to Japan and been promised arms by General
Ricarte and that the Japanese fleet would land the arms on the east coast.
The patriot unit in each *bayan* municipality would overthrow the police,
Constabulary, and collaborators and then join the march on Manila. The
Japanese fleet would destroy the U.S. fleet in Manila and Subic. The
Japanese, as Asian brothers, would then depart from a free Philippines.
This mythical sequence shared by the Ricartista, Tanggulan, and Sakdal
insurrectionists, "corrects" the sequence of 1898 when the United States
provided guns to Aguinaldo and destroyed the Spanish fleet but then
turned on the Malolos Republic.

Dionisio Macapagal says that on the night after May Day 1935 his
unit assembled, went down to the highway, and cut the telegraph wires.
They sent a runner north to Gapan to hasten delivery of the guns. The
messenger returned to say that there were no guns on the way and all
was quiet to the north. They began to worry. Word from the south said
that the rising would go ahead in San Ildefonso, but the Sakdals there had
only a handful of shotguns.

Dionisio Macapagal says that it was married men like himself who
first became wary, then afraid. Without modern rifles, it would be suicide

to attack the police barracks. They went home. He says he hid his uniform and went to bed for two days to hide his shame. Next day, news came of 2 or 3 Sakdals shot dead and "100" arrested at San Ildefonso and "50" dead at Cabuyao, Laguna.

About 1934, the national Palihan ng Bayan was founded by Eusebio Godoy, a Manila politician opposed to Quezon. It included rich and poor opposed to the U.S. Tydings-McDuffie Act, which would delay independence and extend U.S. trade privileges with the Philippines. The *palihan* refers to the anvil on the reverse of the one-peso coin. The organization's main activity was to "buy Filipino," boycott U.S. goods, and listen to speeches about independence. Dionisio Macapagal signed with blood from a finger.

After the 1935 debacle of Sakdal, Dionisio Macapagal stayed with KPMP on agrarian issues but looked elsewhere for his nationalism since the union did not address the indignity of colonial rule. He became the local leader of the radical pro-Japanese Ganap, along with his wife's brother, Ninoy Morales. The HDP says that Pinambaran, of which Buga was still a *sitio*, was the stronghold of Ganap.[20] They received propaganda about the Greater East Asia Co-Prosperity Sphere of Japan and looked to their Japanese Asian brothers to liberate the Philippines from the white U.S. colonialists. Japan would then leave the Philippines as an independent Asian nation in a free Asia. In the late 1930s, Mang Dionisio waited for the Japanese liberators. But in electoral politics he supported Frente Popular, a coalition of leftist groups. It was anti-Nacionalista, anti-Quezon, and, in Mang Dionisio's eyes, continued the goals of General Sandiko's leftist-populist Democratas.

Japanese Occupation

When the Japanese landed, Dionisio Macapagal had been the appointed *teniente auxilyar* of the *sitio* of Buga since about 1928. He was made village president of Ganap and village headman. But the real power in Buga was in the hands of his cousin and fellow member of the Kapatiran/KPMP, Kardeng de Guzman. At the beginning of World War II, when U.S. forces abandoned a base near Sibul Springs, Kardeng carted away hundreds of rifles and much ammunition, arming supporters to form his own unit of the U.S. Armed Forces Far East (USAFFE). He distributed some guns and ammunition to allies like Dioscoro de Leon of Gapan and some to his brother, Andron, who was a member of the emerging KPMP-based Hukbalahap. In the first year of occupation, Kardeng and Dionisio worked together to maintain Buga as a *katahimikan*, or place of peace.

In late 1943, Mang Dionisio went to Manila and found work as a *kapatas*, a foreman of a labor gang working in the port area under Japanese officers. He is adamant that he did not become a Makapili soldier for the Japanese or an informer. Rather, his observations of the Japanese in San Miguel and Manila disillusioned him about the promises of independence. Their strict military discipline and the activities of the secret police, the Kempetai, were oppressive.

In 1944, U.S. bombing raids on Manila intensified. Speaking in English, the lingua franca, a Japanese officer friend told Mang Dionisio: "Soon the Americans will come back. Look at all the aeroplanes they have. All Japanese will die here. I will never see my family again. Here is all my money. You have children. Go away to your homes quickly." He gave Mang Dionisio and his men a pass written in Japanese that ordered them to go to Caloocan. They walked there through burning Manila and parted ways. Mang Dionisio walked home to Buga.

Other San Miguel Ganap members were more committed to the Japanese cause or had reason to fear vengeance for their deeds during the occupation. They stayed with the Japanese and retreated north to the last stand of the Japanese army at Quiangan. None are known to have returned alive.

Liberation and the Huk Rebellion

In Buga, Dionisio was left alone by the Hukbalahap leaders, Amando Batumbakal and Losio Santos under Kumander Andron de Guzman, who was then in control of the area.

When "USAFFE" member Kardeng de Guzman was released by the Americans from his dungeon in Fort Santiago, he kept Dionisio under "house arrest" at night for his own protection.[21] Ganap members were being picked up by USAFFE forces that had laid low in the mountains throughout the war. The Bagro brothers, two well-to-do Visayans who had been refugees in Buga, were forced to dig their own graves and buried alive. Other local Ganap members were picked up and taken to a camp near Sibul. Unless an influential person spoke up for them, they were executed within two days.

Dionisio and Miguel Macapagal and Ninoy Morales had hoped that Japan would send the guns for an insurrection to liberate the Philippines from the Americans and the tenants from the landlords. In 1945–46, the configuration of forces was changed. The realities of occupation by the Japanese army and Kempetai had chastened the patriot imagination. It was Douglas MacArthur who had returned with guns as a liberator. After the United States granted independence on schedule on 4 July 1946, it was no longer an issue that could arouse peasant patriots to contemplate insurrection.[22]

When independence in effect detached the agrarian issue from nationalism, a more intense class conflict emerged. During the war, the

Hukbalahap guerrilla army, based on the KPMP peasant union, had contested the countryside against the "puppet" Bureau of Constabulary and
the Japanese army. At night and away from the roads, Huk village committees and units were the de facto government in much of Central
Luzon during the last two years of the war.

After the war, the Pambansang Kaisahan ng Magbubukid (PKM)
peasant union was enormously popular. It had the same members, leaders, and goals as the prewar KPMP. But now the peasants had arms, military experience, and proven wartime commanders plus widespread support in the face of the attempt by the U.S. Army, the landowners, and the
government to disarm the Huk and forcibly disband the PKM.[23]

Dionisio Macapagal supported but did not join the new PKM union.
His Ganap background made him suspect to both the Huk and USAFFE
anti-Japanese guerrillas. Moreover, at age forty, with five children, he had
other priorities. He farmed in the wet season, and in the dry season he concentrated on a new enterprise that had emerged after the war—logging.

Logging Entrepreneur

Burned-out Manila was hungry for lumber to rebuild, and the Sierra
Madre forests were made accessible by military vehicles. Dionisio
Macapagal "bought" a 6 x 6 truck from American soldiers and went into
business hauling logs from the mountains. Until the Sierra Madre was
stripped bare of trees, logging would remain an important industry in
Central Luzon. In Buga, some fourteen men had logging trucks. A majority had connections with Kardeng de Guzman's USAFFE unit. When they
began logging in 1945, the forest fringe was only a couple of miles away.
Rubeng de Guzman recounted in 1980 that he had recently revisited
ridges where in 1948–50 there had been so many springs that even in the
dry season it was impossible to drive the six-wheel-drive trucks unless
one laid a corduroy of saplings. In 1980, in the same season, the ridges
were arid *kogun* grassland, and his party had to walk two hours down
into the valley to get water.

In the 1946 presidential elections, Dionisio rejected the PKM policy
that all Huks should vote Democratic Alliance (DA) for Congress and for
the Nacionalista candidate Sergio Osmeña for president against the
wartime collaborator Manuel Roxas. He stuck to the position that the
Nacionalista Party was the unreformed party of the rich. He was happy to
vote for the DA candidates for Bulacan: Dr. Jesus Lava, head of the
Communist Party, and Colonel Alejo Santos, a famous USAFFE guerrilla.
Since prewar times, he had always voted anti-Nacionalista, selecting candidates opposed to Quezon and Osmeña: for the Democrata of General

Sandiko and Judge Sumulong, for the Sakdal Party in 1935, and for the Frente Popular on the eve of World War II. Roxas was the only non-Nacionalista, and he would vote for him even if this meant voting for a man as conservative and antipeasant as any president could be. Moreover, Manuel Roxas's wife, Doña Trinidad de Leon, was a member of the landed family with whom he was at lifelong odds. The decision was personally dangerous, as the election involved armed coercion on both sides. As an ex-Ganap, it was extremely impolitic to draw attention to himself by campaigning for the collaborator, Manuel Roxas.

The PKM and Huk campaigned vigorously for Osmeña against Roxas but for their Democratic Alliance congressional candidates against the party mates of both presidential candidates. Both the Huk faction that hoped to follow the parliamentary road and that which saw no alternative to armed revolution were determined to make a national show of strength.

Mang Dionisio said in 1972 that the Huk had put an end to many of the abuses against which he had fought in the 1920s and 1930s: *buhat-bahay* landlord coercion to vote as directed or be evicted; household services; abuse of tenants' women; compulsory loans; high interest; and high rents. Many landlords deserted the towns during the Huk Rebellion and never came back, so eventually the farmers came to control the municipal government.

But in 1946 the Huks were "like martial law." Their units came to the villages and said: "Whoever votes for Roxas will have their heels cooled" or "will be taken to where the swamp cabbage grows" — euphemisms for being tied up and thrown into a watercourse to drown. Both sides used coercion and terror. The landlords' armed overseers, police, and military used terror more often and more indiscriminately because most peasants supported the PKM/Huk. As the 1946 election approached, Kardeng de Guzman (by then an overseer for Doña Trinidad de Leon, in one of his roles) and Dionisio Macapagal could muster only seven votes for Roxas. They were meeting in the *bisita* one night when the Huks came and took away Nilo Jigon, holding him three days before killing him.

The logging days, therefore, were also the *panahon ng Huk*, or "Huk period," for Mang Dionisio. President Roxas declared martial law and sent the national military, backed by artillery and aircraft, to break the Huks. The military used *zona*, or operations of forcible concentration. Buga was forcibly evacuated for three months beginning in September 1948. All rural barrios of San Miguel and nearby towns were cleared of residents while the army conducted search and destroy operations in the countryside. Only Civilian Guard units, which were financed equally by the landlords' association and the army, were allowed to remain in the villages. Forcibly concentrated in the township, the men were screened by intelligence agents. Anyone seen outside the township or taken to the army camp near Sibul could be shot. Many bodies floated in the river.[24] In 1972–73, people spoke of this period as "real" martial law compared to the locally mild form imposed under Marcos.

Mang Dionisio's cousin, Eduardo de Guzman (Kumander Andron) was the most effective local Huk leader from 1946 to 1948. His brothers, Kardeng and Graciano de Guzman, overseers of estates owned by relatives of President Roxas's widow, Doña Trining de León, arranged his surrender in person in late 1948 to President Quirino. San Miguel peasants were then allowed to return to their farms, which they found to be in miserable condition: rice was overripe and rat-damaged and abandoned livestock had died or been slaughtered by contending forces. When confined to the township, peasants had little food or shelter, according to Dionisio. Big landlords, like the de Leons, did not let even their own tenants camp in or obtain well water from their yards. Several children and old people died of privation or unsanitary conditions.

Kumpadres Fall Out: The Case of the Cursed Buffalo

In the logging days, Mang Dionisio camped in the mountains with his boyhood *kabarkada*, and later *kumpadre*, Jose Lazaro. They played and worked together, hauling from the same cuts to the same sawmills. When logging stopped during the wet season, they exchanged farm labor by swimming buffaloes across the river to plow and harrow the other's field. With the proceeds of logging, they bought land side by side on the left bank of the river in a salient of smallholder land wedged between three lots of the Hacienda de Leon. In 1957, Mang Dionisio began to build a big, solid house only two hundred meters from Jose's. But the *kumpadres* had by then fallen out in a rift that became the basis for a factional alignment that lasted a quarter of a century, from 1956 to 1980.

Around 1955, Jose had acted as guarantor for a crop loan taken out by Dionisio. The creditor was threatening to foreclose on Jose's security for Dionisio's loan. Jose was in the river scrubbing a buffalo. When his *kumpadre*, Dionisio, came up, they exchanged greetings and news. Jose asked Dionisio when he was going to pay the debt, as he was being pressed.

Dionisio joked that the creditor could wait. Just then the buffalo trod on Jose's foot. Jose says he shouted in pain the stereotypical Tagalog swearwords that double as insult: "Your mother is a whore!" Dionisio took the words as an insult directed to him. He swore back in the same terms. They parted enemies.

In the etiquette of Filipino life, the everyday *bati*, or greeting, is to ask the other: "where are you coming from" (or going to)? The *kumpadres* ceased to exchange such greetings. Each studiously ignored the existence of the other. If they were walking toward each other on a village track, one would step aside into the paddies and pretend to urinate, rather than greet the other. If one walked into a room or gathering, even at a wake for the dead, the other would leave. The two proud men severed their business and farm relations, avoided each other, and forbade their families to exchange visits. Jose, an expert carpenter with a reputation for helping others to build during the dry season, did not join *bataris* parties to help build Dionisio's new house when in 1957 he moved across the river to his new farm. Likewise, Dionisio did not help build or see the inside of Jose's impressive bungalow, built in the 1970s, though he had to walk past it whenever he went to the village center or town.

Postwar: Small Proprietor and Village Notable

Before the war (*nuong pistaym*), Mang Dionisio played a leading role in getting the village to build its own small *bisita* as the first step to independence from Pinambaran. After 1946, he was a *lider* for the Liberal Party (LP) and from 1957 to 1963 the appointed *teniente auxilyar* of Buga. In 1958, he was able to persuade Don Cecilio de Leon to donate a site and the mayor and congressman to allocate funds to build an elementary school in the village, so that small children would not have to walk to Salacot or Pinambaran. In 1964, NP mayor Felipe Buencamino had the *sitio* recognized as a barrio. As the position of barrio *kapitan* is elective, Mang Dionisio stepped down.

Although his older brothers, Guillermo and Miguel, were alive, they were not active politically. Dionisio was *pinakamatanda*, "the one who serves as (political) elder," of the *angkan* of the numerous Macapagals. In disputes with other families, dealings with the government, or legal cases, he represented the Macapagals and his political allies. In return, the *matanda* (elders) of those households promised to deliver votes to his candidates. His reputation for delivering a large bloc of votes allowed him to get favors for kin and allies from elected LP officials of the village, municipal, provincial, and national governments. He aligned himself with the de Guzman faction, which voted consistently Liberal.

When the *kumpadres* fell out, Jose, in the logic of faction, aligned himself with the anti–de Guzman faction. Consistently a minority in the face of long de Guzman control of the village, the anti–de Guzman faction voted Nacionalista (later the Kilusan Bagong Lipunan, or KBL, the dictator Marcos's New Society movement) from 1946 to 1980 in village, municipal, and higher-level elections. Jose remained on good personal terms with his cousin, Kardeng de Guzman, and his formidable sons, having been a member of Kardeng's USAFFE unit during the Japanese occupation and a fellow logger. Throughout the Huk rebellion (1946–53), Dionisio, Kardeng, and Jose were pro-PKM and collaborated with the Huk, though Kardeng was at one time an overseer on the de Leon hacienda and led a Civilian Guard unit. Thereafter, they continued to support what the Huk had fought for — land reform — though each had bought some second-class land with his logging proceeds.

Prosperous Village Notable, Small Landowner

In the early 1950s, Dionisio Macapagal bought two farm lots totaling about four hectares with money from hauling logs and a soft loan from kin who had shared the Macapagal brothers' house in the 1920s. On his new land, Dionisio erected a substantial house made of concrete blocks and lumber. He bought a big diesel engine and set it up on the river levee to run a circular saw, a *kaskarador* (rice mill), and a pump to irrigate his fields. The rice mill and saw paid for themselves until the forest was exhausted, and improving village roads allowed farmers better rice recovery at *kono* (mills) on the highway.

In 1957, Mang Dionisio's political activism paid off materially. Through a relation who was a surveyor, he learned of some twenty-four hectares of land abandoned during the peasant war by a bankrupt Chinese. Through LP contacts, Mang Dionisio made applications for homestead farms (two hectares each) for twelve kinsmen and allies, including himself, a son, a son-in-law, and his vice-*teniente*, Adong Feliciano. The land was on the edge of Candaba Swamp in the barrio of Manaul, Candaba, and overgrown with *talahib* and *kogun* grasses. Though useful as loan collateral, the farms were distant, flood-prone, and rat-infested. They were worth farming only if the irrigation schedule allotted water for a crop in the nonflooding dry season.

Diosdado Macapagal, an LP party mate with a similar name, was elected in 1961 as president of the Philippines. He had announced a land reform program to distribute "idle and abandoned lands." Among Mang Dionisio's treasures was a photograph of himself in the president's office being presented with a homestead title.

Financing Children's Education: Debt and the Land

In the 1950s and 1960s, Dionisio Macapagal was a prosperous and influential village elder. His older children had grown up in hard times: the days of the Depression, peasant unions, World War II, and the peasant war, but he had ambitions for the younger ones. He transferred his Morales farm to his eldest daughter's husband. His eldest son, Ruding, finished high school, joined the army, and saw service in Mindanao and

Palawan. Ruding says that, on discharge, he worked Dionisio's two farms because the house was a *munisipyong munti*, or mini–city hall, as Dionisio helped family, neighbors, and allies with their official and legal problems.

The second son, Lorenzo, found a job as a carpenter at the American military base in Olongapo. He invested in a jeepney that allowed Ruding to drive sixteen students to and from high school in town. They paid four *cavans* of *palay* per head, per year, due at the main harvest. Ruding paid the sixty-four *cavans* per year to Lorenzo for the jeep. Between the school runs and on non–school days, he drove the jeepney as a bus along the highway and kept the cash earnings.

Dionisio could not provide farms for his three younger children, who were born after World War II. Like many Filipinos, he sought to provide for them by capitalizing them with an education. He put his third son, Pablo, through high school, then his fourth and youngest daughter, Guadalupe, through teacher's college. Then he put two granddaughters through college.

To pay for college fees, Mang Dionisio took out loans against his farms in Buga. This was a risky strategy. In similar fashion, Kardeng de Guzman, who had bought fifteen hectares of land with his logging profits, borrowed against his title to put his three youngest children through college and to support one of them in an election campaign for town councilor. He was unable to repay the loans, lost the land, and was left with a farm held as tenant. Much of the land in San Miguel that changed ownership after 1945 was mortgaged by smallholders to finance their children's education. While prewar villagers had commonly lost their farms to predatory landlords, after the war such reverses sprang more often from villagers taking risks to secure their children's future in a changing social landscape. A series of bad crops in the 1960s and 1970s made it difficult for Mang Dionisio to repay his loan. When I arrived in the village in 1971, gossip had it that Mang Dionisio was *nabaon sa utang*, buried in debt, and would lose his land.

In 1971, Dionisio Macapagal, then sixty-five, was a vigorous local notable at the crest of his political trajectory. The mayor, Marcelo de Guzman-Aure, was a cousin. His ally, Kardeng de Guzman, had died in 1969, but Kardeng's eldest son had been barrio captain since 1968 and his third son, Raul de Guzman, a town councilor since 1967. Longtime congressman Rogaciano Mercado, although nominally a Nacionalista, was allied with LP mayor Aure. As a *matanda* elder of the LP for San Miguel, Mang Dionisio had good access to him, as well as to municipal, provincial, and national officials, prosecutors, and judges through his LP links and a lifetime of making and servicing contacts. Each year he planted some *milagrosa*, a fine-flavored, aromatic, highly priced variety of rice. A sack of *milagrosa* or a goat delivered to an influential's house helped to open or strengthen contacts that he might want to use then or later.

Eclipse under Martial Law

In late 1971, the favorable political conjuncture began to come apart. Mayor Aure won reelection in November, but municipal councilor Raul de Guzman lost. Barrio Captain Rubeng de Guzman took a job in Cabanatuan City as a minor overseer with his uncle, Graciano de Guzman, manager of de Leon estates in Nueva Ecija. Barrio elections were called on short notice for January 1972. The recently settled Parang *sitio* of Buga, east of Dionisio's farm, had already its own *bisita* and school. In December, its leaders successfully applied to secede and form a new barrio, Sapang. Deciding that he could not live in Cabanatuan City and be a successful barrio captain, Rubeng de Guzman resigned just before the election.

The succession struggle between the first and second councilors, each claiming he had been promised the succession, split the de Guzman LP faction in Buga and sharpened the rift between Mang Dionisio and his estranged *kumpadre*. The NP faction was organized first, with Mang Jose Lazaro as its candidate for captain.

With only ten days to go, LP mayor Marcelo de Guzman Aure came to a village LP caucus meeting at night. After the rival aspirants had presented their cases, he took them apart, persuading each candidate to step aside and support the other for the good of the party. Each said that he could muster more votes for the LP if nominated but if passed over he would run as an independent. Mayor Aure made a judgment of Solomon: let them test which could get most votes for the party but as councilors! He gave the *kapitan* nomination to an unwilling Dionisio Macapagal.

The campaign was bitter because the anti–de Guzman faction scented blood. Jose Lazaro, Mang Dionisio's estranged *kumpadre*, had a large *angkan* and was probably the richest man in Buga from the proceeds of his eleven-hectare farm plus remittances from a son working on the American military base. He was widely respected as a helpful and kind neighbor, courteous but rather shy. Dionisio Macapagal was reputed to be *makahari*, imperious and undemocratic, and he had offended a number of people due to his forceful personality and abrasive manner. Moreover, he had an ongoing dispute with members of the tightly disciplined Iglesia ni Cristo, which could deliver some 32 of the 325 votes. Some NP members argued that his daughter, Guadalupe, acting headmistress of the village elementary school, could not fairly supervise the vote or handle the grading of children whose families opposed her father. Don Cecilio de Leon recommended that his tenants vote against Mang Dionisio, for he resented the latter's support for those who had dared transfer from share tenancy to leasehold under the 1963 land reform Act 3844 of President Macapagal and the current 1969 land reform Act 6389 of incumbent President Marcos. The brief campaign was made more difficult because the two candidates for captain continued to studiously ignore each other at meetings.

Jose Lazaro won by a comfortable margin, but all his NP candidates for councilor lost. Teofilo Castillo felt vindicated because he had topped the winning all-LP slate of councilors with more votes than his rival or either captain candidate, confirming his claim to the next captain nomination. Dionisio Macapagal was humiliated but tried to take a continuing role as elder of the Macapagals rather than withdrawing into his farm and family. His nephew, Melencio Macapagal, eldest of Miguel's sons and leader of the biggest branch of the Macapagals, was elected third councilor with a vote higher than Mang Dionisio's. He began to assert himself more independently as leader of the more numerous branch of the Macapagal *angkan*.

During the rest of my stay, until May 1973, Jose Lazaro presided as executive barrio captain, but his meetings with the opposition barrio council were perfunctory. From July to early September, when the whole of Central Luzon was devastated by a succession of three typhoons that flooded the lowlands for weeks and wiped out the main crop, there were the usual accusations that the incumbent had manipulated the distribution of relief goods, keeping some for himself and his close allies, at the expense of more needy families. Just after the floods receded, President Marcos declared martial law.

Martial Law and Millenarian Discourse

In 1971, I was surprised at the grasp villagers had of national-level politics. They knew the names of political figures at all levels and carefully watched microshifts in the alignments of congressmen and senators, high-level army officers, and politicians at the provincial and municipal levels. Villagers compared, evaluated, and debated the significance of different news sources each evening at *tsismisan* (gossip spots) in the village. Politics was a spectator sport more popular by far than cockfighting.

There was a feeling that great changes were at hand. There had been massive leftist-nationalist student disturbances in Manila beginning in 1969, and repeated demonstrations and marches for land reform by priests, activists, and peasant leaders were backed by a permanent embassy of peasants outside Congress. A Constitutional Convention was debating the fundamental law of the nation. The half-senate and local elections were marred by a bomb blast in late 1971 at the Plaza Miranda in Manila, killing and injuring a number of people, including several LP senators. A breakaway Communist Party of the Philippines had been formed, and its armed wing, the New People's Army (NPA), had renewed the insurgency. Muslim rebellion was growing in the south, and in early 1972 President Marcos suspended the writ of habeas corpus.

In the village, there was intense "rational" interest in following political issues, personalities, and their implications, but this was complemented by a millenarian mode of thought. The "rational," or pragmatic, mode was skeptical, cynical, and took the form of a colloquium of political experts evaluating news and constructing *realpolitik* scenarios. At first, I associated the pragmatic mode with older men and the millenarian mode with older women, given their greater religiosity, lesser interest in political detail, and the influence of the Union Espiritista, a spirit-medium cult whose followers were mostly older women. As my grasp of Tagalog and range of acquaintances extended, I realized that my first impression was mistaken and the millenarian mode is more like an idiom, an alternative code that older people could switch on or off according to the topic or turn of discussion. The sense of national political crisis, coupled with floods in mid-1972, brought the apocalyptic mode of discourse to the fore.

On the eve of the declaration of martial law, all news media were suddenly seized by the military. On the morning of Saturday, 21 September 1971, many people shook their silent transistor radios, cursed, and looked for new batteries. When the broadcasts resumed, the media were plainly under complete regime control. Thus, people had to read between the lines, seek out and retail oral news and rumor, or simply speculate. They did so in both the rational and millenarian modes.

I soon abandoned my early impression that millenarian discourse was restricted to members of one age, gender, religious persuasion, or personality type. I thought it more useful to treat it as a kind of dialect, with its own lexicon of signs and its own grammar for relating the signs to each other meaningfully. If that were true, then it could be learned, and the test would be whether I could say new things in it intelligibly. Texts were available in the set of stories that Mang Dionisio and his age mates told about the ideas and practices of the 1920s–40s, peasant unions, and radical nationalist movements. Closer at hand were contemporary conversations in the millenarian mode or dialect. I decided to write full verbatim notes, when possible, rather than outline "the facts" in English and discard the rest as "noise." By the time I had changed my method, many of my notes were in "the facts" mode, and there was too much going on to waste the time of informants going over subjects we had already covered.

The Fake Plebiscite and the Hidden Transcript of Protest

In September 1972, President Marcos declared martial law and personally assumed all central legislative, executive, and judicial powers. He purged the top officers, closed the Congress, dictated to the Constitutional Convention a text that gave him the powers of both a president and prime minister, controlled the media, purged the upper ranks of the civil service, and forced all judges to sign undated resignations. Meanwhile, he purged elected local government officials and tried to construct a one-party state by turning the purged Nacionalista Party into the KBL New Society Movement. The KBL initiation ceremonies owed much to the KKK rites that had been, in turn, modified in the 1920s and 1930s by peasant movements.

In January 1973, Marcos called for a plebiscite to demonstrate broad public approval of his extraordinary powers under the new, dictated constitution. A set of questions was circulated in the controlled press. Marcos attempted to justify dispensing with the secret ballot by decreeing that to enfranchise minorities the illiterate poor, and youth the voting would be by show of hands of all persons over fifteen.

The acting headmistress of the Buga School and Mang Dionisio's daughter, Guadalupe Macapagal, and Kapitan Jose Lazaro had the unwelcome task of conducting the balloting under the eyes of a policeman. The papers were brought by a jeepload of armed Constabulary. When the plebiscite papers were opened, Kapitan Jose and Headmistress Guadalupe read the instructions, which led to a dispute over procedures. Kapitan Jose read the first question in a small and embarrassed voice. It differed from those in the list of questions that had been publicized earlier.

Guadalupe grabbed the paper and read it again in her loud teacher's voice. An uproar ensued. The LP–de Guzman faction, led by Dionisio Macapagal's eldest son, Ruding, his son-in-law Ruding Santos, and his close neighbors, Lauro Calfa-Cruz, Garciano Flores, and Councilor Adoracion Toledo, demanded that before any vote be taken the entire new set of questions be read aloud so they could assess the implications of voting "yes" on the first.

Guadalupe read a list of questions that transferred unlimited power to the president. Each question raised an angry outburst. Kapitan Jose read the first question again and called for a voice vote. Of the 235 voters, some 27 NP backers of Kapitan Lazaro voted "yes," while the rest yelled "no."

Kapitan Jose was plainly embarrassed; he conferred again with Guadalupe, then dropped a bombshell: he had not fully explained the procedure. The instructions required that a "yes" vote could be taken by voice or show of hands. To vote "no," however, every objector must come forward, write out his reason, and sign it. People yelled "*lutong macau!*"

(a fixed-menu restaurant where the customer eats what is available or nothing) and most ran from the school, ignoring a policeman blowing his whistle frantically. Only thirty-one stayed to see the outcome.

Graciano Flores came forward and demanded to exercise his right to vote "no." Watched by his neighbors, Ruding Macapagal, Oreng Calfa Cruz, LP councilor Adoreng Toledo, and the NP/KBL's Tony Yalong, he wrote in Tagalog reminiscent of the Lord's Prayer: "It is not fitting that one man who is mortal should have power without limit and without end," and signed it. Kapitan Jose then consulted those remaining about how he should deal with the other five questions. He said he was required to get a large turnout and a high percentage of "yes" votes. There were only 31 of 235 voters remaining. Kapitan Jose's NP backers advised him to take a vote among those who were left, count the "no" votes, deduct that number from 235, and report the rest as "yes." Amid fist-waving confrontations, Councilor Adoreng Toledo demanded the reverse: those absent had rejected the farce, and their votes should be considered negative. I have photographs showing the angry scene.

Kapitan Jose went home perplexed and embarrassed. He later said that he was afraid to report his failure for fear that it would bring retaliation upon the village. He said that martial law under President Quirino, during the Huk war, had been a time of terror. He erased his neighbor Garciano Flores's words and name. Instead of taking the results to town by 6:00 P.M. as required, he went to bed. He could not sleep. Around 4:00 A.M., armed police arrived, demanding that he bring the results and go with them to the *munisipyo* (city hall). There were four other *kapitans* in that jeep. At the *munisipyo*, about a dozen other temporizing kapitans were waiting to report or for transport home. Mayor Aure had been drinking. He said that he did not want to hear their stories or protests. *Pinuwersa tayo, eh* (We are powerless). Destroying their voting records without looking at them, Mayor Aure gave each *kapitan* a fresh form for his village with ready-made numbers showing 95 percent attendance and 97 percent "yes" voting. He told them to sign and go home. The mayor had radioed the "correct" results from each village and the totals for the municipality to the provincial capital at 6:00 P.M.

The next day, the radio and press reported astounding turnouts and percentages. Some NP/KBL reports said that only Buga was chronically *opo-sisyonista*. But LP supporters exchanged stories of similar frauds elsewhere.

Thinking about rural protest in that twenty-four hours, and about the record of past protest, gives another sense to James Scott's "hidden transcript."[25] Kapitan Jose Lazaro had literally erased Garciano Flores's heroic gesture from the record. He had then tried to conceal the extent of protest by some 80 percent of his fellow villagers. The schoolteacher and policeman neither volunteered nor were asked for written reports. The mayor had pre-erased the record of protest in what he would later say was more than two-thirds of the villages. Perhaps the official record of all past protest is underreported, like domestic violence everywhere or like the intralocal crimes that in the Philippines are processed by means of *areglo* (compromise settlement) rather than the central state's criminal law. Those in local formal authority may choose not to record or report all that they know when that might bring central state repression on their kin, neighbors, and constituents. They may expunge from the record the extent of protest to hide from authorities their own lack of control. Central state authority may know — indeed, may *have* to know — via alternative channels — something of what is afoot. But the central authority itself may depend on the public report and record of protest being muted, so it need neither admit the challenge nor respond to it.

As an anthropologist, I was in both a privileged and a compromised position. Everyone in the Philippines knew that the plebiscite result had been faked. But the media were tightly controlled. If I took the story and photographs to the foreign press, there was a chance this would cause temporary embarrassment to the regime. The probable costs included some danger to the people named and photographed, confiscation of my field notes, and my expulsion from the country for interfering in its internal affairs. I chose to be silent. I had the photographs developed in another town, where the faces were not identifiable.

Opposition under Martial Law

I left the Philippines in May 1973 and did not return until December 1979. In the meantime, I had followed some events by letter. These included the depressing frequency of floods and crop failures and the deaths of old friends.

Mang Dionisio celebrated his *boda de oro* (fiftieth wedding anniversary) in March 1977. I sent enough money to buy a large pig. The ritual had an element of thanksgiving for his wife Felisa's recovery from two expensive operations. His letter focused on the status of those who had sponsored parts of the ritual (my translation):

> We had a great number of visitors. Mr. Jaime Vidal [a National Irrigation Authority (NIA) engineer] became our *ninong* and our *ninang* was the Manager of the Rural Bank of Sta. Ana [Pampanga, where Dionisio's 12 homestead holders borrow for Manaul farms], Mrs. Consuelo Limjoco. There were five large pigs slaughtered so the feast of your mother and me was plentiful. The one who prepared the church was Miss Emma Sta. Ana,

District Supervisor of Elementary Schools. The one who presented the songs at the church was the principal at Kamias Elementary School, Naty Ventura. But if you ask me how life has been since then, we are destitute and I have nothing to spend as my crop was drowned. So we are even buying rice.

That same dry season, two new state services reached Mang Dionisio's house. His schoolteacher daughter, Guadalupe, wrote in English:

> We have already our electric power—we had our installation last May and only few houses here in Buga have not yet their installations. Those who can afford had their lightings already and many were able to buy some electrical appliances. And also NIA has started its project here in Buga. The canal runs in front of our house. But the construction was stopped because father Jose our *Kapitan* is still questioning the passage in our field although grandmother Raquel [Morales] the owner of the land has already sign [*sic*] the permit to right of way. Meantime NIA stopped the construction.

She was more direct about some practical benefits of the choice of ritual sponsors. Some were her own professional superiors.

> Luckily our eldest sister's husband Ruding is employed in NIA as truck inspector and receiving a salary of P450 a month, which is really a great help to them since his eldest daughter is taking up nursing. So when the construction was started in our place, he was in-charge of the trucks. Father's *ninong* [NIA engineer Vidal] is truly powerful. Otherwise Ruding would have been laid off because of his educational background: he is only a high school graduate.

When I returned for three months of research in December 1979, I focused on two projects: the implementation of Marcos's 1972 land reform decree and a political history of the municipality. The decree made share tenancy "contrary to national policy." Operation Leasehold "compulsorily" transferred all tenants of rice and corn land to a fixed rent based on 25 percent of the average normal harvest of the last three normal crop years before the October 1972 decree. Operation Land Transfer gave tenants of any landowner who owned more than seven hectares the right to buy their farms in installments over a fifteen-year period. As they had done in all previous attempts at land reform, the landowners set out to overturn, weaken, and evade the law. Without a Congress, they could not water down the law itself. But they could use the courts to protest, appeal, and delay land transfer and use "everyday resistance" to evade, obstruct, delay, and sabotage every step necessary for the reforms to take effect.

Several landowners with whom I spoke vilified tenants who went along with the reform as ingrates and receivers of stolen property. They complained that now that the government had sided with the tenants and eviction was impossible the tenants had become rude. They no longer called at the house with presents of fruit, no longer used the respect enclitic *po* in addressing owners, and would pass them in the street without a greeting. Both large and medium-sized owners argued that the reforms transformed to a cold contractual basis what had traditionally been warm mutual consideration between landowner and tenant: "We treated them like members of the family." The history of dissent belied this gloss. This landlord version of the patron-client model did not correspond to the reality of tenant life except for a minority of big-house courtier favorites.

Most tenants welcomed the reforms in principle but temporized in practice: if the dictator Marcos had ordered it and set up a bureaucracy to implement it, then they would accept the benefits. But they would not stick their necks out to be the first to get them. Marcos was mortal. If he fell and the reforms were reversed, they did not want to be evicted. Meantime, they still had to get credit to plant crops and support their families. The decree said nothing about writing off ancestral debts to the landowners.

Mayor Aure had been removed from office and replaced with Juan de la Cruz, an NP councilor who had placed third in 1971. The first farmer to become mayor, he was relatively young and had strong support in the villages. In Buga, Kapitan Jose Lazaro had been retained in office like most NP (now KBL) elected or installed officials. He was now a vigorous seventy-four, still shy and mild, but he did not consult his LP council and had delegated much power to his appointed secretary and 1972 backers. They had accumulated the usual resentment that is due to unelected, overlong incumbents, plus the usual rumors of corruption.

Dionisio Macapagal was firmly opposed to Marcos on principle because he had usurped the constitution, overthrown democracy, and now ruled as a *diktador*. Moreover, Marcos was NP, and Mang Dionisio still thought of politics in two-party terms, wherein he was LP and therefore opposed to the NP/KBL. Anyway, he was proudly *oposisyonista* in character.

However, he supported the regime's land reform program. That was what the Kapatiran Magsasaka, KPMP, Tanggulan, Sakdal, and PKM had struggled for. He had nothing to gain from it, as he owned his own land. It was a matter of *prinsipyo* and *karapatan*, the right of the farmers.

Under martial law, Mang Dionisio continued to support his neighbor Lauro Calfa Cruz's epic legal case, which had begun in 1964. Lauro Calfa-Cruz was the last of a batch of de Leon share tenants who had applied for transfer to fixed-rent tenancy under President Macapagal's RA 3844 of 1963. Among the first were Mang Dionisio's nephew, Juan Macapagal,

and son-in-law, Ruding Santos. In the face of threats of harassing coun-
tercharges by the estate, many tenants withdrew. Some of the harassing
charges against Lauro Calfa-Cruz were grounds for eviction and imprisonment. Dionisio Macapagal helped his neighbor by putting up a bail
bond. The tenant had to report to the police three times a month. In
revenge on this tenant who had gone to the law and asked for lease
rental, attorney Don Cecilio de Leon had used the law as well. He restricted Calfa-Cruz to the bare thousand square meters houselot set by the
law, drawing its boundaries to exclude bamboo and fruit trees that the
tenant had planted on land unusable for rice, and evicted from their
houses the tenant's kin. Then he charged the tenant with theft for cutting
bamboo sticks within his farm but outside the legal houselot.

In 1978, Lauro Calfa-Cruz began pressing the system to explain why,
after eight years of Operation Land Transfer, no Certificate of Land
Transfer (CLT) had ever reached him. Totoy Palomo, the son of a de Leon
overseer, was the municipal team leader of the Department of Agrarian
Reform (DAR). Palomo claimed that the CLT had not been released by
the head office. Lauro Calfa-Cruz's son, Tomi, who had graduated as an
agricultural engineer, used his skills and contacts as a field technician for
a rural bank to follow up Lauro's application. He started at DAR's Manila
office and persisted until he got a signed document that stated the date
the CLT had been released and sent to the province. The provincial team
leader in Baliuag signed a document indicating the date the CLT was sent
to San Miguel. Since Palomo still denied that his office had it, Tomi now
pressed administrative charges against him for withholding the CLT. In
a separate case he had filed with other tenants, he charged that Palomo
had embezzled and malversed the release and collection of farm credit.

As they had done in Lauro Calfa-Cruz's case, Buga's two haciendas
used the law to resist every step of the land reform process. They reject-
ed land valuation by the PD27 formula and demanded market prices.
They demanded valuation and payment in *palay* directly to the landown-
er, not through the Land Bank of the Philippines. Maximally, the
Association of San Miguel Landowners, Inc., using the legal strategy of
top corporate lawyer Juan T. David, set out to overturn one by one in the
Court of Appeals and the Supreme Court the key elements of the reforms.
Those precedent judgments are binding on lower courts and officials.
Since the tenants had no strategy and were represented by free Bureau of
Agrarian Legal Assistance lawyers, newly graduated and easily bribed,
the owners were sure to win the important precedent-setting cases.

The PD27 formula gave a low valuation of P5,400 per hectare with
irrigation, P3,600 per hectare without, and P3,200 per hectare on the
stony *lupang galas* soil. The valuations were well below the market price

of about P10 to 17,000 for irrigated land. Dionisio Macapagal commented that the formula produced too low a result: he had been offered P14,500 per hectare for his own irrigated land. But that was the valuation set in strict accordance with the decree and implementing instructions by a Barrio Committee on Land Productivity (BCLP). The BCLP was composed of two representatives each for the owners of land in the barrio, the tenants, the owner-cultivators, and the Samahan Nayon (a precooperative set up as a credit channel), plus the barrio captain and a Department of Agrarian Reform secretary. Dionisio Macapagal, as one owner-cultivator representative, acted as the chair. The two landowners' representatives came once but refused to produce records or participate.

Having ignored the BCLP valuation process, the San Miguel landowners then filed charges against those tenants who paid amortization to the Land Bank. Their grounds were that their protest and appeal on the valuation was subjudice and so, until a decision was handed down, the old conditions should continue. The precedent was set in 1979, when my *kumpadre* Manuel Caballero, tenant of Buga's Hacienda Sevilla de Leon, was charged with failing to pay lease rent to the estate. He had paid the due amortization installment to the Land Bank of the Philippines. The hacienda Sevilla de Leon claimed that he must continue to pay lease rent directly, in *palay*, as long as the valuation was under protest. When Caballero lost before Judge Estrada, the landowners used the precedent to file charges against other tenants who had not paid lease rent.

They then protested and appealed every means proposed to set a valuation. The large landowners refused to release their records. In later protests and appeals, they refused to recognize the tenants' carbon copies of the harvest reckoning signed by their own overseers, challenging each signature. The strategy was plain: to obstruct and delay legal transfer until such time as the regime would fall or give up. In demanding that rent and valuation be based on years after 1972, they hoped to capture windfall gains from the increase in harvest due to high-yielding crop varieties and the new irrigation system.

Reconciliation of the Kumpadres: Using the Millennial Dialect

I returned to Buga in November 1990 as floods receded following a typhoon. Aside from the underlying cause, deforestation of the Sierra Madre, the floods in this locality had been made deeper and longer by the silt obstructing the drainage. Anguish at its effects impelled me to interfere to reconcile Dionisio Macapagal and his estranged *kumpadre*, Kapitan Jose Lazaro. My brief role change from observer to participant had unforeseen results that influenced the direction of politics in the village.

I was then staying with Bernabe de Guzman, whose late father Kardeng's empty house I had rented in 1971-73. On my second day in the village, I walked the two kilometers or so upstream to call on the two old men — as a courtesy to the incumbent Kapitan Jose and out of affection for him and Dionisio Macapagal.

I was upset by the degree of flood damage in the depression between the river levee and rising ground in the northeast sector of the village. The typhoon had caught the crop ripe for harvest. One farmer's crop, reaped and left on the bunds to dry, had been completely washed away. The flood had been deepened and prolonged because the drainage channel had been allowed to accumulate silt until it was above the land it should drain — including the farms of both Kapitan Jose and Mang Dionisio. I asked other distressed farmers why the drain had been allowed to fill with silt. The hacienda de Leon, through whose land the lower half ran, had no further interest in the size or security of the harvest under fixed rent and amortization. But the farms of the two elders were affected. Why had neither used the opportunity, when earthmoving equipment was building and maintaining the NIA irrigation extension, to borrow a front-end loader to clean the canal? Some said that everyone knew the problem, but Buga's affairs were chaotic, without *kaisahan* (unity). Kapitan Jose had the formal authority to request the NIA and other appropriate authorities to clean the drain, but he was *mahiyain* (shy). Mang Dionisio is *matapang*, aggressive about chasing up business with officials, but he had no authority. So the opportunity had been missed. Now, with the drain about 1.5 kilometers long and 1 meter wide, and with about 1 meter of silt to be removed, it was too big a job to be done by hand by the eight affected farmers.

I walked around to inspect the damage with Mang Dionisio, taking photographs that he and other farmers might use with the bank to claim a crop-loan write-off for disaster. When we were about twenty meters from Kapitan Jose, Mang Dionisio stopped and turned his back. I greeted the *kapitan* and photographed the damage to his farm. He spoke to me with his back turned to Mang Dionisio, who was studying the sky. Confronted with a village that was unable to help itself because its leaders were at odds, I became concerned enough to cross that line between observer and activist and become involved, for just a few days, in village affairs.

Over lunch, I asked Mang Dionisio how their feud began, getting the story of two *kumpadres* who had been estranged for twenty-five years. On the way home, I called on Kapitan Jose, who told of the cursed buffalo. Instead of listening without comment as I had always done before, I now made some remarks about the darkness and division within Buga and how it was slipping behind other villages. Since its elders lacked *kaisahan*, or unity, there was *gulo* (chaos) among the people. Neighbors who could not work together for the common good were flooded together. Elders could not expect to solve problems among the youth when they could not swallow their pride to put aside old grudges and do what needed doing. But when the night is darkest, I added, using the rhetoric of prewar brotherhoods, the dawn is close. Surprisingly, neither laughed.

That night I put the problem to Rubeng de Guzman and separately to his uncle, Kumander Andron, who had recently retired to the village after thirty years spent as an armed guard for LVN Movies. Spotting an opportunity where I had naively seen only a drainage problem, Rubeng seems to have conceived a wider but compatible project—the restoration of his own family's political fortunes. That night it was decided to begin secret negotiations with each old man, to reconcile them and get the village moving.

For the next couple of nights, we negotiators set out about 10:00 P.M., when most villagers are long asleep, to hazard our ankles amid two kilometers of yapping dogs and go upstream to the houses of the feuding elders. When the dogs and the visitors' calls woke the households, the negotiators entered, asking to discuss serious matters. Keeping himself and his own agenda in the background, Rubeng introduced me as a disinterested outsider who had returned from afar only to find darkness preventing peace in the village. Taking my cue, I spoke of brotherhood, unity, progress, and reconciliation and how putting things in order and achieving peace must begin with the elders. Neither old man had been warned of our first visit, but each caught its implications immediately: reconciliation with a long-estranged *kumpadre*.

The first night they listened closely to the negotiators. Their wives nodded at our words and may have reinforced them after we left. We were home before the earliest riser. The second night, Kapitan Jose burst into tears. He said he had not seen the inside of his *kumpadre*'s house since it was built twenty-six years ago. He asked us to make the reconciliation and make it soon. We had projected a long siege only to find the gates flung open.

The peace emissaries had previously agreed that it would be important to win the consent of each elder before they met, thereby sparing either the embarrassment of having an overture publicly spurned. Rubeng told Kapitan Jose that, if Mang Dionisio also agreed, he would like to make an event of it: have Jose and Dionisio brought together by their own kin to meet on neutral ground in the manner of a bride and groom. Jose said no, the fault was his, he had cursed: "If he will receive me, I will go to his house."

Elated at this breakthrough, we mediators woke Mang Dionisio after midnight. The cacophony of baying dogs had stirred kin and neighbors from their sleep, wanting to know what was afoot. Mang Dionisio and Nana Pitang listened again to our speeches. Dionisio began to cry, saying that he wanted to reconcile with his *kumpadre* Jose. But he would not wait for some ceremonial. This had gone on for twenty-six years; let it end now. He said that, as the original debt was his, the fault was his as well, and he would visit Jose in his house. By that time, it was about 2:30 A.M., the whole family was up, and everybody, including the emissaries, was crying. A few minutes later, Rubeng slipped out to tell Kapitan Jose and soon returned with him and his wife.

The emotional release intensified as the elderly couples embraced. Neighbors wakened by the dogs arrived. All had been embarrassed or forced to take sides because of this long feud. In the midst of the crying and embracing, the two wives confessed that they, as *kumadres* and neighbors, had met discreetly at wakes, funerals, and friends' houses to maintain their friendship when their husbands were not present.

A few days later, Rubeng arranged for the *kumpadres* to greet each other and embrace publicly — at his house. With his gaze fixed on future elections, Rubeng was working overtime to organize his preferred outcomes. Under his deft leadership, conversations shifted subtly from reconciliation to plans for a "new" village government. The *kapitan* and his council, everyone agreed, would retain formal power until Marcos called for new elections.

Rubeng, as it turned out, was happy enough with the council: all were elected from his own LP slate, from which he had withdrawn, purely for personal reasons, in late 1971. But reactivating the council would, on its own, exclude influential members of the other side. Their energies would be better harnessed if they went along than if they turned against the "unity" team. Kapitan Jose was ready to move forward, but his secretary bore too many grudges and was unpopular.

Kapitan Jose went a stage further with unity than I had anticipated: he acted as if his captaincy was joint with Dionisio Macapagal. The two joined together to advance the business of their village, calling a special assembly at the *bisita* on 6 December 1980, two days before Concepcion, the annual harvest festival. Kapitan Jose gave the chair to Mang Dionisio, who led the singing of the national anthem, "Lupang Hinirang"; the regime song, "Bagong Lipunan"; and a Christmas carol, and then led a long oath about new life and unity. Amando Batumbakal, an old Huk hero, spoke on unity and struggle. Mang Dionisio invoked a list of founders of the *visita*, household heads who around 1922 had taken the first steps to win Barrio Buga's independence from Barrio Pinambaran. Councilor Adoreng Toledo predicted that from unity would come progress. Then Councilor Teopilo Castillo led a prayer for unity and the discipline to build a new life and a new *barangay* in the New Society. Kapitan Jose foresaw unity and from it success in the new day ahead. Mang Dionisio then gave back the chair so formal business could proceed, since he had no official position.

Kapitan Jose then had the incumbent secretary read the minutes of the special barrio council, which had called for the appointment of new barrio officials plus a steering committee of ten to advise the elected council. Jose nominated, and his council approved, the new set unanimously: Dionisio Macapagal, secretary; Patricio Francisco, treasurer; Hapon Manalili as *tanod* (village policeman), and Ninoy Morales as judge. From there, two old rivals, Teopilo Castillo and Simeon Manalili, the first and second councilors, showed their command of meeting procedure. Their nominations for the ten advisers surprised me, for about half were cross-factional. I cannot recover from my notes the source of this unexpected combination — whether it from the euphoria of reconciliation, a strategy of cosmetic unity, or alliance building among key vote leaders.

The unity wagon kept rolling for about a year while the leaders who had jumped on it maneuvered to grab the reins. Kapitan Jose and Mang Dionisio accomplished a great deal during the remainder of Jose's term as village leader. They were able to mobilize village energies and harness those of the rival younger aspirants to the captaincy. Buga's reform raised some eyebrows with the municipal government and the Ministry of Local Government. There was a spate of resolutions and delegations to the *municipio*, the *capitolio* in Malolos, and the regional capital in San Fernando, Pampanga. With unity, the village had once again become *sikat*, shining or outstanding.

All Change Partners: The de Guzman Resurgence

By 1981, villagers all over the Philippines were fed up with the incumbents elected in December 1971 and January 1972 and wanted new elections. Too long immune to popular pressure, many officials had become lazy, corrupt, and even physically abusive.

In 1981, Marcos announced village elections but declared that, as the *barangay* was like a family, it should not be divided by party politics. Therefore he prohibited any "party" from running a slate. Since the KBL was a "movement" and not a party, he was free to maneuver. However, the Ministry of Local Government and Community Development (MLGCD) surveys showed that if incumbent KBL *kapitans* ran then most would lose.[26] Marcos let those run who would but without the official label. It would be impossible for observers to add the results or determine whether his KBL had won or lost overall. It would also make campaigning difficult for any organized opposition.

In Buga, Kapitan Jose Lazaro retired. The KBL put up a slate led by those who had backed Jose in 1972 plus some younger men who had decided that the KBL was certain to win one way or another. Rubeng de

Guzman ran for the National Union for Liberation (NUL) opposition party. His unity theme and some imaginative organizational practices helped him win handsomely.

In 1984, Rubeng de Guzman told me that all the winning *kapitans* were called by MLGCD to a five-day seminar at Malolos, the provincial capital, to instruct them in their rights and duties. He was surprised to find that a majority of the 550 *kapitans* were from the opposition, like himself. Most had won against KBL incumbents. On the second-last day, the *kapitans* were told that buses would be provided to take them home at 1 P.M. on the last day. At 2 P.M., there would be a mass oath taking for the KBL. The KBL *kapitans* would be introduced to KBL cabinet ministers from the province and instructed in how to make applications for *mehora* (village public works). That night, Rubeng and a fellow oppositionist drank together to their undying loyalty to the anti-KBL voters who had elected them and to their principled opposition to the dictator. They boasted how they had beaten the KBL once and could do it again. Next day, both were at the KBL oath taking. Both had read the message correctly: no KBL oath, no pork barrel for your village.

Back in Buga, Rubeng called together his council (elected on an anti-KBL ticket) plus the LP/NUL *angkan* leaders. They swore to stick together, *alang alang sa mehora*, out of respect for the infrastructure improvements then promised. Rubeng took them to Mayor de la Cruz, who welcomed the prodigals into the regime party. As KBL members and the elected incumbents, they became ex officio the KBL leaders in the village. The mayor showered Buga with discretionary projects.

The military assassination of Senator Ninoy Aquino in August 1983 dismayed Dionisio Macapagal, like most other Filipinos. I returned in December 1983 for a few weeks and found Bugans as absorbed then in the Agrava Commission hearings into the assassination as Americans were with the trial of O. J. Simpson. They claimed special knowledge because Roly Galman, the man that the army alleged was a communist assassin and had shot the senator, had lived about two kilometers downstream in Bagong Silang. They said that Galman was a minor gunman who occasionally held up service stations. One Friday evening upon adjournment, Commissioner Agrava announced to the television camera that on the following Monday she would call Galman's common law wife as the next witness. Rubeng de Guzman gestured to me with a finger across his throat: "Now Lina will be killed." Around 8:00 P.M., word came upstream that men with short haircuts in a military jeep had "invited" Lina Galman and one Taruc, her boyfriend. A few weeks later a male and a female body were found buried in a paddy near Baliuag, just off the highway to Manila.

Since 1981, Dionisio Macapagal had accepted pragmatic politics. Hitherto a lifelong *oposisyonista*, he had discarded some principles and old allies to join the winning team.

He considered the death of Aquino to be *marumi*, or dirty, but he did not give way to moral scruple nor connect that death to all the others and the regime's assaults on democratic legality. There were elections coming in 1984, and the pragmatic slogan *alang alang sa mehora* prevailed over morality. Melencio Macapagal had come to his own terms with the regime: two of his daughters had married members of Marcos's Presidential Guard. Just being seen in their uniformed company helped him in business. His eldest son, Liber, had been made a policeman and decorated for bravery for actions against the NPA.[27] The alliance held firm, and again Buga got pork barrel benefits from the 1984 elections.

Caught on the Losing Side

I was in Chiang Mai, Thailand, when the regime came unglued in the aftermath of the scandalously manipulated February 1986 presidential elections. I watched the EDSA demonstrations, with fascinated Thai, and felt that I was in the wrong place. In Buga, my friends found themselves on the wrong side. When I arrived home, I found an early de Guzman letter that recounted triumphant election tactics despite splits in the coalition. Some village families, fed up with Marcos, had defected, while others switched out of gratitude for legal favors from a younger generation of de Leons who had returned to San Miguel firmly opposed to the dictator and ambitious to place themselves in a post-Marcos regime.

Dionisio Macapagal's letter arrived later. He recounted how the incumbent de Guzman–Macapagal faction had achieved unprecedented unity and an excellent count for Marcos. Then the dramatic events unfolded on the EDSA highway between the two military camps. He wrote that when Marcos fled they were sitting around a television late at night: "We cheered with tears in our eyes, we who had voted for the *dambuhala* [monster]."

The new regime swiftly purged Marcos-era local officials from the provincial and municipal governments, replacing them with anti-Marcos organizers of the Aquino campaign.

In San Miguel, Tikboy de Leon–Lipana was appointed as officer in charge (OIC) mayor. He dismissed the KBL town council and a majority of the "KBL" *barangay kapitans*, including de Guzman. In their place, he appointed people who had helped the Aquino campaign or appeared to control significant parcels of votes.

Retirement and the Succession Problem

When Aquino came to power in 1986, Dionisio Macapagal was eighty years old but still vigorous. When I last saw him, in late January 1995, he was nearly eighty-nine, still clear minded but physically frail. In the meantime, because he had held onto control of his land and the Macapagal *angkan* for so long, the ambitions of his close male kin had been frustrated. Since 1984, his sons had been trying to wrest control of farm and family from him and each other, of the *angkan* from him and his nephew Melencio, and of the village from his lifelong allies.

Someone who heads a farm or other family enterprise does not retire all in one day like an employee: he drops some heavy jobs but retains key skilled tasks and decision making as long as possible. Surrendering control of the farm means becoming dependent on what a successor sees fit to dole out. That leaves a double succession problem, involving the control of farms and the control of family and village affairs. Where the farmholder maintains control of a farm past about age fifty, his successor apparent has to find another farm or source of income to support his own family. There are potential conflicts if the successor, already heading his own household, has to remain subordinate for many years as the old man reluctantly relinquishes one by one the managerial tasks of the farm and the right to dispose of the harvest.

The problem is prolonged when the farmer remains vigorous into his seventies and eighties, as did Mang Dionisio and his *kumpadre*, Jose Lazaro. In 1995, both were nearly ninety years old. Their first-born children are in their sixties and have been heads of their own households for nearly two generations. Even their last-born children are already middle aged. Older children have loaned money to their parents to redeem the farm from mortgage, for subsistence after a bad crop, and for emergencies like medical operations. They feel a moral right to claim the farm. The younger children who stayed on as farmhands feel that they have supported the old couple for years and thus have the customary succession right of the last born and also, having no other income, a claim to the farm by need.

The old couple delay handing over the farm, for thereafter they must ask for every measure of rice and every penny by the grace and favor of the new farm wife. That reversal of dependency hurts the proud.

Families that own their own land or have a CLT under land reform have no landowner to blame for perceived unjust successions. They alone have to deal with the competing claims of siblings for sole succession to farm holder or must decide how to divide the farm. One device to avoid, mitigate, or at least postpone conflict among siblings has been to leave the legal farm under one title but divide it extralegally into blocks, each operated by one child. There remain problems of how to apportion responsibility for outstanding debts, the annual land tax, irrigation fees, and amortization and how to apportion the use of beasts of burden, machines, grazing, straw, the right to borrow cheap institutional credit, and the right to mortgage usufruct of a farm portion to outsiders. Operation Land Transfer did not cause the succession problem, but it posed it more starkly.

The other succession problem is the *pinakamatanda*, the political leadership of the *angkan* in the sense of the led kindred of siblings, cousins, and their families and spouses. There is no rule dictating who should lead or follow whom and no law of succession: the *pinakamatanda* is the "one who acts as elder," that is, the one with enough political skills, contacts, and energy to be put forward to represent kinsmen in dealings with nonkin and officials.

Mang Dionisio very nearly lost his land to foreclosure in the early 1980s. A friend of the family helped redeem the land in 1983, under the condition that the youngest son, Amang, who had no other occupation, would succeed to the farm. By 1984, crop failures and medical expenses had caused Mang Dionisio's debts to grow again. His eldest son, Ruding, had remittances from his adult children working abroad. He redeemed the home farm and took it over. Mang Dionisio wrote me that his younger son, Amang, had the other village farm. All he had left for himself was the unreliable Manaul farm. He had to ask his children for rice and money.

Then Ruding did the unthinkable: in 1991, he split the Macapagal *angkan* and the Macapagal–de Guzman alliance and sided with the faction and party of the de Leons in order to run for *barangay kapitan*. Rubeng de Guzman had resigned as *barangay kapitan* in 1988 to run successfully for municipal councilor. He had, however, stayed in office so long that his able but frustrated allies had changed sides or left the village. Rubeng left a weak successor whom he thought he could control.

By 1991, remittances had made Ruding Macapagal one of the new rich of the village. He and his family had become—in the eyes of those unable to afford a car, a new bungalow-style concrete house, or other consumption items—*mga sosyal*, or socialites. They attended parties and picnics with businesspeople in town and were courted as village leaders by the de Leon camp. The political numbers counted. The Macapagals were the most numerous surname. Moreover, the wife of the *daikon* of the Iglesia ni Cristo sect, reputedly able to deliver an assured 10 percent of the vote, was a Macapagal. Ruding headed the opposition slate as its *kapitan* candidate. His cousin, Melencio, stayed with the de Guzman camp, aligned with the mayor, governor, and congressional candidates who were opposed to the de Leons. In the 1992 elections, that alliance defeated the de Leon candidates but found itself outside the party of the new president, Fidel Ramos. As Rubeng de Guzman had done in 1981, alliance members switched to the party of the *administrasyon* after winning the election in order to get access to the pork barrel.

Mang Dionisio remonstrated with his son about breaking up the Macapagal–de Guzman coalition, which had held together since the days of the Kapatiran Magsasaka in the 1920s. He went to Rubeng de Guzman in tears to say he had no option but to vote for his son Ruding but would not campaign for him. Ruding was beaten for *kapitan*, but Melencio won as a councilor. In 1992, an aging Rubeng de Guzman, almost blinded with cataracts, lost reelection for the town council and retired from active politics. Proud men do not run for an office lower than their last win or candidacy. In the *barangay* elections of 1994, Mang Dionisio's youngest son, Amang, ran for the office of *kapitan* against Rodi Lacanilao, longtime councilor and the de Guzman candidate. Lacanilao won. Once again the Macapagal name alone could not win a plurality for *kapitan*, but both Melencio and Ruding won as councilors.

Conclusion

By 1995, Dionisio Macapagal has lived long, almost ninety years. The frailties of age had forced him to hand over management of farm and family politics to his sons. He has seen, and played a part as logger in, the retreat of the forest of the Sierra Madre, and as a farmer he has suffered the consequences in the form of floods and drying streams. He has lived through several regimes: American Commonwealth, Japanese, Philippine Republic, Marcos's dictatorship, and the restored democracy. Ideas of justice led the young Dionisio into radical nationalist conspiracies and antilandlord unions. The millenarian story that a new day of liberty, equality, and fraternity was about to dawn in the East persuaded him in his youth to be initiated into oath-bound brotherhoods sworn to die to redeem the land and win freedom.

Though a lifelong *oposisyonista*, he has never, so far as I know, fired a shot in anger. Like other small farmers, he married early. With a wife and children as "hostages to fortune," he had to move between the millennial discourse of the ideal and the common sense world of making the best of life in the world as it is.

Getting to know him and his fellow villagers disabused me of any notion that there is a single peasant worldview or mentality or that it makes sense to talk about a dominant ideology. Peasants, like professors, are collectors of ideas and "explanations" of society.

The more reflective could outline, as might a student in a seminar, the ideas of millenarian nationalism, Marxist-Leninist revolution, a labor theory of value account of landlord and capitalist exploitation, the corporatist idea of the need for mutual cooperation between labor and capital; they could compare the Greater East Asia Co-Prosperity Sphere, U.S.-style constitutional democracy, Marcos's Revolution from the Center, People Power participatory democracy, liberation theology, and half a dozen Christian denominations. But to be able to recount and explain a set of ideas does not require that one believe in or be committed to any. Nor does the revelation of a new idea to explain what is wrong with society somehow erase from memory all others. The ability to use the language of one ideology does not mean one cannot switch codes, as company, topic, strategy, and the turn of conversation require. Mang Dionisio took up a number of such truths, serially. More interesting, he held several, and those apparently contradictory, all at once.

Mang Dionisio's account and those of his neighbors and the HDP indicates that ideas can change the perception of the justice of taken-for-granted relations and/or whether and how it is possible to change them. Ideas, leaders, and forms of organization from Manila helped spark and articulate peasant unrest in the provinces close to the capital. They did so at least a decade before the Great Depression of the 1930s.

It is not true that history is written only by the winners: much of it is written by opposition intellectuals. In the last fifty years in the Philippines, those have been predominantly "nationalists." They see the past as a prelude to the inevitable class and national victory of the armed socialist revolution of the laboring masses of workers and peasants led by Marxist-Leninists. Postwar nationalist historians dismiss as rightist ultranationalists those peasants and workers who looked to guns from Japan to free themselves from what they perceived as an alliance between landlord politicians and the U.S. colonial regime. Armed with teleological hindsight and the postwar politics of the separate issue of elite collaboration with the Japanese occupation regime, they project backward the political correctness of 1946 and make peasants and party permanently and presciently anti-Japanese.

Thus, Mang Dionisio's tale is confirmed by Capadocia's account of radical politics in the 1930s. Both accounts show overlapping leftist and nationalist strands of radical politics grappling with the problem that had beset nationalists since the 1890s: where could they find an ally to supply the guns needed to defeat landowner and occupier?[28] In an earlier age, both American and Irish patriots who rebelled against the

English crown looked to France for guns and a fleet. Dionisio Macapagal, like many Filipino rebels, hoped for guns from Japan, not to submit to a new colonial power but to win freedom.

Notes

I wish to thank James C. Scott and the Agrarian Studies Program at Yale University for their hospitality while I wrote the first draft of this essay for the 1995 Asian Studies Conference in Washington, D.C., and to acknowledge the support of Macquarie University for granting me leave. Drs. Sumit Guha and Heinzpeter Znoj, fellows of the ASP, and Dr. Alfred W. McCoy of the Center for Southeast Asian Studies at the University of Wisconsin-Madison generously commented on an earlier draft. During the subsequent editing Vina Lanzona and Al McCoy made judicious cuts in an overlong manuscript.

1. Cumulatively, I have spent about three of the last twenty-five years in Buga. I am grateful to Mang Dionisio Macapagal for his patience, friendship, and guidance and to Mang Bernabe de Guzman and his family for generous hospitality, friendship, and kindness.
2. Carl H. Lande, *Leaders, Factions, and Parties: The Structure of Philippine Politics* (New Haven: Yale University, Southeast Asia Program, 1964).
3. Renato Rosaldo writes about this issue in relation to Ilongot historicity in *Ilongot Headhunting, 1883-1974: A Study in Society and History* (Stanford: Stanford University Press, 1980). In sum, Rosaldo sees these oral devices as a particular way of authorizing "historical" accounts in oral societies. He goes on to discuss its implications for Ilongot historicity, a historicity that bases "truth" on direct experience.
4. Frank Lynch, *Four Readings on Philippines Values* (Quezon City: Ateneo de Manila University Press, 1973).
5. Brian Fegan, "Entrepreneurs in Votes and Violence: Three Generations of a Peasant Political Family," in *An Anarchy of Families: State and Family in the Philippines,* edited by Alfred W. McCoy (Madison: Center for Southeast Asian Studies, University of Wisconsin, 1993).
6. The social history of the locality is outlined in Brian Fegan, "Social History of a Central Luzon Barrio," in *Philippine Social History: Global Trade and Local Transformations,* edited by Alfred W. McCoy and Edilberto C. de Jesus (Quezon City: Ateneo de Manila Press, 1982); and Fegan, "Entrepreneurs."
7. Historical Data Papers (HDP), "History and Cultural Life of San Miguel, Bulacan," typescript, ca. 1950-51, in the collection Historical Data Papers of Bulacan (copies held at San Miguel High School and the Philippine National Library, Manila). The HDP barrio and municipal histories were compiled by municipal committees of teachers and informed citizens in 1950-51 under the direction of the Ministry of Education.
8. Cecilio de Leon, interview with the author, Quezon City, 1980.
9. Rodolfo Apolinario, interview with the author, Poblacion, San Miguel, 1980; Cecilio de Leon, interview with the author, San Vicente San Miguel, 1980; Bernardo Sempio, interview with the author, San Vicente San Miguel, 1980.
10. Rodolfo Apolinario, interview with the author, Poblacion, San Miguel, 1980.
11. Dionisio Macapagal's account fifty years after the event may have overlooked the degree to which a rise in the market price of *palay* exacerbated resentment over landlords' low valuation of it in 1918-20. The wholesale

price of milled rice rose from around P6 per *cavan* in 1911–16 to P8 around harvest time in 1917, P10 around harvest time in 1918, and then a record P16 from then until the harvest of 1920. See Bureau of Commerce and Industry, *Statistical Bulletin of the Philippine Islands: Seventh Number, 1924* (Manila: Bureau of Printing, 1925). The prices of other foods and consumer goods rose markedly in the same years, apparently as a delayed effect of the 1914–18 war.

12. Benedict Kerkvliet, *The Huk Rebellion: A Study of Peasant Revolt in the Philippines* (Berkeley: University of California Press, 1977).
13. HDP, "Historical and Cultural Life."
14. Herminigildo Cruz, "Labor Movement in the Philippines Islands," *Labor: Bulletin of the Bureau of Labor* 8, no. 26 (March 1927).
15. Guillermo Capadocia, "The Philippine Labor Movement," typescript, Military Intelligence Service (ISAFP), Manila, Personal File: Guillermo Capadocia (ca. 1950).
16. See also Joseph R. Hayden, *The Philippines: A Study in National Development* (New York: Macmillan, 1942).
17. Capadocia, "Philippine Labor Movement."
18. Interviews with the author, Buga, San Miguel, 1972.
19. David Sturtevant, *Popular Uprisings in the Philippines, 1840–1940* (Ithaca: Cornell University Press, 1976).
20. HDP, "History and Cultural Life."
21. Fegan, "Entrepreneurs."
22. Small numbers of urban intellectuals, economic nationalists, and Marxists would mobilize from then until 1991 against continuing U.S. treaty rights to economic privileges and military bases, seen as infringements on national sovereignty. To peasants, the 1946 Parity Amendment to the constitution, which gave U.S. citizens the same economic rights as Filipinos, was the last major nationalist issue.
23. Kerkvliet, *Huk Rebellion*, provides a detailed account of the peasant war of 1946–53.
24. Jose Hernandez and Adong Feliciano, interview with the author, Buga, 1980.
25. James C. Scott, *Domination and the Arts of Resistance: Hidden Transcripts* (New Haven: Yale University Press, 1990).
26. Mr. San Gabriel, interview with the author, Caloocan City Hall, 1984. Born in Barrio Pinambaran, he became an official of the Ministry of Local Government and Community Development, then OIC mayor of Caloocan City following a disputed election.
27. Brian Fegan, "Requiem for a Cop," *Canberra Anthropology* 11, no. 2 (October 1988): 72–77.
28. Josefa Saniel, *Japan and the Philippines, 1868–1898* (Quezon City: Ateneo de Manila University Press, 1969).

BIBLIOGRAPHY

Capadocia, Guillermo. "The Philippine Labor Movement." Military Intelligence Service (ISAFP), Manila. Personal File: Guillermo Capadocia. Ca. 1950. Typescript.

Cruz, Herminigildo. "Labor Movement in the Philippine Islands." *Labor: Bulletin of the Bureau of Labor* 8, no. 26 (March 1927).

Fegan, Brian. "Entrepreneurs in Votes and Violence: Three Generations of a Peasant Political Family." In *An Anarchy of Families: State and Family in the Philippines*, edited by Alfred W. McCoy. Monographs, no. 10. Madison: Center for Southeast Asian Studies, University of Wisconsin, 1993.

Fegan, Brian. "Requiem for a Cop." *Canberra Anthropology* 11, no. 2 (October 1988): 72-77.

Fegan, Brian. "Social History of a Central Luzon Barrio." In *Philippine Social History: Global Trade and Local Transformations*, edited by Alfred W. McCoy and Edilberto C. de Jesus. Quezon City: Ateneo de Manila University Press, 1982.

Government of the Philippine Islands, Department of Commerce and Communications. *Statistical Bulletin of the Philippine Islands, 1924*. Manila: Bureau of Printing, 1925.

Hayden, Joseph R. *The Philippines: A Study in National Development*. New York: Macmillan, 1942.

Historical Data Papers. "History and Cultural Life of San Miguel, Bulacan." Typescript, ca. 1950-51. In the collection Historical Data Papers of Bulacan. Copies held at San Miguel High School and the Philippine National Library, Manila.

Kerkvliet, Benedict T. *The Huk Rebellion: A Study of Peasant Revolt in the Philippines*. Berkeley: University of California Press, 1977.

Lynch, Frank. *Four Readings on Philippine Values*. Quezon City: Ateneo de Manila University Press, 1973.

Saniel, Josefa. *Japan and the Philippines, 1868-1898*. Quezon City: University of the Philippines Press, 1969.

Scott, James. *Domination and the Arts of Resistance: Hidden Transcripts*. New Haven: Yale University Press, 1990.

Sturtevant, David. *Popular Uprisings in the Philippines, 1840-1940*. Ithaca: Cornell University Press, 1976.

Manuela Santa Ana vda. de Maclang, April 1996, at home
in Barangay San Ricardo, Talavera, Nueva Ecija Province.

Benedict J. Tria Kerkvliet

D ressed in a shapeless, plain dress that hung over her skinny frame
down to her ankles, her graying hair tightly drawn behind her head,
Manuela Santa Ana vda. de Maclang spoke distinctly through a micro-
phone to a crowd of about 250 people. They were assembled for a meeting of the local cooperative known as the "KB." Before she had begun to
speak, people had grown restless. It was nearly noon. They had been sitting for nearly two hours. Though the sun was relatively mild that day, 8
February 1985, and tall acacia and sampaloc trees partially shaded the
clearing in the village of San Ricardo (Talavera, Nueva Ecija), where the
meeting took place, people were hot and sweaty. They were also growing weary of speeches and reports by KB officers and other speakers. But
after she had been speaking for a few minutes I looked around and
gauged that now people were listening attentively. They followed her
every move as she emphasized points with her hands and shuffled from
one part to another of the hard packed dirt "platform" from which she
spoke. While many listening had had their disagreements with her and
some had opposed outright the things she had said and done in the past,
few denied that she was a sincere person who had given much of her life
to public service. She spoke confidently and often eloquently, altering the
pitch of her voice to fit each part of her message and pausing at strategic
intervals to give listeners a chance to absorb what she was saying. For
forty-five minutes she held the audience in rapt attention.

Elang, as she is usually called, has lived most of her life in San Ricardo,
a rice-growing village in Talavera, Nueva Ecija. She has never been involved
in national politics in the conventional sense of the term and never, so far as
I know, has she aspired to do so. Her political world has been mainly in the
small rural towns and villages of Nueva Ecija on the margins of national
political life. Her political style is also marginal to what popular media and
most academics say about Philippine politics. Many of her actions and motivations do not correspond to the way politics in the Philippines is usually
portrayed and the way political leaders are said to act and think.

Yet in other senses I would not see Elang Santa Ana as marginal. In the village of San Ricardo and the municipality of Talavera, she has been a prominent person for decades. It is not that she is rich or highly educated or a high official in municipal government. She has been none of these. Rather, she has been a central figure because of her persistent and long involvement in land reform, economic development, and other vital social issues in the area. I also suspect that her brand of politics is not as remote as the conventional literature would suggest from much of Philippine political life. She represents a type of political leadership that is probably more widespread in the country than the mass media would suggest. Hence, a discussion of who she is, what brought her to that February 1985 meeting, and why people respect her also pertains to an important perspective on Philippine political life.

Conventional Views of Philippine Politics

I see three prominent interpretations of Philippine politics. One is the patron-client, factional argument that the country's politics revolves around personal relations and networks in which people are primarily driven by personal obligations, exchanges of favors, and a hunger for power and money. These networks and motivations, according to this view, are particularly apparent during elections, although they are also at the heart of most other political activities in the country. A second interpretation is that of the patrimonial or elite democracy. It, too, emphasizes that patron-client relations are central to political life, but it adds that intimidation, coercion, and violence are also widespread. In addition, this view argues that the political system, though it has democratic-looking institutions, is essentially run by members of an elite who use their connections, wealth, power, and brute force to control the country's resources. One lucrative way to acquire personal fame and fortune is to hold public office, which is why the elites fight among themselves to get elected, manipulating voters and abusing the formal rules in the process. A third view, which might be labeled the neocolonial or dependency analysis, agrees with much that the second interpretation argues but qualifies the power of the Filipino elite. According to the dependency argument, foreign businesses and, at least until very recently, American military interests have long dominated the country in many areas. Consequently, members of the elite are often clients of these foreign interests.

All three of these interpretations are frequently valuable in making sense of politics in the Philippines. I have often used them, especially the first two, in my own work, and in so doing I have contributed to the perpetuation of these interpretations.

Yet I am also uneasy with these views and have been for some time. A great deal of political life in the country cannot be squeezed into one or even all of them. Limiting analysis to these conventional views means that values, motivations, aspirations, and relationships other than those undergirding them are deemed unimportant. Consequently, Philippine politics and its society and culture generally are portrayed in an overly simplistic and untextured fashion. Similarly, Filipinos for whom other concerns, beliefs, and values greatly matter are reduced to mere caricatures of their fuller, more complicated selves. And a great many people and events are marginalized because they do not conform to the prominent theories on Philippine politics.[1]

Manuela Santa Ana is one person who comes to mind when I am musing about the limitations of the conventional views on Philippine politics. Many things she has done and her reasons for doing them fall outside the parameters of the usual ways of analyzing political actors in the country. Several other people who appear in the narrative that follows, including some who were at odds with her, are in a similar position vis-à-vis those dominant interpretations. Hence, I do not think she is unique or even terribly unusual, though demonstrating that is not the purpose of this essay. My purpose is to tell about a person who has been politically engaged in vital political issues and, in so telling, to convey an often neglected dimension of Philippine politics. Obviously, my account of her politics is not going to be "complete." I do not claim to know everything or even most things that she has done or why she did them. I only know some, based primarily on what she has told me and, equally important in my view, what others, especially many who have known her for years, have said about her. I also observed her while I was living in and visiting San Ricardo.[2] Though incomplete, I think my understanding of her is enough for readers to appreciate my point, that her life—her politics—is more than what the usual analyses would lead us to expect. While family and other personal relations have been important for her political involvement, as significant if not more so are her beliefs that rural people should live better and that they must organize to make the political system work for them.

Early Years: Living in Rebellion

When still only a teenager in the late 1930s, Elang Santa Ana was politically engaged. She had joined a local chapter of the Ligang Kabataan ng Pilipinas (LKP), a youth group promoting nationalism, primarily, as she recalled, through parades and demonstrations in Talavera and Cabanatuan City (the capital of Nueva Ecija). The group opposed both the government

of the United States, which still ruled the country, and of Japan, which had
already invaded China and whose mighty military machine cast an omi-
nous shadow over the Philippine archipelago. But Elang's more immediate reason for joining the LKP, she said, was to help her father, Amando
Santa Ana, a prominent local leader of peasant organizations (particularly the KPMP in the late 1930s) who had been involved in two peasant
uprisings—the Tanggulan (1932) and Sakdalista (1935).[3] He was frequently harassed by the police, she said, had been arrested from time to time,
and was regularly asked by tenant farmers to assist them in their conflicts
with their landlords. Joining the youth group struck her as something she
could do to support her father. She recalls that the league's activities were
also often enjoyable, bringing together young people like her from villages all around the province.

Elang was born in 1924 in San Ricardo, the village to which her
maternal grandparents, the Valdezes, had migrated from other parts of
the province a dozen or more years earlier. Her grandparents and other
Valdez families who had moved with them and cleared land to farm rice
may at one time have held legal title to several hectares. By the late 1920s,
however, none of the Valdez households had much land. It had been
"lost," according to various descendants' recollections, on account of
swindles by larger landowners and because the Valdezes sold it bit by bit
in order to pay their debts. The debts were the consequence of two problems: the family having to borrow in order to meet farming expenses but
being unable to repay due to bad harvests and because some males in the
family overindulged in gambling and other vices. For a time, Elang's parents shared three hectares with other relatives on her mother's side, but
in the early 1930s financial hardship forced them to sell. Afterward, the
Santa Ana family lived primarily by working for others, foraging for food
in fields and waterways, and gleaning in the fields. In the late 1930s,
Elang's father also received occasional income from the provincial KPMP
chapter, in which he held an elected position.

Amando Santa Ana, originally from the municipality of Quezon, had
met his wife-to-be while working odd jobs in Talavera. They married in
1921, settled in San Ricardo, and between 1923 and 1938 had six children,
five daughters and one son. Much of the child rearing was done by
Elang's mother and the older children. Elang, who was the second eldest,
recalls that she quit school after the third grade in part because she had
to help her mother with family chores, especially the washing and looking after younger siblings. Also, she added, it was not common in those
days for children, especially girls, to finish primary school.

Shortly after the Japanese army invaded the country in December
1941, reaching Talavera shortly after Christmas that year, Elang's father

went underground with the first group of men in the area to resist the new foreign government. It was the third time in ten years that he had left his family to join a rebellion. It was also the last time Elang saw her father alive. Two years later, in March 1944, he was killed during one of the most vicious battles between the anti-Japanese Hukbalahap guerrilla forces, in which Amando was a squadron leader, and Japanese soldiers and their Filipino troops. Recognizing his body to be that of the local guerrilla leader, Japanese troops severed his head and displayed it in Talavera's *poblacion* as a trophy of their victory.[4] That act stiffened the resolve of many people for miles around to continue to oppose the Japanese military regime. Among them were two of his children, Elang and one of her sisters, who were also in the Hukbalahap.

In early 1942, Elang had received a message from her father that he needed to see her. She set out to meet him but due to the turmoil and logistical difficulties of guerrilla warfare they never managed to rendezvous. Meanwhile, she joined the resistance movement, too. In March 1942, she was instructed to go to a place near the Nueva Ecija–Bulacan boundary where she would be given an assignment. But shortly after arriving she was struck with appendicitis and rushed to Malolos, Bulacan, where a doctor sympathetic to the resistance movement operated on her. As she recuperated from her brush with death, she fell in love with Federico Maclang, a Bulakeño who was also in the resistance. For the next thirty-eight years they lived as husband and wife, although they never married because Federico already had a wife (and two children) from whom he was separated. Their respective responsibilities in the Hukbalahap often took Elang and Federico in different directions. He was a leader in the guerrilla organization's regional committee (Reco) responsible for parts of Bulacan, Pampanga, and Bataan provinces. Elang was in the mobile school, teaching new supporters and recruits about the purpose of the anti-Japanese movement, training other teachers, and helping to establish more schools for the resistance. She was frequently moving in Nueva Ecija, Bulacan, and Pampanga provinces.

After the Japanese were defeated, she returned without Federico to San Ricardo. The war had greatly disrupted the Santa Ana family, not only because the father had left and been killed and Elang and another sister had been away but also because family members who remained behind frequently had to hide and move from place to place to avoid the persecution of the authorities, who knew that some family members were in the Hukbalahap. Now that political conditions had settled down, Elang wanted to help her mother, brother (then not yet ten years old), and youngest sisters to resettle in San Ricardo. Together the family built a small thatch-roofed house to replace the one that had fallen down and began to bring some order to their lives. In January 1946, however, Elang was called away again and would not return to San Ricardo to live for another six years.

She had received word that Federico wanted her to join him in Santa Cruz, Laguna, where he was involved with a tenant farmers' organization. Upon arriving there by bus, she heard that a few hours earlier a gunman hired by a local landlord had shot Federico. There was some confusion as to where he was. He had managed to escape the would-be assassin but was bleeding badly when last seen. Tenant families later led her to a village near Pila, Laguna, where Federico lay, bandages covering his torso. Word was that the landlord's hired guns and the local police were tracking him down; he needed to leave quickly. Late that night friends ferried Elang and Federico by *banca* across the Laguna de Bay and found refuge for them on the other side. A few days later, they slipped into Manila and took shelter within the network of Federico's friends. It was the beginning of another episode in Elang's life of rebellion.

Federico Maclang was born in 1914 in Bulacan, Bulacan, one of thirteen children. After three years of formal education, he had quit school in order to work and help his family. His parents farmed a small piece of land and took care of a large fish pond owned by another family. Federico recalled observing that, although his parents worked extremely hard, they earned little in return. This led him to wonder about economic and political matters and to teach himself more about Philippine history. By 1928, aged fourteen, he was working in Manila, going from job to job as a low-paid laborer. Through his older brother Emilio, who had preceded him to Manila, and his distant uncle Jacinto Manahan, he was introduced to union activists and began to get involved in the growing labor movement. He was particularly influenced by a large strike at the Minerva cigar factory in 1934. He had also met the founding leaders of the Partido Komunista sa Pilipinas (PKP), including Vicente Lava and Crisanto Evangelista. His brother Emilio was a PKP member and ended up being one of the few sent to the Soviet Union to observe the Communist Party there. Federico joined the PKP in 1934, by which time the American colonial government had declared the party a subversive organization and imprisoned several of its leaders, including Evangelista. For the next seventeen years, much of Federico's work revolved around his underground PKP activities. In 1944, he was elected to the party's Central Committee. Between early 1946 and October 1950, while he and Elang lived in Manila, he had high-level party responsibilities, particularly in the realm of organizational matters, supplies, and communications. In 1948, he was elected to the party's Political Bureau.

Because he could not tell her much about his activities, Elang was not terribly knowledgeable about what her husband did while they lived in

Manila. She never joined the PKP, in part, she explained, because she could not see herself living the regimented, single-purpose life that was expected of party members. While Federico went about his "movement and revolutionary work," Elang said, she set up housekeeping and earned money to support the two of them and their first child, "Junior," who was born in January 1947.

They initially rented an apartment in Manila's Tondo District. She sold roasted corn and sweet potatoes in front of the nearby Rizal School, across the street from Alhambra cigar and cigarette factory. In the evening, while she prepared the corn and sweet potatoes, Federico made little bags from old newspapers in which to put them. One of the most difficult aspects of being a sidewalk vendor was dealing with the police. To avoid arrest or being forced to leave, she learned from other vendors how to win a policeman's sympathy with stories about having an unemployed husband and no other means of support; she also learned how to bribe the police as a last resort. Gradually she switched to selling meat, from which she could earn more, and eventually secured a meat stall in a local *palengke* (open market). She managed to save enough from her earnings and Federico's winnings at cockfight betting (his weekend hobby, she smiled, "even while he was making revolution") to have a small hollow-block house built on the fringes of Tondo.

Meanwhile, the Huk rebellion was raging in her home province and other parts of central Luzon. Although Elang was not involved, she was very concerned, especially for her many relatives and friends in San Ricardo and elsewhere who supported the uprising. She also knew that the PKP was now even more deeply immersed in underground activities and that her husband's work was becoming as dangerous as it had been during the Japanese occupation.

One day in mid-1948, Elang returned home from her meat stall to be informed by her younger sister, who was staying with them, that some men had been inquiring about Federico. Later that afternoon, while Elang was doing laundry, the same men returned. They asked if she was the wife of Ambrosio Reyes (Federico's alias). Yes, she replied. Immediately she suspected that the men were police. Asked where Mr. Reyes was, she answered that he was having his glasses repaired. Her father-in-law, who was also staying with them at the time and was suspicious, interjected that, no, Ambrosio had done that already and had gone off someplace else. Her father-in-law was trying to confuse the visitors. As the men left, one of them said to tell Mr. Reyes that his friend Reynaldo Conrado had stopped by.

That message confirmed her suspicions; Reynaldo Conrado was the alias Federico had used while in the anti-Japanese resistance movement. In the evening, she intercepted Federico on his way home and told him what had happened. They quickly decided that he should stay someplace else for a while.

The next day the men returned. Her husband, she told them, had not come home. "'Maybe he's with number two or number three,'" she recalled telling them to fabricate a story. "'After all,' I continued, pointing to my big stomach because at the time I was very pregnant with our second child, 'look at me. He can't do it with me, so he's probably with number two or number three.'" She added that her husband had not even left her the money to pay the doctor. By the time the men left, Elang recalled with a smile, they had taken pity on her and given her money for her medical expenses.

That day, her father-in-law, sister, and she decided to leave Manila immediately. They feared that the house would be raided and the family harassed, even imprisoned and tortured. She told her *kumare*, who was not involved in the movement, that a family emergency required her to move.[5] She asked the woman to sell the house and all its contents. With a basket of belongings and her one-year-old son, Elang set out by bus for a friend's house in Bulacan.

She was there more than a month before receiving a message from Federico. Cautiously, they began to correspond and devised ways to meet. One of those occasions, fortuitously, was the evening she gave birth to their daughter, Evelyn. Meanwhile, she had received P4,400 from her *kumare* for the sale of their house and belongings in Manila.

In late 1948, she and Federico decided that it was safe to live together again in Manila. They rented an apartment in Santa Cruz District near the San Lorenzo race track. She got a job in a garment factory. One of her sisters lived with them to help look after the children. From time to time, her mother also visited from San Ricardo. Life was back to normal—as "normal," anyway, as it ever became during the time of Federico's revolutionary activities.

Police knocking on their apartment door on the night on 17 October 1950 threw their lives into disarray once again. For some days, Elang had suspected that her family was being watched. Earlier that afternoon, as she and Federico returned from shopping, she had sensed that they were being followed. Federico was not worried, however, and suggested that they see a movie. She was eager to get home, but he insisted. They saw "In Despair," she said, with a touch of irony in her voice.[6] Federico watched intensely, but she could not concentrate on the film. She kept thinking that the people sitting near them were agents. As they left the Life Theater, Federico was in high spirits and wanted to have *miryenda* at the nearby Ma Mon Luk eatery. She was extremely nervous. "Everyone on the street looked like an agent to me," she recalled. She begged her husband to go straight home. After they had retired for the evening, she awoke hungry and thought of some sweet potatoes her mother had brought that day from Nueva Ecija. She boiled some and was eating when she heard the knocking. From a bedroom window she could see armed police in front of the apartment building. She went to the second bedroom and saw more armed men in the back. She awakened Federico. He immediately decided to escape through a side window. As he was leaving, she went downstairs and opened the door. The uniformed man standing there asked politely if her husband was home. Just as she replied no, Federico was led from around the corner by policemen. His attempted escape had failed.

After several hours of questioning Federico in the apartment, during which time Elang tried to stay calm and even served sweet potatoes to the interrogators, the military captain in charge announced that he had orders to bring her husband to the Philippine Constabulary's Camp Crame for detention. Elang asked that she be allowed to accompany him. She had heard of similar cases in which people being taken to military camps were killed along the way. The officer refused. She insisted. After calling his commander, the captain said that now he was told to bring everyone in the house to the detention center. Elang and Federico objected but to no avail. Their two young children, Elang's sister, her brother (who had been visiting them), and a friend also staying with them were loaded together with Elang and Federico into an army truck. The only good thing, Elang recalled, was that her mother was not included because she had spent the night with friends.

Upon reaching Camp Crame in the early hours of 18 October, Federico learned that other PKP Political Bureau members had been arrested in simultaneous raids that night. With much fanfare, the government publicized the arrests and began preparing for a trial that lasted nearly a year. The captives were convicted of subversion, rebellion, murder, and other crimes and given lengthy sentences. Federico served more than twenty years. He was released in early 1971 but was rearrested in 1972 after President Ferdinand Marcos declared martial law. In 1974, following negotiations between the Marcos government and PKP leaders, Federico was freed again along with other party members.

Family, Work, and Politics

The next twenty-four years of Elang's life, from her husband's arrest in 1950 until his release in 1974, revolved around raising her son and daughter, earning a living to support her family (including her mother), and politics. Whenever possible she and her children visited Federico. But because he was incarcerated in prisons near Manila visits were irregular. In early 1952, she and the children had returned to San Ricardo, more than a hundred kilometers away, after she had tried for more than a year to work and reestablish a household in Manila. The factory where she had been employed before Federico's arrest would not take her back; the odd jobs and street vending she then did brought in too little income, and besides the police often hassled her. For a few months, around the time her husband's trial was ending, she lived in Bulacan with her in-laws. About that time she also became very ill, mainly from exhaustion. After she recovered, she and her in-laws decided that she should return to San Ricardo.

She missed Federico, but she did not miss Manila. The countryside, she believed, was a better place for her children, and living in her native village boosted her morale enormously. She and her mother moved in together after building a modest house on a lot that had belonged to her maternal grandparents, adjacent to where her older sister and other relatives lived. Once again, she was among old friends, especially several women with whom she had grown up and who had also been active in the Hukbalahap. Some had been involved in the Huk rebellion as well, which by 1952 was winding down in central Luzon. She spent a lot of time in those first few months back in San Ricardo talking with these old friends, whose experiences and political views during the last decade resonated with hers.

Initially, to make ends meet, she worked as she had when young — planting rice, harvesting, and gleaning in the fields. Often she joined groups of workers that included some of her sisters and her brother, who like her were landless. It was hard work and intermittent, barely providing enough income to put food on the table. She began looking for other ways of making a living.

In 1953, she became an agent for Insular Life Insurance, one of the insurers at the time that was reaching into rural communities for new markets. She traveled around Talavera and neighboring municipalities to find customers, leaving her children in the care of her mother and sisters. As her sales increased, her income from commissions grew. After a couple of years, a rival company, Sterling Life, enticed her to become its agent by promising higher commissions. She worked for that company until she stopped selling insurance in the mid-1960s. She figured that she earned more from selling life insurance than she could from any other work that she might have been able to do at that time. One of her goals was to have enough money to send her son and daughter to college. She succeeded. Both Junior and Evelyn graduated from provincial colleges and found employment, Junior as a public servant in the government and Evelyn as a teacher in Talavera's high school.

Her main asset as an insurance salesperson was her honesty. This is the view of many who knew her at the time, including those who bought policies from her. Insurance agents, as a group, had bad reputations because some of them absconded with the cash payments that clients entrusted to them for delivery to the company's provincial office in Cabanatuan City. Milking clients in this manner could go on for years because agents could also issue phony documents claiming that clients' policies were paid up. Clients often would not discover that they were being cheated until they filed a claim or checked with the provincial office or the head office in Manila—which, given the cumbersome transportation system in rural Nueva Ecija, was not easily done. By that point, the agent responsible had made a considerable sum of money and often was no longer around. Consequently, Elang's reputation for being straight both increased her sales and improved the image of her line of work.

Though she was busy earning a living and raising her children, she felt something was missing in her life. She wanted to be involved more directly in the political issues still swirling around Nueva Ecija. She was keen, she recalled, "to be of service" to the people around her, particularly small landowners, tenant farmers, and agricultural workers—people with whom she had deep affinity because of her background and the activism of her father.[7] The peasant-based Huk rebellion had died down, but tenant-landlord relations and agrarian issues remained controversial. The nation's new president, Ramon Magsaysay, elected in November 1953, had helped focus attention on tenancy reform legislation. Locally, landlords had resumed searching for ways to reduce their obligations to tenants and even get rid of tenants altogether by replacing them with machinery and wage laborers. Some large landowners were recruiting workers from elsewhere, raising the ire of local tenants and seasonal agricultural workers. Meanwhile, local interest in electoral politics was renewed on account of the elections of 1951 and 1953, which were much cleaner and less violent than those that had taken place in the second half of the 1940s.

Elang wanted to get involved in organizations dealing directly with rural problems, but there were none to be found due to the political climate at the time. In the twilight of the Huk rebellion, most people were extremely skittish about forming organizations that might be suspected of being "communist" and vulnerable to police and military harassment. Elang began attending meetings of Nacionalista Party (NP) supporters in San Ricardo and Talavera town. Partly what attracted her to the NP was that several villagers active in it were former Hukbalahap like herself. Another reason, she said, was that the alternative major political party at the time, the Liberal Party (LP), "stunk too much" (*masyadong mabaho*) on account of the sordid record of the LP politicians then in office, most prominently Elpidio Quirino, the nation's president from 1947 to 1953.

By 1955, NP leaders in Talavera had nominated Elang as a candidate for the Talavera's Municipal Council. For several weeks prior to the November election day, she traveled with other NP nominees to most villages in the municipality, becoming, she recalled, a more confident public speaker than she had expected. Her speeches to villagers emphasized issues regarding land, landlord-tenant relations, and such public needs as transportation, electrification, and sanitation. The latter were local concerns about which she had become increasingly aware after returning to San Ricardo from Manila and traveling around the province selling insurance. Her speeches, she said, were usually fairly direct and serious; she was not good at telling jokes, clowning around, singing, or doing other things to entertain audiences. Some residents remember, however, that she was an effective, often amusing storyteller, using her own and other people's experiences to engage people while making a point. Finances for her campaign were meager. Elang recalled using "a few hundred" pesos of her own savings, but most of the costs for travel, food, and leaflets—her three principal expenditures—were paid by the municipal branch of the NP and by donations. She did not try to buy people's votes, and, as far as she could recollect, neither did other Municipal Council candidates. Mayoral candidates may have, she said, but that was not widespread and probably had little influence on the outcome, an assessment shared by most people who recalled the campaigns for local office during the second half of the 1950s. The 1955 election campaign was also rather peaceful. There were few reports of voters being coerced or threatened by armed men supporting certain candidates. Armed bodyguards were often present at campaign rallies, though none were for Elang specifically. They were usually employed by candidates for mayor or, more often, candidates for provincial governor and the national House of Representatives when those candidates were in the same neighborhood as the candidates for municipal offices. "Guns, goons, and gold," Elang said, were not prominent then in Talavera's electoral politics. They became more evident in the late 1960s, many local residents recalled when I asked them in 1978–79, although even then campaigns for municipal and village offices, as distinct from provincial and congressional races, were generally nonviolent.

Elang's campaign organization was also minimal. For logistical arrangements, she relied heavily on the local NP infrastructure, which included leaders in most of Talavera's villages, who prepared venues and schedules for speaking events. A few people in San Ricardo and other villages voluntarily worked specifically for her election, mainly by talking to neighbors about her but also by collecting contributions to help pay her campaign expenses. Supporters included relatives, but most were people whom she knew from her Hukbalahap days and through selling insurance. Others had known and admired her father. Family relationships and friendships, she said, were "of course, important" in getting supporters and votes, but, she added, they were not enough to win. As a candidate, she believed she needed to get people to vote for her on the basis of her views, background, and abilities. She tried to convey those qualities in her speeches and through meetings with small groups of people as she went from village to village.

As best as she and others could recall, the main issue against her in that campaign was "communism and subversion." Because her husband was in jail as a subversive and a PKP leader, her father had been a leader in peasant organizations and the local Hukbalahap, and she had been in the Hukbalahap, "my opponents," she said, "continually accused me of being subversive and a communist." She basically argued that joining the Hukbalahap had been illegal only in the eyes of the Japanese government at the time. She also said that, even though her husband was in the PKP, she had never been and had no desire to be. As for her father, she emphasized the sacrifices he had made to assist poor tenant farmers and the fact that he had given his life fighting to oust the repressive Japanese military regime.

This issue was the flip side of one of her main assets. She was already well known in Talavera precisely because of her Hukbalahap involvement and her father's. Moreover, many voters in Talavera had been in or supported the Hukbalahap. On balance, she felt her Hukbalahap involvement and her father's reputation helped her campaign.

She received the largest number of votes of all contenders for the eight at-large council seats and became the first woman ever elected to a municipal office in Talavera's history. Winning that 1955 election, she recalled years later, was one of the most joyous events of her public life. She had entered the race somewhat hesitantly, unsure of how to campaign and not confident about winning. Indeed, initially she considered herself a long shot. As the campaign picked up, she began to entertain thoughts of winning but never expected to garner the most votes of all. Her mother, she said, was very proud of her, and she thought her father would have been, too, even though electoral politics had probably never interested him.

She served as a Municipal Council member for four years, from January 1956 to December 1960. During that time, the municipality was divided into eight districts and she was assigned to look after one that included San Ricardo and several other villages in the eastern part of Talavera. But she was not restricted to matters concerning that district. For example, she sponsored resolutions and ordinances to assist squatters in the *poblacion* of Talavera who were being evicted from land on which a new municipal hall was to be built. She was also deeply involved in the council's successful effort to prevent the provincial authorities from giving to a neighboring municipality some of Talavera's land. Like other council members and the mayor and vice mayor, much of her official duties involved trying to get financing for municipal projects like roads and sanitation. Tax revenues were woefully inadequate, and the taxing powers of municipalities were extremely limited. The best hope for funding local projects was to approach provincial and national government offices. Several times she accompanied mayor Teodosio Valenton to Manila to follow up the Talavera council's petitions to congressmen and senators asking for money to complete the municipal hall, build more classrooms in village schools, construct bridges, and even paint San Ricardo's elementary school.[8]

An issue affecting many parts of the municipality in which she was often involved concerned landlord-tenant relations. Peasants from many villages asked her for advice, to intervene in disputes with their landlords, and for assistance in getting help from relevant parts of the government. Sometimes by talking to both parties she could help to resolve disputes, but often amicable solutions were not possible. Her official position gave her no formal power to do much more because the municipal government had virtually no legal jurisdiction over such matters. Landlord-tenant relations, tenancy conditions, land use rights, ownership rights, and so on were in the realm of national government agencies and the court system. One important role she did play was to help tenants to use the newly established Court of Agrarian Relations. An early example involved residents in San Ricardo and three nearby villages.

They were tenants of Manolo Tinio, who owned two hundred hectares of rice land. He had embarked on a program, set in motion in the early 1950s, to replace all forty-five of his tenants with machinery and hired laborers. By 1955, he had already managed to remove tenants on forty-five hectares. In 1956, he targeted another fifty-five. In February of that year, he sent a letter to the twelve tenants on the land saying that henceforth he would be farming it with machinery and their services would no longer be needed by 1957. Shortly thereafter, he had his tractor drivers plow that land and form long contoured fields, destroying in the process the boundaries and dikes (*pilapil*) of his tenants' fields. Angry and upset, several tenants appealed to Elang for advice and help. She went to Tinio's house in Cabanatuan City but could not persuade him to change his mind. He insisted that he was within his rights. After further investigation, she arranged for a sympathetic attorney in Cabanatuan to counsel the tenants for a small fee. They ended up lodging a case against

Tinio in the Cabanatuan branch of the Court of Agrarian Relations. It became the first of numerous court cases in a protracted struggle between Tinio and his remaining tenants, which lasted from 1956 to 1972. In this particular skirmish, the court facilitated a settlement that allowed Tinio to reshape the fields but left the tenants to continue farming them.[9] The agreement, however, broke down a year or so later when Tinio escalated his pressures to remove these and more tenants.

As Elang's term in office drew to an end in 1959, she sought the Nacionalista Party's nomination for vice mayor, a stepping stone to the mayorship, the office to which by then she really aspired. She failed, however, to win the nomination at the Talavera NP's preelection convention. She thinks some delegates who originally said they would support her were lured by money to support a rival candidate. She was not prepared, she said, to play that kind of politics. Another strike against her may have been her open support for the tenants, which displeased some NP delegates who were landlords. In any event, that was the end of her ambitions to become mayor or even vice mayor.

She also decided not to run again for a council seat. Losing the vice mayor nomination had greatly disappointed her. She was also run down, and she needed to spend more time selling insurance, still the principal source of income for her family. As a council member she was paid only a small amount, about P50 per month, depending on the number of council meetings.[10]

The new mayor elected in November 1959, Lucio Aquino, a fellow NP member, appointed her municipal librarian for four years. And in 1964, the next mayor, Romeo Maliwat, also of the NP, reappointed her for another four years. The position did not require much of her beyond normal working hours and it paid P120 per month, more than what she had received as a council member. The library was tiny and had a small budget, hence running it was an easy assignment. On weekends and in the evenings, she sold insurance. She and her mother were also raising a few pigs, which they sold for additional income. By 1960, she had moved with her children and mother to Talavera town, which was more convenient for her work and for her son, who was a student at the municipal high school. They lived in a small house typical of families with modest means at the time, with bamboo walls (sawali) and a thatched roof. They stayed there until 1972, though they frequently visited San Ricardo.

During her second term as municipal librarian, she became active in a newly formed peasant organization, the MASAKA, commonly referred to in Talavera as the Samahang Magsasaka (Peasant Association).[11] Her involvement began when a friend asked her to go with him and others from Nueva Ecija to the MASAKA's founding convention. The friend had worked with her father in the prewar peasant organization, the KPMP. She readily agreed to join the group. Her efforts to assist tenants while she was on the Municipal Council had led her to appreciate the need for an organization that would speak for the peasants' interests. The MASAKA's primary purpose, she said, was to pressure the government to implement the 1963 land reform law. In particular, it sought to prevent tenants from being unjustly evicted and help them become owners of the fields they farmed. The organization also advocated better wages for agrarian workers and other social and political improvements.

At the founding convention, held in Cabiao, Nueva Ecija, in late 1964 or early 1965, she was elected to the MASAKA's National Council; a few years later, she was reelected for a second term.[12] During the first couple of years, her major responsibility was to organize MASAKA chapters (balangay) in Nueva Ecija. She began in Talavera, assisted by relatives and friends in various parts of the municipality. She got the permission of village (baryo) captains to explain MASAKA. Usually the captain called a general meeting of residents at which she and others would explain the origins of the organization and what it was doing. After forming chapters in seven villages, she organized a convention, which established a municipal chapter and elected officers. Some of these leaders had been active in the Hukbalahap or the Huk rebellion; others were new to peasant organizations. They then worked with her to form more village chapters. By the late 1960s, nearly all villages in Talavera had MASAKA chapters, usually with more than fifty members each. The municipality as whole had more than a thousand members. Meanwhile, Elang was repeating the process in other municipalities, working with people from those areas. After several municipal chapters had been established, she helped to form a provincial office for the MASAKA.

Because her deepening involvement with MASAKA required so much of her time and energy, she stopped selling insurance. The MASAKA paid most of her travel expenses and gave her a modest monthly stipend, although it was less than her insurance commissions.[13] Her librarian post, which she kept until the end of Maliwat's term as mayor, and the pigs she and her mother raised remained her family's main sources of income.

When organizing MASAKA chapters, she and those with whom she worked encountered two main obstacles. One concerned communism. Some villagers hesitated to get involved with something that might be a communist organization or be seen by others as communistic. At that time, communist organizations were illegal and there was a lot of anticommunist rhetoric in the media and coming from government officials. That her husband had been a ranking PKP leader added to some people's anxiety. Elang explained to all audiences — villagers, government officers, and the military—that the MASAKA was not a communist organization and had no connection with the PKP. Some MASAKA members may have been PKP; prospective MASAKA members, she said, were not asked whether they were or were not in the Communist Party. She was not. A second problem was the view among many tenants that fixed rent tenancy (*buwisan*), which was the form of tenancy the 1963 agrarian reform law endorsed and the MASAKA advocated if a tenant could not own his or her field, was inferior to a good share tenancy (*samahan*) arrangement. In the former, tenants had to pay a specific amount in rent each season regardless of the yield; they also had to pay all production expenses, and the landlord had no obligation to give production loans. In the latter, a tenant's rent was a percentage of the crop (usually half), tenants and landlords shared production expenses, and landlords were supposed to give low interest loans. To Elang and other MASAKA leaders, the preference for the share system was the result of tenants "leaning on landlords" (*nakakasandal sa may-ari*) for so long that they had a hard time imagining themselves standing on their own two feet. Over time, however, most tenants, she said, saw the advantages of the fixed rent system.

As a MASAKA leader, she also helped organize demonstrations for land reform and on behalf of tenants being threatened with eviction in various parts of Nueva Ecija, in other parts of central Luzon, and in Manila. From Talavera, she said, she could quickly organize 250 to 500 people to attend these events. Demonstrations in Manila were often staged in front of the president's residence, Malacañang, because the law stipulated that the president must declare a place a land reform area before the tenants could begin the process of becoming owners of their fields. In Talavera, she often confronted landlords who were trying to evict tenants or take more than their legal share of the harvests. One incident in 1966 involved Manolo Tinio, who was still using various legal and illegal methods to evict his remaining tenants. In this case, he claimed to have court authorization to take the land of a tenant who had not plowed his field on time. The tenant had not been able to plow because his carabao had been stolen, something many villagers suspected Tinio had arranged. Elang helped persuade numerous MASAKA members from several villages to show up early one morning with their carabaos and plows. By midday, she said, the threatened tenant's two and a half hectare field had been prepared, thereby undermining Tinio's excuse for eviction. Another Talavera landlord with whom she had several run-ins was Dr. Dominador Ferry, who, she said, referred to her as the "attorney" (*abogada*) in a sarcastic tone of voice. In their first confrontation, in which he insisted that his tenants use his rice-threshing machine (*tilyadora*) even though it cost more than another one that the tenants had arranged for, he boasted that he would surely win. Otherwise, Elang recalled him saying, "'one of my balls will be pulverized'" (*madudurog ang isang itlog ko*). On the appointed day for the threshing to be done, hundreds of MASAKA members from around Talavera backed up Ferry's tenants as they used the other machine. It was the first of three encounters in which Elang's side prevailed. So, Elang smiled, "Ferry has no more balls" (*wala nang itlog si Ferry, tatlong beses pang durog*).

Beginning in 1969–1970, Elang reduced her MASAKA involvement, in part because of splits within the national leadership over direction, policies, and personalities, but mainly in order to have more time for a new organization, the Samahang Progresibo ng Kababaihang Pilipinas (the Progressive Association of Philippine Women, or SPKP), in which she had become involved.[14] By the late 1960s, she was a member of its national board. In pressing for women to have the same rights as men, the SPKP sought, for instance, equal pay for men and women doing the same. Another objective was to get women into employment that was generally reserved for men. She helped organize SPKP chapters in Nueva Ecija, including one in San Ricardo in which the principal activists were women who had been in the Hukbalahap.

By this point, Elang had declined the offer of the new mayor, Bonifacio de Jesus, to continue as the municipal librarian. She was still raising some pigs and she had a little store (*tindahan*) in front of her house in Talavera. Her son Junior had finished college, was working, and was contributing to the family income. A few years later, her daughter Evelyn also finished college and began teaching in Talavera's schools. Soon Junior married and established a separate household. Evelyn remained single and continued to live with her mother; she became the principal provider for the two of them and, after his release from prison, her father.

But before Federico got out of jail, Elang was put in. On 23 September 1972, armed Philippine Constabulary (PC) soldiers "invited" her, she said, to their provincial headquarters in Cabanatuan City. There she saw several other Nueva Ecija MASAKA leaders, whom the PC had also "invited." They were told that President Ferdinand Marcos had declared martial law the day before. That explained, Elang realized, why the radio stations had not been broadcasting any news. Neither she nor her fellow MASAKA leaders were terribly surprised at Marcos's actions. Martial law had been in the wind for many months; the MASAKA had even joined with other groups to demonstrate in Manila against it. From the moment she was arrested until she was released sixteen months later, her guards did not explain why she and other MASAKA leaders had been imprisoned other than to say that they were following orders. The line of questioning during several interrogation sessions implied that officials considered the MASAKA to be a subversive organization, but that was never made a formal charge as far as Elang knew.

She spent two months behind bars in Cabanatuan, eight in Talavera, then six more in the PC's Camp Olivas in Pampanga. Prison life, she said, was mostly "boring—sleeping, standing around, sleeping, reading, lying down." One big disappointment, she recalled, is that not a single peasant whom she had helped in the past, including MASAKA members, visited her while she was incarcerated. She understood the reason why—they were scared—but it was hard to accept nevertheless. Before being transferred to Camp Olivas, she had been the only woman prisoner. At Camp Olivas, she was with other women whose backgrounds ranged from political prisoners like herself to pickpockets, prostitutes, and thieves. After a period of considerable mistrust, she and her fellow prisoners learned to talk to each other and established a close community. They elected her "mayor." The evening of the day in February 1974 when she was told that she would be released within twenty-four hours her fellow inmates gave her a farewell *despedida* (party) during which, she recalled, "we were all crying."

With Best Intentions: Land for the Landless

The next phase of Elang's political life, 1974–85, revolved largely around trying to get Tinio land for landless villagers. She did not plan it that way, but that is where her political interests led her under circumstances that unfolded in San Ricardo and its vicinity.

Upon returning to Talavera from prison, she found Federico. He had been released from prison shortly before she had been. Though he was sickly, frail, and suffering from rheumatism, it was a happy family reunion for the couple, their children, and other relatives. He was sixty years old; Elang was fifty. They had no employment, no savings, and few material possessions. They both needed to rest and recuperate. For financial support, they would have to rely heavily on their two grown children, at least for a year or two. They decided to return to San Ricardo, moving into the simple *sawali* house on stilts that Elang had entrusted to relatives when she had relocated with her mother and children to Talavera in the late 1950s. Their son Junior, his wife, and their first grandchild were there. Their daughter Evelyn moved with them; she would commute by jeepney and bus to her teaching job in Talavera town. Elang's aged mother also remained with them. Life would continue to be simple and frugal, but for the first time in years it also held the prospect of being soothing and peaceful, allowing Elang and Federico's bodies and spirits to mend and for the couple to get to know each other again.

She would not be scurrying from meeting to meeting, demonstration to demonstration. In any case, the political climate of those early years of martial law were too stern and stifling for that. The MASAKA had been expunged, the PKP had sworn it would not make waves, and the villagers generally were extremely wary of getting involved in anything that hinted of trouble with the military or civilian authorities.

By 1977–78, both Elang and Federico's lives had become absorbed again in politics. Although still partly crippled with rheumatism, Federico was tired of resting. He wanted to do something to help relieve the conditions of the large number of landless families he was living among. Elang's long interest in the land politics was also being rekindled as fellow villagers talked to her about their situations and solicited her advice. Many of them she had met while traipsing through rice fields selling clothing to harvesters, the means by which she contributed to her household's income.

Two other circumstances seemed to open up possibilities for some concerted effort to bring tangible benefits to local landless people. The first was what the two biggest landowners in the vicinity were doing with their fields. Manolo Tinio, Elang's longtime adversary on agrarian matters, had died in 1977, leaving his 200-hectare hacienda to heirs who could not agree among themselves on how to farm it or even whether to keep it. Consequently, beginning in 1978, the land sat idle. Many people, including Elang and Federico, began to ponder how land-hungry people in the area, especially the nearly one-third of households that were totally landless, could get access to that huge area. Adjacent to Manolo's hacienda was another 117 hectares virtually going to waste, at least from the point of view of poor and landless villagers. It belonged to Manolo's half-brother Vivencio and his two half-sisters, part of a much larger hacienda they had inherited from their father. Vivencio and his sisters had mechanized this portion in the 1950s–60s and produced rice. But in 1975–76 they abruptly switched to sugarcane and no longer seemed attentive to the fields. Many people in San Ricardo and neighboring villages saw that land as another vast area that local people could use much more effectively and beneficially.

The second circumstance was land reform. Marcos's martial law regime promised land reform on a scale not previously seen in the country. While implementation was slow or nonexistent in many parts of the nation, it was picking up in Nueva Ecija. And Department of Agrarian Reform (DAR) officials in the province seemed to be serious about implementing the 1971 law and Marcos's decrees, including the prohibitions against landlords evicting tenants. One feature of land reform was the requirement that people who qualified as beneficiaries or expected to qualify should join their local Samahang Nayon (Village Association, or SN), an organization being established by the government.

Many in Nueva Ecija, including numerous residents of San Ricardo and neighboring villages, did not take this organization seriously. They figured it would be a flash in the pan, like other top-down rural organizations imposed by governments in the past. But Elang, Federico, and a few others in San Ricardo began to see possibilities for this legal organization, especially at a time when nongovernmental organizations were highly suspect, to be a vehicle for advocating land redistribution and aiding both tenants and landless households.

Federico became involved in San Ricardo's new SN and began attending meetings in villages throughout the municipality. In 1977, he was elected president of Talavera's association of SN chapters. He and Elang helped tenants of landlords whose lands clearly fell within the scope of the land reform law. They worked with or pressured provincial DAR officials (one of whom by then was their son Junior) to speed up the complicated redistribution process. The process involved the government investigating, surveying, assessing, then buying the fields of large owners and afterwards reselling them to the former owners' tenants, who would pay the government in annual installments over several years. Elang and her husband helped to organize countless meetings to explain the land redistribution procedures and assist tenants when they encountered problems with landlords and DAR officials.

Meanwhile, Federico and Elang were also pursuing courses that they hoped would bring mechanized, untenanted land into the land reform picture. This was a major obstacle to overcome in order to get access to lands like the two Tinio haciendas. The laws, including Marcos's decrees, applied only to tenanted land. Landowners like the Tinios, who earlier had removed tenants and farmed with machinery and wage workers, were not vulnerable to land reform, even if their land lay idle. As early as 1976, Federico had been writing to national government officials, including President Marcos, about the plight of landless villagers, requesting that the mechanized Tinio properties be subjected to land reform. In 1978–79, he and other villagers sent many more letters and had numerous meetings with municipal, provincial, and national officials, especially those in the DAR and the Land Bank (from which came government funding to buy the lands of landlords for resale to tenants).[15] Federico and Elang also met with Manolo Tinio's heirs and with Vivencio Tinio and his sisters, trying to persuade them to voluntarily sell their lands to the government. By this point, Elang was almost as deeply involved as her husband, in part because Federico's health was failing again. In early 1979, they worked with local SN officers to prepare a list of poor villagers living adjacent to both Tinio haciendas who most qualified for fields. Around 70 percent of the nearly three hundred people they listed were landless; the rest were small landowners and tenant farmers.[16] At a series of meetings organized by SN leaders in April 1979, Federico told these people about the progress being made in negotiations with the government to buy the Manolo Tinio and Vivencio Tinio haciendas. They were also told that in order to remain on the list of potential recipients of Tinio land they should join the SN. Most did, although several did not, largely because they could not afford the P25 membership fee and P100 annual dues.[17]

Hopes of a breakthrough rose in September 1979 when Federico was informed that Marcos had endorsed a recommendation of provincial DAR officials that the Land Bank buy the two Tinio haciendas.[18] But shortly thereafter hopes fell when the villagers learned that only Vivencio and his sisters were interested in selling. Heirs to the Manolo Tinio hacienda would not sell. Even worse, Vivencio Tinio and sisters would sell only if they were paid in cash. The Land Bank was authorized to pay only a small fraction of the price in cash; the rest would have to be paid in bonds, an arrangement that Tinio and his sisters rejected. In retrospect, this marked the beginning of the strong disagreements and disputes that increasingly divided those who had started out united by their objective to get Tinio land for poor villagers, especially the landless. The conflict became most vivid and confrontational in April and May of 1981.

By that point, a sizable group of poor landless villagers believed that the course Elang and other SN, and now "KB," leaders were following was actually leading further away from rather than closer to the landless getting Tinio land.[19] The KB (the Kilusang Bayan sa Paglilingkod ng Talavera, Inc., or People' s Movement for the Service of Talavera, Inc.) was an organization of aspirants to the Tinio land formed in late 1979 upon the advice of provincial DAR officials. It was to be the entity that would actually purchase the land from the Land Bank once the government had figured out how to buy the Vicencio Tinio property. The KB was led first by Federico and then by Elang. Many landless KB members as well as numerous others who had not joined (again because of its membership costs) had become extremely dubious that the hacienda could be obtained through negotiations and the other methods used by the KB and SN leaders. Moreover, they reasoned, in the leadership's effort to accommodate the government's requirements and Tinio's demand for cash, the project was increasingly excluding the very people who were supposed to be the principal beneficiaries — the poor and landless. The KB, as one poor man recalled, "was becoming an organization for those with money." Others said it was an organization "for the rich."

For several months, these disillusioned villagers had been quietly discussing the possibility of unilaterally farming some or all of Vivencio Tinio's land. On 26 May 1981, having judged that the time was ripe for direct action, more than one hundred families, virtually all of them landless and from San Ricardo, took over seventy hectares of the mechanized portion of that hacienda. They divided the area among themselves and began to prepare their new fields for planting. Earlier they had composed a petition justifying their actions. A delegation from the group had also asked Elang and other KB leaders to join them or at least endorse their objectives. The delegates stressed that the KB's effort to purchase the Tinio property had failed and even were it later to succeed only those with money, not poor landless villagers, would benefit. To get the land for the landless, they argued, they should start farming it, not with the idea of owning the fields but of becoming Tinio's tenants. It was a tense and trying exchange between representatives of the two now starkly different positions. They knew each other well and had been on the same side in many previous struggles. Spokespersons for the group advocating a land takeover included Elang's brother-in-law, a *kumpare* and *kumare*, and several longtime compatriots from her MASAKA and Hukbalahap days. But Elang and other KB leaders were not swayed; they urged the group to abandon their petition and take no further action lest their delicate negotiations with the Tinios and government officials be jeopardized.

The land takeover lasted one week. Then the Talavera police and soldiers from Cabanatuan forced the people to leave the fields and arrested their spokespersons. Later all charges were dropped on the condition that the leaders swear in writing not to attempt anything like that again.[20] The takeover had failed. Many of those involved were even more bitter than before, feeling that they now had two enemies: the landowner and the KB. Those involved in the takeover had learned that KB leaders had actually told authorities that the KB opposed the action. From the point of view of the takeover participants, the KB had in effect sided with Tinio and the police.

Elang has acknowledged that the KB opposed the other group's actions, not because she and other KB officers agreed with Tinio and the authorities but because they believed that the takeover could scuttle ongoing efforts to find a viable solution to a major dilemma, especially if the KB failed to disassociate itself from the unilateral action. The dilemma was how to pay Vivencio Tinio for the hacienda in cash while at same time getting the land to those most in need of it. Trying to solve it had become Elang, Federico, and other KB leaders' preoccupation. In the process, on 21 December 1980, Federico died. His worn, tired, and bent body finally got the better of his energetic and visionary spirit. Within a few weeks of burying her husband, however, Elang and other KB officers had resumed their efforts.

The best prospect, which seemed quite possible in 1981, was to get a presidential exemption to the law so that the Land Bank could pay Vivencio Tinio in cash. For the next two years, Elang and other KB leaders pursued every angle imaginable to make this happen, but without success. Then, in early 1984, Vivencio Tinio and his sisters put their land on the market. Within weeks several buyers had expressed serious interest in the property, among them the Manila Bank and the wealthy Puyat family. The latter reportedly offered P40,000 per hectare, P10,000 more than the price that Tinio, the KB, and the government had agreed upon if they could close the deal. Now hard choices stared Elang in the face. Either the KB had to come up with the money locally or a wealthy buyer would get the land. Neither option was what Elang and most villagers wanted because both in effect excluded poor landless households. What participants in the 1981 takeover had warned against was now happening. The Vivencio Tinio hacienda was not going to the landless and poor.

Elang and her fellow KB officers decided that the least unsavory course was to find people locally who could afford Tinio's price. At least that would keep the land in the hands of San Ricardo and other Talavera residents, including several tenants and small landowners who could afford to buy a hectare or two each. And the local rich who bought would likely be hiring nearby landless families to cultivate and harvest their fields. In addition, Elang and other officers estimated that the KB might be able to initiate business activities that could employ some of the underemployed villagers. In July 1984, Vivencio Tinio and his sisters agreed to sell to the KB at P30,000 per hectare provided payment was made in full by 15 December. For the next five months, KB officers scrambled all around Talavera and even beyond to find new KB members who could afford Tinio's price. By the deadline, the KB had collected enough from its members to pay the Tinios most of the required P3.5 million. The Tinios then agreed to an extension, allowing the KB to pay the balance in two installments in February and April 1985.[21]

This achievement was the topic of Elang's speech at the February 1985 meeting with which this chapter opened. She and the other KB officers had recently given Tinio the second installment and were confident of paying the final one in April. In a way, Elang was delivering a victory speech. But as she elaborated the details of the numerous negotiations and meetings and extensive correspondence that had transpired since the late 1970s she was also trying to justify, and indirectly apologize for, not living up to the land-for-the-landless dream that she too had had at the outset. She was aware of local criticism of the route that she, her late husband,

and other activists had taken. Subsequent conversations with her that month convinced me that the criticism hurt her. She was also angered by rumors that she had personally profited from the whole affair, pocketing KB money for herself or getting a "kickback" from the Tinios. Some people, she said, believed that is how she was able to afford in 1984 to replace her old house with a hollow-block, tiled-floor one. In fact, she insisted, her daughter had paid for the house with savings and a loan.[22] At the same time, Elang understood why many landless people were disappointed and criticized her. In her speech and on other public occasions, she strove to convey the enormous constraints that the law, the government, and the Tinios had imposed on the entire effort. In the end, she was sorry the outcome was not as good as many, herself included, had originally hoped, but she was satisfied that it was the best one possible under the circumstances.

About 65 percent of the Tinio land purchased in 1985 was acquired by households in the middle range of the community's social structure. They were not rich, a point emphasized by Elang and other defenders of the KB leadership's course of action. But they were not poor either, said those critical of what had happened. Most of those buyers already had other fields to farm. Moreover, critics said, ten of the households were definitely wealthy. Those ten bought nearly half of the Tinio land, and five were closely related. Hence, a sizable fraction of the former hacienda went to a wealthy clan.

During the second half of the 1980s and into the 1990s, the KB became a significant institution in San Ricardo and its vicinity. People inside and outside the organization give Elang a lot of the credit for its success, including its financial integrity. For a few years, she was the chairperson of the KB's fifteen-member board of directors, although she later stepped aside. Her role in the early 1990s was general manager of the cooperative enterprises that the organization had developed. It stockpiled members' paddy (*palay*) to await favorable selling prices, then shared the profits with the members. The KB also provided low-interest loans and other services to members. It established a store, a canteen, and a granary with a modern rice mill. These three businesses employed a few of those landless members who could not afford to buy Tinio land. By the early 1990s, criticism of the KB and what its officials had done a decade earlier could still occasionally be heard, but it had largely dissipated as animosities had faded. Cordial, even friendly relations had been reestablished between Elang and most of those involved in the attempted takeover, including her brother-in-law.

The KB was the focus of Elang's public life throughout the 1980s and into the 1990s, although in 1987 she again became a member of Talavera's Municipal Council. Romeo Maliwat asked her to serve when he was put in charge of forming a council during the reshuffle of local governments following the collapse of the Marcos regime in 1986. Maliwat, one of the two mayors in 1960s who had appointed her librarian, had been an outspoken Talavera supporter of Aquino during the 1986 presidential election. Elang had supported Marcos, mainly because she figured he would be more committed to agrarian reform than Aquino, although she was not particularly active in that election campaign. Despite having been on opposite sides in the 1986 presidential election, Maliwat explained to me that he wanted Elang on the Municipal Council because he respected her and figured she would add credibility to his appointed municipal government, thereby reducing the sharp political divisions of the time. That she and Maliwat were close ritual relatives (*kumparing/kumaring buo*) was not a particularly important consideration for him, he said, for he had such relationships with hundreds of people.

When local elections were reestablished in 1988, she easily won a seat on the Municipal Council, and in 1992 she was reelected, though with far fewer votes.[23] In each election, she was one of only half a dozen women running for the council and the only one to win. Her campaign themes in 1988 included the importance of stabilizing democratic institutions and maintaining peace and order. She was critical of attempted coups d'état against the Aquino government and the frequent military abuses of the time. She also emphasized her record of speaking out on behalf of the peasants and agricultural workers. She campaigned with other council candidates on Lakas Party ticket, headed by Maliwat (who was running for mayor), going from village to village, and often house to house, much as she had in her first campaign in 1955. Her organization was built on relatives, associates from her previous political activities, and friends. As in her previous campaigns, her financing came primarily from her own family, supplemented by small contributions from relatives, friends, and other supporters, including some who had opposed her during the Vivencio Tinio hacienda purchase. Unlike many other candidates, she did not give money, rice, or other material inducements to voters or leaders of blocs of voters. Such campaign practices, she believes, corrupt the election process.

As a council member from 1986 until mid-1995, she was particularly involved in matters pertaining to agriculture, land, rural cooperatives, and education. For several years, she was the chair of the council's committees on agriculture and cooperatives. Tenant farmers from many parts of Talavera frequently asked her to help solve problems with their landlords. She explained the options, clarified the meaning of the land reform laws, put them in touch with attorneys, and contacted relevant government officials. Because of her reputation for advocating full implementation of agrarian reform laws, tenants from other municipalities in Nueva

Ecija also sought her assistance. And she was appointed by provincial authorities to the Provincial Agrarian Reform Commission, a body composed of representatives from various relevant social sectors and agencies (such as landlord groups, peasant organizations, the Land Bank of the Philippines, and the Department of Agrarian Reform and Agriculture) that was to help resolve problems arising in the course of implementing land distribution and other agrarian reform laws.

Although she was an agrarian reform advocate, she was not automatically on the side of every peasant who was having problems with government officials or their landlords. She particularly objected to tenants who did not themselves abide by the agrarian reform laws. For instance, she scolded land recipients who did not make regular amortization payments to the Land Bank, who pawned (*sinangla*) the fields they had received under the land redistribution program, or who drank or gambled excessively then complained that they could not repay their loans. She also took issue with some peasant organizations in Nueva Ecija and elsewhere that argued that the agrarian reform laws were virtually worthless because too many concessions had been made to landowners or that wanted land to be given to tenants free of charge. Her view was that, despite its limitations, the agrarian reform laws that had accumulated over the last two decades were significant advances over what tenants had faced in the 1940s–60s, and if fully implemented they would improve the standard of living and quality of life for their beneficiaries. Moreover, she argued, the "genuine land reform" that the far left advocates is not in the realm of possibility in the Philippines. Rather than constantly pressing for something that is not possible, she preferred to press for full implementation of what is already on the books.

Her salary as a council member was modest—P7,500 per month during her final term, roughly what a provincial high school teacher would make. But she kept only a small fraction of that for herself; much of it she gave to a variety of causes for which people asked monetary contributions: P200 to help a village youth group purchase volleyball equipment, P250 to another village's health clinic, P300 to a poor family in yet another village whose child had been killed in an accident, and so forth. Every month people would come to her—as they did to other council members—for aid. Unlike the mayor and vice mayor, she explained, councilors had no budget for such things, so it was either turn the people down (which she also did sometimes) or dip into her own pocket.

By the end of her council term in 1995, Elang was weary. She was in her seventies and wanted to concentrate on the KB cooperatives. Yet she could not bring herself to completely let go of public office. The solution was found when she and others persuaded her daughter, Evelyn, to run for the Municipal Council in the May 1995 elections. This was also a significant economic sacrifice because it involved Evelyn retiring early from her teaching position at Talavera High School, as the law prohibited government employees from holding elected office. Evelyn's salary had been an important income source for the Santa Ana–Maclang household, which consisted of Elang, Evelyn, Evelyn's husband Olive, and their two young daughters. Whether she won or lost, the household would be relying mainly on income from half a dozen pigs and one hectare of land (which Olive looked after), Evelyn's meager retirement pay, and the stipend Elang received as the KB's general manager.

Elang was keen for Evelyn to run. She saw it as a "test" to gauge how voters in Talavera thought of her own public service record because Evelyn's campaign would be pitched heavily in terms of perpetuating the work that Elang had been doing. Elang went village to village with Evelyn, especially in the first half of the campaign, telling people why she was retiring from public office and wanted them to vote for her daughter.

Elang was extremely gratified by the results. Evelyn won, hanging on to eighth place in the field of fifty-three candidates (nearly all of them men) for the eight council seats and becoming the second woman in Talavera's history to become a municipal councilor. Evelyn described her victory as a "minor miracle," for she was a neophyte campaigner, had spent far less than most other council candidates, and was the only winner who was not on the Lakas Party ticket (she had run on the Philippine Democratic Party ticket). To Elang, the win was testimony to voters' appreciation for what she had stood for and tried to do as a council member beginning in the 1950s and continuing in the 1980s–90s and as a political activist generally from the time she was a teenager to the present.

Conventional Views Revisited

One cannot rely on patron-client analysis to understand Manuela Santa Ana vda. de Maclang's political life as presented in this essay. With the material I have drawn upon, it would be impossible to characterize her as a client of some higher, larger, more powerful person or family. It would be difficult, as well, to understand her political behavior in terms of factional struggles and jockeying or of intimidation and coercion. Nor can one readily depict her as a patron in her own right, cultivating clients to follow her and dispensing or withholding rewards to keep people in tow. One hears San Ricardo residents talking about so and so being a *bata* (underling) of another person or someone making a habit of cultivating *bata*. But I have yet to hear that kind of language about Elang—or about her husband Federico. I would not claim that patron-client relations and the calculations that accompany them have played no role in her life. I concede the possibility that they have, perhaps, for instance, in her relationship with Romeo Maliwat. As indicated at the outset, I do not know all there is to know about her politics. But much that I do know does not fit within a patron-client framework. This is a vital point. Patron-client and patrimonial analyses of Philippine politics are not wrong. But they are very limited, a feature that is often forgotten. Consequently, relying exclusively on those frameworks results in people like Elang being shunted aside or important aspects of their politics being ignored.

True, family and other personal relationships have influenced her political life. She joined her first political organization when still a teenager in part because she wanted to help her father. Her election campaigns drew heavily on relatives and friendships. During her first run for elected office in the mid-1950s, she had name recognition in part because of her father's local prominence. When organizing MASAKA chapters, she initially turned to relatives and people she knew from her earlier political involvement. And in 1995 she promoted her daughter to succeed her on Talavera's Municipal Council.

At the same time, values beyond personal relationships and her own material well-being, for that matter, have influenced her political choices. She could have had an easier, more comfortable life, even by rural Philippine standards. As a young woman, she opposed foreign rule of her country, going so far as risking her life by joining an underground resistance movement against the Japanese. Thereafter, major social and political issues in her part of the country—particularly tenant-landlord relations, land distribution, and poverty—deeply concerned her and animated her activities, which were often controversial. Many times she sided with tenants against their landlords. Her prominence in the MASAKA organization not only led to numerous confrontations with large landowners but to imprisonment. Back in San Ricardo after being released from jail and rejoining her husband for first time in more than twenty years, they both soon became involved in a project stretching over many years that aimed to help landless villagers. In that and other political activities, Elang made choices that put her at odds with others involved in the same struggle. Their differences were largely matters of judgment on strategies and tactics, not personal rivalries or animosities. Few doubted her integrity. Indeed, one of the hallmarks of her long political life has been her reputation in most quarters for being an honest, public-spirited person with strong views about social and political issues.

Cumulatively, the themes I see running through Elang's public life reflect a type of politically involved person about whom too little has been written in the Philippine studies literature. First, her standards of what constitutes appropriate and inappropriate behavior guide her use of leadership positions to serve interests that she and many whom she represents believe are often ignored or marginalized in a political system biased against people of modest social and economic backgrounds. Second, she is troubled by problems confronting average villagers— chronic poverty, unemployment, little or no land to farm, and vulnerability to people with economic and governmental power. These are not abstract matters for her. She knows about them from firsthand experience and from people she has lived with all of her life. Third, she assumes responsibility for trying to figure out how these circumstances might be remedied in both the short and the long run. She does not sit on the sidelines. Fourth, in taking the responsibility for doing something, she uses whatever avenues are available within the political system. Apart from her membership in the anti-Japanese guerrilla movement, her pursuit of improved conditions for villagers has been through legal channels, ranging from electoral politics to local and national rural-based organizations. Though for her the political system has numerous shortcomings, she has persisted in using it as advantageously as she can to advance the causes that have animated her life.

NOTES

1. I have elaborated on this matter in "Toward a More Comprehensive Analysis of Philippine Politics: Beyond the Patron-Client, Factional Framework," *Journal of Southeast Asian Studies* 26 (September 1995): 410–19; and "Contested Meanings of Elections in the Philippines," in *The Politics of Elections in Southeast Asia,* edited by R. H. Taylor, 136–63 (Cambridge: Cambridge University Press, 1996).

2. I met and talked to her for the first time in April 1970 while I was staying in Talavera and conducting my initial research in San Ricardo. From June 1978 to May 1979, my wife Melinda and I lived in San Ricardo while we studied political life there. We had several opportunities to chat with "Nana Elang," as we came to call her; to talk with her husband, Federico Maclang, and other members of their family; and to learn about her from other people. In January 1985, Melinda and I lived in San Ricardo for another four months, during which time we again had long conversations with her. Brief trips to San Ricardo in 1987, 1989, 1991, 1994, and 1996 have provided opportunities to keep in touch with her activities. Unless otherwise referenced, most of the details in this essay come from conversations with her and other people in San Ricardo and neighboring villages.

3. Elang told me about her father's Sakdalista involvement. A newspaper article lists Amando Santa Ana among ten Tanggulan members who attempted to "sack" Talavera's Municipal Hall on 3 May 1932 (*The Herald,* 10 June 1932, 1). KPMP refers to the Kalipunang Pambansa ng mga Magsasaka sa Pilipinas (National Society of Peasants in the Philippines).

4. *History and Cultural Life of Talavera and Its Barrios* (N.p: Bureau of Public Schools, Historical Data Papers, ca. early 1950s).

5. *Kumare (kumpare* for a male) refers to a relationship between two people established by virtue of one of the persons being a godparent to the other person's child (also called a *kumareng buo* or *kumpareng buo* relationship) or a godparent to a child of the other party's relative.

6. The full title of this Tagalog film is *In Despair: Sa Kawalang Pag-asa,* directed by Lamberto V. Javellaña for the prominent LVN movie studio and starring Mila del Sol, Jaime de la Rosa, and Ben Rubio (*Manila Times,* 16 October 1950, 7). I am told the title comes from a popular song of the time.

7. Her terminology was *paglingkuran,* literally "to serve someone," and *paglilingkod,* "being of service" or "doing work for another person."

8. My search for records of the 1956–60 municipal government in Talavera uncovered only a few. The documents I found included minutes of seven council meetings between January and June 1957 and a handful of resolutions also from 1957. Most of the matters discussed in these records concerned the municipal government's lack of funding and requests to congressmen and senators to finance public works projects out of their "pork barrel funds"— the term actually used even in documents written predominantly in Tagalog. When I asked Elang in 1979 if she had any records from her council term, she said no. Whatever records she had kept were lost or destroyed, especially on the several occasions when her house was badly damaged by monsoon winds and rains.

9. Besides Elang's recollection of this event, I am drawing on what several tenants who were involved told me in 1978–79, my conversations with Manolo Tinio in 1970, and a few surviving court records from Court of Agrarian Relations,

case no 138 NE 56 (1956), found as exhibits N and O in Court of Agrarian Relations, case no. 2,975 NE 62, *Tinio v. Buenaventura et al.* For more on the struggle over Tinio's land, see my *Everyday Politics in the Philippines: Class and Status Relations in a Central Luzon Village* (Berkeley: University of California Press, 1990), 34–36, 117–29.

10. In the late 1950s, P50 was equivalent to about two and a half sacks of rice (*bigas*) of fifty kilograms per sack. That is, a kilogram of *bigas* in Nueva Ecija cost about forty centavos (worksheets of prices, Department of Economic Research, Central Bank of the Philippines, Manila, 1978).

11. MASAKA stands for Malayang Samahang Magsasaka (Free Association of Peasants). It was active from about 1965 until 1972, primarily in the central Luzon provinces of Nueva Ecija, Pampanga, Tarlac, and Bulacan; it also had chapters in provinces such as Zambales, Quezon, Laguna, and Batangas (Felixberto Olalia, founding president of the MASAKA, interviewed by me, 6 May 1978, Mandaluyong, Metro Manila).

12. The length of a term on the National Council was probably two years. She did not recall whether it was in 1968 or 1969 that she was no longer on the council. Her name is among the thirty-one National Council members on the MASAKA's National Independence Day Program, which was held in Malolos, Bulacan ("Pagdiriwang sa Araw ng Kalayaan," Malayang Samahang Magsasaka, 12 June 1967, 3). Judging from the first names, I would say she was the only woman on the council. Regarding the date of the organization's founding convention, she said it was late 1964. Felixberto Olalia, founding president of the organization, recalled it being January or February 1965 (interviewed by me, 22 April 1978, Mandaluyong, Metro Manila).

13. The MASAKA's funding, she said, came primarily from the annual dues of P3.60 that members were supposed to pay, although many did not. Ten percent of the dues stayed with the member's barrio chapter, 20 percent went to the municipal one, 30 percent to the provincial office, and 40 percent to the national office. The organization's president, Felixberto Olalia, said that irregular and unreliable contributions from members posed a serious problem for the MASAKA. He could make "beautiful budgets," he laughed, "but they were only paper" because he could not plan on actually getting the income (interviewed by me, 22 April 1978, Mandaluyong, Metro Manila).

14. The reasons for and outcomes of divisions within the MASAKA require more analysis than I can provide here. Elang's explanations emphasized some members' dissatisfaction with several national leaders, including Felixberto Olalia, who appeared to them to be aloof and careless with the organization's funds. Olalia claimed that certain PKP leaders split the organization when they started trying to take it over after they were released from prison in 1969 (interviewed by me, 6 May 1978, Mandaluyong, Metro Manila).

15. Documentation of Federico's activities includes: Federico Maclang, Sr., to President Ferdinand Marcos, 17 April 1978; Federico Maclang, Sr., to Conrado F. Estrella, Minister of Agrarian Reform, 2 May 1979; Eugenio Bernardo, Officer in Charge, Agrarian Reform, Nueva Ecija, to the Honorable Minister [Estrella], Agrarian Reform, 2 August 1979; and Memorandum to President Ferdinand Marcos from Conrado F. Estrella, 18 October 1979. These and other records are in the KBP's *Talavera v. Tinio* folder, Nueva Ecija District Office, Cabanatuan, Ministry of Agrarian Reform.

16. The list is part of a letter to Conrado F. Estrella from Federico Maclang, Jr.,

dated 1 April 1979 (KBP, *Talavera v. Tinio* folder, Nueva Ecija District Office, Cabanatuan, Ministry of Agrarian Reform).

17. Because I was living in San Ricardo at the time, I was able to attend the meeting and observe and hear people's reactions.

18. Memorandum to Minister Conrado Estrella, MAR [DAR], from Presidential Executive Assistant Jacobo C. Clave, Office of the President, Malacañang, 21 September 1979 (Tinio Estate folder, Talavera Municipal Office).

19. For an extended analysis of the events summarized in this and the next several paragraphs, see Kerkvliet, *Everyday Politics*, 182–98, 291–93. In that account, and elsewhere in the book, the pseudonym Nora Dison refers to Manuela Santa Ana Maclang.

20. Some of the signed *salaysay* (testimonies with promises), dated 1 June 1981, are in the Tinio Estate folder, Talavera Municipal Office.

21. Vivencio Tinio, To Whom It May Concern, 27 July 1984 (letter); "Kahilingan ng Kilusang Bayan sa Paglilingkod ng Talavera," addressed to Vivencio Tinio, 10 December 1984; receipt of payment, signed by Vivencio H. Tinio, 21 December 1984; Vivencio H. Tinio to Elang, 30 January 1985 (all documents are in KBP, *Talavera v. Tinio* folder, Nueva Ecija District Office, Cabanatuan, Ministry of Agrarian Reform).

22. Also circulating in San Ricardo at the time were some uncharitable speculations about how she and her son and daughter had been able to buy a hectare, making them some of the very few landless who got any of the Tinio land. Most people, however, even those who had clashed with Elang and other KB officers over the issue, knew that she and her children had borrowed money in order to make the purchase. My sense in 1985 and on subsequent visits to San Ricardo was that few people held such suspicions. Elang and her daughter have continued to live in a modest manner similar to that of many other households in the middle strata of village society.

23. In the January 1988 local election, she received 12,576 votes, the highest of all candidates running for the eight council seats. In the May 1992 election, she got 5,935 — sixth place out of eight (Canvass of Votes, Municipal Board of Canvassers, Talavera, Nueva Ecija).

"Rafael" in his pre-NPA days, checking the payroll
as the overseer of Hacienda Milagros,
Negros Occidental Province, 1977.

Changing Sides in Revolutionary Times: The Career of a Lower-Class CPP-NPA Leader in Negros Occidental

Rosanne Rutten

If there is a virtue in the collection of individual stories, perhaps it is as an antidote to overbroad generalizations."[1] This statement is certainly relevant to the study of workers in the sugarcane hacienda region of Negros Occidental. Biographies of lower-class political actors may well correct a persistent stereotype of this hacienda society. A dominant image of Negros Occidental—a province whose population of 2.2 million sustains one of the largest sugar-producing complexes in Southeast Asia—is that of a two-class society with a wealthy class of "sugar barons" (planters and millers) lording it over a voiceless and helpless class of hacienda and mill workers.

Though it is right in stressing planter power and domination, it is wrong in denying workers the potential for sustained political action of their own. It may lead observers to the mistaken view that Negros is a "social volcano" with an amorphous mass of socially isolated and politically helpless workers suddenly exploding into violent protest whenever they are unable to bear their oppression.[2] The spectacular expansion of the revolutionary movement CPP-NPA (Communist Party of the Philippines–New People's Army, hereafter NPA)[3] in the hacienda lowlands in the 1970s and 1980s is often interpreted in those terms.

By viewing hacienda workers, instead, as political actors, and by tracing the careers of some of these actors, a more complex image of Negros hacienda society emerges. First, it shows that workers have made, and are making, connections with power groups and organizations other than their planters: progressive factions in the Roman Catholic Church, labor unions, the NPA, the military, and other government authorities. The political role of workers is not confined to that of clientelist voters linked to planter candidates who merely "jerk on [these] lines . . . and haul in the votes," as Benedict Kerkvliet[4] has paraphrased the factional model of Philippine electoral politics.

Second, it shows a vast expansion of these connections since the imposition of martial law in 1972, when labor unions and progressive clergy intensified mobilization among hacienda workers, followed by the NPA, and followed, in turn, by the military and civilian authorities with an attempt to countermobilize.

Third, it draws attention to the enterprising poor who are central in making these connections: hacienda workers and *empleados* (salaried employees such as truck drivers, foremen, and overseers) who have developed the skills, contacts, and commitment to organize constituencies—and organize them, so they say, to improve workers' living conditions. They are leaders of individual Basic Christian Communities (Kristianong Katilingban, or BCC), presidents of hacienda union chapters, NPA activists and party branch secretaries on the hacienda level, presidents of hacienda cooperatives established as part of the government's counterinsurgency drive, and, on a lower level still, the women and men who perform supportive organizational tasks. In addition, they are the hacienda workers and *empleados* who have risen within the various movements' hierarchies to occupy supracommunity positions, in particular within the NPA.

In the course of their careers, these worker activists have integrated themselves into larger social networks, expanded their "activity fields"[5] far beyond hacienda boundaries, adopted or developed "collective action frames"[6] that set out a course of action to mobilize their constituencies and gain concessions, developed a sense of efficacy, and increased their leadership skills—such that they presently form a large category of experienced local mobilizers with more potential for lower-class political action than ever before in Negros history.

To make this category of local leaders visible, we need to move beyond a focus on electoral politics and the personalistic leader-follower model of Philippine political strife and view hacienda workers as part of a wide political arena in which activist organizations, as well as the state, seek to mobilize the poor to reshape local configurations of power. I refer here to popular mobilization that is issue oriented, that involves the institutionalization of community leadership within the framework of regional or national organizations, and that includes a deliberate "reframing" of people's perceptions about the causes of their poverty and the solutions for which they should strive. It is these mobilization campaigns, spurred by nationwide power contention in the case of the NPA and government authorities, that produced new opportunities for hacienda workers and *empleados* to develop positions of community leadership independent of planter control.

This essay discusses the career of one such local leader. Son of a hacienda foreman and houseboy of his planter, he became, consecutively, hacienda overseer, union organizer, local NPA leader, ally of the military in its counterinsurgency campaign, and leader of a municipal organization of "rebel returnees" that engages in electoral politics.[7] Switching to new regionwide power contenders in the course of his career, he covered a wide range of leadership positions in the process. His biography, then, sheds light on the emergence of new types of local leadership in Negros hacienda society during the wave of left-wing mobilization in the 1970s–80s and countermobilization in the 1980s–90s. It places this process in the context of regional and national power contention, on the one hand, and lower-class community mobilization on the other.[8]

"The Telling of History within Life History"[9]

Biographies may illuminate "what a person . . . enmeshed in this [particular] society was able to do as an individual, and what . . . he was not able to do," Norbert Elias noted, provided that they consider "his interdependence with other social figures of his time."[10] Biographies may also shed light on what an individual was able, and unable, to think.[11] It is the potential to lay bare both the twists and turns in the actions, relations, and perceptions of individuals in the course of their life careers, and (the shifts in) the social constraints on these actions and thoughts, that can make the biographical approach such a powerful complement to other forms of social and historical analysis.[12] Reconstruction of individual life careers may show how individuals maneuver within and across social networks, move in and out of communities, and readjust their social orientations as they cope with social and cultural changes to which they, in turn, also contribute. It may help explain apparently dramatic changes in people's loyalties and perceptions. Tracing in more or less detail the sequence of relevant choice situations, one can explore how individuals perceived those situations, what motivated their actions, how the social configurations in which they were embedded constrained their actions, and how they developed new perceptions and commitments in the process.[13]

Here I discuss a man's life with two related ends in mind: first, to explain the remarkable career of a lower-class actor who rose to some prominence and whose career was marked by successive shifts in loyalties; and, second, to explore how the changing configurations of Negros hacienda society enabled and constrained his actions and perceptions so as to shed light on changing opportunities for political action among the rural proletariat of Negros Occidental.

Social historians depend on written sources that favor elites and top leaders of popular movements; people of the lower classes primarily surface in the state's "archives of the repression" as troublemakers and subversives.[14] Anthropologists and oral historians may cover wider ground:

they can trace the political careers of ordinary people whose actions were not (or were only partially) recorded by the police and other authorities. This allows them to include a wide range of nonsubversive forms of local leadership and action and to follow the careers of local leaders in and out of confrontational activities.

The biographical sketches and autobiographical accounts available on Philippine popular politics deal primarily with national and regional leaders of unions and revolutionary movements from the late-nine-teenth-century anticolonial Katipunan to the peasant-based Huk movement of the late 1940 and 1950s (the Hukbong Mapagpalaya ng Bayan, or People's Liberation Army) and to the NPA and its related National Democratic Front (NDF) in more recent times.[15] The backgrounds of these leaders are mostly urban, educated, and middle class or elite. Local leaders primarily surface through the accounts of their superiors. Only some authors have been interested and able to capture the accounts of lower-class leaders and activists in peasant, revolutionary, and religio-political movements. They rely on extensive anthropological fieldwork, one-time interviews, or written sources such as personal diaries.[16]

The local leader who is the subject of this biography, and whom I call Rafael here, was the overseer of a sugarcane hacienda in north-central Negros Occidental when I did my first fieldwork there in 1977–78.[17] When I returned to "Hacienda Milagros" (a pseudonym) for a short visit in early 1985, Rafael was "away in the hills," serving the NPA as a political officer. During my second long stay in Hda. Milagros in 1992, Rafael was a "rebel returnee" living within the compound of a small military detachment at another hacienda, where he was working as an overseer and from which he operated as a countermobilizer for the military. When I returned for some additional research in early 1995, he was living in a small shack on a distant hacienda in Northern Negros with a new wife and child. He had abandoned his family, was jobless and sickly, and was, in that period at least, politically marginalized.

His biography relies primarily on two sources: Rafael's own account, relayed in interviews I had with him; and other people's accounts of him, in particular those of his former hacienda mates.[18] I took notes rather than tape-recording the interviews since I'm most comfortable with that method and, as some data were sensitive, it was the least obtrusive. Quotes are therefore, by necessity, short.

Reconstructing a person's motives and actions is tricky business, even on the basis of firsthand information. A person's life experiences are interpreted twice, first by those recounting them to the writer, then by the writer herself.[19] Since current positions shape perceptions of past events, it is important to specify that I rely primarily on interviews I made in two periods: in 1977–78, when the NPA had barely started to organize in the fieldwork area; and in 1992 and 1995, several years after Rafael's surrender to the military. Undoubtedly, Rafael readjusted his view of his NPA career in the period before and after he changed sides.

Moreover, in 1992 Rafael appeared to have a ready-made story about his conflicts with the NPA regional leadership and consequent shift in loyalty. Having been interrogated at length by the military, interviewed by the media, invited by a Senate committee to testify on the (counter)insurgency in Negros,[20] and even asked by a film director to sell his life story (which he refused)[21]—all of this shortly after his surrender to the military—he may have constructed a specific version of his life story for public consumption. Finally, Rafael presented himself, in his recollections to me, as master of his own thoughts and actions, deftly maneuvering through the power configurations of hacienda society as he followed his own principled plans to reform society and uplift the poor. This may be the perspective of a typical leader, which stresses efficacy and initiative and downplays structural constraints. Talks with others, particularly his former hacienda mates, provided valuable additional views, which either tallied with Rafael's self-image or presented him in another light.

My own contact with Rafael developed into a very cordial one, helped along by his relaxed, considerate manner and sense of humor. As a hacienda overseer, he had been supportive and slightly amused by my research at Hda. Milagros in 1977–78; he let me inspect the weekly hacienda payrolls, talked confidentially about his problems as an overseer, and did not join in the rumors spread about by other supervisory personnel that I was linked to the "subversive" Catholic nuns in town who had introduced me to the hacienda. In 1992, we spent four days talking at his overseer's house within the enclosures of a small paramilitary detachment in his new area of residence several kilometers from Hda. Milagros. Finally, we spoke for one day in 1995 when I visited him at his remote dwelling in the north. He appeared to enjoy the talks and value the interest of a familiar Westerner in his career. He was serious and straightforward and keenly aware that I was writing a book in which he might figure prominently. I had the impression that the interviews allowed him to justify, both to himself and to the outside world, the shifts in his loyalties and convictions.

Changing Opportunities for Local Leadership in Negros Hacienda Society

In the hacienda lowlands of Negros Occidental, local leaders have long been able to exist and thrive only by the grace of planter (or miller) protection.

Planter families closely controlled, and still try to control, power relations on their haciendas. The several thousand haciendas that the province presently counts, ranging from twenty to more than a thousand hectares, are still primarily owned by families, which live in the provincial towns, Manila, or abroad. The haciendas employ some 200,000 resident wage laborers in total, plus casual and migrant workers. Since the development of commercial sugarcane agriculture in the province in the mid–nineteenth century, planters, and later sugar mill owners too, controlled the provincial government, mayors and *barangay* captains, police, and the judiciary. Parish priests depended on their largesse. On the haciendas, planters could stifle incipient protest and independent leadership by withholding access to work and credit or by calling in the municipal police.

The hacienda overseer (*encargado*) was the prime community leader, with the hacienda the smallest political community. Overseers were appointed by planters, and their power depended on planter backing. Government authorities, political parties, and the Roman Catholic Church depended on overseers as their local brokers and apparently refrained from cultivating their own network of local leaders on the hacienda level. Overseers were expected to disseminate government directives (handed down by *barangay* captains), lead workers to voter precincts, and act as the local arm of the municipal police; they were sought by political candidates as local *liders* in election campaigns; and, on planter request, they arranged that the parish priest would say Mass in the haciendas regularly. Workers, for their part, channeled their demands and requests to various authorities through their overseer. The roots of this local power structure probably date back to the period of hacienda formation in Spanish colonial times, when, according to Alfred McCoy, "autonomous villages were few and the planter served as the agent of the Spanish colonial regime with the *de facto* power to administer justice and call upon *Guardia Civil* troopers to enforce his authority."[22]

Intraelite contention produced opportunities for worker mobilization and new local leadership positions. With planters and millers fighting over the terms of milling contracts and the control of elective posts in the 1920s and 1930s, elite factions were keen to use worker organizations (mutual aid societies and a labor union) as political clout.[23] Where mobilization of hacienda workers took place without elite support, those who took the initiative were messianic leaders who claimed to possess magical powers. Most notable were the former hacienda laborer Dionisio Sigobela (better known as "Papa Isio"), whose movement operated from the mountainous peasant hinterlands around the turn of the century, and, in the 1920s, "Emperor" Florencio Yntrencherado, a former fish sauce trader from the neighboring island of Panay.[24] Little is known, however, of the hacienda-based mobilizers of these various organizations and movements.

In more recent times, the following mobilization campaigns produced new hacienda-based leadership positions for hacienda workers. This holds true for at least part of the province, including the home region of the subject of the present biography.

A. *Conservative Catholic mobilization* of hacienda workers and other provincial poor by the Barangay Sang Virgen movement (1950s–70s), the "Community of the Blessed Virgin," a Catholic revitalization movement that was established by sugar planter Antonio Gaston in the 1950s. The movement attributed the lack of progress among poor families to the weakness of character of the poor, a "wrong sense of values," and "materialistic aspirations" and proposed as a solution a "spiritual renaissance," a "basic, solid re-education in values" by means of "a return to Christ in the truest sense."[25] In the hacienda lowlands, this movement was sponsored by planters, who regularly sent their workers to the movement's three-day Sa-Maria retreats, which were aimed at personal repentance and conversion to Christian values. The retreats were the poor man's version of the Cursillos de Cristianidad, adopted from Spain and popular at that time among planters and other wealthier, better-educated persons. Apparently, by sponsoring worker participation planters hoped to counter the influence of unions that were active in the 1950s among peasants and sugar mill workers and that attempted to penetrate the haciendas, in particular, from the 1960s onward. Though Columban priests in Southern Negros Occidental introduced a more progressive version of the Sa-Maria, the retreats in the north remained focused on spiritual renewal.[26]

Training "leaders for Christ" among the rural poor was one of the movement's goals. Hacienda workers and supervisory personnel attended leadership seminars and were expected to keep the faith alive in their communities through prayer groups and recruit more people into the movement. These leadership positions were backed by the planters and carried status through the link with the Church.

B. *Left-wing Catholic mobilization* of hacienda workers and upland peasants by clergy inspired by Vatican II and liberation theology (late 1960s–present). Progressive priests and nuns sought to empower the poor to resist local forms of oppression by organizing Basic Christian Communities in haciendas and villages. In the lowlands, conscientization of workers through seminars and weekly worship meetings conducted by lay leaders in the haciendas formed the backbone of the movement, and workers used the hacienda-based BCCs to discuss and protest injustices. Supported by the bishop, the movement counted by the 1980s some 2,700 BCCs in the province, with a total membership of almost two hundred thousand women and men.[27] Though it was soon opposed by planters, the support of the Church hierarchy lent it some protection.

Again, special seminars and leadership positions within each Basic Christian Community produced a new category of hacienda-based leaders throughout the province. In contrast to the Barangay Sang Virgen movement, these local leaders functioned independent of planter control, were exposed to planter repression, and apparently included more workers than supervisory personnel.[28]

c. Mobilization by *moderate labor unions*, attorney led, which sought to obtain workers' legal due through court cases (1960s–present). Such union mobilization increased significantly after the declaration of martial law in 1972, when President Ferdinand Marcos made a show of supporting the workers' cause by legislating new minimum wages and expanding the provincial office of the Department of Labor to deal with workers' complaints. Effective government support was seriously lacking, however, and planters successfully thwarted litigation by means of delaying tactics or intimidation of workers.

Workers began to take up positions as presidents and officials of hacienda-based union chapters, but their activities were usually limited to visits to the district office of the Bureau of Labor Relations of the Department of Labor in Bacolod City.

D. Worker mobilization by the *left-wing union* National Federation of Sugar Workers (NFSW), established in 1971 by progressive Catholic clergy in the province and enjoying some Church support (1970s–present). Despite state and planter repression, the union expanded during the Marcos regime, partly by organizing through the networks of Basic Christian Communities in individual haciendas. One of the strenghts of the union was its organizing strategy: given the powerlessness of workers in court, the union encouraged them to stage informal collective actions to gain concessions from planters and to organize for hacienda-based union certification elections and the negotiation of collective-bargaining agreements. This called for intensive hacienda-based mobilization.

The union developed, among hacienda workers, a cadre of organizers, union chapter presidents, and lesser officials. These hacienda organizers bore the brunt of planter repression and police surveillance, in particular when some organizers linked up with the NPA and the union was branded as "subversive."

E. The *CPP-NPA* (1970s–present). The CPP-NPA (or NPA) in Negros Occidental traces its beginnings to a handful of student activists who were sent from Manila to Bacolod City in 1971 on an expansion mission and started to organize among the provincial student population linked to the Marxist Kabataang Makabayan youth movement (Patriotic Youth).[29]

Seeking refuge in the remote southern uplands after the declaration of martial law in 1972, the local student activists linked up with their erstwhile adversaries, students involved in Christian-socialist movements, who facilitated their access to supportive members of the Catholic clergy and to local organizers of Church-supported farmer organizations and labor unions. After establishing their first rural base in the southern peasant uplands through links with several progressive clergy in the 1970s, NPA cadres expanded recruitment to the hacienda lowlands in the late 1970s and 1980s.[30] They targeted in particular local BCC leaders and organizers of the union NFSW in order to facilitate entry into the haciendas. By 1986, the NPA had mobilized islandwide in 586 haciendas and 352 villages, organized more than a hundred thousand hacienda workers and peasants into mass organizations, established 251 party branches, and counted some four thousand (candidate) party members. It had twenty-seven guerrilla squads spread across the island and a community-based militia with more than five thousand members.[31]

NPA influence in the hacienda lowlands began to decline in the late 1980s. The Aquino government launched a concerted counterinsurgency drive, and in 1988 part of the regional NPA leadership (the so-called splittist group, which sought to make use of the enlarged democratic space in the post-Marcos era) quit the movement out of disagreement with the party's shift toward hard-line tactics. The latter portended the nationwide rift in the NPA, based on disagreements about strategy and leadership, that surfaced in 1992–93. In Negros, a large number of leaders and cadres sided in 1993 with the so-called rejectionists, who resisted the mainstream faction headed by CPP leader-in-exile Jose Maria Sison.[32] By 1992, the number of NPA-influenced villages in Negros as a whole had dropped to an estimated 125 and by 1995 to 71; the number of guerrilla fighters had declined from an estimated 976 in 1989 to 430 in 1992.[33] However, NPA influence appeared to increase again from 1995 onward, as most of the government army units had pulled out of the island and had turned over the responsibility for counterinsurgency to forces of the Philippine National Police, which were ill equipped for this task, and as the two NPA factions sought to regain popular support in villages and haciendas. The remarkable defection of the former Negros island commander, retired brigadier general Raymundo Jarque, to the pro-Sison faction of the Negros-wide NPA in October 1995 gave the NPA a further boost.[34]

Highly institutionalized, NPA mobilization involved workers in a variety of hacienda-based committees, each with its own leaders and subleaders. Within each organized hacienda, a select few eventually formed the hacienda party branch. NPA cadres gave intensive local training in leadership and organizational skills besides the standard ideological seminars for the "organized masses" and local activists. The power of the local leaders depended on backing by the political and military apparatus of the NPA.[35]

F. Countermobilization by *military and civil authorities*, assisted by "rebel returnees" (late 1980s–present): In Negros Occidental, at least two attempts were made, with the support of planters, to neutralize the NPA mass base and dismantle its political structure in haciendas and villages. The first was initiated by the provincial commander of the Philippine Constabulary and Integrated National Police (PC-INP), Col. Miguel Coronel, during the early years of the Aquino administration in the absence of a nationwide counterinsurgency plan. Coronel tried to recapture the "hearts and minds" of NPA supporters through a massive campaign of anticommunist propaganda and selective terror by PC and paramilitary personnel.[36]

The second attempt was led by the army and was part of a nationwide strategy of community-based countermobilization, coupled with an amnesty program. So-called Special Operations Teams were trained in psychological warfare and approached the NPA's civilian mass base with a mixture of persuasion and tacit coercion. The Special Operations Teams combined forced community "mass surrenders" with civic action, a strong military presence, recruitment of a local paramilitary force, and funding of livelihood projects for rebel returnees. The army coordinated this relatively nonviolent approach toward civilians with violent offensives against suspected guerrilla fighters. In 1987–94, almost twelve thousand "rebels" surrendered to the authorities, according to police sources, including party members, mass activists, and sympathizers.[37]

Several local NPA leaders who were either captured by or surrendered to the military became an important asset in this countermobilization campaign. Cooperating with the military by force or choice, they provided essential intelligence information and facilitated the official — though not always actual — surrender of their former constituencies.[38] Government-funded cooperative livelihood projects for rebel returnees provided some new leadership positions in the haciendas, which were backed by government agencies.

To summarize, prior to the 1960s, hacienda-based positions of local leaders were primarily backed by the planter, in particular the positions of hacienda overseer and local leader of the short-lived conservative Catholic Barangay Sang Virgen. By the 1970s, mobilization by labor unions and progressive clergy had produced local leadership positions for workers independent of, and contentious toward, their individual planters. Backing by unions and Church could not guarantee protection from planter repression, however, and hacienda overseers remained influential executives of planter power. As the NPA gained control in many parts of the hacienda lowlands in the early and mid-1980s, hacienda workers developed positions of power within the political structure of the NPA. Eventually, the armed force and punitive capacity of the NPA neutralized the power of hacienda overseers, limited planter repression, and more or less guaranteed the effective exercise of power by its hacienda-based leaders, which involved gaining concessions from planters in the form of wage increases or subsistence farm lots. Government counterinsurgency programs in the late 1980s and early 1990s, in turn, isolated local leaders from the NPA's political and military organizations while creating new positions of some influence for rebel returnees and others.

The Setting

The locus of the present case is a municipality some twenty kilometers from the provincial capital Bacolod City in the heart of the province's sugar belt. The town itself bears marks of the recent history of contention in the area, and some of its spaces have gained particular significance. A small *convento* next to the Roman Catholic church and presbytery, built in the 1970s for progressive nuns active in the Basic Christian Communities program, has been abandoned. The Ave Marias currently transmitted loudly in the early mornings over the town and surrounding haciendas by a sound system connected to the bell tower signal the Church's return to a more conservative practice of the faith.

In the 1980s, several suspected NPA organizers suffered torture at the police station in the Town Hall. On the cement pavement next door, bodies of suspected NPA sympathizers were carelessly dumped by the military for identification and public warning. At the marketplace, a chief of police was killed by NPA snipers while having coffee, and NPA supporters painted slogans on the walls at night, later covered with anti-NPA posters by police. The plaza, where hacienda workers traditionally converged for Catholic processions and patronage-type election rallies, became for several years also a space for left-wing rallies where hacienda worker crowds provided a show of strength with clenched fists raised and red banners waving. In the late 1980s, military jeeps, trucks, and an armored vehicle from the nearby military detachment were added to the regular traffic around the plaza. Today, the office of the left-wing union NFSW sits precariously in a side street, with military informers lounging at *sari-sari* stores nearby.

Hacienda Milagros, located several kilometers from the town center and bordered on all sides by other haciendas, is owned by a family corporation consisting of four siblings. It is managed by one of these siblings (henceforth called "the planter"), who lives in Bacolod City. It covers 134 hectares, and has some sixty families living and working on its land as *dumaan* (resident workers) and *empleados*. They form clusters of extended families. They share a history of worker mobilization, which, in their own view, involves a chronological link between organization by the Church, the left-wing union, and the NPA. What has reinforced this view is that several local leaders moved through these institutions and pulled at least part of their constituencies with them. Rafael was one of them.

From Houseboy to Hacienda Overseer: Gaining Power as a Planter's Dependent

Rafael was born around 1949 in Hda. Milagros. His father was a hacienda truck driver who hauled cane to the sugar *centrals* in the area and later became a foreman (*cabo*) when his hand was paralyzed. His mother was an occasional field laborer in the hacienda, with a small trade on the side, selling snacks and palm wine to migrant workers during the milling season. Both parents were born in nearby haciendas and had moved to Hda. Milagros in 1937 after their marriage, invited by a close relative, in search of better labor conditions. They enjoyed some social prominence in the hacienda: Rafael's father was an *empleado* with a secure wage income year-round and some authority as a foreman, and he owned a small statue of San Roque, which was carried around the hacienda in a procession during San Roque's feast day every August.

Still, the family was part of the hacienda worker population. Rafael's mother and siblings worked in the cane fields as wage laborers. The family lived in a small bamboo house with a thatched roof (provided by the planter) similar to those of worker families. His siblings' career opportunities were as limited as those of worker children: they had only a few years' elementary education (except the younger ones, as Rafael's overseer salary paid for their high school education), and they became either hacienda laborers in Milagros or housemaids or factory workers in Manila. Rafael himself had reached only fifth grade in elementary school.

Rafael's upward mobility was based on his parents' loyal service to the planter as well as his own talents. At sixteen, he was employed as "houseboy" at the planter's family home in Bacolod City. Intelligent but physically frail and unable to do strenuous work, he was later appointed foreman in Hda. Milagros and promoted to the position of overseer in the early 1970s. He was in his early twenties then and would soon marry a young woman from Milagros of hacienda worker background.

The position of overseer in Hda. Milagros had long been occupied by a poor relative of the planter, Tio Pedeng (a first cousin of the planter's mother). It was apparently common practice for planters to place a some-what poorer relative in the hacienda to manage daily affairs and ensure good communication with the planter and efficient control of the work-ers. Lower-class and poorly educated locals were seldom chosen. For twenty-four years, Tio Pedeng was the undisputed power figure in the hacienda. From the modest "big house" (*balay dako*) in the hacienda's cen-ter, where he lived with his family, he monopolized contacts between workers and the planter (all requests for wage advances had to pass through him), occasionally shouted at workers who had a complaint about labor conditions or income (and thereby smothered their protests), and carried a handgun when supervising work in the fields (though workers later recounted that he never used it). His wife monopolized the retail trade in the hacienda by pressuring several women workers who had tiny stores at home to stop their trade. Considered a kind man by some, the overseer was generally feared and "respected." Workers knew he could call in the planter and municipal police to deal with workers who were *reklamador*. In the 1960s, workers tended to blame periods of extreme poverty in the hacienda on the overseer's mismanagement of funds, but they were hesitant to complain to the planter about him. Overseer Pedeng finally migrated with his family to the United States in the early 1970s, facilitated by his status as a U.S. Army veteran.

By appointing Rafael as the new overseer, the planter opened up this leadership position to local families. He had a specific reason for doing so: he preferred a trustworthy lower-class employee with little formal schooling, he later explained to me, in order to avoid being deceived. Apparently, Tio Pedeng had claimed several hectares of the planter's land as his own, often serving as a dummy for the planter in registering the ownership of that land.

As the overseer, Rafael functioned as a channel through which the planter, government, and Church sought to reach the workers. He dele-gated, supervised, and paid for the work in the fields and relayed the planter's response to workers' complaints; he informed workers of coming elections and ensured their participation; and he assisted the parish priest when the latter said Mass in the hacienda. For the workers, in turn, Rafael was their mouthpiece vis-à-vis the planter and the chief allocator of scarce hacienda goods such as rice credit, light work, and house repair materials.

Situated between planter and workers, Rafael's position was highly ambivalent. Like every overseer, he needed to maneuver between the opposing roles of planter executive and workers' spokesman. The previ-ous overseer, Pedeng, socially an outsider, tended toward the first role. Rafael, rooted in the hacienda and with a large network of relatives, friends, and ritual kin among the workers, tended toward the second.

Whatever his own inclinations, workers expected him to defend their interests vis-à-vis the planter. Of the forty-six households in Hda. Milagros in 1977, twelve were related to him through kinship or marriage. He participated in the *tuba* drinking sessions on Sundays at workers' homes, invited them to the birthday parties of his children, chatted with them in the cane fields during rest periods, and so was closely attuned to their problems and needs. Workers generally considered him a "good" overseer: considerate, approachable, and willing to plead the workers' case. Soft-spoken, he treated workers with respect and familiarity.

On the other hand, Rafael's personal tie with the planter was marked by a considerable debt of gratitude. Rafael "owed" the planter a lot, as one worker commented, and hence had to be available to him whenever he was called. But he also developed a friendship with the planter on more equal terms, in particular during the latter's yearly birthday party when the planter provided workers with *letson* (roast pork) and drinks and spent the day in the hacienda drinking beer with Rafael and a befriended tractor driver.

Rafael, then, was a modest advocate of workers' demands who opted for nonconfrontational solutions such as raising piece-rate income by manipulating the payroll, increasing the degree of difficulty of certain tasks. Moreover, he did not favor all workers equally. He was culturally pressured to favor his kin, friends, and ritual kin in the distribution of such hacienda resources as light work, scarce work in the lean season, and house repair materials. This produced factional tensions between Rafael's kin and friends, on the one hand, and the rest of the worker families on the other.

To maintain his position, Rafael needed to maneuver between these conflicting loyalties between planter and workers, kin and nonkin. At the same time, he had to cope with fellow *empleados* who eyed his position as overseer and made slanderous remarks to the planter about him. His ethos, like that of his hacienda peers, was marked by personal loyalties and reciprocal obligations, adapted to the configuration of personal dependencies, personalized access to scarce resources, and patronage.

In the early to late 1970s, the planter sent *empleados* and workers (women and men) to several consecutive Sa-Maria retreats of the Catholic Barangay Sang Virgen movement. These were emotional affairs aimed at personal repentance, self-purification, abidance by the Ten Commandments, and love for one's fellow men, including one's employer. Rafael joined the retreat three times and became the community leader of the movement. He was little attracted by the movement's advice to "just pray" and turn to Dios when suffering from hunger, he later recounted, but he appreciated the focus on peace and unity. He headed a group of Sa-Maria singers in the hacienda charged with keeping alive the Christian feelings of harmony and brother-hood produced by the retreats, and he initiated the singing of Sa-Maria songs at social gatherings and special serenades. Whatever the pacifying aims of the planter, Rafael and other Sa-Maritanos evoked, by means of song, strong emotions of community and solidarity among workers and *empleados* of the hacienda. At the same time, Rafael added a religious-moral element to his local leadership role.

Disengaging from the Planter

A turning point in the career of Rafael was his conflict with the planter in 1977–78 and his eventual dismissal as overseer in 1978, which set him on the track of left-wing worker mobilization. Facilitating this move was his gradual involvement in left-wing networks, a gradual reframing toward nonpartisan class activism, and his experience and status as a local leader. These changes took place in the context of increasing mobilization of workers and peasants in Negros Occidental during Marcos's martial law regime.

Organization of workers into a Basic Christian Community and a chapter of a moderate labor union in the early and mid-1970s produced new leadership positions in the hacienda that were confrontational toward the planter. Left-wing priests and nuns in the parish, newly appointed, opened the doors of the presbytery to hacienda workers and recruited hacienda youths to organize Basic Christian Communities in the haciendas. A worker's son of Milagros and the daughter of an over-seer of a small neighboring hacienda became such lay leaders. Though the clergy first operated through overseer Rafael to gain permission for the worship meetings and to select participants for the seminars organ-ized by the nuns in town, they soon bypassed him as they began to rely on their own lay leaders. This coincided with a more confrontational stand in the meetings. Workers of Milagros began to discuss their collec-tive problems on the basis of the gospel during the weekly meetings of their Kristianong Katilingban (Basic Christian Community) and staged small-scale collective protests against the planter. When the government accused the parish priest of subversive activities, the planter's wife—tra-ditionally in charge of religious affairs in the hacienda—ordered the meetings to stop. Informally, a number of workers retained close contact with the clergy.

No doubt inspired by the organizing experience of the BCC, several workers organized a local chapter of the National Union of Sugar Industries (NUSI), a moderate union whose radio program informed workers of their legal rights and called upon them to join the union to get their legal due. With the union's help, they filed a complaint in 1975 with the Department of Labor in Bacolod City concerning nonpayment of obligatory bonuses. Vulnerable to planter reprisals, workers endured a miserable outcome at first: the planter countered by delaying the court case, locking out militant members, and reducing work for the others. Though the workers finally obtained their benefit payments, the NUSI union chapter slowly disintegrated. Of the four local leaders in this union (all married workers), two women would remain local activists and two men would quit (one was accused by his companions of embezzling their meager funds). With the eclipse of the NUSI in the hacienda, the local lay leaders began to organize the workers of Milagros for the left-wing labor union NFSW, which was supported by left-wing clergy.

Rafael was sandwiched between workers' attempts at class mobilization and the planter's attempts to repress it. Moreover, his kin, close friends, and fellow *empleados* took the planter's side. They viewed unionization as a threat to the overseer, on whom they depended for a few meager privileges and whom they felt obliged to support. The rift between Rafael's circle and the other workers deepened. Slander and veiled threats were hurled to and fro. Rafael's faction warned workers that their contacts with the "subversive" nuns in town would lead to trouble. The organized workers, on the other hand, labeled the people of Rafael's faction as being "on the side of the *amo*" (master, employer).

Rafael himself performed a balancing act between the different interest groups. He implemented the minimum repressive measures that the planter expected of him as an overseer but did not interfere with the actual mobilizing work. He distanced himself from the worship meetings of the Basic Christian Community in the hacienda when the lay leaders moved from God and the gospel to labor conditions and the right to organize, but he did not actively move against them. He did refuse work to militant NUSI members in the hacienda when ordered to do so by the planter. But he did not try to stop the subsequent organizing by the left-wing NFSW.

The sugar crisis of 1976–79 posed new dilemmas for Rafael. In 1977–78, the planter passed on his losses to the workers and lowered laborers' rice credits, work assignments, and wages. Every payday, Rafael had bad news for the workers who converged at his house. He felt extremely distressed about it, which made his head reel, he said. He tried to help them by tinkering with the payroll and suggesting, unsuccessfully, that *empleados* share part of their wages (including his own) with the workers. He felt responsible for improving worker conditions but helpless to do so. Protest against the planter did not yet figure in his repertoire. He just felt like knocking off.

Moreover, the sugar crisis led to management changes that cost Rafael his job. Pressured to rationalize the production process, the planter attracted new management to improve production methods, reduce labor costs, and exercise greater control over the work performed. He appointed an administrator with a college degree in agriculture and early in 1978 a new overseer with a high school education; both were newcomers to the hacienda. Rafael, with only a few years of elementary education, was demoted to foreman.

Faced with many collective complaints and actions in the hacienda at that time, the planter began to reprimand Rafael for not sufficiently controlling the laborers, and he decided to employ a security guard—with blue uniform, rifle, and all—to guard his property against possible theft and destruction and to keep an eye on the workers. While living in the hacienda, the guard and his family were soon incorporated into the worker community and his activities were mostly limited to loitering.

A crisis of loyalty preceded Rafael's demotion to foreman. As the planter had accused him of various wrongdoings, Rafael's initial concern was to repair the relationship. When the planter gradually shifted most of the overseer's tasks to the security guard (before the new overseer was appointed), Rafael and his kin group directed their anger at this alleged competitor and a truck driver suspected of spreading slander about Rafael. Relations were tense in the hacienda; everyone was speculating about Rafael's position. In the evenings, Rafael would discuss his plight with trusted persons or get himself soundly drunk to escape the rumors. He mellowed toward the planter when the latter approached him in a friendly manner, and he accepted his demotion on the condition that he would retain his salary. When the planter gradually lowered his salary, however, Rafael and his kin group felt thoroughly humiliated, and his mother referred to the planter as "kicking" them all.

In this period in Hda. Milagros, new social networks and ideological frames were available through which Rafael could express and address his grievances. The standard option for employees in case of a "misunderstanding" with a planter had been to move out and settle elsewhere. Instead, Rafael sought contact with the clergy's lay leaders at the *convento*, through a befriended overseer of a neighboring hacienda whose daughter was a lay leader herself, and he moved closer to the teenaged lay leader in Milagros. The lay leaders assured him that the organized workers in the hacienda would support him if he lost his job.

Ideologically, he was attracted to the concepts of social justice and the collective fight against landlord oppression, which were central to the "conscientization" efforts of clergy and the left-wing union. Soon Rafael began to invite lay leaders to hold seminars in the hacienda about workers' rights, and he signed up for the nuns' seminars in town, bringing *empleados* along. The nuns and the NFSW considered his shift to the left a great success, and they asked him to help them carry out their expansion program. Rafael became a part-time union organizer in the hacienda and its surroundings.

When the planter had him locked up in the provincial jail in 1979 on charges of padding the payroll, Rafael cut his ties with him completely. Set free when the union posted bail, he returned to the hacienda, quit his position as foreman, became a full-time union organizer, and moved from the planter's payroll to that of the union. His support for workers' protests incited the planter to accuse him of the burning of a hectare of cane field (the action was planned by the union, but Rafael denied personal responsibility) and theft from the warehouse.

The factional rift between Rafael's kin and nonkin in the hacienda dissolved as Rafael moved closer to the progressive clergy and the NFSW. His relatives, perceiving his demotion and imprisonment as an insult to the whole kin group, and having lost their preferential access to scarce hacienda resources, had little reason to remain loyal to the planter, and their interests now coincided with those of the other workers. Eventually they all joined the NFSW.

From Union Organizer to NPA Party Boss

Rafael rose from the position of union organizer to the powerful post of district secretary of the underground movement, following a career path already laid out by the NPA when Rafael made his choices. The trailblazers were the clergy's lay leaders in the parish, who formed a tightly knit group of committed hacienda-born organizers. These young men and women first doubled as union organizers for the NFSW, with the nuns' blessings. They regularly assembled at the nuns' *convento*, discussed the frustrated attempts of workers to gain concessions from planters, talked about "genuine liberation," and developed contacts with student activists and NPA organizers. Eventually, and against the will of the nuns, they responded positively to the recruitment efforts of their NPA friends and became NPA organizers themselves. Such choices in favor of the NPA were made by lay leaders and union organizers provincewide, as the NPA targeted specifically the cadres and contacts of Church and union in their recruitment work. When Rafael entered the picture, this network linking legal and illegal spheres was already established. People used the term *hublag* (the movement) to refer to the composite of NPA and above-ground organizations they perceived to be supportive of the NPA.

Rafael mentioned to me the following reasons for entering the *hublag*: his keen awareness of *inhustisya* (injustice), in particular the poverty of the workers and the failure of the authorities to respect the rights of the poor; the inability of the progressive clergy to show convincingly how to change the system of oppression; and the persistent recruitment efforts of one man, a lay Church leader and union organizer from another hacienda who became an NPA organizer and eventually recruited Rafael for his team.

According to his own account, Rafael began to work for the NPA in 1978 above ground through the union, organizing in Hda. Milagros and surrounding haciendas. He took his oath of allegiance to the party (CPP) as a candidate member in the late 1970s and went underground in 1984. After heading a party section committee, he was promoted to the position of secretary of a district committee, the district to which Hda. Milagros also belonged (a section covers one municipality, a district three to five municipalities). As such, he could attend the meetings of the Regional Party Committee.

When still a union organizer, Rafael was instrumental in expanding and consolidating the union membership in the hacienda, developed earlier by the lay leader and several union activists. He focused on the youth and those who had initially opposed the union, including his own relatives and fellow *empleados*. He soon began to organize for the revolutionary *hublag* as well. Under his leadership, the hacienda was by the early 1980s one of the most successfully "consolidated" haciendas in the municipality.

Banking on his social status as a former overseer and his moral prestige as a former Sa-Maria leader, and using his pivotal position in a large kin group and in dense cross-community networks as well as his charisma as a soft-spoken, trustworthy leader, Rafael was a skilled organizer. He was, for instance, a persuasive speaker at the ideological seminars of the NPA, which were held regularly in one of the hacienda houses. These were intensive social affairs that lasted from one day to more than three, live-in. The seminars—which ranged from beginner to advanced stages and were based on standard texts provided by the NPA leadership— were the primary means of introducing people, by stages, deeper into the movement. With Rafael as one of the main seminar *instructors*, who also personally invited people to participate, initially hesitant people were pulled over the threshold. He was also instrumental in inviting interested adults and youths to take up tasks in the movement.

Besides using organizing methods devised by the NPA leadership, he indigenized the recruitment work by appealing, on his own initiative, to symbols and values familiar to the people of Milagros. In organizing the youth of Milagros and two neighboring haciendas, he used the songs and concept of the Sa-Maria serenade (*harana*) but changed the texts to more revolutionary messages that called for unity and brotherhood/sisterhood in the light of the "struggle." Rafael "rode on the idea of Dios," one of the members of the youth group later said. Moreover, in persuading reluctant supporters, he appealed to local values of honor, reciprocity, and familial responsibility. He told an older male worker: "You have grown old working in this hacienda; did you get a *medalya* [award] from the owner, or any other favor?" knowing well that the answer would be negative. Against parents reluctant to let a child join the movement as a full-time activist, he argued that to cede a child to the struggle was the only way to ensure a truly brighter future for all their children and grandchildren (a prime cultural value), thus recasting familial sacrifice and loss as contributions to future family uplift.

By organizing areawide raffles among union members, with festive draws held at Hda. Milagros, he appealed to community feelings but widened this community to include supporters of the *hublag* from other haciendas in the area. Hundreds of people were present at the drawings, including many from other haciendas whom Rafael had come to know well through his organizing work. In his speeches, Rafael would depict the crowd — after the joint singing of *Bayan Ko*, the national anthem of the Left, with raised fists — as "one large family" and the raffle as a means of mutual aid among the workers.

As Rafael developed his career in the NPA, he followed a string of seminars that led into the inner sanctum of party ideology and also acquainted him with the practicalities of guerrilla warfare. At the same time, the NPA collectives in which he operated, in particular the Propaganda Organizing Team, section committee, and district committee, in that order, became his new reference groups and contributed to the internalization of the new ideology, albeit only in part.

He gradually renounced religion, for instance, though he later claimed that inwardly his faith lingered on. As NPA influence in the hacienda increased, he dropped the Sa-Maria music and shifted to purely revolutionary songs. He was taught as a cadre that the culture of the Church was backward and putrid, that religion was like a business, and that it offered no solution to people's problems. Those who continued to attend church were called "backward" (using the English term). Once, when he crossed himself in the presence of regional party leader Frank Fernandez, a former priest, Fernandez chided him: "Comrade, as if you've lost your faith in dialectical materialism!" Visiting cadres made sneering remarks about the many *santos* at the family shrine in his home in Milagros: a Santo Niño, Lourdes, Virgin Mary, Sagrada Familia, the image of Jesus and the Last Supper, and two Bibles. Rafael's wife (herself an organizer) gave away some *santos* and threw away the rest, to the dismay of some neighbors.

Eventually, as a mobile political cadre, Rafael's influence in the organized haciendas of his district covered the many grounds of a party boss heading a local section of a shadow state: taxation, recruitment of personnel, ideological work, protection, policing, intelligence, administration of justice, and moral engineering. He was supported by the hacienda-based party branches of the NPA, which consisted of male and female worker activists. Rafael's power position was backed by the NPA's armed force: he could send armed fighters to unwilling supporters in the haciendas to threaten them into obedience (a standard procedure in the NPA) and to neutralize opposition by overseers.

Following the guidelines of his superiors, Rafael issued directives about, for instance, monthly rice and cash contributions for the *hublag* per household, a ban on gambling in the organized haciendas, or a ban on local activists participating in public dances, which were considered denigrating for women. He selected prospective NPA cadres, and some teenagers eagerly awaited Rafael's letter of invitation. He checked the intelligence reports of the many part-time eavesdroppers in the haciendas and untangled cases of personal enemies accusing one another of being an informer for the military. He judged cases of young cadres having a love affair without the consent of the movement and advised what they should do to qualify for marriage within it. As a district secretary, he performed marriages for cadres in solemn ceremonies, and with his district committee members he had the authority to issue the death penalty for suspected informers (primarily itinerant vendors) and other suspected enemies of the people (in particular, abusive overseers and policemen).[39] He also helped coordinate livelihood projects with "legal" organizations, thereby tapping such organizations as quasi–line agencies for development work. These were the powers and opportunities the NPA provided to people in Rafael's position.

In Rafael's own account, his goal was primarily to improve the lot of hacienda workers by fighting landlord oppression and military repression. The NPA provided the means to do so. The organization and collective actions of the workers, which he helped to guide, provided tangible benefits: better wage deals, subsistence farmlots for worker and *empleado* families, and the planters' acknowledgment of the workers as an assertive party whose interests they should take into account. Moreover, the coercive power of the NPA was used to the workers' advantage: the NPA backed workers' demands by burning cane fields and the trucks of planters who were unwilling to cooperate.

In this context, Rafael formed a mediating link between the NPA and the planter of Hda. Milagros. Around 1984, he wrote the planter a letter, "from the hills," as he recounted it. In it, he professed innocence concerning the payroll-padding incident and blamed the new management for having "sabotaged" him. He ended the letter with so-called suggestions. The planter should, he wrote, appoint an old-time resident of Milagros instead of an outsider as an overseer, provide his workers with small subsistence farm lots, and show some affection for the people of Milagros (*palanga-on ang mga tawo*). The planter heeded the advice: he appointed a local worker as overseer, yielded several hectares to the workers as subsistence lots at the start of the new sugar crisis in the mid-1980s, and continued to pay legal minimum wages and benefits. In return, Rafael exempted him from forced NPA taxation and protected his property from destruction when he was late in giving in to demands.

The planter's son later remarked that his father had a good relationship with Rafael. "If not, our tractors might have been burned just like those of neighboring haciendas." As the NPA consolidated its control over the area and most planters stopped visiting their haciendas, the planter of Milagros continued to visit the place by jeep several times a week, at six in the morning, bringing a bagful of *pan de sal* with him to distribute, as usual, among the workers he happened to see. He claimed he had nothing to fear.

The rapprochement between Rafael and the planter was more than instrumental on both sides. The planter strongly opposed President Marcos (whose government monopoly of the sugar industry spelled financial distress for many planters), disliked the military, and sympathized with the NPA in its anti-Marcos stand. Besides, the planter and his wife continued to feel a personal bond with Rafael despite the years of conflict. Later, when reminiscing about Rafael's years in the NPA, they described him in positive terms as "very idealistic." Rafael still felt a personal attachment as well. He recalled with affection how he had a chance meeting with the planter on a dirt road in Milagros at the time of the anti-Marcos uprising in Manila in 1986. The planter, from his jeep window, had embraced him and slipped him two hundred-peso bills.

Like any political leader, Rafael cultivated a social network of protection and support. As he rose in the NPA hierarchy, this network expanded across municipalities and classes. It included not only the regional party leaders of (urban) middle- and upper-class background but a wide range of cadres on the district and section levels as well as members of the *masa* (organized lower-class supporters) on whom he often depended for food and shelter. It also included provincial union leaders and human rights lawyers from his days as a union organizer as well as sympathetic members of the business community who provided some material support (which safeguarded them against NPA actions) and were called in movement jargon "alliances." Such alliances were produced through personal ties. There was, for instance, an old Chinese storekeeper in Bacolod City who apparently provided Rafael with rice and other foodstuffs, a cassette recorder, payment of the schooling costs of one of his children, and an occasional hiding place in the city. The link was made through a member of Rafael's security forces, who was the brother of the young wife of the Chinese businessman. This widening of social networks, on a lesser scale, was also true of low-level activists in the hacienda.

In addition, Rafael developed a support network of close relatives and friends within the movement. His wife became a local organizer and seminar instructor. A sister-in-law became a youth organizer in the hacienda, was a talented instructor, and eventually became a full-time member of the District Education Committee. His younger brother suc-ceeded her as youth organizer and eventually rose to the position of provincial head of a theater group linked to the movement. Another sis-ter-in-law became the head of the women's group in the hacienda. Sons of friends acted as armed guards for Rafael and other NPA visitors to the hacienda and were eventually recruited as full-time guerrilla soldiers or snipers. Daughters of friends were recruited as youth organizers and financial officers. This resembles the particularistic style of Philippine political practice. But, like other NPA organizers in the hacienda, Rafael soon moved beyond his trusted circle, following the NPA policy of gain-ing the support or compliance of all the members of a community.

Though poor and propertyless, always on the move, depending on a small allowance and whatever food people were willilng to offer him, and with a wife who worked in the cane fields to support the family, Rafael was still widely viewed as a man of power. People of Milagros valued his positive leadership traits, his charisma and kindness, and willingly gave him rice, sugar, and coffee whenever a courier relayed his requests. But some also mentioned negative traits generally attributed to powerful males in Philippine politics: favoritism and illicit affairs, both explicitly condemned by the movement. Some alleged that he had indulged in a love affair with a hacienda girl working at the NPA's district level, that his relatives were favored in the allocation of workers' farmlots, and that his wife profited from his access to financial support and regularly returned home from the town market carrying "a large can of powdered milk and a kilo of pork," as a female worker recalled with envy.

Broker or Party Agent? Conflict with the NPA Leadership

Strategic differences that began to split the NPA in the post-Marcos period — between those opting for a continued rural people's war, those placing more emphasis on an urban insurrectionary approach, and those insisting on more participation in the legal political sphere—came to a head in Negros after the collapse of the nationwide cease-fire agreement in February 1987.[40] Apparently following the national line, the Negros regional leadership took a more insurrectionist stand.[41] It cut its ties with politically moderate allies (dating from the period of the broad anti-Marcos alliance), stepped up large-scale military actions (raiding army detachments and municipal halls), and intensified its campaign of liquidating policemen and confiscating hacienda property. So-called moderates among the regional leadership, who sought to make use of the enlarged democratic space, disagreed and "reached the limits of their tolerance," as one of them later said.[42] They began to resign from the movement in 1987, were arrested in 1988, and subsequently were granted amnesty. One was Nemesio Demafelis, former secretary of the Regional Executive Committee of the Negros Island Regional Party Committee. After NPA snipers killed one of their group in 1988, some of these returnees formed a vocal anti-NPA lobby.[43]

Rafael was one of the moderates in the lower party echelons and was close to Demafelis. Moreover, he had strong ties with the labor movement in Negros, in whose ranks influential cadres preferred an emphasis on legal union struggle rather than rural guerrilla warfare.[44] His own conflict with the dominant faction in the regional party leadership can be reconstructed as follows.

He joined the NPA as a broker between workers and the movement. To an important extent, he served the movement and used its organization and sanctioning powers to advance the interests of the people he considered his constituency—initially the workers of Milagros and eventually the poor population of the whole district. During his own recruitment, he did begin to identify with the NPA organization as well, and his ideas changed about the best strategy to help his constituents (shifting toward armed revolution), but his primary identification remained with the *pumuluyo*, "the people," the poor. The movement's top leadership, on the other hand, expected its local leaders to be agents, not brokers, and to carry out party directives, not use them as they saw fit, let alone shape them.

Given the system of "democratic centralism," dissenters had limited influence. Party policy constrained local leaders' room to maneuver. In the mid-1980s, however, this maneuvering space expanded somewhat: opting for a broad anti-Marcos alliance, the regional party leadership approved of alliances with "middle sectors" and politically moderate organizations and nongovernmental organizations (NGOs). This allowed Rafael to tap such contacts in a truly entrepreneurial manner in order to deliver tangible benefits to his constituencies. But the change in regional party policy toward an all-out confrontational approach after the collapse of the cease-fire negotiations in 1987, during the Aquino administration, narrowed this room to maneuver considerably. Brokers were pressured to be party agents above all and felt compelled to implement directives against the collective interests of their constituencies.

When, in Rafael's view, the regional leadership sacrificed the immediate interests of the poor to those of the armed struggle, his conflict with the leadership took shape. It was a matter of "food" versus "arms," he said, and he squarely chose the former. For him, the main goal of the NPA was "to solve the economic problems" of the people. His confrontation with his superiors centered on two issues: the regional party leadership decided, at a regional party plenum in 1987, that people in NPA-controlled areas should cut their ties with NGOs that were not sympathetic to the NPA line; and it ordered Rafael and others to disband a hacienda-based organization of overseers and foremen that aimed to gain concessions for the workers through negotiations with their planters.

Both decisions damaged the economic interests of Rafael's worker constituency. In his district, a politically moderate NGO (the Philippine Business for Social Progress, or PBSP) financially supported government-approved land reform projects of workers on foreclosed hacienda land. Probably unknown to the NGO, local cadres cooperated with it on terms designed to retain NPA control over the beneficiaries. "We could handle it," as one of them said. Some workers of Hda. Milagros, including the party branch secretary, were beneficiaries of such a project on a neighboring hacienda. But the head of the regional party committee, Frank Fernandez, and several other regional leaders saw danger. According to one well-informed person, they considered the PBSP (which apparently received some American funding) to be a CIA organ that was infiltrating NPA areas. Moreover, they argued that the beneficiaries were becoming too preoccupied with their economic interests and were turning away from the political struggle.

When Rafael heard about the proposed change in policy, he organized a meeting on the district level at which the party branch secretary of Milagros was among those who forcefully defended cooperation with the PBSP: "Let him [the regional party leader] immerse himself in the masses and experience what such a project actually means to the people!" Rafael rallied the district committee behind him in support of continuing cooperation with PBSP, but he lost out against other district secretaries at the annual regional plenum. Beneficiaries of the project in Hda. Milagros were eventually able to link up with a left-wing NGO to fill the void.

Second, the order to disband the organization of overseers and other *empleados* in 1987 affected one of Rafael's pet projects. This organization was established in the area in 1984 when the sugar crisis (which also spelled financial trouble for planters) and broad anti-Marcos protests were toning down the NPA's antiplanter actions. Its founders, Rafael and another former overseer, argued that workers and overseers should make an alliance to increase unity in haciendas and that overseers be used to negotiate with their planters on behalf of the workers. They justified this viewpoint through some creative ideological work: they argued that overseers are not instruments of planter control, as standard NPA ideology has it, but are in a sense workers as well. Their organization of *empleados* helped to remove overseer resistance against the NPA, further consolidated local NPA control, and helped workers to gain concessions from planters. Such was the effect, for instance, in Hda. Milagros, where Rafael organized a branch.

According to Rafael, regional party leader Fernandez ordered him to disband the organization "because he wanted to incite the conflict between workers and management rather than help improve the situation of workers through a better worker-management relationship." The majority of the regional leaders branded the organization's approach "reformist" since it was nonconfrontational and included negotiation. Rafael kept this disagreement to himself so that the workers "wouldn't lose morale."

He became convinced that the party short-changed the workers in other ways as well. When the NPA began to tax planters on a sizable scale, Rafael "struggled" unsuccessfully with party leaders to let hacienda workers share in the "taxes" paid by their own planters on the grounds that the workers had helped to create the product. The tax income went to party coffers, however.

Summarizing his resentment, he stated that the higher-level leaders "have only theoretical knowledge; they have no experience of the practical life of the workers." Former professionals, priests, and college students predominated among the leaders of the Negros region, and Rafael was one of the few district secretaries with a hacienda background and little formal education. The party rules by directive, he said, and memoranda from lower-level or lower-class cadres may simply be disregarded. To these class-based grievances he added that his superiors and fellow district-secretaries acted "superior" toward him and some expected "high-class food" even if that required asking dirt-poor *masa* for some extra pesos, something Rafael observed during a regional plenum in a hacienda in his district.

Rafael's views were probably reinforced by his close interaction with people equally disenchanted with the regional party leadership. These included members of Rafael's district committee, some of whom would either surrender to, or be captured by, the authorities in 1988, the year of his own capture/surrender. According to military sources, one of them told newsmen after his surrender that "he planned to give up . . . after realizing that the program of the movement is not really for the welfare of the masses."[45] Regional leaders such as Ed Federico and Nemesio Demafelis held similar views.

The final event that added to Rafael's estrangement from the party leadership was the failure of the movement to help him when he was seriously ill. He suffered from tuberculosis and other complications, aggravated by malnutrition and a heavy workload, but, contrary to movement policy, responsible cadres did not pay for his medication. "My best companion did not help me, but my worst enemy did," Rafael said to me in 1992, referring to the military, which paid for medical treatment after his capture.

A Career as a Countermobilizer

Rafael fell into government hands in late July 1988. In the preceding months, he had been faced with new constraints and opportunities provided by the changing power balance in the province. His risks in the movement increased as police and the army intensified their counterinsurgency campaign and as planters teamed up with the military by providing financing and space for paramilitary detachments in haciendas. Capture and surrender of a growing number of cadres and regional leaders improved military intelligence. One cadre from Milagros was tortured and killed within the hacienda in early July 1988 by paramilitary men from a nearby detachment guided by a police informer, a traumatic experience for the people of Milagros that signified the increasingly vulnerable position of NPA cadres. The military was hot on Rafael's trail, people in the hacienda recall.

On the other hand, the government advertised amnesty and some financial help for NPAs who surrendered, argued that with the ouster of Marcos and the restoration of democracy the fight for the uplift of the poor no longer required armed struggle, and provided funds for the establishment of cooperatives for returnees to show its good intentions. Opportunities and pressures to switch "to the other side" (*sa pihak*) thus increased. Though members of the Philippine Constabulary and paramilitary forces were doing the dirty work of torturing and killing suspected NPAs (in particular, low-level cadres in 1987–88), high-ranking police and army officials were providing protection to those willing to surrender, in particular to high-level cadres with significant counterinsurgency value.[46] The experiences of several high-ranking returnees in the province in 1987–88 testified to this. Some of these returnees, moreover, publicly denounced the NPA as "a new tyrant dressed in revolutionary cloth"[47] and formed a countermobilizing network linked to the government's new counterinsurgency program.

Former NPA cadres and the military became interdependent once the cadres were in military hands. Many higher-ranking returnees feared NPA retaliation and opted for military protection. The military, in turn, depended on former NPA leaders to help wean their (former) constituencies away from the NPA.[48]

Rafael's surrender was, in his own words, "accidental." People of Hda. Milagros had different versions of the story. Some said it all happened because of his illness: unable to cope, he wanted to "rest" and hiked to Bacolod City with his wife to get medical help. He stayed at the house of a first cousin, who notified a colonel who was her relative. Rafael refused to surrender at first but was arrested, brought to an army camp, and surrendered afterward. A relative and household helper of Rafael's cousin gave a different account: Rafael had long wanted to quit, and he surrendered to a high-ranking military to ensure protection against trigger-happy troopers. Others claimed that a "treacherous" relative of Rafael, the overseer in Milagros at that time, who was generally disliked because of his aggressive behavior, set a trap for him at his relative's house in order to get the P70,000 price on Rafael's head. Rafael denied the latter version and affirmed the first. Whatever the true account, he did eventually surrender. As he said in 1992, he did so because he disagreed with the new hard-line approach of the party and because his illness and the movement's failure to help him left him with no other option. He stayed for a year at the 301st Army Brigade headquarters in Hinigaran under the custody of Col. Rene Cardones, head of the Negros Island Command, who saw to it that Rafael received proper medical treatment. His wife and children moved in with him in a small house made of bamboo and nipa leaf.

Cut off from NPA contacts, Rafael found himself in the company of nationalist reformists among the military with whom he discussed the ills of the country, he recalled, "for nights on end." There was a meeting of minds. These were military officers charged with undermining the NPA mass base through propaganda lectures, organized mass surrenders, civic actions, and a display of correct behavior. Rafael found common ground in their populism, nationalism, and antilandlord attitude. He became a proponent of a strong regulatory state that would discipline planters and benefit the poor, and he was attracted by the apparent determination of the provincial government and the military (in the post-Marcos era) to make a concerted effort to address the problems of the poor. Apparently, he adopted the views of his captors, anchoring them to his own reformist and NPA dissident views.

In his own account, he started to work for the military voluntarily. When he had recovered from his illness, he recalled, "Colonel Cardones told me I could return home. But I answered that my wish to help the *pumuluyo* [the poor] was not yet fulfilled. I said, 'If you have programs for the good of the people, then I'll help.' Cardones was delighted and said we would together make a program to my liking." Though Colonel Cardones was soon transferred and the program did not materialize as planned, Rafael stayed on to take advantage of the opportunities available.

He became a countermobilizer whose organizing work resembled that of his NPA days. Linked to the Special Operations Team (SOT) of the Eleventh Infantry Battalion, which settled in a military detachment close to Hda. Milagros, Rafael became a regular speaker at mass surrenders staged by the SOT, sought to pressure planters to comply with labor laws, and mediated in favor of government-funded livelihood projects. He organized a paramilitary group composed of former comrades in the movement who had followed him out. This particular group, a Civilian Armed Forces Geographical Unit (a paramilitary group supervised by the military), was, under Rafael's guidance, generally regarded as nonabusive. Moreover, he established a small "cultural group" of youthful returnees, which staged songs and sketches with an anti-NPA message at mass surrenders and on other occasions. Rafael composed its songs and accompanied the singers on the guitar.

Eventually, he became overseer in Hda. Ramones (a pseudonym), a hacienda several kilometers from Hda. Milagros in the heart of former NPA territory, where he lived with his family within the compound of a small military detachment. He remained on the payroll of the military as a public speaker at mass surrenders and paramilitary training courses. Always an organizer, he mobilized the workers in this hacienda to thresh out problems with the planter, this time keeping union and NPA at bay.

Once he defined himself as belonging on the government's side, he apparently set himself three tasks. First, he urged the military to discipline its ranks, treat the poor with respect, and refrain from using violence against the NPA's civilian base, and so he embarked on a *mission civilisatrice* within the military camp. The insurgency, he argued, would not be put down by killing civilians but by eradicating poverty. He told the military that "99 percent" of the NPA members and supporters did not know what communism is, that they supported the NPA because of their poverty, and that the military should help solve the problem of low wages and income. He defined NPA supporters and rank and file not as enemies of the authorities but as people deceived by the NPA leadership—a view that the military's Special Operations Teams also promoted. Moreover, he introduced the NPA's "criticism/self-criticism" sessions among the members of the SOT with which he cooperated to help improve and discipline their behavior. Provincial military officials, groping for ways to improve counterinsurgency methods at that time, were highly interested in the views of Rafael and other high-ranking returnees.[49] In retrospect, Rafael credited himself with causing a decline in military atrocities in the province.

Second, he became a broker between his former constituency and the military. Again, he had primarily the interests of the workers in mind, he said. He mediated the contact between the Special Operations Team and the workers of Hda. Milagros in preparation for their official mass surrender, assuring them that the military would treat them well, which they did, and linking the workers to relevant municipal government agencies for material assistance, in particular the Department of Agriculture and its farm lot project. He made sure that the leaders of the SOT were invited to a fiesta organized by workers of Milagros after the surrender. Moreover, he arranged that captured or surrendered NPA activists from Hda. Milagros (and other acquaintances) would come under his protection, and he helped several to obtain jobs in the hacienda where he was overseer at the time. He warned parents when a son or daughter appeared on the military's order of battle as a wanted NPA and tried to arrange for the child's surrender. He also informed former comrades who were thinking of quitting the movement that he could have their names removed from the order of battle if they would contact him. He helped found an organization of returnees in the municipality and managed to get funding for a cooperative livelihood project for its members through the provincial vice governor. In short, he provided his former constituency with protection from possible military violence and some access to government resources through counterinsurgency channels. At the same time, this brokerage helped military and civil authorities to make inroads in NPA-controlled areas and so facilitated the demobilization of part of Rafael's former constituency.

Third, Rafael sought to undo the popular convictions about the NPA that he had helped to ingrain. Convinced that the NPA was not the solution to problems of poverty, the message of his speeches and songs was simple: poverty bred the insurgency, but the problem of poverty could be solved through government assistance and the poor should claim access to it. He denounced the "corruption" of the NPA, the relative comfort of its high-ranking leaders, and the propaganda that hid from the *masa* its communist agenda. The NPA, he claimed, did not place the interests of the poor first. And he made an emotional appeal to stop the "killing of Filipinos by Filipinos." He presented the same view in the private talks I had with him, and it appeared to reflect his personal convictions.

People in Hda. Milagros were highly ambivalent about Rafael's new role. They feared he would inform on them but also realized that he was strategically placed to give them protection. Their main concern at the time of his surrender in 1988 was the potential for military violence. The hacienda was then still controlled by the NPA, with a sizable core of active members and people in local leadership positions, but the military was closing in. Members of the 331st PC Company, which was responsible for counterinsurgency in the area at that time, used informers or hooded returnees and captured insurgents to pinpoint NPA members in hacienda communities who were then questioned under torture and sometimes killed. This happened to a man from Milagros several weeks before Rafael's surrender. An NPA sniper, he was savagely killed by PC paramilitary troops in full view of the hacienda workers, leaving them shocked and extremely fearful. Three men of Hda. Milagros were killed in other places by military or paramilitary forces.

But Rafael's surrender coincided with a shift in counterinsurgency strategy and personnel in Central and Northern Negros in 1988–89. In dealing with the civilian mass base and political apparatus of the NPA, policy changed from the selective terror of the PC to the relatively nonviolent approach of the army's Special Operations Teams. NPA activists in the hacienda first suspected Rafael of riding military helicopters to pinpoint houses (Rafael wrote them a letter denying this). They also thought he had provided the army's SOT, which took over counterinsurgency responsibilities in the area in 1988–89, with information about their activities for the NPA since they had been singled out for interrogation and found the military well informed. On the other hand, they credited Rafael for their nonviolent and polite treatment by the SOT. Under this army unit, the hacienda residents were spared arrest and torture as part of the SOT's persuasive approach. Though some were aware of the SOT's nonviolent strategy, others ascribed it to Rafael's efforts: "Rafael taught the military," they said, "he was there at the detachment."

Loyalties in the hacienda split, set in motion by Rafael's countermobilizing activities against the background of the power shift in favor of the military. Rafael's close relatives quit their positions as local activists and lost faith in the movement. Besides, they were considered potential military informers by fellow activists, as were other close kin of Rafael. A former NPA cadre from Milagros, held in custody for a while under Rafael's protection and later returned to Milagros, came under similar suspicion. Obviously, security was a major preoccupation of the worker activists in the hacienda, in particular as small armed bands of fighters and other NPAs continued to pass through the hacienda. As the activists equated close ties with Rafael with potential informership and *sabotahe* (sabotage), their contacts with workers linked to Rafael became particularly tense.

Among other workers whose commitment to the NPA weakened under Rafael's influence were several anxious parents of full-time NPA cadres. Rafael persuaded them to urge their children to surrender under his protection, and for them he was a lifeline to their children. Besides, marginal NPA supporters who were not part of the local NPA apparatus valued peace above all, abhorred "trouble" (violence on both sides), and appreciated the accommodation with the military that Rafael could provide. Finally, reluctant NPA supporters, pressured to provide support in the days of NPA control, now felt they had enough backing to openly distance themselves from the organization.

A core of local NPA activists countered Rafael's influence, however. These women and men among the hacienda's worker population were firmly embedded in wider NPA networks, which fostered continuing loyalty. They dismissed Rafael as a traitor (trajidor), claimed that the government livelihood projects were "fake," and interpreted Rafael's countermobilization activities as attempts to "brainwash" them. For instance, they stopped an attempt by Rafael to mobilize teenagers in Hda. Milagros for staging anti-NPA propaganda. Rafael had recruited nine of his relatives to join the cultural group he had established among returnees in the nearby detachment, which performed anti-NPA sketches and songs at mass surrenders and Labor Day rallies. The girls and boys, who had been too young to experience the NPA cultural group that was active in the hacienda before, thought it fun and earned an allowance besides. Claiming that the youths were being "brainwashed" by the military, NPA activists eventually stopped their participation. Moreover, when Rafael tried to recruit two of his nephews in Milagros as paramilitary members, the boys were willing but the activists successfully advised their parents against it.

Still, there was a feeling of loss and lowered morale among these remaining activists. They resented Rafael because he had recruited them and then turned against the movement, because he was now safe and financially secure while the remaining full timers suffered danger and destitution. In particular, the personal sacrifices he had persuaded them to make, as a moral exemplar, now seemed "useless," as one female worker of Milagros said. She remarked bitterly that Rafael had recruited her son as an NPA sniper: "He is now six feet under the ground [killed by the military], while Rafael is alive and well." It was primarily Rafael who had fostered a sense of moral community in the hacienda, with songs and plays that acknowledged the value of sacrifice for the movement. With his defection, an important part of the moral support group fell away. Another woman commented scornfully that she had needlessly worried about her oath as a party member to provide life-long service to the *hublag,* "since now even Rafael has surrendered."

Activists' previous attachment to Rafael and their later ambivalence and resentment are reflected in two images they projected of him: One pictures him as being held by the military, still trying to defend workers' interests within the severe constraints of his captivity ("Held by a colonel! What else could he do but what the colonel told him to do?"). The second pictures him as ideologically transformed, materialistic, devoid of his social consciousness and idealism, "wearing fine clothes," and having "many vices—chicks, drinks . . ." Sometimes I heard the same people voicing both views on different occasions.

There was, then, a tense and awkward interdependence between Milagros activists and Rafael by 1992. They feared his potential informer activities, needed his protection, and risked falling out of the NPA network if they associated with him too closely.

Lider in the 1992 Elections: Factional Politics with a Difference

By 1992, had Rafael entered electoral politics as a *lider,* a person who mobilizes votes among personal acquaintances for certain candidates in return for collective or individual favors. Candidates sought him out as a vote broker and visited him for negotiations at his home in Hda. Ramones, where he was overseer at the time. His own objective was to push a reformist agenda in local government by working the traditional system of factional politics.

Opportunities were favorable for newcomers in the electoral political arena. The nationwide election campaign of 1992—which concerned all elective posts from national president to mayor and municipal councilor—saw an unprecedented scramble for local *liders.* The post-Marcos era had produced a multiparty system in which presidential contenders established their own personality-centered parties. Factional alliances on all levels were more fluid than before (and included left-wing factions), and more candidates apparently entered the race per electoral position than in previous elections.[50]

Moreover, in Negros Occidental, reformist rebel returnees had political clout because of their (assumed) mass following and economic clout because of government financial support for rebel returnees' cooperatives. Gubernatorial candidate Lito Coscolluela, the incumbent vice governor, was an active funds dispenser for livelihood projects of rebel returnee associations as well as other rural cooperatives, in line with national development and counterinsurgency policies. Furthermore, Coscolluela's rhetoric was reformist and favorable to the poor, which made Rafael's own reformist agenda look feasible.

With other returnees, Rafael established a municipality-wide organization of rebel returnees and allied persons. This organization entered the elections as a political machine, with campaigners in villages and haciendas. Rafael was one of its main *liders*. Its "people's agenda" was decidedly progressive and focused on the following interests of the poor: empowerment, starting with influence in the Municipal Council through sectoral representatives;[51] welfare by means of cooperatives, livelihood projects, and full implementation of the government land reform program; and involvement in politics as well-informed, organized, political actors rather than clients of political patrons. The organization, its leaders argued, was principled and opted for long-term involvement in electoral politics.

Its strategy was not to have its members elected to office but to have them appointed as sectoral representatives in government councils, thus gaining influence in local government through the back door, so to speak. The newly introduced Local Government Code provided an opportunity to do so. Though the rules for the selection of sectoral representatives were not yet fully specified, Rafael's organization assumed that the vice mayor had the authority to appoint the representatives of workers, peasants, women, and others in the Municipal Council and therefore focused on supporting a vice mayoral candidate. In return, this candidate would, if elected, fill all sectoral seats with members of the organization. The candidate was the uncle of a former student activist who had been a close associate of Rafael in his NPA days. Garnering only 28 percent of the vote, however, he lost.

Other candidates supported by the organization included gubernatorial candidate Lito Coscolluela, with whom Rafael was personally acquainted because of his assistance to rural cooperatives, and several candidates for municipal councilor, one of whom was a former NPA organizer and chairman of a rural cooperative at the time. The gubernatorial and vice mayoral candidates both ran under the banner of the party of presidential candidate Fidel Ramos, Lakas-Edsa, which was President Aquino's choice. Through the contacts of the former student activist, the organization also linked up with the Partido Demokratiko Sosyalista ng Pilipinas, a small national party, which according to Rafael was "against imperialism, feudalism, and military abuses" but supported the party of Fidel Ramos during the elections.

Politically, Rafael and the organization's other leaders tried to steer a middle course. They made an agreement of noninterference with the NPA and generally avoided traditional clientelist politicians. Some political candidates, who suspected they still maintained ties with the NPA,

shunned them. Others, who tried to profit from their assumed large following among previous NPA supporters, eagerly sought their support.

It is hard to gauge the actual electoral support they were able to
mobilize among previous NPA constituencies. Rafael's electoral influence was weak in Hda. Milagros. There his sub-*liders* had to compete
with the NFSW union, still firmly embedded in the hacienda, which had
its own preferred candidate for vice mayor. Most workers of Milagros
supported the union's candidate: she was a familiar figure in town politics, unlike Rafael's choice, and workers considered her helpful because
she had financially assisted the municipal union chapter in the past.

A specific conjuncture facilitated Rafael's new electoral activities.
There was, first of all, the presence of former local NPA leaders, who
brought with them into the electoral arena vast experience in grassroots
political organizing, an issue-oriented political agenda, an organization
of returnees, links with government funding agencies because of their
returnee status, and links with (former) constituencies among poor rural
populations that had been more or less cut off from traditional politicians
during the years of NPA control. Government recognition and access to
government funds enhanced their reputations and their political clout.
Moreover, Rafael could profit from a fluid political configuration in
which the military and the civil government were regaining control over
previous NPA-controlled areas, and political candidates—from traditional to left wing—were trying to gain access to these electorates
through local vote brokers.

Marginalized and on His Own in a Period of NPA Decline

In 1993–94, Rafael's life took another turn with the convergence of professional setbacks and personal tragedies against the backdrop of a further shift in the power balance in favor of the military and civil authorities in the province. He lost his job as an overseer, quit his work for the
military, and was deserted by his wife because of alleged adulterous
behavior. He eventually moved, with a new young wife and her young
children from a previous marriage, to a hacienda in Northern Negros
where one of his close relatives lived. By 1995, Rafael was jobless and
again suffering from tuberculosis, and his new family barely survived on
his wife's earnings as a vendor of lottery tickets. They lived precariously
in a small, ramshackle, bamboo/nipa house along a riverbed in a remote
corner of the hacienda. His first wife found a job as a cook for Catholic
sisters in a *convento* close to Bacolod City, where she lived in with her
youngest children.

Again, several versions circulated about the causes of this twist in
Rafael's life. In line with his self-image as a social reformer, he explained

to me that he had antagonized landlord interests and been neglected by the military. He was fired by the planter of Hda. Ramones, he said, because he had informed the workers about their legal benefits and supported a mass meeting with the planter to claim their thirteenth month's pay. On its part, the military brigade that employed him became so negligent in paying his monthly allowances after a change in command that he decided to go AWOL (absent without leave). When the military authorities located him in Northern Negros, they gave him some medical and food assistance. But they no longer sought his services. "I told them, if you need me to lecture at [mass surrender] seminars, I'm available. But I've never been asked. Maybe because of my poor health," he said. And he suggested that he made the offer primarily to earn money to support his family. Though the military battalion that descended on his new home town was the same one that had previously employed him as a countermobilizer, the officers with whom he had been close had been replaced by then, and neither he nor the new officers felt committed to each other.

Markedly different stories circulated in Hda. Milagros. In one version, Rafael had sold some sugarcane on the side and pocketed the proceeds and was therefore sent away by the planter of Hda. Ramones. It was rumored that he had embezzled the funds of the rebel-returnee project and fallen out of grace with the military. But what damaged his image the most, in particular among the hacienda women, was his attachment to another woman who by 1995 had borne him a child and was pregnant with a second. Activists and former comrades who had admired Rafael as a model NPA cadre deplored his loss of sexual self-restraint, while his kin bewailed the misery it had brought to his wife and children and himself. Various people claimed that Rafael felt thoroughly ashamed toward his relatives as well as others. According to one of his friends, shame kept Rafael from rejoining the *hublag* when a former comrade invited him to do so. A relative claimed that it also kept him from accepting assistance offered by a member of a prominent planter-politician family in his new hometown, an old acquaintance who had been a sympathetic ally of the NPA when Rafael was an influential cadre in that area.

His social marginalization, whatever its personal causes, took place in the wider context of a decline in NPA influence and an increase in government control over the countryside. His case suggests that planters and the authorities no longer needed rebel returnees as much as they used to, though Rafael's tarnished reputation may be partly responsible for this latest turn in his career. Apparently, his planter employer at Hda. Ramones, located in former NPA territory, eventually felt secure enough to do without Rafael, and the military has made no effort to attract him back.

Conclusion

Rafael's career illustrates a change in the power structure of Negros hacienda society: the virtual power monopoly of planters in the haciendas in the province — epitomized by the position of the hacienda overseer as prime community leader — has given way to a more multifarious power structure with new positions of community leadership independent of planter control.[52] In an effort to break the powerful alliance of planters, state, and conservative Church and change the power balance in favor of the workers, labor unions and progressive clergy set in motion a sequence of community mobilizing and countermobilizing efforts in which the NPA and the state soon joined. This mobilization wave opened up new opportunities for local leadership with backing from organizations other than the planter.

One might say that Rafael, as one such local leader, remained the eternal lower-class dependent, for his influential positions always derived from powerful backers, be they planters, Church, union, revolutionary movement, or the state. From his own point of view, however, he was using opportunities for lower-class organization and empowerment to the fullest and increased his bargaining power as he developed constituencies and as the various mobilizing institutions came to depend on skillful organizers like him.

Rafael's career as local leader for Church, union, and NPA, in that chronological order, was not exceptional in Negros Occidental. The specific sequence of mobilization in his hacienda, as in many others in the area, which had started with the Church, provided workers the means for developing local power positions that gradually became more independent of planter control, more confrontational, and more powerfully backed. The progressive clergy cooperated with the left-wing union in the province, and the NPA deliberately recruited among local leaders of Church and union.

Much less common, but again not truly exceptional, was Rafael's shift to the side of the government and military after his capture and surrender. Personal interviews and reports in provincial newspapers about similar cases suggest that military coercion was not a decisive reason. Coercion of middle- to high-ranking NPA officials in the province appears to have been negligible, as the military were keen to attract captured or surrendered NPA cadres who could broker the surrender of their former constituencies persuasively. Other considerations were in play: disaffection with the NPA leadership, personal grudges, a conviction that the movement was on the wrong track and causing more harm than good, and fear of NPA retaliation because of their own vocal dissidence (in particular after the NPA killing of one such dissident) and hence their need for (military) protection.

Though Rafael changed sides — from planter, to union and NPA, to the military — his case is different from that of the *balimbing*, the turncoat

so common in Philippine factional politics, who shifts sides out of expediency. His personal experience of planter repression and his participation
in the mobilization campaigns to increase the power of the poor and
improve their lot constituted a learning process that changed his understanding of society as well as his self-image and political style. From a
clientelist broker he became a confirmed social reformer and in the
process developed a commitment to the larger class of hacienda workers
and even, though fainter, to the Philippine rural poor in general. Besides,
he increased his potential for independent political action as he developed
leadership skills, widened his social networks, increased his influence,
and expanded his knowledge of the Philippine social and political scene.

Rafael's story suggests that he easily combined his reformist agenda
with the revolutionary goals of the NPA as long as he was convinced that
true reform and revolutionary struggle went hand in hand. He lost his
commitment to the NPA when he felt that reform had been sacrificed to
the armed struggle, and once in military custody he linked himself to the
professed reformism of the government's counterinsurgency program.

With the decline of major left-wing mobilizing institutions since the late
1980s and the related "restoration of planter power"[53] in Negros Occidental,
the power constellation on the hacienda level has not reverted to its premo-
bilization state. There is now among the hacienda worker population a large
group of experienced local leaders whose skills, networks, and commitments
might be reactivated when wider political opportunities are favorable.

The case of Rafael, despite his recent marginalization, suggests the
potential for lower-class, reformist, political organization that may build
on former NPA networks—including links with urban intellectuals and
other members of the provincial middle class—possibly under the aegis
of a populist reformist party. In 1995, such scenarios circulated among
rebel returnees on the municipal and provincial levels, including former
regional leader Demafelis.[54] However, returnees are a mixed lot who lack
a strong provincial organization and whose political clout may be wan-
ing. Moreover, local leaders who are still in the left-wing camp appear
hesitant to cooperate with them. These local leaders, in turn, split among
themselves following the rift in the NPA in 1992–93 and in the wider left-
wing movement since. With fragmentation rather than consolidation the
present trend among reformist and revolutionary local leaders, the
effects of their presence may be felt most on the level of individual
haciendas, where many persistently and almost imperceptibly work,
with varying success, to reach collective bargaining agreements, achieve
land redistribution among workers under the present Comprehensive
Agrarian Reform Law, or produce improvements for workers through
informal claim-making.[55]

GLOSSARY

Barangay Sang Virgen: Community of the Blessed Virgin, a conservative Catholic revival movement for the lower classes that originated in Negros Occidental in the 1950s.

BCC: Basic Christian Community, a community-based group of lower-class Catholic worshippers who hold priestless worship meetings and provide mutual help. Intended as a means of involving the rural poor more closely in the Church, in many areas progressive clergy and lay leaders, from the 1970s onwards, shaped the BCC into a vehicle through which the rural poor could discuss community problems and facilitate nonviolent collective action.

CPP-NPA: Communist Party of the Philippines–New People's Army.

convento: presbytery.

empleado: employee with a fixed monthly salary such as a hacienda truck driver, foreman, or overseer.

hublag: literally, "the movement;" a term used by hacienda workers and villagers in Negros Occidental to refer to the composite of CPP-NPA plus those legal organizations they perceive to be supportive of it.

lider: a local leader in electoral politics who mobilizes his or her social network for a candidate for elective office.

masa: "organized masses," that is, lower-class persons who support the CPP-NPA but do not themselves have tasks in the organization.

NFSW: National Federation of Sugar Workers.

NPA: New People's Army, the armed force of the Communist Party of the Philippines. In popular parlance, NPA often stands for both the political and military wings of the revolutionary movement.

PC: Philippine Constabulary.

rebel returnee: a former member of the CPP-NPA who has officially "returned to the folds of the law" and has pledged allegiance to the Philippine Republic.

Sa-Maria: retreat of the Barangay Sang Virgen movement.

Special Operations Team: counterinsurgency unit of the Armed Forces of the Philippines that specializes in nonviolent strategies to capture the "hearts and minds" of the civilian mass base of the NPA.

NOTES

This research is part of a larger project on the rise and decline of the CPP-NPA in two communities in Negros Occidental. It was financed through a grant from the Royal Netherlands Academy of Arts and Sciences. While in the Philippines in January though November of 1992, I was affiliated with the Institute of Philippine Culture, Ateneo de Manila University. I thank Charles Tilly and members of his Proseminar on Political Mobilization and Conflict at the Center for Studies of Social Change, New School for Social Research, New York, who offered a very inspiring environment where I could discuss some of my research findings in 1993–94. I am also grateful to Lodewijk Brunt and John Wiersma for their suggestions concerning the biographical approach.

1. Alexander Stille, Benevolence and Betrayal: *Five Italian Jewish Families Under Fascism* (New York: Summit Books, 1991), 16.
2. For a critique of the "volcanic model" of revolutions, see Rod Aya, *Rethinking Revolutions and Collective Violence: Studies on Concept, Theory, and Method* (Amsterdam: Het Spinhuis, 1990), 21–49.
3. In calling the CPP-NPA simply NPA, I follow popular parlance in Negros Occidental. Most people referred to both the political and military wings of the revolutionary movement as the NPA and often included as well several legal organizations that supported the movement and were linked to the National Democratic Front, the underground united front organization controlled by the CPP.
4. Benedict J. Tria Kerkvliet, "Understanding Politics in a Nueva Ecija Rural Community," in *From Marcos to Aquino: Local Perspectives on Political Transition in the Philippines,* edited by Benedict J. Tria Kerkvliet and Resil B. Mojares (Quezon City: Ateneo de Manila University Press, 1991), 244.
5. Joan Vincent, "Agrarian Society as Organized Flow: Processes of Development Past and Present," *Peasant Studies 6* (1977): 56–65.
6. David A. Snow and Robert D. Benford, "Master Frames and Cycles of Protest," in *Frontiers of Social Movement Theory,* edited by Aldon Morris and Carol Mueller (New Haven: Yale University Press, 1992), 133–55.
7. A rebel returnee is a former member of the CPP-NPA who has officially "returned to the folds of the law," as the government terms it, and pledged allegiance to the Philippine Republic.
8. Kerkvliet's study of the Huk peasant movement in Central Luzon brings to the fore a similar category of local leaders from the ranks of the rural poor, some of whom rose to higher positions. See Benedict J. Kerkvliet, *The Huk Rebellion: A Study of Peasant Revolt in the Philippines,* rpt. 1977 (Quezon City: New Day, 1979), 262–63. He notes a similar continuity in the leadership careers of some villagers, which spanned consecutive local leadership roles in peasant unions, the revolutionary movement, and government-supported organizations. See Benedict J. Kerkvliet, *Everyday Politics in the Philippines: Class and Status Relations in a Central Luzon Village* (Berkeley: University of California Press, 1990), 186–87.
9. The expression is borrowed from Sidney W. Mintz, "The Sensation of Moving While Standing Still," *American Ethnologist* 16 (1989): 791.

10. Norbert Elias, *Mozart: Portrait of a Genius*, edited by Michael Schröter (Berkeley: University of California Press, 1993), 14, 15.

11. See, for example, Carlo Ginzburg, *The Cheese and the Worms: The Cosmos of a Sixteenth-Century Miller* (London: Routledge and Kegan Paul, 1980).

12. As Charles Tilly reminds us, an interactionist analysis with an eye for the social constraints on individual action is essential to avoid writing narratives that "assume self-propelled units, the explanation of the behavior of which lies entirely in their conscious confrontation with changing environments" (*Roads from Past to Future* [Lanham: Rowman and Littlefield, 1997], 21).

13. Good examples of such biographies are Sidney W. Mintz, *Worker in the Cane: A Puerto Rican Life History*, rpt. 1960 (New York: W. W. Norton, 1974); and June Nash, *I Spent My Life in the Mines: The Story of Juan Rojas, Bolivian Tin Miner* (New York: Columbia University Press, 1992). Studies of "deviant careers" by sociologists of the Chicago School provide a fine example of a biographical approach that combines sequential, situational, and interactionist analyses. See, for instance, Barbara Sherman Heyl, *The Madam as Entrepreneur: Career Management in House Prostitution* (New Brunswick, N.J.: Transaction Books, 1979); and Carl B. Klockars, *The Professional Fence* (New York: Free Press, 1974).

14. Police records in France allowed, for instance, the piecing together of what Tilly calls "collective biographies" of nineteenth-century activists as well as the reconstruction of the careers of terrorists during the French Revolution. See Charles Tilly, "Retrieving European Lives," in *Reliving the Past: The Worlds of Social History*, edited by Olivier Zunz (Chapel Hill and London: University of North Carolina Press, 1985), 22–25; and Richard Cobb, "The Biographical Approach and the Personal Case History," in *Reactions to the French Revolution* (London: Oxford University Press, 1972), 63–75.

15. See, for example, William Henry Scott, *The Union Obrera Democratica: First Filipino Labor Union* (Quezon City: New Day, 1992); Santiago V. Alvarez, *The Katipunan and the Revolution: Memoirs of a General*, trans. Paula Carolina S. Malay, with an introduction by Ruby R. Paredes, rpt. 1927–28 (Quezon City: Ateneo de Manila University Press, 1992); William J. Pomeroy, *The Forest: A Personal Record of the Huk Guerrilla Struggle in the Philippines* (New York: International Publishers, 1963); Luis Taruc, *He Who Rides the Tiger: The Story of an Asian Guerrilla Leader* (London: Geoffrey Chapman, 1967); Edicio De la Torre, *Touching Ground, Taking Root: Theological and Political Reflections on the Philippine Struggle* (Quezon City: Socio-Pastoral Institute, 1986); and Benjamin Pimentel, Jr., *Edjop: The Unusual Journey of Edgar Jopson* (Quezon City: KEN Inc., 1989).

16. See, for instance, Brian Fegan, "Entrepreneurs in Votes and Violence: Three Generations of a Peasant Political Family," in *An Anarchy of Families: State and Family in the Philippines*, edited by Alfred W. McCoy (Madison: Center for Southeast Asian Studies, University of Wisconsin, 1993), 33–107; Kerkvliet, *Huk Rebellion*; Joseph Collins, *The Philippines: Fire on the Rim* (San Francisco: Institute for Food and Development Policy, 1989); Glenn A. May, "Private Presher and Sergeant Vergara: The Underside of the Philippine-American War," in *A Past Recovered* (Quezon City: New Day, 1987), 129–49; and Reynaldo C. Ileto, *Pasyon and Revolution: Popular Movements in the Philippines, 1840–1910* (Quezon City: Ateneo de Manila University Press, 1979).

17. I lived in Hda. Milagros for a year and a half during several periods of field-work in the years 1977–95. The research in 1977–78 dealt with women,

worker families, and collective actions. Starting in 1992, I began focusing on
the rise and decline of the NPA in Negros Occidental from the perspective of
workers in Hda. Milagros and villagers in a southern upland community. See,
for instance, Rosanne Rutten, *Women Workers of Hacienda Milagros: Wage Labor
and Household Subsistence on a Philippine Sugarcane Plantation*, Publication Series
South and Southeast Asia, no. 30 (Amsterdam: University of Amsterdam,
Anthropological-Sociological Center, 1982); "Courting the Workers' Vote:
Rhetoric and Response in a Philippine Hacienda Region," *Pilipinas*, no. 22
(1994): 1–34; "Popular Support for the Revolutionary Movement CPP-NPA:
Experiences in a Hacienda in Negros Occidental, 1978–1995," in *The Revolution
Falters: The Left in Philippine Politics After 1986*, edited by Patricio N. Abinales,
110–53 (Ithaca: Southeast Asia Program, Cornell University, 1996); and
"Religious Revival and Revolutionary Mobilization in a Philippine Plantation
Region," in *Religious Revival in Southeast Asia*, edited by Bernhard Dahm
(Singapore: Institute of Southeast Asian Studies, forthcoming).
18. I used this "triangulation" method not only to compare Rafael's account with
other sources but to gain insight into how others perceived him. See also
Heyl, *The Madam as Entrepreneur*, 4.
19. See Vincent Crapanzano, *Tuhami: Portrait of a Moroccan* (Chicago: University
of Chicago Press, 1980), 8.
20. In June 1989, Rafael and other former high-ranking NPA cadres in Negros were
invited to testify at a Senate hearing in Manila on private sector involvement
in counterinsurgency in Negros Occidental (since 1988, planters had made
regular payments to the "Sugar Development Fund," which financed paramilitary groups in the hacienda region). The PC-INP commander of Negros
Occidental, Col. Miguel Coronel, had promoted their testimony so as to clar-
ify to the Senate committee the actual strength and threat of the NPA in the
province (*AFP Negros News and Features*, 2 May 1989, 6 June 1989).
21. Rafael refused to sell his life story to a film director because, he said, people
might think he was primarily after financial gain.
22. Alfred W. McCoy, "A Queen Dies Slowly: The Rise and Decline of Iloilo
City," in *Philippine Social History: Global Trade and Local Transformations*, edited by Alfred W. McCoy and Ed. C. de Jesus (Quezon City: Ateneo de Manila
University Press, 1982), 325.
23. John A. Larkin, *Sugar and the Origins of Modern Philippine Society* (Berkeley:
University of California Press, 1993); Alfred W. McCoy, "Sugar Barons:
Formation of a Native Planter Class in the Colonial Philippines," *Journal of
Peasant Studies* 19.3-4 (1992): 106–41.
24. Alfred W. McCoy, "Baylan: Animist Religion and Philippine Peasant
Ideology," *Philippine Quarterly of Culture and Society* 10 (1982), 141–94.
25. *The Barangay Manual: Barangay Sang Virgen* (Manila: Barangay National Center
Office, 1960), 2, 6. See also Nanette Dungo-Garcia, "Changing Social Relations
in the Negros Sugar Hacienda: The Eroding Relation of Patronage between
the Hacendero and Worker in the Context of Developments in the Wider
Political Milieu," Ph.D. diss., University of the Philippines, 1993, 169–70.
26. See also Modesto P. Sa-onoy, *A Brief History of the Church in Negros Occidental*
(Bacolod City: Negros Occidental Historical Commission, 1976), 110–13. On the
more progressive version of the Sa-Maria retreat, see Niall O'Brien, *Revolution
from the Heart* (New York and Oxford: Oxford University Press, 1987), 17–21.
On the significance of the Barangay Sang Virgen movement for the development of local leadership in haciendas, see Rutten, "Religious Revival."

27. *Primer: Basic Christian Community (Community Organizing)* (Bacolod City: Diocesan Pastoral Center, Diocese of Bacolod, 1989).

28. For more information on Basic Christian Communities in Negros Occidental, see O'Brien, *Revolution from the Heart*; and Niall O'Brien, *Island of Tears, Island of Hope: Living the Gospel in a Revolutionary Situation* (Maryknoll, N.Y.: Orbis Books, 1993). On planter and state repression of progressive clergy and lay leaders in Negros Occidental, see Alfred W. McCoy, *Priests on Trial* (Vic., Australia: Penguin, 1984).

29. A first, aborted attempt was made in 1969. See Primo Esleyer, "Social Justice and the Thompson Sub-Machine Guns," *Sugarland: A Magazine for the Sugar Industry* (Bacolod City) 6.8 (1969): 39; and John Howard Adkins, "Land Control and Political Behavior in the Philippines: A Comparative Assessment of the Impact of Land Usage Patterns on Socio-Political Relationships and Behavior in Occidental and Oriental Negros," Ph.D. diss., University of Michigan, 1975), 224–25.

30. Leonardo S. Nicdao, "History of the Establishment of the CPP/NPA in Negros Occidental," typescript; Gregg R. Jones, *Red Revolution: Inside the Philippine Guerrilla Movement* (Boulder: Westview Press, 1989), 92–93.

31. The source here is the "KR Comprehensive Report" (comprehensive report of the Negros Regional Party Committee), with figures as of October 1986, a document captured by the military after the seizure of a large NPA camp in Barangay Gawahon, Victorias, in July 1987. The figures are cited in Miguel G. Coronel, *Pro-Democracy People's War* (Quezon City: Vanmarc Ventures, 1991), 658, 664–65.

32. Nationwide, the CPP-NPA split into the faction of CPP leader Jose Maria Sison (the "reaffirmists"), which dictated the strategy of rural-based protracted people's war, and the faction opposed to the line of Sison (the "rejectionists"), which placed more emphasis on legal struggle (using the expanded democratic space of the post-Marcos era) and/or urban insurrectionist activities and which deplored Sison's stifling of party debates. The split materialized in Negros when in 1993 the Negros Regional Party Committee sided with the rejectionists, and all the people connected to the movement, down to the village and hacienda levels, were expected to take sides. The rejectionist faction claimed a majority following in Negros, in particular among guerrilla forces, but it was weakened when its top leaders were captured in January 1994. The two factions staked out their own territories on the island. The split was carried over to legal mass organizations, which became visible with separate demonstrations in Bacolod City on Human Rights Day and Labor Day. The left-wing union NFSW sympathized with the reaffirmist faction, but part of its staff split off and founded in 1994 a rival union more sympathetic to the rejectionist side (the Democratic Association of Labor Organizations, or DALO), apparently taking a number of organizers and organized haciendas with them in the north and south of the province. See *AFP Negros News and Features* (Bacolod City), 6 and 8 October 1993, 12 January 1994, 9 February 1994. On the split in Negros, see Jaime Espina, "Inside the Negros Rectification Movement: Special Report," *Today News-Views* (Bacolod City), 19, 20, 21, 25, 27 April 1994 and 3, 7–8, 14–15 May 1994. On the nationwide split from a viewpoint sympathetic to the "rejectionist" side, see Joel Rocamora, *Breaking Through: The Struggle within the Communist Party of the Philippines* (Manila: Anvil, 1994). See also Kathleen Weekley, "From Vanguard to Rearguard: The Theoretical Roots of

the Crisis of the Communist Party of the Philippines," in Abinales, *The Revolution Falters*, 28–59.

33. *AFP Negros News and Features*, 27 June 1989, 2 September 1992, 30 September 1992; *Today News-Views* (Bacolod City), 13 February 1995.

34. Retired brigadier general Raymundo Jarque said he joined the NPA in Negros in October 1995 because "there is no other way of finding justice under the present system." In his view, he was unable to successfully defend himself against false accusations of various crimes, including theft (on the basis of charges filed against him by a Negros sugar planter) and masterminding the failed murder of an ombudsman. His is another fascinating case of a person "changing sides" within the shifting provincial power configuration. In 1989, Jarque had led the massive military counterinsurgency "Operation Thunderbolt" in Southern Negros, which had forced more than 35,000 people to evacuate. By 1997, he was a consultant for the revolutionary National Democratic Front during peace talks in the Netherlands between the NDF and the government. See *Visayan Daily Star* (Bacolod City), 11 October 1995; and *Sun Star Bacolod Daily*, 2 March 1997.

35. Rutten, "Popular Support."

36. Amnesty International, *Philippines: The Killing Goes On* (London: Amnesty International, 1992). For an analysis of this counterinsurgency campaign in Negros Occidental by its main designer, see the study by the former provincial commander of the Philippine Constabulary, Miguel G. Coronel, *Pro-Democracy People's War*, pt. 6: "Testing and Evaluating The Holistic Formula and Pro-Dem People's War: The Negros Counterinsurgency Campaign, 1986–1989," 647–747.

37. Rosanne Rutten, "'Mass Surrenders' in Negros Occidental: Ideology, Force, and Accommodation in a Counterinsurgency Program," paper presented at the Fourth International Philippine Studies Conference, Australian National University, Canberra, 1–3 July 1992; *Visayan Daily Star* (Bacolod City), 8 November 1994.

38. For instance, one former female NPA cadre helped stage the mass surrenders of hundreds of people in various upland communities where she had been an organizer before. See "CPP-Linked Folk Return to Gov't Fold," *Visayan Daily Star* (Bacolod City), 27 May 1987; and "CPP Men, Sympathizers Return to Gov't," *Visayan Daily Star*, 20 July 1988.

39. According to the rules, the district committee decides on death penalties on the basis of intelligence information provided by lower cadres; in practice, lower cadres sometimes act without the sanction of their superiors.

40. On the rift within the CPP-NPA during the Aquino period, see Gareth Porter, "Strategic Debates and Dilemmas in the Philippine Communist Movement," *Pilipinas* no. 13 (1989): 19–40.

41. *AFP Negros News and Features*, 28 January 1988.

42. "'Majority of Rebels Planning to Resign,'" *Visayan Daily Star*, 17 March 1988.

43. Killed was Jose "Joe" Tanpinco, a former official of the National Federation of Sugar Workers. See "Rebel Resignees Condemn Slaying," *Visayan Daily Star*, 5 July 1988. Shortly afterward, several returnees (former high-ranking cadres) publicly condemned CPP-NPA policies at a press conference in Bacolod City, and later formed the Brotherhood of Organized Resignees (BORN), which called for the NPA to pull out of legal organizations.

44. This stand of revolutionary cadres in Negros labor unions is mentioned in "On the Mode of Production: The Negros Enigma," *Diliman Review* 36.4 (1988): 16.

45. *AFP Negros News and Features*, 12 July 1988.
46. To ensure a safe transfer to the military through trustworthy intermediaries, NPAs who surrender individually try to do so through personal ties. This is a common pattern. Low-ranking cadres seek contact with a policeman or Constabulary officer through their own kin or friendship networks. High-ranking cadres of elite background may have access to higher military officials. An extreme example is the surrender of Silvino "Macao" Gallardo, who was the commanding officer of the NPA Regional Operation Command in Negros in September 1991. His family contacted Defense Secretary Renato De Villa, "a close family friend," who "sent a presidential plane to fly the rebel leader to Manila where he was left in the custody of Brig. Gen. Carlos Tañega, chief of the Armed Forces intelligence service" (*AFP Negros News and Features*, 11 September 1991). Gallardo's grandfather had been a provincial PC commander in Negros Occidental. Some NPAs take another route to cross safely to the other side: they contact reporters of the provincial radio station *Radyo Bombo*, who witness the surrender and thereby provide some protection.
47. *Visayan Daily Star*, 9–10 July 1988.
48. The careers of former NPAs in the counterinsurgency movement often reflected their careers in the NPA. Some former NPA political organizers, like Rafael, became active propagandists for the government and speakers at mass surrenders or joined the newly formed anticommunist union DIWA (Democratic and Independent Workers Association) as organizers. Some former fighters or snipers joined paramilitary teams, including the notorious Eagle Squad of Bacolod City's Police Chief Nick Torres. Others joined the ranks of police informers and loitered at bus stations, jeepney stands, and the Bacolod passenger ship terminal to spot familiar NPA cadres.
49. For instance, provincial PC-INP commander Col. Miguel Coronel had long talks with returnees so that he might better "know the enemy." These informed his counterinsurgency manual *Pro-Democracy People's War*.
50. On the 1992 election campaigns in a Negros Occidental municipality, see Rutten, "Courting."
51. These are the representatives of workers, peasants, women, and others who occupy the five sectoral seats on the Municipal Council (in contrast to the eight elected seats).
52. See also Dungo-Garcia, "Changing Social Relations," 329–32.
53. Alfred W. McCoy, "The Restoration of Planter Power in La Carlota City," in Kerkvliet and Mojares, *From Marcos to Aquino*, 105–42.
54. Nemesio Demafelis, interview with the author, Bacolod City, 17 March 1995; Napoleon Dojillo, interview with John Wiersma, Bacolod City, 20 February 1995.
55. See, for instance, Romana P. de los Reyes and Sylvia Ma. G. Jopillo, *Pursuing Agrarian Reform in Negros Occidental* (Quezon City: Ateneo de Manila University, Institute of Philippine Culture, 1991); and Raymundo T. Pandan, Jr., ed., *The Agrarian Reform Process in Negros Occidental: A Program Review and Analysis* (Bacolod City: University of St. La Salle, 1991).

Patricio N. Abinales is an associate professor at the Center for Southeast Asian Studies, Kyoto University. Born in Mindanao and educated at the University of the Philippines, he worked as a staff researcher at the university's Third World Studies Center, specializing in the military, before entering the doctoral program in politics at Cornell University. After returning to his native Mindanao as a field researcher, he completed his doctoral dissertation on the island's modern politics, "State Authority and Local Power in the Southern Philippines, 1900–1972" (1997).

Michael Cullinane is a historian of the Philippines and associate director of the Center for Southeast Asian Studies, University of Wisconsin-Madison. After six years of Philippine fieldwork in the mid-1970s, he completed his doctoral dissertation at the University of Michigan on "*Ilustrado* Politics: The Response of the Filipino Educated Elite to American Colonial Rule" (1989). He has continued to publish widely on the social history of Cebu and the political history of the Philippines.

Brian Fegan has recently retired as a senior lecturer in anthropology at Macquarie University. After fieldwork in Barrio Buga, San Miguel de Mayumo, Bulacan Province, in the early 1970s, he wrote his doctoral dissertation at Yale University under the title "Folk Capitalism: Economic Strategies in a Philippine Wet-Rice Village" (1979). Drawing upon his continuing fieldwork in San Miguel, he has published a series of articles on the politics and economics of Filipino peasant life. Apart from this academic research, he has worked extensively in applied anthropology as a consultant and external reviewer for Australian aid projects from Bangladesh to the Philippines and Manchuria.

Benedict J. Tria Kerkvliet is professor of political and social change in the Research School of Pacific and Asian Studies at the Australian National University in Canberra. After extended fieldwork in the Philippines in 1969–70, he completed his doctoral dissertation at the University of Wisconsin-Madison, which he published under the title *The Huk Rebellion: A Study of Peasant Revolt in the Philippines* (1977). After additional fieldwork in 1978–79, especially in Barrio San Ricardo, Talavera, Nueva Ecija Province, he commenced a study of routine rather than revolutionary politics entitled *Everyday Politics in the Philippines: Class and Status Relations in a Central Luzon Village* (1990). Currently, he is also researching agrarian politics in Vietnam.

Vina A. Lanzona is a Ph.D. candidate in history at the University of Wisconsin-Madison, where she is currently completing her dissertation on women in the Huk rebellion. After graduating from the Ateneo de Manila University in 1989, she completed her M.A. in social theory and European history at the New School for Social Research. In

1996–97, she returned to the Philippines for dissertation fieldwork, which included extended interviews with female veterans of the Huk movement. In 1998, she completed her dissertation research in London with a series of extended interviews with Celia Mariano-Pomeroy, the senior woman in the Communist Party hierarchy during that period.

Alfred W. McCoy is professor of history at the University of Wisconsin-Madison. After field research from 1973 to 1976, he wrote his dissertation at Yale University on the regional history of the Western Visayas, "Ylo-ilo: Factional Conflict in a Colonial Economy" (1977). Through regular research trips to the Philippines, he has published a series of essays on the country's modern political history. His latest book on the Philippines, a history of the armed forces, was published by Yale University Press in 1999 as *Closer than Brothers: Manhood at the Philippine Military Academy.* In addition to his Philippine work, he has written on the political economy of the Southeast Asian opium trade and is author of *The Politics of Heroin* (1991).

Resil Mojares is professor at the University of San Carlos in Cebu City. He completed his Ph.D. dissertation at the University of the Philippines in 1979 and later published it under the title *Origins and Rise of the Filipino Novel* (1983). He is a leading specialist on Philippine literature and social history. Among his publications are *Theater in Society, Society in Theater: Social History of a Cebuano Village* (1985), *The Man Who Would Be President: Serging Osmeña and Philippine Politics* (1986), and *Vicente Sotto: The Maverick Senator* (1992).

Rosanne Rutten is a lecturer in anthropology at the University of Amsterdam. Her first study of social conditions in Negros Occidental, *Women Workers of Hacienda Milagros: Wage Labor and Household Subsistence on a Philippine Sugar Plantation* (1982), was based on extensive fieldwork for a master's thesis. She did her doctoral research in Aklan and Albay and published the dissertation as *Artisans and Entrepreneurs in the Rural Philippines: Making a Living and Gaining Wealth in Two Commercialized Crafts* (1990). She has since returned to Negros periodically for field research on insurgency and social mobilization in the province and has reported these findings in a series of articles.

John Sidel is a lecturer in politics at the School of Oriental and African Studies in London. He has been conducting research in the Philippines since 1985 and has completed his doctoral dissertation on politics in Cavite and Cebu Provinces at Cornell University. It was published by Stanford University Press in 1999 as *Coercion, Capital, Crime.* Currently, drawing on extensive field research in East Java, he is writing on Indonesian politics.

Index

Center for Southeast Asian Studies
University of Wisconsin-Madison
MONOGRAPH SERIES

After the Galleons: Foreign Trade, Economic Change and Entrepreneurship
in the Nineteenth-Century Philippines
by Benito J. Legarda, Jr.

Voices From the Thai Countryside: "The Necklace" and Other Stories
by Samruam Singh, edited and translated by Katherine Bowie

Population and History: The Demographic Origins of the Modern Philippines
edited by Daniel F. Doeppers and Peter Xenos

Sitti Djaoerah: A Novel of Colonial Indonesia
by M.J. Soetan Hasoendoetan, translated by Susan Rodgers

Face of Empire: United States – Philippines Relations, 1898–1946
by Frank Hindman Golay

Inventing a Hero: The Posthumous Re-Creation of Andres Bonifacio
by Glenn May

The Mekong Delta: Ecology, Economy, and Revolution, 1860–1960
by Pierre Brocheux

Autonomous Histories, Particular Truths: Essays in Honor of John Smail
edited by Laurie J. Sears

An Anarchy of Families: State and Family in the Philippines
edited by Alfred W. McCoy

Salome: A Filipino Filmscript by Ricardo Lee
translated by Rofel Brion

Recalling the Revolution: Memoirs of a Filipino General
by Santiago Alvarez, translated by Paula Carolina S. Malay

Anthropology Goes to War: Professional Ethics and Counterinsurgency in Thailand
by Eric Wakin

Voices From the Thai Countryside: The Short Stories of Samruam Singh
edited and translated by Katherine Bowie

Putu Wijaya in Performance: An Approach to Indonesian Theatre
edited by Ellen Rafferty

Gender, Power, and the Construction of the Moral Order
edited by Nancy Eberhardt

Bomb: Indonesian Short Stories by Putu Wijaya
edited by Ellen Rafferty and Laurie J. Sears

Aesthetic Tradition and Cultural Transition in Java and Bali
edited by Stephanie Morgan and Laurie J. Sears

A Complete Account of the Peasant Uprising in the Central Region
by Phan Chu Trinh, translated by Peter Baugher and Vu Ngo Chieu

Publications Committee:
Carol J. Compton; Daniel F. Doeppers (chair); Ian Coxhead;
John Eichenseher; Alfred W. McCoy; R. Anderson Sutton; Janet Opdyke (editor)